Shirley Conran went to St Paul's Gi[...], [...which taught]
her how to maximize time, followed by a finishing school in Swit-
zerland, which taught her how to waste time. She then trained as a
painter and sculptor at Southern College of Art, Portsmouth. Until she
was thirty she worked as a textile designer and colour consultant, and
she has designed her own paint range. She was one of the selection
committee for the Design Council for eight years. She was the first
women's editor of the *Observer* colour magazine and a women's editor
of the *Daily Mail*, where she launched 'Femail'. She handled the publicity for the Women in Media campaign for legislation against sex
discrimination. She was formerly married to design tycoon Sir Terence
Conran, and they have two sons, Sebastian and Jasper, both of whom
are designers; fashion designer Georgina Godley is her daughter-in-
law. Shirley Conran now lives in Monaco.

Shirley Conran has also published *Superwoman* (1975); *The Superwoman
Yearbook* (1976); *Superwoman in Action* (published in hardback as *Superwoman 2*, 1977); *Futurewoman* (with Elizabeth Sidney, published in
hardback as *Futures*, 1979); *Forever Superwoman* (1981); *The Magic
Garden* (1983) for beginner gardeners; and, for children, *The Amazing
Umbrella Shop* (1990). Penguin also publish her bestselling novel *Lace*,
its sequel *Lace 2* and *Savages*. Her latest novel is *Crimson*, forthcoming
in Penguin.

**When first published, *Superwoman* was an instant international
bestseller:**

'Shirley Conran has thought of everything. It is the best book on
household management . . . as compulsive a read as any good novel'
– **The Times**

'A wise and witty book . . . Jam-packed with all manner of
household hints and endless useful advice . . . It would make a
splendid wedding present' – **Sunday Express**

SHIRLEY CONRAN

DOWN WITH SUPERWOMAN!

EVERYTHING YOU NEED TO KNOW
ABOUT RUNNING A HOME

CHAPTER-HEAD ILLUSTRATIONS
BY RAYMOND TURVEY

PENGUIN BOOKS
IN ASSOCIATION WITH SIDGWICK & JACKSON

Sidgwick & Jackson Ltd
1 Tavistock Chambers
Bloomsbury Way
London WC1A 2SG

PENGUIN BOOKS

Published by the Penguin Group
Penguin Books Ltd, 27 Wrights Lane, London W8 5TZ, England
Penguin Books USA Inc., 375 Hudson Street, New York, New York 10014, USA
Penguin Books Australia Ltd, Ringwood, Victoria, Australia
Penguin Books Canada Ltd, 10 Alcorn Avenue, Toronto, Ontario, Canada M4V 3B2
Penguin Books (NZ) Ltd, 182–190 Wairau Road, Auckland 10, New Zealand

Penguin Books Ltd, Registered Offices: Harmondsworth, Middlesex, England

Superwoman first published by Sidgwick and Jackson 1975
Published by Penguin Books 1977
Down with Superwoman!, a wholly revised and updated edition,
first published by Sidgwick & Jackson, in association with Penguin Books, 1990
Published in Penguin Books 1991
1 3 5 7 9 10 8 6 4 2

The publishers acknowledge with gratitude the poet's kind permission to reproduce
on p. 262 'Women Enough', copyright © 1979 by Erica Mann Jong.
All rights reserved

Text illustrations by Sands Graphics

Printed in England by Clays Ltd, St Ives plc

For my mother
IDA PEARCE
with love and thanks

Contents

DOWN WITH SUPERWOMAN!

DOWN WITH SUPERWOMAN!

Acknowledgements

People are always surprised to discover how long a book takes to write and how many people are involved in it. The original manuscript work took me two years, I then worked on the individual international editions for two years and this update has taken a further year – a total of five years' work.

I would like to thank the many people who helped get this book to the point where you are now reading it: these include my supportive publishers, WILLIAM ARMSTRONG and PETER CARSON; my editor, GERALDINE COOKE, who first suggested this edition and who supplied many carrots and a few sticks; and MARGARET HICKEY for her careful research and editorial work. I would also like to thank FELICITY GREEN and ANN QUEENSBERRY for so kindly reading and criticizing the complete final manuscript.

In my office, NIKKI MANWARING and NICOLE PROETTA have shown great enthusiasm and been very supportive; their meticulous hard work is greatly appreciated, as was the help of EVA CLEYDON and ROSELYN HAUDBERG.

For their kind help, expertise and criticism I would like to thank BRIAN STAPLETON, HEATHER GODLEY, DR DENNIS FRIEDMAN, RICHARD MACLELLAN, STEPHEN MILSOM, DR BETHEL SOLOMONS, KEITH WELLS, DR JAMES CYRIAX, ELSE DRUYF-D'HOLLOSY, ROLAND CASTRO, PETER KERTESZ, LIZ DRUMMOND, DAVID MCNEILL and CATHERINE SLAYTOR.

I am also grateful to THE DUCHESS OF BEDFORD, LADY ANTONIA PINTER, JACQUELINE GRAHAM-PELHAM, ANNE BEHAR, JANET COHEN, ROSIE BLACKMORE, KATHY GILGUNN, VANESSA GAYLE, PHOEBE ATKINS, BETTY PETERS, BERYL MANN, MAGGI WILLIS, MAGGIE MCCOURT, IAN HALE, JACK WATERHOUSE, CHRIS DANIEL, HELEN CRISP, TIM KAHN and MR LLOYD of Meecher Higgins & Thomas.

Many organizations have also helped me. For their kind help I would particularly like to thank the Institute of Chartered Accountants in England and Wales, The Law Society, the National Consumer Council, Parent Network and Exploring Parenthood.

I would also like to thank MARY QUANT for egging me on throughout and for writing the original introduction, and KATHARINE WHITEHORN, GEORGE SEDDON, NIKKI WOOD and PAULINE HORRIGAN for reading the original manuscript and suggesting improvements and additions. I must also thank the editor of *The Observer* and the editor of the *Daily Mail* for their permission to include material written when I was a woman's editor on those newspapers.

I would like to thank MARGARET LECOMBER for typing on and on and on with interest and enthusiasm, CELIA BRAYFIELD for two weeks' research work, DEE WELLS and JENNIFER WARE for their criticism, and AUDREY SLAUGHTER for her patience.

I am also grateful to LADY MEDAWAR, LIZA KENDALL, IRIS WADE of Elizabeth Arden, BARTY PHILLIPS, JEAN SOUTHERN, BETTY JAKENS, RUTH FRANCIS,

DOWN WITH SUPERWOMAN!

JANET SEED, BARBARA KELLY, PAMELA LEWIS, LOTTE BERK, SHIRLEY LOWE, SHEILA BLACK, JANET FITCH, PRUDENCE RAPER, PHOEBE HITCHIN, DORIS GRANT, BARBARA SUSSMAN, ALEXANDER WEYMOUTH, SID FIELD, DR JONATHAN GOULD, SEBASTIAN CONRAN, JASPER CONRAN, ROBERT LACEY, JOHN LAUGHTON, MICHAEL BATEMAN, TONY FAIRHURST, PHILLIP DALTON, TONY WILKINS, ALAN MURPHY, ALBERT LOCKE, NOEL RITCHIE, British Gas, the British Standards Institute, the Press Association, the Automobile Association, *Do-It-Yourself* Magazine, the Food Information Bureau, the Metropolitan Police, the RSPCA, St Thomas's Hospital, Messrs Sandersons and the many other people and organizations who were kind enough to help me.

OUR MOTTO: Life is too short to stuff a mushroom

The reason why

What is a home? A home is a myth. A home is the Forth Bridge, one damn never-ending cleaning job that nobody notices unless you don't do it.

No matter what they claim, no one can tell you how to make washing up a sensuous experience, but until some inventor produces a mechanical housemaid, *somebody's* got to do the dirty work.

Down With Superwoman! is for people who have to housekeep but who prefer to do something more interesting. It will help you do all the housework that you can't avoid, as fast and painlessly as possible. It tells you how to run a home in which everyone (including you) can enjoy living, without feeling guilty every time you put your feet up.

I don't pretend that housework is fun because on the whole it isn't, although there are some aspects of it that are pleasant. Getting up early, preparing breakfast, setting the table, darning, spring cleaning and arranging flowers would never be a strain for me. But I find routine cleaning tedious at the best of times and clinically depressing at the worst.

Because housework is so dreary, it is quite easy to forget to do it, or even forget *how* to do it. Thirty years of blood, sweat, toil and tears haven't helped me to eliminate housework, but they have taught me a few tricks to lighten the load.

This is the basic minimum of household information that you can get away with. However, it is also a COMPREHENSIVE* reference work, and SHOULD CERTAINLY PAY FOR ITSELF BEFORE YOU'VE FINISHED READING IT.

Some sections are thoughtfully labelled SKIP THIS UNTIL YOU NEED IT. When you read one of these, read it slowly. Do not allow your eyes to skim over it. Be prepared to read this section twice – it might save you a lot of money by clarifying the intricacies of insurance when moving or by explaining how your electricity meter works. It certainly won't be riveting literature, but I hope it's easier to understand than anything else you may have tried to read on the subject.

By the way, I have mentioned prices and costs as little as possible because, no matter what the politicians say, Old Mother Conran predicts that world prices will continue to go up and up and up. However well the Government fudges its figures, we all know that inflation is much higher than it is officially supposed to be and it won't go away; all the things *I* buy seem to have gone up ten times in the last fifteen years. The official cost-of-living index doesn't seem to include things like marmalade or school coats, heating oil or first homes.

Parts of this book are taken from my own home notebooks, a few bits are from specialist books I've written and parts are the summed-up experience of ten years as a home editor on leading British national newspapers. Where there is an excellent book on a subject that I cover briefly, I recommend that book for

* Which is why information is occasionally duplicated if it is needed in two places.

further reading, but only if it is exceptionally good. When I mention a book that is out of print, it's because it's really worth pursuing at your library.

What are my qualifications for writing this book? Sadly, I have learnt how to do things right by first doing them wrong. I hope you benefit from my expensive experience.

As with housework, 'he' and 'she' are interchangeable within this book. When meaning 'a person', I have used the gramatically correct 'he', unless I feel that what I am saying is particularly applicable to women, when I have used 'she'.

Incidentally, I was surprised by the number of men who bought the first edition of this book. At first I thought they were buying it to teach their wives to scrub floors better (swine), but no – *they very often were buying their own copies*. They pointed out that many men *have* to do housework, if they are bachelors, divorced or widowed, and that sometimes a single, *male* parent has to look after the children.

I hope that new readers will find this updated edition useful and that old friends will like the new sections and the new title, *Down With Superwoman!*, which states my message more clearly.

The original title, *Superwoman*, was used ironically to demolish a myth. I had noticed a growing anxiety and depression among ordinary women as the result of media propaganda about females who effortlessly organize a career (not 'job'), home, husband, children and social life, while simultaneously retaining a 24-hour-perfect hairstyle and doing something esoteric, such as learning Japanese, in their spare time.

But I suspected that no one could achieve everything that the *traditional* woman was *supposed* to do, let alone this demanding, exhausting, super-achiever that threatened to depress our lives. I christened this impossible creature SUPERWOMAN, and in due course

the SUPERWOMAN syndrome became a medical reference. Psychiatrists prescribed the first edition of this book for patients who couldn't cope. Perhaps they were expected to cope with too much. Perhaps they were the ones who expected.

To get the best out of this book it's important to forget SUPERWOMAN. Instead, remember your own limitations, allow for your understandable weaknesses and ignore the impossible milk-and-honey standards of the trivia-obsessed media housewife.

Use this book to check on your workload, your system and any human help you can find. (Could it be lying next to you? See 'How to get help in the home', p. 262.)

A real achiever isn't a woman who can do anything, but a woman who avoids doing too much. She knows her own limitations and sticks happily within them. She realizes that life is untidy and so are the children in it. She knows that perfection is hell to live with, and her standards are her own rather than the idiotic unrealistic ones set by TV, magazines, mothers-in-law and lying friends. (Inter-woman competition can be as cruel, gruelling, and unnecessary as any competition in the traditional male rat race.)

Any sensible woman knows in her brain that it's ridiculous to feel guilty about un-done housework. It is *not* the natural state of woman to feel, whenever you're enjoying yourself, that what you *should* be doing instead is going home to clean the oven; this guilt has been forced on you by centuries of conditioning by people who *don't* want to clean the oven. Housework doesn't make a home – generally, a happy woman does. And no happy woman wastes time worrying whether the door knobs are clean enough.

One good reason to avoid housework is in order to have more time for *yourself*. Remember that a mother, as well as being the supporting cast of the entire family show, **IS THE ONE AND ONLY STAR OF HER OWN LIFE**. Therefore, avoid overwork and look after yourself, so that you are in good shape to look after all the people who depend on you.

It took me years to acquire the discipline, control and iron will that was necessary in order to stop doing things for other people and start doing things for myself. At first I told myself that I didn't have the time. But then I worked out that if you work a regulation 40-hour week and sleep 8 hours a night, you still have 72 hours a week left over (which is almost twice as long as a working week) in which to do something stimulating and rewarding, or at least just SOME-THING.

It is quite difficult (to begin with) to do as little housework as possible. You have to be well organized to keep housework in its place, which, as far as I'm concerned, is firmly underfoot. Good organization doesn't just happen naturally, any more than good sex. You have to learn how to do it and then put in a lot of practice, like the piano.

I make no secret of the fact that I would rather lie on a sofa than sweep beneath it, but you have to be efficient if you're going to be lazy.

Some may suggest that women don't have to be well organized in order to be efficient, but I know of no job, whether it's bathing a baby or running a nightclub, that isn't easier, quicker and more enjoyable if you think about the logical way to do it in advance – and that's a simple definition of organization.

Over the last few years housework has become easier, thanks to such time-savers as nutritious pre-prepared supermarket meals and the microwave oven. However, in an increasingly stressful world that seems to be spinning faster and faster, the *organization* of a home has become more difficult. Arguing with inexorable computers, puzzling credit-card interest rates and slotting the children's time-tables into yours are problems that your mother may never have known. Running a happy home today requires a lot more self-awareness and a bit more organization.

Many women don't like organizing themselves because it involves a little forethought and self-discipline. But organization needn't mean a rigid plan brought to the fine pitch of a royal visit. There must be a plan, but keep it a loose plan, one you can scrap or alter whenever it doesn't fit in with reality. Life is like a British summer – you have to grab it quickly, before it disappears. This means being flexible enough to drop everything and get out into the sun while it's still shining – which it never does on schedule.

A plan helps you to know what you *haven't* done. You might also find out what will galvanize you into action to get that work done – what cunning carrot will coax you into doing it. The writer Katharine Whitehorn asks friends in at least once a week because that's the only empirical method she knows of getting herself to tidy up the home. In half-an-hour's whirl of activity – which she enjoys – she does it all; it then becomes not a boring routine but a double-bonus activity. Of course, if you like your home tidied daily, this could get a bit expensive and you might even run out of friends.

Her methods are not mine. My methods are probably not yours. There may be those who find my methods appalling. Fine. What works for me might not work for you, but one of the tricks of sorting out what's best and fastest for yourself is to criticize someone else. Then, SHAZAM! You may have suddenly analysed and perhaps improved your own system. *So please deface this book.* It is a working book. Add to it, cross things out, make notes and scribble your own ideas in the margin.

Some women think that some of the

things I suggest are too simple to write down. I disagree. You never know what you don't know. A sensible woman *aims* at simplicity: simplicity in organizing and living her life, in doing without things that (accumulatively) threaten to take over her life.

Some men have asked me how I *dare* write a book about what women already know. This sort of man believes that he was born with a total and unquestionable knowledge of the combustion engine, how to grill a steak and how to make love, whereas his womenfolk were born only with a built-in knowledge of housework.

Well, who *did* traditionally teach women to do housework? Obviously their mothers. Well . . . who taught them? And when? And where did *they* go for their refresher courses? And when?

In any case, these days housework is not confined to one sex or one class. We *all* have to do it. Luckily, many modern men are willing to help with what *they* call the system-support work (a face-saving, space-age phrase used in rocket construction), and all boys should be taught to do so. (Don't stop at potty training: teach them how to *totally* clean up after themselves.)

But even when the man does his fair share of the housework, it's still the woman who is responsible for seeing that the background to family life runs smoothly. It's this responsibility that causes the anxiety that can lead to stress – hence the new chapter 'How to survive life'.

It's doubtful whether all the advice in this book will apply, or appeal, to any one woman, for it was not written for a specific woman, and, in any case, a woman's circumstances constantly change. (My own circumstances have changed since I first wrote this book: I no longer live hand-to-mouth in a city basement, but by the sea in sunny Monte Carlo. And I now have a much-loved daughter-in-law and grandson, Sam.)

Whatever their circumstances, some women go out to work full- or part-time, some don't; a few start some kind of business on the side. Some have husbands, some have lovers, some have both. Many have children but some don't. Some women have no husband, no lover, several children and a full-time job. Some women have none of these. For this reason I have tried to cover problem areas and their solutions from mild to extreme. For instance, in 'How to spend money' my suggestion that you try having two purses may help you sort out a housekeeping-money muddle. The same section also shows you how to do basic accounts.

So dig into this book as you need it. It is a concentrated course on how to get things done. Try my ideas one at a time – not in a bunch at once. Don't try too much or nothing will work, and you risk overloading the brain and blowing a fuse. Don't, without trying them, decide that my strange ideas don't work.

Finally, no one should waste her life on the treadmill of housework. So decide how much you're prepared to do and when. Four hours a day? One day a week? No time at all? (A high aim, I feel, but good luck to you.) Decide how much mechanical or human help you want, how much it will cost and how you're going to get the money to pay for it. I see no reason not to hire human help if you can afford it and if some people want to do it. Some people would hate my job as much as I hate housework.

Don't use any human help to raise your housekeeping standards. Use it to create more free time to get out and enjoy yourself. There is *always* something better to do than housework.

Whoever's doing it, remember that the whole point of housework is to keep the place functioning efficiently as a cheerful background for living – so live! Decide on something positive, or simply pleasurable, to do for *yourself* with the time you save. Otherwise life . . . just . . . slithers . . . a-w-a-y . . .

How to save time ~ and money

The only way that never fails is to get up earlier, but if this is too difficult, try cutting out anything that isn't essential. The secret is *elimination*. So make your list of things that no one will care much if you don't do. (Some of these suggestions need money, so they might have to be tucked away at the back of your mind until the piggy bank is feeling stronger.) No one is forcing you to give up anything, but if something has to go, *consider* these *money-* or *time-savers*.

* DON'T waste money on expensive beauty products; make your own (see 'Mix your own beauty kit', p. 303).
* DON'T wear nail varnish.
* Keep your nails short and they won't break. You won't look like the Queen of the Typing Pool, but you will look like HM the Queen.
* DON'T wear jewellery.
* DON'T keep pets (unless you live alone).

* DON'T have a car, have a bike.
* DON'T have a telephone.
* DON'T write letters, only post-cards.
* DON'T polish floors; seal them.
* DON'T scrub the bath. Unless anyone in your family is allergic to detergent, keep a bathroom bottle of liquid detergent and get everyone to pour in a capful before turning on the water.
* DON'T dry dishes. Buy a second drainer and stand it in front of the first, or else spread tea-towels on the table or a trolley to provide more drip-dry surface.
* In fact, if life gets unbearable, DON'T wash up at all. Get the family to wash up, Elizabethan style. That is, each person has his own mug, plate, knife, fork and spoon and manages with these, then washes them up and resets his own place for the next meal. This always happened in our family

7

DOWN WITH SUPERWOMAN!

towards the end of the school holidays.

* DON'T lay a tablecloth or use table napkins.

* DON'T make beds. Use continental quilts or sleeping bags.

* DON'T scrub dirty collars and cuffs. Wet them and dip in a saucerful of detergent; leave for ten minutes, then wash.

* DON'T buy any children's clothes or household linen that isn't drip-dry or non-iron.

* DON'T iron handkerchiefs (it's more hygienic to use disposable paper tissues) or nightclothes (smooth and fold them).

* DON'T sew. Mend sheet tears with iron-on tape. Stick patches on with Copydex.

* DON'T shop with a friend.

* DON'T go to the sales (with or without a friend) unless it's for something you decided to buy at least three months ago.

* DON'T shop for food when you're hungry.

* DON'T shop for food with more cash than you intend to spend.

* DON'T pay for food by cheque or card.

* DON'T pay the manufacturer's recommended retail price without checking around first (especially for air fares) and *tell* the people you check with that you are comparative shopping.

* DON'T buy clothes for exotic sports in exotic climates except in those exotic climates, or you'll buy the wrong thing.

* DON'T join a health club. Do yoga, skip, jog, walk, exercise or swim with a friend – then you'll both keep it up.

* DON'T buy anything that eats, leaks or needs maintenance (especially boats and swimming pools).

* DO cover kitchen shelves with self-adhesive, wipe-clean plastic. You will save cleaning time.

* DO line the grill pan and the tray under the gas burners with aluminium foil.

* DO roast in foil, which cuts out basting and oven cleaning; unwrap for the last fifteen minutes to brown nicely.

* DO use non-stick pans (unless you're a Green), which cut the horror out of washing-up, as well as a lot of the time.

* DO get your family to tidy up after themselves or else stand a cardboard box under the kitchen table and dump everything you find in this lost property office. After a bit they prefer to tidy up their own possessions rather than sort them out of the tangle.

* DO close any charge accounts at shops.

* DO shop by telephone whenever possible if your weakness is impulse buying. You pay for the call and maybe a bit more for the food, but it cuts out those expensive impulsive purchases.

* DO be carefully inefficient. Start running out of things (but never lavatory rolls).

* DO squash lavatory rolls so that the centre is oval, not round. Then the paper doesn't roll off ten yards at a time.

* DO consider easy maintenance your first requisite when buying anything from flooring (good bets are sealed cork and wood in mid-tones) to dishwashers.

* DO invest in time switches for electrical equipment, from electric blankets to immersion heaters and lights in the back room to ward off burglars when you're away on holiday.

THE SIMPLIFY LIFE CHECK-LIST

Consider this check-list for ways to drastically simplify and uncomplicate your life-style. It should be a life (yours) and style (yours), not some souped-up form of living beyond your means that may be dictated to you by other people. Check that you are not unnecessarily overspending in terms of emotions and energy (mental and physical) as well as time and money.

Ask yourself: do you want it? Do you need it? Can you live without it? Will discarding it save you money? Time? Worry? Upkeep? Insurance? In the list below I've starred my own crossed-off items, just to give you something to argue about.

* Jewellery
* Big parties (going to or giving)
* Theatre
* Cinema
* Concerts
  Excess furniture
  Excess rooms
  Personal transportation
* Inessential home equipment (Conran's Last Law says there's always one machine not working and in need of attention)
  Houseplants (very, very reluctantly)
  Pets
* Snacks
  Three meals a day
  Excess clothing
  Lower temperature central heating
  A second house
  A second anything (or anyone)

However, what may be taking up your time may not be the case of material possessions but excessive demands on your emotional strength. Perhaps you happily submit to these demands? If so, learn to say NO (with no qualifications) and then learn not to feel guilty about it. Guilt is a pointless waste of time.

HOW TO CUT DOWN ON HOUSEWORK

Conran's Law is that housework expands to fill the time available – plus half an hour. So you will *never* get it finished. Therefore, keep it to the minimum and keep it underfoot. No one's going to strangle you if the mantelpiece is dusty. Your man doesn't love you because you can tell the difference between whitest and whiter-than-white. Your children won't remember you with love in twenty years' time because your floors had such a fantastic shine.

A TV producer and mother of two small children once asked me, 'Now that I can afford some home help, how much cleaner should my home be?' I was astounded. A home should be as clean as you can get away with. On the whole, nobody except you cares how the place looks. If somebody does, then press him into service. Always, charmingly, press any critic into service: they either help or stop criticizing or, ideally, both.

I don't believe in being too organized. Many women are quite rightly suspicious of time-and-motion methods suggested for running the home like a factory. A home is not a factory (thank heaven) and it cannot be organized with the same methods. You are often doing three things at once in a home and it's just when the dog has been sick (because it ate your slipper) that the doorbell rings.

One fairly painless way to cut down on housework is to apply the principle of reverse thinking. Instead of calculating how much there is to do, decide how much time you are prepared to devote to it – and when. This is one way of sorting out your priorities almost without thinking about them. I used to hire myself on Saturday morning from 9 to 11 a.m. and when my time was up, like the cleaning lady, I stopped. The work that was left over had to wait until the next Saturday morning, or for ever.

9

DOWN WITH SUPERWOMAN!

I also firmly believe that every mother should have household help and the people who should help are the people who are making the work in the first place – the rest of the family. So in my home we *all* work on Saturday morning (together with any guests). From 9 to 11 a.m. is a good time if you have teenagers: get them at it any earlier and they'll complain that you're getting them up at *dawn*; keep them at it any later and they'll howl that you're taking up the *whole weekend*. But most teenagers will work hard for two hours a week, provided that they are not asked to perform extra little chores simply because, like Mount Everest, they are *there*.

A friend of mine has a variation on this theme. Every morning after her family has charged off, she sets the kitchen timer for one hour and when it pings, she stops.

DAILY LICK AND SPIT

AIM to get through the routine housework in the minimum time. Try to keep a routine, which starts with getting up at the time you planned. If you get up late, you'll probably do everything late all day and snap at people.

Decide how long your daily routine will take and realize, if you are overrunning, that you will either have to abandon the job unfinished or sacrifice whatever other, possibly more enjoyable, occupation you had planned for the afternoon.

It's amazing how much better a room looks if you *don't clean it at all* but simply tidy it, straightening the cushions, emptying the ashtrays and shoving every odd thing into a large basket and standing it in a corner. Making the bed makes a bedroom instantly look tidy.

Allow time after breakfast to empty waste-paper baskets, ashtrays and kitchen dustbin; put everyone's clothes where they ought to be; throw away dead flowers, renew water if necessary, water your plants, wipe washbasins, sweep the kitchen floor, make the beds – do this only for very young children.

In spite of my mother's traditional horror, although I clear the table, I always do last night's washing-up the next morning, because I haven't the strength to cope with it after the evening meal (see 'How to wash up', p. 32).

SUGGESTED ROUTINE

Highlight what you want to do weekly and leave the rest for a monthly check.

On Monday Clean up the kitchen after the weekend, defrost the fridge (if it doesn't have an automatic defroster), clean the oven, scrub out dustbins and deal with any other strictly kitchen jobs, plus household desk work. Don't do the washing.

On Tuesday Do the clothes washing and mending and shopping, including a trip to the dry cleaners.

On Wednesday If you insist on ironing, do it in the company of the TV or radio. You'll risk backache, if not a slipped disc, if your ironing board is too low and you have to stoop over it. Consider getting a cordless iron.

On Thursday Clean other rooms. If you can get away with it, this is the day you can take off with a free conscience. Use it for odd jobs such as turning out cupboards, washing down paintwork, cleaning ceilings (light fittings and cobwebs), cleaning the pram, polishing the silver if you have any and so on. Or just leave the house at 10 a.m. and do something interesting.

On Friday Do the weekend shopping; clean the bathroom and lavatory thoroughly; clean one room (see 'How to be a housemaid', p. 19) or passages or hell holes such as a basement area full of dustbins.

If you're doing a full-time job you probably won't have time for a daily routine, but rely on one thorough weekend cleaning swoop – in which case, still use this routine, and for further ideas turn to 'How to be a working wife and mother', p. 241.

The general idea is to do *one* chore (or related chores) each day, rather than a daily smorgasbord of activities.

SPRING CLEAN FASTER

Spring cleaning is rarely necessary if you stick to a good weekly schedule. But one day when you are feeling strong and rich you might:

* Finger through the *Yellow Pages* and get a professional carpet cleaner to estimate for cleaning your carpets and upholstery. It's amazing what they can achieve.
* If you use open fires, call the chimney sweep.
* Send all the curtains to be cleaned. In London you can telephone specialists Pilgrim Payne to collect them (081-960-5656).
* Look at your list of things to be mended, things to be bought and things to be overhauled.

I try to do this work in the first week of January. It's anticlimax time and the weather is nasty, so you might as well do the nasty jobs now and try not to do any more for the rest of the year. Nobody seems to notice. The rest of the year I just make notes in the back of my diary of things to be mended or replaced as the home inexorably disintegrates about my ears. Don't do anything that can be postponed until spring-cleaning time.

Not everyone agrees with me but, temperature permitting, I believe that the best private spring-cleaning outfit is a bikini. You can always wriggle into a sweater as well if you're not warm enough.

Spring clean with a friend (who doesn't talk *too* much) to spur you on, cheer you up, patch you up or wipe you down and – ideally – complete the job for you when you get stuck or bored. Do the same for her.

Warning! Mutual help is best done on an hourly basis. Her home might be twice as large and take twice as long.

Plan a methodical campaign

Decide what you can afford to do in terms of time, money and interest.

1 Inspect your home, yet another notebook in hand, and list all the things you'd like to see clean – you'll feel so virtuous when you tick them off as each job is finished. You'll feel virtuous just making the list and doing nothing.
2 Decide what to clean and what to renew. It's only a little more trouble to paint a wall than just to scrub it. Paint costs more than water, but achieves more exciting results.
3 Check if any small jobs, such as mending electric plugs or sash cords, or chimney cleaning, have to be handled by professionals and, if so, arrange for them to be done before anything else.
4 Check that your ladder is strong and firm, that the first-aid box is full and that your paint brushes are not stiff.
5 Check your cleaning cupboard. Are your brooms balding? Is your vacuum cleaner listless? Have you got enough dusters, a feather duster (vital) and a ceiling broom?
6 Decide in which order the rooms will be cleaned. Clean one room at a time, because you can stop right there if time runs out or you get bored. *Stop* half an hour before you had planned, because then you won't be too exhausted to clear up properly.
7 Plan the simplest catering for your family, but don't live on bread and

cheese – a grilled chop and salad is almost as easy to fix and better for you.

8 Tell your nearest – who won't even have noticed that you are spring cleaning – that you'll expect him to provide a night out, say next Monday, and you'll be having a bubble bath and going to the hairdresser beforehand.

THE TRUTH ABOUT HOUSEHOLD CLEANERS

As with beauty products, manufacturers of cleaning products sell them by playing on a woman's chemical ignorance, her feelings of inadequacy, her guilt and her wish for eternal guaranteed happiness and approval.

They sell you a pretty bottle of Swipe, implying that if you're not loved or approved enough then it must be because your floors have a yellow waxy build-up or because you're not working hard enough at being a good housewife.

DON'T fall for the ads and DO learn what's in the cleaning products so that you don't duplicate-buy.

'Detergent' comes from the Latin for 'to cleanse', so any cleaner can claim to be a detergent. Soaps and modern detergents have a similar cleaning effect, but soap has an organic base whereas modern detergents are synthetic (man-made).

Nearly every household cleaner – whether soap, scourer, detergent, spray cleaner or floor polish – is based on either soap and sodium carbonate (washing soda) or sodium phosphate (TSP), or a mixture of both with a few additions. These additions might be washing soda, bleach, ammonia, alcohol, caustic soda, vinegar, paraffin, turpentine and paraffin wax, which are also used in other cleaning products. There's not much more to it than that except for packaging and advertising.

Household cleaners can work in one of three main ways, or in combinations of the three. They can:

1 Dissolve the dirt with a solvent
2 Float off the dirt with oil or soap and then float off the oil or soap with water
3 Use an abrasive or rubbing action to rub off the dirt; this can be as simple an abrasive action as a washerwoman's rub, or as strong an abrasive action as using steel wool to rub off dirt from cooking pots.

Soaps, detergents and general-purpose household cleaners dissolve dirt and float it off the dirty surface, either by themselves or combined with water.

The stronger the chemical, the more likely it is to dissolve the dirt – but also the more likely to damage the surface (such as your antique table) from which the dirt is being removed. So you need some weak cleaners and some strong cleaners, and you need to know which to apply where.

Of course, you can buy only one basic, strong cleaning solution and weaken it yourself for the more delicate jobs (for my recipes, see p. 14). Incidentally, when a manufacturer says, 'kind to your hands', he means 'weak solution'; *nothing* is kind to your hands except rubber gloves. (Get them really big, then they're easy to slip on.)

The purest soaps and detergents (such as Ivory soap, Dreft powder) have basically nothing added to them, but they are used only for delicate jobs like washing-up or handwashing lingerie.

Soaps and detergents for laundry are basically the same but have added ingredients to improve the cleaning action.

Dishwasher detergents are mainly harsh abrasive TSP with added borax to soften the water.

Household cleaners (such as Jif) are composed mainly of TSP or washing soda (sodium carbonate). Whether they are a powder, liquid or spray, they are essentially the same, differing in strength and suitable for most washable surfaces.

Abrasive powder cleaners (such as Ajax and Vim) include the same basic ingredients but with a little added abrasive powder. 'Abrasive' is Latin for 'scraping off', which is what it does, rubbing off the dirt as well as dissolving it off; one of the first historical abrasives was powdered pumice stone. Sometimes bleach is also added.

Soap pads (such as Brillo) are made of fine steel wool (a *very* strong abrasive) soaked in a liquid soap and then dried.

Metal polishes also contain a very, very, very fine abrasive and probably some ammonia, which makes glass and non-tarnishable metal shine and sparkle.

Liquid metal polish is generally a more efficient tarnish remover than a powder polish. Something like Brasso cleans all metals except silver, for which you need a finer abrasive.

Window-cleaning liquids and sprays contain ammonia, because this makes glass shine and sparkle. When independently tested (by the British Glass Economics Division) my home-made recipe (see p. 15) was considered to be as good as any on the market, so why not use that?

Oven, toilet bowl and drain cleaners (such as Lysol) are based on a corrosive (a chemical abrasive, or eater-off) called lye, so always USE RUBBER GLOVES, keep them away from your face and eyes, and if the latter accidentally come into contact with one of these cleaners, wash off immediately with lots and lots of cold water rinses.

CLEANERS TO BUY

You really need only five basic household cleaners – a mild soap, a strong detergent, an abrasive cleaner, a metal cleaner and ammonia – but here are the maximum

number to consider; don't buy more than you need.

Manufacturers tend to recommend that you use far more of their product than is necessary. You could halve or even quarter the amount of powder you put in your machine and your wash will come out just as clean. Try it.

WARNING! Keep all these liquids away from children.

1 **Household soap**, in solid bar or flakes.

2 **A biological washing-machine detergent**, such as Ecover. As it is biodegradable, it doesn't kill animal life when it leaves your drain. If you care about the pollution of the earth, the rivers and the sea, please write a note to the manager of your local supermarket and ask him to stock only biodegradable detergents, such as Ecover, which is *not* biologically harmful. You can use detergent for almost anything that's washed with water, and for soaking off burnt saucepans and tidemarks and dingy unreachable bottoms in narrow-necked vases. Incidentally, it's the *soaking* that is most effective in removing dirt, not the 'biological action'.

3 **A cleansing powder that contains bleach**, such as Vim or Flash.

4 **Washing-up liquid**, such as Fairy Liquid. Alternatively, get a gallon can of Teepol concentrate, which you can dilute.

5 **A dishwasher detergent**, such as Finish.

6 **Steel-wool scouring pads**, cut in half to last longer.

7 **Household ammonia** Add to water for cleaning windows, picture glass, mirrors. Also adds sparkle to silver.

8 **Washing soda** Add 1 tablespoon to warm water and detergent to wash paintwork. Add 2 tablespoons to water when soaking burnt saucepans or oven racks.

DOWN WITH SUPERWOMAN!

9 **Household bleach** Bleach removes colour and acts as an antiseptic and deodorizer. Use cautiously to whiten yellowed, scorched, mildewed or stained cloth (see 'Hello, goodbye washday', p. 48). Useful for cleaning any surface that it will not damage (such as the lavatory or china, or earthenware cups and teapots).

Peroxide is a mild bleach; buy 20 volume (4 per cent hydrogen) peroxide. If you dilute this 50/50 with water, you will have a very mild bleach to use for removing stains from delicate fabrics and china (see 'Stain removal', pp. 41–5).

Shop-bought household bleaches, such as Brobat, are a strong mixture of chlorine bleach and disinfectant and should not be used for stain removal.

10 **Disinfectant**, such as Dettol.
11 **A non-aerosol oven cleaner**, such as Kleen-Off.
12 **Floor polish**, such as Mansion.
13 **Furniture polish**, such as Johnson's Pledge.

Note: on all cleaning products look for the ozone-friendly sticker or sign on the lid.

CLEANERS TO MAKE YOURSELF

There's no reason why you shouldn't make your *own* household cleaners. Just try my window-cleaning recipe, which you can make faster than a cup of coffee; or the White House furniture polish, which one antique dealer brews up 5 litres (1 gal) at a time.

To make a good selection takes less time than baking a cake. It took me sixteen minutes to make my first six cleaners; what is tedious is the thought of tripping out to the DIY store for the ingredients, but, in fact, it's quickly done.

Half an hour spent making cleaners

Great Grandmother's Secret Recipe Home Cleaner

every six months and you will not only save wads of money, you will also get an *instant* reputation as an old-fashioned, real homemaker. Men step inside the door and say, 'This smells like an old-fashioned farmhouse.' It's the cleaning equivalent of making your coffee with freshly ground beans – it's the *smell* that gets you the reputation.

You can decant your cleaners into your *own* matching jars and bottles, bought from the DIY store along with the ingredients. I have a set of amber glass chemist's bottles in all sizes. Buy pretty, stick-on labels, as for presents, and insert your own house brand names.

Be very careful to label them 'poison' and not to keep them with your food or drink. You could dot the tops of your cleaning jars with red paint or nail varnish.

Partly out of interest and partly because of the high cost of convenience cleaners, I've included throughout this book quite a lot of simple, cheap 'do-it-yourself' ideas as used by Great-grandmother.

It's no more dangerous to make these cleaners than to use what's under your sink at the moment! Wear rubber gloves, but the only recipe to make with great care is the cooker cleaner. Wash utensils *thoroughly* after use: you don't want your sauces to taste of paraffin.

Washing-up liquid You might acquire a jar to put chopped-up bits of left-over soap, topped with boiling water. This results in a soft soap jelly for washing-up.

Window cleaner Mix 1 cup paraffin, 1 cup water and 1 cup methylated spirit. Shake well and bottle. Rub on glass, polish off when dry. This recipe is a real winner.

Polish for chrome and paintwork Mix 2 cups paraffin with 1 cup methylated spirit. Rub on with damp rag.

Non-slip linoleum polish (don't make near a naked flame) Place a wide-necked jar in a bowl of hot water, add 560 ml (1 pt) methylated spirit and 85 ml (3 fl oz) brown shellac, stir until dissolved, then tightly screw on lid. Wash and dry linoleum, then brush on polish and leave to dry.

To remove grease stains and dirt from furniture Mix $\frac{1}{4}$ cup methylated spirit, $\frac{1}{2}$ cup vinegar, $\frac{1}{2}$ cup turpentine and $\frac{1}{2}$ cup paraffin. Bottle and shake. Apply with rag and polish off immediately. First test on an inconspicuous part of anything old or valuable.

Great-grandmother's furniture polish Mix 1 cup turpentine, 2 cups linseed oil and 1 cup water. Takes a lot of rubbing, but you get a good shine.

White House furniture polish 1 cup turpentine, 1 cup linseed oil, $\frac{1}{2}$ cup methylated spirit, $\frac{1}{2}$ cup vinegar. Mix together and shake well before using. For leather and furniture. Apply with soft rag, then polish with duster.

Cooker cleaner Dissolve 1 tablespoon caustic soda in 250 ml ($\frac{1}{2}$ pt) hot water. Separately mix 1 tablespoon flour and a little water to a thick cream. Add to soda solution, stir and bottle. Apply to cooker with mop.

Warning! Take great care not to spill mixture. Wear rubber gloves and don't bend over it.

Scouring powder Wood ash that is left after a fire makes a good scouring mixture and can remove stains from metal and china. Keep a jar near the sink.

Silver cleaner (given to me by a canny Scots housekeeper) Mix 1 table-spoon ammonia, 1 tablespoon powdered whiting, 560 ml (1 pt) boiling water. Leave for fifteen minutes. Don't bend over mixture, because it fizzes and fumes. Saturate a piece of old towelling in it and let it drip dry. Instead of using an ordinary drying-up cloth, dry your silver with this and it will rarely need cleaning. (If you can't be bothered, use Goddard's Long Life Silver Cleaner.)

Tip from the Ritz The Ritz cloakroom has the most sparkling silver hairbrushes in London. 'Use a spot of meths by itself on a piece of cotton wool to brighten up silver in a hurry,' says the cloakroom lady.

DON'T WRECK YOUR PLANET

As with vegetarians, there are different degrees of Green, from mild (not wearing fur or ivory) to strict (no leather shoes or non-stick saucepans). Many people are now ecologically aware. Many people want to look after their environment, but they still want to clean with minimum effort. Having a clean ecological conscience means avoiding aerosol cans and products that contain phosphates and enzymes.

Aerosols

Many of the cleaning products are packed in aerosol cans, which are believed to damage the Earth's ozone layer, which filters out the harmful, ultraviolet rays of the sun and prevents lethal levels of radiation from reaching us. Unfortunately, scientists have discovered a hole, about the size of the USA, in the ozone layer.

Phosphates

Phosphates discharged through sewers into rivers and lakes kill fish and animal life there. In some countries the level of phosphates in detergents is strictly regulated, but in Britain it can be difficult to find a phosphate-free product. If the packet doesn't say it's phosphate-free, it won't be.

Enzymes

In the USA and Canada the two major detergent manufacturers, Procter & Gamble and Lever Brothers, have stopped adding enzymes to their brands because of consumers' concern about harmful effects on their health and the environment. Unfortunately, enzyme powders will still be sold in Britain by some irresponsible manufacturers until people decide not to buy them.

A range of products called Ecover, made by a Belgian company, can be found in many health-food shops. Ecover market washing powder, washing-up liquid, cream cleaner, lavatory cleaner, fabric conditioner, wool-wash liquid, floor soap and heavy-duty hand cleaner; all are rapidly biodegradable, made from natural substances, **do not contain phosphates, bleaches, enzymes or other harmful substances** found in most commercial equivalents and *are not tested on animals*. (If you can't find a supplier in your area, write to the distributors: Full Moon, Charlton Court Farm, Steyning, West Sussex, tel: 0903-879077.)

Ecover and Ark cleaners are sold as ecologically sound – fully biodegradable with no enzymes or phosphates. However, as with other Green products, they are considerably more expensive than other cleaners and will be until pressure is put on supermarkets by Britain's 18 million Greens. *Please, please write to your supermarket and complain that prices are too high.*

If you care enough about your children's future to buy safe products, write to the Friends of the Earth (26–28 Underwood Street, London N1 7JQ, tel: 071-490 1555), enclosing an SAE, for a detailed list of products that they recommend, from cosmetics to garden insect killers. You might buy their handbook, entitled *Friends of the Earth Handbook*. They also publish *The Good Wood Guide* to ideologically sound suppliers (including Traidcraft and Habitat). This is important because 95 per cent of hardwood imports deplete tropical rain forests.

Among good books is *Blueprint for a Green Planet* by John Seymour and Herbert Girardet, published by Dorling Kindersley, which covers subjects such as safe housekeeping, water pollution, food for health, dismantling the rubbish mountain, the hazard-free home, gardening without chemicals and car pollution. Another excellent book is *The Green Consumer Guide* by John Elkington and Julia Hailes, published by Gollancz, which clearly explains the environmental issues and lists goods to buy as well as goods *not* to buy.

Note: Recycled paper is sold by W. H. Smith, Oxfam and Friends of the Earth.

FLOWER POWER

After you've finished cleaning, what makes a room look fresh and cherished is – flowers. No matter how broke I used to be, I always had flowers in my sitting-room; they add sparkle to your furniture and when I didn't have furniture – only mattresses on the floor – they cheered me up.

No arrangement is too small or insignificant to look pretty: two big daisies in an egg-cup, some snowdrops in a wine glass.

Containers

Choose helpful vases. A helpful container is one that is the right size, a good shape and solidly balanced. Vases that open out like large trumpets and bulbous pots with narrow necks make whatever flowers you put in them look weedy and undersized; all jugs and decanters are fine; most bowls are charming, if they're deep enough and you have flowers to fill them.

Keep your containers simple. If there's a line to the container, follow it. Use cylindrical glass vases or tumblers (very good for a single flower with one leaf). Use everyday kitchen objects as vases: a celery glass, soufflé dishes, glass jam jars, water jugs and carafes, earthenware kitchen jars, plain white china kitchen jugs, empty green glass bottles.

Don't bother with crumpled chicken wire to hold your flowers in place; either do without and let the flowers fall naturally where they will, or buy those crumbly green bricks of foam 'oasis' from a florist, then cut a chunk to fit.

When arranging the flowers, make sure you have plenty of counter space, a chopping board, a sharp pair of secateurs, a heavy hammer for bashing thick stalks, scissors for soft stalks and a water jug with a good long spout for adding water to the container after you've arranged the flowers in it.

A quick way to cut flowers to the length that looks all right in the container: put the container on the table, hold the bunch of flowers against it, *in front of the table* and raise or lower them until the proportion looks right. Then snip the stems to the required length. Don't be afraid to cut down long stems drastically (the shorter the stem, the longer the flower will last) and try breaking up sprays into single flowers.

To preserve cut flowers in water

For daffodils, other bulb flowers and **thin stems**, cut 2.5 cm (1 in) off stem, cutting at an angle.

For **hard-stemmed** flowers, such as chrysanthemums, bash bottom 10 cm (4 in) of stems, or they can't absorb water.

For **very hard stems**, such as lilac or rose, strip off any thorns from stem. Split or crush end of stem with a hammer or heavy rolling pin. Snip up the centre of stem for 5 cm (2 in). Plunge to neck in cold water.

If leaves are left on the flower stems below the water-line, your glorious creation will soon stink unappealingly of stagnant weedy water.

Keep the water pure by adding a drop of bleach, a teaspoon of salt or an aspirin. Make the flowers last longer by adding a pinch of PHOSTROGEN (fertilizer powder used in the garden).

Susan Pulbrook, who arranges the flowers at Buckingham Palace, says don't bother to change the water, but *top it up* with fresh water, daily if you can.

Don't stand flowers in a draught or near a radiator or they will open very fast and your creation will start getting overblown before you've had a good look at it.

To revive a wilting flower arrangement, re-cut ends of stems and stand in 2.5 cm (1 in) of just boiled water for a few seconds, then give the flowers a long drink, up to the neck, in cold water for two hours.

Incidentally, Interflora strongly suggest that when you ask your florist to send flowers to someone you specify the number and colour (say, 'one dozen white short-stemmed roses') and mention anything you don't want included – for example, 'no gladioli'.

HOW TO BE A HOUSE-MAID

I can't claim to be a comprehensive cleaner. I would no more want to read a comprehensive domestic encyclopaedia than I would want to write it. For thoroughness and idiosyncratic problems with a faint aura of mothballs I recommend *Modern Domestic Encyclopaedia* by Dorothy V. Davis, published by Faber and Faber in 1970. Just to pick at random from the index, it covers such useful specialist cleaning areas as hamster urine stains; elastic corsets (shouldn't go for two weeks without washing, she advises); knickers, weighty; panama hats; piano, ivory keys to whiten; serge, to remove shine from; teddy bears; swansdown; suspender belts; and wedding dress, clean to store (never know when it might come in useful again).

I learned most of what follows from a parlourmaid called Louise, who had been in service after the First World War at Panshanger, one of the great Edwardian houses of England. A few of her tips were:

1 Work at a steady, rather fast pace. Time yourself to work up to it. A steady worker does the work in half the time.
2 When you have finished cleaning a room, stand in the doorway and look round it, slowly and critically from right to left, from top to bottom.
3 Always work from right to left around a room and from top to bottom.
4 Stick to your routine.
5 Organize your equipment before you start.
6 Put everything that you don't want to carry around with you all the time in a place that is easy to get at and where people won't fall over it, such as the hall. This includes a good quality sponge mop (cheap ones break), long-handled broom, dustpan and brush, an upholstery brush, real feather duster – like a French maid in a farce – vacuum cleaner and extension cord on roller (with a 15-m (50-ft) extension cord

you can vacuum all over the house without unplugging and replugging).

HOW TO SAVE TIME WHEN YOU'RE CLEANING

1 **A gardening apron** has lots of pockets. Alternatively, sew a strip of tough material around your apron and subdivide it into pockets. Turn yourself into a walking housemaid's basket: put as many small cleaning tools into the pockets as possible, in an orderly manner, so you can reach down for the Windolene without looking when you recall the mirror that needs cleaning.

Try decanting some of your cleaners into smaller plastic (labelled) bottles. Carry a toothbrush (for cleaning round the taps and fiddly jobs), and razor blade for scraping off anything that you feel tempted to scrape with your fingernail.

2 As you clean, carry a bucket or basket containing all the things you will need and a screwtop jar to empty ashtrays into (then wipe them with a clean sponge). Keep the jar in your cleaning basket and empty it straight into the dustbin.

Alternatively, carry a plastic rubbish sack into which to tip cigarette butts, dead flowers and the rest of the debris.

3 Carry your tools in a bucket – a housemaid's bucket with subdivisions or an ordinary bucket that contains: 2 scrub pads with a sponge on one side, a dry sponge, dustpan and brush, oven cleaner, heavy-duty cleaner such as Liquid Ajax for baths and sinks, powdered cleaner such as Vim, Windolene (or my home-made cleaner, see p. 15) for windows and mirrors, ammonia, furniture polish, floor cleaner, floor polish, carpet cleaner, several cleaning cloths (old cotton nappies or a cut-up T-shirt?), J cloths and traditional yellow dusters.

4 **Use the feather duster for** cobwebs, ceiling mouldings, light fixtures, mirrors, picture frames (including tops), blinds, window frames, table lamps and light bulbs, door handles, table surfaces, ornaments, books, furniture (especially the legs), plants, telephones, radiators, electronic equipment, skirting boards.

Use your feather duster slowly and use it to *wipe*. Don't shake it or you'll shake the dust in the air and it will fall back on the furniture. Don't dust around the fire (this work is for a small brush) or you'll ruin your feather duster.

5 Always have a spare drive belt for the vacuum cleaner.

CLEANING A ROOM

Basic routine

Close all doors and windows. Deal with fireplace if necessary (see p. 20). Use real feather duster for doorknobs, door surrounds, overhead lights, lamps, light switches, bookshelves, plants, curtain rods, blinds, electrical equipment. Brush upholstery. Use toothbrush on upholstery piping. Check overhead and side lights, telephones, heating apparatus, drawer tops and knobs.

Dust with soft cloth folded into a pad so that there are no loose corners to catch. Carry damp spongecloth in left hand to remove dirty or sticky marks. Dust from top downwards (highest surface first), *before* you sweep or vacuum, then use a feather duster for tops of bookshelves or picture rail.

Wash paintwork if necessary. You are supposed to wash paintwork from the bottom up, but I've never understood why and, gravity being what it is, I've always done it the other way. Use two pails, one for warm water with detergent and a spongecloth, one for rinsing with a bit of old towelling. Don't fill either pail more than half-way. It may be too heavy and the water may slosh over. No matter where you're cleaning, do the floor last. Vacuum, swab or sweep it. Finally, check that all the pictures hang straight.

Vacuum floors from right to left. Keep one hand free to move objects out of your way and don't replace them. Always vacuum *away* from where you're standing. Vacuum stairs, starting at the top. Stand on one end of a rug, so it doesn't slip when you vacuum it. Finally, replace the items you moved.

Rinse out cleaning cloths after use and hang to dry. Don't leave damp cloths in a cupboard or they will smell sinister.

Hang brushes up *on hooks*. Never stand a brush on its bristles or the bristles will turn sideways. When brushes are dirty, wash in warm water with detergent and rinse thoroughly in clear, warm water, then cold water.

The fireplace

Rake out ash (unless it's a wood fire, in which case leave it to build up a good base for your fire through the winter), and remove anything solid with tongs. Brush soot from grate, remove ash pan, put in old newspaper and carry to dustbin. Sweep hearth and wipe with spongecloth.

To light a fire (or lay it ready for lighting) You need matches, newspaper, twigs, old wooden boxes or cardboard, logs or coal or smokeless fuel. In a smokeless zone you must use a smokeless fire lighter. The method I was taught came from a Girl Guide, who insisted that fire lighters are smelly and not always to hand.

Put *loosely* screwed up newspaper balls on top of the cinders. Lay a lattice of kindling on top and around the sides. Pile on wood or coal, keeping it firmly balanced so it won't topple out of the grate. Light paper at bottom in several places so that it burns evenly. The trick is to get lots of air into the paper and kindling. Never leave a fire when it is starting.

Warning! Always use a fireguard in front of a fire, whether coal, electric, gas or oil stove. After visiting a children's burns ward I wouldn't have an open bar electric fire or oil stove in my home.

WINDOWS AND WALLS

To clean windows Take down or draw back the curtains. Clean frames first: dust them, then wipe clean with warm water and Flash. Wipe with clean water and dry.

If window glass is very dirty, use a little warm water and 1 tablespoon methylated spirits, plus a sponge, finishing off with a dry chamois leather. If not very dirty, use Windowlene, which also cleans mirrors and picture glass. Better still, make your own! Try Old Mother Conran's amazing window cleaner (for recipe, see p. 15).

For luxury window cleaning there's an instrument with an adjustable handle that lengthens your reach by 60 cm (2 ft). It has a hinged sponge head that adjusts to clean all sizes of window.

Curtains Dirty curtains will rot, so remove hooks, release gathers. Soak overnight in the bath in lukewarm water and detergent. Let water out and refill bath with cold water to rinse. Let water out again, gently squeeze surplus water out, then, if necessary, wash in the correct way for the fabric.

If you allow room enough to run a rod through the bottom of your hems, net curtains will hang straight, drip dry and possibly not need ironing.

Curtains that are interlined should be taken to a dry cleaner.

Blinds To clean venetian blinds *wear gloves*, rubber or otherwise, as you can hurt your hands, especially with metal blinds. Clean with warm soapy water and sponge. Dust holland blinds. Wipe specially treated blinds with detergent and water.

Don't send delicate blinds to the laundry. My coffee-coloured lace ones were wrecked by London's most expensive hand laundry. You'll do better washing them gently by hand yourself in lukewarm water. (That's all *they* do.) Rinse clean.

Wallpaper Goddard's Dry Clean, which is an aerosol powder, works wonders on greasy marks. If that doesn't work, rub the stain with white bread or a soft india rubber. It's possible to cover a badly stained part with a patch of the pattern torn (not cut) to fit and pasted over, but the wallpaper may have faded so the new patch may not exactly match. In fact, this is undoubtedly what will happen.

FLOORS

Tiles and sheets

Ceramic tiles, terrazzo or marble Sweep. If necessary wash by hand or mop, using hot water and synthetic detergent such as Surf.

Remove stubborn marks on quarry tiles and terrazzo with fine scouring powder (such as Vim) or fine steel wool.

Use Cardinal liquid polish for unglazed tiles, brickwork and cement.

Linoleum Wash with Flash and very hot water and don't leave it soaking wet, as it will crack. Dry with mop or cloth.

Cork Sweep, vacuum or damp mop. Occasionally mop with warm water and Flash. If it has been sealed, don't polish it. Otherwise use a non-slip wax polish, using a little polish and a lot of buffing. If sealed, it can be resealed as required. A tough abrasive will rub off the costly sealed layer, so don't use one.

Remove a yellowing build-up of old wax polish with a lot of elbow grease, fine steel wool and white spirit, or Liquid Ajax with ammonia. Leave fifteen minutes. Rinse, dry and rewax. Alternatively, it can be sanded by machine (for nearest sanding firm look in your *Yellow Pages*).

Rubber, thermoplastic or vinyl Sweep, vacuum or mop. Avoid rubber solvents (such as dry-cleaning fluid) and coarse abrasives. Use warm water for washing, and polish with wax or plastic emulsion polish. For special cleaning use scrubbing brush or mop with hot water and detergent. Carefully remove stubborn stains with steel wool and scouring powder, then repolish. Remove a build-up of wax polish on vinyl as for cork.

Wood

Wood (pine, deal or parquet) Sweep, mop or vacuum. Wash with as little warm water as possible, with detergent. If *oiled*, sweep or use an oil-impregnated mop when required. If *wax-polished*, remove build-up of wax as for cork. If *sealed*, you can sweep or damp-mop with water and detergent. Reseal as required. Allow about two years for heavy wear, as in a kitchen, longer in a sitting-room. Can be sanded by machine.

White wood Scrub, using hot water and detergent. Rinse with cold water, then polish when dry.

Carpets and rugs

Fitted carpet Use a good underlay. Don't use rubber underlay for a seamed carpet because it drags the seaming. Don't use it where you have underfloor electric heating.

Vacuum regularly. Use the little vacuum cleaner attachment on the edges of the carpet or they will get exceedingly grubby. You're not supposed to vacuum or carpet-sweep a new carpet for two weeks in order to allow the loose fibres to bed down: brush it gently, if you feel you must.

Expect a static problem (as in a mild electric shock) from newly laid carpet; it may take up to six months to stop.

To wash a carpet Test trial patch with shampoo. Move furniture, then:

1 Vacuum carpet.
2 Use proper carpet shampoo, with a hired proper carpet shampooer, which stops the carpet getting too wet.
3 Start at wall farthest from the door and don't replace furniture until dry.

For bad stains call a professional carpet cleaner; I've seen them work wonders.

Here's how to make *your own carpet shampoo*. (This tip was given me by a famous carpet manufacturer.) Put a generous amount of lathering detergent into a bowl with warm water. Add 1 dessertspoonful of ammonia and stir it up to get as much froth as possible. Spread *only* the froth over the whole carpet. Leave to dry, then vacuum. Any marks *still* showing after this can be treated with a dry-cleaning fluid.

Carpet stains Remove normal stains fast with mild detergent, such as 1001, rinse well, then dry by hitting carpet with your fist wrapped in a towel. For oil, paint, polish or tar, soften stain with a little eucalyptus oil, then try a cleaning solvent such as Beaucaire. Start at the outside edge of stain and work inwards. If stain doesn't shift, try Liquid Ajax or the following carpet stain solution, which can be used for alcohol, coffee, tea, wine, food, soot, ink and fruit stains.

Carpet stain cleaner Add 1 teaspoonful white vinegar to 560 ml (1 pt) of water with carpet shampoo added according to instructions on pack. Lather with sponge. Rub gently until stain has gone. Rub gently with clear water.

For owners of unhouse-trained puppies or babies who are still at the stage of being amiably sick over your shoulder, there is one thing that will get rid of that rancid smell: soda water. If you take your whisky neat during this stage and don't have any soda water, just dip your handkerchief in Alka Seltzer solution or bicarbonate of soda and rub it on the spot.

To repair fitted carpet Cut a square of damaged carpet and remove it. The golden rule is always to work from the back. Cut a square from the 45 cm ($\frac{1}{2}$ yd) of extra carpet that you thoughtfully ordered when you bought it. Cut a square of hessian 2.5 cm (1 in) larger all round than the carpet square. With Copydex, stick the new carpet centrally on the hessian square and leave to dry for five minutes. Now cover the surrounding hessian with Copydex, lift the fitted carpet square with a finger or a knife blade and slide it into place. Then put a newspaper on top and sit on it for five minutes. The patch may look newer than the rest of the carpet, because, of course, it is. You could try rubbing a little dirt around to blur the joins.

Old, valuable carpets Antique shops don't shampoo them; they hang them over a line and beat them. (Sorry about that.) Seriously, if you have an expensive rug, don't risk washing it yourself. Send it to real experts (look in the *Yellow Pages*), who will wash it with Johnson's baby soap and rinse it in gallons of specially purified water, then put it on a special rack to dry.

Cleaning long-haired rugs Hand-wash in lukewarm water using a mild detergent. Rinse thoroughly with a fabric softener and allow to dry naturally (it will take ages). Brush pile gently.

How then do you clean a fur rug such as white sheep or goat skin? Don't immerse in water; just sponge the surface, a small area at a time, with a rich soap-flake lather. Rinse and dry each section before going on.

FURNITURE

Wood

If you put antique or modern wooden furniture too near any heat source, it may crack or shrivel. This often occurs after installing central heating unless humidifiers or bowls of water (with flowers in them, perhaps) are placed in the room. In a centrally heated home always stand a jug of water by a bowl of flowers. Then you can dash forward and top it up as necessary.

If you put wooden furniture in a damp atmosphere (such as a bathroom), it may swell. Drawers might therefore be difficult to pull open. Rub soap or candlewax on the runners of the drawers that stick.

Dust wooden furniture and occasionally wipe clean with a damp chamois leather followed by a dry duster. To remove stickiness or fingermarks use a damp chamois cloth or a cloth wrung out in warm water and detergent.

If you buy **a really dirty antique** that has a build-up of dirt, clean it by dusting, then rub with a hot damp cloth wrung out in soapy hot water. Rinse thoroughly and immediately pat until it's dry. Make sure it's really dry – leave at least a week – before putting on any protective polish, if necessary.

DON'T put polish on a damp surface or white patches will appear.

Wood is very absorbent and must be treated with a finish that protects it from moisture, grease and dirt. These protective finishes determine the final texture of the wood – whether it has a high gloss, a dull gloss or a matt look.

Much modern furniture is not solid, but uses a sandwich of wood veneer on plywood or blockboard (which is built-up strips of wood). Plywood is particularly useful for curves and blockboard is unlikely to warp.

For mass-produced wood finishes, apart from satin, matt, oiled or french-polished surfaces, occasionally rub with a soft cloth and a cream or liquid polish.

Don't polish a **satin** or **matt** finish or it may become glossy.

Wax-polished furniture is treated with beeswax made into a stiff paste with turpentine and rubbed well into the wood.

You can use a standard wax furniture polish instead.

An **oil finish** is good for an open-grained finish on oak, teak and other hardwoods. It is generally achieved with linseed oil and turpentine rubbed into wood.

If you want to keep the same appearance, you should continue to dust, then rub with an oily rag. Alternatively, use a good quality teak oil such as Johnson's teak cream. Don't use much. Try not to use any other oil, as it goes horribly sticky.

If a **permanent seal** finish has been applied, then don't waste your time polishing it. You know if it's got a permanent seal because it will never *look* as though it needs polishing. Continue to ignore it, polishwise, especially if it has been **french polished**. Layers of shellac dissolved in spirit have been built up and rubbed down to that gleaming finish. If your furniture has a permanent finish (whether french polish or polyurethane varnish), then you only need to dust it.

To remove polish from furniture use a solution of 1 tablespoon vinegar to 560 ml (1 pt) warm water. Dry and re-polish.

How do you clean the **brass inlay on a polished antique** when you don't want to use some vicious modern brass cleaner for fear of what it might do to the surrounding wood? Use a neutral shoe cream, such as Meltonian.

Painted furniture can be washed with detergent and warm water.

DOWN WITH SUPERWOMAN!

Non-wooden furniture

Perspex and acrylic Clean with spray-on Windolene.

Plastics Can be washed with warm water and detergent. Don't rub dry, because this increases static, which collects dust. Remove stains by rubbing with a damp cloth dipped in bicarbonate of soda.

Slate Clean with warm water and detergent. When dry, rub with a rag moistened in cooking oil, then rub off with a dry cloth.

Marble Clean immediately. Can stain because it's porous, so wash quickly after putting coffee cups and wine glasses on table-tops and mantelpieces. Clean with soapy water; whiten by rubbing with a lemon. Treat light stains left by glasses with 2 teaspoons of borax in 250 ml ($\frac{1}{2}$ pt) of water. Dry and polish. Clean with Bell's 1967 Cleaner (1). Polish with Bell's Marble Polish (2). For stained marble use Rustic Marble Cleaner, but this will dull the polished surface, which can only be restored by expert polishing. All from A. Bell and Co., Kingsthorpe Works, Northampton (tel: 0604-714808).

Wickerwork and cane Wash in hot water and detergent (in the bath is a good place) and rinse three times more than you thought necessary, otherwise the cane will quickly split.

Upholstery

Leather Clean with a soft cloth dipped in warm soapsuds, followed by a soft cloth wrung out in clear water, then dry with a soft cloth. Leather is skin and needs polishing with furniture cream to keep it supple and prevent cracks. Or use saddle soap.

Suede This is a very difficult fabric to clean and I would never try. In fact, much as I love it, I would never buy suede. Take to a specialist dry cleaner.

You can try to remove greasemarks with a dry-cleaning solvent, then restore the nap by brushing with a special suede brush.

Imitation leather or plastic Use a car upholstery cleaner such as Groom or Valet from Halfords. Don't use abrasive cleaners on any plastics, as they may scratch. Reinforced plastics can be repaired with car body repair kits, then repainted with polyurethane paint.

Fabric-covered upholstery Clean by taking out the cushions and vacuuming or brushing out the corners. Shampoo periodically with a carpet or upholstery shampoo or a detergent with warm water and gentle scrubbing brush, working on one area at a time and being careful to overlap each area with the next. Avoid using too much water.

Loose covers Dry clean if possible, as they are less likely to shrink. Otherwise wash in lukewarm water. Make sure washing powder has dissolved before putting in fabric. Treat gently. Squeeze or spin damp-dry. Don't twist or wring. Iron, on wrong side if possible, while still damp and immediately replace on chair while the seams are still slightly damp; they will then stretch out. (I never bother to iron.)

Furniture stains removal

Ink stains Rub with finest dry steel wool or with a cloth wrapped round your finger and dampened with methylated spirit. If the stain persists, dab it with a weak solution of oxalic acid. This will remove both colour and polish, so rub in linseed oil to darken the patch, leave it to soak in, then after a day or so, give it a coat of polish and buff well. It's best to try this out first on a bit of the wood that doesn't show.

Rust stains Remove with a proprietary remover such as Moval from Boots.

White rings and heat marks on a french-polished surface Try a very little methylated spirit rubbed on with a soft cloth. Repolish with brown shoe polish while the surface is still soft.

Cigarette burns Rub down with fine steel wool. Then rub in linseed oil and proceed as for ink stains (above).

Wine or spirit marks You can rarely remove these if they have been left on a table too long.

Candlewax Scrape off as much as possible with a blunt knife. If the grease is on the carpet or upholstery, cover it with tissue or blotting paper and hold a hot iron just clear of the paper, so that it warms the wax, which you blot, using a fresh bit of tissue each time. If it is on fabric, place between two bits of blotting paper and iron. Then clean with dry-cleaning fluid. Work from middle of stain to edge.

Grease marks on sofa backs and arms or bedheads Rub gently with cloth and dry-cleaning fluid. Work from outer edge of stain inwards. Then (if necessary), repeat with chamois leather wrung out in a solution of warm water and a liquid detergent. Rinse well.

To remove scratches White shoe polish or white typing fluid can hide scratches on white woodwork. For dark scratches, try touching up with iodine or shoe polish. Try to eliminate bad marks by rubbing down gently with finest steel wool, then resurfacing. Alternatively, try darkening with iodine or olive oil on the end of a cotton bud. A much scratched item can be professionally sanded and resealed, and this will be expensive.

To destroy woodworm You can either buy a special insecticide and apply it or holler for help from an expert, such as Rentokil. I wouldn't take any chances here, as woodworm spreads very fast to other furniture, window frames, floorboards, beams, etc. Never import any bit of furniture into your home without checking it for those sinister tiny holes with tiny beige piles of wood dust beneath.

LIGHT FITTINGS AND PICTURES

If possible, remove **electric fittings** to clean. Alternatively, get a steady stool or ladder if the fittings are at ceiling level. Wear rubber gloves. Turn off switch. Wipe bulb. (You can lose 25 per cent of your light with a grimy bulb.) Dust with a feather duster, especially paper shades. Try to remove dirt marks with an india rubber or a just-damp cloth. Wash acrylic shades with warm soapy water (I wash them in the bath). Let them drain on a towel; don't rub them or you will increase static, which attracts dirt. (It's worth telling you this twice.)

Clean **glass and frames of pictures** with a chamois dampened with methylated spirit.

BEDROOMS

Cupboards and drawers Empty cupboards, wipe with spongecloth dipped in detergent and warm water, then wrung out. Don't get the wood too wet. When dry, line cupboards and drawers with paper to prevent bottoms getting dirty again; wallpaper or lining paper can look pretty. If you haven't much storage space, stack shoes on plastic racks piled on top of each other, as in a shop; keep underwear and small articles in clear plastic bags; hang hooks inside doors and stretch elastic between two drawing pins to hold ties and belts. Visit John Lewis stores to check their numerous ingenious storage items for maximizing wardrobe space.

The best way to keep a wardrobe dry, and therefore mildew-free, is to fill a cloth bag with 350 g (12 oz) of diatomaceous earth granules (available for a few pence from a chemist). Hang it in the lower half of the wardrobe. When the bag is about double its original weight through absorption of moisture, empty the granules into an aluminium pan and bake in a 200 °C (400 °F/Mark 6) oven for an hour or so. Then refill the bag.

Mattresses Take the polythene wrappings off mattresses and pillows or they may eventually mildew. A flock, feather or hair mattress should be turned from end to end daily (thought I'd let you know). A spring interior needs turning only once a month.

Clean mattress stains with upholstery shampoo, then rinse and dab with a towel until damp dry. For urine stains, spot clean with a solution of ½ cup white vinegar and ½ cup cold water. Blot dry. Apply solution of ½ cup liquid detergent in lukewarm water. Leave 10 minutes. Blot dry, rinse with cool water. Buy cotton mattress covers, from John Lewis for example, if your mattress is clean but you can't get the stain off.

Sheets Mark the corner of each sheet 'S' for single, 'D' for double, 'K' for kingsize and so on. Although you can feel the difference in weight, one has days when one isn't certain of *anything* and they certainly aren't improved by unfolding and folding up clean sheets for half the morning.

Reasonably, the middle of a sheet is the part that somebody puts his foot through first, when it's wearing thin (the sheet that is). Try to anticipate this. When sheets are showing signs of wear but before they get too thin, cut them down the middle and join the two outside edges together with a flat seam, then hem the two new outside edges.

Mend holes in sheets by sewing a square patch on either side, considerably bigger than the hole.

Sheets can yellow through too-warm storage. Send them to the laundry with a note or wash using a mild powder bleach, not a strong household bleach, which might rot the fibres.

Blankets Before washing, soak really dirty blankets in the bath in cold water with added softener such as Calgon. Blankets can be turned sides to middle, like sheets, when they have become thin and worn. Another use of aged blankets is this old camper's trick: use three thin blankets underneath the bottom sheet and you will never need an electric underblanket.

Duvets Only those filled with synthetic fibre can be washed and you may need to go to a launderette for a machine large enough to cope. Don't send them to the laundry. Down and/or feather duvets can be cleaned by specialist firms. Avoid having to clean duvets by always using slip-covers that can be taken off and washed. (See also 'How to be a laundrymaid', problem corner, p. 53.)

Hair brushes Wash in warm water with detergent, but expensive wooden-backed teak, rosewood or ebony hair brushes shouldn't be *immersed* in water. Rinse in clear warm water then finally slosh in cold water to harden the bristles, and wave fiercely and quickly to flick the water out, before lying on their backs to dry, away from direct heat.

How to have lavender-scented sheets Get some lavender water (only a good quality one, such as Yardley). Put in a plastic bottle with a spray top (from your local Body Shop) and after making the bed, spray once, gently, over the turned back top sheet.

BATHROOM CLEAN-UP

With Liquid Ajax, scrub shower/bath/basin. Use toothbrush around taps. Rinse all immediately with shower spray. Scrub Liquid Ajax on tiles. Clean lavatory inside, then outside, with Liquid Ajax.

Moving right to left, spray mirrors, wipe top of medicine chest (which shouldn't be in the bathroom) with damp cloth, shine chrome with clean, dry cloth. Clean floor with vacuum (for carpet) or mop cleaner/polisher on tiles.

Allow 20 minutes minimum.

Owners of small children might find it worth keeping a brush, dustpan and waste-paper basket in, and exclusively for, the bathroom, so you can deal with those sweet papers, old lavatory rolls, empty bottles and toothpaste tubes.

Remove hair spray from mirrors with a cloth soaked in surgical spirit. Wipe mirrors with Windolene spray.

The bath I find a hand shower invaluable for bathing children, getting boys to wash themselves and rinsing hair, but *especially* for cleaning the bath.

More backs have been put out cleaning baths than in any other activity. If you have serious stain problems that just won't yield to elbow grease, these tips may help.

Don't use a fierce abrasive cleaner on the bath, because it may scratch the surface. Try Liquid Ajax or dry detergent powder. Never use lavatory cleaner in the bath, it's too harsh.

For general grime and dinge run a full hot bath and empty washing powder into it. Leave the foamy mess for at least six hours, then rinse out the bath with cold water.

For coppery green and tan stains, cut a lemon and smear the juice (citric acid) on the offending areas. Leave for a couple of minutes and wash off thoroughly.

Jenolite or Oz removes even lime stains as well as scum and rust.

Clean chrome bath taps with cloth and soapy water. Polish with a soft cloth. If stains persist, rub on dry bicarbonate of soda with a damp cloth. If that doesn't work, use Duraglit.

If your shower starts losing power, it may be because you're in a hard water area and a lime deposit is building up in the showerhead and blocking the water exits. Remove head, soak for ten minutes in vinegar and then rub off the deposit.

Wash showerhead in warm soapy water, then rinse, dry and replace.

The lavatory Keep your lavatory brush in water with a little disinfectant. You don't have to buy a smart holder. I keep mine in a stone marmalade jar. Wash the lavatory brush by holding it in the lavatory bowl, then flushing.

Clean the lavatory by lifting the seat and pouring down a bucket of hot water with bleach or detergent and a disinfectant such as Dettol. Scrub with the long-handled lavatory brush and swab outside of lavatory and seat with spongecloth. A dirty lavatory pan can be cleaned with shop-bought Harpic or chlorine bleach (never both, because together they produce chlorine gas vapour). Alternatively, for very bad stains on lavatory or bath, use RB70 from Selfridges or plumbers' merchants. As a last resort, wipe with 1 part spirits of salts to 5 parts water. *Wear rubber gloves*, as this can be dangerous. Rub stain quickly with a mop or brush dipped in spirits of salts, which can then be thrown away. Flush three times.

Dissipate unwelcome odours by opening a window. Avoid fresheners (un-Green).

Lavatories are meant for human waste and nothing else. Anything else – and that includes large wedges of toilet paper, newspaper, sanitary towels and tea leaves – is likely to block a lavatory. If your lavatory gets blocked, holler for a plumber (in *Yellow Pages*).

Similarly, exterior **drains** must be kept unblocked. Don't let leaves block them up. If they threaten to do so, get a wire cage (a bit like a bee-keeper's bonnet) fitted round the drain. Occasionally *flush it by pouring boiling water* with a handful of washing soda down it. If there seems to be something badly wrong or a smell that gets worse, or you see a rat (or smell one), telephone the local town hall and ask for quick help from the sanitation department.

DOWN WITH SUPERWOMAN!

KITCHEN CLEAN-UP

Put food away, tidy larder or food cupboards. Set mop inside kitchen door and put carry-all bucket on right of sink. With heavy duty squirt cleaner (such as Liquid Ajax), remove fingerprints from cupboards and working surfaces, clean fridge top and air vent, areas around cooker (use toothbrush as well). Clean windows, using Liquid Ajax if greasy. Clean sink with Liquid Ajax, use toothbrush round taps. Vacuum floor, then mop with mixture of ammonia and water or a cleaning polish.

Allow 40 minutes minimum.

Large appliances

To clean a gas or electric cooker Turn off electricity at mains or all gas pilots. Turn off taps or switches, remove any utensils. Half fill sink with hot water and detergent. Remove grill pan, burners, shelves and trays and put in sink to soak if there is room. Wipe enamelled parts with warm damp spongecloth. Use Liquid Gumption for stubborn dirt on cooker enamel (and sinks). You're not supposed to use a harsh abrasive or a caustic cleaner on enamel areas or the inside of an oven, but if you are faced with a filthy oven, buy a cleaner, such as Easy Off, or make your own (see p. 15). Otherwise clean oven with hot water and detergent. Scrub burners (if you have a gas cooker), grill pan, shelves or trays (if you have an electric cooker), rinse and dry, and then replace. Remember to light gas pilots and test, or turn on electricity at the mains.

To clean a solid-fuel cooker Wipe up spills immediately. Regularly brush out oven. Wipe enamel parts with damp cloth and rub dry, or use Liquid Gumption or a spray cleaner if really dirty.

Cleaning a grill pan Unable to find out how to clean the exterior of a really filthy oven and grill pan, I eventually telephoned the manufacturers. 'You shouldn't have let it get filthy,' they chided me severely. Apart from it being none of their business, it was an unhelpful answer, because I had just bought the filthy oven along with the filthy flat.

If the handle is plastic, remove it. (You may need a Phillips screwdriver. Remember, they hitched it on somehow; all you have to do is find out what they did and reverse it.) Now attack with Flash and Brillo pads and to hell with those gentle warm-water instructions.

Dishwasher Clean as you would a stainless steel sink, with hot water and dishwashing liquid. Do not put cast iron, pewter, bone-handled or other hollow-handled knives, anything gilded or antique or hand-painted in your dishwasher. *If in doubt, don't put it in.* As with birth control, crossing your fingers and hoping for the best might easily lead to disaster.

Refrigerator care A refrigerator won't do its job of keeping food fresh if you leave the door open or jam in so much food that the cold air can't circulate around it. If the cooling unit gets clogged up with ice, it can't do its job efficiently.

Don't leave a refrigerator shut if you turn off the gas or electricity when you go on holiday. The inside may be spotted with nasty green mould when you open it on your return and the rubber ice trays may have perished.

Always buy rubber ice trays, which allow you to take out one cube when you feel like it without holding the thing under a tap or hitting it on the bottom with a hammer.

Don't put food away in ceramic bowls (they may easily break) or brown paper bags (because you can't see what's in them). Wrap all food in polythene bags or keep in covered boxes or bowls, or wrap and cover with cling film; otherwise the kippers may impart their flavour to the raspberry mousse, which may in turn add an interesting *je ne sais quoi* to the

Camembert, which you shouldn't keep in the refrigerator anyway because it is a soft cheese.

If you haven't an automatic defrosting refrigerator, you should defrost the fridge once a fortnight. Turn off the refrigerator. Take all the food out and throw away anything from the back that is growing whiskers or looks too small to survive. Now take out the shelves and empty the ice tray. Wash the shelves and plastic boxes and bowls with warm water and a little bicarbonate of soda. You shouldn't use detergent, because it can leave a soapy smell if you don't rinse it off thoroughly.

Wait for the ice to melt. You can hurry this up by leaving the door open and putting a washing-up bowl of hot water in the middle of the refrigerator. You had better put a tray or folded towel or both on the bottom shelf, or melted ice will run all over the kitchen floor. Don't be tempted to dislodge the ice with a knife – you may pierce the shell of the refrigerator and you will then have to buy a new refrigerator.

Good tip: if you have an old-fashioned hair dryer with a hose attachment, plug the dryer into the nearest socket and put the hose end into the freezer.

Air-conditioner Wash or change the filter every month, or even more often. Reusable filters can be washed in soapy water, rinsed in clean water, then dried and replaced.

Sinks

Porcelain Sprinkle detergent, then add a few centimetres/inches of warm water and 4 tablespoons of chlorine bleach. Rub, leave ten minutes, rub again. Rinse well. For stubborn stains mix 2 tablespoons baking powder with enough hydrogen peroxide to make a paste. Apply with a rag. Leave overnight.

Stainless steel Clean the sink with hot water and washing-up liquid. Don't use a scourer on a metal sink or you may scratch it. If dull, wipe with vinegar on a sponge, then wipe dry. Clean the sink outlet by dissolving a handful of washing soda in warm water and pouring it down the sink and the outside drain. Alternatively, you can use household bleach. Do this once a month.

Anything, except water, is likely to block a sink (unless you have a fitted electrical waste disposal). That includes matchsticks, tea leaves and vegetable peelings. So use a plastic sink drainer and buy a sink plunger, which is a stick with a black rubber hollow breast shape on the end of it.

If the sink blocks, turn to 'How to unblock a sink', p. 174.

The kitchen floor

Brush, mop or wash. By all means have a sponge mop, but when operating it from standing height, you will not be able to see clearly how dirty the kitchen floor is. (Perhaps that's what you want?) Again, disregard the magic ads on TV. So what do you do? Scrub it when it's dirty like your mother did, but now with Flash, which is the eighth wonder of my world. (See also 'Floors', p. 81.)

Larder and food cupboard care

Don't put away jars or tins with drips on them. Clean floors and shelves with warm, damp spongecloth. Fold packet tops over *before* putting away and regularly wipe out bread, cake and biscuit tins.

Small electric equipment

Never put electrical equipment in water and always unplug it before cleaning.

Toaster Hold it upside down and gently shake out any crumbs. Use a baby's brush to clean difficult-to-reach areas. Swab gently with a sponge and detergent, then rinse. Soak stains over-

DOWN WITH SUPERWOMAN!

night with a runny paste made of warm water and a presoak, such as Bio-tex.

Food mixer Fill it two-thirds full with hot soapy water, put the lid on, and switch it on for thirty seconds. Then rinse out under the tap.

Electric fan Wipe the blades, base and grill with a damp cloth. Then wipe with a cloth wrung out in soapy water and, finally, with a cloth wrung out in clean water. Towel dry.

Pans and dishes

If you are left with a nasty burnt mess in your saucepans, try soaking them overnight in lukewarm water and 1 tablespoon of detergent. Before using a pan for the first time, wash with spongecloth and warm soapy water, or whatever you cook first may taste rather odd. Don't put pans straight on to a high heat. Don't leave empty pans on burners or in the oven.

Non-stick pans (Green purists don't use them.) Don't use abrasives and scourers or you may remove the non-stick surface. Don't use metal implements such as spoons; use wood or plastic ones. Don't store non-stick pans in each other or they may scratch. When using for the first time, put 3 tablespoons oil in the pan and gently warm it on the cooker for a minute, then wash normally.

If Teflon pans discolour, try mixing 2 tablespoons baking soda, ¼ cup of household bleach and 1 cup water. Boil solution in the stained pan for five minutes. Wash, rinse and dry. Wipe with oil before using.

Aluminium pans (Green purists prefer to use stainless steel.) Don't scrape with a metal spoon, as it scratches the surface. Don't use washing soda, which is bad for aluminium. Don't use a harsh scouring pad. If you shove a hot aluminium frying pan into water, it will hiss and perhaps buckle, so cool it first. If food has been burnt or fish cooked in it,

boil up a little water with washing-up liquid in it *before* you take it off the stove. If the insides of aluminium pans discolour, boil up some water in them with a squeezed lemon or some rhubarb.

Stainless steel pans (such as Prestige) and enamelware Don't use abrasives or harsh scouring pads. Use hot water and detergent to clean. If the inside discolours, fill with hot water and 2 tablespoons bleach and leave overnight, then wash thoroughly.

To clean **stainless steel cutlery**, put neat bleach in a bowl and dunk cutlery for about an hour or longer. Then rinse. They will sparkle like new.

Cast-iron cookware If vitreous-lined, use *only hot water and detergent*. If not vitreous-lined, clean as quickly as possible after using with warm water and detergent. Dry, then rub with oil on a paper towel to discourage rusting.

Clean rusting cast iron by drying it thoroughly and rubbing an oiled rag over it. If your cast iron is really rusty, scour thoroughly with fine steel wool, then wash with dishwashing liquid and hot water. Dry thoroughly by popping into the oven for a minute. Oil thoroughly with a rag. Then bake (empty) on lowest possible oven temperature for an hour. On no account use this method to treat cast-iron pots that have enamelled interiors.

Copper pans Should be lined with silver, nickel or tin. Unlined copper develops poisonous verdigris, so reline when necessary and use wooden spoons for stirring. Antique shops can often quote for relining copper pans.

Clean copper with half a lemon dipped in salt and vinegar and rubbed on. Alternatively, use Goddard's Long Term Brass and Copper Polish. You don't end up with a smelly rag to throw away if you use Duraglit wadding metal polish (it also cleans pewter).

Rub corrosion spots with salt and vinegar or a lemon rind dipped in salt, then wash. Treat bad marks with fine steel wool and liquid polish.

Ovenproof dishes Not necessarily *flameproof*, so don't use on top of the cooker unless you are certain. (I lost a wonderful Worcester fish dish that way.) Play safe and always use a metal heat-diffuser mat on an electric hob, but on no account do this on a naked gas flame because the cooker enamel could be damaged.

Always check whether your dishes are ovenproof. Unless they are stamped 'ovenproof', assume they are *not*, however ovenish they look.

Don't put anything plastic or with plastic handles in the oven or it will probably start melting.

Hot dishes and plates straight from the oven can mark wood, plastic, table-cloths and painted surfaces. Don't *ever* risk it. (Plastics aren't magic and can scratch, burn and chip.) Buy cheap, natural cork table-mats.

Pyrosil ware Not non-stick, but you can freeze dishes in it and then take it straight from a freezer to a hot oven and the dish won't crack – that's why they make rocket nose cones with the stuff. There's a hook-on handle, which enables you to use dishes as saucepans.

Cleaning ornaments and utensils

Brass and bronze If it's lacquered, it doesn't need cleaning, only dusting. If it isn't lacquered and not for cooking, why not lacquer it with brass lacquer? Ask in a hardware shop for cellulose clear lacquer. It dries very fast – in about ten minutes – and hardens in an hour.

If the brass is for cooking, treat as copper pans. Clean with Brasso or Antiquax Copper and Brass Polish.

Pewter For heavy stains on ordinary pewter (not antiques), try cleaning with a brass polish, such as Brasso or Bluebell. Don't use silver polish. For general cleaning, polish with whiting and a little household ammonia, but don't do this more than a couple of times a year.

Silver Goddard's Long Term is an excellent fast silver cleaner. Alternatively, make your own (see p. 15).

If possible, keep a silver bag, which postpones tarnish and means that silver is stored in the minimum space. Smart stores like Harrods sell these yard-long baize bags with divisions for each different implement. You might make your own.

Never let bleach get near silver; the result is a disastrous stain impossible to remove.

Brides have been known to burst into tears as yet another wedding gift, thinly silver-plated sauceboat turns irrevocably, uncleanably black before the first anniversary. Having had the same trouble myself, I won't bother you with pages of tedious chemical reasoning. Eventually, after rubbing my sauceboat with all sorts of never-fail quick-clean preparations, I had it replated.

If you wish your sauceboat to gleam when its donor comes to dinner, then you should always wash the relevant item as soon as possible after the meal. *Never* leave sauce in a sauceboat; no gravy; no mayonnaise; no vinaigrette. Similarly, never leave sauces in any other silver container, such as a bowl, or on spoons. I lost a lovely rat-tail teaspoon through leaving it in a jar of chutney: the silver was eaten away.

Get egg tarnish off silver by using Goddard's Silver Dip for quick results. For general cleaning, however, try Goddard's Long Term silver polish.

To clean a silver teapot, fill it with boiling water and add 1 teaspoonful denture cleaner. Leave overnight and rinse well.

Cutlery Vinegar, lemon juice, egg and salt can mark silver cutlery, so wash as fast as possible.

Keep a bag of alum of camphor in the drawer to dissuade silver cutlery from going black.

DOWN WITH SUPERWOMAN!

Keep **knives** in a drawer or jar by themselves and you are less likely to cut yourself or scratch other implements. Don't leave ivory or plastic-handled knives in hot water or put them in the dishwasher. Carbon steel knives should be wiped clean after use and rubbed with cooking oil before putting away. Remove stains with emery paper. Sharpen on carborundum stone.

Don't use Silver Dip on stainless steel because it pits it. Instead, put bleach in a bowl and dunk cutlery for an hour or longer if necessary. It will sparkle like new.

Don't use abrasive powders on **trays** with a printed pattern (especially tin trays) or you risk scratching the pattern off. Use warm water and washing-up liquid.

China and glass Don't pile things in a cupboard unless they are designed to stack. China is at risk if stored too high, too low or too far back in a cupboard. Things that are difficult to reach are more likely to get broken.

Remove tea stains from china with a damp cloth dipped in bicarbonate of soda, borax or bleach solution.

Butlers clean **glass decanters** and narrow-necked glass vases by swilling them round with brandy and lead shot. *You* can soak them overnight in detergent and warm water. Best to avoid stains by rinsing out the decanter as soon as possible after use.

Wash glass and crystal with soapy water. Then rinse again in a bowl containing 1 cup vinegar to 6 cups water. Air dry, don't rub.

Natural materials are not static. They expand with heat and contract with cold and damp according to the way they are treated. If you hold a glass under the hot tap, it may crack. If you pour hot water into a glass, put a metal spoon in first to absorb the heat.

Wooden bowls, plates, chopping boards and worktops Don't leave in too warm a place. Don't dry near direct heat, as they may split. Don't use abrasive powders or steel wool. Don't leave damp. Never leave to soak or the wood will quickly split. Dry immediately. When dry, rub lightly with oil on a paper towel.

If a **salad bowl** gets smelly, wash quickly in warm, soapy water, rinse thoroughly and dry immediately. Don't put it in the dishwasher. Scrub chopping boards with dishwashing liquid and hot water and dry immediately.

Natural, untreated wood surfaces To clean your table or chopping block, wipe with a cloth sprinkled with dishwashing liquid. *Rinse well, repeatedly*. With a cloth, apply a half-and-half solution of chlorine bleach and water. *Rinse well, repeatedly*. If there are knife cuts or other marks, rub down the surface with steel wool or sandpaper (first use a heavy grade, finishing with a light one), then rub with a rag dipped in mineral oil and wipe dry.

How to wash-up

Note: When using a dishwasher, never put in antique or precious glass, hand-painted or valuable china or bone-handled knives or wood or plastic anything. (It's worth telling you this twice.)

Read the instruction book *before* using the dishwasher for the first time.

Wash-up without a dishwasher and save energy

With two sinks, or a sink and a rinsing bowl, and two washing-up racks, you rarely need to dry, although you might need to polish glass and cutlery.

If you are right-handed and planning a kitchen from scratch, remember that you will wash-up from right to left, so plan to have the draining surface on the left.

Breakages happen if too many things are crowded into the bowl or piled up to drain. If there's only one drainer and not much space round the sink, use a nearby table or pull up a trolley behind you (or to one side) upon which to stack the dishes: glasses and cutlery, plates and cups on top, serving dishes on lower shelf and cooking pots beneath. As you clear one surface into the sink, use it for draining. Spread a towel on any drying surface that doesn't drain into the sink, or the china won't drain dry.

If you say, 'But trolleys are the sort of thing my *grandmother* had,' I would say, 'If you can get hers, grab it fast.' Use it as a push-around, extra work and storage space. I use one when I'm writing books, in the office, painting (pictures), cooking in tiny areas with little storage space, sewing and sometimes when doing a repair job.

Washing-up starts with *proper stacking*. Some would-be helpers (often male) tend to pile things into a sink, higgledy-piggledy, run warm water on them and then leave them. These people probably never have to reach into the greasy cold water to remove the dishes in order to put in hot water to start actually doing the washing-up. These people also tend to ignore the goo on the undersides of plates and they think that saucepans, baking tins and vegetable dishes don't count or get done by leprechauns . . .

Empty coffee grounds or tea leaves. Scrape bits off plates and stack crockery and utensils according to size and greasiness.

Put cutlery and table silver to soak in a jug or saucepan of hot water and detergent. Keep bone or wooden handles out of water.

Wash articles in this order: glass, silver, cutlery, non-greasy china, non-greasy serving pans, greasy china, greasy serving pans, cooking pans.

Wash glass in warm water and detergent and rinse in clear warm water. Use a soft nail-brush or old toothbrush for cut glass.

Keep party china or rarely used china

in plastic bags, so that you don't have to wash it again before using it.

Clean sink outlet. Wipe cooker top and grill pan, drainer, sink. Rinse dishcloth and spread to dry.

For the cheapest possible washing-up liquid buy a 5-litre (1-gal) can of Teepol concentrate and decant it into a bottle or squirt container. If you want to make it 'kind to your hands', dilute it with water.

Getting rid of the rubbish

An electric waste disposal unit in the sink eliminates the sludgy, smelly stuff. Get the sort that unclogs itself when you push a button, otherwise you may have to call a mechanic every time it clogs itself up. Whatever brand you use and however careful you are, you will need four times as many teaspoons as you had before: it seems to trap them, like an insect-eating orchid.

I love a Trashmasher **electric rubbish compactor**. It is invaluable if you live in the country and have to get rid of your own rubbish, although the sacks are expensive. Depending on what you dump in it, it can reduce eight sacks of rubbish to one sack; it's quiet (except when crushing bottles – if you can't get to a bottle bank) and will eat almost anything. Hide the key so that the baby can't compact whatever it cares to throw in. From Harrods.

Pedal bins drive me scatty because they generally have inadequate base balance, and so are unsteady and tip drunkenly towards me every time I tread on the pedal. And they don't take enough of my rubbish. Swing-top bins are just as irritating. I keep knocking the lid off, get my hand caught in the flap or, getting the timing wrong, leave more food smeared on the lid than in the bin. **Use a waist-high bin with disposable plastic sacks.**

Metal **dustbins** make a noise and get

bent; plastic ones get split: hence my choice of kitchen bins. Paint your name on them (use emulsion paint) if you don't want them pinched. I wash mine in the bath with warm water and detergent and a stiff brush, rinse with clear water and disinfectant, and then tip them upside down to dry, still in the bath.

Keep a pack of plastic dustbin liners in your kitchen paper drawer for those moments when all your dustbins are full and you need a sack for further rubbish. Or use them instead of dustbins, if animals can't get at them.

GETTING RID OF NASTY SMELLS

How do you get rid of a persistent nasty smell, such as in a bedsitter that seems to have housed a dozen cats? It's amazing to think that our ancestors dealt with this problem before anyone thought of disguising the odour with synthetic daffodil spray. They used to open windows and doors to create a draught, and you can continue the tradition. To help the smell on its way squirt *eau de toilette* into the air, burn incense, perfumes from Floris and Mary Chess or scented candles.

Avoid those nasty cut-out circles in windows, which are expensively let into the glass and create draughts, by installing an electric ventilating fan in your bathroom or kitchen (get a strong one).

How to get rid of common household odours

Cat or dog Air the place. Open all doors and windows. Turn on all fans. If the animals are still resident, bathe them. Then wash whatever rugs they lie on and swab all upholstered surfaces with a cloth wrung out in warm, soapy water. Dry with a clean cloth. Train your animal to sleep in its own place (basket and/or rug). Wash this *at least* once a week. Change

the cat litter box daily and sprinkle 1 tablespoon of baking soda on the bottom of the box before adding new litter.

Cooking and tobacco To rid clothes of these odours, hang them in the open air for several hours. To get rid of **general cooking smells**, boil a few cloves in a cup of vinegar.

Drain Every time you use the sink, flush out the drain with hot water and, once a week, put $\frac{1}{2}$ cup of washing soda down it, then flush again with hot water. If you think something smelly is stuck in the U-bend or trap, try using a plunger, then flush with hot water. If that doesn't work, unscrew the bolt in the U-bend in the same way as if you'd lost your diamond ring down it (see 'Fast maintenance', p. 174).

Garlic Wrap a bit of waterproof Elastoplast around the handle of a kitchen knife that you keep *only* for garlic, then you won't use it to cut (and taint) anything else.

Onion and fish To remove either of these smells from knives, push them up to the hilt in earth (e.g., your kitchen window-box of herbs). Add 1 teaspoon mustard powder to the dishwasher to get the smell of fish off **silver**. Add 1 teaspoon of vinegar to the dishwasher to remove a fishy smell from **china**. If you can't get rid of a smell in a **saucepan** try boiling a little vinegar in it for a minute. To stop **stock for soup** smelling vile, add 1 tablespoon of vinegar.

Paint When you're painting, cut an onion in half and put it, cut-sides-up, in the room. Afterwards, throw it away fast so you don't accidentally use it for cooking.

Perspiration To get rid of this smell in clothes wash, rinse thoroughly in warm water with a little added vinegar, then rinse in clear luke-warm water and dry, if possible, in the open air.

Rubbish Empty the kitchen bin every day (evening is best). To prevent the bin or pail getting dirty, use bin liners. When dirty, clean bin by squirting dishwashing liquid into it, adding ½ cup of chlorine bleach and half filling with water. Sponge sides, pour dirty water down the sink, then rinse the sink.

Smoke After a party or poker session, place a cup of vinegar in the room.

AVOID PESTS

Often, as with New York cockroaches, the pest problem infects the cleanest and highest in the land. There is no shame involved, even in having bedbugs: they also travel in taxis.

I learned the hard way about the horrors of pests in the home when we bought a charming old stone French farmhouse hung with vines and surrounded with lime trees. Our kitchen equipment was rudimentary (we were camping in): a tin bath for the water, two bookshelves for the food and crockery and a sort of pale blue, jazzed-up bucket that called itself a field toilet. On the first day the ants appeared, followed by the flies, then the spiders and the mosquitoes, then the bats and finally, on the fifth day, a sweet little fieldmouse. The mouse multiplied over the weekend and on the seventh day we rested not, because the rats had arrived. Our dream house was like being in the middle of an army training range with everything zeroing in on us. It is difficult to sleep with rats running all over the place; if you throw books and boots at them, you quickly run out of books and boots and they always miss the target.

On the eighth day, aided by the next-door farmer, we ruthlessly invested in rubber gloves, assorted pesticides and tins in which to keep the food. There is *nothing* like a plague of rats to make you pest-conscious for ever more. Pests (even the pretty little fieldmouse) carry disease, often bite and can take over the place incredibly fast if you allow it to happen.

Prevention is better than cure Keep the home clean, avoid damp, meticulously clean up food spills, keep dustbin lids on tightly and avoid having piles of rotting animal and/or vegetable matter in the garden.

If you find you have a pest, empty and clean all shelves, throw away affected food, such as rice, flour or noodles. Spray shelves with insecticide and leave for half a day before replacing contents. In future keep food in airtight tins.

Don't keep food or grain in the open, at floor level, in the kitchen or the larder. Keep the floor crumbless. Regularly clean out food cupboards.

When you're using a spray insecticide, don't spray it on food, drink, animals or children. Don't breathe it in yourself and don't spray near an open fire. And don't throw a used can into a fire unless you think that an explosion might enliven your afternoon.

Mice In spite of precautions you may be afflicted by mice. They shred and chew things such as newspapers, corners and clothes, gnaw wire and leave droppings, which are like tiny brown seeds. Cheese in a trap works for only one mouse at a time and they seem to breed as fast as the trap shuts. Telephone the public health department of your town hall. They will kill the mice. Sad indeed, but you can't afford to be squeamish.

Rats The first time I saw a rat in an empty house I jumped on a chair, held my skirt round my legs and gave a quavery little scream, just like a cartoon. You don't need me to tell you what a rat looks like – your racial memory will inform you.

Rats carry very nasty diseases, so if you see a rat call the town hall and ask for the pest controller or rodent exterminator or public health inspector or whatever he's called this week. If you can, avoid dealing with the rats yourself. If you can't, telephone to ask the inspector's advice about which poison to

DOWN WITH SUPERWOMAN!

use to pattern-trap the regular rat run. Ugh!

Fleas and bedbugs Don't panic. These are not necessarily associated with dirt, although they thrive in unhygienic conditions.

Each type of **flea** likes a different sort of host: horses, cats, rats, dogs, humans. Animal fleas will bite humans; some people seem to attract them far more than others. Their bites leave itching red spots on the skin, which (counsel of perfection) you should not scratch. They like darkness and warmth, tend to lay eggs in floor cracks and appear in warm wet weather, viz. early summer and early autumn.

If they are infesting something such as the cat's bed, burn it. Buy Bob Martin's Pestroy aerosol and spray the floor, any other places where a lot of dust collects and anything that is infected, such as your bed. If two days later you still have fleas, repeat the process. If in four days you still have fleas, call the public health inspector.

Bedbugs can enter your home via secondhand books and furniture, as well as beds. They are about 5 mm ($\frac{1}{4}$ in) long, roundish, brownish and flattish. Their irritating bites leave large red patches and possible swelling. They suck human blood at night and lay eggs in cracks in the woodwork and behind wallpaper. You will need to damp-spray the mattress thoroughly with insecticide (top, bottom *and* sides) and the frame, springs and slats of the bed. Also spray the surrounding floor, the skirting boards and any cracks in the walls or floor, then seal them. Repeat this performance the next day. Don't sleep on the mattress till it's dry. If this doesn't work, call in an expert, who will fumigate the room by blocking all windows, ventilations, cracks and keyholes. The room is then left sealed for some time before being aired and cleaned.

Cockroaches, silver fish and other flying or crawling insects Cockroaches love moist warm dark places and silver fish love damp, so watch water pipes. Spray with a suitable insecticide, sprinkle insecticide powder liberally where you suspect their 'run' is, and if necessary holler for the public health inspector to trace the source of the trouble.

Flies and wasps It has been reported that Vapona strips are impregnated with nerve gas. *Which?* does not recommend them. Use old-fashioned sticky fly paper.

How to make a wasp trap. Take a plastic bottle and cut off the top two-thirds of the way up. Invert the top and fit it into the bottom. Mix $\frac{1}{2}$ teacup of red wine with 1 tablespoon of jam and pour the mixture into the bottle. Your trap is now ready. The wasps dive into the sticky mixture and then can't get out, so they drown. Stand it by the table if you're eating in the garden.

Flies love decaying food. Get rid of it.

Moths It's the grubs, which like dark, warm places, that do the damage. They attack wool, fur, skin and feathers. They don't attack rubber, man-made or vegetable fibres, such as cotton or linen. Watch the following for moth damage:

1 Woollen clothes.
2 Blankets, quilts and rugs.
3 Carpets and underfelt.
4 Upholstered furniture and curtains.
5 Stuffed animals, birds, fur and feathers.

All stored articles should be cleaned, frequently inspected and protected by a moth deterrent such as naphthalene, camphor tablets or paradichlorobenzine. Hang the mothballs or crystals as high as you can in the wardrobe, so that the vapour descends from above; it's heavier than air, so cannot rise.

Where grubs have attacked an item, such as a stuffed bird, you should burn or otherwise dispose of it. If possible send other items to the dry cleaner. If

TERMITE

FLEA

FLY

WASP

MOSQUITO

CENTIPEDES

COCKROACH

SILVERFISH

POWDER-
POST BEETLE

ADULT
CLOTHES MOTH

BLACK CARPET
BEETLE LARVA

FIREBRAT

ANT

BEDBUG

BLACK WIDOW SPIDER

HOUSE MOUSE

RAT

you have moths in your clothes, empty your wardrobe and hang the clothes on a line to air in the open. Spray wardrobes and chests with insecticide, also skirting boards, walls and floor cracks, shelves and clothes rails.

Mosquitoes Their nasty Brrr can herald a sleepless night for all the wrong reasons. They breed near stagnant water, such as a slimy pond, and in damp leaves that collect in gutters. Use a special spray-can repellent.

37

DOWN WITH SUPERWOMAN!

Ants Be especially careful in the summer months, when they are likely to invade a ground floor kitchen from the garden. Leave no food spills unwiped, especially if sugary. Keep fruit in a bowl in the middle of a basin of water: ants can't swim. Use a special ant killer from garden shops.

Furniture beetle (woodworm) Lays its eggs (which take three years to hatch) in cracks and crevices of *unpolished* wood, such as the undersides of chairs, backs of wardrobes and chests of drawers, flooring and wooden panels. The baby beetle bites its way through to the open air leaving a tiny exit hole. Wood dust beneath a piece of furniture is a sure sign of 'woodworm'. Don't allow into the house any secondhand or 110th-hand furniture that has tiny holes in it, unless you are sure that it has been professionally treated: you risk infecting your other furniture.

You can treat furniture with a woodworm insecticide. The best time is April and May, because then you can get the babies (fiendish chuckle), but DON'T WAIT for April to come round. Brush the insecticide well into the peppery-holed surface. Treatment may discolour light woods.

All insecticides should be available from big stores, ironmongers (fast dying out) or some do-it-yourself shops.

Dry rot is not dry. It is a sinisterly science-fictionish fungus that grows and lives on wood and finally reduces it to a dry, crumbling state that sounds 'dead' when hit with a hammer and has a nasty mouldy smell. It starts in damp, unventilated places such as under floorboards and behind wood panelling. It spreads by thin root-like strands, which creep over non-nourishing brickwork to reach more appetizing wood. It produces flat growths rather like a cross between a pancake and a mushroom. If you suspect that you have dry rot, immediately call a surveyor or a wood preservation firm.

The first part of treatment consists in discovering the causes. These could be:

1 A damp-proof course rendered ineffective because someone has piled up coal, earth, sand or gravel or something against an outside wall.
2 A broken damp-proof course.
3 No damp-proof course in your home.
4 Not drying out wet boards before laying a floor covering such as cork or linoleum.
5 Faulty plumbing that keeps floorboards damp, particularly hot water pipe joints behind a bath panel.
6 Faulty, leaking drain pipes; possibly combined with worn pointing.

Once the cause has been analysed all rotten wood must be cut away and immediately burned for 1 m (3 ft) beyond the infected area. All nearby brickwork must be sterilized with a blowlamp then, when cool, treated with a preservative. The timber can then be repaired with new timber, which should also be treated with a preservative.

Wet rot Not so serious as dry rot, as it is easier to arrest. It is a timber fungus that grows in a *really* damp, wet place where you get leaking water, such as a cellar, shed or Rachmanite bathroom. The fungus, which rarely shows itself on the surface, makes the damp wood darken.

Treatment consists of checking the source of moisture and thoroughly drying the timber, which might have to be treated with preservative. Badly decayed timber should be cut out and replaced.

Expert treatment If your house timber has woodworm, or wet or dry rot, get expert treatment from a specialist such as Rentokil. It's extremely expensive, but not so expensive as to have the old homestead crumble about your ears.

On no account go only to one firm. Get several quotes. (I have found one firm *ten times* more expensive than another.) If the job promises to be expensive, you may find it economical to employ a surveyor to advise you and possibly supervise the work. I did.

To stamp out woodworm thoroughly they will heave up floorboards, replacing any that are unsafe, and spray the lot with woodworm-killing fluid. All reputable companies give a guarantee – usually twenty-five years. Don't try to tackle extensive woodworm yourself; you can never be sure you've done a proper job, and have no guarantee to produce if you sell the house.

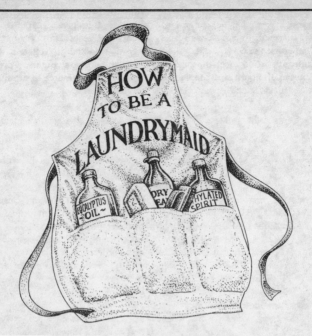

CONFESSIONS OF A DRY-CLEANER'S DAUGHTER

Speaking treacherously as a dry-cleaner's daughter, I would say you can save yourself a lot of cleaning bills if you equip yourself with a stain-removal kit (see p. 42). Keep it in a drawer out of reach of children. Label all bottles.

Whatever the stain, if there's nothing available with which to treat it, act immediately by soaking in lots of *cold water*. If cold water doesn't remove the stain, try using lukewarm water and ordinary soap. *Never use hot water or you may permanently set the stain*.

If you act fast enough, you can remove most stains with a towel, a bar of soap, a cup of lukewarm water and a nail-brush used *very gently*. Damp the cloth and rub the soap in until the stain comes off, then put the damp cloth between two sides of a towel and thump it until it is damp-dry. I have whipped a blouse off a duchess, a shirt from the back of a football star and the entire suit from my doctor when he spilt blood on it (mine). So *if* you act immediately, you can ignore most of the following advice.

The seven golden rules of stain-shifting

1 Treat stains as fast as possible.
2 Never use hot water.
3 Treat from the wrong side of the fabric, if possible, so that the dirt needn't be pushed right through it.
4 If coloured, check effect of remover on an unimportant part of the fabric. Test all chemicals first on an inconspicuous area.
5 After using a chemical, rinse well in lukewarm water.
6 Use a weak solution several times, rather than a strong solution.
7 Avoid leaving a ring in place of the

stain by this old trick I learned at my Daddy's knee, known in the trade as 'spotting'. When using a chemical, always make a ring larger than the stained area, then gradually work in towards the stain, never vice versa. Treat potential water rings in the same way. After treatment with water or a chemical, place the still-wet article on a towel and thump the fabric dry with another towel, working *round the edge* of the treated area and towards the middle.

STAIN-REMOVAL TREATMENTS

The theory of stain removal is either to dissolve the stain or wash it out. If you don't know a specific treatment, choose one of these four main rough-and-ready treatments in this order; in other words, if 1 doesn't work, try 2, then 3, then 4.

1 **Water-soluble items** (from kindergarten paint to toothpaste) Sponge or rub gently under cold, or at most lukewarm, water. If persistent, try soap and lukewarm water.

2 **Protein stains** Soak for several hours or overnight in cold water in which has been dissolved a little biological enzyme powder (such as Bio-tex). This breaks down the protein molecules in urine, sweat, blood, milk, egg, tea, coffee, fruit, vegetable and wine stains. Enzymes are ineffective in water hotter than 60 °C (140 °F) (hand-hot water is 50 °C (122 °F)).

Warning! Wool, silk and fabrics that are flameproof or not colour-fast shouldn't be soaked. Wash quickly in a solution of warm water and enzyme detergent.

3 **Fat, oil and grease stains** Dab with a cotton-wool pad soaked in Beaucaire (which is simply dry-cleaning fluid) applied to the dry fabric. Dry-cleaning fluid dissolves rubber, so don't use on

rubber-backed items, such as a raincoat. Work near an open window so that slight fumes evaporate fast.

Don't use a grease solvent on plastic or expanded polystyrene items, as they may dissolve. Try washing in a solution of warm water and synthetic detergent.

A friend of mine, who runs a hotel and whose life is filled with nameless stains, always tries a dab of eucalyptus oil on **unknown, old, dried-out stains** and leaves it to 'lift' the stain, then removes the eucalyptus oil with dry-cleaning solvent.

If you haven't any dry-cleaning fluid and the fabric isn't 'dry clean only', try working liquid detergent into the stain. Rinse well with lukewarm water and thump dry with a towel.

4 **Stubborn stains such as scorch, mildew and make-up marks** Test bleach on part of the fabric that won't be visible when worn, then damp garment and immerse it in a 50/50 solution of peroxide and water. Watch it: don't walk way. Wash thoroughly, then rinse and dry. Once I scorched a beautiful pink suit, gave it to a friend for Oxfam and, to my chagrin, saw her wearing it the next week without the scorch mark.

Bleach should never be used on a fabric that has a special finish, such as drip-dry.

How to remove stains with bleach Shop-bought household bleaches are a strong mixture of chlorine bleach and disinfectant and *should not be used for stain removal*.

Use chlorine bleach. Mix 2 tablespoons bleach and 1 litre (2 pt) water. Apply to *small stains* with cotton bud. *Large stains* should be soaked in the solution. Leave five to fifteen minutes. Watch it: *don't go away*, don't answer the phone or the doorbell; bleach is fierce and must be treated with respect. Rinse well and repeat treatment if necessary.

If any stain disappears and you are left with a yellowish stain, apply a *mild* bleach solution and rinse carefully.

Warning! You can't use chlorine bleach on silk, wool, polyester, acetate, rayon or special finish fabrics such as drip-dry cotton. Instead, try a solution of 4 tablespoons ammonia to 4 tablespoons water. Damp stain with solution and repeat until stain disappears. Rinse in cold water, then rinse in cold water with vinegar (1 litre (2 pt) water and 1 tablespoon vinegar). Rinse with clear water.

If you don't know what a **mystery stain** is and you don't want to risk removing it yourself, take the garment to a dry cleaner, point out the stain (otherwise it may not be noticed and it will be returned to you) and firmly state that that stain is the only reason you want the garment cleaned. If you are on friendly terms with your dry cleaner, ask him how he's going to treat it. At least he will have to stop and think about it. Try to patronize a cleaner who cleans in his own shop; then you will also know where that lost button is likely to be.

Never buy anything white that *must* be dry cleaned; it will always come back from the cleaners pale grey, because dry-cleaning spirit isn't white in the first place, and when your Wimbledon-white wedding dress has been whirled round in a machine with a lot of seeming demob suits, it will never regain its first virgin bloom.

STAIN-REMOVAL KIT (a real money saver)

General A bucket and a box containing the following: packet of tissues; two small sponges; two old handkerchiefs; ordinary clothes brush; wire clothes brush (use gently, it's a ruthless weapon); Sellotape (for wrapping round knuckles, sticky side out, then dabbing at fluff on a dark suit); spray can of Goddard's aerosol dry-clean spray (removes spots without leaving a

ring, and is especially good for ties); heavy pudding basin (not plastic); biological detergent. Of course, you may not want to use spray cans or biological detergent for ecological reasons.

Water soluble stains Bicarbonate of soda; bottle-washing soda; small jar of soapless detergent; salts of lemon or Movol; Steradent false-teeth cleaner.

Fat, oil and grease stains Methylated spirit; glycerine; turpentine; eucalyptus oil; Polystrippa (to soften hard paint); Polyclens oil-paint remover; grease solvent such as Beaucaire (use near open window to blow away fumes).

You may also need the following: india rubber (for wallpaper); blotting paper (for sealing wax); acetone (for nail varnish and various types of adhesive); don't use acetone on acetate rayon.

HOW TO SHIFT THE STAINS IN YOUR LIFE

(Please forgive some repetitions, I want a quick, comprehensive reference.)

Don't use those little specialist tubes; you don't need them. Furthermore, there is an urge, if one doesn't work, to try another one. My dry-cleaner brother says that these things are making him a fortune because he has to deal with the mess people make with them on their clothes.

If a stain doesn't come out with dry-cleaning fluid or soap and water, before you do anything else, try soaking the stain in a basin of cold water overnight (particularly good for fruit stains).

Alcohol (Drink stains after a party.) Spot with clear alcohol. On acetate fabric, dilute 1 part alcohol in 2 parts water.

Animal messes Sponge with borax solution (560 ml (1 pt) water to 1 dessertspoon borax). Won't smell as much if you squirt the area with soda water. White vinegar and water (mix 50/50) is good on pee and cat-spray.

Antiperspirants Sponge with mixture of detergent and warm water. Try sponging with ammonia. For silk and wool, dilute with water 50/50.

Ballpoint pen Soak with methylated spirit.

Beer Sponge immediately with plenty of clear cold water.

Bird droppings Dissolve a handful of washing soda and 1 tablespoon soapless detergent in half a bucket of warm water. Scrub the droppings with it.

Blood, meat juice, gravy Act as fast as possible. A carpet cleaner once told me that he'd just had an emergency call. Some man had had a spat with his wife. Smashed a hammer across her head, in fact. Then, as it was all white wall-to-wall, the man had had the presence of mind to call the carpet cleaner *immediately*. That's what I call sang-froid.

If still wet, wash out stain in cold salt water. Once dried, especially by heat, blood is very difficult to remove. Try soaking article in warm solution of Biotex, then wash according to fabric. If stain persists, try soaking in a solution of hydrogen peroxide and a few drops of ammonia (but don't leave longer than five minutes, or the fabric will rot), and be careful to soak it all off.

Candlewax Although any manicurist or Latin lover will tell you never to use them as weapons, scrape as much wax as possible off with your fingernails. If the wax is on wood, do the best you can by rubbing with the fingernail and ball of finger. If the wax is staining a cloth, place blotting paper over the stain, iron over it with a hot iron and attack any remaining stain with dry-cleaning fluid.

Carbon paper On fingers or clothing. Use dry-cleaning fluid.

Chewing gum To freeze-harden the gum, rub with a cube of ice (in polythene bag to prevent wetting the material), scrape as much as possible off with a fingernail, then use dry-cleaning fluid.

Chocolate Work liquid detergent into the stain, then rinse off well with lukewarm water.

Coffee, tea and curry Instant action essential. Sponge with borax and warm water. If the stain persists, try detergent and warm water.

Cosmetics Mostly coloured grease. Remove even the powder round your neckline by 'spotting' with dry-cleaning fluid on the dry fabric, followed by lukewarm water and soap.

Dandelion Use biological detergent, if your conscience permits.

Emulsion paint See Paint.

Felt-tip pen Water-soluble. Soak immediately, then use soap and water.

Fruit (including tomato sauce) Wash out immediately in cold water, then warm water with biological powder. Wash delicate fabrics in cold water, then work glycerine into stain and leave for one hour to 'float' the stain off, then wash out with detergent and warm water. On non-washable fabrics leave glycerine for several hours, then sponge with liquid detergent and water. Better still, like the sensible French, always tuck your napkin in your neck when eating spaghetti or peaches, regardless of the company, because a fruit stain is potential disaster. I once dined with a theatrical tycoon. She touched my blouse and said 'silk', she touched my jacket and said 'cashmere', then she rang a bell and asked her maid to bring me a big child's bib from the pile she thoughtfully kept for guests.

Grass or seaweed Spot with methylated spirit, then wash thoroughly.

Grease Soak cotton wool in dry-cleaning fluid and 'spot' the stain.

Hair lacquer (on mirror) Wipe with methylated spirit.

Human beings Try clear acetone for stains you can't get off your skin, such as Elastoplast residue, latex paint or tar on feet.

Ice cream Use dry-cleaning fluid and then wash.

Iron mould Drip on a solution of salts

of lemon (2 teaspoonfuls to 280 ml ($\frac{1}{2}$ pt) warm water), rinse well, then wash. Dispose of any of the solution that's left over – it's poisonous. Or use Movol, from Boots.

Jam Soak in warm borax solution (560 ml (1 pt) water to 28 g (1 oz) borax), then wash.

Latex adhesive Can be removed with special remover made by Copydex.

Lipstick Use dry-cleaning fluid, followed by soap and warm water.

Make-up See Cosmetics.

Mildew Brush off as much as possible, then sponge with hydrogen peroxide and rinse thoroughly.

Oil See Grease.

Paint If you are painting, buy 1 litre (2 pt) Polyclens or white spirit – when you need it, you need it quick and plentiful (as when you've upset a tin of paint on the Chinese carpet).

A pool of paint First spoon up all you can of the spilt liquid, working from the edge inwards so as not to enlarge the area affected. Then mop with newspaper, then tissues.

Emulsion paint Wash *immediately* with lots of cold water. If stain has set, try methylated spirit, but I don't hold out much hope on an old stain. You could pick at it with a comb or thumb and forefinger.

Emulsion or oil paint that has set Cross fingers and apply a little Polystrippa – this will quickly soften the paint. It may also soften everything else as well, so stand by with lots of water to stop the rot. Once softened, old paint stains can be treated as fresh paint stains. Polyclens is wonderful stuff for taming oil paint (and varnish, polyurethane sealers, etc.). The only snag is that it dissolves any plastics and adhesives, so if you don't watch out you can really come unstuck. It is also good for cleaning paint brushes – just dunk thoroughly in Polyclens for five minutes, then hold under the cold tap.

Oil paint on artificial fabrics and most plastics (including patent floor tiles) Soak with white spirit until all traces of paint are gone, then wash with lukewarm water and detergent.

Oil paint on natural fibres Mop up. Soak immediately and liberally with Polyclens, then wash with lots and lots of cold water. If you have no Polyclens, remember the way an artist cleans oil brushes: wipe with newspaper, rub with a rag soaked in turps or white spirit, then wash in warm soapy water.

Perspiration See Antiperspirants.

Rust Dab with a commercial rust remover such as Movol, from Boots. Otherwise, for mild stains on cloth, stretch the cloth over a mixing bowl full of boiling water (you need the steam action) and squeeze fresh lemon juice on it. Or try this special formula. Mix 20 g ($\frac{3}{4}$ oz) potassium persulphate in 560 ml (1 pt) water and soak the spot in it. Rinse. Repeat if necessary.

Scorch marks Rinse immediately in cold running water, sponge with borax and water. If this has no result, try a weak solution of hydrogen peroxide.

Seawater

1 **On fabrics** Sponge with warm water to dissolve salt. If stain persists, spot with methylated spirit, then launder or dry clean.

2 **On shoes** Try 2 teaspoons methylated spirits to 1 dessertspoon milk. Rub on, leave to dry, then repolish. If unsuccessful, buy and apply overall shoe dye of the same colour.

Soot Brush off excess and sponge with dry-cleaning fluid.

Tar Scrape off with the back of a knife or thumbnail. Swab with turpentine, then dry-cleaning fluid. If you get **tar in your hair**, get someone to wash it off, a hank at a time, patiently, with liquid detergent, then give hair an oil treatment (see 'Bodywork', p. 305).

Float tar off a dog or cat's paw by

rubbing in eucalyptus oil, leaving for half an hour, then washing off with warm water and detergent. Repeat until tar is completely removed.

Tea

1 **Inside the teapot** Fill the teapot with boiling water, add 1 teaspoon denture cleaning powder and stir. Leave for several hours, then rinse thoroughly. Alternatively, fill with water, add 1 tablespoon bleach and leave overnight. Or don't let anyone look in the teapot.

2 **On china or glass** Wipe with a damp cloth dipped in bicarbonate of soda and rinse. Or soak in a detergent. Or treat overnight with bleach solution.

Ties Treat as appropriate, but treat whole tie, not just the stain. Swab with dry-cleaning fluid, then thump dry with a towel, upon a towel. Press into shape with your hands or under a damp cloth. *Never* send another tie to the cleaners, especially not an expensive, lined one. The more expensive a necktie, the more easily a dry cleaner ruins it.

Tomato See Fruit.

Urine Sponge or wash in warm water. Sponge remaining stain with a solution of vinegar and water (1 tablespoon vinegar to 560 ml (1 pt) water).

Vomit Sponge with borax solution. If on a carpet, remove vomit with a cloth, then squirt with soda syphon to get rid of smell.

Wallpaper marks Try to avoid cleaning wallpaper – nobody minds a spot here or there (could you hang something over it?) and you risk leaving a large, obvious 'clean' patch, which will show how grubby your wallpaper is. If spongeable, wipe with a damp cloth or sponge. Otherwise, try a soft india rubber or a piece of soft bread. For grease marks, use dry-cleaning fluid.

Wax crayon Try liquid detergent, rinsed off with lukewarm water. If it persists, try a mild bleach solution and rinse carefully.

Wine Stretch the stained bit of fabric over a pudding basin and keep it in position with a rubber band or a bit of string. Push material down into borax and water solution in the basin for half an hour. Then launder or dry clean.

WHY NOT DYE A LITTLE?

You don't need much equipment to transform all your underwear and become a scarlet woman. With a little effort you too could sleep between coffee-coloured sheets like a film director, or make sure that all your towels match by dyeing them French blue. I once dyed all my sad white nylon underwear Madonna Blue, which is a bit stronger than baby blue, but not as dark as the standard Vatican shade.

You'll need only a plastic bucket or a sink for cold dyeing. For hot water dyeing, you will need a wooden stick or spoon, rubber gloves and a flameproof bucket, although any big tin container will do; I use an old Victorian fish kettle.

Know what fibre you are dyeing before you start. If you aren't certain what fabric you are hoping to dye . . . DON'T GUESS.

Just in case you're confused by mad scientist trade names, see guide on p. 46.

I doubt whether you are going to cut bits out of your underwear to identify it, but if you want to know what you should use to dye those curtains that look like silk, but which you suspect to be rayon and which actually turn out to be terylene . . . send a snippet of fabric and have it analysed *free* by Dylon's laboratory. Write to Annette Stevens, Consumer Advice Bureau, Dylon International Ltd, Worsley Bridge Road, London SE26 5HD (tel: 081-650-4801).

As together we dyed an assortment of coloured tights to a hopefully alluring black, Annette told me the mistakes that women make most frequently.

Fabric guide

Fabric	Fibre group	Fabric	Fibre group
Acetate Rayon	Acetate	Leacril	Acrylic
Acrilan	Acrylic	Linen	Natural
Bri-nylon	Nylon	Lycra	Elastomeric
Canvas	Natural	Neo-spun	Acrylic
Cashmilon	Acrylic	Nylon	Nylon
Celon	Nylon	Orlon	Acrylic
Cotton	Natural	Perlon	Nylon
Courtelle	Acrylic	Raycelon	Viscose Rayon
Crimplene	Polyester	Sarille	Viscose Rayon
Crimplene/cotton	Polyester mixture		(usually but not
Dacron	Polyester		always)
Dacron/cotton	Polyester mixture	Sayelle	Acrylic
Darelle	Viscose Rayon	Shareen	Nylon
Delustra	Viscose Rayon	Silk	Natural
Dicel	Acetate	Spanzelle	Elastomeric
Diolen	Polyester	Tendrelle	Nylon
Dralon	Acrylic	Tergal	Polyester
Elaston	Polynosic (a re-	Terlenka	Polyester
	generated viscose)	Terylene	Polyester
Enkalon	Nylon	Terylene/cotton	Polyester mixture
Enkasheer	Nylon	Trevira	Polyester
Evlan	Viscose Rayon	Tricel	Triacetate
Fibre-glass	Glass fibre	Tricelon	Triacetate
Helanca	Nylon/Polyester	Vincel	Viscose Rayon
Lancofil	Acetate	Viscose Rayon	Viscose Rayon
Lancola	Acetate	Wool	Natural
Lancolene	Acetate	Zantrel	Polynosic
Lansil	Acetate		

As always, the main complaint is that women *don't read the instructions*. I submit that that is because the instruction books are generally badly written, unclear, boring and confusing.

* DO wear rubber gloves.
* DO weigh your article and obey the instructions for that weight.
* DO thoroughly wet the item before dyeing it.
* DO wash the garment first (unless you're using Wash'n Dye, of which more later).
* DO remove all stains beforehand or they will dye a different shade from the rest of the item.
* DO stir constantly with a wooden stick or spoon when you are dyeing by hand. Take the telephone off the hook and don't answer the door.
* DO expect to blend colour. If you

dye a yellow nightdress with blue dye, it will not turn blue ... it will turn green.

Colour arithmetic

Red + yellow = orange/red
Blue + yellow = green
Yellow + pink = coral
Green + yellow = lime
Light brown + medium red = rust
Red + blue = purple
Pale blue + pink = lilac
Yellow + brown = golden brown
Dark brown + light red = reddish brown

Dyeing patterned material is tricky and I personally wouldn't do it. In over-dyeing patterned material, the *strongest colour in the pattern should be used as a guide*. For example a red, yellow and pale green pattern would be suitable for over-dyeing in red, this being the strongest of the three colours named.

* DON'T use a too-small vessel or the colour will be patchy.
* DON'T dye glass fibre or acrylic, which simply won't absorb the dye. Some acrylic trade names are Courtelle, Acrilan, Dralon, Orlon, Neospun, Leacril, Sayelle and Cashmilon.
* DON'T expect magic. Your beat-up, worn-out, old, cheap sweater won't be suddenly transformed into a new, fresh, smart, expensive-looking, different coloured sweater all for 95p. It will still be old and beat-up but a different colour.
* DON'T try to overdye a dark colour with a light colour. You can't transform a dark blue bra into a pale peach one, although you can metamorphose a yellowing white one into palest peach. You can also turn it white again by using Dylon Super White.

The following advice refers to Dylon dyes because they are easily obtainable and simple to use. There are four basic dyes: Dylon Cold, Multi-purpose, Wash'n Dye and Natural Fabric Dye.

BEWARE special finishes such as drip-dry, which can result in blotchy home dyeing.

Warning! Don't wash home-dyed articles with biological powder, such as Ariel, or the colour will come out. Use a detergent soap powder.

For dyeing wool do not use Dylon Cold unless you want a very pale shade. Use Natural Fabric Dye hand-size pack. You can use Super White for whitening wool.

Dylon Cold For all natural fibres (except wool). Dye fading cotton, towels, jaded tea-towels, boring bedspreads and sheets, over-familiar blouses. You simply buy a little tin with a packet of dye fix. Mix the dye powder with water and add

4 tablespoons salt to each tin of dye. Dissolve the dye fixer in boiling water. Add both to a bowl of cold water. Now submerge the item for 60 minutes, stirring for the first 10. Then wash, rinse until water clears and dry as usual. It shouldn't bleed afterwards. ('Bleeding' is when the garment discolours the water.)

Multi-purpose A tiny tin of dye powder intended for the odd pair of gloves, tights or pants. Check weight of garment before using it. After using this dye, always wash a garment immediately, to make sure that it bleeds thoroughly.

You dissolve the dye by stirring in boiling water, add 1 heaped tablespoon salt, then the garment, simmer for 20 minutes, rinse thoroughly, wring and dry away from direct heat or sunlight.

Wash'n Dye For using in a washing machine because it washes as well as dyes the article. Useful for big items, such as rayon curtains or sheets or loose covers.

You just chuck in the dirty items and follow the directions. Don't add soap powder. Run the machine for 12 minutes (or the full cycle on automatics), rinse, then dry away from sunlight or direct heat. Will dye up to 1.25 kg (2½ lb) dry weight.

Warning! Terylene, Tricel and Crimplene will need three times the dye quantities and you can still dye them only to pale shades. You can't dye polyesters.

Natural Fabric Dye Dylon's newest product comes in two packets, one for hand washing (do wool and silk by this method), and one for machine washing. With a washing machine, you empty powder into the drum, add 1 kg (2 lb) salt and throw in articles to be dyed. Fill the machine with cold water (or set lowest temperature programme till machine is full), then switch to 60 °C (140 °F) programme. When dyeing cycle is over, add your usual washing powder and run a 95 °C (200 °F) programme.

DOWN WITH SUPERWOMAN!

SWIFT SEWING BOX

I used to have a great big EFFICIENT mother-type sewing box with pretty rows of different coloured cottons and so forth. I used to have a basket grandly labelled SEWING, which was generally overflowing with grey flannel school clothes that I couldn't summon up the energy to attack.

Then I realized that when travelling on business I took a tiny travel sewing kit and always immediately repaired anything that burst. So I put this kit on the television in the sitting room and pointed it out to the men of the family, and thereafter anyone who had anything to sew went and did it themselves.

One of the greatest favours you can do for your male children is to teach them how to sew at an early age, before their little fingers lose their dexterity. I just didn't sew for anyone over 7, but I *did* see that the sewing kit was stocked up. If the men in your life travel, get them a pocket sewing kit – they are inexpensive and don't take up any more room than a passport. I once gave one to each of the men in my life and you'd have thought I was dishing out gold cuff-links; they seemed pathetically grateful. I almost felt guilty.

Basic sewing kit

Needles, large and small
Tin of pins
Small scissors
Thimble
Tape measure
Reels of cotton in black, white, brown, beige, colourless
Black button thread
Thin elastic
Trouser band hooks
Hooks and eyes
Seam ripper

I also have a transparent plastic button bag and an odd sock bag, and keep an old pair of jeans to cut up and use for patches.

Zip tip Zips are less likely to stick if you close them before cleaning the garment. If your zip sticks, it might be because a thread has caught in it. On the other hand it might need lubricating; try a light touch of cooking oil or grease – even your face cream might unstick it.

If your zip won't stay up, and it's not because a garment is too small for you, pull up zip end, slap a bit of Sellotape horizontally across it, or vertically up the zip, as a temporary measure.

Sewing tip I once worked with Charlotte Altmann, an exquisitely dressed architect who made all her own clothes (including tailoring) and her own furnishings. She only ever used one stitch: a running stitch with three stitches, then she over-sewed the third stitch. I had no confidence in her method but I tried it – and I have used no other stitch for all sewing jobs for the past twenty-five years.

HELLO, GOODBYE WASHDAY
(short guide to the weekly wash)

How to lose your laundry efficiently

Laundries are wonderful if you are rich enough, even though they can beat hell out of your linen. Decide which things always go. I currently send sheets, big towels and shirts. I have to face the fact that I'm not a ravishing redhead, I can't speak six languages and I can't iron shirts.

Sort into piles: white shirts, coloured shirts, sheets. See that everything is marked with your initials, using an indelible laundry pen. Write in laundry book as you put in laundry box. Always mend shirts before laundering, for even a small tear may return a major calamity.

All over Britain laundry vans are collecting the wrong boxes and taking them back to be mechanically rubbed on stones at the riverside (explains how the holes get into the sheets), then redistributing them back to even wronger doorsteps. When it comes to chasing a missing load, you have no proof *because the laundry list is in the lost box.* So I bought a little office duplicating book, the sort that leaves you carbon copies, which I keep with a ballpoint pen in the bottom of the laundry basket, where nobody nicks it to keep the bridge scores.

Not since the invention of double-entry bookkeeping in the fourteenth century has there been such a revolutionary idea. I write the laundry list in my book, tear out the top copy and send it with the laundry, and tick off the items in my book when they are returned. If anything is missing, I report it to the laundry immediately and, as my laundry is a member of the Association of British Laundry, Cleaning and Rental Services (ABLCRS for short!), they play the game properly and make fair compensation for anything that they've lost.

I've also started to use this book for when I take a load to the dry-cleaning shop, as those easily lost little slips with their mad hieroglyphics mean nothing to me.

How to be a laundrymaid

Don't do it on a Monday when you have all the clearing up from the weekend. Use gloves to protect your hands when laundering – a must if your skin is sensitive to washing powders.

To eliminate washday blues Do what I was taught at my Daddy's knee: however desirable and alluring a garment looks or makes you look, if it is going to be a cleaning problem, DON'T BUY IT. Don't buy anything that can't be washed in a machine. Don't buy anything that isn't colour-fast, shrink resistant and non-iron.

Always buy clothes from reputable stores, such as Marks and Spencer, and not the hippy stall in the local market.

Always read the care instruction label on a garment.

Don't wash:

1 Angora or cashmere sweaters. Dry clean.
2 A pleated skirt, unless the label says you can. Dry clean.
3 Anything cheap that you like in crêpe, satin or corduroy. You risk the garment losing shape. Dry clean.
   The rule is: if in doubt, dry clean.
4 Ties. Wash unlined cotton or wool ties in warm water and detergent, rinse well and pat dry in towel. Press under damp cloth.

By far the best way to clean a tie (especially an expensive silk one) is to do it yourself by swabbing the entire thing with dry-cleaning fluid and pressing it into shape to dry. This is the *only* way to clean a tie with a lining.

How and what to wash by hand

I used to be very mean with water when hand-washing. Then an Italian laundry maid saw me in action and told me that you can never get anything clean if you wash it in grubby water. Simple, really. She told me to keep on rinsing until the water is clear, otherwise you risk a grubby wash, a soapy smell and a sticky feel.

Use mild liquid dishwasher detergent, which is as mild as, and cheaper than, special soap-flakes.

Always hand wash **anything expensive and delicate, such as woollens or lace,** unless such garments are definitely marked otherwise. Wash in cold water with Woolite. Do everything gently. Rinse in cold water, squeeze gently, then press damp-dry in a towel. Damp-dry an item by gently squeezing the water out of it (wringing can ruin the shape), spreading it on a towel and rolling the towel up. Stand on it barefoot for a moment. Repeat the process with a dry towel.

Don't hang up **woollens**: lay them out on a towel, pull into shape and leave to dry over the back of a sofa, or on the table or somewhere else flat and warm, but not hot. Never on radiators.

Many garment manufacturers now produce treated wool garments. You can wash such an item in a washing machine and spin-dry it and it will still retain its shape. Be careful to obey the manufacturer's washing instructions.

Wash **elasticated underwear** in lukewarm water, never boil. Don't iron. Don't let it get too dirty. Don't wring it out: pat dry in a towel and proceed as for woollens.

How to get the best from your washing machine

Before washing Empty pockets, mend tears and remove stains. Hot water sets stains so they cannot be removed. *Ever*. Sort clothes into piles of:

1 White cotton and linen.
2 Coloured cotton and linen.
3 Nylon and other synthetics.
4 Rayon and silk.
5 Woollens.
6 Items whose colour you suspect might run.

Choose the appropriate programme and push the button.

Use *very* hot water for white and colour-fast cottons (cheap cottons are not always fast). Use hand-hot water for synthetics, warm water for woollens and anything you're dubious about.

However, there's a bit more to it than that. Perhaps you had better find the time to finish this chapter *before* washday.

For which washing machine to choose,

see 'How to buy the best and cheapest equipment', p. 61.

Don't put more things in the washing machine than it will wash. You don't pack it like a suitcase. If you don't feel like weighing the sheets or you haven't anything to weigh them on, fill it two-thirds full, as a rough guide. Always put stockings, tights, lace and underwear in a pillow case, so they don't catch in the machine.

After using a washing machine, rinse it with clear water, disconnect it from the electricity supply unless it is permanently installed, *then dry it inside and out with an absorbent cloth*. Through not doing this and not using the machine for several months while I was away, I turned a trusty into a rusty seventeen-year-old twin tub and had to scrap it.

Fastness Wash all black things separately; it then won't really matter if they're not fast. Never wash pale colours with dark colours in case the colours bleed. Never wash white with any other colour. Coloured sheets and towels should be washed separately for the first few times, as surplus dye may come out. (It doesn't mean that they will get paler.)

You can tell whether or not a colour will run by wetting a corner of it in hot water and squeezing it in a white towel. Anything brightly coloured or printed might run. Graceful ethnic fabrics don't only run, *they gallop*.

Which washing product?

They really ought to print the washing powder instructions on the cornflakes pack because everybody *reads* the cornflakes pack. For washer-women who are bewildered by manufacturers' claims, descriptions and instructions, here are the encapsulated facts about washing products.

The word 'detergent' is derived from the Latin for 'to cleanse'. Pure soap was the original detergent for washing people, clothes and homes. Synthetic detergents are a mixture of chemicals, each one with a different purpose, such as scum-inhibiting.

You would use a soft, good quality solid soap on your face rather than a harsh, household soap, which you might use on the tougher, dirtier floor. Similarly, you should use two sorts of cleaner: a detergent (such as Ariel) for heavy-duty cleaning in the machine of fabrics such as cotton, and a cold water wash (such as Woolite) for more delicate materials, such as silk.

Since 1980 manufacturers of detergents have been obliged by law to make their products 80 per cent biodegradable.

Unfortunately, most detergents in Britain still contain phosphates, which help to remove dirt from clothes. They also help to destroy animal life in lakes and rivers. So if you want to wash with an ecologically clean conscience, you should use only pure soap or else one of the products referred to in 'Don't wreck your planet' on p. 15. Pure soap tends to leave a scummy residue in hard water, so use Calgon powder as well to soften the water.

There are four *textures* of cleaner: solid, powder, flakes and liquid. They all do the same job. I prefer to use a liquid cleaner, such as Ariel.

How much to use Whatever you use, it is important when washing clothes to maintain a good lather throughout the wash, except for special, low-lather products used with front-loading automatic washing machines. On no account use high-lather products in these or the machine may leak.

Enzyme pre-washes (such as Ariel) Green purists do not use these products, which break down proteins by chemical action during soaking so that the garment can then be washed by detergent in the normal way. Natural body proteins include blood, sweat and urine as well as

most food stains, such as egg yolk and cocoa. (Stubborn old stains may need several soakings.)

NEVER soak wool, silk, fabrics that are not colour-fast or specially finished fabrics, such as drip-dry.

It is important to remember that enzymes need time to act. The longer the soak, the cooler the water can be. Generally speaking, soak garments overnight, eight hours in cold water with biological powder, or soak for an hour in hand-hot water ($50\,°C$ ($122\,°F$) to be precise). If the water is too hot, the enzymes will not act. You may find it easiest to soak in the bath overnight.

Some people say that you can add a cupful of enzyme pre-wash to the detergent in your machine, but, as an enzyme pre-wash loses its power if used in hot water, it seems a crazy thing to do.

There's a rumour that one person in five is sensitive to enzyme pre-washes, so make sure you dissolve it properly to begin with and rinse it out thoroughly and off your hands.

Good tip: You can use an enzyme pre-wash powder or liquid (such as Ariel) to soak overnight such kitchen irritations as burnt milk or scrambled egg in saucepans or for cleaning narrow-necked decanters or vases.

Cold-water detergents (such as Woolite) *Advantages.* Permanent pleats stay pleated, wool doesn't shrink, colours don't run, white nylon stays white, silk blouses don't reduce you to tears, and you can save a substantial amount a year on your fuel bill.

Try cold water laundering, unless you are in a hard-water area or using a public laundrette (where there is a bacteria risk) or where cold water is less than $0\,°C$ ($32\,°F$) in winter.

Disadvantages. They can leave a residue on fabric and washing machine unless used in *cold* water.

I travel with a small bottle of Woolite.

Warning! Stick to the times given in the instructions, or the colour may fuzz or fade.

Fabric softeners Fabric softeners can be a lot of extra bother. If you use them, follow the manufacturer's instructions to add to the wash water, the final rinse or the dryer. They work by coating the fibres with a thin, invisible layer, which includes silicones and thereby prevents the fibres from adhering to one another. This tends to make each item feel soft and fluffy as opposed to thick, compressed, and 'felted' (a bit like blotting paper). Fabric softeners now come in both liquid (Lenor) and sheet (Bounce) form. Good for blankets.

Boiling Boil nasty handkerchiefs, or baby or invalid linen or similar in a boiler, an old saucepan or something big enough.

Boiling for about ten minutes will often get out stains that ordinary washing won't and it also kills germs by sterilizing, so is good for face flannels, dishcloths and tea-towels. If you have a stubborn stain, send it to a good laundry with a note safely pinned to the item.

When to use bleach
* To disinfect both the wash and the washing machine.
* To lift off heavy soil, stains and residues of stains.
* To whiten and brighten fabrics.
* To remove stains from sinks or baths; deodorize sinks and toilet bowls; remove stains from coffee pots, teapots and cups; disinfect chopping blocks, wells and swimming pools; and remove mildew, etc.

How to use bleach
* Don't use chlorine bleach on silk, wool, permanently treated clothes, mohair, leather, acetate or rayon.
* Use bleach carefully according to directions, but remember that bleach shortens the life of any fabric.

* Don't mix bleach with any other chemical or cleaner. It could be dangerous.
* Use chlorine bleach for whites and an oxygen bleach for colours (this is a preventive bleach that stops colours looking dingy rather than making them white).
* Don't add liquid chlorine bleach directly to the wash at the beginning of the washing machine cycle or it may cancel out the optical brightener in the detergent.
* If you want **to make your own chlorine bleach**, the famous French Javel water (merely a chlorine bleach solution) is based on a mixture of 450 g (1 lb) washing soda to 2 litres (4 pt) cold water, with 200 g (8 oz) chloride of lime (from the DIY shop) added and stirred.

Tips to save money and increase efficiency

If you're not using a liquid detergent (such as Ariel), which is less harmful for your machine, always *thoroughly dissolve* soap or detergent powder before adding clothes. If the detergent hasn't been properly dissolved, you risk a patchy garment, so never sprinkle washing powder on clothes.

For a hand wash Try using diluted liquid dishwasher detergent, which is as mild as, and cheaper than, special soapflakes.

For a cheap wash Unless you're washing silk, wool or something delicate, try saving money and softening water by using 2 parts soap powder to 1 part washing soda.

For really dirty clothes such as workman's overalls, try 3 parts detergent to 1 part washing soda.

In hard-water areas, where soapy water goes scummy and whites look grey, always use hot water and soften the water by adding washing soda *before* the soap is added (otherwise you will still get the scum). If you're using a machine, fill it with water, add soda, agitate to dissolve soda, then add soap and dissolve. Then add laundry.

Problem corner

If you have anything too big to go in your machine, use the bath. I wash a huge, white cotton broderie-anglaise-covered quilt with a synthetic filling by filling the bath with lukewarm water and detergent. The quilt soaks overnight. In the morning I scrub by hand its tedious yards of lace frills, then let the water out. To rinse the quilt, I fill the bath twice with lukewarm water, then drain all the water out. I stamp barefoot on the thing to get out as much water as possible. I hang the quilt over the edge of the bath, still dripping into it, and leave it for a couple of hours. I spread it on towels on the floor and I stamp again. Then I drag it out into the sun and dry it over towels.

If you have a treasured item, wash it yourself, in sink or bath. You are insanely optimistic if you hopefully wash a treasured garment in a washing machine.

If you have children's nightwear, these garments by law must be flame-resistant, but if they are not washed with phosphate detergents *they lose their flame resistance*. If you use non-phosphate detergents, soak clothes afterwards for an hour in a bucket of cold water and one cup vinegar, then rinse in clear water and dry.

If your drip-dry items wrinkle, don't wash heavy and light items together, don't overload washing machine or dryer. Take out of dryer immediately it stops or (if you don't want to be hanging around the dryer *waiting* for it to stop) drip-dry the garments into the bath or shower tray, squeeze the bottoms, then gently pull them into shape.

If your wash is looking scummy, try once a month putting it through the washing machine as usual, only without adding soap or detergent to the water.

Washing in soft-water areas
* Try a cold water wash.
* Use soap powder.
* Clean whites with a ten minute pre-soak in bleach water ($\frac{1}{4}$ cup for 18 litres (4 gal) of water).

Washing in hard-water areas
* You can use Calgon powder to soften the water, or install an expensive water softener. Otherwise . . .
* If soap is used in a hard-water area, a limestone scum will form.
* Synthetic detergents generally work very well in hard water.
* Try a *cold-water* wash with a non-phosphate detergent and rinse very well.
* **Warning!** Non-phosphate detergents can clog your machine with calcium deposits if used with hot water.
* If a **new washing machine** isn't giving as good results as hand-washing and you are in a hard-water area, check the washing instructions on the package, to be sure you're using the right washing agent for your machine and your local water, and if you are, then try using a lot more of it.

Drying clothes

If you dry your washing outdoors (using free energy), wipe the line first and stand with your back to the wind so the wet things don't flap in your face.

I bought a drying machine in the years when it rained 361 days *somewhere* in Britain (meteorological department figures). Without a garden, I find a dryer more important than a washing machine. A good tumble dryer can also reduce ironing by 90 per cent. Clean out the lint filter every time you load the dryer and check the exhaust duct once a year (see p. 62 for points to check when buying a dryer).

Drip-dry items Pillows and other feather-filled objects can be washed whole and tumble-dried.

Starching Buy a powdered starch, such as Robin, and mix exactly as it says on the container. Spray starch tends to leave a nasty brown deposit on the base of the iron, which you then transfer to the next white blouse. So do spray starch items last. Then unplug the iron, cool it and clean the base with a special iron cleaning cloth or a sole plate cleaner, which won't scratch the surface.

Use plastic starch if you want a rock-hard finish like nurses' cuffs.

Ironing

The secret of ironing is to avoid it. I learned this by accident when, fifteen years ago, I ironed a shirt. It took two tear-sodden hours and I scorched it (some say, carefully). Since then it has been understood in my family that Mother Doesn't Iron (like Mother Doesn't Speak German, Mother Doesn't Play the Guitar and Mother Isn't a Redhead). In my family we are all allowed a few idiosyncrasies per person: we choose our own and respect everyone else's. Anyone who wants his shirts ironed does them himself and this is regarded by me as idiosyncratic.

If you like ironing (my mother finds it very soothing), put the iron on something flameproof, such as a metal stand or heat diffuser on the end of the ironing board. Any old ironing board will do. My mother uses a cheap wooden one, which she covers with a pretty material, sticking it on with drawing pins.

Get a sleeve board: you can't iron a sleeve without it unless you mess around folding clean tea-towels into arm-shaped pads.

If you're going to iron, do so while the clothes are still damp. If you can't iron

at once, either roll up the clothes while still damp (I once accidentally left some sheets like this for a week and they went grey-green in parts) or else, just before you iron, wet with a flour shaker filled with water: the very best thing for damping-as-you-iron is a pressure sprayer, like that bottle gadget you squirt to clean plant leaves.

It is important to know *what* you're ironing. Read the label first. Silk, or any synthetic, can fall apart under your eyes if you use too hot an iron. If you *know* it's cotton or linen, use a hot iron. If you don't know, take it gently. Start ironing on a part that won't show in case you're about to burn it.

Always try to iron clothes through a damp cloth. Many cheap fabrics, such as boutique crêpe and satin, should always be ironed through a damp cloth so the iron marks don't show.

The point of ironing on the wrong side is that ironing makes the material shiny. On the other hand, it's fiddly to turn things inside out and back again and you risk creasing them more than they were in the beginning.

Never iron velvet or velvet ribbon; steam it. Put on your electric kettle of water and, when boiling, point it at that which you wish to de-crease. Wear rubber gloves or you may steam-scald yourself. If you haven't a kettle, try hanging the velvet in the bathroom over the hottest possible bath (also a good, quick way to de-crease a suit when travelling) and if that doesn't work, take it to the dry cleaners.

Pressing is the same as ironing, only you do it over a damp cloth and push hard. I know a TV personality who always presses his trousers before wearing them – every single time – because it stops them knee-ing and bagging.

Airing If you put ironed things away when warm but still a little damp (which is very easy), mildew will sprout (see 'Stain removal', p. 44). In addition, damp clothes are unhealthy. So air things after ironing them, in the sunshine (best of all – but not for white woollens or you will probably have yellow woollens) or in the dryer. Don't air things in front of a fire, even with a guard. Shall I tell you how fast you can burn to death? In fifteen seconds.

How to buy the best and cheapest equipment

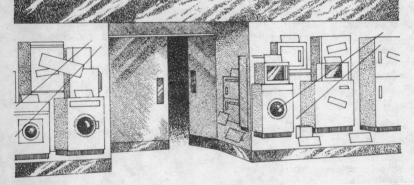

Good tip: Get sticky labels off shop purchases with methylated spirit.

ARMCHAIR SHOPPING
(mail order)

In favour of mail order

Buying by mail order saves time and trouble when choosing the goods. Instead of the misery of bus stops, crowded car parks and even more crowded stores, you can study the catalogue in the quiet of your armchair and you can ask other opinions; if you have ever stood on one leg and agonized in a store before buying what your mate turned out to hate, you will appreciate the advantage.

The goods are delivered to your home, which saves wear and tear of back, arms and temper.

You can return mail-order goods if you're dissatisfied. With reputable firms,

this is a genuine offer: they reckon that the bother of getting the goods back to them would be carried out only by someone with reason.

Mail-order goods can be cheaper than store-bought ones, because the savings on expensive retail stores (the wages of those indolent store assistants with insolent eyelashes) can be passed on to the customer. Stores in a high-rent area usually have higher overheads than a mail-order warehouse in a cheap-rent area where labour is plentiful.

Disadvantages of mail order

It can be difficult to judge from a photograph what the goods really look like and whether the quality is up to standard. However, some reputable firms try to deliver merchandise that is *better* than it looks in the catalogue, rightly reckoning that then they will have a delighted customer who'll come back for more, rather than a disappointed one who won't.

If you hate putting pen to paper, it can be a drag to write off for a few catalogues, fill in coupons and make out a cheque. But you probably pay by cheque in a store and paying up is never pleasant anywhere.

There is often a delay in the arrival of the goods . . . but so there is when getting 'instant' delivery from stores these days.

If the goods fail to give satisfaction, it's even more bother to pack them up again and send them back. But that argument also applies to retail stores: I have waited six weeks for a store to collect something they delivered to me by *accident* and left to clutter up my hall.

If you return the goods, there could be a delay in returning your money if the company is not a reputable one, so CHOOSE YOUR COMPANY WITH CARE. Usually advertisers in big reputable newspapers are a safe bet, because most reputable newspapers keep a careful eye on their advertisements – they don't want dissatisfied readers.

HOUSEHOLD MACHINERY

I took my first unconscious step towards female emancipation and away from martyrdom when I decided that, instead of teaching the au pair girl to cook for the children, it might be a better investment of time to teach the children to cook for the au pair. After all, I didn't change the children every year. For the first time they always ate what was put before them and they eventually asked to do the shopping, a task that they performed far more frugally than I.

The next step was to find a new job for the au pair and to invest the money saved on her wages in anti-drudge machines. One was the fridge-freezer, the other was the dishwasher, and any working woman with a family could regard these as business investments to offset against her wages in the family budget. The cost of both machines was equivalent to the au pair's wages for eighteen months, not taking her keep into account. Furthermore, I never had to do the freezer's homework and the dishwasher didn't have an affair with my husband.

You need all the help you can get and afford, but even if you can pay for it, manufacturers don't make it easy to choose, blinding you with marketing science and glittering extras that you probably won't need. You can get along without a surprising amount of equipment.

Before buying

Do not be swayed by glamorous advertisements. Before buying household machinery, trot along to your local library to see which model is recommended by *Which?* If you want to subscribe to *Which?* the address is: Consumers' Association, 14 Buckingham Street, London WC2N 6DS. Alternatively, write to the Good Housekeeping Institute (enclosing an SAE), which publishes fact sheets on various domestic appliances as well as on subjects such as insulation. The address is National Magazine House, 72 Broadwick Street, London W1V 2BP.

When buying machines don't forget to consider four points:

1 **Installation** Will it need new wiring, plumbing, or a ventilation fan and if so, is it possible and how much will it cost?

Will the shop you're buying the machine from arrange to have it installed, or will you have to arrange it yourself? If so, who does the maker recommend in your area?

2 **Maintenance** Is this the responsibility of the shop or the maker? If the latter, how long is it likely to take

Life expectancy of household appliances

Appliance	Years
Washing machine	11
Spin dryer	10
Clothes dryer	14
Refrigerator	16
Freezer	15
Oven, electric	16
Oven, gas	16
Vacuum cleaner	
upright	18
tank	15
Sewing machine	24
Toaster	10
Television, black and white	11
Television, colour (figures vary, but approximately)	7–8

for repairs to be done and how much might they be?

3 **Guarantee** *Always read the guarantee*. The time to read the boring, fine, grey print is BEFORE you buy, not when something goes wrong. Remember that there is no such thing as an 'unconditional guarantee'. The important point is to find out what is *not* covered by a guarantee; if you have doubts, ask the seller for answers *in writing* to the following questions:

* Is the entire product covered, or only parts?
* Is the shop or maker guaranteeing your purchase?
* How long does the guarantee last?
* Does it include the cost of spare parts?
* Does it include standard 'visit' charges and VAT?
* Who pays for the labour costs during the guarantee period?
* Is there an authorized service representative nearby?

Before you buy anything ask to see it demonstrated.

4 **Repairs** Stand over the man who's repairing your tumble dryer and see what he does and make a note of what was wrong with it. Also the date and what it cost. This might be useful ammunition with which to write to the manufacturer if the machine develops the same fault three times a year; or it might eventually teach you to empty the lint bag of your tumble dryer.

Basic equipment

Most people, however biased, would like certain basic equipment, such as cooker, dishwasher, refrigerator, freezer, vacuum cleaner and washing machine.

Cooker Choose your cooker with care because you'll probably be spending over 500 hours a year at it, cooking 1,000 meals a year. The basic choice is gas, electricity or solid fuel, such as an Aga.

It is possible to buy a second-hand cooker (reconditioned) through your local gas or electricity showroom, although they don't always like to own up to this. Insist and persist.

All the professional cooks I have ever met use **gas** cookers when possible because the heat of the burners is instantly adjustable. The top of a gas oven is hotter than the bottom, which can be a culinary advantage because you can economically fill the oven with foods to cook at different temperatures. I would not recommend a Gaggenau, because they are such a bother to light.

The advantages of **electricity** are the lack of fumes and an even oven temperature. The disadvantages of electricity are clumsily controlled heat, possible danger to children if you can't see that the burners are switched on and non-performance during power strikes.

A **solid fuel** cooker is cheap to run, can heat water and provide limited central heating, and is delightfully cosy to have in the kitchen. But they are comparatively large and dirty, are clumsily controlled and have no grill.

Other points to look for in all cookers are: size of grill, size of oven, self-cleaning oven, time-switch, spit, roasting thermometer, number of burners, simmerstat (so that milk or sauces simmer instead of boiling over), see-through oven doors with light-up interiors. Always buy a self-cleaning oven, if possible, because it eliminates a filthy job.

Eye-level grills (providing your eye is on that level) often mean red-hot grill-pan handles, but you can have a grill fixed apart from your oven. You can also have a gas and/or electric hob separated from your eye-level oven.

Double ovens are a good idea, especially if you are cooking several meals at once. They also ensure enough warm plates. Remember that if you choose a coloured oven, you will be stuck with that colour even if at a later date you want to change your kitchen colour scheme. I wouldn't do it.

Microwave ovens These are now used by many people who swear by them as great time-savers – the kitchen complement to a freezer. Unlike gas or electric ovens, which cook by the direct application of heat, microwave (radar) ovens generate electromagnetic waves that heat food far faster than conventional methods. The cooking can be done on paper plates, plastic, glass and ceramics – anything but metal – and does not mess up the oven. The fast-cooking process helps preserve the natural flavour and colour of food, and – according to the industry – cuts cookery bills by over 50 per cent. Against this saving you should measure the cost and the space it occupies. However, microwave ovens don't give the food a lovely brown colour – it comes out the same colour it goes in; if you want to make work for yourself, you can always brown it in your conventional oven or get a dual purpose oven, so that you defrost, then cook by

micro, then brown by conventional heat.

You really have to re-educate yourself to use a microwave oven. You can't just make your Aunt Sarah's casserole recipe and stick it in hopefully. You have to use a special cook-book (a good one is *Microwave Cooking for Health* by Beverley Piper published by Penguin Books), learn how to use the microwave and carefully follow the instructions that come with it. Be prepared to experiment, be prepared for one or two failures and be prepared not to show off your microwave to visitors until you've really tamed it. But you *can* totter home at night after a hard day over a hot typewriter and defrost a frozen steak in fifteen minutes or cook a baked potato (very comforting) in a few minutes.

Slow cookers Better known as crock-pots, because the cooking surface is an inner ceramic pot. For the woman in a rush a crockpot makes it possible to prepare long-cooking dishes like stews in the few minutes it takes to get ready the ingredients. You put the food in the pot in the morning, set the control at low, about 100 °C (200 °F) and go about your business. No stirring, no peeking, no worry about burning. They cost only a few pence a day to operate (as much as one burner, not one oven), and the slow-cooking method is particularly good for tenderizing cheaper cuts of meat.

One disadvantage is that the sealed-in heating element cannot be repaired if it breaks. The other disadvantage is that in order to get the family show on the road, you might be performing like an eight-armed Indian goddess before breakfast and not be able to spare even those few minutes to prepare the ingredients. In which case I suggest that you prepare it the night before, when cooking the evening meal (*not* after eating it, when the Inner You tends to run down).

DOWN WITH SUPERWOMAN!

Margaret Drabble told me that Victorian writer Mrs Gaskell was once asked how a woman could be a successful writer. She pondered, then answered, 'Get a slow casserole cooking first thing in the morning, then you can concentrate on your work.' Were she living today, I'm sure she would have an electric crockpot.

Extractor fan Every kitchen should have an extractor fan, preferably with a ducted range hood. Apart from the not necessarily delightful odours of cookery, a cooker can put out as much as 90 kg (200 lb) of grease-laden moisture a year. Much cheaper to buy and install is a *ductless* hood, which does not expel the air but filters and recirculates it. Grease and odour filters trap a lot of kitchen smog, but do not cool the atmosphere. Don't forget that they have to be cleaned regularly.

Dishwasher The advantages of having a dishwasher are many: your washing up gets done better and is also sterilized; you might save up to an hour a day at the sink; your guests don't feel that they have to offer to help you wash up. A dishwasher uses about two units of electricity for a single wash – about the same as it costs to run a fridge for a day.

Don't expect a dishwasher to dispense with your dishwashing, but it will halve the job and also seems to provide a painless, built-in discipline for tidying up immediately. People with dishwashers always seem to have tidy kitchens. Some hardy types claim that after scraping the dishes and pots you might as well wash 'em. However, if you have a good-sized family and/or like to entertain, a dishwasher is definitely liberating. A dishwasher requires only ten minutes of your time to stack a load that would take at least forty-five minutes to do by hand.

Most dishwashers have several cycles, and many of them wash saucepans too.

The water should be between 55 and 60 °C (130 and 140 °F). The machine must be carefully loaded, the dishes should be scraped, a special dishwasher detergent must be used and, although these machines generally do a good job, they will ruin wood, bone, horn, hand-painted or delicate china, cut or etched glass and most plastic (although Melamine is supposed to be dishwasher-proof). A rinse aid is necessary to ensure that the final rinse leaves no smears on the dishes that would otherwise be wiped off with a cloth when drying. You may also need to add salt to the machine's water softener every now and again.

If you've never had a dishwasher, this sounds like a lot of trouble, but within a week, you'll be hooked on it. I have *two* dishwashers because when I have people to stay there's too much for one load. Don't buy an expensive one; like racehorses, these machines seem to be highly strung and the more sophisticated the machinery, the more expensive the repair. Buy from the cheap range at John Lewis. Stick a label on the door saying 'No wood, cut glass or plastic'.

If you don't eat at home much or have a small family, don't get a dishwasher; get two wooden dish drainers from Habitat, which fold flat when not in use.

Refrigerator When buying the first time, people always buy a too-small fridge. The average family needs about 0.3 cu. m (12 cu. ft); minimum 0.11 cu. m (4 cu. ft) even for a bachelor.

Absorption models are silent but use twice as much electricity as compressor machines, which purr.

Useful things to have in a refrigerator are:

1 Well-organized, back-of-door storage, with enough height for hock bottles.
2 Adjustable shelving.

3 Plenty of room to make ice.
4 A worktop, if you need only a small model.
5 Deep-freeze space, if you're not buying a freezer.

Ignore ridiculous egg holders. (You shouldn't keep eggs in the refrigerator or they will crack when you boil them, and you can't always make mayonnaise with them unless you take them out half an hour before using them.)

The extra cost of a frost-free or self-defrosting refrigerator is a worthwhile investment over the ten- to fifteen-year lifetime of the appliance. Otherwise, it will have to be defrosted manually every two weeks.

Deep freeze See 'Food', p. 134.

Vacuum cleaner There are basically three types of vacuum cleaner:

1 **An upright model** has a revolving brush to sweep the carpet and is good if you have acres of fitted carpet. Although you can get kits of attachments for vacuuming stairs and hard-to-get-at places, an upright is awkward to lift.
2 **A cylinder or canister model** is easily stored, especially good for rugs and stairs, with special attachments for curtains and upholstery.
3 **A heavy-duty wet/dry model** on castors will follow you like a dog. I use this because it's light to lift and cleans *everywhere* easily. The drawback is that it needs more room for storage.

Don't bang a vacuum cleaner about, it's a sensitive machine. Pick up hairgrips or pins by hand because they might damage the engine. Empty the bag before it's full. Service it regularly, because repairs are expensive, and *stop using it* if you suspect that it's faulty.

Washing machine Here we are in the fog-index area. Pay no attention to TV advertisements. Basically, you have three alternatives.

1 **A twin tub**, with one tub for washing and the other to spin dry, after which clothes are dried in a tumble dryer or on the line. It needs constant attention, but it used to take me two hours to do my family laundry for four and the *lot* got finished in that time.
2 **An automatic washing machine** washes, rinses and spin dries, leaving you to dry the load by some other method. Only buy the sort of machine that does this without any further attention from you in order to rinse and spin dry.
3 **A washer-dryer** will wash, rinse, spin dry and tumble dry without any further attention while you watch a film; the load will take much longer to deal with than with either a twin tub or an automatic. The advertising may well cheerily advise you to 'spread the load and banish washday'. In fact, this seems to mean doing some washing every day, instead of the lot in one go.

To summarize, an automatic washing machine does *not* tumble dry.

It *is* possible to buy a fully automatic machine in which you can fling your dirty clothes and later remove them completely dry. On no account buy a washer-dryer unless it does this in one operation – i.e., you flick the appropriate dials and switches at *one time only*. Unfortunately, my AEG washer-dryer will not do this, so that it means instead of coming home to dry clothes, I come home to damp clothes and have to then programme the machine a second time.

When my son left home, I gave him a Miele, which he called the automatic Mum. Not cheap, but twelve years later it is still working.

You have to bend down to a **front-loading** machine, but you have to lean over a **top-loading** model and heave out the damp load. Short girls with weak

DOWN WITH SUPERWOMAN!

backs should avoid them. Obviously you can't build a top-loading machine into a laundry 'wall'. I prefer front-loaders.

Tumble dryers A tumble dryer is essential if:

* You have small children and a lot of washing to do.
* You live in a flat with nowhere to hang your washing to dry.
* You live next to an industrial area or near a motorway.
* You hate going to the clothes line in winter.

Tumble dryers tumble damp clothes in warm air until they are dry, with a cold tumble afterwards to prevent creases. Dryers can be very sophisticated, with several operating thermostats to provide a variety of temperatures and drying cycles to accommodate different types of fabric.

Tumble dryers must be vented to allow the damp air to pass out of the room, otherwise you will have severe condensation problems. But you needn't have a permanent venting system that runs through an outside wall. Venting kits, which come with most tumble dryers, have a venting hose that can be hung out of a window, so long as the machine is near enough.

Sewing machine A sewing machine is a wonderful slave for plain sewing, mending, making alterations, seaming fabrics to make curtains. If you haven't learned to use one, take a few lessons. (Almost all stores that sell sewing machines can tell you where to learn to use them.) The kind of machine to buy depends on the kinds of sewing for which you will use it.

The 'Mini' versus the 'Porsche' The simpler the better to start with. A really complicated machine may awe you into inaction. If you don't want to produce elaborate stitches, buy a simple model.

A **portable** machine comes in a carrying case. A **non-portable** machine is a piece of furniture. A portable in a carrying case requires storage space and also a sewing box. Before deciding on a portable (which is really only portable if you're an amateur weight-lifter), remember that the machine will have to be placed on something for sewing. Card tables aren't strong enough and dining tables can be a bit high. I used to wham away at my desk.

A lightweight portable is not suitable for sewing heavy fabrics. If you are planning to stitch loose covers or winter woollen coats, you had better get a heavier machine (but not otherwise).

Don't buy a sewing machine that has plastic parts. Your best buy may be a second-hand, reconditioned machine. These usually come with guarantees and can give excellent service. Before buying you should test the actual machine you're purchasing.

Sewing machine check-list
* Is the control – foot pedal or knee lever – comfortable?
* Is the light in a good position? Is it easy to change the bulb?
* Are the markings on the machine for tension and stitch adjustment clear? Are these adjustments easy to use?
* Is the machine quiet?
* Is it easy to insert the bobbin and to wind the thread on it?
* How is the machine oiled?
* Is the wiring protected?
* If the cabinet has a hinged lid, is it properly supported when open?
* Are the spare parts for the machine readily available? (For that reason alone it is inadvisable to buy an unknown brand; repairs may be difficult.)

Maintenance A sewing machine should

last more than twenty years (in fact, more like a hundred years if the parts are not plastic), but the machine needs some care. Lint should be removed as it accumulates. The tension discs, bobbin case and levers should be wiped with a soft cloth. The moving parts should be oiled unless the machine is self-oiling. The machine should be cleaned periodically.

To buy or not to buy?

Always cut out machinery where possible; there is then that much less to go wrong and more available kitchen space. Here's my biased list of what and what not to buy, and what to look for when you decide to invest in further helpful equipment.

AND SO TO BED

Cooking apart, what a bride needs to know most about – and generally knows least about – is what to look for when buying a double bed.

Apparently most people make three big mistakes when buying their first double bed.

First mistake They economize. Most of the cost of a mattress is inside, where you can't see it. Women will buy a good bedspread because they – and their friends – can see what they're getting for their money. But faced with two beds that look alike and are the same size, they don't see why one should cost more.

Second mistake Newly-weds buy too small a bed.

To buy	Why?
A good radio	It entertains and informs when you're doing the washing-up and says good morning cheerfully.
Continental quilts	They simplify bed-making and are lighter and cosier than traditional bedclothes.
Good quality, drip-dry, non-iron bed linen, underwear and shirts	They save time and trouble.
A self-cleaning oven	It eliminates a dirty job.
A front-opening deep-freeze	Top-loading ones can be awkward and confusing to use.
A tumble dryer	It rained in Britain somewhere or other on 350 days one year and a tumble dryer gets things bone dry.
An electric trashmasher	If you live in isolated country.
A cordless steam iron	One thing less to trip over.
An adjustable ironing board to suit your height	Otherwise you will get backache, or worse.
A shower in the bath	A shower uses less water than a bath; it makes hair washing easy and comfortable; children love it; it encourages people to clean the bath and a cold shower is invigorating.
Mixer taps	For painless temperature control.
Electric blender or food processor	It makes soups, purées and puddings in a trice and grinds coffee as well. Escoffier would have given his *sous-chef* for one.
A combined microwave/conventional oven	If you can afford it, this little wonder works out the time to defrost, the time to cook and you can brown a joint without shifting ovens.
A good steady stool that converts to a stepladder	You'll use it constantly.
Anglepoise lamps	For close work, study, shaving, make-up and even washing-up.
A solid, non-rickety trolley	It's a movable, working or stacking surface for the kitchen, study or work-room.
A double sink with swivel mixer taps	It's half-way to a washing-up machine.
An electric coffee grinder	If you haven't got a blender and enjoy coffee.
An electric kettle	. . . because it boils in a trice.

Inexpensive gadgets worth the money

To buy	Why?
A pair of cheap sunglasses to keep in the kitchen	For peeling onions.
A one hour timer – clock-work, not battery	Useful for timing anything, not just cooking.
A take-any-size bottle top opener that looks a bit like a pair of nutcrackers	If you don't have Superman wrists.
A Pyrex measuring jug or Talaware tin measurer with ancient British measurements as well as metric ones	For using pre-metric cookbooks and for converting continental and American recipes.
Fold-flat wooden drainers with shelves for cups (from Habitat)	Cuts out drying dishes by hand.
A cutlery drainer basket	Cuts cutlery drying time.
A good, bendy fish slice	Fish won't break as you serve.
A small steak hammer	For bashing steak and flower stems.
A good (wooden, not plastic) pepper grinder	Plastic ones slip their grinding wheels.
A kitchen paper dispenser	For holding rolls of aluminium foil, clingfilm, kitchen roll, baggies and kitchen notebook.
A frying-pan cover	To braise food.
A wok	Because men and children love to use it.
A self-cleaning garlic press	It reverses to press out its own squashed left-over bits.
Electric knife sharpener	If you need knives, you need sharp knives. Blunt knives are dangerous.
Three good kitchen knives	They are basic kitchen equipment.
Cheap non-stick saucepans, casserole and frying pans	They take the strain out of washing-up.
A Cooper's roasting thermometer	You'll never overcook a joint again.
A pair of kitchen tongs	To save your fingertips.
A shopping basket on wheels	To save your back. Shop in luggage shops for a good-looking, fold-up bag on wheels with a shoulder strap.
Rubber ice trays	Plastic ones break. With these you can remove one cube at a time without hitting the thing or holding it under a tap.

Not to buy	Unless
An electric floor-polisher	You have acres of parquet, PVC or linoleum floor.
A water softener	You can't work up a lather in your house. A water softener is necessary in areas in which the water is so 'hard' (loaded with minerals) that it reacts with soap to leave rings of sludge around the tub, besides making the coffee taste terrible.
Electric frying pans } Electric toasters }	You want to accumulate mechanical clutter in the kitchen.
Tupperware	You can't find cheaper plastic containers at your local large store.
Exercise machines	You know someone who's used one for over a year.
A waste-disposal sink unit	You live in a seventeenth-storey flat with little room for a dustbin.
A flimsy lightweight dish drainer	You don't mind the lot crashing to the floor.
Plastic colanders	You don't mind replacing them regularly. They seem to melt disgustingly before your eyes.

Third mistake They buy a bed because they like its cover, although they see it only when they're turning the mattress.

So what do you need to know about buying a double bed?

What is a bed? A bed is a mattress

supported by a base, which may be of open coiled springs, wire mesh or laminated wood, which is generally specified for slipped-disc sufferers. If the base is upholstered, it is made of covered coiled springs.

How long? A 1.8 m (6 ft) man needs over 4 cm (1.5 in) at his head and feet, yet standard beds are 1.9 m (6 ft 3 in) long. Customers rarely ask for anything longer. A bed should be 15 cm (6 in) longer than the taller occupant.

How wide? Sleeping alone you need 90 cm (3 ft) width, but two people together need less than 1.8 m (6 ft) because, as one expert said, 'Whether or not it's deliberate, there's a certain amount of animal magnetism when two people sleep together.' But unless they snuggle up like a couple of puppies they need a bed at least 1.5 m (5 ft) wide and not the traditional 1.35 m (4 ft 6 in).

How high? Expert opinions vary between 45 cm (18 in) and 50 cm (20 in). Elderly people find it easier to get out of a high bed and it is certainly easier to make. A bed that consists of a mattress on the floor is very difficult to make, unless used with a sleeping bag; if so, this should have an inner sheet or sheet bag, otherwise the sleeping bag will smell fusty. If you buy sleeping bags, get the sort that can be unzipped to use as a quilt or zipped to each other to make a double sleeping bag – you never know.

Castors can be fitted to a bed in order to make it easier to pull out and make, and easier to clean underneath; buy them from a hardware store.

Which mattress is best?

Latex foam on a laminated wood base has a disadvantage in that restless sleepers generally hit base. These mattresses are generally 15 cm (6 in) deep and don't need turning, don't make fluff and don't attract moths or vermin.

Foam plastic mattresses have the same qualities and keep their shape and resilience better than they used to. In case you smoke in bed, these may burst into flames.

Interior sprung mattresses are made of coiled wire springs, well padded with cotton waste, coiled hair and rubber or plastic foam. Beware of those that are over-sprung: one bed almost threw me out every time I turned over.

Pocketed sprung mattresses – the most expensive – are built to last a lifetime. Each of the hundreds of springs is sewn into a separate pocket, which ensures independent suspension. Everyone moves in bed about four times an hour, and a man and a woman rarely weigh the same. Consequently, unless the mattress has independent suspension, the lighter partner often slides downhill. But not on a pocketed sprung mattress.

Flock mattresses are to be avoided if possible. They are made from wool waste, or flock, which may quickly become lumpy.

Look for a mattress with a BS (British Standard) label.

How long can you expect a mattress to last? Of course it depends on a lot of variables, such as the weight of the people who lie on it, how often it is used, and how good it was in the first place, but a rough life expectancy might be as follows:

Flock (considered unsatisfactory by bedding experts because of a tendency to lump) 6 or 7 years.
Latex foam 15 years.
Spring interior 15 years.
Pocketed spring 20 years.

Heal's have a special mattress-making department, which will give free, specific quotations for remaking old mattresses. 196 Tottenham Court Road, London W1P 9LD (tel: 071-636-1666).

DOWN WITH SUPERWOMAN!

All you need to know about a futon

A futon is an alternative to a conventional bed or a converted sofa bed, and is especially useful in bedsitters. Originally from Japan, it is basically a 7.5-cm (3-in) thick cotton mattress that folds into three parts and looks like a sandwich, or two parts with the third used as a sofa back.

Futons are made by machine-blowing raw cotton into sheets about 2.5 cm (1 in) thick. The sheets are cut to size and three sheets are inserted into a cotton case through an open seam. The layers are then teased to the edge of the case to ensure a smooth and even surface. The seam is sewn up and the futon is tufted with cotton thread to hold the layers securely in place. You can also buy wool-mix futons (70 per cent cotton, 30 per cent wool), which are slightly softer to lie on.

You can sleep on a single futon or stack two on top of each other, directly on the floor or on traditional tatami mats. You can also buy a wooden base to raise it off the floor, making it more like a conventional bed.

Futons are space-saving; when not in use, they can be rolled up and put in a cupboard; they make a convenient spare bed; they give firm and comfortable back support, so are good for orthopaedic use; they provide good insulation and children can't fall out of a futon.

The disadvantages of a futon are: it is awkward for the old and arthritic, who find it difficult to heave themselves up from a low bed; it takes a while to become used to sleeping on a firmer surface than that to which you are accustomed.

How to clean a futon Remove fresh stains, such as spilt coffee, by dabbing with a tissue or paper cloth to absorb as much liquid as possible. Next, wipe with a wet cloth, without soaking the material, then air it to dry. Remove any remaining stain with a spot cleaner, such as Goddard's Dry Clean.

As with a duvet, you can use a cotton cover to protect your futon, which can easily be removed for washing. My futon is dark brown and doesn't often need washing. I use it as a sofa and spare bed.

Bed dress

Pillows Down is soft and light and expensive. Feathers are heavier and cheaper. Foam is less yielding, more springy, doesn't last as long as down or feathers, can make your neck feel tense and I can't stand it. Comparative shopping is essential with pillows because there are amazing price variations. John Lewis and British Home Stores give good value. Buy at sale time.

Buying bed clothes When buying sheets or blankets, a generous allowance is the width plus 45 cm (18 in) to tuck in on all sides.

Sheets Having impulsively and creatively bought patterned bed linen over the years, I gloomily admit that the glamorous, glossy-magazine, bed image that I originally had in mind has been shattered. If you scorch a pillowslip here and lose a sheet there, you end up with one rosebud-strewn pillow, one scattered with teddy bears, a multi-striped top sheet and a brilliant blue undersheet.

If you want to simplify life, buy only white bed linen, which always looks crispest, is easier to launder if badly stained and is *cheaper* anyway. Cheap sheets can be full of filling, which makes them feel less thin but which comes out with the first wash. Look closely at your sheets and check that you have a tight, firm weave by crunching a corner between your fingers: you can then see if there seems to be a lot of starchy filling.

Wait to buy linen until the summer or winter sales, then go to stores with a good reputation. Habitat and John Lewis stores provide excellent value and a great range of colours. They also take enormous trouble over any complaints. For inexpensive linen get the Limerick's catalogue from 117 Victoria Avenue, Southend-on-Sea, Essex (tel: 0702-343486).

Buying blankets Warmest and lightest are fine merino wool, then pure wool, then Acrilan, which is moth-proof, easy to wash, quick to dry and will not shrink or 'felt' – that is, get thick and stiff. Some synthetics can feel funny – it's difficult to describe, but a bit as if they'd been made from sticky candy floss – and they are not nearly so cuddly as wool. Wool-and-rayon mix blankets are less warm and don't wear as well as most all-synthetics, but they feel better. Wool-and-cotton mix blankets are generally cheapest and hard-wearing but they are heavy and not so warm as all-wool blankets. Buy at sale time. Comparative shopping essential.

Below is a guide showing metric bed sizes and the correct sheet and blanket size for each. Take it with you when you shop for sheets and blankets and don't let shop assistants persuade you to buy sheets that are too small for your bed.

Any larger bed or round bed requires special sheet and blanket sizes, which are fantastically expensive and, as they're generally specially made, they generally take months to arrive.

All you ever wanted to know about a continental quilt

A continental quilt almost eliminates bedmaking. A good continental quilt (or duvet) can be the equivalent of at least three blankets, and can cost and weigh considerably less than conventional bedclothes.

You're supposed to make the bed using only a bottom sheet and a quilt cover, but I use two sheets traditionally and keep the quilt in its special cotton case until spring-cleaning time comes round, when I wash the case only.

What, you may wonder, is the

Bed and bed linen sizes

Bed size	Sheet size
1 **Very narrow** 76 × 190 cm (2 ft 6 in × 6 ft 3 in) Don't buy it; it's too narrow	150 × 260 cm (60 × 102 in)
2 **Small single** 90 × 190 cm (3 ft × 6 ft 3 in) Minimal comfort for one 3 **Standard single** 100 × 200 cm (3 ft 3 in × 6 ft 6 in)	180 × 260 cm (70 × 102 in)
4 **Small double** 135 × 190 cm (4 ft 6 in × 6 ft 3 in) Minimal comfort for two 5 **Standard double** 150 × 200 cm (5 ft × 6 ft 6 in) Also called Queen size	230 × 260 cm (90 × 102 in)
6 **King size** 180 × 200 cm (6 ft × 6 ft 6 in)	275 × 275 cm (108 × 108 in)

Blanket size
Blankets should be the same width as sheets, but they can be shorter, although never less than 250 cm (100 in).

Continental quilts
Don't buy too small (everyone does the first time)! Minimum quilt width for one adult is 135 cm (54 in) and for two adults, 180 cm (72 in). Buy small double-size for a child in a 90 cm (3 ft) wide bed; the overhang on the recommended size is too small. Buy the largest possible size for a double bed to avoid overhang disputes or cold bottoms.

DOWN WITH SUPERWOMAN!

difference between an eiderdown and a continental quilt? The eiderdown is tightly packed and crushed down and there are no air pockets to trap the warm air round you, which is what the quilt does, on the same principle as a string vest.

Can you use a double-bed eiderdown as a single quilt? No.

What should you look for when you buy a quilt? Inspect the label. Make sure it has the number and year of the latest British Standard for continental quilts. *Example*: BS 5335:1990. A quilt should also be labelled with the following: the manufacturer's name and trademark, a description of the filling material, an appropriate washing or dry-cleaning symbol, the length and width of the quilt in centimetres, the claimed thermal resistance of the quilt (measured in togs), a description of the fibre content of the casing material.

The seven questions to ask before buying a continental quilt are:

1 Is it large enough to keep the sleeper covered?
2 Is it light enough?
3 Is it warm enough? The thermal resistance of a quilt – in other words its insulation value – is measured in togs. The best merino blanket might have 9 togs and a Terylene P3 quilt has about 11 togs. Quilts rated 4.5 or 6.0 togs minimum are suitable for summer use; from 7.5 togs minimum up to 12.0 togs minimum are warm; over 12.0 togs are very warm. Down quilts vary between 10.0 and 15.0 togs.
4 Does it 'drape' well, settling snugly round the sleeper in order to trap the body's natural warmth?
5 Is it free from 'cold spots' caused by movement of the filling (i.e., collecting in a bag at the bottom of the bed)?
6 Is it constructed from good quality materials so that it stands up to the wear and tear of continual use?
7 Can it be easily cleaned?

In order to prevent edge draughts, a continental quilt must be large enough to overlap the sides and bottom of the bed while covering the sleeper.

Width Forget about the bed width. The minimum width quilt for one adult is 135 cm (54 in) and for two adults it is 180 cm (72 in). Two sleeping on a wide double bed *could* use a single quilt each, as they do in Austria. But it doesn't sound very friendly.

Length Forget about the bed length and think about the person. Again, don't skimp. Children grow fast and the same person might not always use that quilt. Minimum 200 cm (6 ft 6 in) to 210 cm (7 ft) for tall people.

Stitching There are several sorts of stitching, but there's no mystique about it. Some channel across, some channel up and down. It doesn't matter how it's stitched as long as there is stitching every 20–30 cm (8–12 in).

Synthetic fillings There are basically two types of synthetic filling: fibres and staple fibre. Staple fibres are chopped fibre bonded with an adhesive to produce a wad, like cotton wool. Staple fibre hasn't a good warmth-to-weight ratio and doesn't snuggle closely round you.

Buy only where you see the ICI Terylene P3 green label standard or the pink label for people who feel the cold more than most or live in a very cold house or district.

Synthetic filling is produced to a uniform density and placed between two cover cloths, which are stitched through in such a way as not to disturb the filling; this is where it scores over feather filling, which can move fairly freely up and down to lump inside the quilt. But synthetic fillings do not absorb moisture and many people find that synthetic quilts make them uncomfortably sweaty.

Feather fillings Old feathers aren't as efficient as new feathers. In time they turn to dust. The life of down feathers *in careful use* is forty years.

Down is from the breast of the female eider duck and there's no quill in it, which is why it is very soft. **Feathers** must also come from water fowl. In **mixtures,** what counts is the first word. **'Down and feather'** has to be 51 per cent down. So watch for this.

To clean No one expects you to clean a synthetic quilt often, if at all, during its working life. Should you have an accident, synthetic quilts should be washed. A quilt doesn't weigh very much, so any suitable washing machine or launderette machine will take it: what's easiest is to send it to the laundry. *Don't dry clean it.* Down and feathers have to be professionally cleaned. Send them to the Danish Express Laundry, 16 Hinde Street, London W1M 5AR (tel: 071-935 6306).

If you get a stain on a quilt cover, just push the filling out of the way and sponge the stain as fast as possible with cold water, or lukewarm water and washing-up liquid, rinse well and mop with a towel.

Beds might be quicker to make with quilts, but when made by me, they tend to look a bit wobbly and lumpy, as if there were still someone in there. Heavy-weight cotton bedspreads smooth them out nicely.

Do-it-yourself quilts Quilts are cheaper by about one-seventh if you buy them in a do-it-yourself kit, in down, feather or Terylene P3. There are several different sizes. I've tried a single: it's easy and quite quick.

Most merchandise mentioned in this chapter can be bought from stores in the John Lewis Partnership.

How to be a Successful Designer

TRUST YOUR OWN TASTE
(how and why you should develop your own decorative style)

Although money can't buy it, anyone intelligent can learn to have good taste. Otherwise you can spend like a drunken film star, but you risk an expensive clutter that hasn't quite come off. If you pay someone else to design your home, you risk something pretty expensive, lifeless and unlived in or, alternatively, an exuberantly camped-up setting with mouldings picked out in white and in which you feel uneasy.

So the first rule is: do it yourself. Because otherwise you'll never learn.

Discovering your own good taste is an unpeeling process, eliminating the layers that other people have impressed upon you. One of the easiest ways to **find out what you like** is to get a pinboard and start sticking up anything that takes your fancy – a scrap of lace, photo-graphs, postcards, a colour swatch, a cartoon.

Then start to **decide what you like best**, because good taste is the result of severe and constant pruning. Your taste develops and crystallizes. You create your own perfect environment by cutting out everything else.

You might like several styles – art deco, art nouveau, Bauhaus, functional and cottage modern – but, unless you're very sure what you're doing (and very few people are), stick firmly to one style.

Look at the way you dress: the colours of your clothes will also suit your room, which will then also suit you. If you're a brown and cream woman, go for that sort of room. If you're a silk girl, choose silky rayon. If you're a tailored type, so should your room be.

Use self-discipline For instance, in a bedsitter or small flat start with one colour theme and allow yourself only two subsidiary colours and two patterns – at the most. If you have a flat, using one overall colour scheme will make it more co-ordinated and pulled together, so will one floor colour throughout.

If you've got a badly shaped room complicated by writhing pipes or oddly boxed-in areas, use a dark colour all over walls and ceiling to simplify the area.

If you've got a horrid little box-shape, low-ceilinged room, pull it together with a small but strong traditional pattern over walls and ceiling.

In a dark basement have light walls and floor. Smartest basement I've seen yet had white ceramic tiles throughout.

Be realistic Just as you can't wear belts if you haven't a waist, or milkmaid smocks if you're six feet tall, you may not be able to indulge in ornate Victoriana in a modern flat, or pristine chrome and glass and fragile ivory figurines if you have five children and two labradors, or bright pink anywhere.

Be ruthless This applies to presents, however kindly given, if they are somebody else's taste and not yours; sell them, swop or hide them, because if you don't really like them, they only distract **your** style. Say, 'I'm saving it until I've got a bigger place!' or 'My mother's looking after it for me.'

No one's forcing you to be ruthless, but that's the only way to get the best effect.

Don't compromise Don't settle for second best. Don't have anything that is **nearly** all right. It should be the best or an obvious stand-in; if you long for a glass and chrome TV table, don't settle for one that your mother offered you with cabriole legs. Stand the TV on an orange box or on the floor.

Lack of money need not cramp your emerging style. For ten years I was a designer, producing rooms for other people. However, apart from one antique chandelier, my personal life has mostly been lived on exultant street-market bargains, chain-store furniture, cheap beds

that broke, prototypes that fell apart and painted junk. But as Mae West never said, money isn't everything. The decorative jobs that I've been most pleased with have always been my cut-price rooms.

Don't accumulate Apart from lights, carpet and curtains, the more you remove from a room the better it tends to look.

Analyse your fatal weakness and stamp it out, whether it is for Tudor chandelier light fittings that look as if Errol Flynn should be swinging from them, or a passion for making your own lampshades (I've never seen a home-made lampshade that didn't look wrinkled, tired or slightly drunk).

Stamp out your pretensions You can go out looking like a million dollars when you aren't worth a bus fare and people will only applaud, but you can't fool anyone in your home. Whatever your pretensions – intellectual, social, financial or moral – they will soon show up in your personal setting.

Finally, know what you're good at and emphasize it Don't try anything else. If you're a patchwork-and-homemade-scones girl with good child-bearing hips, you won't give an authentic impression of yourself in an incense-fuddled 'hippy' boudoir. But if plants just grow for you, have banks of massed ferns; if you've got an eye for little objects, collect tables of them. The trick is to know what you're bad at and **not** do it; to know what you're good at and **emphasize it**. I've **never** been made to work harder than when, for a short period, I was assisting David Hicks, who reputedly charges thousands of dollars an hour in New York for interior design advice. Here are some planning tips for those of you who can't afford him.

Never take any book on home design too seriously. Your taste and problems might be different from those of the author. And you want to end up with

DOWN WITH SUPERWOMAN!

something that *you* like living in and that looks as if it was meant to be lived in, not photographed.

The civilizing influence in my first home was a small puppy that swiftly grew to the size of a small sofa. By the time the dog had chewed her way round for a week, the place looked far less formal and more relaxed.

As space gets more valuable and you have less of it, you have to be more ingenious in planning. You may have just one room in which to eat, pay bills, watch television, sew on buttons, sit, drink and entertain. A designer will make amazing lists of all the activities your room is used for (recreational area . . . drinking space . . .) and then divide it up accordingly, but you can't divide what isn't enough in the first place.

Whether you're thinking of cheering up a bedsitter or planning a complete conversion, home design needs careful planning and involves four major practical decisions.

1 What you would like.
2 What must be done.
3 How much you can do yourself.
4 How much you can afford to have done by somebody else.

Start by making a list of what you hope to do and a secret list of what you think are other people's mistakes. Plan to spend only 60 per cent of your money, leaving 20 per cent for 'contingencies', which translated means mistakes or things you forgot to include. The other 20 per cent should be retained for things that turn out to be far, far more expensive than you ever expected. In ten years spent with a good design firm I never saw one job finished under budget. If your original decorating budget covers your final finished work, I'll happily buy **your** book.

If you are a muddler, plan the minimum furniture, never save souvenirs, and keep no newspapers or magazines.

Be lavish with your budget when it comes to storage space; in order to keep sane and tidy you need lots of drawers, shelves or bags to shove things into.

PLANNING

Get some graph paper and decide on a scale, whatever suits you best. 1:20 cm (metric) or $\frac{1}{2}$ in:1 ft is relatively easy to handle.

Make plans of your rooms, each to scale; then measure your furniture and draw that to scale. Write the name on each piece of it, for example, 'grandmother's rocker', and cut out the pieces. You can now juggle the furniture around the plans of the rooms.

You need far more space than you think (for instance, allow 75 cm (2 ft 6 in) depth of chair space round a dining table, because you have to pull the chairs out in order to sit on them).

Even when a plan looks perfect you will find that the room, once filled with furniture, looks far smaller than you imagined and **different** from the way you imagined it. The more you take out of a room, the bigger it looks. There is no exception to this rule.

Work out a colour plan. The less ambitious you are with colour, pattern and texture, the more likely you are to be successful. Stick to one basic colour scheme – i.e., beiges, browns and creams, or black, greys and white – then everything will flow into everything else. To get the colours right when choosing fabrics and carpets, see them under natural as well as artificial light.

When you go shopping, take a list of the items you need and **buy only those**, no matter how many fantastic bargains you see on your rounds.

Your financial order of preference should be warmth, light, comfort, decoration.

Your decorative planning sequ-

ence should be plumbing, heating, lighting, carpentry, built-in furniture, paintwork, curtaining, furniture, accessories.

If you live in a furnished flat, try to avoid spending money on fixtures that you can't take with you.

If your home is big, you need more furniture to fill it or it may feel self-consciously empty.

If your home is small, keep it uncluttered. Have plain, light-coloured walls with matching curtains, a pale, but practical, uniform coloured floor and mirrors.

Living-room can mean three separate rooms, or a kitchen/dining-room plus a sitting-room, or an open-plan kitchen/dining-/sitting-room. This last arrangement can be rather beat-up or very grand, but it's the least exhausting plan for a woman with no home help.

Many couples start with two small rooms, knock down the dividing wall and turn them into one big room. But unless you have a ridiculously narrow house, never knock the hall passageway wall down as well or you will suffer from draughts, dirt and a lack of privacy, while the sofa will always be strewn with raincoats if not satchels.

The Golden Rule for all small living-rooms is: the more space in the middle of the room, the better. Channel the traffic of comings and goings and site a telephone where it won't disturb the general conversation. Put the TV where you don't have to shift the furniture round when you want to watch it, or else have it on a trolley. Have small furniture that looks light and is easy to move, but don't buy a small two-seater sofa because invariably only one person sits on it; it may be better and cheaper to have easy chairs and no sofa.

Space-making

Circular dining tables save space. For parties, have a cheap, larger wooden top made, which is hinged and folds in the middle so can be kept under a bed. If you haven't much room, buy space-makers such as stacking chairs, stacking side tables, stacking stools, bookshelves and china.

If a table is also used as an office desk, buy an office cabinet on castors that can tuck away under the table when needed as a desk-drawer unit or be used as a bedside or telephone table. Also buy versatile furniture, such as flap-up, fold-down or otherwise expanding tables, a kitchen stool that converts to a small step-ladder, and children's beds of different lengths and heights on castors so they can slide under each other during the day. Buy dual purpose furniture, such as convertible sofas or beds with drawers beneath or beds with more beds beneath. Use built-in furniture where suitable.

Avoid sliding doors on cupboards in kitchen and bedroom unless you're desperately short of space and money. They tend to be the cheapest to make but the doors often jam and it's always difficult to get to the middle of the cupboard.

Shallow drawers are easy to keep neat. Keep deep drawers and cupboards tidy by subdividing them with knife boxes, shoe boxes, cheap trays, deep plastic cat-litter trays or seed boxes. These are good for make-up, bottles, jewellery, sewing kit and all kitchen storage because you can pull them out to get at the back items. They are also good for keeping underwear, children's clothes and small toys.

Use the backs of wardrobe doors to hang compartmented shoe bags for belts, scarves, gloves, handbags, ties, tights and shoe-cleaning equipment. It may even be possible to construct a 5 cm (2 in) deep wooden frame for the back of the wardrobe door and fix hardboard trays across it to hold small items. Stick a hanger through your laundry bag and hang it on the back of the bathroom door.

If you're chronically untidy (or if they are), you need not only a place for everything, but also an extra, empty space in which to fling what's left when you are caught on the hop. Keep an empty drawer or cupboard or buy a big laundry basket for a quick temporary tidy-up (or keep a grocery box under the kitchen table).

Maintenance

From now on buy everything with an eye to maintenance. And when buying furniture, lie on beds and sit on chairs and at tables to check that they fit you comfortably.

Upholstery is so expensive that you should silicone spray it and don't expect *that* to work magic. Loose covers are a great investment. Avoid loose weaves, which will hole quickly or hang unevenly in curtains. And avoid regular patterns, such as a houndstooth, because these show every mark. A dark or patterned fabric with a dark background is easily the most practical for upholstery. When you're looking at it in the shop, imagine that sofa with two ineradicable small coffee stains on it and you may see what I mean.

Curtains When buying materials, allow 10 per cent extra length for shrinkage **and** wash the material before you start (send it to the laundry).

Ask the shop assistant to calculate for you because you're almost bound to make a mistake. Allow 30 cm (12 in) hems in case you move and the next place has bigger windows. There's nothing more irritating than hems a little bit too short.

Lined and interlined curtains are nicest, but horribly expensive and difficult to make. If you're starting, it's easier and cheaper to make unlined curtains. Use a simple tape suspension method. I don't like using pinch-pleat removable prongs because they fall out so easily and are so difficult to put back. I find the easiest, trimmest method is Rufflette's Regis. It is a neat, smart shirr heading with wide tape and drawstrings. Some people don't mind hand-hemming curtains after they've been hanging a month. Other people prefer to take their curtains down five years later to find the pins irrevocably rusted into the hems.

Walls Always save a jar of paint for emergency touch-ups in every room you paint – and label the jar. When not wielding it, hang your paintbrush by the handle. Stand a paint tin on paper plate or circle of aluminium foil. **Never** hope that the paint won't splash. Clear up half an hour before you intended. Exhaustion suddenly paralyses you when decorating.

Sound equipment

Housing the family sound equipment is a simple, practical problem liable to be complicated by unpredictable human elements such as the chooser of the sound system, who tends to be male, fussy, blind to decorative considerations and immune to reason. Of course, the sound system should be part of the rest of the room, and not a walnut-veneered blot on a Philip Johnson landscape, but you'll never convince the serious stereo enthusiast of this unless you can also provide the essential environment his equipment needs. It should be:

1 On a level, solid base, not attached to the floor, because slamming doors, stamping feet and mass bopping tend to create bad vibes for stereo.

2 In a draught- and dust-free atmosphere.

3 Easy to get at.

4 Provided with proper storage for records, cassettes, cartridges, CDs,

videos, tape or any other audio-visual extravagances.

Always stack old LP records upright. I know a pop concert impresario who stacks them between full Coca-Cola cans.

HOW DO YOU MEASURE UP?

How deep is the ocean? How high is the sky? It doesn't really matter to you; what matters is whether you can hang your coat in the wardrobe or get the right number of knees under the dining table.

What follows is a summary of standard measurements. Remember that nobody is standard, so make allowances if you are an exquisite miniature and your husband is a giant, or vice versa.

Furniture

Dining and desk chairs Allow 60 cm (2 ft) width per person and 75 cm (2 ft 6 in) depth to allow for pulling chairs back from table before standing. A dining chair should be 45 cm (18 in) from floor to seat for eating at a table 75 cm (2 ft 6 in) high.

Dining table and office desk height Average table height is 71 cm (28 in). Narrowest width for dining table to seat people on both sides without unavoidable knee-brushing, 60 cm (2 ft). You may want an extending, folding table, but see that the legs and cross-bracing allow room for human beings. A round table with central pedestal saves space, saves knee-knocks and is the best shape for general conversation. However, if the room is long and narrow it may be better to choose a rectangular table.

Bookshelves Allow minimum 30 cm (1 ft) height per shelf (bigger for art books) and 30 cm (1 ft) depth.

Bookshelves should be supported by brackets or uprights every 60 cm (2 ft) or

they will sag under the weight of books. Shelves can be supported on a frame system or on metal adjustable brackets slotted into narrow, upright, metal strips that are fixed to the wall.

Wardrobes Never build or buy a clothes cupboard less than 60 cm (2 ft) deep. Average masculine shoulders are 45 cm (18 in) wide and hangers need breathing space to avoid bunching up.

A Swedish designer calculated that the average man needs 1.05 m (3 ft 6 in) minimum width for clothes hanging space, but I prefer to put my trust in the American designer who calculated that the average well-dressed man needs 1.9 m (6 ft 4 in) of well-designed closet, but that the average well-dressed woman needs almost twice that amount of space – 3.6 m (12 ft) – to keep well organized. That includes drawer space and out-of-season clothes space. He didn't define what he meant by 'well-dressed'. As far as I'm concerned that's Widow Onassis's level, but it's useful to quote to a man when you're sharing out the personal storage space.

Bathroom You need about 95 × 95 cm (3 × 3 ft) for a shower, approximately 170 × 70 cm (5 ft 6 in × 2 ft 4 in) for a bath, 70 × 80 cm (2 ft 4 in × 2 ft 8 in) for a basin, 70 × 80 cm (2 ft 4 in × 2 ft 8 in) both for lavatory and bidet.

NOT MUCH MONEY, EVEN LESS SPACE

The minimum living equipment is less and cheaper than you imagine. You can do without anything new except for divan beds and window blinds. Carpet, chairs, tables, storage items, all can be acquired cheaply secondhand.

There's no problem if you are living alone in one room, provided you have no belongings. This means, in fact, that there's **always** a storage problem. Solve it with a storage wall of shelves and stacking bins. John Lewis have inexpensive, folding, stacking, white-painted bookcases in their whitewood departments. Dexion maxi-bins – sometimes found in hardware shops – come in various sizes and bright colours and can hold anything. So can rows of plastic shopping bags or shiny black plastic dustbin liners (don't overweight them).

You could economize and use industrial shelving, or make instant shelves (for books, tennis balls or cornflakes) with planks of wood supported on bricks piled up in double rows, i.e., two bricks to each column. Expect to support your planks every 90 cm (3 ft). This also works (with broader planks) for fast mass seating.

Scrub, scrape, strip, paint or polish the floorboards; cover the centre with cheap Indian cream rugs (small ones; big ones are very hard to clean, something you don't realize until you've tried to heave a large, wet Indian rug out of the bath. Use lino paint to cover nasty-coloured linoleum.

You can get furniture cheaply if you know where to look, in junk shops, builders' yards, street markets and furniture marts, but you have to be prepared to wait. You'll never find what you want if you're in a hurry. Don't advertise for furniture or answer advertisements for furniture. You can waste a lot of time and money. Instead, haunt the auction rooms.

For new furniture that doesn't cost a fortune, QA (quick assembly), KD (knock down) and Demountable are all furniture kits that you assemble yourself. Sofas, desks, wardrobes, chairs, tables, dressers and even beds are available. Most pieces are designed to be put together with nothing more than a hammer, screwdriver or wrench: some come with a specially designed 'key' to tighten bolts or recessed screws. If buying on the spot, always ask a salesperson to demonstrate the assembly method because some of them would tax Einstein's brain.

Beware of over-elaborate KD or QA furniture. I once bought two screw-it-to-the-wall bookshelf-with-built-in-desk units for my sons. I actually assembled one and screwed it to the wall, an invitation for a boy to **prove** that it wasn't **properly** screwed-to-the-wall. After it had been torn out of the wall three times, I gave the other kit to the postman and **he** didn't do anything about it except sigh heavily when I asked.

Wicker furniture is a good buy; it's light to move around, has a pleasant summery look to it and is unlikely to disintegrate unless used outside. But it's unstable, it often squeaks, snags your tights and can be ripped apart by cats. Men don't like it because they can't throw themselves into it comfortably.

Perspex furniture is durable, lightweight and easy to clean, and comes in attractive colours that are added when the plastic is in liquid form, so it cannot fade or peel. There are two disadvantages, however. When you dust it, a static charge builds up and this makes dust cling, so pale Perspex furniture can tend to look grubby. The other drawback is that it scratches very easily – and stays scratched; you can't rub it down with half a Brillo pad. It doesn't mellow with age, like wood. You can sometimes file it down and oil it, but that can leave a nasty blob instead of a scratch.

Whitewood furniture is generally the best buy; sturdiest furniture that's the least trouble. You can always paint it. It needs a coat of primer to seal the porous wood; don't try to skimp this or the result will be blotchy and rough. On the other hand, it needs only one coat of clear varnish, or use Ronseal's pinewood shade polyurethane varnish to make it look like smart pine furniture; I've seen a whole whitewood kitchen successfully treated in this way.

There are only two things to say about

junk. First, never buy it if there's a suspicion of **living** woodworm. You can tell by the minute pinhead holes (scattered like grapeshot) and the tiny piles of wood dust underneath. Lots of lovely furniture has been successfully treated for wood-worm, but if in doubt – don't buy it.

My second point is that most junkshop owners are well behind current trends. You have only to look at the cut of their jeans to know that they don't spend their evenings with their nose in *Vogue*. It's therefore not difficult to buy just a little ahead of the trend and pick up really pretty things cheaply, as well as enjoying the thrill of the chase and restoration.

With aged upholstery, learn not to be put off by the guts spilling out of sofas, large burnt areas or a profusion of stains. Instead, look at the basic shape and remember that **anything** can be cleaned, re-covered or repaired; but always check for moth, woodworm and split frames. Buy upholsterer's rubber webbing to replace any springs that have gone ping. After removing the springs, tack the webbing across the frame: north to south, then east to west, or vice versa. If you're buying new upholstery, measure the space before you visit the shop or open the catalogue in order to make sure that there's room to get a four-seater sofa through the door and up the stairs and round the corner . . .

The is one problem that you don't have if you buy unit furniture. I personally find unit seating uncomfortable because the units tend to push apart and leave you sinking floorwards. But there's a lot to be said for it. The whole idea of unit seating is that you buy a piece at a time as you can afford it, and once you have enough you can always reassemble it in different ways, different rooms or different houses. Always buy units with removable covers, or the new ones will make the old ones look shabby. Always choose a big, established manufacturer

who doesn't look as if he's going to go bankrupt next week (in which case you'll never get the end of your sofa) and always choose solid, heavy furniture that doesn't skid about.

Be imaginative: if you want a huge coffee table, you could cut the legs off a cheap kitchen table and possibly cover it to floor level with a felt throw-over cloth. I discovered this trick after letting my flat to a nice American journalist, who sawed down the legs on my kitchen table, **then** told me and said that he hoped I didn't mind. I was speechless, but when I saw that instead of a cheap-looking white kitchen table I had a sumptuous coffee table, I forgave him.

A good example of comfortable one-room living on a next-to-nothing budget is an attic that once belonged to Jamaican politician Barbara Blake. Her priorities were a telephone, two good locks on the door plus bolt, chain and peephole, all of which she fixed in place herself. The fitted, dark-brown carpet was top priority, because she loved walking barefoot, because everyone she knew sat on the floor against big cushions (which she made from foam off-cuts) and because the floor was in such bad condition that it had to be covered with something.

'I spent all my money on the carpet, the cushions, paint and a tool kit,' she told me. 'If you have a good tool kit, you can do most small carpentry jobs yourself, and anyway you darn well have to these days, you just can't find any odd-job men, they've died out like pterodactyls. I covered almost the whole of one wall with an instant mural – a huge tree-against-the-blue-sky poster, which was an advertisement for a bank; I wrote to them and asked for one, then cut their name off the bottom.'

Some modern designers say who needs furniture anyway, even if you have the money to buy it? Why not a foam pad or old mattress (covered along with the floor by a deep-pile carpet) on which you doss down at night under a duvet. A foam pad platform with a shaggy carpet over it and bright cushions can make a casual recliner or bed or provide seats for a crowd, for the girl who collects the whole football team.

You might have a series of slab cushions that you, or any teenagers you try to look after, can use for sitting or sleeping on or building up to suit the purpose of the moment. The occasional visitor can be seated on these fabric-covered, semi-rigid foam pads, which can be used as individual low lollers, piled up for seating at a low table, or laid out side by side for overnight guests. Storage boxes can be used as side tables or else can have foam-padded tops when used as occasional seats. It's a thought, especially for the young and supple-kneed.

CONSUMER'S QUICK GUIDE TO FLOOR COVERINGS

Flooring is a big investment. If you're one of those people who move house every few years, putting in costly flooring or wall-to-wall carpeting is apt to be a rotten investment. You can't take either with you and the next owner of your home may not share your taste, so he won't want to pay for it. Another warning: a scramble of pets in your house can make a few hundred pounds' worth of wall-to-wall carpeting look, to put it politely, like a dog's breakfast in only a few months. (I've known a kitten wreck a fitted carpet before I'd even had the bill for it.) If you want to keep a decent fitted floor covering, as well as pets, use any other kind of surface. Coco matting is not a bad idea, so long as it's fitted like carpet, but it looks sleazy if it curls at the edges.

Don't have white or very pale floors of any sort – paint, carpet, rugs, linoleum, tiles – unless you're prepared for cleaning headaches. The exception is pale wood

or ceramic tiles in a dark basement, because the light-reflecting quality is worth any extra trouble.

Wood

There are two sorts of wood floor: hardwood, such as parquet or tiles, and softwood, such as pine. If you have an old house with wooden floors, you're lucky. Minor disadvantages are that wood scratches when heavy furniture is moved or children with metal tips on their shoes run across the floor, but it does resist ordinary wear and can be quickly cleaned with a damp mop.

If you have an old, heavily varnished, dingy, wooden floor, you can either strip it and revarnish it, or repaint it with yacht paint. I love the look of a well-sanded wooden floor sealed with polyurethane. This is a tough, long-wearing, plastic surface coating that eliminates the need for waxing. You can sand and seal a floor yourself, with a hired sander, but if you can afford it, have it done professionally since sanding is exhausting work and sealing needs a long drying time. **Two polyurethane coats are needed** (don't economize here).

My husband and I once laid a 9 × 6-m (30 × 20-ft) floor of pale birch squares and although we did it in a fairly sloppy manner (it was our first attempt), it really looked terrific. The polyurethane finish was great; the floor wasn't waxed once in ten years. However, we did it in the evenings after office work and the effort nearly killed me. I'd never do it again.

A wood-tiled or parquet floor with a varnish seal and a wax finish should never be washed with water (although you can damp-mop it occasionally). The frequency of waxing depends on wear as well as on your time and enthusiasm. Don't think you can get away without waxing. In time it will crumble like shredded wheat.

Carpeting

Rugs or carpets add warmth to a room, protect the floors and muffle sound, which can be more important in a flat than in a house. You'll get a good spacious effect with wall-to-wall carpeting and it is easy to maintain (although currently un-chic). All you need to keep it clean is good vacuum cleaning and a professional shampoo every two years (amazing clean-ups are possible). Make sure that wall-to-wall is professionally laid, on good underlay, otherwise floor-boards may show and seams come apart; also you may lay the pile the wrong way.

If you have half-way good-looking wooden floors you might use rugs (this is a chic look), but even if they're rubber backed they tend to slip and old ladies tend to break their legs on them. An almost room-sized piece of broadloom can be cheaper than a big rug.

Weaves and textures 'Wilton' and 'Axminster' describe the weave of a carpet. 'Broadloom' just means that it was woven on a loom over 1.8 m (6 ft) wide.

There are five basic carpet textures: cut pile velour (which looks like velvet), cord and twist pile, shag (which looks shaggy like a sheepdog) and carved (which has a textural, 3D pattern and is otherwise the same as velour). There's also Saxony, which is somewhere between velour and shag.

Velour looks grandest but shows footprints and traffic patterns.

Cord is easy to clean, robust and comparatively cheap. It wears best because of its relatively flat surface, but doesn't feel luxurious or bouncy underfoot.

Shag can look floppy, can flatten in patches if the tufts are too long, and high heels can snag in it. Otherwise it looks good. I find it very difficult to clean but, because of this, it's also easy to disguise stains. A tufted construction is traditional, but nowadays there is often a latex

backing to stop it stretching and to give it a good 'lay'. Bonded carpets are not looped under the basic weave; instead the fibres are bonded into place. This can save up to 30 per cent of the fibre, but they won't last so long. However, they're fine for bedrooms and other light-traffic areas.

You need best quality carpet where it gets the hardest wear (hall and stairs). You can get away with cheaper in the bedroom. Check whether your carpet is moth-proof or will burn easily, and what it's made of and how to clean it. Underlays double the life of a carpet, add warmth and a lush ankle-straining bounce, and lessen noise.

Try to avoid having a fitted carpet under the dining table; it will stain very fast indeed. If you have fitted carpet, put a patterned rug on it – easier than the carpet to take away and clean.

Solid-colour carpeting shows more stains than the tweedy or patterned kinds, but looks more luxurious. Theoretically, a medium-intensity colour shows less dirt than a **very** light colour or a **very** dark one, but my experience is that the colours that least show the dirt are dark green and dark brown. Most carpet stains seem to be in various shades of brown, so if you start off with a brown carpet they are least likely to show up. Other dark carpets (especially black) show up every cat hair, speck of dust and thread of white cotton.

Stair carpets Carpet that is the full width of the stairs and continues round the stair turns looks best, but is extraordinarily extravagant as it will wear on the edge of the treads and you will not be able to move it up a bit because it won't fit the turns, so it will wear out about **six times faster**. Keep your stair carpet as wide as possible (for good looks) but the same width throughout. Then allow an extra 45 cm (18 in) rolled under at the bottom and the top of the stairs so that you can move it up or down as it starts to wear. Use the best contract quality that you can afford and have it professionally laid if you can. After a lifetime spent trying to skimp on stair carpet, I promise you that money saved here is money fast wasted. It's the only carpeted surface in the house on which you shouldn't economize. If you can't carpet your stairs sensibly and expensively, don't do it at all. Cover them with matting or stain the treads, which will then be very noisy.

There's a lot to be said for carpet tiles. They're easy to lay (millionaire author Frederick Forsyth laid them himself to take his mind off writing *Day of the Jackal*) and easy to trim, and you can shift the worn ones around and rip out the unsavoury ones. You can replace them cheaply. The only thing to be said against them is that they look institutional and dreary, although the quality and colours are improving, and I've seen some really terrific geometric designs.

Why do you need carpet underlay? For quiet, for extra underfoot bounce and resilience and to make the carpet last longer, which it certainly does (sometimes, in my experience, up to twice as long). Always buy good underlay – it's a good investment, and it'll certainly last far longer than the carpet. It should be laid over an extra paper lining (called padfelt in the trade). There are three basic carpet underlays:

Old-fashioned felt, which can stretch and shred and isn't very clean.

Foam rubber, which gives a good 'bounce' and is often attached to the back of the carpet at the factory.

Waffle sponge rubber, which comes in different thicknesses. Don't pick an excessive, ankle-breaking thickness.

Carpet fibres

Wool Wears like an old soldier, is easy to clean, resilient, warm, comfortable, resistant to abrasion. What more can you ask? Alas, at present wool is very ex-

pensive. Some of the synthetics are almost as serviceable and attractive, especially if blended with a percentage of wool, but they attract dust, so pale colours cause a cleaning problem.

Acrylic Resembles wool, is far cheaper, resistant to soiling, is durable, resilient, can't mildew or be attacked by moths. Various acrylic fibres have trade names, such as Acrilan and Courtelle.

Polyesters Fibres such as Dacron can have the weight and luxury of wool, but are shinier and less resilient, with poor stain resistance.

Nylon This is the best wearing of the man-made yarns. It is tough, cleans easily and is comparatively reasonably priced. It has one problem: static electricity. This means that you can get little electric shocks off metal furniture or even other people. Some manufacturers now incorporate anti-static in the fibre, which eliminates the problem.

WARNING! Street-market carpet sellers can be as slippery, devious and downright crooked as they're traditionally supposed to be. If you can wait, some of the best department stores in the country have money-saving carpet sales that come close to matching the fringe operators' prices. Be wary of 'warehouse' stores. Be wary of the relics of warehouse fires, which appear in the ad columns with a relentless monotony that should alarm fire brigades and insurance firms. Be sceptical of 'factory-to-you' advertising. For carpeting, as with any other important investment – I can't emphasize this enough – go to a reputable dealer who will stand by his product, and **haggle** with the man who runs the shop (I never thought I had the nerve until I didn't have the money). Tell him that you can afford £x a square metre or yard, choose a carpet (which may be twice as much) and keep saying that you want that colour and quality, only cheaper, to fit your budget. You may have to walk out and come back a couple of days later.

Resilient floors

If you really want an easy-to-care for floor, cover it with a water-resistant material that can be washed with a mop and detergent and water. Some need waxing to maintain a shine, but Moses didn't come down from the Mount saying that a shine was absolutely essential. In any case, resilient floors can most practically be used in kitchens, bathrooms, dens, playrooms, nurseries, utility rooms, basements and halls. Some of the handsome, new, textured vinyl floors look good in any room. I have found those cream or white pockmarked vinyl tiles surprisingly effective and surprisingly easy to keep clean (in spite of my earlier warning aginst light flooring).

Resilient surfaces include linoleum, vinyl, cork and rubber tile. A pattern shows less dirt than a solid colour, but dirt can collect in embossed or textured patterns.

Linoleum is inexpensive and will last several years, depending on the quality chosen and wear given. It is grease-resistant and easy to lay, but needs to be waxed to protect the surface. Linoleum is made in various thicknesses; light duty (1.1 mm) for general use, heavy duty (3.2 mm) for playrooms, kitchens or downstairs passages.

Inlaid linoleum indicates that the pattern goes through to the backing, while in ordinary linoleum the pattern has been printed on the surface and **is likely to wear out**. Inlaid linoleum needs polish.

Vinyl in sheet or tiles makes the most resilient floor covering, is quiet and easy to clean, but is easily marked. Scuff marks can be removed with Flash; black heel marks or cigarette burns can be buffed off with fine steel wool (half a Brillo pad); then repolish the area.

Sheet vinyl is generally produced in rolls of 1–2 m width (3–6 ft) × 2 mm quality for domestic use. There is a wide choice of patterns and colours. Sheet vinyl with a cushioned backing is an effective sound-absorber and very soft for walking, so it is good for kitchens.

Vinyl tile is easier to lay than sheets, particularly if you buy the self-adhesive (peel-and-stick) type. As with carpet tiles, a badly scarred or stained section can be easily, and invisibly, replaced. Vinyl tile comes in 23- or 30-cm (9- or 12-in) squares. Get thickness of 1.1 mm for general domestic purposes and 2 mm for heavy duty.

Rubber tile is made of synthetic rubber. It is softened by petroleum products, so don't try to get marks off with nail-varnish remover or dry-cleaning fluid. The surface becomes slippery when wet, so it is not now used often in the home.

Cork tile is soft, warm underfoot and sound-absorbent, but is broken down by heavy traffic, grease and alkalis, so is considered unsuitable for kitchens by purists, although many people have it. The best cork tile has a clear film of vinyl applied to it to improve durability, water resistance and ease of maintenance. It's available in strips or squares of varying size, and thickness varies from 4.5 mm (general domestic purpose) to 6 mm (heavy duty). Wicanders have a good selection (Stoner House, Kilnmead, Crawley, West Sussex, tel: 0293-27700).

Non-resilient flooring

This includes brick, ceramic and clay tile, quarry tile, stone, slate, marble and terrazzo – all expensive and difficult to install but good-looking and should last longer than you. Ceramic and clay are used mainly in bathrooms and kitchens because, if properly laid, they are waterproof, easy to wash and hard to stain or dent, and can be easily disinfected. Good for terraces, gardens, patios and kitchens, though it is hard on dropped glassware and does feel rather unyielding: I dreamed I dwelt in marble halls and they were terribly hard on the feet.

Flooring guide

Cost†	Material	Suitable for	Possible advantages	Possible disadvantages
1–2	Brick	Ruggedly brutal interiors; workman-like areas	Hard to hurt, porous	Wears and chips quicker than you'd expect
3–10	Carpet, wall-to-wall*	Everywhere except kitchen and play room	Warm, sumptuous, sound-absorbent	Easily stained; don't lay it yourself, if possible
3–10	Carpet, squares	Everywhere except kitchen and play room	Easy to lay, moves with you	Easily stained
2–5 2–4	Ceramic tiles* Clay tiles*	Mainly kitchen/bathroom	Easy to clean, hygienic	Hard on feet for long periods of standing, cold, noisy
5–8	Cork tiles (vinyl treated)	Everywhere, but mainly kitchen/nursery/bathroom	Warm, easy to clean, yielding, sound-absorbing; get it pre-sealed	Dirt shows easily on darker surface; choose caramel!
1–3 1–2	Linoleum tiles Linoleum sheet	Everywhere, except over uneven floor-boards, because it will crack and split. In this case, first cover floor-boards with sheets of hardboard.	Cheap, easy to lay, wide variety of finish	Only moderate wear unless it's inlaid
8–10	Marble slabs*	Everywhere except kitchen	Sumptuous, easy to clean, durable	Hard on feet for long periods of standing, cold, noisy
6–8	Quarry tiles*	Mainly kitchen	Easy to clean, durable	Hard on feet for long periods of standing
3–7	Rubber tiles Rubber sheet	Heavy-duty areas where you're standing, e.g., kitchen	Resilient, warm, sound-absorbent	Slippery when wet; not much choice of pattern
6	Slate slabs* Terrazzo*	Everywhere except kitchen (too hard on feet)	Durable, sumptuous, easy to clean	Hard on feet for long periods of standing, cold, noisy, can crack if you drop a really heavy object on it
3–7 3–7	Vinyl tiles Vinyl sheet	Everywhere	Easy to clean, relatively cheap, wide variety of finish; tiles easy to lay	Easily marked by indentations and abrasions unless vinyl throughout
2–4 4–10	Woodstrip* Wood block (parquet)	Everywhere except damp areas such as bathroom, kitchen, conservatory, utility rooms	Can look elegant, soothing, traditional; good with antiques, long life	Expensive; not suitable for rooms with water

† Relative guide on 1–10 scale. * Moderately expensive to install.

SPREADING THE LIGHT

Except for designers, photographers and lighting experts, no one believes that lighting can make a bad interior look good and a good interior look bad. But it's true.

The best lighting system is the one that you don't notice as a lighting system. You don't notice cords coming down from the ceiling, you don't trip over spaghetti junctions on the floor and you don't notice ugly shadows as in early Ealing films.

Some light fittings can be really beautiful. Tiffany shades, art nouveau flower petal designs or bluebells on stalks and almost anything in Christopher Wray's Chelsea emporium.

Lighting is either general and diffused (overall), or specific, to illuminate a certain area. Specific light is needed for precision work, writing, sewing and eating, and should be concentrated lighting from one source, which can be an adjustable spotlight or one of the many Anglepoise models. When you left home for a bedsitter, your first investment for life should have been an adjustable table lamp, and every student should have one.

A ceiling light might be a spotlight fixed in the central rose, a ceiling pendant or a classic globular paper Japanese Noguchi lantern; or one of those Thirties-style inverted umbrellas of pearlized glass. But the average ceiling light is neither unobtrusive nor good-looking and there's a lot to be said for converting a central fitting into a ceiling track (which is a relatively simple wiring job) for more versatile lighting. This system can be very useful in a kitchen, if the areas where you need light (preparation-cooker-sink) are near each other. If they are not, then use wall-mounted spotlights.

Spotlights suspended from overhead, or from a wall-fixed track are a good method of illuminating a row of pictures or display shelving. In an office they are a neat way of providing specific light from the same power source for more than one person. In a nursery they are out of the reach of everyone except you.

Indeed, a series of spotlights can be a cheap and easy way to solve most lighting problems for a whole home. Don't expect them to provide an even, overall level of light because their purpose is the reverse; never place a spotlight so that it shines directly into someone's face, because the light is too glaring. Bounce it off the ceiling or the wall or an especially beautiful object, such as your brass Buddha, a vase of daffodils or a dramatic scarlet wall.

Spotlights multiply the effect of a room's highlights and conceal its deficiencies. (This is why the dress you saw last night from the bus looked better in the shop window than it does on you.) A few pools of light in a room can make a tranquil atmosphere in which to soak, as though you were in a bath, at the end of the day, while your mind unravels. In fact, I always have spotlights in the bathroom. Most spotlights are of the Edison screw variety, not the push-in-and-wiggle sort that have bayonet fixings. Some miniature bulbs have different diameter fittings. For simple shopping, always use one size of bulb with one sort of fixture.

Halogen lighting provides a lot of light from one source. I use halogen plain brass standard lamps and halogen spotlights to illuminate antiques.

The most flattering and relaxing light for a dining table is **candlelight**; not really very expensive or much bother. Otherwise, I like diffused wall lighting and I detest pendant lights over a dining table. In order to avoid headaches and glare they have to be pulled to below eye-level; this big, black shape looms between you and the person across the table and every time you pass the salt you risk hitting it.

Wall-fixed or ceiling-fixed diffused lighting can be provided by a simple circular translucent plastic shade, as plain as possible. There are special outdoor models to welcome mosquitoes to the patio or illuminate the Jehovah's Witness at your front door. You can also get outdoor spotlights, as well as indoor ones, to floodlight the syringa.

Concealed lighting is flattering and looks expensive, although it needn't be. Try fitting a bulb in a shop-fitter's cheap light cradle (like a fencer's mask). Stand it on aluminium cooking foil for extra safety and put it on the back of a high cupboard, armoire or other high furniture, or behind a stereo speaker, where the light can't be seen. You get a 10-megawatt luxury impression.

Low-level lighting that comes from below-knee level also looks positively exotic and amazing. Glamour is further achieved by using a dimmer switch, which enables you to increase or dim the light according to your mood, as in cinemas. It's not much more complicated or expensive than an on-off switch (and I have them everywhere, especially in the bathrooms).

If you intend to make up and/or shave in the bathroom, fix a strip light on either side of the mirror, rather than above it (depressingly, it will underline every line on your face). Always make up in daylight for daylight; it's really being cruel to be kind to yourself.

The bulb you use in your fitting controls the brightness and quality of the light you get; clear glass gives a brighter light, pearl glass gives a softer effect and silvered reflector bulbs are both bright and soft. The higher the wattage, the brighter the bulb and the more electricity it consumes.

A night light (called a nursery bulb) is dimmest of all at 5 watts. Miniature bulbs for old-fashioned lights are 25 watts. Unless they are the major light source in a room, table lamps take 40- or 60-watt bulbs. Working lights and principal sources of light should take 100- to 150-watt bulbs, depending on your requirements, and some central lights take an even higher wattage. The most popular bulbs are 60 or 100 watts. If using fluorescent tubes, look for tubes marked 'colour 27 de luxe warm white'. Don't fall for anything labelled merely 'natural' or 'daylight' or 'warm white', because you will look greenish or bluish.

If you are wiring a house for the first time, or rewiring, check:

1 That you have enough socket outlets in the right place. (You always need more than you think; perfection is a pair per wall.)

2 That the switches are where you need them – by the door, by the bed and at the top and bottom of stairs and long passages. Two-way switches are essential for the last two so that you can switch them on and off as you walk about or go up or down the stairs.

3 That wall and light fixings are in the ideal position, too high for children, low enough to change the bulb easily (with stepladder, if necessary) and to avoid glare. Remember to allow for tall men, if you've got any.

How to buy a classic table or standard lamp and shade

1 Try to buy both together, from the department manager or an assistant who knows what he's talking about. The John Lewis group and Habitat have excellent lighting departments.

2 Buy the carrier (that little wire construction that the shade sits on) at the same time as the shade.

3 Take the base with you when you go shopping, no matter how difficult it is to carry on the bus.

4 Buy a shade that you can easily clean yourself.

5 Don't buy too small a base to a table-lamp, because it will look ridiculous. Don't buy too large or too small a shade for the base. It's very difficult to judge these proportions and the wrong choice can easily look faintly ridiculous, which is why you may need an expert second opinion.

Shop around for cheap fixtures. For instance, you can get almost everything electrical (flexes, bulbs, switches, as well as major appliances) at a trade discount from British Distributing Company, 590 Green Lane, Haringay, London N8 0RA (tel: 081-881 2001).

MAKING AN ENTRANCE

First impressions always count, so yours had better be good. The smaller your hall, the easier and cheaper it is to get it looking great. The problem is that it's generally too small and uncomfortable or boring to take seriously. And think of all the necessary junk that it might have to house, for instance:

Mat/Dog leashes/Rubber boots/Scarves/
Skates/Gloves/Briefcases/Hats/
Telephone/Chair/Writing pad with
pencil/Umbrellas/Newspapers/Mail/
Magazines/Coats/Messages.

To this I would add a waste-paper basket; where else can you shove all unsolicited junk dropped into your mailbox?

If your hall needs a face-lift, first decide whether you want it to be functional or an amazing surprise, or both. If it is cramped or dark or faces north, paint it a brilliant, rich burnt orange or tomato juice red or some colour with warmth and impact. Avoid pale, cold colours, such as pale blue and lavender, which tend to look dull, anaemic and chilly.

The hall is one place where you can have a bold wallpaper without getting sick to death of it, because you are generally passing through instead of sitting there. However, blessed with filthy children, I preferred to paint my hall rather than paper it. A small hall takes such a lot of hard wear and it's easier to repaint than to repaper (and the children might do it themselves).

All hall junk is divisible into that which hangs, that which stands and that which simply sits. Use hooks for the first and a tall bookshelf for the rest. All you then need is a mirror.

A hall may be a good place for a stop-in-your-tracks bulletin board or to show off a collection. I know a girl who used to hang her collection of antique keys in the hall and another who used a long 90-cm (3-ft) wide passage as an art gallery for her etchings.

No floor will get dirtier than that in your hall, so avoid plain, pale shades. If you're using carpet, go for something dirt-coloured (such as earth brown); remember that no doormat is ever too big, and the Royal National Institute for the Blind will make special sizes for you (RNIB, Alma Road, Reigate, Surrey RH2 0AS; tel. 07372-244701).

KITCHEN SENSE

The farther and more separate the kitchen is from the sitting-room, the farther the cook is from (a) conversation, (b) help and (c) television. Do you want your kitchen just for preparing food, as a sociable place where the whole family will tend to assemble, or even as a place to entertain – as more and more people are doing these days? Whichever it is, it's a factory capable of producing up to 1,000 meals a year, so, if you're starting from scratch, plan it with factory efficiency before adding the indoor plant in copper saucepan.

You can often improve your kitchen efficiency without spending a penny, simply by checking on your basic plan as follows, to avoid unnecessary walking or doubling back on your tracks.

1 The **layout** for a kitchen is food storage/ refrigerator/preparation counter/ sink/preparation counter/cooker/oven/ serving area.
2 The best **storage** grouping is as follows:
   food near preparation counter or table;
   coffee and tea near kettle;
   seasonings and saucepans near cooker;
   work table within reach of sink and cooker;

DOWN WITH SUPERWOMAN!

Four basic kitchen designs

china and glass near eating area (and sink, or dishwasher, if possible).

Four basic, owner-driver kitchen designs are:

1 Galley, lined on two sides with working units. The minimum useful size for cooking family meals is 4 × 2.60 m (13 ft × 8 ft 6 in) wide. A one-sided galley kitchen shouldn't be narrower than 1.60 m (5 ft 3 in).
2 L-shaped working area, with units on two touching sides of the room and table in the remaining corner, which can be used for eating.
3 U-shaped plan on three touching walls (this provides more storage and working space). Doors and any table for eating should be on the remaining wall.
4 Room divided for cooking and eating by a waist-high peninsular unit. A peninsular kitchen is a good idea for a mother with young children, especially if divided by a half door to keep the children out of the work area.

Many accidents and illnesses are caused by awkward working heights and badly placed storage area: your kitchen is probably the most accident-prone area of your home.

Correct working heights for the average woman, who is 1.60 m (5 ft 3 in) tall, are given below. Subtract from, or add to, them according to whether you're smaller or taller, and you'll have a tailor-made kitchen.

To obtain the **one vital measurement** stand up straight against the wall in the shoes you usually wear in the kitchen. Get someone to mark the distance from the floor to the flat of your hand when, with arms straight at your sides, you hold your hand parallel to the floor. This measurement is the height that the **bottom** of your sink should be if you want to avoid stooping over it.

To calculate the height of the counter top, add 15 cm (6 in) – approximate depth of sink – to the palm-of-hand measurement. You will then be able to stand at the worktop without the slight stoop that is the worst possible posture, resulting in tension, backache or a slipped disc.

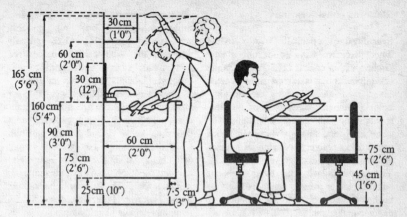

Correct working heights for the average woman

If you are the average woman and your extended palm is 75 cm (2 ft 6 in) above floor level, your sink **bottom** should be 75 cm (2 ft 6 in) and your worktop should be 90 cm (3 ft) from the floor. Builders generally make both too low – I can only assume that such men are midgets, or that they don't do any of the cooking or washing-up.

Other general measurements are:

* 165 cm (5 ft 6 in): height for top shelf in unobstructed wall unit;
* 160 cm (5 ft 4 in): height for top shelf set back over worktop;
* 90 cm (3 ft): height for standing at a worktop;
* 75 cm (2 ft 6 in): table or sit-down counter top height for eating or working when sitting on standard chairs;
* 45 cm (1 ft 6 in): height for chairs and benches;
* 25 cm (10 in): height for lowest storage shelf;
* 7.5 × 7.5 cm (3 × 3 in): toe recess necessary. Add 7.5 cm (3 in) to counter top if there isn't a toe recess.
* 60 cm (2 ft): depth for general storage;
* 30 cm (1 ft): depth for china storage;
* 30 cm (1 ft): minimum height for splashback behind counter and sink.

I used to work with the international architect and kitchen designer John Prizeman. We argued a great deal because the main thing I learned from him over the years is that **there is no such thing as a perfect kitchen**. What is the right layout for one kind of situation is the wrong layout for another.

Prizeman says, 'There is a certain tendency, especially in magazines, to treat a kitchen as a gallery for attractive junk. But however pretty it may be to imagine that one is really in a nineteenth-century farmhouse, the basic necessity is to make the kitchen as efficient as possible for cooking. Afterwards, add decorations to an efficient kitchen, rather than efficiency to a culinary museum.'

If you really have a country kitchen, plan for a kitchen that is a sociable meeting and eating place. When choosing a floor, remember that dogs and children have muddy feet. Make sure that the working part of the kitchen is planned so that it cannot become a general circulation area. Protection from the outside climate and dirt is vital; if possible, arrange to enter the kitchen through an outside lobby or 'mud room' for stripping off coats and boots.

DOWN WITH SUPERWOMAN!

Planning considerations

Standard or specially made units?
There are two ways to fit out a new kitchen: either choose the standard range of equipment that is nearest to your needs, or go to a specialist who can custom-tailor a kitchen exactly to your requirements. The cost may well be about the same and the harassment should be about equal (non-delivery of standard units versus non-appearance of carpenter). The best standard units have one clear advantage: the overall design is likely to be better than the average carpenter or cabinet-maker can produce unaided.

As all kitchen units and equipment are made in different heights and depths, a group from different manufacturers can look a real mess. You can almost always easily adjust the depth of the units to stand in one neat line by getting a carpenter (or doing it yourself) and building a narrow 10–15-cm (4–6-in) counter shelf to be fitted at worktop height behind your units. Where you have a very deep bit of equipment, you simply saw a bit out of your shelf to accommodate it neatly.

You can use a similar principle to line up units of different heights, standing them on plinths, painted to match floor, wall or cabinets (this is a job for an experienced carpenter).

It's sensible to seek an experienced, independent designer's help, and he should at least save his fee in ensuring that the plan is economical and that you choose the best equipment through him at maximum discounts.

Alternatively, many kitchen-unit firms have their own design service, which is often amazingly cheap and provided with no obligation to buy the firm's units.

The kitchen floor should be tough, washable, non-slippery and non-noisy (you're going to make enough clatter with the pans) and not too hard on the feet. Good materials are linoleum or vinyl (see 'Resilient floors', p. 81).

Kitchen walls might be horizontal tongue-and-groove boarding, possibly stained a brilliant colour to cover badly uneven walls. Walls can also be covered with paint, steam- and condensation-proof vinyl, or plastic-coated wallpaper.

There's no material that's suitable for all **worktops**. Laminated plastic is standard, with wood chopping blocks or a chopping area. All sink and worktop splashbacks should be at least 30 cm (1 ft) high and should be water-, grease- and detergent-proof. Any of the materials suitable for floors or worktops can be used. Use ceramic tile, treated wood, linoleum or Formica plastic panels.

Ventilation is doubly important if you plan a sociable kitchen. Ideally, every kitchen should have a good-sized exhaust fan; a cooker can put out as much as 100 kg (200 lb) of grease-laden moisture a year. In old houses a ducted hood can sometimes be let into the chimney. It is much cheaper to buy and install a *ductless* hood, which does not expel the air but recirculates it. The grease and odour filters trap a lot of kitchen smog but, of course, do not cool the atmosphere.

Electrical work A fully equipped kitchen needs a lot more electrical outlets than you would think, but never as many as designers tell you. Six socket outlets is a comfortable minimum, ten is luxury. One cooker outlet is needed, or two if split-level units are used at some distance from each other. Waste-disposal units need a separate outlet and should be earthed for safety.

Lighting Working areas, sink and stove need to be especially well lit. Use spotlights or fluorescent lighting over working areas; I prefer spotlights, as they are more flattering – I am at my least glamorous in the kitchen and need all the help I can get. Fit strip lights under kitchen cupboards to illuminate working surfaces. Lighting circuits may also have to allow for ceiling, worktop and cupboard lights. If you can't afford to buy all the electrical equipment needed in one shopping swoop, spare capacity should optimistically be left.

Sinks A double sink with two drainers is, to my mind, vital, almost the equivalent of a dishwasher, and uses far less energy. Most sinks are stainless steel (noisy but wears well and doesn't rust), vitreous enamel (can scratch and start rusting) or earthenware (can chip and is now hard to get, but I like it best). You can get a Perspex sink specially made in wonderful colours: it won't chip but scratches easily. Ideally there should be draining surface on both sides of the sink, grooved to drain into the sink: otherwise have one on the left if you are right-handed, or vice versa.

Dishwasher The best place for a dishwasher is probably under the sink. Don't get a small dishwasher. Buy a reputable make (*not* British) and one that isn't too complicated to operate.

Chair If you want to relax in a big kitchen while someone takes your photograph, there's nothing to beat a rocking chair, but for ironing and sewing, cooking and chopping, writing shopping lists or just flopping into, the best kitchen chair is the adjustable, secretarial typing chair. It's on wheels, the seat goes up or down to fit you, the back automatically adjusts to yours; get one with an easily cleaned fabric or plastic seat. Then sit *well back* in it. (I didn't write the last sentence: the typing agency added it.)

Designing an efficient and low-cost kitchen is only a matter of deciding what can be dispensed with if you aren't going to get it anyway. Everyone's priorities are different, but in my opinion the minimum essential kitchen consists of a cold tap, a double sink, a cooker, a refrigerator, a freezer and two tall bookshelves (one for china and pots, one for food in packs or tins).

Useful ideas

1 Instead of shelves, use one outsized odd bit of furniture – what the French call an *armoire* and the British call a wardrobe. The fashion designer Jean Muir bought, for next to nothing, a huge, ugly, carved-everywhere Indian *armoire* and painted it white: it has the look of an elegant frosted cake and holds *everything* she needs for the kitchen.

2 In my kitchens, instead of kitchen cupboards, shelves above the double sink hold all glass, china and cutlery in a knife box: guests can wash up without asking where things go.

3 I fit a counter-height, 90-cm (3-ft) wide cupboard with two doors, in which I keep the kitchen rubbish bin, any ecological sort-out bins and all emptied boxes that otherwise pile up in a corner of the kitchen.

4 I fit spacesaving 45-cm (1 ft 6-in) wide pull-out racks that act as shelves for food storage. It's easy to get at everything. Include one by the cooker for all near-cooker necessities, such as spices and the salt tin.

5 I always plan a gap for trays.

A classic micro-kitchen kit is simply a wallful of wooden shelves that gives suitable storage for everything, keeps clean through constant use and cuts out the expense of doors and drawers, etc. The shelf at waist height should be deeper than the others (to act as a counter) and be given a waterproof varnish (from hardware stores). A small, round, stainless-steel sink can be let into it and a garbage pail can stand near by or underneath it. I find this system works very neatly in a small, basic, country kitchen.

How to design your own kitchen

1 **Decide how much you're going to spend,** remembering that labour-saving equipment is the working woman's first investment. *Check measurements of the room*, including diagonals and ceiling

DOWN WITH SUPERWOMAN!

heights. Mark position of existing drainage, gas, water and electricity fixtures. *Decide equipment* and subtract cost from original budget sum. Don't forget installation costs.

2 Draw sketch designs at a scale of 1:20 (metric) or ½ in:1 ft. Use tracing paper over graph paper; it's easiest.

3 Consider where things are to go. For instance, do you want your sink in front of the window so that you can look out, or against a wall so that you can have storage space over it? If possible, allow for the worktop space: 90 cm (3 ft) for preparation and dirty dishes; 75 cm (2 ft 6 in) for clean dishes before storing; 60 cm (2 ft) for serving from oven and burners; 45 cm (1 ft 6 in) for countertop near refrigerator.

4 Check that each work area has adequate related storage space.

5 Check that you have allowed at least 120 cm (4 ft) for a person to pass between standing equipment.

6 Then, if possible, mark with chalk where each piece of furniture will be placed on the actual floor of the new kitchen and play-act cooking, serving and clearing up a meal to see whether it works.

7 Check easy access to related rooms such as dining-room, laundry, children's areas.

8 Check the place for food delivery (where you dump the shopping bags when you stagger in with them).

9 Check that any pets have somewhere to be fed where you won't put your foot in the cat's milk or fall over the dog.

10 Choose materials and colours. Remember that anything on display and not in constant use will get greasy.

11 Remember that you'll probably never get it perfect; a kitchen just isn't a factory assembly line, thank heaven.

YOUR BATHROOM

A bathroom is the last bastion of privacy in today's intrusive world. Provided you have no children, it's possible for your bathroom, however small, to be a little sybaritic paradise with scented water and soft music (only your transistor), soothing and regenerating in every way.

If you share it with three children, it's more likely to be a sleazy mess of squashed ducks, submarines and a sagging towel rail. Forget all dreams of elegance, and hope only to keep it shipshape. Have somewhere near the bath to store those damned ducks, even if it's only a cheerful plastic play bucket. Have one big toothpaste for everybody, otherwise the floor will be covered in tube tops. Fix lots of plastic-covered cup hooks to hold tooth mugs and towels. If there's room for shelves, put them up wherever you can.

If you are designing or redesigning a bathroom and have plenty of room and plenty of money, you have no problem. You trot along to some smart pop star's ablutions consultant and supplier of gold taps to sheikhs and have your fantasy bath – circular, sunken, double or twin. Most people's problems are more likely to be lack of space and money combined – with conspicuous presence of damp, draughts and unflattering plastic bathcaps.

Always make a list of your requirements, whether you're buying a few pounds' worth of face-lift or a complete new bathroom. Even a small amount of money goes farther in brightening up a bathroom than in any other room in the house. Buy pictures (prints or reproduction line drawings), choose one or two indoor plants that thrive in the damp and try to co-ordinate your towels (dye them all dark purple, chocolate or maroon – white towels get dirtiest fastest and most publicly, black towels look sordid; cigar-brown, burgundy, French blue or olive green towels are a splendid idea for a family with young children. I always buy pale grey, because they never look grubby).

If you are creating an entirely new bathroom, either a first or a second, plan it as near as possible to the water supply and drains in order to save money on plumbing. For the same reason two bathrooms are best placed side by side or on top of each other, or next to the kitchen, or on top of it. But there are many other possible places: in part of a hall or landing, in the empty well over a staircase, over a porch or garage. I've made a bathroom (with shower, not bath) from a 60 × 180-cm (2 × 6-ft) niche on the stairs and converted one from a coal cellar (pale blue it was, with tiled floor and silvery spotlight, like an Italian trattoria). I've also had a bedroom in which the bath and basin were behind louvred doors, flush with the louvred wardrobe (WC was separate). This is a really good, space-saving, private bath idea if your bedroom is big enough. Or you might add a bathroom with one of the very good, do-it-yourself home extensions, but this is more expensive.

Building regulations lay down that a lavatory, or bathroom that contains a lavatory, must *not* open directly into a kitchen, workroom or living room; you need a lobby or a passage in between. The exception to this rule is when a bathroom opens off a bedroom or dressing-room, provided that the lavatory isn't the only one in the home. If you haven't an opening window or skylight, you must have a mechanical extractor fan wired to the light switch to prevent condensation and smells.

Overflows from baths and cisterns can be plumbed back into their own waste-pipes, thus avoiding soaking brickwork. You should always be able to get at your water tanks, stopcocks and pipes.

A bathroom ideally might contain a bath, WC, possibly a bidet, handbasin, possibly a dirty linen receptacle, chair, storage cupboard for towels, plenty of cupboard space for make-up and other supplies, plenty of counter space to stand things on and possibly display shelves for one or two decorative objects.

Having decided what you want, decide where you want to put it in the bathroom and draw up a scale plan.

The **floor** should be waterproof; do make sure that your flooring is stuck down with the correct adhesive. Use pad-felt lining under a foam- or rubber-backed nylon carpet for the bathroom; any other sort of carpet rots very fast, probably within two years.

Walls may be tiled or painted with emulsion or silk vinyl, which is more durable. If you have wallpaper, back the bath and basin with transparent sheet Perspex.

If you have a very small bathroom, you can get an extremely pretty effect by covering walls, ceiling and any fitted cupboards with flowered wallpaper (the smaller the flowers, the prettier it will look). But buy only a waterproof paper (try Sanderson's American papers or Cole's French and Portuguese ones) and don't mess about trying to varnish one yourself.

Pine panelling is also very effective and cosy in a small area. With the current price of wood and carpenters, it might be cheaper to use gold leaf, but if you have walls in bad condition it's a quick way to hide them and simultaneously cut down the condensation.

You need efficient **light** for morning make-up and shaving and I like soft light for a relaxed evening bath (see 'Spreading the light', p. 82).

Make sure that you can **heat** the room up quickly. Fit a single-bar electric radiant heater over the door (it must have permanent wiring and a pull-cord switch).

If there's room, install **baths** 30 cm (1 ft) out from the wall so that you have a convenient surrounding counter at bather's level. A bath should also have generous elbow-room, side-fitting taps (two children can then bath at one time), a shower spray and mixer taps if you can afford them.

Fix safety handgrips for the very old or very pregnant, screwed into the wall at an angle at two different heights to help people hoist themselves in and out. Have a non-slip tread mat to stick to the bath bottom. Glass fibre baths are cheaper, not cold to touch, often have non-slip bottoms, are impossible to chip and have more exciting colours than the traditional ones. They also scratch easily. A dark-coloured bath can look downright sleazy, and it never looks clean.

Basins should have a flat top with recessed draining areas for soap, and there should be at least one mirror over the basin. Since children swing on a basin and workmen stand on it, get a pedestal basin, not wall-fixed, so that it can stand up for itself and can't be pulled out of a wall. The plumbing should be hidden in the pedestal. There are now some very, very tiny basins for you in your small corner (try Ideal Standard or Adamsez) and there are also showers that fold flat against the walls.

You can get small fitted **shower** cabinets made especially for tiny rooms; I had one 50 cm (20 in) wide.

Hot and cold water should reach the shower at the same pressure, so make sure that the plumber doesn't tap the cold in straight from the mains (a favourite trick) because you'll have a lot of trouble getting water at the right temperature and flow. A thermostatically controlled mixer valve cuts down danger of accidental scalding. Always have a shower curtain or you risk soaking the carpet, which soaks the floorboards, which can then rot without your noticing. Keep the curtain tucked into the bath or shower tray or the water will run down the curtain to the floor. Get the biggest shower tray available in metal, plastic (warm to naked feet) or ceramic.

WCs should be as near silent as possible. Low-level siphonic suites are quieter than the traditional type.

If you're fitting a **bidet** (which is intended for washing the bottom but can be used for anything, such as giving the hydrangeas a good soak), you don't need the sort with a fountain in the middle. Plumbers tend to look furtive when discussing 'biddies'. Make sure that your plumber knows how to fit one. I have seen a bidet fitted with the fountain connected to the cold tap only, which could give you a nasty surprise. I have also seen a bidet fitted flush to the wall, as if for one-legged ladies.

If you have the space and building regulations permit, it's a good idea to keep the washing machine out of the busy, messy kitchen and have it in the bathroom instead. But keep the medicine cabinet *out* of the bathroom, so that no tiny tot can lock itself in with the aspirin.

HOW TO ENJOY BEING IN BED

The ideal adult bedroom should be designed like a living-room, but with a bed and bedside storage. It should be warm, restful, seductive and cheerful to wake up in and sunny in the morning. (Try Chinese Yellow walls or window blinds if you face north.) It should have adequate storage, two socket outlets by the bed; and, if possible, a desk and chair.

As well as sleep, a bedroom is a place for quiet, privacy and fantasy. You may see yourself in a froth of frills, luxurious furs or black leather. Your getaway image may be that of a demure Victorian maiden, a luscious Colette overblown rose, the sultan's favourite or Modesty Blaise. Whatever your fantasy, your bedroom is where you can happily indulge it. There are just one or two practical considerations to bear in mind.

To allow for an easy change of fantasy, try to keep the background neutral.

Don't use a small, patterned wallpaper over ceiling and walls unless it's a small room and you're going for a cosy look. Use a mid-tone background colour for the carpet.

To switch your moods as inexpensively as possible use different bedspreads, cushions, loose covers on chairs and change pictures when you feel like it.

Incidentally, if you have a guest bedroom, you should sleep in it yourself for two or three nights to check that its standard of comfort is similar to that of your own. You may be amazed to find how much it lacks.

Bedheads The point of a bedhead is for decoration and comfort and it's no use having the first without the second. I once bought an exquisitely carved wooden Jacobean fireplace for a friend's bedhead. She was delighted until she found that she couldn't sit up in bed without the carved wood digging into her spine. Your fantasies may be more practical, but the logic of a bedhead is to have something to lean against when you sit up in bed – a sort of fixed cushion. This might be one of those pale pink padded creations (incidentally, grease marks from hair accumulate on these in no time and ruin the Mae West sexy image) or a 10-cm (4-in) thick slab of synthetic rubber cushion, which measures the width of the bed and has a zippable cover for cleaning. It can be hooked to matching fabric loops suspended from a brass/chrome or wooden strip fixed at a suitable height above the bed.

Electric blankets In old, cold houses without central heating there's nothing to beat the luxury of an electric underblanket, except perhaps an electric overblanket. Double-bed models have individual temperature controls so, should you wish, you can swelter while he merely smoulders. Electric blankets are safe; the nervous can reassure themselves with the thought that no reputable firm

wants to be sued by lot of sizzled corpses, and anyway a low-voltage blanket wouldn't have the strength to kill you. BUT make sure that the electric blanket that you buy complies with *British Standard regulations*, and get it serviced yearly by the firm that manufactured it. The only drawback to an electric blanket is that it involves yet another electric flex to trip you up as you stagger into bed.

Mirrors These can add sparkle, glitter, depth and interest to a bedroom. Moreover, every woman needs a full-length mirror in her bedroom in which to take a severely appraising look at herself when dressed, and an even more severe look at herself when undressed.

Mirrors are now made in metric sizes only. The imperial sizes, which they have replaced, are shown in brackets:

76 × 44 cm (30 × 18 in)
120 × 60 cm (48 × 24 in)
120 × 36 cm (48 × 15 in)
152 × 44 cm (60 × 18 in)

Lighting As well as general lighting, there should be adjustable lighting at the dressing table and on each side of a double bed, where suitable shades should shelter the insomniac's light from the eyes of a sleeping companion.

Although lined and interlined curtains are generally an unnecessary extravagance, bedroom curtains should be heavy enough, or lined, to cut out all light so that a light sleeper doesn't inevitably wake up at dawn.

Storage Bedside tables should be bedside chests. What's romantic about the nosedrops, box of tissues, notepad or whatever is your necessary bedside comfort?

Ideally, a dressing table should be in the bathroom (by the washbasin) and the mirror should be surrounded by bulbs like that in an actress's dressing-room – and for the same reason. If your dressing table is in your bedroom and you can't afford a built-in unit, try fixing a flat wooden panel or a plain flush door over two whitewood chests with space beneath in which to tuck a stool or chair. This can then also act as a desk. You might cover it with a cloth.

However you plan to house make-up, it always ends up looking a mess. If you're having a swish built-in dressing unit (in a bedroom or bathroom), flap-up counter tops are useful for storing deep bottles that fall about when you open drawers. Allow 35 cm (14 in) depth, which will house the deepest hairspray.

Have a line of containers, whether they're silver christening mugs or jam jars, to hold cotton wool, make-up brushes and tubes of make-up, combs, manicure sticks and buffer. Use plastic knife boxes to subdivide drawers.

CHILD-PROOFING THE HOME

Planning the children's quarters in a family home is the most important problem if parents are to remain civilized, even-tempered adults.

Respect your children's need for privacy and you may teach them to respect yours. If it is possible to have one, a child's room is not a luxury, it is a necessity so that a mother can retain her individuality and sanity. In many houses where the dining-room is seldom used, it might be better employed as a children's sitting-room or bedroom.

If your space is very small, it's best to remember that if you can't beat 'em, join 'em. Make up your mind to live in a cheerful litter and, until the last one is 12, don't expect to be civilized before bedtime, when lots of storage space is the answer to tidying up. Luckily, children like shabby, worn rooms with bright colours and chipped paint in which they can run amok, within reason. This is by far the easiest sort of room to let them have, so don't waste money on children's furniture: buy junk furniture, paint it

the mad colours of their choice and don't worry about the damage.

It is unfair to children to have fragile, valuable articles in rooms that they use. If you must have delicate things about, keep them 122 cm (4 ft) above the floor, but, as children tend to throw things, they will probably get broken anyway. Whether it's curtain fabric or a doll, don't buy anything for a child's room that you would mind seeing wrecked.

Walls Plain painted walls show every mark of every starfish hand. Assume the walls are there to be drawn on. I don't believe in carefully painting one portion of the children's room with blackboard paint. It will be the one area guaranteed never to inspire a *natural* child (as opposed to a designer's child) to pick up a crayon in creative malice. A pin-board is essential for sticking their paintings, photographs and pictures of their heroes on. Make it as large as possible and paint it the colour of the walls.

Floors You need a swabbable floor covering, which cuts out carpet but not short-pile rugs (for older children only, as young ones sometimes slip). Avoid wooden boards, which can have splinters unless they are well sealed. Cork is comfortable, feels warm to little bare feet, but is expensive. I like linoleum in a not-too-light, not-too-dark shade (ideal background surface for crayon drawings) and I never bother to polish it, as it has to be mopped so often, and little children might slip on it.

Furniture There's plenty of nursery furniture on the market. I naturally believe in push-chairs that can convert into beds or carry-cots, old fashioned high chairs that convert into low chair and table, and play-pens, but, apart from these items for under-2s, I believe in buying sturdy, kickable, grown-up furniture for children. They grow out of their clothes at a depressing rate: curb your maternal instincts and don't buy kiddy-size furniture that they will also grow out of. Buy sturdy child-proof furniture. Pick zipped, upholstered furniture that is easily cleaned, on a strong metal frame.

Bunk beds certainly save space and children love crawling over them. I scrapped ours because I couldn't bear standing on tiptoe to make the top bed and crawling around on hands and knees to make the bottom one, but continental quilts make things easier, and so do fitted bottom sheets. Incidentally, it's very difficult to make a room look smart with bunk beds, unless it is designed on the lines of a ship's cabin (which isn't a bad idea for a tiny room to be shared by two children in a small modern house). I prefer Habitat's two proper single beds, in two different heights, which slide under each other during the day, leaving the maximum play space.

Storage I have tried drawers, cupboards, toy boxes, wardrobes and specially designed kiddies' storage units and I find that the easiest way to keep children's junk tidy, whether it be teddybears, books or pocket calculators, is on adjustable open shelves built across one wall of the room. If you have the space to run adjustable shelves for toys and books right along one wall, make one shelf 60 cm (2 ft) deep, which will provide a practical desk or play bench for puzzles and constructional work and perhaps cut out the necessity for a space-consuming table. Tiny toys on which you break your neck, or collections of such dangers as marbles, can be kept in plastic washing-up bowls, cat-litter trays or stackable boxes. I keep them in two nine-drawer, cheap wooden office filing units, which measure 45 cm (18 in) high × 45 cm (18 in) deep × 90 cm (3 ft) wide and also act as seats and low tabletops, as well as the North Pole or a space rocket.

When the toys get too much for the shelves to hold, I make the children sort out for themselves what they want to

throw or give away (after all, you expect them to respect *your* possessions).

I don't believe you can ever expect a young child to tidy up its own mess unless you supervise, which means that clearing up takes twice as much of your time as if you had done it yourself in the first place. But they'll never learn unless you do that. And as I've said before, the one rule they learn to respect is 'if you leave anything on the floor, you must expect it to be trodden on by clumsy grown-ups'.

Safety Never leave a young child alone in the bath and always test the water temperature with your elbow before popping him in. Never let a baby have a pillow in case he accidentally smothers himself. Never leave a hot water-bottle in a small child's bed in case it leaks or he opens it and scalds himself. Don't give small, swallowable toys to small children. Never let young children get within reach of matches, razor blades, soap or hot drinks: in many hospital wards you can see small children with terrible burns – from only one spilt cup of tea. Don't use a tablecloth, which they can pull over on themselves. Never leave the kitchen if anything is cooking in a pan of deep fat and *always turn saucepan handles so that they don't protrude beyond the cooker*. Keep the first-aid kit in the kitchen, not the bathroom, where a child might lock himself in with it. You're supposed to keep it locked, but who can ever find a key in an emergency? I prefer to keep it in a high cupboard. Don't keep poisonous cleaners under a sink, where a child could sip the Teepol or the turps – put these, too, in a high cupboard and keep your china under the sink.

If you have any glass doors that a child could run into, criss-cross coloured tape across them (it looks horrible, but then so does the gash in a child's forehead). Make sure that doorways, stairwells, passages and landings are properly lit, with light switches at the top and bottom of the stairs. If you have a crawler, fix a safety gate at the top and bottom of the stairs and at entrances to the kitchen. Lock up the garden shed. And if you don't put *anything* on a mantelpiece (or a mirror above it), then a child won't be tempted to reach or climb near a fire to get it.

(For general safety ideas, see 'Self-preservation', p. 189.)

WHAT TO DO

Only those who have tried converting a house will know that I speak the truth when I say that a conversion is absolute hell, and that every conversion is a different sort of hell. Debutante converters don't want to hear this; instead they turn to those case histories in the glossies, which invariably end 'and six months later, we were holding our first candlelit dinner party'. In fact; it is far more likely that six months later you will have a nervous breakdown because the builders are still on site, settling in for the winter and showing no sign of nervous strain.

Nevertheless, converting can be exciting, creative and rewarding, so don't be put off by what follows. But forewarned is forearmed: you're much more likely to be having that candlelit dinner party to schedule if you are prepared for the worst.

Improving your home is one of the few ways left to increase your capital assets without being taxed.

How you start depends whether you want to improve the place you live in now or whether you are thinking of buying a place and then improving it. If you're buying, you are now allowed to see the building society surveyor's report; formerly they wouldn't let you do this even though you had to pay for it. Pay enormous respect to it and study it with the utmost pessimism. A report on an old building is necessarily somewhat vague; it is often not possible to find out exactly what condition the building is in without almost tearing it apart.

Ideally, you should experience your building in all weathers before making decisions (this should take about a week in Britain). This is the time to change your mind, because later it will become very expensive.

Before you start, decide roughly what

you want. It's important to distinguish between an improvement, which adds value to your house, and an indulgence, which doesn't, no matter what it costs. Don't decide to turn the house back to front just for the hell of it. The last occupant probably lived there quite efficiently and happily in its present condition.

WHAT TO AVOID

Victorian houses, with rooms on many levels, bay windows and thick walls, can be very difficult to convert. Georgian terrace houses are comparatively easy, because the windows are regular, the floors on one level and internal partitions are of light construction. Often the main reason for change is that there are only two rooms to a floor. This can probably be altered to three rooms a floor by building a small extension on the back to make kitchen and bathrooms.

Don't finally decide what you are going to do before showing your lists to your builder or architect, and hearing what he has to say about the expense and complexity of the work involved. Anything structural is going to involve a lot of money, and plumbing seems to cost more than emeralds. So don't set your heart on installing an extra lavatory as far away as possible from the present plumbing arrangements just because *you* find that this is the most convenient place for it. Some items, however, only *seem* to be as permanent as the foundations: it is often possible to move the stairs and the kitchen if you have some good reason for doing so.

WHAT TO SPEND

Having decided how much you can afford, you should consider whether you are justified in spending it as an invest-

ment: whether, should you want to sell later, your house will fetch the price you paid for it, plus the cost of conversion. If not, you may still decide to go ahead, but you should again consider whether you really want to rip out the walls, go for a substantial open-plan scheme, knock two floors into one and build a 4.5-m (15-ft) high cage for tropical birds in the middle (as Vanessa Redgrave did), because you might then end up with a property that would make an estate agent wince. On the other hand, you don't want to lose confidence and do something dull. In order that you don't spend more money on your home than you would recoup with a sale, before starting building work, find out the going rate and maximum prices for houses like yours in your area. Ask a local estate agent for a rough price.

Your first spending priority should be to protect your investment rather than improve it (you don't want your home to *lose* value). Get a surveyor to check that the house is watertight and has a sound roof, chimneys, guttering, pipes and drains, and to look for damaged brickwork, rising damp, rotting door or window frames. Get several estimates and a written guarantee if you're installing a damp-proof course or removing dry rot.

WHAT ADDS TO THE VALUE OF YOUR HOUSE

* Modernizing it altogether.
* Modernizing the plumbing.
* Modernizing the bathroom.
* A second bathroom.
* A second lavatory.
* Modernizing the kitchen (but don't regard more than £1,000 spent on this as adding to the value of your house).
* Rewiring, if your electrical system is over thirty years old.

HOW TO RUN YOUR OWN BUILDING SITE

* Making another bedroom by enlarg-
ing the attic or by adding a room on
top of a garage, or with a prefabricated
back extension (but it may not add to
the investment value if you spend
more than 20 per cent of the present
value of your house).
* Repainting.

**Possibly a good investment,
depending on how it's done**

* Building a wall to make one large bedroom into two small ones.
* Knocking down a wall to reorganize the living space.
* Moving the stairs.

**What improvements may NOT add
to the value of your house**

* Spending a lot on the kitchen.
* Adding a sunroom, conservatory,
garage or carport.
* Knocking down the hall wall so you
walk straight into the living-room.
* Knocking two rooms into one.
* Don't plan too small a new bathroom. Just as newly-marrieds always
buy their first refrigerator a couple of
sizes too small, they are also blissfully
unaware of the amount of space that is
needed for a baby, folding bath, baby
chest and duck collection.

Personally, I'm against building-in all
cupboard space, because doing so often
destroys the proportions of a small room
and leaves no space to move furniture
around, and what woman doesn't like to
do that occasionally? However, if you
build wall-to-wall storage units, an important point is to add a polystyrene ceiling moulding (cove) along the top to
match the rest of the room. It costs little
and avoids that ugly sawn-in-two look.
What not to do yourself, because
it's dangerous and you need a skilled
expert: any major job involving roof,

walls, damp-proof course, plumbing, loft
floors, central-heating boilers, gas or electrical appliances, dry rot or woodworm,
bricklaying, plastering or drains.

A major conversion is not much cheaper (it may cost even more) than a new
home. Generally speaking, the shell represents one-third of the cost of a new
house; finishes, services and equipment
account for the other two-thirds.

GETTING EXTRA ROOM

If you can get more room by building an
extension, I would do this any time:
moving is more expensive and more unsettling than you ever allow for, and the
money involved is money down the
drain, whereas a well-planned extension
(and there are several really good prefabricated systems available) can be a
sound investment. Choose between a
package deal and a *standard extension*.

A package deal is the design and construction of a tailor-made extension
which provides one or two extra rooms
in the attic or at ground level at the back
of the house. It might be to enlarge your
kitchen or add a WC, bathroom, granny
apartment or another bedroom. A
package-deal system should do all the
work for you, involving initial con-
sultancy (free), design, survey, drawings,
liaising with the local authority, plumbing and electrical work.

A standard extension is not tailor-
made, but there's a choice of good lightweight, prefabricated construction systems. You are responsible for providing
the concrete base slab on which to erect
the walls and roof. Pay particular attention to the insulation.

**GETTING THE MONEY TO
PAY FOR IT**

1 Try asking your building society for

99

DOWN WITH SUPERWOMAN!

an additional mortgage. Tax relief is normally allowed on part of the mortgage (this must be for a main or only residence).

2 Tax relief is also allowed on a bank loan for home improvement (so make sure that your loan is so labelled), but not on money lent for home repairs or general maintenance.

3 Ask your local council for a loan at mortgage rates.

Can you get any free money?

You may be able to get a local government grant to help improve an old house, if you go about it in the right way and comply with council conditions. Thoroughly investigate the possibilities of a grant: be persistent and don't be put off by having to swim through bureaucratic treacle.

You can almost certainly get a grant if your house has no proper drainage, damp-proof course, bathroom or kitchen. Grants are not supposed to help you to improve a modern house or add on extra bedrooms, but to improve and extend the life of old housing. You can't get a grant for a building that was built or converted after 1961.

There are four types of grant. An **improvement grant** is yours *as a right* to improve old houses, provided you comply with certain conditions.

An **intermediate grant** is to provide a house with standard amenities for the first time, including replacements or essential repairs, such as installing a hot or cold water supply or a sink or a bath. This is *also your right*, and the grant will help pay for new amenities or for repair or replacement work.

A **special grant** is a discretionary grant for landlords to improve bedsitter accommodation or a house shared by people not in the same family. You get this only if you are *not* converting the building into flats.

A **repair grant** is a discretionary grant for houses within a Housing Action or General Improvement area.

Find out about grants at the home improvement office of your town hall or through your architect (one who knows the local ropes can be of great help there). My local builder advises you to telephone the grant application office at the town hall. Allow four to five telephone calls daily over two weeks to get the permissions. Fifty telephone calls isn't much for thousands of pounds tax free. Here's what you have to do to get it.

1 Prove your ownership at the Land Registry Office.

2 Get permission from your building society.

3 Get agreement from any sitting tenant.

4 Get planning permission from the local authority; this involves simple before-and-after plans, not necessarily architect's plans.

5 Get permission from the sewage department.

6 Comply with fire prevention regulations if the building is to be subdivided.

The drawbacks

1 The great drawback to obtaining a grant is the time it takes to get a decision. After you have all those proofs and permissions, and have applied for a grant, it may be six weeks before an official comes to inspect your place and another six to eight weeks to process your application. And if you've already moved in, you won't want to hang around with three children and no lavatory for three months.

Don't book a builder until you have a grant, because he won't want to hang around waiting for a yes or no from the council. When you do get a yes, you may then have to wait for the builder.

On no account go ahead with putting in the damp-proof course, or whatever, in a reasonable manner, before you have a decision. You may not get your grant. Bureaucracy discourages efficiency. Most local authorities will give you permission to go ahead after their initial inspection, but at your own risk and in no way committing themselves to giving any grant.

2 Once you have a grant you can expect regular inspections to make sure you're complying with building regulations. That's reasonable.

3 The grant will usually cover only up to *half the total cost* of the work, although some local authorities will lend you the other half on mortgage terms. In the case of houses within a Housing Action or General Improvement area, the half may be increased to 75 per cent and 60 per cent respectively.

4 Generally the grant won't be paid until the work has been completed to the authority's satisfaction, so you may still have to organize a bridging bank loan to cover payment of work until it has been completed.

CHOOSING YOUR EXPERT

(surveyor, architect, builder, direct labour)

If only for an initial consultation you should invest in a professional adviser and I can't stress this too strongly. Never ask a friend for professional advice, if only because you haven't a legal leg to stand on if things go wrong. Moreover, professionals generally resent giving free advice, and paying for it can be cheaper than losing a friend.

A surveyor can advise you if you're thinking of doing work yourself (for instance, you want to know which walls are load-bearing, if you're thinking of knocking any down). Generally you should ask for a full structural survey, which will include structure, timber, main fittings and approximate cost of any recommended repairs. But don't ask for a valuation unless you need it, because this is expensive.

You will have to ask and pay extra for a report on drains, electrical wiring and central heating; get a heating engineer to check on that.

A surveyor's report is a document of doom that makes you feel as if the house is about to crumble around your ears. Treat it calmly but with respect. Perhaps you can use it to beat down the price of the house by deducting from the asking price the amount that will be needed for repairs, according to this survey. One man I spoke to complained because the drains cost him an extra unscheduled £850. His surveyor's report had said, 'Drains not tested and do not look satisfactory', but he crossed his fingers and hoped for the best. The best is not going to happen in your conversion, either. You can't be too pessimistic.

There is no set survey fee, so make sure you start out your conversion career by agreeing one. Get a qualified surveyor from a local reputable estate agent or the Royal Institution of Chartered Surveyors (RICS).

At a later stage a surveyor can also draw plans to get local authority consent, write the specification, get tenders from builders and supervise site work. He won't do this work for nothing, so check how much it's going to cost you. Don't consult an interior designer if any structural work is involved. He may not have had the necessary training and experience, he may not be insured and you won't have the twelve-year comeback that one has against architects. The more complicated your job, the more essential it is that you consult an expert.

DOWN WITH SUPERWOMAN!

Never convert for the first time without consulting a good, experienced architect. A consultation to discuss the problem on site should not cost much. He should be able to recognize the full potential of the building for your needs. You may think that you can do this unaided, but a good architect can (because of his training and experience) usually suggest better ideas, and also ways to save money. He doesn't impose his taste on yours: he translates *your* taste.

Architects' fees should be paid according to the standard scale in the RIBA's Conditions of Engagement. Get a copy from RIBA Publications Ltd, Finsbury Mission, Moreland Street, London EC1V 8VB (tel: 071-251 0791).

The cost will vary according to the service you want – preliminary advice; plans; a scheme design with plans, outline specifications and estimated cost (expect a charge of around 5 per cent of the estimated total cost); or a full architectural service.

The full fee for conversion work is about 12½ per cent of the total cost of the job. If you don't want the architect to supervise you can knock 3 per cent off that but in my opinion it would be sheer folly to do so. The supervision work is the part that makes strong women weep and marriages split. The full service consists of analysis of your requirements; relating these to the existing structure; drawing the designs; getting planning approval and building regulations approval; drawing up the specification of work to be done; putting the job out to tender to different builders and choosing the best quotation; drawing up the building contract; checking that the work is done and up to standard.

The difficulty of finding a good architect to handle a conversion is that most good architects don't want to do this sort of work. It is not considered creative, the client's personality and furnishings are bound to be dominant, the budget is always tight, and there is a vast amount of supervisory work and site visits involved for a very small creative and financial return.

Many architects prefer not to work for friends or agree to suspend the friendship for the duration of the contract; the chances that you will never be friends again are high. Things can go badly wrong through no fault of yours or his, but any bitterness can persist as long and as sourly as between the divorced. If the work is disastrous, or never gets completed, you won't like to sue a friend. But it is accepted as part of the deal that you can sue your architect and he is, as a matter of course, insured against this possibility. Remember that architects remain legally responsible for their work for twelve years afterwards.

If you have a friend who is an architect, the best thing to do is to ask him for a recommendation. He should both understand and respect this attitude. Alternatively, find a satisfied client. If an architectural practice is recommended, make sure that you are going to deal with the same partner. Or you can write and ask for a list of qualified architects in your area from the Client Advisory Service of the Royal Institute of British Architects (RIBA), 66 Portland Place, London W1N 4AD (tel: 071-580 5533). Make it clear what sort of work is to be done and how much you are thinking of spending. If you merely want an extra bathroom you won't want an architect who specializes in running up blocks of flats. It isn't absolutely necessary to use a local architect, but a local architect probably knows the capabilities (or otherwise) of local builders, electricians and carpenters.

A newly qualified architect will probably be brimming over with ideas, and will put in hours of love and care on the detail drawings, but my attitude is that I can't afford to train a new architect on my job. It's too expensive, and the men on the site will probably be able to run circles round a novice.

If the architect needs any specialist advice, perhaps from a structural engineer or quantity surveyor, he chooses them and you pay them.

Tell the architect your *real* budget. Do this in writing and make it clear that you can't get your mitts on one pound more. Do not go back on this. An architect once asked me despairingly why it is always so difficult to get a client to say how much he wants to spend. One of the reasons for the caginess of the client may be that he believes architects to be artistic chaps who are vague about money, so he wants to keep a little something in reserve. This is bad practice, because one of the architect's professional responsibilities is to stick to the mutually agreed budget, and he can be legally held to this and made to pay up for any extra incurred by him without your written approval.

There are three major causes of extra expense:

Mistakes, such as measuring up a room 10 cm (4 in) short, so that a new set of panelling has to be bought. The firm who makes the mistake should pay the extra cost.

Changes of mind on the part of the client, such as deciding to install central heating when seven-eighths of the work has been completed. The client pays for this and the extra redecorating and making-good involved.

Nasty surprises – known as contingencies. Even after the best surveys unexpected snags are apt to come to light as hidden faults in the old structure are exposed. Allow 15 per cent for contingencies alone. As some builders tend to find extras up to the contingency sum allowed, put 10 per cent in the contract and be prepared to go 5 per cent over the top. This is a secret between the architect

and the client that the builder should not know about.

The contract, which is drawn up between the builder and the architect, can settle on a fixed price, although this naturally does not cover changes of mind or extras.

A lawyer who has been through it all asked me particularly to add that it cannot be taken for granted that an agreement exists between architect and builder. In conversion work or, indeed, in any work, there is often an appalling lack of the kind of specification that anybody could understand and rely upon (or indeed any specification at all). It cannot be stressed enough how vital it is that the builder is made to explain, in much greater detail than he is willing to, what exactly will be provided. And the same applies to an architect. It is also vital that the architect's drawings should be discussed and *fully understood by the client*, and that elementary questions (such as whether there is sufficient fall in the land to allow for a sewage pipe) have been considered by him before he devises his plans.

YOUR BRIEF, THE SPECIFICATION AND THE PLANS

The next job is to discuss with the architect what you want. Make sure that well in advance of this meeting you and your mate have *thoroughly* discussed (a) what you want and (b) how much you can spend. Arguments in front of the architect are expensive for you and bewildering for him. Decide which of you is to deal with the architect. *Don't both of you do it.* And don't appeal to him as umpire to decide whether a dishwasher is more important than a second lavatory (as always in conversions, the answer is 'it depends'), or whether pink would be best although Fred prefers beige.

DOWN WITH SUPERWOMAN!

Crystallize your ideas by collecting a folder of scraps and ideas, including other people's conversions, cut out of magazines or technical journals. This will probably amount to ten different styles, but at least it's a talking point from which to narrow down to one brief. Get what you want down on paper. You might start by writing three little lists.

Phase 1 Necessities; these might be to reroof or to straighten out Dickensian plumbing.

Phase 2 Subsequent priorities; these might be changing a window into glass doors or refitting the kitchen.

Phase 3 What you'd like to do if or when you can afford it; this might be fitting a sauna bath in the cellar.

You will be truly astounded by the architect's estimate of the cost, but it is likely to be a fairly accurate one. You then scrap Phase 3 and the architect prepares his brief. This is a summary of what you want the finished scheme to look like and provide. It will probably be illustrated by simple diagrams and perhaps drawings. Keep a copy of everything for checking against what actually gets done.

Once you've approved this, the architect draws up a **specification**, which he puts out to tender, to get prices for the work from different building firms. You then scrap Phase 2, having got a clear idea of what you can't afford. You then decide on a builder and go through the specification again in an effort to make savings on his price.

You and your mate slash it savagely. The architect then does an even more vicious hatchet job. You then revise the specification after considerable argument and a few tears over essentials that have been demoted to luxuries, such as the cleaning cupboard. You now realize that a lot of your necessities are, in fact, luxuries. You may even decide that the architect and the building firm are luxuries and say goodbye to them. You

will, of course, have to pay the architect for his services so far.

It is important to realize that an architect can be legally entitled to be paid his full fee (i.e., a percentage of the total building costs) whether or not the building work actually takes place, and whether or not he does any useful supervision. Do not take the latter for granted. Make sure you get it in writing.

Your sketch plan

You need some sort of sketch plan of the floor layout to help you sort out your ideas, discuss them with builder and architect and, perhaps, to get planning permission. It helps if you can get copies of the house plans either from your deeds or from plans that may already be in the possession of your local authority. If not, a builder, surveyor or architect's assistant can produce them quickly and fairly cheaply. Don't try to do *accurate* plans yourself. It will take ages and you risk inaccuracy.

When looking at the plans remember that:

* The top of the page is north (unless otherwise stated).
* The thick black lines are the walls.
* New brickwork has a ⟍ diagonal line pattern.
* Dotted lines are walls that may be demolished.
* Two thin parallel lines are windows, the cheese wedge is a door and the stripes are stairs.
* A little ○- or ▽ shows individual power and lighting points.

All people overestimate the amount of room in a sketch plan, and the finished rooms are always smaller than they envisaged. There is always less room to move among the furniture than there seemed on paper. This is because they forgot to allow for their own size. You take up more room than you think. You

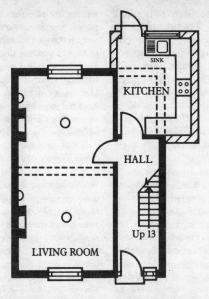

are at least 45 cm (18 in) wide and need another 30 cm (12 in) to allow for elbow room. To get a better idea, cut out a bit of paper the size of an armchair (on plan), label it 'self' and push it around the drawing.

Whether for plans or anything else on your job, never use student labour. This is *not* cheaper. It may seem cheaper before you start but you are far more likely to get slower work and mistakes: he is *not* qualified or experienced.

HOW TO HANDLE A BUILDER

If you haven't a local architect or surveyor, the best way to choose a builder is by recommendation from someone who's employed one (recently). Otherwise, look in the *Yellow Pages* (*always* follow up references) or get suggestions (without responsibility) from the National Federation of Building Trade Employers (NFBTE). A small builder is generally far cheaper and easier to deal with than a large builder because you deal with the productive people at only one remove and there are rarely any unproductive people.

Never ask a builder to estimate without a written specification. If you have to arrange this without professional help, write 'For total work and materials involved' after each item. That 'total' is all-important. Never leave *anything* to the discretion of the builder: this is asking for trouble. You must write down in clear language (which need not be technical) every single step of the job, from beginning to end.

Type four copies of your specification and get three firms (at least) to quote. Estimates are always free. You may be surprised to find that one builder's price may be double that of another.

Apart from the price, the vital thing to confirm is your builder's start and finishing dates. I also like to ask for their dated progress plan so that I can then check by how much (not if) they are falling behind – not for any legal, binding reason but because it means, at least, that the builder has to give some thought to advance planning, instead of plucking a date out of the air. The time to ask for this plan, which he won't want to give you, is just before signing the contract – your moment of maximum power. It's reasonable to ask for it – you merely want to know the date and work progress calculations that the builder made in order to arrive at the final finishing date. If you don't get this time plan before the contract is signed, you are unlikely to get it afterwards.

Dates of payment should also be arranged in advance. A small job lasting only a few weeks is generally paid upon completion. Anything bigger generally involves stage payment in monthly arrears. Arrange that this is done in accordance with a 'time-and-work-completed schedule'. I don't suppose that you will mind paying them earlier if the work is completed faster than anticipated; I doubt if you will be called upon to do so.

You or (more likely) your architect may be able to arrange a penalty clause if the work isn't finished on time. I have had such an arrangement: the penalty sum wasn't very big but I suspect that had the arrangement not existed I would still be without door-knobs, locks, window-panes, etc.

An architect should also be responsible for approving interim payments. He issues the builder with a certificate of work inspected and approved (check that he has inspected it). The builder gives you the certificate and you pay up, by pre-agreement.

A small part of the payment should always be withheld until the job has been completed to your satisfaction, say 10 per cent for six weeks after both sides agree that the job is finished, or 2½ per cent for six months. This means that you have more chance of getting those tedious little time-consuming finishing touches completed and anything broken along the way mended.

Once chosen, your builder should

write a formal letter on the firm's writing paper, giving his total price for the job *and* materials excluding extras, which are to be accepted by him only on a written, signed and dated order from the client, Mrs X or Mr X (but not two people). Get the builder to also write his price on the final page of two copies of the specification, together with his name, the name of his firm, the date and their stamp.

It's reasonable for a builder to cover himself in a quotation by stipulating that it doesn't allow for decayed timber, defective brickwork and other – literally – unforeseeable items. Do not regard these as an added expense. Allow for them in your budget as an unforeseeable expense. Always get the cost of any such extra work agreed in writing before the work is put in hand.

Once you have accepted your builder, *always* try to cut down on his estimate before finally accepting it. (Again, this is far easier if you have an architect or surveyor.) In order to do this you will have to know what each item costs, which means that the builder will have to price it, which he won't like doing at all. But, again, you can sweetly point out that he must know what each item costs in order to arrive at the finished price. Once you have a detailed, itemized list you can always cut things out or cut to cheaper finishes, and you will be in an even better position when it comes to arguing about extras at the end. (It always comes to arguing about extras in the end.)

One woman, a home editor married to a brilliant international designer, told me that the conversion point at which she nearly tottered into a nursing home was when she saw the bill for extras. 'You have to argue about things that seem insane, such as whether the price of a central-heating system described as "all inclusive" should include the flue,' she said. 'Builders have an amazing capacity to leave things out of a voluminous specification and then invoice you for them afterwards, as if they had planned the extras right from the beginning.' *Moral*: check the specification not only for what's on it but for what might have been left out. Professional advice can be invaluable at this point. I had a bad experience when an architect took my briefing on a conversion (luckily I kept all my notes and they were dated) but accidentally omitted many points on the architect's specification to the builder; as these points had to be included, they later cost me a hefty sum. So in future I would go to a lawyer to draw up the contract with the architect; which would cover this point.

Never pay a builder in advance for anything, ever. If he can't run his business so that he has enough money to pay for a few bricks and other advance materials, then you don't want to entrust your money to this fellow. If you have to pay for special fittings, then pay the firm that supplies them *direct*. Get the invoice sent to you and *see* the fitting before paying for it. The building trade is notorious for bankruptcies.

Before signing the contract ask your builder to confirm on his firm's headed writing paper (dated and signed) that the firm is properly insured for third party liability, otherwise you might be responsible if the scaffolding collapses on the plumber or a carpenter is electrocuted. You should also tell your own insurers (recorded delivery) that you are indulging in building work and make sure that your existing policy covers fire damage to work in progress and is perhaps increased to cover the new value of your building.

Agree with the builder who will be responsible for your work and to whom all instruction, queries and criticism can be directed – in other words, who's the foreman. Specify in your contract that a working foreman should be on site during *all* normal working hours, and that any extra or different work is to be done only if signed and dated instructions are given by one of you to this foreman.

Never change your mind or add one single extra after building work has started, unless some major error becomes apparent. Such changes are not only very, very expensive (because you're at their mercy and have to agree to their price) but – much more important – they will mean that the work will take longer and this will give the builder a perfect excuse for not sticking to his time plan. Not sticking to the time plan is what is most likely to drive you to depression, drink or despair.

DEALING WITH DIRECT LABOUR

I don't think you can do this, as a matter of course, if you have a full-time job outside the home. I *have* done it (and in another country at that) with no problems, but I'm still amazed, and it can be attributed to luck. In general it is as likely to happen as HRH Prince Charles dropping in to help with the bricklaying.

However, if you are available and can be called on at any time, if you are prepared to regard dealing with direct time labour as a proper part-time job, if you have had previous experience (preferably bad) of a conversion job, if you can discipline yourself into having the necessary firm, tough, untrusting nature and are prepared to forget the words 'kind' and 'reasonable', I don't see why you shouldn't run your own contract. This might save up to 40 per cent of the basic cost of the job, which is what the building firms slap on for overheads.

It is possible to use a small builder for the foundations, concrete, brickwork and plaster work, and *then* directly employ electricians, plumbers, central-heating engineers and installers, carpenters and decorators (generally in that order). Hire them to specification and get that dated, signed and a written price for it. You should also get these specialist sub-contractors to buy any necessary materials at wholesale or discount prices. See the goods on site and the (dated) bill before paying it.

But don't make a major move without having a survey, a specification, a set of plans and a price in advance from your direct labour that is clearly stated on paper. If you decide to use direct labour, let your surveyor or architect know this before he writes the specification; he can then separate it into a separate specification for each subcontractor.

With the exception of plumbers, with whom I've had dreadful, dramatic and expensive experiences dating back over the last twenty years, I like dealing with labour direct. You make payments in stages, they submit bills for materials, you check that the materials have been used (count the doorknobs) and generally keep track of what you promise them and what and when you pay them, writing it in one simple exercise book *always* dating the entries and getting them to sign for money you have paid. All you need is this one book, in which everything, but *everything*, is written down.

The only difficult part, of course, is organizing them all to come at the right time and, believe me, this can be more difficult than organizing a debutante ball. Again, a consultant architect or surveyor can be a great help in planning this timing sequence. Always contact them to check several days before they are due to start and *never* behave well if they don't.

Once your workmen have started the job, don't you be understanding or stiff-upper-lipped or anything but tough and straight. Certainly if you're in charge of the job, don't threaten to tell your husband. They don't care a bit and it weakens your position for ever.

Before they all appear on site, decide:

* Where they are going to put their equipment (ladders, concrete mixer, masses of dusty dust sheets, etc.).
* Where they are going to have their meals and make their tea and get any water.
* What the lavatory and washing situation is.

No two buildings are the same and it's obviously not possible to encapsulate all the sequences of building work in one paragraph (which is what I'm about to do), but you might use the following sequence as a guide. Discuss it first with your architect, surveyor, building inspector or local planning department. Although the latter can be a bit of a pain, they can also be very, very helpful.

Demolition, foundation digging, prepare for sewage, damp-proofing or dry-rot treatment, brickwork, laying solid floors, walls and structural repairs, roofing and guttering, internal walls, plumbing, heating, electrical (remember telephone), plastering, glasswork, painting and decorating.

This list isn't all-inclusive and it probably isn't in the right order for your job, but at some point you've got to work out that the sewage obviously has to go in at the same time as the foundations and before the solid floor, and all the other operations must be similarly planned. Use a critical path method (see further on) to co-ordinate the right sequence of events for your job, whether it be new work, an addition or a conversion.

MEN AT WORK???

Make two resolutions when you are ready for the workmen to move in. Do not go away while the work is in progress, and don't make plans for after it is finished. I have known some builders drink the cellar dry, use a new sofa as a carpenter's bench (a favourite trick, this) and wreck a newly finished kitchen (newly finished by them). Try to get your job done in summer. Of course, everyone else is trying, but it is so much more endurable to be unexpectedly without heat, light, water or lavatories for long periods in the summer.

Be prepared for broken promises, poor workmanship, non-appearance of such star performers as the electrician, new goods that arrive damaged or are quickly damaged, new goods that are immediately installed in the wrong place or the wrong way. Always discreetly check on work done *after* the builders have left for the night and always bring up any queries with the foreman the very next morning before work starts again.

YOUR CRITICAL PATH

This is a sort of time plan on one sheet, like a school timetable. Buy a piece of cardboard, about 50 × 75 cm (20 × 30 in), tough enough to withstand constant handling for several months, and mark it off in squares. Divide it vertically into weeks and horizontally into the people you are about to be served by, or possibly do battle with: *Architect, Plumber, Electrician* and so on, right down through the list of subcontractors. Fill in the dates when these people say that they will be arriving to do something at your place and when they say they will have left, having done it. These people can be fey and elusive. You may find it extremely difficult to pin any of them down to a given month, let alone day, but it is very important that you do this before work starts. (If you have an architect, he should do it anyway, but you can still be checking.)

Pin this board in front of your telephone (or somewhere central, if you haven't got one) and attach a diary to it

to use as a log-book for making notes. Record in the log-book all instructions and dates of arrival of important materials and fittings. If you suspect that the men aren't turning up as arranged, jot down the number of men that turn up daily – if this tends to be only from 11 a.m. to 12.30 p.m., you can argue with your builder from a strong position (although be prepared for him to imply that this log-book of yours is sheer fantasy, a cunning attempt on your part to force him to doubt his own sanity, like Ingrid Bergman in *Gaslight*). This book will also be useful if you have to resort to law (and if you have to, don't threaten – do it). However, the more you prepare for trouble, the less likely it is to happen, because the builder realizes right from the beginning that you are a force to be reckoned with.

The plan and diary log-book will not only help you to keep track of what isn't happening, it will also somehow absorb your spleen and keep you sane. It is also useful if you finally get on to the solicitor, because he will be impressed by your accuracy, so long as you sound forty degrees cooler than you feel.

Buy a large office duplicate book in which to scrawl all relevant letters, then you automatically have a date-order filing system. *And* confirm all site conference decisions in it. Keep every scrap of paper relating to the job, even notes made by the electrician on the back of a dirty envelope.

When dealing with workmen you must be polite, controlled, relentless, pessimistic and trust to your own powers of reasoning, however inadequate these may be considered. If you don't understand what it is they're asking your permission to do, don't *ever* tell them to do what they think is best. Make them keep on explaining until you understand the logic of it – or lack of logic. You may feel embarrassed at first when insisting on one-syllable explanations, but remember who is footing the bill. And if they can't explain it, the odds are that it isn't logical.

Be prepared for men who come to mend one thing to break another before leaving. One woman I know who spent £6,000 on a conversion had to have double glazing panels replaced three times. Carpenters hammered a nail through the same water pipe three times in succession. The vinyl tile floor, laid by experts, oozed bitumen for weeks afterwards. All the towel rails fell off the walls. None of the locks locked. The men who came to treat the woodworm knocked a can of dark brown, smelly, ineradicable liquid over the newly tiled hall floor. Also mice ate through the PVC cable and fused all the lighting, but I count this an Act of God.

Be tough, but keep calm at all times, because temper will get you nowhere when commenting on non-coordination of deliveries ordered months beforehand. Contractors have a habit of ordering things a week before they need them, when the items are on a three- or four-month delivery. Check this doesn't happen in your case. Check, and be seen to check, the delivery date quoted on all items, and put the delivery notes on your Critical Path.

HOW YOU CAN HELP THEM

Finally, which of *your* actions most madden those to whom you have entrusted your conversion?

Architects don't like those who have no idea of the true cost of building work and who stagger back, disbelievingly, clutching their breasts when informed of the facts.

Instructions should come from either husband or wife, but not both. You and your husband should act with the builders and architect rather as you should in front of the children. Keep a calm,

united front and always back each other. Do not argue in front of the workmen. Bottle it up until they've gone home.

Nobody likes changes of plan once work is in progress, even if you are willing to pay for it.

No one can stand a client living on the job or moving in on the date that the job was supposed to be finished, even when she has had to move out of her previous home on that date. However, my own view is that if you don't move in, they will never move out.

HOW TO CONVERT AND STAY SANE

Of course, there *are* wonderful workmen, who finish the job on time and are a positive pleasure to have around the house, singing as they go, like Snow White's seven dwarfs. If that's the sort of artisan you have, he won't mind a progress check: 'Ho ho, we're two days ahead of schedule,' he will chuckle, peering indulgently at your Critical Path, as he makes you a cup of tea. But you can't rely on it, so remember the Scout's motto and BE PREPARED – for THE WORST!

In many conversion jobs there comes a point at which women start to break down and marriages start to break up. So be quiet but firm *right from the beginning*. No fluttering hands, no pretty little wails of, 'Oh, but it *must* be finished by the 27th because . . .' This simply doesn't work. They don't *care*. Furthermore, they see through this old-fashioned, female 'charm-the-artisan' gambit.

The 'British worker' is an optimist, especially when it comes to work. He always undercalculates the time it will take. Before he starts your job he has arranged to take on another one six weeks later with another lady who is going to feel exactly the same as you do about getting the job finished. And there's another poor soul waiting after that one. So he works hard on the start of your job, but then mysteriously disappears, then turns up for two hours, or for a quick cup of tea, then dashes back to his other job. Then he's off to Mrs No. 3, like a sort of Latin lover, awash with tea. And remember, there was another woman *before* you who is probably still waiting for him.

On the whole, British workmen seem to think that a woman's time is less valuable than theirs. They will not make exact appointments. They are *really surprised* if you reproach them for not turning up on the day that they said they would; they expect *you* to take time off from your work (perhaps losing money by doing so) or hang around the place the whole week just in case they turn up a few days after they said they would.

Abroad, this attitude is called the British Disease. Prepare for it with your logbook and your very visible, pinned-up-on-the-wall Critical Path (do a copy before you start, in case the first mysteriously gets destroyed), which you will use efficiently to keep track of their inefficiency.

Your chart will not *cause* any trouble unless some artisan tries to use it as a magic scapegoat. It will not *prevent* any trouble. It is merely an accurate record of what was arranged, what has happened and what has not happened, and without it you will be *sunk*, with not a leg to stand on (which is why some artisans take exception to it).

Inefficient people do not like having their lies and broken promises calmly recorded. It makes them uneasy. Be prepared for a little male chauvinist flak, because it is very important that you recognize it as such or you may start to doubt your sanity. Your husband will probably side with the builder, architect, designer or whoever it is because he is an *expert* and you are not.

Don't assume that the professionals are the good guys – the architect or that chap from the builder in the decent suit. The architect may be gullible and the foreman just tell you a different, upmarket brand of lie. The situation may easily deteriorate into a difficult-to-pin-down situation, when they gang up on you. You are 'difficult' if you expect things to happen as arranged; they prefer not to visit your place, they explain to their boss as if you had chicken-pox. No, they never say why, but this idea may *also* get subtly put across to your husband. He may even tell you to stop being 'difficult'. If so, what you should do is have a look at your Critical Path and give the following thought a try: *You are not crazy; they are!* You are chief victim and star witness. This is important, because this is the point at which you are (understandably) likely to get 'hysterical'.

This is the point at which you start to feel there *is* no point. You wish you'd never thought of it, you can't think how you got into it and you want to get out of it and never see the builder again. At this point, DON'T sack your builder and hand the job over to your husband, or you will probably be in a *worse* situation. Better the builder you know than the builder you don't know. The next lot will be just as bad; nobody likes finishing someone else's job, and if they do, they have a marvellous built-in excuse for getting it wrong.

Your husband may at this point feel impelled to take over. I don't know your husband, but what I do know is that:

1 If he had been 'in charge' of the job, whatever has just happened would probably have happened anyway.
2 If he is able to handle contractors efficiently, he would probably have done so in the first place.
3 If this job somehow got delegated to you in the first place, he will probably to some degree resent taking it over, and resent it even more if he can't get better results than you. His tedious male machismo is then at risk.

DOWN WITH SUPERWOMAN!

The inefficient resent the efficient. In particular, men who are lazy in the head (which is the most common cause of inefficiency) resent an efficient woman. But efficiency is your *only* form of self-protection, when your money and sanity are involved, on a conversion job. There are three things to remember if chaos is (perhaps) to be avoided. The first is, as I've said earlier, to write into the contract an on-site, supervising foreman *at all times.*

Second, don't avoid your first showdown. Remember, right from the beginning, that the first showdown will probably occur and prepare for it: don't get familiar with them. Be pleasant and polite but keep your log-book and your distance; it's much more difficult to have a five-star row with a man you've been charming deliberately. You *must* be taken seriously and they are not used to taking women seriously and, sad to say, if you're on your own, with no back-up feller, then you will be taken even less seriously.

Your first showdown is an important stage in your conversion programme. Like teaching puppies not to wet the carpet, never let them get away with it the first time. Give them an inch and they'll take a liberty. Make the biggest, showy, all-star fuss you can: this is the first battle and if you win it hands down things will be much easier in future.

Third, your weapon is the only thing that you've got and they want – money. So hang on to the money. They'll come whining to you when the payment is due but the work has not been done. Refuse it. Therefore never arrange payments on a date alone, but for work completed by that date. And never pay in advance or your workmen may simply disappear.

There is only one way to *try* to get the job finished. That is by keeping the same builder, keeping cool, keeping informed, keeping track of what happens and (most important) keeping as much money as

possible in *your* hands until it is ALL FINISHED.

WHERE TO GET AN EXPERT

If you don't know where to start looking for an expert, you can get in touch with your local house maintenance improvers and repairers through the following professional bodies:

Royal Institute of British Architects, 66 Portland Place, London W1N 4AD (tel: 071-580-5533)

Royal Institution of Chartered Surveyors, 12 Great George Street, Parliament Square, London SW1P 3AD (tel: 071-222-7000)

National Federation of Roofing Contractors, 24 Weymouth Street, London W1N 3FA (tel: 071-436-0387)

National Federation of Building Trade Employers, 82 New Cavendish Street, London W1M 8AD (tel: 071-580-5588)

National Association of Plumbing, Heating and Mechanical Services Contractors, 6 Gate Street, London WC2E 3HP (tel: 071-405-2678)

Institute of Plumbing, 64 Station Lane, Hornchurch, Essex RM12 6NB (tel: 04024-45199)

Electrical Contractors Association, Esca House, 34 Palace Court, Bayswater, London W2 4HY (tel: 071-229-1266)

National Inspection Council for Electrical Installation Contracting, 36–37 Albert Embankment, London SE1 7UJ (tel: 071-582-7746)

British Wood Preserving Association, Building Number 6, The Office Village, 4 Romsford Road, Stratford, London E15 4EA (tel: 081-519-2588)

There is no professional body that deals with *house deterioration*. Get advice from your local town hall or a chartered surveyor. Get quotations from firms such as Rentokil for damp-proofing, dry rot, pest control and insulation.

ADVICE AND CONSENT

Building regulations and local by-laws can be complicated and they differ from place to place.

Never start altering, improving or building anything extra without first checking whether any permission to do so is needed. If it is, then get it. Otherwise you may be forced to demolish the work you have just done.

Ask your town hall to advise you (ask for the building control office). Allow at least six weeks for getting permission.

Planning permission is not concerned with interior work unless you are changing the use of a building or dividing it into flats. It is concerned with the way land is developed and the juxtaposition of buildings – generally speaking the look, amenities and population density of the area. Once given, planning permission is valid for five years. You don't need planning permission for an extension that doesn't increase the size by volume (as it was in 1948 or when built) of your building by more than one-tenth, or 115 cu. m (150 cu. yds), which should be big enough for most extensions.

Building regulations deal with safety and hygiene. They don't affect certain outbuildings, such as a garden shed, a porch or greenhouse of the approved size. Once given, approval is valid for three years. Approval is needed for:

alterations to structural work;
alterations to walls or ceiling;
new or extended rooms;
new or altered stairways;
new or altered drainage or flue pipes;
a new lavatory.

Make sure the builder has obtained any necessary consents if you've arranged for him to do this, if you haven't an architect, because it's *your* responsibility to comply with local regulations.

You may have other private restrictions, so *check the deeds*. They may prevent you from having a window that overlooks a neighbour's or from building in the garden. *Check the mortgage conditions*.

If you are making any alterations in the **plumbing**, you will need permission from your local public health department, which will also check your drains if you have any doubts about them. The local authority is generally very helpful about advising you on any plumbing or draining problems.

All new **electricity, gas and water systems** should be checked by the appropriate local board. The local electricity board should be able to advise you on electrical appliances, wiring and rewiring. If you're not satisfied that they're doing this job properly, write direct to ask for action to the Marketing Department of the Electricity Council, 30 Millbank, London SW1P 4JA (tel: 071-834-2333).

THE CONVERTER'S CREED
(to summarize . . .)

Our motto: extras are always extra expensive

1 Always get a recommendation in writing from the professional or trade organization of the fellow you're about to hire. This includes *everyone* from the architect to the subcontractors. Make sure they're not being recommended by their mother or sister; speak to the recommenders, rather than write.

2 Always get the price for *anything or anyone* in advance, *in writing*, dated.

3 Always get a guarantee where applicable.

4 Always try to deal with experienced,

well-established firms or people. You can't afford to train people on your job.

5 Never pay anything in advance.

6 Never arrange the payments on a date basis; insist on work progress payments related to time.

7 Never pay up totally until a few months after the job has been completed.

8 Never trust anyone to do what has been arranged when it has been arranged. Check immediately beforehand *and afterwards*.

How to MOVE HOUSE

Expect everything to go wrong and you won't feel quite so bad when it does.

As part of your moving budget plan some selfish treat for yourself after the first week in your new home. Think of this grimly when things get bad. Be prepared for sadistic friends who delight in breaking bad news. Remember your private treat to come and fork out your notebooks: tears will get you nowhere.

WHO TO USE

For reasons beyond my control (briefly, money) I once moved five times in eighteen months. The first time I hired a lad and a van and the agony took three days and the breakages were appalling. My slipped disc alone cost a small fortune to repair. The second, third and fourth time I hired a specialist firm now called Pitt & Scott Ltd (20–24 Eden Grove, London N7 8ED, tel: 071-607-7321 or 267-1131).

A team of five men, used to working together, moved steadily over the house like locusts, leaving a trail of newspaper in their wake. They packed and moved me out in two hours and were into the new place and unpacked in two hours more and the whole drama was most enjoyable.

The fifth time I couldn't be present, but I engaged the moving department of one of Britain's most famous and expensive stores. A bunch of decrepit, gnarled, near old-age pensioners turned up. My husband lost my moving plan and the whole mess took weeks to clear up.

The moral of the story is: if you can afford it, use specialists. Only the best seems to be cheap enough.

Pickford's, the largest removal firm in the UK, and Pitt & Scott both provide good leaflets **which include the difficulties of moving abroad** and other non-straightforward moves. Look up Pickford's nearest offices in the telephone book. Large removal companies can be cheaper than small companies on long distance moves because additional unloading staff can be made available from nearby branch offices at the other end.

If you can't afford specialists, haven't got anything difficult to move and aren't moving far, the cheapest way is to hire a van (you can drive a van up to 3.5-tonne capacity using an ordinary driving licence). Hire of van plus a man costs a little more.

For anything more elaborate: **choose your mover carefully and book well in advance, preferably six weeks before** (I got the gnarled dwarfs because I didn't do this).

Surprisingly, removal men have peak demand periods: the period before the day the rent is due, at the end of the month or on quarter days, and during the spring and summer – especially in the school holiday period. So these are the most expensive times to move. The cheapest time of the year to move is probably on a Monday in mid-February.

Get the leaflet (send an SAE) published by the British Association of Removers (277 Grays Inn Road, London WC1X 8EB, tel: 071-837-3088) – if nothing else, it's a good thing to wave at the removal men. Furthermore, if you hold it in your hand on The Day, you can't hold anything else in your hand, i.e., interfere.

Estimates and contracts Get quotes from three firms. You may be surprised how much they vary (up to 50 per cent in my experience). It can literally be a shattering experience to discover on the day of the move why the price from the firm you accepted is so low, because of their inefficiency.

If there's not enough furniture to fill a van, you will get a cheaper quotation. Some items can be moved as a 'part lot', which means that the firm will fit it in when they have a van in that area, but you must be prepared to wait up to ten days for delivery.

Draw the estimator's notice to any antiques, which will need specially careful handling.

Find out what the conditions of the contract are. In other words, find out what you're getting for your money, and **check that it covers insurance** while packing and unpacking, loading and unloading, and in transit, and whether insurance covers damage to clocks and electrical equipment. The removers won't be responsible for the safety of jewellery, money or documents, so you should pop these in your bank or sew them into your stays or whatever before you move.

Whether it's two students with a bashed-up van or an elaborate convoy, ask to be sent, recorded delivery, written proof that they are insured for damage to your goods and check with your insurance agent, again by recorded delivery, perhaps after a telephone call to sort out the problem. Many firms have contracts limiting their liability to, say, £10 per item or the cost of repairing or replacing it, whichever is the smaller. If this is the case, extend your own house-contents insurance to cover the move.

Discover whether tea chests and packing materials are provided by the removal firm. Also packing and unpacking. Fixing curtains and carpets will certainly be extra. Find out how many men there will be on the job and ask for separate estimated times of arrival, loading, journey and unloading. Ask if there will be any extra costs.

Read your contract carefully; there are limitations to the contractors' liability. Briefly, the conditions of contract should cover the following points:

1 Acceptance of estimates.
2 Accessibility of premises.
3 Delays caused by events beyond company's control.
4 Responsibilities of a client.
5 What an estimate does not include.

6 What cannot be removed or stored.

7 When charges are to be paid.

8 The company's rights when charges are not paid.

9 Extent of company's liability.

10 The submission of claims.

11 Arbitration procedure.

12 Use of subcontractors.

Naturally, you will get confirmation of these points in writing, together with a written estimate. When you confirm the estimate, send it by recorded delivery, and ask for a receipt and make sure that you get it or *you risk being liable for any expensive drama*.

There's generally a time limit – and it's generally seven days – in which to claim or complain. I have endeavoured to avoid boring legal jargon in this book; I stick it in only when it is *vital*. It's so easy for the eyes to glaze over and the brain blank out at paragraphs like the one in bold print below. Only when your Ming is in bits, your saucepans have lost their handles, the crate of your best china is missing and one piano leg has disappeared may you see the point of it.

IMPORTANT LEGAL POINT: Normally, if a Party 'A' (that's you) accuses a Party 'B' (that's the Removal Firm) of negligence, the burden of proof lies with the Accuser. When Party 'A' is the Client (called the Bailor) and Party 'B' is the Remover (called the Bailee for reward), the burden of proof is transferred to Party 'B', who must show that any loss or damage to belongings did not arise through his fault. It is sufficient for Party 'A' merely to claim that the damage was done by Party 'B' and not to establish how, why or where it was done. It is also necessary for Party 'B', if he is to be successful in rebutting the charges of 'A', to prove that he has not been negligent.

If you're moving, that interesting little point is worth the cost of this whole book. It can mean that instead of your having to prove that the removers broke your Ming, they are responsible unless they can prove that they didn't.

When they broke my antique chandelier, Pitt & Scott paid promptly without argument. We'd had the arrangement beforehand when I wanted the chandelier disassembled, but they insisted that they would be responsible for it only if they crated it.

R. Wilkinson & Son (39–45 Wastdale Road, Forest Hill, London SE23 1HN, tel: 081-699-4420), who repaired it (they also repair HM The Queen's chandeliers), told me that they get a lot of repair work from people who insist on crating chandeliers. It's fascinating to watch an expert unhook all the bits of a chandelier, wrap them in newspapers and lay them flat in a small box, the size of a laundry box. As when taking machinery to bits, you start at the top of the box and lay from left to right, then reassemble in reverse order.

THINGS TO ARRANGE IN ADVANCE

Traffic restrictions If any, such as double yellow lines, apply to the area to which you are moving, tell the contractor well in advance so that he can ask for police co-operation.

Fixtures and fittings Make sure you have, in advance, ascertained what fixtures and fittings will be left at your new home. Get it in writing from the old owner of the property.

Amazingly, rose bushes, hydrangeas and doorknobs come into this category, as well as curtain rails, light fittings, fireplace fittings, TV aerial and fitted cupboards. I have suffered from finding all the above items surprisingly missing upon my entry, and very tedious it was at the time. No use hollering for a lawyer when dusk is falling and you are roaming in the gloaming on a Friday night with no doorknobs and nothing to hang your clothes on.

Also, check the type of sockets at your new home to ensure that cookers, refrigerators and lamps will work on the day.

Services Gas and telephone offices must be notified of your move a week beforehand (although British Gas *can* cope with forty-eight hours' notice). Electricity and water authorities can be notified forty-eight hours beforehand. Ask for services to be turned on the day before you arrive at your new home (or on the actual day if entry is impossible before you arrive), and turned off and the meters read at your old home on the morning of the day you leave. Be there to see that they are, and complain if they're not. Keep carbon copies (dated) of your letters and send all letters recorded delivery because you can no more assume that the service industries are efficient in your new, unknown area, than they were in the old one.

It is wise to get, and file, a letter from the gas, electricity and other authorities confirming that you will not be responsible for bill payments after the move. I speak as one who was billed for six months by a single industry for *hundreds of pounds* currently due on houses that I left respectively two and three years ago. It may be relentless maniac computers, but it's still unsettling, time-consuming and very expensive in legal fees.

Locate the local doctor, hospital, bank and police station in your new area, with telephone numbers and addresses. Don't forget to contact the milkman too. Ask your neighbour which one she uses – a good way to meet your neighbour.

Electrical and gas fittings, etc. Instruct the local authorities to disconnect fittings such as gas cookers, gas fires,

water heaters and electrical fittings, which should be removed only by a qualified electrician. Removal men won't disconnect any electrical or gas apparatus or take down electrical fittings if wired up to the mains. Nor will they take down or erect TV aerials, so arrange separately for this.

Refrigerators should be defrosted before loading. And you should start to run down any freezer supplies (i.e., eat the stuff) as soon as you know you're going to move, because a freezer is a heavy, delicate item and should be empty when moved.

Change of address Visit your local post office to tell them of your intended departure. Fill in the forms to ensure that they forward your letters (*everyone* in your household to whom a letter may be addressed must sign the forms); you pay a fee for this service (currently £2.75 for one month, £5.50 for three months, £14.00 for a year).

Send change-of-address postcards to your friends, the magazines you subscribe to, the income tax people, your insurance company and all firms where you have a charge account.

Notification of new address for premium bonds should go, together with serial numbers held, to Bonds and Stock Office, Lytham St Annes, Lancs. Similarly, savings certificates should be re-registered at the Department for National Savings, Mulburne Gate House, Durham DH99 1NS.

Unwanted items Make an inventory of what you want to (a) move, (b) sell and (c) throw away. Call a rich charity (poor charities don't have transport) to collect unsaleable items or just leave them on the doorstep with a notice saying 'Please help yourself'. You'll be amazed how fast your junk disappears. Alternatively, telephone the town hall and ask for the refuse department to come and quote for removing the stuff.

Remember that no charity or hospital

is thirsting for your broken television set, empty bottles or beat-up old armchair.

On-the-spot removal instructions Write two copies, one for you and one for the foreman.

Make a neat plan of the dear old home, in red, numbering each piece of furniture. Get sticky trunk labels and stick the number on each piece of furniture, with a letter indicating its site in the new home. Make a neat plan of the new home, using blue pencil, with a letter attached to each room. Write the appropriate letter on the label on each piece of furniture. Each item should end up something like 'Ground floor scullery: Room G, Item 29'. This is the moving plan that my husband lost on the moving day with such disastrous results.

Sleeping and eating arrangements Organize yourself and family for sleep, preferably in someone else's house, such as that of the nearest grandmother or friends (big present afterwards to hostess). If, as is highly probable, you can't afford to move the family into a hotel during the drama period, fix a list of friends whom you can move to in emergencies. Perhaps you won't like the idea of imposing on them, but plenty of people don't mind putting a sofa or spare room at your disposal for a night. I have often offered mine to friends about to move; they've never taken advantage of the offer (and I refuse to list possible reasons) but it's reassuring to know that you have an emergency plan.

Plan meals also, whether it's a box of sandwiches, a picnic basket or a restaurant – and remember that you will need cash for the latter.

Children and pets Do your best to get rid of the children. Ruthlessly use a grandmother, a Universal Aunt or student at almost any cost. Check parks, cinemas and babysitters in your new area. Keep a predetermined place for a box of placebos: soft drinks, toys, games, books, TV.

One removal expert stresses that parents must be extra kind and considerate during the whole of the removal period. Let calm and patience be the keywords, advises this obviously childless fellow. Keep babies, young children and pets out of the way. Removal men don't like stepping on or tripping over them.

Domestic animals can become unusually aggressive because they are upset by a change in routine and environment. The RSPCA (look them up in the telephone directory) provide cheap cardboard carrying cartons for transporting cats, puppies and tortoises. Birds should be taken in a covered cage or a cardboard showbox with airholes punched in, then they won't flap around and risk injury. Carry fish in water in any waterproof container for a short journey, or sealed plastic bags with plenty of air to water. For anything larger consult your vet because, unlike children, pets can be tranquillized for a journey.

ON THE DAY

When the moving men arrive, go round the house with the foreman. Point out to him anything extraordinary that might need special attention. Don't forget outside items such as plants, statues, wire fencing. Give instructions only to the foreman.

What you must remember about removal men is to keep your plan simple, keep out of the way and communicate only with their chief wizard. I may be cynical, but budget for half of a generous tip in advance, give it to the supervisor and hint that the other half may be forthcoming upon your final departure. Allow £5–£10 per removal man per day.

A good removal firm packs everything – books, china, saucepans, toys, EVERYTHING. (In larger homes the delicate stuff, such as china, glass and small items, may be packed the day before the move.) Bedding should be folded and left for the removal men to pack. Their tasks include taking apart and reassembling large bits of furniture such as bedsteads, wardrobes, desks and kitchen drawers. They take down curtains and take up linoleum. However, they do not rehang or relay it at the new home, except by previous arrangement. Nor do they refix wall fittings such as mirrors.

Very small valuable items, such as miniature carvings, should be packed in cotton wool in a box by the owner. Stereos and hi-fis, say experts, should be specially packed in the cartons in which they arrived. As you will have thrown them away when you originally unpacked them, such items should be carefully packed in tea chests after screwing down various screws on the turntable and playing arm, according to the manufacturer's instructions. I wrecked a good stereo by not doing this on my last move.

Don't pack anything dangerous or inflammable, such as matches, chemicals or a battery gas lighter.

Leaving the old home Check that you have left your home as neat and clean as possible; as you would hope to find your new one, in fact.

If the old house is likely to be empty for a few winter days, it is advisable for the mover to drain pipes and tanks, which you do *after* the water supply has been turned off by the water board, by taking out all the plugs and turning on all the taps until the water gives out.

Lock the door after you finally leave and make sure that your removal impresario has a key to your new home as well as the address.

Upon arrival Stick large letters on the doors of every room in your new house, according to your plan. Check that every piece of furniture carried in bears a number and a letter. (Tie or tape your furniture keys to the piece to which they belong.)

Your main job It is your job on the day to keep especially silent. Don't moan, it doesn't help. Don't carry anything, save your strength for cleaning up.

Do *not* bend with the remover to remove. The most exasperating clients, say removal men, are those who tell them their jobs. Keep calm and keep within range, but out of the way.

You should:

1 Keep track of two sets of keys. Keys to the old home and the new should be kept in your handbag, and, if possible, the chief removal wizard should also have a set.
2 Make notes. Make a note of anything that's been forgotten, lost or broken.
3 Make tea. The last things stored in the first van (and therefore first out) should be the electric kettle, mugs, milk and tea-bags (cups always get broken and anyway never hold enough tea).
4 Keep hold of the emergency survival suitcase.

Emergency survival suitcase Should contain essential items, other than food and drink, such as washbag, toothpaste and toothbrushes, lavatory paper, soap, towels, tin opener and corkscrew, rubber gloves, sleeping pills if you take them, aspirins, a rubber sink plug, coat-hangers, a torch, a couple of spare light bulbs.

Keep your head when making, agreeing and checking your list of possessions upon arrival, and getting the removal chief-in-charge to sign it at the in and out stages. This avoids later argument as to whether the Jacobean loving cup wasn't in three pieces when they packed it.

It's the packing crates or orange boxes that make the muddle, so if you're moving without professional help, move them into the new home first and keep them in one room near the front door. Stick a numbered label on each case listing its contents, and keep the copy list of contents clipped to that dratted notebook as well, because then you'll know what's in the packing case that mysteriously disappears. Do not unpack crates until the furniture is in place. Move heavy furniture, such as gas stove and washing machine, before the lighter stuff.

Check that the sink, stove, lavatory, bath and basins work correctly. Check all curtain hanging apparatus is ready and working. Move curtains and carpets. Check light bulbs, light shades and electric plugs.

If all services have not been turned on, telephone and *complain*. Keep cool and reasonable when complaining, do not sound harassed, or you will be written off as a hysterical woman (which, of course, you now are). Always sweetly ask for the name of the person you are talking to at the other end of the line and insist on getting it. You may want to complain about *them* later – which is, of course, why they are reluctant to divulge their name.

Get to know the neighbours fast, so that you can tap them for water, extra milk and tea-bags. Just take a deep breath and knock on the door; then smile hopefully.

The friendliest way to greet a new harassed neighbour is to offer your telephone and tea-bags. Also, if you can afford it, give them a bowl of fruit or a bottle of wine on the evening of the first (always worst) day.

The day after Complain again. Catch up on everything you thought you would be able to finish faster than was in fact possible.

LONG-TERM STORAGE

If all or some goods are being moved into storage, ask in advance what the cost of storage and insurance will be and how goods in store will be covered for loss or damage through fire (for any reason) or flood. You are responsible for seeing that your goods are insured during the storage period, but the storage contractor can arrange this. Also ask how quickly your goods can be got back to you.

By far the safest, cleanest, most trouble-free – and expensive – form of long-term storage is the relatively new concept of container loading. This involves prepacking the goods into standard size plywood containers, which are sealed with metal clamps, stacked in a warehouse and unsealed only when you want them.

Ask the remover to supply 'Keep Forward' labels to paste on to a *few* items in store that you might need earlier than the rest, such as a desk or a bed or a pram. Once the goods are stored away it can be expensive to locate separate items.

If you pack any woollen garments, blankets or fabrics in trunks and chests, liberally scatter moth deterrent. Storage contractors are not responsible for moths. It's best if carpets and rugs are cleaned before storage and also treated with moth deterrent.

Don't store anything liquid or inflammable.

MOVING ABROAD

Be ultra careful about the insurance arrangements of your mover. I have moved abroad a great deal, but only on the cheap, driving the van myself.

If you're moving on business to somewhere really *foreign*, say Saudi Arabia, try to specify the removal firm (in writing) to the people that employ you.

The Queen uses Pitt & Scott, and I do as well (see their address and telephone numbers on p. 115). They have a worldwide network and can offer a door-todoor removals service to any part of the

DOWN WITH SUPERWOMAN!

world (no matter what size your possessions are). Your household contents are carefully wrapped and packed in containers that are then sealed. Pitt & Scott will handle the documentation, arrange customs clearance and insurance, and will try to steer you clear of unnecessary red tape. The goods will be delivered to your new door. Anything you don't want to take with you can be stored for as long as you like at reasonable cost at one of their warehouses.

How to buy the best and cheapest
FOOD

HOW TO SAVE TIME AND MONEY SHOPPING

Save time for yourself by cutting your shopping down to twice a week maximum – preferably on Tuesday and Friday, never on Monday because there is less choice and not all the food in the shops is fresh. Also, the more you keep away from the shops, the less money you'll spend. You can't afford to see shopping trips as social occasions – it's too temptingly expensive.

The earlier you visit the supermarket, the less crowded it will be and the less time you'll have to waste queueing at the check-out.

Try to avoid carrying shopping bags, because they will tire you. Buy, borrow or beg **a bag on wheels**. Not a basket: they take up too much room and snag your tights, and the basket doesn't lift off from the supporting frame. John Lewis sells a good selection of bags on

wheels that zip up flat and have an adjustable shoulder strap (for lifting the bags up steps).

Bulk-buy as much canned and dry goods as you can afford in terms of money and storage.

Make a shopping list, and try to stick to it. Keep a spiral notebook in the kitchen as a **shopping book** with an attached pencil – shopping lists on old envelopes tend to get lost. (You might, like me, also use this notebook for planning meals. Work out menus on the left-hand page: on the facing page write down what you need to buy in order to make them.)

Before you shop, run your eye over your standard food list to check what you might need. Always jot down 'marmalade' just *before* you finish the jar.

Make a standard food list by writing down what's in your cupboards *now*. Star weekly necessities like this, *, and divide

123

the list into fishmonger, chemist, super-market, baker, sweet-shop, or whatever your tastes dictate.

Pin your standard food list on the back of the larder door (I also tape one in the back of my address book). If you haven't a larder, pin it on the back of the kitchen door.

Stock up with groceries and canned foods once a fortnight, taking advantage of discounts, cut prices or large sizes. Don't be inflexible with shopping. If you see an amazingly cheap treat, like juicy mussels, that isn't on your shopping list, then get it. *But knock something else off it.*

SHOPPING CHECK-LIST

Jeer if you must, but I've used this check-list for twelve years, with or without someone to shop for me.

Starred items are staples for quick weekly check.

If you do all your shopping at one supermarket, so much the better. I always write out a shopping list from my check-list because otherwise I impulse buy.

I sometimes don't make up menus until I've returned from the shops. Instead I put down on the list something vague like two fish dishes, three meat items.

Cross out or add to these lists as you please.

Cleaning materials

spongecloths, dusters, matches, Brillo scouring pads, Domestos bleach, washing-up liquid, oven spray, Duraglit brass, copper and chrome, Pledge spray polish, Goddard's Long Term silver polish, Dettol disinfectant, Ariel biologi-cal detergent, Stergene, Flash, Liquid Ajax, shoe-cream, Liquid Gumption, An-tiquax, plastic dustbin liners, plastic

baggies, cling film, aluminium foil, paper towels, rubber gloves

_____

_____

_____

_____

Chemist

*lavatory paper, *soap, *toothpaste and powder, sponges, toothbrushes, *tam-pons, Elastoplast, tissues, vitamin tab-lets, *shampoo, *razor blades

_____

_____

_____

_____

Baker

*loaves: Edinburgh, rye, Prewett's stone-ground; croissants, rolls, cake

_____

_____

_____

_____

Dairy products

*milk, cream, cheese, *fromage frais*, yoghurt

_____

_____

_____

_____

Petshop

*dog food, *cat food, *cat litter

_____

_____

_____

_____

Greengrocer

*parsley, *mint, *salad vegetables: lettuce, cucumber, tomatoes, white cabbage, spring onions, radishes, celery, endive, water-cress, beetroot
* *Basic British vegetables:* mushrooms, onions, potatoes, cabbages, cauliflower, turnips, swedes, leeks, carrots
Other vegetables: avocados, peppers, courgettes, sweet corn
* *Fruit:* oranges, apples, bananas, lemons, pineapple

_____

_____

_____

_____

_____

Fishmonger

shrimps, cod, herrings, mackerel, sole, kippers, mussels, crab

_____

_____

_____

_____

Butcher

This list is for when my dazed mind can't think further than lamb chops.

Grill or fry *Beef* Steaks, fillets, top price but tender; rump, the most flavoursome; Porterhouse, the largest.

Veal Best end of neck; fillet, sliced from top of back leg; loin chops; escalopes, to be rolled even thinner and lightly cooked.

Pork Chops, spare ribs; fillet, for splendid occasions; sausages.

Lamb Cutlets, small; loin chops; chump chops – more meat, less bone.

Casseroles and stews *Beef* Stewing steak, chuck steak, skirt, neck, leg, shin, silverside, brisket, mince.

Veal Breast, for pies.

Pork Belly.

Lamb Scrag end for stews and hotpots, breast.

Offal Tripe (beef), sweetbreads (veal or lamb), brains, tongues, liver (lamb or ox), cow's heels, pig's trotters, kidneys (lamb's, calf's, pig's or ox), heart (lamb or ox), calf's head, pig's head.

Roasts *Beef* Rib on the bone or boned and rolled for easy carving; sirloin; topside.

Veal Leg or half-leg; shoulder or half-shoulder; best end of neck.

Pork leg or half-leg; loin; hand or shoulder (juicy and cheaper).

Lamb Leg or half-leg; shoulder or half-shoulder (fattish); best end of neck – to carve in 'chop' portions; breast, boned, stuffed and rolled; saddle, more meaty than best end of neck.

Also Chicken, turkey, duck, hare, rabbit, game pheasant, partridge

_____

_____

_____

_____

DOWN WITH SUPERWOMAN!

Groceries

My list of basics * bacon, * bread, bouillon cubes, breakfast cereals, * butter, * cheese, * coffee beans, cocoa, * biscuits, * cream, * eggs, * frozen goods, honey, marmalade, jam, ham, fruit juice, haricot beans, pasta, rice, sugar, tea, flour, sauces, dried fruit, salt and pepper, olive oil, herbs, packet soups, tomatoes (canned and tubed), canned goods, cornflour, nuts, olives.

Vinegars: cider, wine-tarragon; cooking wines, red and white; cooking sherry; brandy essence.

HOW TO TELL IF FOOD IS FRESH

Fruit

Most newspapers tell you what fruit is in good supply and well priced. Handle a fruit gently to decide if it's ripe; don't judge solely by appearance. Never buy more fresh fruit than you can eat, cook, preserve, or freeze within a day or so.

Fish

The scales and flesh must glisten, even the cuts should be bright. This shine applies not only to whole fish but also to fillets, chunks and scallops. If dull, the fish has been around too long. Flesh should be firm, springy and cling to the bone.

How to test for fresh fish

* Try pressing the flesh with your finger; if the mark remains indented, the fish has started to go bad.
* Pick it up by the head or tail; the fish should be firm, not limp and floppy.
* The eyes should be bright, clear, full, bulging and without traces of blood.
* Gills should be reddish pink and free of slime and odour.
* If the fish looks at all slimy (especially a boned fillet), it is deteriorating.
* If a fishtail is broken or brittle, it may mean that the fish is not fresh but has been frozen and defrosted. Don't buy it.

Scallops Check for shininess and firmness. Fresh scallops are pinkish white, soft yellow or orange; if they are grey and milky, they're old.

Prawns They are usually available fresh only in July, August, and September. The rest of the year they're frozen and defrosted. Watch out for any prawn that has a carbolic odour (pick it up to sniff).

Crab The shell should be brown and shiny, not dull.

How to test good meat

Fresh – that is refrigerated, not frozen – beef, lamb, pork and poultry are in abundance everywhere at all seasons.

Each variety of meat has different indications as to its age and quality. Generally speaking, it should be neither dark nor pale. It should be firm and elastic to the touch. It should not be unduly flabby or moist, and it certainly shouldn't smell. Cheaper cuts are as nutritious as the more costly cuts, but you have to spend a longer time preparing and cooking them.

Beef Choosing good beef isn't easy, because so much depends on how it has been treated before it reaches the counter. The best beef comes from young animals that, after slaughtering, are hung, head downwards, for a few days in order to tenderize the meat with minimum loss of weight. Properly hung lean meat is moist and red with a brownish tinge, marbled – the fat between the lean should be firm and cream or pale yellow. Quality meat should include little or no gristle. Bones should be shiny and pink, with perhaps a bluish tinge. With imported beef, the fat is nearer to white and the meat is pink.

Bright red meat hasn't been hung long enough. Brownish dry-looking meat could well come from an older, tougher animal, but is suitable for slow casserole cooking or braising.

Pork It should not be excessively fat. The fat should be firm and milky white, not soft or oily. The meat should be pale pink, firm and smooth, with little gristle. A fresh cut looks slightly moist, not dry. Bones are pinkish, tinged with pale blue. The skin should be thin, pliant, smooth and hairless, not thick and coarse.

Bacon Should have firm, moist flesh and white or creamy fat, untinged with yellow or green. It comes from the body of the pig; ham comes from either the side or underbelly (the bacon usually sold in packages), or the back.

Both are soaked in brine for four days, then left to mature for up to ten days. At this point bacon is called *cured bacon*, with pale rind, pink flesh and a delicate flavour. Subsequent smoking results in *smoked cured bacon*, which is darker pink and has a golden rind.

Veal Look for soft, moist, fine-grained delicate pale pink flesh with little, if any, fat. Young veal has bubbles on the surface. Avoid flabby, wet, dry brown, blue tinged or mottled veal. There should be gelatinous tissue around the meat. Bones should be soft. Imported veal is a creamy colour.

Lamb Is a sheep under 15 months old. Meat from young animals is rosy pink, although hill lambs are darker. An older animal has dark-red meat. Fat should be creamy white, never yellow, which indicates a rather ancient animal. With frozen lamb, the lean is paler and the fat is white and crumbly. Blue-tinged, glistening bones come from a young animal.

Mutton (which generally means sheep over a year old) Has white flinty bones.

Offal is the edible parts of an animal that are left after the carcass has been cut up: head, feet, tail, sweetbreads, tongue, liver, kidney, brains, heart. These meats are often cheaper compared to more popular cuts. They contain little wastage in bone or gristle and seldom require long preparation or cooking. Much of this is delicious and excellent nutrition and, as it's easily digestible, is good for children and invalids. Depending upon which country you're in, offal is classified as gourmet delicacies (France) or low-status scraps (Canada).

Liver Calves' liver is the most delicate in flavour (and expensive), followed by lambs', pigs' and ox liver (the most pungent and cheapest). Fresh liver is wobbly and moist, not hard and dry. Calves' liver is creamy brown, ox liver is dark.

Kidneys Lambs' kidneys are best, then calves' kidneys (scarce), pigs' kidneys and ox kidneys, which are largest and coarsest and probably tough, suitable only for slow cooking, casseroles and pies. Always remember to snip out the cores before cooking or you may sniff an ammonia-like smell.

Tongue Generally ox or lamb; pig's tongue is always sold with the head and calves don't seem to have tongues, or perhaps they're so delicious that the butchers eat them. Tongue should be soaked overnight in slightly salted water before boiling, and skinned before serving.

Brains Calves', lambs' or pigs' brains should be soaked in cold water for a couple of hours to remove blood before cooking.

Hearts There's no such thing as a tender heart at the meat counter. They require long slow cooking and are delicious.

Sweetbreads Are not what is sometimes rumoured but glands from the throat and chest cavity. Lambs' sweetbreads are considered most delicate, then calves'; ox sweetbreads are larger, tougher and stronger, and taste very different. Skin before cooking, like kidneys.

SEASONAL FOOD GUIDES

With the help of a Covent Garden wholesaler and a hotel caterer, I've listed the food in a calendar because if it's June and you want to know what's fresh and cheap, you don't want to start sorting it out for yourself from an alphabetical index.

Food is not generally cheapest at the start of the season, but in the middle, so the food calendar has both a seasonal chart and a good-time-to-buy guide – when there *is* a predictable good time to buy. In order to simplify, I haven't necessarily mentioned when imported, as plentiful availability is what is most important.

I have also included an alphabetical list of some seasonal foods (see pages 132–4), so that if your man lusts for fresh grouse, you can tell him he can't have it until 12 August.

LOOKING FORWARD TO A FREEZE-UP

Freezers can greatly improve your cooking and cut down the time spent on it, as well as saving money on bulk buying. Stocking up a freezer at certain times of the year can be a better investment than putting your money into the building

society: some people reckon that up to 20 per cent of a family's food cost can be saved by bulk buying, cutting down on shopping trips and bulk cooking, for both family meals and entertaining, especially of large groups or at short notice.

When my freezer is full, I feel a warm, housewifely glow. It's the nearest I can get to an old-fashioned larder with marble shelves, rows of bottled fruit and hanging ham. I used to feel guilty about this before I went to France to interview French farmers' wives and found that the things they were most proud of were their corpse-sized freezers. And they didn't have half an ox inside either. They were stuffed with French pastries. *Tiens.* Of course I prefer fresh meat and vegetables but there are eight good reasons why I have a freezer:

1 It saves money and effort.
2 It cuts waste. Left-over portions get frozen as a meal for one, not produced the next day to a chorus of groans.
3 It saves cooking time and shopping time.
4 It enables me to enjoy cooking far more, because I do less of it.
5 It helps me entertain without anxiety or exhaustion.
6 I am always ready to produce a meal in emergencies.
7 I rarely run out of everyday food. (I even freeze a sliced loaf in case I run out of breakfast toast. You can toast the bread while still frozen.) You can also freeze milk and butter, and coffee beans.
8 Because I am a microwave oven enthusiast. The microwave and the freezer are perfect partners, particularly useful for small families or someone who lives alone.

A good specialist cookbook, with concisely written and easy-to-follow recipes, is *Microwave Cooking for Health* by Beverley Piper, published by Penguin Books in 1987.

Seasonal food chart

Month available	Meat, fish and game (including imports)	Vegetables (including imports)	Fruit (including imports)	Preferably cheapest time to buy

All year	beef
	lamb
	mutton
	pork
	rabbit
	sucking-pig
	veal
	
	cod
	dab
	haddock
	halibut
	herring
	mackerel
	plaice
	prawns
	salmon
	scampi
	skate
	sole
	trout
	turbot
	whiting
		artichokes
		asparagus
		aubergines
		avocados
		beans
		  (broad, French)
		beetroot
		broccoli
		cabbage (hard
		  white or red)
		carrots, old
		cauliflower
		celery
		chicory
		cress (salad)
		cucumber
		garlic
		green pepper
		horseradish
		lettuce (round)
		mushrooms
		onions
		parsnips
		peas
		potatoes
		spinach
		spring onions
		tomatoes
		turnips
		turnip tops (taste
		  like spring onions)
			apples
			bananas
			grapefruit
			grapes
			lemons
			melon
			nuts
			oranges
			pineapple
			strawberries
			tangerines	

January		broccoli, white
		  (until Aug.)
		Savoy and spring
		  cabbage
		  (until May)
		spring greens
		  (until May)		

February	whitebait
	  (until June)
			lemons, best
			  (until Oct.)
			rhubarb
			  (until Oct.)	

March	crab
	  (until Oct.)
	fresh trout
	  (until Sept.)
		broad beans
		  (until Sept.)
		dwarf beans
		  (until Dec.)
		turnip tops
		  (until July)
				spring
				greens

April	fresh lamb
	  (until May)
	sucking-pig
	  (until May)
	veal
	  (until May)
		cucumber
		  (until Sept.)
		Jerusalem
		  artichokes
		  (until Dec.)
			Charentais
			melons
			  (until May)
			ortaniques
				salmon
				broccoli

DOWN WITH SUPERWOMAN!

Month available	Meat, fish and game (including imports)	Vegetables (including imports)	Fruit (including imports)	Preferably cheapest time to buy
April (*contd*)	herring (until Jan.) mackerel (until June)	spinach (until Oct.) spring onions (until Nov.) sweet potatoes (until Sept.) Webb's Wonder lettuce, hooray! (until Oct.)		
May	red mullet (until Sept.)	asparagus (until July) Cos and Webb lettuce (until Nov.) mange touts (until Aug.) marrow (until Oct.) mint (until Nov.) peas (until Aug.) radish (until Oct.) summer cabbage (until Sept.) turnips, new (until July)	gooseberries (until July) strawberries (until June)	mackerel plaice salmon trout whitebait rhubarb
June		mint (until Oct.) new potatoes (until Aug.) new turnips (getting positively rare) (until Sept.) parsley (until Dec.) runner beans (until Sept.) broad beans (until Aug.) French beans (until Aug.) new carrots (until July) globe artichokes (until Oct.) cauliflower (until Oct.) kale (until Sept.)	apricots (until Aug.) blackcurrants (until Aug.) cantaloup melons (until July) cherries (until Aug.) gooseberries (until Aug.) raspberries (until Aug.) redcurrants (until Aug.)	red mullet salmon trout artichokes asparagus cucumber carrots dwarf beans new potatoes gooseberries raspberries redcurrants strawberries cherries
July	halibut (until Dec.)	courgettes (until Oct.) endive (until Sept.)	apples (until Feb.) blackcurrants (until Aug.)	salmon trout turbot

130

Month available	Meat, fish and game (including imports)	Vegetables (including imports)	Fruit (including imports)	Preferably cheapest time to buy
July (contd)		fennel (until Sept.) parsnips (until March) shallots (until March)	loganberries (until Aug.) peaches (until Aug.) plums, cooking (until Oct.)	asparagus new potatoes peas spinach black- currants cherries
August	grouse (12 Aug.– 10 Dec.) hare (until Feb.)	aubergines (until Dec.) beetroot (until Feb.) cabbage, red and hard white (until Jan.) celery (until Feb.) corn on the cob (until Oct.) cucumber (until Sept.) leeks (until April) old potatoes (until June) onions, Spanish and pickling (until Nov.) sorrel (until Oct.) tomatoes, English (until Oct.)	fresh figs (until Sept.) limes (until Sept.) plums, dessert (until Oct.) watermelons (until Sept.)	crab halibut trout broad beans marrow radishes (until Sept.) spinach plums
September	hake (until Jan.) skate (until April) partridge (until Feb.) mutton (best and cheapest from now until Feb.) mussels (until April)	broccoli, purple (until Oct.) Brussels sprouts (until March) celeriac (until Dec.) celery (until Feb.) red peppers (until Nov.) swedes (until April) turnips, old (until March)	apples, English (until March) blackberries (until Oct.) grapes (until Dec.) honeydew melons (until Nov.) pears (until Jan.)	haddock mutton (until Feb.) rabbit cauliflower corn on the cob mushrooms parsnips runner beans tomatoes turnips, new apples blackberries pears
October	pheasant (until Feb.)	chicory (until May) new parsnips (until March) primo cabbage (until Feb.) swedes (until April)	apples, cookers (until April) dates (until March)	cod mussels rabbit carrots, old cauliflower mushrooms parsnips spinach turnips apples blackberries

DOWN WITH SUPERWOMAN!

Month available	Meat, fish and game (including imports)	Vegetables (including imports)	Fruit (including imports)	Preferably cheapest time to buy
November		Brussels sprouts (until March) Jerusalem artichokes (until March) shallots (until Dec.) sea kale (until May)	satsumas (until March) dried figs (until Feb.) dried muscatels (until Jan.)	hare mussels all root vegetables celery leeks sprouts
December		broccoli, white (until April)		hare all root vegetables sprouts

Alphabetical list of food in season

Food group	Name.	Plentiful	Imported
Meat, fish and game	beef	all year	all year
	cod	Oct.–May	all year
	crab	March–Oct.	
	dab	June–Feb.	
	grouse	12 Aug.–10 Dec.	
	haddock	June–Dec.	all year
	hake	June–Jan.	
	halibut	July–Dec.	all year
	hare	Sept.–Feb.	
	herring	May–Jan.	all year
	lamb	April–May	all year
	mackerel	April–June	all year
	mussels	Sept.–April	
	mutton	Sept.–Feb.	all year
	partridge	Sept.–Feb.	
	pheasant	Oct.–Feb.	
	plaice	April–Oct.	
	pork	all year	all year
	rabbit	Sept.–Feb.	all year
	red mullet	May–Sept.	
	salmon	Feb.–Aug.	all year
	skate	Oct.–April	
	sole	April–Jan.	all year
	sucking-pig	April–May	all year
	trout	March–Sept.	all year
	turbot	June–Dec.	all year
	veal	April–May	all year
	whitebait	Feb.–June	
Vegetables	artichokes (globe)	June–Oct.	May–Jan.
	artichokes (Jerusalem)	April–Dec.	
	asparagus	May–July	all year
	aubergines (import)	Aug.–Dec.	all year

Food group	Name	Plentiful	Imported
Vegetables (*contd*)	avocado pears (import)	Dec.–May	all year
	beans (broad)	June–Aug.	March–Sept.
	beans (dwarf)	July–Aug.	March–Dec.
	beans (French)	July–Aug.	all year
	beans (runner)	July–Sept.	
	beetroot	Aug.–Feb.	
	broccoli (white)	Dec.–Aug.	
	broccoli (purple)	Sept.–Oct.	
	Brussels sprouts	Nov.–March	
	cabbage (hard white)	Aug.–Jan.	all year
	cabbage (primo)	Oct.–Feb.	
	cabbage (red)	Aug.–Jan.	all year
	cabbage (Savoy)	Jan.–March	
	cabbage (spring)	Jan.–May	
	cabbage (summer)	May–Sept.	
	carrots (new)	June–July	March–June
	carrots (old)	all year	
	cauliflower	June–Oct.	Dec.–May
	celeriac	Sept.–Dec.	April–July
	celery	Aug.–Feb.	all year
	chicory	Oct.–May	June–Dec.
	corn on the cob	Sept.	Aug.–Oct.
	courgettes	July–Oct.	April–Dec.
	cress (salad)	all year	
	cress (water)	April–Dec.	
	cucumber	April–Sept.	all year
	endive (frise)	July–Sept.	June–Nov.
	fennel	July–Sept.	
	garlic	all year	
	horseradish	all year	
	kale (curly)	June–Sept.	
	leeks	Aug.–April	
	lettuce (cos)	May–Nov.	
	lettuce (round)	April–Nov.	all year
	lettuce (Webb's)	May–Oct.	
	mange touts	May–Aug.	
	marrow	May–Oct.	
	mint	May–Nov.	
	mushrooms	all year	
	onions	Sept.–May	all year
	onions (pickling)	Aug.–Nov.	
	onions (Spanish)	Aug.–Nov.	July–Jan.
	onions (spring)	April–Nov.	all year
	parsley	June–Dec.	
	parsnips	Oct.–March	
	peas	May–Aug.	
	peppers (green)		all year
	peppers (red)		Sept.–Nov.
	radish	Aug.–Sept.	
	sea kale	Nov.–May	
	shallots	July–March	Jan.–Oct.
	sorrel	Aug.–Oct.	
	spinach	April–Oct.	
	spring greens	Jan.–May	
	swedes	Oct.–April	
	sweet potatoes		April–Sept.
	turnips (new)	June–July	
	turnips (old)	Sept.–March	
	turnip tops	March	
	tomatoes (English)	Aug.–Oct.	
	tomatoes (import)	May–Oct.	all year

DOWN WITH SUPERWOMAN!

Food group	Name	Plentiful	Imported
Fruit	apples (cookers)	Oct.–April	
	apples (English)	Sept.–March	
	apples (import)		all year
	apricots	June–Aug.	Jan.–Aug.
	bananas (import)		all year
	blackberries	Sept.	
	blackcurrants	July–Aug.	
	cherries	June–Aug.	
	dates (dried, import)	Oct.–March	
	figs (fresh, import)	Aug.–Sept.	
	figs (dried, import)	Nov.–Feb.	
	gooseberries	June	
	grapefruit (import)	Jan.–June	all year
	grapes (import)	Sept.–Dec.	all year
	lemons (import)	Feb.–Oct.	all year
	limes (import)	Aug.–Sept.	
	loganberries	July–Aug.	
	melons (cantaloup, import)	June–July	
	melons (Charentais, import)	April–May	
	melons (water, import)	Aug.–Sept.	
	muscatels (dried, import)	Dec.	
	oranges (import)	Oct.–June	all year
	ortaniques (import)	April	
	pears	Sept.–Jan.	all year
	plums (cooking)	July–Sept.	
	plums (dessert)	Aug.–Oct.	
	raspberries	June–Aug.	
	redcurrants	June–Aug.	
	rhubarb	Feb.–Oct.	
	satsumas (import)	Nov.–March	
	strawberries	May–June	
	tangerines (import)	Dec.–Jan.	

I also serve pre-prepared food (good quality only) and Findus's Slimline dishes, to which I am addicted. Into the microwave they go, while I lay table or tray and remember the bad old days, when I used to stagger home from the office to start peeling the potatoes and was too tired to enjoy the meal by the time it was ready to serve. Had the microwave existed when I first married, I suspect the marriage wouldn't have broken up.

Deep-freezing is the simplest natural way of preserving food. Clarence Birdseye started doing so commercially after a holiday visit to the Antarctic. Food-destroying bacteria won't live at very low temperatures and most food, correctly stored, can safely be frozen for months. A deep-freeze will store shop-bought food for up to one year (I know an American designer who shops only once a month), and home-made frozen dishes are as different from shop-bought frozen dishes as home-bottled peaches are from canned ones.

You can also freeze your own or neighbourhood soft fruit and young vegetables, and a glut needn't rot – it goes straight in the freezer. My father used to fish in the summer and shoot in the winter, and the products of his hunting efforts were all immediately frozen. If you live in the country you can, perhaps, profit by buying and freezing local produce when plentiful.

Buying and stocking a deep-freeze is generally a major housekeeping investment. So what do you get for your money? Briefly, I found that I recouped the initial cost within two years. From then on I started to actually save money (up to 30 per cent: the biggest saving is on meat).

The first filling can be a heavy expense, but I stocked mine gradually. Others prefer to buy the lot at once, empty it, then start again. I know an architect's wife who got a bank loan to buy a freezer and stock it. She bought a dozen chickens, half a lamb, half a side of pork and half a side of beef. She reckoned she cut her costs by half, after not being able to afford beef for years.

However, it's not necessarily the *folie de grandeur* of laying down a complete cow that tempts a housewife, it's just the thought of having a stock cupboard reserve of extra peas and beans, a positive cornucopia of fish fingers and hamburger meat.

A freezer saves time, and it also means the difference between cookery as drudge work (three times a day, non-stop, a thousand meals a year) and cookery when I choose, in concentrated wedges of time, when it is possible to cook a batch of dishes. I've accumulated the current cooked contents without even noticing that I was cooking, simply by cooking more than enough for one meal or by cooking double quantities of everything freezable, such as stew, for a week or two.

It's also a good idea to keep lots of food that's quickly thawed and easily warmed up for pop-up children: chops, pizzas, egg-and-bacon tarts, pies. This means that in the holidays if they are doing something more interesting, older children can miss a meal or cook something simple for themselves when they deign to turn up.

Unexpected guests can always be fed without difficulty or mental arithmetic. If more than expected turn up for a meal, I put the meal I had planned aside and unfreeze something larger, perhaps *blanquette de veau* or *coq au vin*, thawing it out in a double saucepan. Pre-prepared food can be thawed out quicker than a joint or poultry.

If you have a particularly busy or harassing period, or if you are ill, the freezer enables your family to be well fed on balanced meals, whatever the weather or the crisis.

Novelist Mary Stewart told me that when she goes away on lecture tours she leaves a fortnight's supply of prepared, home-frozen food for her husband, with a careful menu for him to follow. Shortly afterwards I followed her example and stocked up on some trial shop-bought gourmet frozen dishes – *canard à l'orange, ratatouille, boeuf bourguignon, fruits de mer* – that sort of thing. In fact, as soon as my back was turned, my husband was invited out every night, so I had the accumulated delicacies for lunch to cheer me up whenever this book looked as if it would never be finished.

I list freezer contents in the back of my menu book, noting date frozen. It's easy to write it all in the book as it goes in because I generally do that in big batches, but it's more difficult to remember to tick them off as you remove them, unless you tape your list in the freezer door. I use the freezer list as a menu book. But 'Would you like smoked haddock, soufflé or grouse this evening?' can be embarrassing if you've run out of grouse and not ticked it off.

Types of freezers

The frozen-food compartment within a refrigerator (meaning one that does not have a separate door or control) is *not* an adequate food freezer. If the temperature is kept cold enough to maintain the frozen foods, it is too cold in the rest of the refrigerator and you are likely to end up with iced milk and frozen eggs.

There are basically three types of freezers, all of which can be bought on HP: 1 Chest of drawers (front-opening). 2 Cabinet with a lift-up top. 3 Combined fridge with freezer on top (not to be confused with a frozen food compartment).

DOWN WITH SUPERWOMAN!

In many ways there seems little to choose between them – they are just large white reliable boxes.

A top-opening freezer would seem to invite frozen fingers and slipped discs. You may have to dive in and burrow like a dog at a rabbit for whatever frozen packet you want, which may be right at the bottom under everything else. You will then have to repack the thing. A top-opening deep-freeze is said to let in less warm air than a front-opening one, but pay no attention to this fact. Buy a front-opening chest of drawers type and shut it fast.

Some freezers have very useful narrow shelves inside the door, some have adjustable grid shelves, some have pull-out drawers. These last are, of course, the easiest to find your food in. You can get freezers with security locks, quick-freeze switches, thermostatic temperature settings, warning lights and interior lights.

Sizes

In general they vary from around 0.11 cu. m (3.5 cu. ft) – the size of a washing machine – to about 0.56 cu m. (17.5 cu. ft). The storage volume of a freezer is measured in litres. An average upright freezer stores about 200 litres, but chest freezers have a capacity of up to 350 litres. If you buy one of the very small ones, once you've got the knack of freezing, you may find it too small for bulk buying.

If there's no room in your kitchen, you don't have to keep your freezer there. You can keep it anywhere that's cool and dry and near a suitable electric socket, even in the garage.

There are manual-defrost freezers, automatic-defrost freezers and frost-free units. Frost-frees are more expensive to operate than the others, and because fans continually circulate cold air through them, some food may dry out if not placed in moisture-proof containers. I would get an automatic. However, you may feel that it is hardly worth the extra use of energy and the extra initial cost. Since a freezer needs to be defrosted only once or twice a year (and it's a good idea to check on the older contents), you may do better with a manual-defrost – one in which you have to turn a switch off to start defrosting and then turn it on again when the process has been completed and the freezer washed.

What's the running cost? Some models are much more efficient than others (check *Which?* magazine in your local library before you buy), but an average upright freezer uses one to two electrical units a day.

To run a freezer economically

1 Check that the thermostat isn't set too low.
2 Choose a cool site, if possible, and certainly insulate if the freezer is placed near any hot appliance, such as a stove.
3 Ensure adequate ventilation both around and beneath the unit.
4 Keep motor unit and condenser grille free from dust.
5 Never overstock with warm food.
6 Keep the freezer full: freezing air is expensive.
7 Never leave the fast-freeze switch on for more than twenty-four hours.
8 Open door as little as possible.

What happens if there's a power cut? The food may stay safe for twenty-four hours, if the door isn't opened. In a well-filled freezer it is possible for food to stay frozen for thirty-six to forty-eight hours. If the freezer is only half full, it may not stay frozen for more than half a day. Dry ice can be packed in, but open the door as little as possible. Cover the food with newspaper and place heavy cardboard over it, with the dry ice on top. It probably also helps to cover the freezer with blankets, placing newspaper between the freezer and the blankets. Don't open your freezer for two hours after the power cut is over and you have switched on the fast-freeze button.

If there's a longer power failure (insure against this as well as against mechanical failure), put on a pair of thick gloves and work fast, wrapping the food in old newspapers. Cover the lot with a blanket. If you can get dry ice, it will protect food for three days but, touch wood, power cuts don't generally last that long.

How to defrost

A collection of frost on freezer walls or shelves causes the temperature to rise. If the frost is scraped away with a wooden or plastic putty knife when it forms, the freezer will need to be defrosted less frequently. But please be careful. My mother once jabbed too hard with a steak knife and had to buy a new freezer.

Defrost completely before the frost reaches a depth of 1 cm ($\frac{1}{2}$ in) over a large area of the surface. Also defrost if frost begins to accumulate on packages that have been stored in the freezer for only a few hours. If possible, defrost when the amount of food in the freezer is low because all food will have to be removed from the freezer during defrosting. To get the food as cold as possible before defrosting the freezer, set the temperature at its coldest setting overnight. Then remove the food and defrost and clean the unit. The inside should be washed with 1 litre (2 pt) of cool (never warm) water containing 1 teaspoon of baking powder. Be sure to wash the gasket. The outside of the freezer should be cleaned by washing with soapsuds and rinsing off. Wipe with a dry cloth and start the freezer again. Set the freezer at its coldest temperature until it is down to −17.7 °C (0 °F) or lower the temperature at which the freezer must be kept. Be sure that there is a thermometer in the freezer, and maintain −17.7 °C (0 °F) in the warmest part. It is also a good idea to keep foods with the fastest turnover in the warmest location and to rotate the food packages so that the oldest packages are used first. You can do this by filling one shelf or basket at a time and always filling from *back to front*.

Refreezing

I would never risk refreezing. Don't even *taste* refrozen food or you risk poisoning yourself.

My younger son once flew hundreds of miles to spend the weekend with me. I gave him what I thought was fresh farm pâté that I had frozen. Alas, it must have been frozen before it got to me: frozen, defrosted and refrozen. We were both violently ill for two days, and my son recovered only in time to catch his plane after what he referred to as 'Ma's poison pâté'.

How to freeze

1 Read the freezer manufacturer's instruction book.
2 Up to one-tenth capacity of the freezer can be frozen at once, say 5 kg (11 lb) in a 4 cubic foot freezer.
3 Freeze only clean, fresh food in good condition, as soon as possible after it has been picked, bought or preserved.
4 Package properly, with moisture, air and flavour proof packaging, such as an ordinary plastic bag. The food must be wrapped so that all air is excluded, but leave a couple of centimetres in

the container for liquids to expand in. (Suck the air out with a straw.)

5 Cool hot foods quickly before freezing. Set the control to the coldest setting two hours before freezing a batch of food (perhaps when you start to work on it).

6 Label all packages. Frozen jugged hare looks very like frozen beef casserole.

7 Don't refreeze food. It could make you ill.

8 Defrost once a year.

DON'T FREEZE:
HARD-BOILED OR SHELLED EGGS, BANANAS, MAYONNAISE (pity), COOKED RICE, POTATOES (except for raw chips, which seem to freeze well), TOMATOES, ANYTHING JUICY LIKE PEARS, MELON, SALAD GREENS, CUCUMBER (a drooping cucumber looks particularly despondent when defrosted).

Pasta can be frozen, but should be undercooked to allow for the reheating. It is never as good as when freshly made.

An opened bottle of wine freezes very successfully – red better than white; the bottle should not be more than three-quarters full, so that it doesn't burst.

Here's my current deep-freeze list. All prepared dishes, soups or sauces are for four.

Drawer 1: *sauces, soups and casseroles*

Sauces 6 bolognese, 6 tomato, 6 onion, 4 cheese, 4 bread.

Soup 4 leek and onion, 2 game, 2 onion, 2 potato, 2 chicken, 4 Scotch broth.

Made dishes 2 tripe and onion, 2 duck and orange, 4 beef casserole, 2 jugged hare, 2 rabbit stew.

Drawer 2: *meat, poultry, game, fish*

3 kg (7 lb) bladebone steak, 2.5 kg (6 lb) pie veal, 21 hamburgers, 12 lamb chump chops, 2 legs lamb, 6 pork chops, 5 grouse, 8 veal escalopes, 3 chickens, 1.5 kg (3 lb) chicken livers, 12 cod steaks, 4 plaice fillets and 4 halibut steaks.

Drawer 3: *bakery*

12 large vol-au-vent cases, 6 flat flans, 12 croissants, 6 dinner rolls, 2 Victoria sandwiches, 20 sandwiches (lemon and sardine, shrimp and cream cheese), 6 pizza pies, 12 chocolate éclairs, 1 sachertorte (already sliced).

Drawer 4: *vegetables and fruit*

4 raspberries, 2 blackberries, 2 strawberries, 6 sweet corn, 2 peas, 2 beans, 2 ratatouille, 4 spinach.

In the narrow door shelves, I keep small items and decent-sized single portion left-overs.

Door shelf 1
2 parsley, 1 mint (just scrunch the bag over a dish and you don't have to chop it), 1 loaf sliced bread, 30 cm (12 in) empty space for left-overs.

Door shelf 2
Ice cream (2 orange sorbet, 4 chocolate, 3 coffee, 2 rum, 3 butterscotch).

Door shelf 3
3 brandy butter, 4 chocolate sauce, 4 frozen pastry, 33 frozen whipped cream rosettes.

Door shelf 4
6 packets prawns, 1 carton cream, 115 g ($\frac{1}{4}$ lb) cheddar cheese, 6 tins frozen orange juice (add a squeezed fresh lemon plus two lemon slices before serving).

PREPARING FROZEN FOOD FOR EATING

Precooked vegetables Don't thaw. Cook in a little boiling salted water. How long? Mr Bertorelli himself told me to take no notice of whatever time the manufacturer puts on the pack. They tend to over-time them. Cook them until *you*

How long can you freeze it?

Food type	Name	Conservation time	Thawing method and time
Bread and rolls		2 months	Room temp.: 1–2 h. Low temp. oven: 15 mins.
Eggs and dairy produce	Eggs (shelled) Long-life milk Butter Cheese (small portions) Fresh cream	6 months 3 months 6 months 6 months 3 months	Refrigerator: approx. 10 h. Refrigerator: 12–18 h. Refrigerator: 10–12 h. Refrigerator: 6–8 h. Refrigerator: 6–8 h.
Confectionery	Biscuits, tarts, etc. Flaky pastry tart Pastry (unbaked)	6 months 1 month 3 months	Directly in oven. Refrigerator: 10–12 h. Refrigerator: 2–4 h. Refrigerator 4–6 h.
Fish and shellfish	Lobsters Shrimps Cod Sardines and other small fish Trout, salmon, turbot, sole	3 months 3 months 2 months 3–4 months 2–3 months	Refrigerator: 5–8 h. Refrigerator: 5–8 h. Refrigerator: 5–8 h. Refrigerator: 5–8 h. Refrigerator: 5–8 h.
Fruits [a]	Apricots Cherries, plums, raspberries, gooseberries, blackberries Peaches, grapes, pineapple Strawberries Stewed fruit (apples, pears) Fruit juices [b]	8 months 10 months 10–12 months 12 months 10 months 10 months	Room temp.: 2–4 h. Refrig.: 10 h. Room temp.: 2–4 h. Refrig.: 10 h. Room temp.: 2–4 h. Refrig.: 10 h. Room temp.: 2–4 h. Refrig.: 10 h. Room temp.: 2–4 h. Refrig.: 10 h. Room temp.: 5 h. Refrig.: 10 h.
Meat	Beef Mutton Veal Pork Fillets, chops Liver, kidneys, other Brain, tongue, mince, sausages Rabbit	10–12 months 6–8 months 9 months 6 months 4 months 10 months 2 months 5–7 months	Refrigerator: 12–18 h. Refrigerator: 24 h. approx. Refrigerator: 24 h. approx. Refrigerator: 18 h. approx. Refrigerator: 12–18 h. Refrigerator: 10 h. approx. Refrigerator: 8–10 h. Refrigerator: 12 h. approx.
Poultry and game	Chicken Turkey (in portions) Duck, goose Hare Partridge, quail Pheasants Game	10 months 7 months 5 months 6 months 8 months 7–8 months 10 months	Refrigerator: 12 h. approx. Refrigerator: 10–12 h. approx. Refrigerator: 12 h. approx. Refrigerator: 12 h. approx. Refrigerator: 12–16 h. approx. Refrigerator: 12–16 h. Refrigerator: 18 h. approx.
Ready-to-serve food	Tomato sauce, stock, vegetables Beef, veal, pork or chicken stews Stewed meat Hamburgers, stuffed peppers, French beans Spinach Fruit salad Sandwiches	3 months 2–3 months 3 months 2 months 2 months 3 months 6 months	Direct heat or *bain-marie* Direct heat Room temp.: 5 h. Refrig.: 10–12 h. Direct heat Room temp.: 5 h. Refrig.: 10–12 h. Direct heat Room temp.: 5 h. Refrig.: 10–12 h. Direct heat or *bain-marie* Room temp.: 5 h. Room temp.: 5 h.

Food type	Name	Conservation time	Thawing method and time
Vegetables	Artichokes, carrots, asparagus, beans, peppers, spinach	12 months	Straight into boiling water
	Cauliflower, cabbage	6–8 months	Straight into boiling water
	Brussels sprouts	6 months	Straight into boiling water
	Mushrooms	6 months	Refrigerator: 2 h.
	Parsley	12 months	Do not thaw, crumble in the hand or bag

Notes: a) The majority of fruit can be frozen when stewed.

b) Orange and lemon juice should be frozen in dark glass containers, in waxed cardboard cartons or in opaque plastic containers to protect it from the light.

It's always best to thaw out in the refrigerator.

Conservation times for the ready-to-serve food will be shorter if pork or fat is added to flavour them.

reckon they are done, just as you would cook any other vegetable.

Meat and poultry When defrosting, it's best to leave these in the refrigerator overnight. The meat must be completely thawed before cooking. Fast thawing destroys the taste and can be dangerous.

Bakery Unwrap and then thaw overnight – although frozen croissants can go straight into a very low oven for ten minutes. Bakery goods freeze extremely well.

Sauces and casseroles May be heated from the frozen state in a double boiler.

Golden Rule Monique Guillaume, the famous French cookery writer, told me that whenever she serves anything frozen, she tries to add *something* fresh, e.g. a lump of butter on peas, a grating of nutmeg on spinach, cream to a white sauce, lemon juice and a little grated peel on fish dishes, and a dash of wine or cooking brandy for any meat stew (well, she's French).

EQUIPMENT AND SUPPLIES

You might prefer elaborate equipment but you can freeze perfectly well with an assortment of plastic bags, elastic bands, transparent wrapping film, deep-freeze polytape (ordinary Sellotape comes unstuck) and wax crayons (ordinary pencil or biro mysteriously dissolves).

An excellent, pithy little guidebook is *Good Food from Your Freezer* by Helge Rubinstein and Sheila Bush, published by Penguin Books.

Look in your *Yellow Pages* for your nearest frozen food supplier at catering prices. You can get a wide range of cooked, frozen and fresh poultry, meats, sea food, vegetables, sausages, fish fingers, fruit, pastries, cakes and ice cream. Vegetables are obtainable in 2.5-kg (5-lb) packs, corn on the cob by the dozen.

MY FAVOURITE COOKBOOK

The cookery book that I give to brides is Delia Smith's *Complete Cookery Course*, published by BBC Books. It's worth buying the hardback because then it will last a lifetime. Delia's 700-page book is beautifully produced, with mouth-watering illustrations; the recipes are clearly laid out and easy to follow. There is step-by-step information to give beginners a working knowledge of the basics of cooking, and the contents include chapters on vegetarian cooking and preserving.

STORE CUPBOARD COOKERY

When, unexpectedly, you have to produce a hostess-type meal and don't necessarily have a deep-freeze, it's generally the challenge and the panic that dismays you. But you are perfectly capable. It's the situation that may be unnerving you unnecessarily. *Looking* serene and prepared is half the secret of being prepared, and let no Scout tell you otherwise.

In an emergency, dress first, then lay the table (shows that they are obviously expected – you can keep guests waiting for food), then start cooking. The worst part of the evening will be the stomach rumbling interlude before dinner, so plan to keep your audience interested. Get your man to bring the boss home via a high grade pub; get the family's five thousand famished friends to help out in the kitchen – they'll enjoy it as long as you pretend it's an enjoyable occasion and do not *bustle*.

The emergencies that send you reeling will fall into two categories. There are the emergencies of quality when the man in your life calls from the office to say he's bringing Mr Big home to sample your culinary splendours, and there are the emergencies of quantity, when all the family invite their friends in at the same time and expect you to perform the miracle of loaves and fishes all over again.

If **emergencies of quantity** are common in your house keep a couple of these in reserve:

1 Cans of ham, tongue, tuna fish, sardines, frankfurters; rice, spaghetti and other pastas.
2 To go with the above: a packet of Parmesan cheese; cans of tomatoes and tomato purée.
3 Cans of soup, especially Crosse & Blackwell's consommé, which can be served cold with a dash of cream or hot with one of the following: a dash of vodka, a squeeze of lemon, a slosh of sherry (and perhaps some green ends of onion chopped small).
4 Packs of long-term carrots or tiny new potatoes (add mint and they'll never know it's Brooke Farm).
5 Bottled and canned whole courses – not instant curries, but delicacies such as Polish stuffed cabbage, French cassoulet or a whole Polish boiled chicken.
6 Fruit and vegetables in cans, especially red peppers and French beans.

Emergencies of quality need those basics and a few extras such as:

1 Canned pâté or bottled gulls' eggs.
2 Canned prawns, shrimps, crab, lobster (to mix with green salad and French dressing or mayonnaise).
3 Hellmann's bottled mayonnaise (decant into a little dish, add a squeeze of lemon and stir hopefully).
4 Lychees and other exotic fruit.
5 Chestnut purée (serve in individual glasses with, if possible, a topping of whipped cream or a dash of brandy).
6 Slowly, one ingredient at a time, build up a collection of herbs, spices, garnish and sauce ingredients – things such as anchovies, stem ginger, crystallized violets, olives, capers, tabasco and a range of dried herbs and spices.

Some things just aren't worth giving shelf space to: most canned minced meats; instant curries and chop sueys; certain herbs, such as chervil and mint, which can't be dried successfully; instant sauces, because making your own with store-cupboard ingredients is almost as quick and the result tastes better. (However, Escoffier Cumberland sauce, heated with the juice and grated rind of half an orange, is well worth trying with most meat or game.)

It helps with emergency cooking if you keep a *stockpot*. While writing this book, I kept one going during the winter, boiled it up every day (the only necessary discipline), then threw it away in the spring.

Don't confuse your stockpot with your dustbin. The only ingredients that you throw into a stockpot are bones, the odd vegetable, herbs and chopped onions. Bones can smell nauseatingly funereal. Disguise the odour by adding chopped garlic and a slosh of vinegar or white wine.

The most important aspect of cooking is knowing what you can get away with and what you can't. What I have found I *must* have fresh are: coffee beans, potatoes, onions, cream and lemons. Also wine vinegar, cooking wine (to add to dishes), butter in which to toss vegetables, and freshly ground black pepper, not that beige dust.

Keep an emergency jar of Nestlé's Gold Blend coffee and Coffee Complement dried milk buried in the depths of your store cupboard. You might also keep some longlife milk and cream hidden at the back of your refrigerator.

Suggestions for meals Canned peas or spinach served straight from the can are pretty uninspiring, but if you take a can of tiny French peas, add butter and spice gently with nutmeg, then serve piping hot with ham or frankfurters, the resulting dish can be delicious. Similarly, serve spinach puréed with cream and grated fresh nutmeg.

Serve noodles tossed in butter or cream with a crushed clove of garlic as a starter/filler.

Serve egg curry, with sliced hard-boiled eggs in a can of Lekari sauce with an added squeeze of lemon and hot fluffy, boiled rice.

CAMOUFLAGE COOKERY

Camouflage is the secret of successful store-cupboard cookery. The principle is simple: use available fresh window-dressing to disguise the unappetizing look, feel or taste of stored food. A few tips . . .

For a fresh touch, try to have a bit of greenery to chop finely on to whatever you're serving. If you leave onions long enough, they will generally sprout. For a chive taste, snip the ends on soups or omelette.

A fresh pepper, whether red or green, lasts about three weeks and tastes delicious shredded into salad. However shrivelled, when chopped into almost any stew dish, it imparts a 'continental' flavour.

A piece of grated lemon peel gives a fresh flavour to almost anything from soup to fruit.

Almost any fresh fruit, from oranges to grapes, tastes delicious when peeled, chopped up, sprinkled with a little white wine, then served in individual wine glasses (any old shape or size) with a dab of sugar sprinkled on and topped with fresh or soured cream. If the cream is canned, whip in a dash of something alcoholic.

JADED COOK

There comes a time in the affairs of women when your mind blanks out, you feel resentful, apologetic, apathetic and mutinous, and you simply can't concentrate on food. Don't worry. *You are a jaded cook.* It was a jaded cook who once said that the best thing about Christmas was that you never had to think 'What shall I give them for dinner?' It was a jaded cook who pointed out that the main advantage of spaghetti is that you don't have to peel it. You could deal with this

A basic fourteen-day meal plan

Cross out anything you don't like to cook, and substitute something you prefer.

Day	Lunch	Dinner
Saturday	pea soup, egg mayonnaise	roast chicken and roast potatoes
Sunday	lamb casserole, baked potatoes and grated cheese	cold chicken and rice, tomato and cucumber salad
Monday	liver pâté, salad, French bread	onion tart, salad
Tuesday	leek soup, baked eggs	spaghetti bolognaise
Wednesday	ham salad	shepherd's pie
Thursday	hamburgers	boiled gammon and mashed potatoes
Friday	omelettes	liver and bacon with onion rings
Saturday	grilled mackerel and grilled tomatoes	steak and kidney pie
Sunday	roast lamb and jacket potatoes	haricot bean salad with hard-boiled eggs and olives
Monday	toasted lamb sandwiches	chicken pie
Tuesday	sausages and chips	baked eggs and vegetable stew
Wednesday	onion and potato soup	lamb chops and spinach
Thursday	egg-and-bacon flan (quiche lorraine)	meat casserole (using cheap cuts)
Friday	cauliflower cheese	cod steamed with bacon, tomatoes and garlic

feeling as calmly as Ethel Kennedy, the widow of Senator Robert Kennedy, who had a fourteen-day family menu plan for her eleven children. It is based on simple roasts, grills, omelettes and salads. When she came to the fifteenth day she simply started again.

The Kennedy secret is **organization**. You, too, can have a food plan.

WARNING! Keep quiet about it. Don't tell anyone, or someone might complain. Keep your plan for when:

* The housework is getting on top of you.
* You're spring cleaning.
* You're studying.
* You're simply lazing, i.e. with your feet up on the sofa reading a bad book.

If anyone *does* notice and upbraids you, make it quite clear that you are no longer the enterprising cook that once you were when newly wed and showing off. Life is too short to stuff a mushroom.

So when you've a spare half hour, try jotting down your own basic fourteen-day plan and *stick to it*. The plan above shows what it might look like. These recipes aren't dull if you serve them prettily. They are no great culinary shakes. They simply stop you going out of your mind and take the minimum time to prepare.

If you have a lot to do one week, or are just very tired, try to minimize the evening cooking with your own variation of the following plan (which I used when I was woman's editor of a daily newspaper and permanently tired).

Prepare for this by cooking not one but two dishes of *anything* that can be frozen and then dished up weeks later. On Saturday cook two dishes, say a casserole and one dish of pasta sauce. Freeze half of what you've cooked. You can then get away with heating up, grilling or roasting for the rest of the week.

Buy good, nourishing food that is

really convenient and involves minimum preparation and shopping, such as ham, smoked mackerel, cheese, fruit, salad, vegetables, yoghurt, special bread such as pumpernickel or rye. Use as many semi-prepared foods as possible.

Monday evening A frozen meal from your freezer (soup or a shop-bought meal)

Tuesday evening Omelette and salad

Wednesday evening A casserole-type dish from your freezer

Thursday evening A pasta dish with sauce from your freezer

Friday evening Grilled fish

Saturday evening A night out (maybe you go to a film and eat a pizza afterwards)

Sunday evening A roast (chicken?)

If at any time during this week you feel too tired to cook *anything*, then serve cold cuts or buy a local take-away, either Indian or Chinese. If anybody tells you you can't afford, or that it's extravagant, to have a pizza or a take-away meal, take to your bed immediately with a severe migraine – and see whether the complainer buys a pizza or a take-away.

A sophisticated version of this plan involves getting your partner to do the cooking for the deep-freeze on Saturday. Alternatively, ask him to cook on one (weekday) evening a week and enthusiastically eat whatever turns up.

Budgets need slimming as urgently as people, so in both these interests I've left elaborate hors-d'oeuvres to your imagination and assumed that puddings are eaten only on festive occasions. Serve fruit or cheese afterwards. The trick with cheese, fruit or salad dishes is to *serve one thing at a time*. A simple bowl of oranges. A dish of bananas the following day. Serve an assortment and you risk the whole family getting jaded by day four.

Puddings

Choose puddings, if you have them, from:

Fruit flan with whipped cream
Chocolate mousse
Sliced oranges with brown sugar
Baked bananas with rum
Lemon syllabub

Salads

Say 'salad' to a jaded cook and she will think only 'lettuce'. Here are more suggestions, because salads are easy and healthy and can certainly stretch a meal.

A salad with a French dressing can be served before, with or after any dish. Choose from chicory, endive, mustard and cress, watercress, cucumber, cauliflower (the flowers only, broken into small flowerets), beetroot, carrot, button mushrooms (slice finely and soak in French dressing for four hours before serving), tomatoes, mixed salad, shredded white or red cabbage.

Combinations Choose from the following:

Lettuce, pineapple and chopped nuts
Watercress, and skinned grapefruit segments
Lettuce and sliced orange
Chicory with peeled grapes
Cucumber, chopped apples, soaked raisins and cold rice
Sliced new potatoes with chopped spring onions
Lettuce and cucumber

French dressing

Ingredients 1 egg-cup wine vinegar, 2 egg-cups oil, salt, pepper, a dash of French mustard, 1 clove crushed garlic, optional. If you are on a no-oil diet, use the juice of 1 orange and 1 lemon instead of oil.

Method Pour ingredients into bottle, flavour to taste, shake until emulsified. Pour over salad immediately, as emulsion is only temporary. Increase quantities, if you wish, to make enough to last a week.

Mayonnaise

If you use a shop-bought one, such as Hellmann's, try squeezing a little lemon juice and garlic into it. It will then taste more home-made, especially if you decant it and hide the jar.

ARE YOU EATING POISON?

'Many people are becoming increasingly worried about today's polluted and degraded foods,' I wrote, fifteen years ago. Now I would delete 'many' and substitute 'most'. Health-food shoppers are no longer regarded as faddists or cranks. It has been calculated that nearly half the people in this country are overweight and undernourished. We are fast becoming a nation fed entirely on canned, potted, instant-mixed, synthetic, dehydrated, freeze-dried, chemically processed food and wonder drugs.

There is said to be a potential danger, both physical and mental, in modern processed food, especially those that use the refined carbohydrates (white flour and white sugar to you). Some people think that this is linked with the increased incidence of coronary thrombosis, obesity and constipation, peptic ulcer and other twentieth-century diseases.

There is reported to be an alarming amount of lead in corned beef, sardines, butter, cheese and apples. Other possible poisons on our plate include salts used in bacon, mercury waste in fish, flour bleach, cyclamates, saccharin and monosodium glutamate. And then there are all those additives with E numbers in packaged food – some of them responsible for making small children 'hyper-active'. Arm yourself with a copy of *E for Additives: A Supermarket Shopping Guide*, published by Thorson, if you are worried about them.

Apart from chemical additives, you can also be poisoned by agricultural and industrial wastes, defoliates, pesticides, detergents, and anything upon which they have been sprayed. My accountant won't eat the skin of baked potatoes, as he once spent a holiday on a potato farm and saw how often poisonous chemicals were sprayed on the plants to kill insects.

In addition to the known effects of these, it is also suspected that there are unknown effects on the body and brain of biologically active substances such as the aforementioned insecticide residue.

What do you do about it?

What health-food experts advise you to eat is compost-grown vegetables and fruit. If you can't manage that, try to stick to fresh meat (although you may want to avoid any you suspect might come from animals that have had hormone injections), fish, dairy foods, eggs, cheese, butter, honey, fresh and dried fruit, fresh vegetables and wheat-grains and raw foods such as salad.

If you don't grow your own fruit and vegetables, you are now advised to peel these before eating or cooking because of the dangerous pesticides and sprays that are used after harvesting to keep fruit and vegetables *looking* good until they get to you. If you don't want to peel them, wash fruit and vegetables in a solution of 2 tablespoons of vinegar to a bowl of water, which will remove some, but not all of the poisonous spray. I wonder if by now you are as alarmed as I am to hear of the poisons that are openly being added to our food.

It has been estimated that the average family throws away per year as many potato peelings as are equivalent to 500 eggs' worth of iron, 60 steaks' worth of protein and 95 orange-juice glasses of vitamin C. Steam vegetables or cook them quickly with their skins on so that the water-soluble vitamins and minerals

DOWN WITH SUPERWOMAN!

aren't lost in the cooking water. Anyway they *taste* better that way. Don't cook them until they are soggy – serve crunchy vegetables.

Don't eat white sugar or white flour.

Use cider vinegar, sunflower seed oil, dried yeast and barbados sugar, and instead of flour to thicken sauces, use gruel, which is a traditional baby food as made by your granny and sold by chemists.

Take a vitamin supplement three times a day, plus specific items for specific problems; I take one 500 mg vitamin C tablet daily, as I am prone to catch cold.

Ignore any idiot who tells you that everyone gets all the necessary vitamins from the average well-balanced diet; he or she is probably under the influence of a food-industry publicity person.

Make your own stone-ground, wholewheat bread and yoghurt.

For years I avoided making my own bread because I thought I didn't have the time. I became scared of making my own bread. For a start, I didn't know what dried yeast looked like or where to get it. I even made my own salt (by dehydrating seawater in Greek rock pools) because I felt so guilty about not making my own bread. Then I did, and turned into an HMB freak.

Grandmother's home-made brown bread

Ingredients
650 g (1½ lb) wholemeal flour
400 ml (¾ pint) water (warm)
12 g (½ oz) salt
12 g (½ oz) dried yeast
12 g (½ oz) sugar

Method
1 Warm a mixing bowl.
2 Put half of the flour into mixing bowl.
3 Add sugar and salt.
4 Cream yeast with 2 tablespoons warm water and add to mixture. Add water.
5 Cover the basin with a clean cloth

and leave in a warm place for 15 minutes.
6 Add remaining flour to make a soft dough, using a little more water if necessary.
7 Knead dough on a well floured surface for 5–10 minutes.
8 Cut dough in half, shape each piece and place in two warmed, greased and floured 450 g (1 lb) loaf tins.
9 Place tins in a warm place, covered with a damp cloth. Leave until dough has risen to about double its size, approximately 30 minutes.
10 Bake at gas mark 6 (200 °C, 400 °F) for 45 minutes.
11 Turn out on to cooling rack.

The Duchess of Devonshire's home-made bread

This is the family recipe. All those 1920 beautiful Mitford sisters, including the Duchess, were brought up on it. It is not only delicious, but easy to make. Use 100 per cent stone-ground wholemeal flour. (The Duchess uses Prewetts.) Quantities given are for two 900 g (2 lb) loaves or four bun loaves.

Ingredients
1.4 kg (3 lb) flour
A little less than 50 g (2 oz) live yeast
1 litre (1¾ pt) warm milk or water
1 teaspoonful sugar
2 teaspoonfuls salt

Method
1 Heap up flour round sides of bowl and put yeast in the middle, a little broken up. Add to yeast the sugar, salt and a little of the warm milk.
2 When yeast is dissolved, stir flour in gradually, adding the rest of the liquid until it becomes a soft dough.
3 Put in a warm place to rise for an hour, covering the bowl with a clean, folded cloth.
4 When risen, turn out on a floured board and knead until it doesn't stick to your hands. Cut in half and knead

each piece separately for some minutes until quite firm.

5 Put into loaf tins and leave for 30 minutes to rise a little more. If you don't have loaf tins, shape the dough into four balls and put on a greased, floured baking sheet.

6 Cook in oven at gas mark 5 (190 °C, 375 °F) for about 1 hour until firm and brown.

Easy yoghurt

Put 2 dessertspoons of a good live yoghurt in the bottom of a large pudding basin. (I like any of the French yoghurts that can be easily obtained in most supermarkets.) Pour on 550 ml (1 pt) longlife milk – unheated, just straight from the packet. Put a plate on top of this and leave in your oven, if it is gas, with a pilot light on. This does *not* mean you light the oven; the gentle heat just contained in it by the pilot light is enough to make perfect yoghurt overnight. If it doesn't, leave it longer.

Put it into a fridge and when cool, eat it. Remember to keep back enough to make your next batch. An airing cupboard or the top of a storage radiator will do instead of a gas oven.

Super rich yoghurt

Ingredients
1.25 litres (2 pt) water
200 g (8 oz) powdered milk
1 large can (400 ml/14 oz size) evaporated whole milk
1 pot plain yoghurt or 3 tablespoons of the last yoghurt you made

Method
In a big mixing bowl blend powdered milk with ½ cup warm water. Blend other ingredients. Cover bowl with cloth, leave overnight where temperature is airing-cupboard hot, between 105 and 115 °C (221 and 239 °F), or leave it overnight in a gas oven with the pilot flame on. If it

doesn't set by morning, the place you put the bowl isn't warm enough.

FOOD HYGIENE

How food is infected

Poisonous bacteria can multiply amazingly fast, amazingly quickly; they reproduce non-sexually by dividing into two, which then divide again, and so on. In a warm, moist place (ideal conditions for bacteria), this can take place every ten minutes.

If a knife becomes contaminated by cutting raw chicken and then, without being washed, is used to cut a cake fresh from the oven, within twelve hours there could be millions of bacteria in that cake and anyone eating it will have food poisoning.

What kills bacteria is a very low or a very high temperature, so store food at a low temperature and cook at a high temperature. Buy food only from clean shops. Supermarket chillers and freezers often have red lines inside: check that the food isn't kept above or outside the red lines. Also check that the temperature dials are in working order: chilled food should be kept at 3 °C (37.4 °F), frozen food should be kept below −18 °C (−0.4 °F).

Check the food pack Don't buy peas or beans in a packet that is a solid lump. If they are lumped together, vegetables may have been partially thawed and then refrozen.

Cans of food should not be dented or damaged at the seam or rim. Dry goods, such as breakfast cereals, should be sold in sealed packages.

Always check the sell-by or eat-by date on can or pack. Never refreeze frozen food. Never assume that prepared food (such as pâté) that you buy at a shop hasn't *already* been frozen – so don't refreeze it, otherwise you will serve Poison Pâté.

Once you've bought it, **store your food** in the kitchen as fast as possible. Don't overload the refrigerator shelves, because this prevents cool air circulation.

Only a freezer with a four-star rating is suitable for home-freezing fresh foods. Fewer than four stars means that the freezer is only suitable for storing frozen food, not for freezing it.

When thawing frozen food, loosely cover it, perhaps with aluminium foil, to prevent cross-contamination.

Don't refreeze food after a freezer breakdown or power cut; instead, insure the contents for a few pounds.

Never put hot food straight into the refrigerator, because that raises the temperature of the refrigerator. However, get cooked food into the refrigerator as fast as possible.

Make sure all food containers are clean. Cover individual items, such as a lamb chop, with cling film (not foil, because then you can't see what the food is).

Bacteria contamination usually occurs on the surface of the food, so cooking separately prepared foods together – for example, stuffing buried deep within a bird – is risky, as the inner preparation may be undercooked. When roasting a bird, cook the stuffing separately, so that it is thoroughly cooked. Don't buy rolled-and-stuffed joints.

One of the ten most common causes of food poisoning is reheated left-overs. Don't reheat left-overs unless they have been refrigerated for a couple of hours, and then make sure you heat them through thoroughly.

Thoroughly heat chilled food, such as cooked TV dinners, to a uniform temperature of 70 °C (158 °F).

Boil shellfish such as mussels; shellfish often feed in waters polluted by sewage.

Raw or very lightly cooked **eggs** are risky: be wary of steak tartare, mayon-naise, hollandaise, *béarnaise* and mornay sauces, zabaglione, home-made ice cream or custard, cold mousses and any other dish made from whipped white of egg, such as meringue or baked Alaska.

Vulnerable people (babies, pregnant women, the sick and the elderly) should not eat eggs, except in baked dishes.

Pregnant women should avoid soft-rinded cheeses (such as Camembert), which might contain listeria; raw meat (as in steak tartare); unpeeled fruit or salad if not thoroughly washed, because this is how you can contract toxo-plasmosis, which carries a strong risk of a malformed baby.

If you want to know more about food hygiene, buy *Safe Shopping, Safe Cooking, Safe Eating* by Dr Richard Lacey, published in paperback by Penguin Books.

Microwave ovens should not be used to heat or reheat food that has been insuf-ficiently cooked to be bacteriologically safe. Microwaves don't have any effect on bacteria that's buried deeper than 2.5 cm (1 in).

NUTRITION

When I set up home thirty years ago, housewives knew nothing about nutri-tion. We had no idea that 50 g (2 oz) of sugar (200 calories) was valueless as food, whereas a 50-g (2-oz) egg (80 calories) was full of nutrients. Nobody told us that giving a child a sugar bun for tea was sabotaging his health. Nobody ex-plained how a poor, well-educated family could eat better (because they would know more about nutrition) than a better-off, uneducated family.

Some good food items, such as stone-ground, wholewheat flour, obviously costs more than the mass-manufactured, bleached supermarket product. But don't forget that (1) a dried apricot is a dried apricot, whatever the label, and (2) the

The protein equivalent of some cheaper food combinations compared with steak

Combination in best proportions		*Steak protein equivalent*
2 cups rice + ¾ cup peas or beans	=	270 g (9.50 oz)
2½ cups rice + ¼ cup soyabeans	=	262 g (9.25 oz)
1½ cups rice + 2 cups skimmed milk	=	219 g (7.75 oz)
1½ cups rice + 70 g (2½ oz) cheese	=	219 g (7.75 oz)
4 slices wholewheat bread + 25 g (1 oz) cheese	=	70 g (2.50 oz)
1 cup wholewheat flour + 1 tbsp non-fat dried milk	=	85 g (3 oz)
1½ cups wholewheat flour + ¼ cup beans	=	130 g (4.60 oz)
1 cup wholewheat flour + ¼ cup soya flour	=	115 g (4.10 oz)
¼ cup non-fat dried milk + 1 cup beans	=	235 g (8.33 oz)
⅓ cup peanut butter + ⅓ cup skimmed milk + 6 slices wholewheat bread	=	285 g (10.10 oz)

best way to procure *real* organic food is to grow your own, an admirable undertaking that will, so to speak, weed out the believers from the doers.

Don't waste money on junk food with no nutritional value for your family – anything bought in a cinema, any synthetically produced food, rubbishy, puffed-up breakfast food, crisps, sweets, chocolate, cakes and biscuits, cola drinks, *artificial* fruit juices.

Buy *fresh* food whenever possible and don't boil away the nutrients. Invest in a steamer and cook vegetables until they are crunchy, not soggy. Wherever possible, eat the skin of vegetables and fruit.

Dr Miriam Stoppard, mother of four, has written a clear, informative book, *Feeding Your Family: a guide to healthy and delicious food* (published by Penguin Books). Dr Stoppard's aim is to make it easy for people to change from an unhealthy way of eating to a healthy one while continuing (occasionally) to eat hamburgers, pizzas, fried egg and bacon.

This book is far more simply written than the HMSO publications on nutrition; Dr Stoppard writes with a zero-level fog index as she explains the basic theory of nutrition and suggests how you can put it into practice; she writes particularly well on children's diet.

QUACK HEALTH FOODS (the new consumer con)

'Organic', 'health' or 'natural' foods are those that have supposedly been grown without chemical fertilizers, fungicides or pesticides. Some chemists call some fertilizers 'organic' even though they are chemical because they are made out of natural minerals, such as lime. However, when you get fertilizers made from by-products of petrochemicals, obviously you are straying a long way from nature.

There's nothing intrinsically wrong with organic food – indeed, the fewer chemicals we ingest the healthier we will be. But the move towards the 'food of innocence' has spawned a world-wide racket. Any old dusty packet of nuts and raisins, essentially identical to the same product available at a supermarket, often sells for twice as much under the magic label 'organic food'.

EASY
ENTERTAINING

HOW TO CUT DOWN ON CHRISTMAS

Christmas has become a huge expense, the result of media indoctrination, and it's high time we rethought it. What used to be a religious service followed by a cheerful family meal has now become a carefully calculated shopkeeper's sales pitch. Alcohol is promoted to the sound of sleigh bells, and banks send you pictures of villages in the snow. On every advertisement, guilt buttons are pushed ('Of course *you* want the best for *your* family') and hope buttons are pushed ('A diamond is forever'), but who gets the best Christmas present? British Telecom, that's who.

Why *should* you exhaust and bankrupt yourself annually because Queen Victoria's husband (who had more money, time and help than you do) imported from Germany all the expensive frills, such as the Christmas tree, of what is now called a traditional Christmas? (If the Albert Memorial wasn't paid for by grateful retailers, then it should have been.)

Nothing could live up to Christmas as it is pitched by the media, so Christmas is often a time of unfulfilled expectations, disappointments and deep depression (sometimes suicidal) – especially for the lonely, who may particularly feel left out of Life's Party on Christmas Day.

Everyone tends to eat too much and drink too much, *you* work too much and it all costs too much. Christmas is often a minefield of family feuds – drunken uncles, exhausting and elaborate visits to mother-in-law (that's not *your* family Christmas, that's *hers*), gifts given to everyone in sight and competitive card-sending ('Bother, I forgot to send *them* one').

So how can you cut down on Christmas without unduly upsetting people? Choose from these suggestions.

First Year Cut down on Christmas cards. Prune your card list. Unless you live abroad (when it's a convenient way of keeping in touch with old friends once a year), forget cards.

Now check your gift list. Instead of gifts, send a card to everyone except your immediate family and godchildren. Remember that only greedy people would want you to spend more on Christmas than you feel you can afford.

Second Year This is the year that almost everyone stops sending gifts to you and instead sends a card (probably with a sigh of relief). Don't send them cards in return. Next year they will stop sending you cards.

Consider rethinking Christmas

Ask your family if they would prefer to do something else. The best and quietest Christmas was one that we had when my sons were 10 and 14. We went to a smart bookshop, each spent a predetermined amount on paperbacks for ourselves, then wrapped them so they couldn't be read until Christmas Day.

For Christmas dinner I served the children's favourite food: red soup, lobster and ice cream. This meal involved no cooking at all; I merely reheated the soup.

Consider cutting out travel Whole families hurl themselves across the country at Christmas, when maximum crowds and minimal services (coming back) provide the worst possible travelling conditions and the highest number of drunken-driving accidents.

So why not choose a different time of the year for a family gathering, one that is *not* a public holiday. My friend Pat (a grandmother) always has her family gathering on the Sunday before Christmas, so that her sons can go off to their in-laws for Christmas Day. Or perhaps you could have Christmas at home and arrange a gathering of the clans on your mother-in-law's birthday?

If you are attending a huge family gathering, a tip to ward off stress is: never do anything that requires concentration, needs finishing or that you want to see the end of, such as a TV programme or a game of Monopoly.

Consider cutting out decorations if you have no young children. If you are going to decorate, focus all your time, money and effort into one Christmas dazzler, either on the front door or the fireplace. A quick idea for a fireplace is to cover the top with crumpled silver cooking foil, stick a row of plain white candles along it and surround the base with holly leaves.

If you decide on a Christmas tree, then stand it on a cloth – a small table-cloth or a big towel; when the tree moults, just pick up the ends of the cloth and shake the needles to the middle.

Avoid drunkenness and poverty by cutting out the selection of drinks to rival the Ritz bar; instead, have a choice of two alcoholic and two really good non-alcoholic drinks. (Home-made lemonade? Proper ginger beer?) Offer spritzer, which is a little white wine and a lot of soda water.

Check the bathroom supplies before Christmas for Alka-Seltzer and aspirin and all the other unfortunately necessary medical extras that are likely to be needed as Boxing Day dawns.

Cut down on Christmas cooking anxiety Most mothers plan their most ambitious meal of the year for the maximum number of guests on the worst possible day to produce it – when all the shops are shut. However, at least this is the only day that you don't have to think 'What shall I give them to eat?'

Avoid overeating by spreading the delicacies over two days, aiming at four marvellous meals instead of one blow-out and three helpings of left-overs.

For minimal effort, buy the pudding (there are plenty of good ones, but I like

DOWN WITH SUPERWOMAN!

Mrs Peak's), buy the brandy butter, buy the mince pies, buy the sausages and stuffing. Then all you have to do is shove the turkey in the oven, with a meat thermometer to avoid serving raw bird: cook the stuffing separately (see p. 148).

Cheap poultry is fed on fishmeal, so it tastes of fish. It's worth making an effort to get a free-range bird from a reputable dealer. I once seriously considered sending our Christmas turkey (which tasted of fish) round to the home of the chairman of a large supermarket chain, with the compliments of the season, because after a couple of mouthfuls, none of my family touched the main attraction of a meal that had cost me a fortune.

A sensible rule (not just for Christmas) is that the cook doesn't wash up.

To avoid a martyred mother doing all the work, lighten the load by spreading it. List your labour force (anyone over 12 who is present) and the work to be done, draw up a rough work timetable and stick it on the kitchen wall. A possible plan is a carefree Christmas morning for him, a chore-free afternoon for her and an evening spent by both of them locked in their bedroom, if only to avoid the teenage party.

Plan to counter-balance conviviality by an occasional breather, a bit of personal peace and quiet for each person.

At any family Christmas, the children don't always behave like the angels on the tree any more than the adults do. Plan times for them to be out of your way. Someone can take them for a walk, and perhaps they might visit a neighbour's children in the morning, in return for which the neighbour's children visit you.

A good outdoor Christmas game for all ages involves a few water pistols and bubble blowers. One person blows the bubbles and the other blasts them with the water pistol.

To save jangling nerves, all musical instruments from whistles to tin drums should be banned after tea. Long may the Sony Walkman be a teenage status symbol.

Gifts

Gifts for you As a reward for cutting Christmas back to where it started, spend some of the money you've saved on a gift for yourself.

Let the under-12s know well in advance that what you'd *really* like for Christmas is a handpainted postcard from them.

Gifts for children The expensive present that bankrupts you is often played with for a very short time and then broken or put to one side to gather dust. What children like as gifts are lots of little intriguing parcels.

Gifts for the rich Nothing expensive. Anyone who is rich and nice doesn't want you to bankrupt yourself by buying something you can ill afford. A personalized something (handkerchief, matches, postcards) always seems welcome.

Gifts for the lonely Nothing is better than a visit.

Gifts for other guests If you are invited to someone else's Christmas dinner, ask in advance how many people will be present and take prettily wrapped but inexpensive gifts for everyone. Try bubble bath for a 2-year-old, a horror mask for any male, a cake of really good soap for any female.

If you particularly *want* to give a lavish present to someone, *don't* give it at Christmas; they may gaze at it with a sinking heart and feel guilty that they haven't given you a gift of similar value.

Wrapping it up

The quickest way to wrap gifts is to decide on one style of wrapping paper. Tissue is the easiest sort of paper to wrap; silver kitchen cooking foil is a good emergency wrap if you've run out of everything else.

Choose one colour ribbon for the females and another for the males. This is particularly useful for standby, emergency, bar-of-soap type gifts. No male likes to receive lily of the valley, no female relishes a bar of Tabac.

Try keeping a permanent gift-wrapping drawer or shoe-box and in it put wrapping paper, scissors, ribbons, a ball of red string and plenty of pretty postcards. Save any charming scraps for decoration – an old earring, a bit of lace, discarded wallpaper samples, twigs that you can spray silver or gold. Stick on your parcels stationers' gold stars, paper flowers, tinsel, folded white lace doilies, chocolate coins and sugar angels.

Having wrapped your present, lay it on its tummy to tie the string or ribbon around. Once tied up, immediately identify your parcel with a name tag; I once wrapped all my Christmas gifts and then realized that I didn't know who they were for, so had to undo them.

MINIMAL ENTERTAINING, MAINLY FOR BEGINNERS

Throwing a party

The first and constant aim of a hostess should be to make her guests feel welcome and relaxed. Be genuinely pleased to see them (and if you aren't, you should never invite them again). A couple should decide beforehand which one is the host and which one dispenses the drink. If you live alone, hire a person to help: you can't do a proper job on your own.

When planning, a hostess ought to consider why people go to parties: if they have no permanent partner (or sometimes if they do), it is often only to meet interesting specimens of the opposite sex. An alternative reason is to show off your new partner to your friends (or your old partner). Some people like to dress up

and flirt, and some just to talk, eat good food, drink good drink and thereby have fun.

Never give a party for a collection of relative strangers, none of whom knows the others. Ideally, ask lots more men than women (women never mind this) and ask several dazzlingly beautiful women (men never mind this). Always introduce bores to each other: that disposes of them and stops party atrophy.

Most nice people feel a bit unsure of themselves before arriving at a party. A good guest should look after himself and other people as well.

Never introduce a newcomer to more than two people at once. Don't drag a couple apart unless you get really frantic distress signals. Try to get people talking in small groups, as a group keeps the conversation going.

If you are a shy host, grab a jug or bottle (any bottle so long as it's full) and walk round offering to refill glasses: this gives you a good opportunity to approach anyone you feel like, when you feel like it, and leave them at your convenience. Apart from this bottle, the host should not be pouring the drinks; his job is to mingle. Ask a friend to pour the drinks or (better) hire a barman.

Drunkenness is easily avoided at any party where an experienced barman's pay is balanced by what he saves you in liquor, and if you don't want anyone to get drunk, simply tell him so in advance. Nobody thinks a host mean if the barman takes his time in giving a drink or gives a weak one when he thinks it's called for.

Another party problem can be getting rid of the last guests. Finish a drinks party by closing the bar and disappearing yourself: the simplest way is to go out to a meal at a restaurant with a pre-arranged group at a pre-arranged time. If, when lingerers see you putting on your coat, they ask if they can come as well, explain that you aren't the host, guiding them towards your front door as you do so.

DOWN WITH SUPERWOMAN!

Meal for up to twelve guests

The two main things to avoid at a party are a harassed hostess, and food and drink running out.

A single cook-host cannot happily cope unaided with serving three courses (even if prepared) for more than six people. It is better to have two dishes rather than more, or hire a waitress. Or try cooking and serving a meal for a friend in her home, then having her do the same for you (same number of guests). It's amazing how much easier it is, when the guests aren't yours.

Warnings! Never try cooking any dish for the first time for your dinner party in case it's a failure. Don't overstretch your limits or you will feel harassed. Don't cook anything that is going to need a lot of last-minute attention, as all your attention should be focused on your guests.

Have plenty of ashtrays (but no cigarettes). You can't have too many ashtrays. Saucers are better than scorch marks.

Make sure your guests are warm. Everyone else feels colder in your home than you do, and nothing freezes conversation faster than draughts.

If you are late on schedule, nobody minds much if you disappear into a smoke-filled kitchen to ease the food disasters, but your guests will feel embarrassed unless they arrive to find the table laid and the drinks ready. So lay the table, get the drinks ready, *then* get yourself dressed, *then* turn your attention to serving the meal.

Encourage people to talk shop – people generally talk with enthusiasm about the subject they know best.

If the meal is going well and everyone is talking freely at the top of their voices, don't risk upsetting the atmosphere by serving coffee somewhere else.

Don't feel the evening is a failure if people leave at 11 p.m. They have to get up the next morning or get back to the babysitter.

Meal for over twelve guests

Bigger parties generally divide into two sorts: the drinks-only affair and the help-yourself buffet.

Don't give a drinks party that starts at 6 and ends at 8.30. It should start at 7 and end at 9.30. After work, people need reasonable time to unwind and freshen up.

Provide a proper place for guests to put coats, even if it means packing your own clothes in suitcases for the night. No one likes to grope for her designer coat under a pile of scruffy duffel coats heaped on the bed.

Lighting + sound = mood at a party. Light should be flattering, low and warm. Turn off any central light fittings. Sound is especially important at the beginning, when only two or three people have arrived and are wondering if they are too early. Buy or borrow six good up-to-date albums (last year's winners will not do).

If, at a drinks party, you serve food, you are assuming that some of your guests may be hungry (especially if they are coming straight from work). Nourishment is not a canapé: serve something you can get your teeth into, such as open sandwiches.

For a buffet supper, choose plenty of pre-prepared food, such as pâté and French bread, salads (not dressed until the last minute), baked potatoes and chilli or some other simple dish that you have prepared the night before, a shop-bought gateau, such as chocolate sachertorte, fresh raspberries or other small berries. Have a dish of hard-boiled eggs nestling in lettuce so that any dieters need not worry about breaking their regime.

Avoid any food that needs cutting, such as smoked salmon, because few of your guests will have three hands.

The sensible reason that everybody serves this sort of meal is that it's the easiest sort of meal to serve.

Party check-list

On the day

* Rearrange furniture as necessary.
* Vacuum carpets.
* Empty wastebins.
* Do the flowers (can be messy).
* Check stereo and albums.
* Check there are enough coat hangers (if not, get some from the dry cleaners).
* Put out cutlery, china, glasses in the eating room. Scatter ashtrays everywhere.
* Check towels, soap, toilet paper.
* If it's a big party, tape the guest list to the back of the front door, or keep it in your hand.
* Lock doors to any rooms that you don't want people to enter and put the keys in a bag in the freezer (it's the only place that nobody gets to).
* Check ice has been delivered in 3-kg (6.6-lb) bags from local off-licence: (some off-licences also hire glasses). Put ice – still in bag – in an empty bath.
* Set up bar. Use a large casserole if an ice bucket unavailable. Check: large spoon for ice, lemons, chopping board, corkscrew, can opener, knives, cloths, Lea & Perrins sauce, Angostura bitters, ashtray on bar, large wastebin behind bar, drinks trays.
* If you have one, put the phone on an answerphone *before you go to dress.* Your job is to give the party, not to answer the telephone.

GUESTS TO STAY

Always sleep in your spare bedroom to make sure that it is comfortable. Provide a basket of essential things that guests may forget, such as cotton wool, razor and blade (if not electric), bath oil and powder, baby oil for removing make-up, hair spray, deodorant, eau de cologne, soap, flannel, towels, tissues, toothbrushes, nail file, shampoo, aspirins, Alka Seltzer, everything that an ailing head or stomach could possibly require. (Alternatively, tell them where to find your medicine cabinet.)

Check that there are plenty of welcoming flowers, books and magazines, paper, pen, envelopes and stamps, a spare blanket, a bedside table with a lamp, glasses and bottle or jug or fresh water, an electric blanket or hot-water bottle, even if it's August and you feel that the weather is mild – other people's homes always seem colder than one's own.

There should be enough room in the spare bedroom for a guest's possessions. When the wardrobe is opened, a pair of cricket pads should not fall out; the chest of drawers should not already contain somebody else's ski clothes.

If your guests bring children, friends or dogs, they should ask your permission in advance and offer you a good escape route, such as 'unless your cat hates children', or 'if you're not allergic to dog hair'.

Whether they are staying overnight or for a month, shortly after your guests arrive, you should tactfully make it clear when you expect them to leave. ('I hope you'll find everything you'll need for five days . . .')

Make the programme of the visit clear and give your guests a chance to slide out of it. For example, 'We eat lunch at one o'clock' means that guests can do what they like in the morning or that you haven't time to entertain them in the morning, or both. 'I thought we might visit the circus this afternoon . . . unless you would prefer to rest' gives a guest a straightforward choice. 'I've booked tickets for all of us at the ballet' means that the guest has no alternative.

Ask your visitors when they want to use the bathroom in the morning, if it is a communal one; otherwise guests might not realize that their simple twenty-minute isometric programme before breakfast and their reading habits after breakfast can cause chaos in the household routine.

When you want to go to bed (which can be at any time), ask your guests whether they would prefer tea or coffee for breakfast. Perhaps offer continental breakfast in bed, which makes a guest feel cosseted and keeps him out of the way until your household is organized.

Unless battalions of staff are clearly visible, a visitor should always make his bed, even on the day he leaves.

A good guest always asks, 'Can I help you?' If a hostess says 'No', that's what she means.

Tipping If there are resident staff, ask your hostess 'What do people usually leave for the staff?' Do exactly what she says and leave any tip in an envelope on the dressing table.

Generally If a guest doesn't know his way around, he should ask his hostess.

A guest always asks if he may use the telephone and pays for his telephone calls. If I'm staying with someone, I list and time my telephone calls. At the end of my stay, I calculate the cost (peak-time rates), double the calculated amount, put the list plus my cheque in an envelope, address it to my hostess and leave it on the dressing table.

If you don't want to return hospitality, simply DON'T. This cuts out all that 'I suppose we ought to have them back' rubbish. It makes it clear that you don't particularly want to see them again. If they want to see you, they will invite you, and then you can politely refuse the invitation.

Suggested reading for hosts and guests Debrett's *Etiquette and Modern Manners* (edited by Elsie Burch Donald, published by Pan Books in paperback) has a good section on visitors and house-guests; it also covers engagements, weddings, divorce, death, business entertaining, and tells you how to answer an

invitation from the Queen. Useful, if a bit ponderous.

PARTIES FOR THE UNDER-8s

Among the few things that can drive you to drink within three hours is a dull or disorganized children's party; they can, however, be more fun than the average grown-up party.

As with a battle offensive, the secret of a good children's party is careful planning. It requires even more effort than an adult party.

Let your children choose their guests and never make them invite someone they don't like, however chummy you may be with the mother.

Invite the smallest number of children you can get away with. Six is the minimum.

Unless the child is under 4, make it clear that you don't want a grown-up escort hanging around it to inhibit you.

Stock printed invitations rarely say exactly what is going to happen, so it can be cheaper and more satisfactory to buy a packet of children's notepaper from Woolworths and write them out yourself, if your child is not old enough to do so. The invitations should firmly state starting and finishing times, and possibly add 'Please don't worry about collecting Ned. We will bring him home.' This avoids awful moments when one child has not been called for and sits in a chair in the hall, getting increasingly upset.

Plan the party as follows:

1 Hire one or two teenage helpers.
2 Start it as late as possible: 3 p.m. is the latest. End it as early as possible: 6 p.m. is the earliest. Divide the three hours into:
   (a) one hour games
   (b) half-an-hour refreshments
   (c) half-an-hour games
   (d) one hour tea

Small children often don't want to play games, so have a selection of small toys in a corner.

Get someone to escort small children to the lavatory on arrival, before and after tea, and before departure.

Dressing up

Girls enjoy dressing up in your (carefully selected and supervised) clothes, underwear and make-up; hats are favourites and any antique laced corsets are sure to make your party a success. This isn't socially acceptable for boys, but field research (mine) proves that they are just as keen. Let little girls use make-up tissues, and make-up; you stand by with large pots of Crowe's theatrical cold cream.

The easiest way to make your party go with a bang is to have a theme. The dressing-up element is almost as much fun if you restrict the dressing-up part to hats plus accessory – witches and wizards; pirates; nurses and doctors, with suitable little black bags; a Wild West party, with hats before tea, guns and caps handed out *after* tea.

While it is a splendid idea to hire ancient Charlie Chaplin movies, do not expect children to sit in silence for a two-hour feature. But a double side-splitter is to show a Laurel and Hardy short film and run it again backwards.

Children do not like being ticked off for jumping on the furniture, tearing their clothes, fighting, quarrelling or being sick on your best carpet. So the good party-giver avoids these things. If possible, remove the furniture from the party room – a drastic but certain way of ensuring that none will be damaged.

The games should be worked out in advance on the basis of a noisy one following a quiet one. The games plan must be written down, because once a good party gets under way, no one – especially not the adult-in-charge – will have time to think. Once lost, control cannot be regained.

Allowing an average of ten minutes a game, it should be possible to keep a group of children happy and interested for a couple of hours. Most parents attempt to keep a party going for too long; it is just as tiring for a child to play party games as it is for an adult to run them.

The equipment needed for each game should be put in a box in a corner of the room before the party starts.

When the first child looks bored, stop the game.

Elimination games, where one winner emerges at the end, are a sure fire way of losing the children's interest.

Everyone must win a small prize if there are to be prizes at all.

Each child should take a gift home, however cheap.

Help-yourself buffet

On easily cleaned floors, buffet parties are a good idea. Give each child a small plate; they love to choose.

Cocktail sausages will disappear at the rate of 186,000 per second. Offer sandwiches and baked potatoes stuffed with grated cheese or crumbled, grilled bacon. Offer tiny sandwiches, tiny cakes, keep everything micro-mini. Label the sandwiches – they like to know what they're getting. Provide a gargantuan bowl of gob stoppers and another of polka dots or brilliant coloured sweets. There must be a birthday cake, but they won't eat it – unless it's ice cream.

This food can be eaten standing and perhaps in the kitchen to avoid having a sticky mess all over your home.

Sit-down meals

The most popular meal is based on the simple sausage, crisps and peanuts. Children love sausage and mash in the style of Billy Bunter, with the sausage sticking up from a small pile of mash. They like tiny hot sausage-rolls or sausages on sticks, or sausages and beans, or sausages with bacon wrapped around. Any sandwiches should be open ones with plenty of topping.

Afterwards, fruit salad is simple, easy, and it doesn't usually make them sick.

The ideal party food (for the giver) is food eaten off paper, so that afterwards you can sweep the whole lot off the table (cloth, mugs, plates, napkins) and into the dustbin. Buy them from Woolworths (cheapest).

Get the children dressed in their outdoor clothes ten minutes before the official closing time as stated on the invitation. Because her child is ready to be collected, you don't have to ask Mrs Jones if she would care for a drink. You don't want to find yourself giving an adults' drinks party *as well as* a children's party.

PARTIES FOR THE OVER-8s AND UNDER-18s

Write down a budget, then let your child do the rest of the work. The child can decide on the number of guests, write the guest list, then write and post the invitations. The child can compile the menu, go shopping for it and then cook it. The child can buy any prizes or other necessary equipment.

Apart from your bedroom (to which you will have moved any adult beverages that you don't want drunk), the cooker is the one thing that should be forbidden to the guests.

Don't be worried by the noise, but by any sudden silence.

You will need: a stereo, as little furniture as possible, as many cushions as possible.

Serve only food that can be eaten in the fingers. Food is perhaps best laid out

in the kitchen, with plenty of tissues to hold savoury food: dozens of small sausages; joints of cold chicken; hot garlic bread; baked potatoes; soured cream or cheese dips, with crisps to dip into them; open sandwiches of salad topped with ham, hard-boiled egg or a strip of cheese or sardine, or all four; fruit in season, with cream, is always finished fast. It's hip to be thin, so enough food should be from the high-protein diet that they are all on. They drink milk, Coke and fruit cup. The older ones drink cider, red wine and they smoke.

Be firm about the hour upon which you intend to repossess yourself of your home and sling out any stray bodies. This must be by mutual agreement with the party giver, but it is a battle that you must win beforehand.

Adults under 15 should be escorted home, whatever they said their parents said. Ideally, hire some suitable conveyance to call at the exit hour and plan an advanced, geographically sensible, dropping-off list. Don't, at this point, assume you will get any help from the sulking host.

Books on giving parties for children say that it is a good idea to have an activity that can occupy children up to 14, such as make popcorn or home-made sweets. *On no account suggest anything so wet or so dangerous* (not only for them, but for you).

PICNICS

If you don't want to waste half a sunny day preparing the picnic and the rest of the day arguing about where to stop the car, decide in advance who's going to choose the picnic spot and don't make over-elaborate preparations, which might be ruined by rain.

Picnics tend to be either a bag of sandwiches or else something a bit more exciting. In which case, take the ingredients and prepare them when you get there. Take nothing sticky or liable to melt or curdle (home-made mayonnaise curdles).

* Instead of butter, use cream-cheese spread.
* Instead of chocolate, take boiled sweets.
* If it's windy or you plan to swim, instead of coffee or tea (which always tastes of the flask), take hot soup.
* Instead of synthetic fruit drinks, take unfrozen orange juice with a squeeze of fresh lemon. Something mildly exciting for children is Peppermint Rock shake. This is cold milk with a dash of Ribena and a drop of peppermint essence.
* Instead of white wine that needs chilling, take red.

Have you ever known a picnic where something wasn't forgotten? If so, use this check-list and add your own special items.

* Paper cups and plates.
* Real kitchen cutlery, because plastic is so bendy.
* Cheap, thick glasses if you're drinking wine (paper cups spoil the taste).
* A kitchen roll to mop up afterwards.
* A wooden salad bowl.
* A plastic container of water, for drinking and wiping sticky fingers.
* Salt, corkscrew, a bottle and can opener.

* At least three empty plastic bags for litter, damp towels and bathing suits.
* Rugs and umbrellas.
* (If you're feeling gracious) cushions, a table-cloth and a wicker basket big enough to carry everything.

Simple meal suggestions

* Hard-boiled eggs, salami, cold sausages, ham, a dismembered fowl – everyone loves eating with their fingers, Henry VIII style.
* Fresh bread (with knife to cut it), rolls or crisp breads.
* Green salad to be dressed on site.
* Fresh, hard fruit or soft fruit in box, cheese.
* Sweet biscuits, but not chocolate ones, which melt and stick together.

Danish open sandwiches, prepared on the spot, need one moist ingredient, such as tomato. Starting with a lettuce-leaf base, add:

1 Slice of cold fried bacon and plenty of fresh ground black pepper.
2 Slice of peeled apple on cream cheese.
3 Chopped radish on liver sausage.
4 A crisp ring of raw onion on sliced cucumber and anchovies.
5 Cold scrambled egg and capers.
6 A slice of tomato and black olive on cream cheese.

RUNNING A PET

Pets are a wonderful idea if you have time on your hands or you live alone or in a superbly staffed country mansion. Pets enhance your lovable earth-mother image. They are comforting. They are friendly. They are loyal. They are fun. Children love them. They love you.

BUT think four times before you buy a pet. Think of:

1 The cost.
2 The amount of time which you'll have to spend on caring for and perhaps exercising your animal.

~~hat will happen if you go away?
~~ou enough space in your home

and are you prepared to have carpets, curtains, upholstery and furniture scratched, clawed and possibly ruined? I once had to patch a fitted carpet four weeks after it had been laid, and before it had been paid for, thanks to an adorable kitten of similar age.

Costs

It costs at least £115 a year to keep a cat in food, milk, cat litter and vets' fees. To keep a spaniel costs twice as much, i.e. £330 a year, calculate the RSPCA. Bigger dogs cost a lot more. A dog likes to eat far more meat than a human being.

Vets are very expensive, although if

you have no money, the RSPCA or Blue Cross will care for your beast. But you may have to trek across town to get to them. You think you won't need a vet? Nothing much seems to go wrong with budgerigars, but kittens and puppies need injections when they're small. To get a cat spayed seems to cost more than a vasectomy. Cats and dogs get fleas, mites, pregnant, into fights and run over. Goldfish get mildew. Hamsters and rabbits get more hamsters and more rabbits.

Going away

You can't go away for a weekend without making arrangements for your pet, either expensively with a vet or kennels, or with a friend. Holidays are worse.

Pets are as much of a tie as children. They need regular feeding, caring and looking after. Young ones tend to make smelly messes, just like babies only without nappies. Unhappiness is a warm puddle.

Puppies chew everything. Your boots, your husband's boots, your girlfriend's fur coat, your mother's best handbag. You may gain in fortitude what you lose in friendship.

Puppies grow into dogs and they bark very loudly in a way that might go right through your head until you yourself feel like baying at the moon.

It is cruel to keep dogs in flats and often in city houses with no gardens. They need exercise. Having for years been dragged horizontally around the park at dawn in the wake of a Weimaraner, I can caution others.

A small but tedious point. Bitches on heat can be very messy and, apart from the blood, you'll find every dog in the district at your front door. How often? Although it varies according to bitch, breed and age, you'll probably have to cope with it twice a year and it goes on far longer than you could possibly imagine. Allow four weeks, but check with your vet.

Kittens grow into cats who look like divine miniature tigers, *but* they can't be put out regularly like dogs, who at least perform like clockwork if well trained. A cat won't do anything you want it to. A cat tray in the kitchen stinks. People are always putting their feet in cats' trays placed elsewhere. The peculiarly pungent lavender-stink aroma of cat hangs ineradicably around the house and you can't disguise it. Get a covered cat-litter tray – like a small dog kennel with a lift-off top – into which the cat can go to excrete. Clean it every day, and use powder deodorant from a pet shop.

Breeding

Another example of false sentimentality about animals that the RSPCA want to discourage is thoughtlessly allowing your pet to breed, then forcing the litter on friends who don't really want them. The result is that at least 1,000 stray and unwanted dogs *a day* are put to sleep by voluntary organizations. In 1986 the RSPCA put down over 54,000 stray cats and unwanted kittens. So if you're an animal lover, make sure that you really are prepared for the responsibility of caring for a living creature.
FINAL WORD OF WARNING! If you have children, never keep a pet if you intend eventually to eat it.

Goldfish I must admit that goldfish are very little trouble and a constant source of pleasure. Give them enough room to swim, change their water once a week and *rarely feed them anything – if you want them to live.* (Having discovered this secret, the mortality rate of goldfish went down rapidly in our home.)

NOW READ ON

Dogs

If you still want a dog you can get a mongrel from a pet store or the RSPCA, or you can buy a pedigree dog from a pet store or an established breeder. Never buy an anonymous dog from a market stall. Get a list of local breeders from the Kennel Club, 1 Clarges Street, London W1. Don't buy a pedigree dog without a pedigree registration certificate.

Don't buy a puppy less than 7 weeks old or more than 12 weeks. Don't buy a puppy that doesn't *look* in good condition, fit and bouncy. Don't accept any explanations for a listless puppy. Don't pick the runt of the litter because it's so tiny and sweet and pathetic. You may be heading for vets' bills.

A pedigree pup should have been inoculated against serious diseases before it's sold and the breeder should provide proof of this. Get a mongrel inoculated. Consult the vet about worming.

Treat your puppy as kindly and gently as you would a baby. Keep him in a blanket-lined box with a ball and a few toys until he's 3 months old, when he can be promoted to a real live dog basket that will catch on your stockings. Only sporting dogs should be kept out of doors in a kennel.

Housetrain your puppy by saying 'no' in a voice that is stern and authoritarian and immediately taking him outside. Exercise him straight away after meals, which is when he's most likely to mess. Dogs need a regular balanced diet, not just meat. Feed a puppy four times a day until he's 6 months old, twice a day until he's 9 months old, then once a day in the morning or evening. Keep to regular times. Give your puppy dog food or finely chopped meat mixed with puppy meal twice a day, and puppy meal or breakfast cereal mixed with milk twice a day, and perhaps a lightly boiled egg twice a week. See he always has fresh water and big bones. Avoid chicken, or fish bones, which can splinter.

he has a collar and an identity keep him on a lead in

Cats

If you've set your heart on a cat, acquiring a kitten seems to be no problem. You just tell everyone you meet tomorrow that you want a kitten and strange kitten owners everywhere will be rushing round in no time. Or you can telephone the RSPCA, buy one from a pet store or get a pedigree cat from a breeder. Again, don't get one less than 7 weeks old. Don't buy a pedigree kitten without a Cat Fancy Registration Form.

Get your kitten checked by the vet and injected as necessary. Spaying or neutering is done 4 to 5 months after birth.

Don't pick up a kitten (or a puppy) by the scruff of its neck or by its paws. Put one hand under his chest and nestle his hindquarters in your other hand.

Feed a kitten four times a day until it's 4 months old, three times a day until it's 6 months old, twice a day until it's 9 months old and then once a day. Start him off on baby cereal mixed with milk and a little chopped liver, fish or good cat food. By the time he's 9 months old he'll need a small can of food a day. Don't feed him fish all the time. As well as milk, a cat needs a constant bowl of clean water.

Housetrain your kitten by putting near his basket a plastic cat tray or ordinary tin tray covered with newspaper, litter or earth. Clean the tray daily. Ugh! Swab it out with hot water and a little disinfectant. You can get a cat panel fixed to your garden door, if you have a garden, or a tiny glass pane which flaps up and down fitted to a suitable window.

CLEAN-UP TIP

Get cat and dog hairs off upholstery with a rotary clothes brush, the sort that has a disposable roll to which hairs and fluff stick and you tear off the dirty bit (obtainable from John Lewis). Alternatively, wrap Sellotape around your knuckles, sticky side out, and collect hairs and fluff on the tape by running your hand over upholstered furniture, clothes, stairs – anywhere. Simply wearing a washing-up glove achieves the same effect.

SIMPLE FIRST AID FOR ANIMALS

A dog or cat that has been run over or seriously injured in any way can be dangerous. The most affectionate pet may not realize that you are trying to help it, and may turn on you. Approach an injured animal very gingerly. Muzzle a dog with a belt or a man's tie or a scarf.

If the pet is bleeding heavily, apply pressure on a sterile gauze pad or a clean handkerchief and tie it down with another handkerchief or strip of cloth. Wrap the pet in an old coat or blanket to keep it warm and prevent it from thrashing round while you rush it to the vet.

Dogs and cats often suffer **eye injuries**. Keep the eye moist by dropping cooking oil into the eye and, if it looks serious, take it to the vet.

Pets can eat **poison** by accident or someone's nasty intent. If it has the shakes, vomits a great deal or gets highly excited, wrap it in a blanket, scoop up (Ugh!) a sample of the vomit (which will indicate what foul substance it has swallowed) and rush pet and sample to the vet.

If you are giving medicine to your cat (by mouth) immobilize the animal by wrapping its body tightly in a towel to the chin. One person should hold the animal between his knees (head uppermost) and gently pull back its head, whereupon its mouth should open. The second person pours the medicine down the back of the cat's throat. If administering a pill, coat it in butter, hold down the cat's tongue and slip the pill down the back of its throat. This is easier than it sounds. Any alternative method may

involve getting badly scratched without the animal having taken the medicine.

Dogs can be plagued with **ticks** and **burrs**, particularly if you live in the country or suburbs, though ticks can breed in a flat. Rub your hands periodically over the dog's body to see if it has ticks. The lumps are easily detected, often under its legpits or ears. Remove these infectious nauseating bloodsuckers by dabbing them with paraffin and then twisting them off with tweezers – counter-clockwise – so making sure that you don't leave the tick's head behind.

Disinfect the bite area with alcohol, burn the ticks and **wash your hands**. Newly acquired **burrs** can also be removed with tweezers, but if the burrs are embedded in the fur, the best thing to do is to very delicately cut them out with nail scissors.

When a pet **limps** badly, or seems unduly bothered by a leg (it may persist in licking a paw), it has probably been impaled by a thorn or splinter. Moving very gently, minutely examine the paw. If the thorn or splinter is still sticking in there, remove it carefully with sterilized tweezers. Then dab the pad with hydrogen peroxide. If the pad has been cut, dab with hydrogen peroxide, to prevent infection.

The dog that constantly roams far from home disturbing other people's lives and rubbish bins is not exactly a first-aid problem, but may quickly become one unless you curb it. If it won't stay home, and you have a garden, the only solution is to run a 30-m (100-ft) wire between trees or poles and attach a running chain to it, to which you firmly attach your dog's collar. However, if you give him good long walks, he may feel less inclined to be the neighbourhood scourge.

However, most pets, if well exercised, properly fed and sensibly treated, seem less likely to get sick than the average human. Come to think of it, they have pretty soft lives.

FAST MAINTENANCE

SKIP THIS ENTIRE CHAPTER UNTIL YOU NEED IT – EXCEPT FOR BUYING YOUR TOOLS.

WHAT EVERY BRIDE SHOULD KNOW

If your man is unwilling, do not force him by any method, whether this be a reproachful glance as you nail your thumb or a list of what your friends' mates do for them (they're probably lying). Men are extremely good at being helpless. The cleverer they are, the more helpless they are, and the cleverest ones prove this neatly by making things *worse*. And you don't want to find yourself patching up a marriage.

The theoretical alternative is to find an odd-job man. In fact, although the odd-job man is not quite as dead as the dodo, he generally has a sense of time

that one can describe only as poetical and knows his scarcity value, which is rather higher than emeralds. In my experience it's quicker, cheaper and less harassing to keep a list of all the jobs that need doing and keep a day completely free to do a lot of them yourself.

Buy a copy of one of many DIY magazines or books available, not only to tell you how to do what, but also to inspire you with enthusiasm and put over the feeling that it's FUN (which for me it isn't). Some of them are especially slanted towards women (too kind) and anything that the do-it-yourself enthusiast can do, from renewing a tap washer to building a home extension or installing your own central-heating system.

Your first purchases should be a radio and a strong firm ladder, and, if possible, don't do anything on top of it unless there is someone in the house to hear you holler for help if you fall off. You will also need a big box in which to keep your brushes, tins, tubes and tools.

HOW TO COPE WITH ELECTRICITY

Do you really save money if you turn off the light bulb on the landing, like Dad says? Or do you only save ½p a month, as your kid brother insists?

Movie director Clive Donner asked me to discover what the yearly bill is for a pilot light, because this is what the miser in him resents paying. He doesn't believe the propaganda that says a pilot light costs nothing a year to run. Other mean, magnificent movie directors might like to know that:

An electric red button, small, neon electric pilot uses approximately half a unit a year, which is less than 3p a year to run.

Make sure that you won't need electro-cardiac treatment next time the bills come in by switching off the appliances that are rather more likely than a pilot light to cause heart flutter . . . These are your HEATERS. All electrical appliances with heating elements (like dryers) cost more to run than those that just have motors (like washing machines), as they burn up a lot more energy. These include toasters, irons, hair dryers and, of course, electric heaters. For example, a 2 kilowatt fan heater, left on from eight in the morning until nine at night would *alone* cost over £50 a quarter.

A *unit* of electricity is the amount needed to produce 1 kilowatt (1,000 watts) of power for one hour. So a 1-kilowatt fire uses one unit in one hour, and a 100-watt bulb uses one-tenth of a unit in one hour.

This is how the gadgets burn up energy

★ 1 kW electric fire: 1 hour = 1 unit.

★ 2 kW electric fire: 1 hour = 2 units.
★ 2.25 kW night storage heater: 8 hours = 5–18 units, depending on charge controller and room temperature.
★ Convector heater: 1 hour = 0.5–3 units, depending on size and type.
★ Water heater: 13.5 litres (3 gal) of hot water for one unit.
★ 100-watt lamp: 10 hours = 1 unit.
★ Small fan: 15 hours = 1 unit.
★ Underblanket for 1 hour a night: 2 weeks = 1 unit.
★ Overblanket used all night: 1 week = 3 units.
★ Vacuum cleaner: 2–4 hours depending on size = 1 unit.
★ Floor polisher: 2.5 hours = 1 unit.
★ 1.7-litre (3-pt) kettle: about 5 boilings = 1 unit, so don't waste money and energy by filling the kettle with more water than you need.
★ Cooker: allow 1 unit for each person in the family each day.
★ Refrigerator: 8–24 hours according to size = 1–2 units.
★ Freezer (0.19 cu. m/7 cu. ft): 24 hours = 2 units.
★ Dishwasher: 1 load = 1 unit.
★ Food mixer/liquidizer: 60 cake mixes = 1 unit.
★ Toaster: 70 slices = 1 unit.
★ Coffee percolator: 10 jugs = 1 unit.
★ Coffee grinder: 1 year = 4 units.
★ Washing machine: average weekly wash = 8–9 units.
★ Tumble dryer: 1 hour = 2 units.
★ Iron: 2 hours = 1 unit.
★ Shaver: 1,800 shaves = 1 unit.
★ Heated rollers (allow twenty minutes per day): 1 month = 1 unit.
★ Colour TV: 4 hours = 1 unit.
★ Stereo: 12 hours = 1 unit.
★ Tape recorder: 15 hours = 1 unit.
★ Sewing machine: 15 hours = 1 unit.
★ Workshop drill: 4 hours = 1 unit.

DOWN WITH SUPERWOMAN!

The electricity bill

Your electricity bill is made up of a standard charge plus the number of units of electricity you use. The cost of a unit varies under different area electricity boards, but at the time of writing it usually works out at 5.45 pence.

To know how much electricity you use in a week, learn how to read your meter

This is much easier than it sounds and modern meters read like the mileage recorder on the car dashboard.

Older meters have six sinister little dials, marked 10,000, 1,000, 100, 10, 1 and $\frac{1}{10}$ KWH per DIV. Ignore the $\frac{1}{10}$ dial. Write down numbers from the other five, working from 10,000 to 1. The hands don't all turn the same way, but they *do* all run from 1 towards 9, so when a hand is between two numbers write down the one it has *passed*.

A week later, read the meter again and subtract the first reading from the second. The result of this calculation will give you the number of units you used that week.

Know your electricity supply

Electricity enters your house through the heavy supply wires of the electricity board, and once inside the house it passes through your fuse box or circuit-breaker panel and is distributed through separate runs of wiring called circuits. Each circuit is rated for the strength of electrical load it can carry.

Circuit breakers and fuses These safeguard your electrical system against overloads that are put on the wiring if you try to draw more electricity through the wiring than it can safely carry. They also protect against fire hazard from flaws within appliances or frayed wires

in the house wiring system that could cause short circuits.

You can save lots of blood, sweat, toil and tears by getting yourself – or rather your home – fitted with circuit breakers in place of fuses. Circuit breakers are switches that trip to 'off' if the circuit is overloaded. To reset you simply have to press a little button – after you have repaired or remedied the cause of the overload.

If you have a 13-amp ring circuit, you will rarely blow a fuse in the fuse box, but the fuse within each plug will give out occasionally (see 'A few things everyone should know', p. 171). Keep a stock of plug fuses, with a list showing what colour fuse serves which appliance. You might keep fuse wire and torch on or in the fuse box or hang them in a shopping bag on a nearby wall.

Use BROWN (13-amp) for all appliances rated 750 watts or more (heaters, irons, toasters, kettles) and RED (3-amp) for all appliances rated at less than 750 watts. Most electrical appliances have a small plate somewhere that tells you the rating in watts.

A 13-amp fuse should not be fitted to a low-powered appliance, as it might overheat and catch fire. Check the amount of current that the appliance uses (it's measured in amps) and when you buy it, ask for the correct fuse.

Be prepared for a power cut Stock up now on alternative methods of lighting, heating and cooking. Hide box of matches, torch, spare battery and candles where your menfolk can't find them, or in your tool-box.

Lighting Candles, oil and hurricane lamps, torches, batteries and bulbs. Candles and oil lamps are too dangerous for young children. Give them a torch each.

Keep two torches in the entrance hall. Get a hurricane or pressure paraffin lamp for the kitchen, together with appropriate fuel. Some families live in the kitchen, if it's big enough, during a power cut.

Heating Oil- and gas-fired boilers use electric pumps or fans, alas. You're safe with open fires. If you buy a paraffin heater, remember that it can be a dangerous fire risk and needs ventilation, but otherwise keep the hot air in as much as possible by not opening windows, which might also create draughts, which can cause fires with candles and oil lamps.

Cooking Pre-cook at non-peak times for later reheating. Refrigerators and freezers are not generally affected, because power cuts rarely last more than a few hours. But keep refrigerator doors shut as much as possible and make sure that a drip tray is in position. Insure your freezer contents anyway.

Dishwashers and automatic washing machines will have to be drained and you will have to start again with fresh detergent when power returns.

Auto-timers on cookers, on central-heating units, heaters or other equipment and electric clocks will need to be reset.

Warning! Electricity cuts increase fire risks. Unplug the television, which is a fire risk anyway if left plugged in overnight, and check that electric bar fires, electric blankets and cooker are switched off.

HOW TO HANDLE GAS

1 DON'T strike a match if you smell gas and DO open all windows immediately. Also extinguish fires, naked flames and cigarettes. Make sure that a gas tap has not been left on accidentally or a pilot light blown out. Turn off the supply at the meter control tap and, even if you are in doubt, telephone Gas Services immediately (look under 'gas' in the telephone directory).

2 Never look for a gas leak with a naked flame. Remember British Gas specialists are the experts when it comes to gas. If there is a leak in the service pipe supplying the meter or in the meter itself, generally no charge is made for repairs. Don't turn the gas on again until the gasman tells you it's safe to do so.

3 A word of warning: don't have your appliances connected by anyone who is not a specialist. Check on anyone who claims to be.

4 Never use a gas water heater fitted in the bathroom while you are in the bath unless the heater is one of the room-sealed type.

5 Never shut the door or window while the water is being drawn from a gas water heater, unless it is a balanced flue type. Of course, water heaters are safe unless you block up vents and close windows and doors so that they cannot 'breathe'.

6 Never, under any circumstances, block up ventilators such as air bricks: they are there to help your appliance breathe.

7 If you have any worries concerning the safety of your gas supply or appliances, telephone Gas Services immediately.

8 Make sure that gas appliances have the British Gas Seal of Approval, especially if you're buying a continental model. So get anything you need from a British Gas showroom.

HOW TO SAVE ENERGY AND CHOP YOUR FUEL BILLS

1 Check that you are on the *correct energy tariff*. If in doubt, ask your local gas or electricity showroom.

2 Have your gas appliances serviced regularly and they will stay at top efficiency.

DOWN WITH SUPERWOMAN!

In the bathroom

3 Fit a 10-cm (4-in) thick jacket around the hot water cylinder; this costs approximately £8–10, and promptly pays for itself. Make sure that the jacket fits snugly. You will then keep your water just as hot but it will cost less.

4 Get *dripping hot taps repaired*. They waste water as well as energy.

5 Fix a *hand shower* to your bath. It will soon pay for itself by halving your bath-water bills. The average bath uses 114 litres (25 gal) of hot water but an average shower uses only about 45 litres (10 gal).

In the kitchen

6 *Don't wash up* unless you have a sink load. Leave small items for a big wash because an average wash and rinse uses 27 litres (6 gal).

7 Never wash up or rinse under a running *hot water tap*; it can run away with 9–13 litres (2–3 gal) a minute.

8 *Descale your kettle* for faster boiling. Descale with a branded product such as Kaydee. Alternatively, fill kettle with cold water, add 1 level tablespoon of borax and boil. Pour away, rub softened deposit with soft scourer. Rinse and repeat.

9 Don't heat more *water* than you need. If you need 1 litre (2 pt) it is throwing money away to boil 1.5 litres (3 pt).

10 Defrost your *refrigerator* regularly and prevent thick ice build-up.

11 Plan menus to make full use of *oven space*. You can cook a whole meal using only the oven burner.

12 Use *grill* to full capacity. It's cheaper to toast three slices at once, instead of two.

13 Use correct sized *saucepans*, not over-large ones.

14 Cover *pans* to keep the heat in and use the hot steam to cook.

15 Adjust flame on a *fast gas ring* to remain under pans and not come up the sides. After a pan has reached boiling point, turn gas as low as possible. Cooking will continue, even on a tiny flame.

Investment

16 Use a *pressure cooker*. It uses less gas and you can cook three sets of vegetables on one burner.

17 Consider replacing old, inefficient or *broken appliances* with efficient new ones, which use less fuel to give the same heat.

Insulation (this applies whatever your heating system)

18 Hot air rises! Keep the heat in. Save up to 75 per cent of your heat loss by unrolling rolls of fibreglass in your loft. Get at least 10 cm (4 in) thickness with loose-fill materials, such as Vermiculite chips, or a thicker layer – about 16 cm (6 in) – for the same amount of insulation roll. This will probably bring it above the level of the joists, making attic storage difficult.

19 Fit plastic or metal *draught excluders* to doors and windows.

20 Apparently 35 per cent of our warm air is lost through the windows. *Double glazing* can reduce this by half. See p. 180 for how to do this on a budget.

Caution! All fuel burning appliances need some fresh air to work safely. Get your local gas service to check your insulation.

Central heating

21 If you are going away for the weekend

or longer, turn off *water heating* switch and lower *thermostat* to minimum.

22 Set the *time clock* to give heat only when it is needed. Systems vary but I suggest you try half an hour before getting up and half an hour *before* going to bed (because the system will take half an hour to cool down).

23 Switch off *radiator valves* and close *warm-air grilles* in rooms that are not being used. Close the doors that lead to them, of course.

Caution! Leave valves and grilles slightly open in very cold weather.

24 Most people could reduce the temperature by a few degrees, wear extra warm clothing and still stay comfortable. So whatever you normally dial – turn it down.

Caution! Don't cut the heat where there are invalids, young babies or senior citizens.

25 Turn a *gas fire* off when you leave the room.

26 Don't open a *window* if a room gets too warm; turn down the heat.

27 Don't draw *curtains* over the radiator or heat will simply be wasted through the windows. If you have full-length curtains either shorten them or don't pull them at night. Fit a matching blind to the window.

28 A panel covered in aluminium foil fitted behind a radiator against an outside wall will reflect heat back into a room that would otherwise be lost. You can buy specially made panels very cheaply but they are not difficult to make yourself, using thick cardboard or polystyrene and kitchen foil.

THE WORKING GIRL'S TOOL-BOX

A good investment is a proper tool-box

fitted with a reasonable set of tools, but I can never fit these instruments back into their neat little places. Instead buy a cheap plastic chain-store tool-box with a handle and several self-raising, subdivided trays inside (the Duchess of Bedford uses one as a make-up box). Make sure to get a strong padlock or lock it away from your friends and children. Alternatively, keep an assortment of your most needed odd-job tools – screwdrivers, hammer, scissors, pliers, adjustable wrench – in a plastic bucket. Take the whole bucket with you when you go to fix something and you'll save that constant running back to get just one more tool. (The disadvantage is that you can't lock a bucket.)

An investment in a tool-box is going to show returns faster than anything else you can buy for your home. I tried to pare down the following list of suggested items, as it's meant to be a tool-box for the inexperienced. 'All the more reason for getting the right tool for the job,' sourly commented a male handyman; however, he did agree that none of the tools listed here is difficult to use.

I've starred the basic essential items for a beginner's tool-kit. Not all items in the following list are traditionally kept in the tool-box, but I can't think where else I would keep them.

★ **A pair of rubber gloves** – never do any electrical work without wearing them. A pair of heavy work-gloves to protect your hands.

★ **Adhesive bandages, ointment for burns, Elastoplast.**

★ **A set of adhesives:**

1 *white glue* for porous and semiporous materials, such as paper, wood, cloth, pottery.

2 *rubber glue* for paper, photographs, leather, plastic.

3 *contact or instant-bonding cement;*

some can be used on just about any material while others are made especially for plastic laminates like Formica.

4 *epoxy glue* for bonding almost anything, including china, glass, metals, wood.

5 *latex-base glue* for fabrics and carpeting. (For further information, see 'How to stick almost anything', p. 183.)

★ Assorted **balls of string, rubber bands, clear plastic tape, picture wire, spare curtain hooks.**

★ **Box of matches, torch and spare batteries, radio, extra batteries, candles.**

★ **A carpenter's level** 45 cm (18 in) long. Vital if you want to hang shelves straight.

★ **Folding carpenter's ruler.** This is easier to use when taking vertical measurements since it does not buckle like a measuring tape.

★ **A centre punch.** A short rod used to start making holes for screws and nails. Also used to drive a nail down flush with the wood without leaving hammer marks.

★ **Chisels.** You will need a 12-mm (½-in) cold chisel for cutting through bolts and nails; one or two wood chisels, 12 mm and 25 mm (½ in and 1 in), for chipping out bits of wood.

★ **Several clamps** in different sizes and a couple of **spring clamps.** They hold things you are sawing, or clamp things you are sticking.

★ **A combination square.** Use for marking and measuring 90° and 45° angles, for measuring, or as a level.

★ **Tap washers** to fit your taps.

★ **A funnel.**

★ **Fuses.** Have an assortment of extras in the proper amperage to match those in your fuse box. Fuse wire.

★ **Hammer.** Buy a good 450-g (1-lb) one with curved-claw back for yanking

nails out. The front is, of course, for crushing rose stems.

★ **Insulating electrical tape and insulated staples** for attaching electrical wire to the top of skirting boards.

★ **A roll of two-wire lamp cord.**

★ **Masking tape.**

★ Assorted **nails**: panel pins, common nails in different lengths, tacks, upholstery nails, drawing pins, picture hangers.

★ **Penetrating oil** for dissolving rust. *Lubricating oil* (a can of 3-in-One) for squeaking doors, window hinges, locks, etc., and for lubricating the sewing machine.

★ **A paint scraper and putty knife.**

★ **A penknife.** I'm not quite sure why, but I feel safer with one around.

★ **A small and a large (35-cm/14-in) pipe wrench** for plumbing jobs.

★ **Plastic wood-filler,** or wood putty, or Polyfilla (water-based cement that looks like flour) for filling screw holes and cracks.

★ **A rubber plunger** (C cup size).

★ **Sandpaper in assorted grades.**

★ **Scissors.** Keep small, large and serrated pairs handy. Serrated scissors grip what you are cutting.

★ **Screws.** Have an assortment in different lengths and sizes, some with flat heads and some with round heads. Also wall plugs.

★ **A wall-plug punch,** for starting holes.

★ **Screwdrivers.** You will need at least one; but even better, get a set of four standard screwdrivers with shanks and tips of varied lengths and sizes and two Phillips screwdrivers for different sizes of cross-topped screws. Get good-quality hardened steel screwdrivers; the tips of inexpensive ones tend to chip off.

★ **Soft lead pencil and rubber** so that when hanging pictures you can mark up your walls in the wrong places and then rub the marks off.

* A heavy **staple gun and staples** (a great short-cut for fastening jobs and swift upholstering).
* Flexible steel **measuring tape**. Get one with metric measurements, with imperial measurements on the reverse side. It should be at least 3.5 m (12 ft) long (6 m/20 ft would be better), marked in metres, centimetres and millimetres (and feet, inches and $\frac{1}{16}$-in markings) for helping to locate studs in walls.
* A **Stanley knife** with interchangeable blades for cutting linoleum and many other materials.
* A **whetstone** for sharpening your chisels, penknife and any other blades.
* An adjustable **wrench**.
* A decent size **tenon saw**. As a tenon saw has small teeth and a stiff back, one doesn't have to be so strong to use it.
* **Pliers** for bending wire, twisting wire, stripping wire, cutting wire and grasping small objects.
* **An adjustable spanner.**
* A **cold chisel** 12 mm ($\frac{1}{2}$ in).
* **Any QA (Quick Assembly) tools** you get when you buy a QA picture frame or chair etc.
* 9 m (10 yds) of **three-core flex**.
* An **electric drill** with an assortment of bits for drilling wood, masonry, metal. You can get a hand drill and this should be your first power-tool. (If you ask for one as a Christmas present, you'll probably get some Chanel No. 5 as well, out of sheer pity.)

Once you have used something, replenish it, so you are not caught in an emergency.

Keep your tool-box where you can get at it.

For a portable work-light, I use an Anglepoise on an extension cord.

Go to any DIY shop and buy an extension cable suitable for the appliance, e.g. lawnmower, vacuum cleaner, iron. Check appliance for amperage.

A FEW THINGS EVERYONE SHOULD KNOW

The hardest part of the simple jobs described in this chapter is to overcome your early conditioning. You were probably brought up to believe that they are not woman's work. But there isn't always a man around when your sink gets blocked, and even if there is, perhaps it's quicker to unblock it yourself than nag him into doing it for you.

Skip this bit and turn to it only in time of crisis. It probably won't make sense until you are forced to do something.

Warning! Most of us know as much about electricity as Thurber's aunt, who feared that her light bulb leaked it. There's only one main thing the average female needs to know and that is that *electricity is potentially dangerous*, so treat it with respect and keep it away from water.

1 Always switch off at the mains before starting a repair job.
2 Never poke a finger or scissors or *anything* into a light-bulb socket or wall socket.
3 Never connect an electric gadget to water, specially not via yourself, or you will risk electrocution. So:
   * DON'T hold a plugged-in appliance with wet hands or if you have wet feet or when you are standing in the bath or with your feet in a bowl of water.
   * DON'T switch a switch with wet hands.
   * DON'T use water to put out an electrical fire in an appliance that is plugged in. Unplug it, then use

DOWN WITH SUPERWOMAN!

a chemical fire-extinguisher (every home should have one that conforms with British Standards). Smother flames with a coat or blanket and call the fire brigade.

When one light goes out it may:

(a) Need a new light bulb, so replace it.
(b) Have a blown fuse, so change it.
(c) Have a broken plug, if it's a standard lamp or table lamp, so change it.

Don't call an expensive electrician until you have checked (a), (b) and (c) above.

The fuse

If you can thread a needle, you can mend a fuse. A fuse is a deliberately weak link. It is inserted into an electrical system to stop it from being overloaded. A fuse blows quite easily (then everything stops), because the bit of wire through which the current passes won't carry a strong load, so it melts. Changing a fuse is just replacing that bit of wire. If it melts, you may have overloaded it with too many appliances. If it goes with a bang, there's usually a fault in one of the appliances, which needs expert attention.

How to mend a fuse When a bunch of lights goes out, you have probably blown a fuse in the fuse box. The cable of a wall light, or any other light that doesn't have a plug, goes back to the fuse box, so if that light blows, then every other light on the circuit will also have gone.

Even if you've never been taught to mend a fuse, you don't have to sit in the dark. All you have to remember is to keep a torch, fuse wire and a small screwdriver in or by the fuse box (or in your tool-box). Switch off the mains current. Pull out and replace each fuse one by one, until you see that one has a broken bit of fizzled wire in the middle. That's where your problem is. With the aid of a

screwdriver, loosen the screw at each end of the fuse and remove the damaged fuse wire. Insert a new wire *of the same thickness* and wind it round the screws until the wire is taut (wind clockwise so that it doesn't unwind as the screws are tightened). Tighten the screws at both ends and replace the fuse.

If you pull out another fuse, you can use it as a guide as to how to twiddle a bit of fresh wire round the broken one. If yours is a new house, you may have cartridge fuses instead of wire. Throw out the old one and put in a new one of the same colour.

Try doing it now. It takes only ten minutes. You've got to know what size wire to put in. Use 5-amp for lighting (thin), 15-amp for heating (thicker), 30-amp for a cooker (quite thick wire). Cartridge fuses are 3-amp or 13-amp. **Don't use the wrong ones.**

If you have a certain type of cartridge fuse that doesn't have visible wires, what can you do? Keep a spare 5-, 15- and 30-amp *new* fuse handy by the fuse box and check each fuse by replacing it with the appropriate new one.

Alternatively, identify your fuses before they blow. Switch on one light only, then remove the fuses, one by one until that light goes out. Then you know that particular fuse feeds that particular light. Continue with this sort of elimination test until all electrical outlets are identified. Label fuses with stick-on labels.

With a modern circuit-breaker (fuse), when there is a fault somewhere, the appropriate button on the fuse will pop out; you simply unplug an appliance, then push in the fuse button to reinstate the fuse. Have these installed if you have your home rewired.

Why did the fuse blow? If you suspect that your fuse has blown because you have *overloaded the circuit* (i.e., plugged too many appliances into one socket), unplug everything running off this outlet before you start mending the

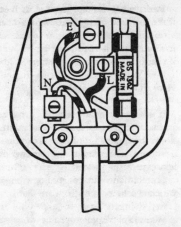

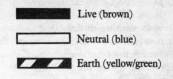

Live (brown)

Neutral (blue)

Earth (yellow/green)

fuse and don't immediately overload it again – leave one appliance off. Otherwise, after you've mended the fuse, it will simply blow again.

If you suspected a faulty appliance, how do you find the villain? You turn off all appliances. You mend the fuse. You turn appliances on again, one by one. When the fuse blows yet again you have found the culprit. Unplug it and mend the fuse *again*, then get an expert to deal with the faulty fitting, which may have a short circuit in its interior wiring. This is an electrician's job, at your stage of maintenance.

How to change or fit a plug

Buy a BSS (British Safety Standards) plug, which comes with wiring instructions. There are two types of plug, one with screws for the cord grip and one with plastic wedges that has no screws and is simpler (this is the MK 13-amp plug, which is slightly more expensive but simpler *and safer*).

Unscrew the plug. It is now in two parts, a top and a bottom. Place the outer case of the flex into the cord grip hole at the base of the plug top. Lay the three wires in the plug bottom in their appropriate terminals, which are marked as follows as you look down on them: neutral (blue) on the left; earth (green or green-and-yellow stripes) at top centre; live (brown) on the right. (The old colours were neutral, black; live, red; and earth, green).

Using a knife, peel off the outer plastic cover of the flex 5 cm (2 in), leaving the three interior wires exposed (make sure you don't cut them). Cut back the covers of the neutral and live wires about 2.5 cm (1 in), leaving the earth a bit longer.

Twist the wires round their terminals in a clockwise direction. Some plugs are fitted with terminals that are loosened with small screws. Loosen them and insert wires in exactly the same order as above, then tighten screws, to secure the wires. Make sure that the wires lie flat in the plug bottom. Prod them so with a screwdriver. Make sure that there are no loose strands of wire. Do not forget to replace fuse.

Replace plug top and screw up. Check cord grip is tight by tugging your flex (hard). Switch off wall socket. Plug in. Switch on socket. Switch on appliance. With any luck there won't be a bang, and, if there is, you've probably got your wires in the wrong place. (See 'How to mend a fuse', p. 172.)

DOWN WITH SUPERWOMAN!

Taps

How to stop a tap dripping If a tap is dripping, it needs a new washer. The replacement washer needs to be the same size as the one in the tap, so it helps to keep a supply of different size washers. Otherwise your local hardware shop will sell you a single one, but you must take along the old washer to make sure of getting the proper size. There is a vast number of different shapes and sizes.

To change a washer, first turn the water supply off at the mains and let all the water run out of the tap. When the tap has run dry, plug the sink so that screws, nuts and washers can't fall down the drain. Remove the top of the tap – the handle part – and the metal cover that fits over the body of the tap. To do this you will need a spanner or wrench; wrap a cloth or adhesive tape round the tap to give a grip and prevent those weapons from marking it.

Some taps have a head that pulls off once a small screw is undone. The screws are sometimes hidden under the covers that say H and C. Get at them by pushing a small screwdriver under the button on top of the tap.

The offending washer and the nuts should be clearly visible now, so all you have to do is unscrew the nut, remove and replace the washer and reassemble the tap.

Alternatively, get a new modern tap. The Supatap has a valve in the middle, so you don't have to turn the water off at the mains to insert a new washer. You just unscrew the top, slip the old washer out, put a new one in, and then screw it up again.

How to stop a tap leaking If water seeps around the top of the tap, you may need to tighten the gland nut.

You needn't turn off the mains water. Just remove the cover of the tap as described, take your spanner and tighten the nut about a quarter turn.

Reassemble the tap and test. If it still leaks, the best thing I know is a cheap little tin of Baswhite filler. You just slap it round the leak and leave it. However, if water still seeps, call a plumber.

How to unblock a sink

Mix together equal parts of coarse salt and soda crystals and force this mixture down the sink hole. Add a shake of detergent and pour down one or two full kettles of boiling water.

If this fails, use a rubber plunger, which can be bought from any hardware store.

Warning! There are two sizes: you want the larger one, the C cup, which is bigger than your sink outlet.

Block up the sink overflow with a damp cloth in order to create a vacuum, grease the edge of the plunger, fit it over the sink hole and pump several times.

If *this* fails, put a bucket under the U-bend in the outlet pipe under the sink. With a wrench, remove the big screws at either end of the inspection cover in the bend and try to scrape out the blockage with a wooden spoon or similar blunt instrument. Carefully push a thick wire or a thin stick *up* the pipe in order to clear it. If you unblock it, replace screw and turn on water to check it's tight *before* removing the bucket. If you absentmindedly drop a diamond ring down the sink, you follow the same routine, because with any luck the ring will have fallen in the loop of pipe under the sink.

How to stop a lavatory overflowing

A lavatory cistern overflows for one of three reasons. Whatever the cause first turn off the water supply to the cistern, remove the top of the cistern and flush the lavatory.

1 If grit has jammed the lever arm. Use a pair of pliers to pull out the split-pin that holds the arm in place. Withdraw the arm and ball and unscrew the valve at the inlet end. Clean and grease the valve thoroughly with Vaseline and put the parts together again.

2 If the ball valve is leaking. Check by removing it and shaking it to hear if there is water inside it. If there is, buy a new plastic one from a hardware store.

3 If there is a defective washer. Remove the lever arm, unscrew the end of cap or piston that connects with the end of the arm and replace the washer.

Pipe safety

Precautions If you are going away for any length of time during the winter, turn off the taps at the water mains, drain all pipes as far as possible, turn off all taps firmly so they don't drip and make sure no plugs are in bath or basin. Pipes and cisterns in the loft, against external walls or under the ground floor are most susceptible to freezing, so make sure that they are properly lagged (insulation should be at least 2.5 cm thick on cisterns and 3.2 cm on pipes).

Alternatively, if you have central heating and are going away for only a couple of days, leave the heating on at the lowest temperature on the thermostat. (I once had a horrendous flood because I forgot to do this.)

Frozen pipes If a tap is not working or the lavatory won't flush, or water won't drain out of a basin and it's 0 °C (32 °F) outside, you probably have a frozen pipe somewhere. Quick action is needed to avoid a burst pipe. Switch off the immersion heater or central-heating boiler and let a solid fuel boiler die down. Turn on taps around the house in turn to try and find out where the blockage is (see above). Once you've located the offending pipe, remove any lagging and apply hot cloths or a hot water bottle to try to melt the ice. You could

also use a hair dryer or a fan heater, but don't use strong heat, such as a blow lamp. Check that the pipe hasn't split – it will start dripping as the ice thaws if it has. Improve the insulation if you don't want it to happen again.

Burst pipes Water expands when it freezes and if it is in a confined space, such as a pipe, that pipe may burst. If you don't do something about it *immediately*, you may have a flood on your hands when a thaw comes. Turn off the main stop-valve, switch off your water heater as above, and turn off all other stop-valves. Turn on all the cold taps in the house to drain the system and hot taps too if the flow of water doesn't stop. Try to find the burst; when you have located it, check if any wiring nearby has got wet. If it has, dry your hands and turn off electricity at the mains. Then call the plumber to fix the pipe.

Leaking radiator pipes or valves An emergency treatment is to wrap a bandage or a towel round the leak and wind string or thin rope round the pipe below the leak and lead the end of the string into a bucket or bowl.

How to hang pictures and put up shelves

For **fairly light pictures and small mirrors** you can use picture hooks made of a bent piece of metal that consists of a hook and a triangular brace through which you drive a nail into the wall to secure the hook. These are available in different sizes and can hold up to 45 kg (100 lb). The triangular brace guides the nail down into the wall at an angle and when the nail has been driven right in and snugs the hook to the wall, it makes a very secure mounting. With very large pictures, it is a good idea to use two of these hooks, spaced about 30 cm (1 ft) apart, because the picture does not work itself askew quite so easily.

Pencil a little **x** on the wall where you

need to drive the nail. (If you have a crumbly plaster wall, stick a piece of see-through tape over the **x** before nailing, and the plaster will flake off less easily.) Then put the nail through the two guide holes on the picture hanger and hold the hanger and nail against the wall so the point of the nail is on your **x** mark. Give a gentle first tap with your hammer and then drive the nail in, gradually hitting harder as the nail becomes more firmly seated in the wall.

Use picture wire to hang pictures; it comes in various strengths for supporting different weights. Don't use natural fibre string or cord, which can rot and drop your picture with a bang. This happened to me once in the middle of the night. Bump, bump, bump down the stairs it went, like a drunken burglar. In bed and terrified I telephoned the police, who, having nothing better to do that night, arrived in three squad cars, with two mounted searchlights and an eager Alsatian dog. This helped me to remember always to use nylon or metal cord for picture hanging.

Shelves and heavy pictures If you are hanging up something very heavy, or putting up shelves that will have to support a great weight, you usually have to use screws and wall plugs to provide a grip. The kind you select depends on the type of wall you have: plaster, wood, plasterboard, concrete, etc. To determine what your wall is made of, you may have to drill a hole in it and analyse the debris that comes out. Don't use an electric drill unless you have practised a bit under supervision from someone who knows how. Otherwise you might break the drill or even your wrist. Be careful, when drilling walls, that you drill only into *wall*. If you drill into water pipes or an electrical conduit you could be in trouble or even dead.

If your drilling produces a white powder and the drill goes right through the wall quite easily, you have some sort of wallboard, usually nailed up over wooden studs. Use toggle plugs, which expand to grip the far side of the board.

Plaster is usually applied over concrete, bricks or wooden lathing. If it is a good depth, use a simple fibre Rawlplug. If it is over a solid concrete or other masonry wall, your drill will not break through; if you scrutinize the dust that comes out from behind the white plaster dust, you can get your DIY man to help you determine the kind of fastener to use to attach the shelves to the wall.

Always insert plugs at right angles to the wall. Use either a plug punch, which you hit with a hammer, or a masonry drill. Make the hole one-eighth longer than the selected plug. Slide the plug in, then screw in the screw. If you choose plastic plugs, pick ones that grip the hole.

If, insanely ambitious, you are trying to hang heavy shelves on a hollow wallboard or plaster-and-lath wall, you should really try to get your fasteners into the studs behind the wall covering. Studs are 5 × 10 cm (2 × 4 in) upright wooden beams to which the wallboard or lathing is attached, and they are generally set 40 cm (16 in) apart (although this is not always the case), measuring from the centre of one stud to the centre of the next. Assuming that there is a stud at the corner of your room, you can measure down 43 cm (17 in) from the corner and with any luck you will be at the centre of the next stud. Drill a hole, using a small bit on your electric drill, to be sure. You can patch up misplaced holes with a bit of Polyfilla and paint. You fasten things to studs with nails or screws, the size depending on the weight of the object you are mounting.

KEEPING THE COLD AND DAMP OUTSIDE

What not to do

The ultimate in do-it-yourselfery is knowing when *not* to do it ... when to get someone else. This applies especially to such potentially dangerous check-up jobs as examining the roof and chimneys, which is really a builder's job. You will probably have difficulty finding a builder who isn't about to embark on his bi-annual Mediterranean cruise, so first make sure that you need his help by checking the roof from outside street level with a pair of borrowed binoculars. You will be surprised how clearly any defects show up.

I also get outside help in the form of an electrician to check all electrical appliances every autumn, whether or not they are giving trouble. Also, check whether you need an electrical time-switch for electric blanket, convector heaters and radiators. Thermostats help too, so you don't waste heat.

Autumn check-list

Look at

The chimney stack (with your binoculars) Are there any cracks?

The roof (again with your binoculars) Check broken or missing tiles and flashings beginning to gape.

The brickwork Does it need repointing?

Interior and exterior walls Check condensation (inside) and cracks (outside). Also basement interior walls and floors, for any sign of moisture that may be news to you. For damp-proofing interior and exterior walls there are solutions such as Aquaseal waterproofer, and Stroma, a damp remover and preventative, which can also be used for rising damp. There's also Synthaprufe, for interior walls, which you apply with a brush. You can then paint on top with oil-free distemper or emulsion paint. There's an Aquaseal damp barrier kit, which is a system for waterproofing damp walls and stopping penetration of damp.

How to mend a window pane It really pays to replace your own broken window panes (or to get him who broke it to repair it, if he's over 10). Professional labour is expensive and difficult to arrange, yet the operation is quite simple for ground-floor windows that can easily be reached from outside. First job is to don work-gloves and remove all the old glass and putty from the frame. Knock the big pieces out with a hammer, making sure that none falls dangerously unnoticed, then take out the glass edges and old putty (best tool for this is an old chisel).

Buried in the old putty you will find a few small nails, partly tapped into the frame. They were to hold the glass in place until the putty set. Remove these with pincers.

The outside ledge of the frame, into which the glass fits (called the rebate), must next be thoroughly cleaned, right down to the wood; the smallest obstruction can prevent the new glass fitting properly. A stiff wire brush is best for this.

Now measure up for a new pane. Care is vital, for glass is intractable and cannot be stretched or trimmed. So measure accurately from side to side and from top to bottom, using a steel tape and measuring from the inner sides of the rebate, which will meet the edge of the glass. Now measure again to check. An old carpenters' saying is measure twice, cut once: measure once, cut twice. *Then deduct 3 mm ($\frac{1}{8}$ in) from each measurement.* The deduction allows for slight irregularities in the window frame or for its being slightly off square. The shop where you buy the glass will cut it *exactly* to your measurements.

There are many different types and weights of glass, so make it clear that you want window glass. Incidentally, if the window you are repairing is a particularly vulnerable one – a playroom window, for example – you may think that buying a slightly heavier grade of glass is worth the extra cost, because it is less likely to shatter again.

DOWN WITH SUPERWOMAN!

You will also need some putty and a few 'sprigs' (small headless nails used by glaziers). If you cannot get sprigs, small panel pins will do: 20 mm ($\frac{3}{4}$ in) is a good size. The best putty is the kind that you buy ready-packed in a polythene sachet. It retains its oil and stays supple.

The next stage of the job is to take a putty-knife or an old table-knife and spread a fairly thin layer of putty right round the rebate on the outside of the window against which the inside of the glass is to lie. (There's a little ledge that you can't see until the putty has been gouged out.) This putty layer is to cushion the glass against the wood.

Now fit the glass in the frame by resting its bottom edge on the lower edge of the frame and swinging it up into the frame. Push the glass firmly against the putty, pressing close to the edges, *not* in the middle of the pane. Some putty will squeeze out on the inside of the glass. It can be cleaned off later.

Now fix the glass in the frame by tapping sprigs or panel pins into the wood close against the glass and leaving them to stick out about 6 mm ($\frac{1}{4}$ in) so that they hold the glass in place. If you use proper sprigs, tap them in with their broader sides against the glass. Use a small hammer for this part of the job, gently tapping the nails and resting the side of the hammer head against the glass during the stroke (if you don't do this, you may break the glass). You need only a couple of nails for each side of the frame, i.e., eight nails per window pane.

Now, using a putty-knife, spread putty into the recess between frame and glass, right round the frame, and trim it to a neat edge. (See how it's done on your unbroken windows.) You really do need a putty-knife for this, and it's also useful to have a jar of hot water handy; if you keep dipping the knife into it, the hot knife will make the putty easier to manipulate, as well as giving an extra-smooth professional finish.

Leave the putty to dry for at least a week before painting it, then give the frame two coats of gloss.

All this relates to wooden window frames. If your windows are metal-framed, there are three small differences of technique.

1 You must use metal casement putty; the ordinary sort will not stick to metal.
2 You will not need sprigs or panel pins, but you will need some glazing clips; these are small spring clips with one arm that goes into a hole in the frame and one that clamps against the glass. You'll see how they work when you remove the old ones along with the old putty.
3 After cleaning out the old glass and putty, you should treat the bare metal of the frame with a rust-inhibitor such as Galvafroid before reglazing.

Defective sash cords are a builder's job, but if you are a do-it-yourself debutante, cotton sash cords should be replaced with nylon cord, which won't rot, or with chain, which won't stretch.

Once you have fathomed the mystery of the double-hung window, it is not too difficult *to replace sash cords*. Each half of the window, top and bottom, is hung on two cords, with one end of each cord tied in a knot that fits into a slot at the edge of the window sash. The other end of the cord goes over a pulley and disappears into the window frame where it is knotted to a heavy weight. The trick is to get at the weights. Prise off the moulding that runs vertically on either side of the window. Use a flat-bladed chisel and brace it against the woodwork with a towel, to protect the paint.

Once the moulding is off, you will see a rectangular 'pocket' of wood held in place in the window frame by two screws. Undo the screws, remove the block of wood and you will unveil the weight. There are, of course, four 'pockets' and four weights per window, one on either side at the top to support the upper window sash, and two below to support the lower sash. To get at the top weights, you will also have to prise off the vertical strip of wood that separates upper and lower sashes. Once you know how, this is *almost* fun to do, but it helps to watch someone else do it the first time.

Persistently rattling window frames and ill-fitting **skylights** should be replaced by a builder.

Plumbing No home can be warm or comfortable if pipes are frozen or burst. Lag internal pipes, especially those in an insulated loft.

Gutters Check gutter outlets, so that autumn leaves or birds' nests don't block them. Put a wire balloon on top (known as a birdcage). It looks a bit like an Edwardian lady motorist's hat and should be sitting atop of all open-ended downpipes and soil pipes.

Check gutters for leaks at the joints. Evidence that water may be running down the outside of a wall may mean that the gutters are broken or blocked at the joints, so that water pours over instead of being carried away. I've only ever met one girl who has mended her own gutter, and she did it painlessly, with Plastic Padding (type 'hard'). You mix a hardener with it and just slap it on the cleaned metal. Sylglas tape gives a good temporary repair.

Crack check

Really large wall cracks (more like splits, which open again when you fill them) These generally spell foundation problems. Get a *qualified* surveyor or consult your local borough surveyor and proceed from there.

Small wall cracks Can be filled with Polyfilla, which mixes like an instant cake mix without the added egg. Be sure to brush out all loose and flaking material before starting to fill the crack. Otherwise your patch might wobble loose.

Small ceiling cracks Can also be filled with Polyfilla.

Cracks where new plaster meets old (the sort that appear when a newly bricked-in fireplace is plastered) The wall looks fine for a few weeks, then cracks appear at the joints between new plaster and old. This happens because the new plaster has shrunk slightly, as is normal. Fill this crack with Polyfilla. If you feel the crack may reopen, wet it with a PVA adhesive such as Unibond or Polybond. This helps the new plaster to adhere to the old. You can also deal with this by mixing Polyfilla with emulsion paint.

Cracks in timber Can be filled with special wood fillers, such as Polycell Woodflex or Rawlplug Plastic Wood, which you squeeze or press into the crack, let dry and sandpaper smooth. Alternatively, use Brummer stopping, which is in different shades to match the most popular woods. Ask for a waterproof exterior grade, if you're using Brummer outside.

Cracks in brickwork or cement rendering Can be sealed with Mortar Mix, which you can get from Marley shops. All you do is add water like a cake mix.

Small cracks in cement Can be sealed with an epoxy compound like Sylmasta. You apply it with a knife or small trowel.

A sudden plague of cracks Expect them everywhere when you have just installed central heating. The timbers dry out and plaster shrinks in the new warm glow. Wait until a whole heating season is over before attempting to deal with them. A humidifier can help reduce the problem and jam jars of water stood on a piano will stop it going honky-tonk.

Gap check

Gaps where the wood is missing (gnawed by gnomes or rats or cats) It's a carpenter's job, because the damaged wood will probably have to be cut away and a new piece glued and pinned into place and repainted.

Gaps between floorboards and skirting (where the draught whistles in) Bridge that gap with a length of quadrant moulding, which, in section, looks like a quarter of a broom handle. Use panel pins to keep it in place because they're very fine and won't split the wood. Fix it to the floor, not the skirting board, so that it moves with the floor.

Gaps between wall and ceiling Structurally it's rarely serious, but it looks a bit impoverished. Filling the actual gaps is usually a waste of time because they may reappear. You might consider fitting a polystyrene-foam cove round the ceiling, available with supplied adhesive from DIY superstores, or get a gypsum plaster cove put up, which looks great.

Gaps between timber window frames and brickwork (because of shrinking woodwork) Fill with a mastic compound, not putty or mortar.

Door and window gaps (which can often be the cause of draughts and rattling) Fix weatherstrip round doors and windows. They still open easily after fitting and in my home I found that weatherstripping unexpectedly cut noise and dirt by an estimated one-third. (See 'Keeping the heat in', p. 180.)

Another method is fixing plastic foam strip around interior doors and windows. I have never found this a permanent fixture myself (don't fall for the ads, girls), but I must admit that it is quick, cheap and easy if you're only there for one winter. You might try using Seal, a white self-adhesive foam weather-strip.

Bathroom gaps between wall and bath or wall and basin Can be sealed with Dow Corning's sealant. I've also successfully used Bostik and Seal-a-Round white plastic tape, which is supplied with its own adhesive.

Remember that draughts are responsible for most heat losses in the average

home. Try checking yours with a wet finger on a windy day.

KEEPING THE HEAT IN

Draught-proofing

There are three basic price ranges. If you don't want to do it yourself, write to the Draught-Proofing Advisory Association, PO Box 12, Haslemere, Surrey, GU27 3AN (tel: 0428-54011), who will inform you of members in your area.

If you want a permanent system, start with the windows. Use a good self-adhesive compression seal around hinged windows. These could be either plastic or rubber in various shapes. On sash windows, which can be very draughty, you may need to use bits of different systems and take the window apart or, much simpler, use good old-fashioned Atomic copper-alloy weather-strip, which can be used all around the window – which you won't have to dismantle. I love this method.

For the bottom of internal doors use a brush or wiper excluder, which is quite easy to fit. Self-adhesive compression seals can go around the sides, but don't seal the top of the door to allow some ventilation. Excluders for external doors need to be more robust; they are generally screwed to the floor and when the door is shut, a flexible seal fits against the bottom of the door or its inside face. *Which?* magazine recommends the Halseal aluminium weather deflector because it was the only excluder they tested that didn't require you to take the door off first for trimming.

An automatic door shutter fixed on top of the door cuts draughts, banging doors and noise, if you don't count my shrill whines of 'Shut that door'.

Double glazing I once met a woman whose only claim to fame was that she had made her own storm windows with something unbelievably called Quick-Fix. It's a plastic channel (into which the double glazing slides) that can be cut to fit (without adhesive) a pane of glass. It is then fitted to your window with special clips that screw to the window frame.

For the chilly, idle and impoverished, there are quicker and cheaper systems that are just as, if not more, effective. Some use magnetic strips or plastic channels to fix panels of glass or plastic sheets of various types to the frame. One of the cheapest and best is Scotch Thermal Seal, a film attached to the frame with double-sided tape, which is then stretched taut by blowing a hair-dryer over it, making it almost invisible. A large benefit of any system, if it seals well, is that it cuts down on draught from badly fitted windows. Some good systems are sold only by mail order – for example, Clip 'n' Stick (DIY Plastics, Lynton Road, Cherey Manor, Swindon, Wilts, tel: 0793-6153-118) and Magnetism (Plastics by Post, Garden Estate, Ventnor, Isle of Wight, tel: 0983-853-114).

Curtain linings These help to keep in heat and interlining helps even more. Milium curtain lining is aluminium backed, and although it looks and feels like a normal fabric it is claimed to reflect heat back into the room.

KEEPING THE AIR FRESH

Once you have your perfectly sealed salon you may have a different problem – *how to avoid a fug-up*. Some might simply open a window, but some might think that if you're spending good money on heating the air, it is better to clean the heated air than replace it with freezing air from outside (which is unlikely to be fresh anyway, more like neat carbon monoxide), which you then start expensively heating up all over again.

Air-conditioners are costly and tend to hum like neurotic bees, but they do deal with condensation, clammy bathrooms, kitchen smells, personal odours and stale cigarette smoke. They also enable you to sleep with windows closed and not wake up with eyes to match.

The Qualitain range by Rootes currently ranges from about £550 for a unit (QWR 095) for a small room. It measures approximately 65 cm (26 in) wide × 62 cm (25 in) deep × 40 cm (16 in) high and has to be fitted into a wall or window. (From Southern Air Conditioners Ltd, 377 Kennington Road, London SE11, tel: 071-735-8662.)

Kitchen or bathroom pongs can be extracted with a Vent-Axia electric fan.

HOW TO BUY SILENCE

As presidents have found before me, this is a very difficult, very expensive and often insoluble problem. You can't do much about traffic, trains or aeroplanes. Whistling errand boys are no longer a problem since they have now died out. And milk carts no longer rattle, they quietly whine away.

Noise pollution can affect your mental health, although this problem is not yet taken seriously by British law. In theory every council has a noise enforcement policy; for instance, Chelsea restricts building work to 8 a.m. to 6.30 p.m. Monday–Friday and 8 a.m. to 1 p.m. on Saturday. No noisy building work is permitted in any other time. Check at your town hall for local conditions. A council *may* take a case to court if there are complaints from more than one household. *But* the builders will probably get a paltry fine, grin and immediately pick up their drills again.

However, if the noise in your own home exhausts you, you might try double glazing and draught-proofing. This, plus air-conditioning, plus contract quality carpet on rubber underlay, so thick you could sprain an ankle, plus lined and

DOWN WITH SUPERWOMAN!

interlined curtains, should make you feel wonderfully protected from everything in the outside world except your bank manager.

There are also some idiotically simple, cheap tricks that you might try. Eventually, I found that the only way to deal with the dreadful noise of the Barbican (London's flat development-cum-cultural centre) was simply to leave the place, but in the final months of our stay I experimented with ear plugs. The wax balls that you roll in your hand until soft and plug into your ear do not harm the ear and they cut down the noise for me, trying to work above a building site, by about half.

There are two disadvantages. One is that someone may come into the room and ask you a question. You ignore it because you haven't heard it. Your silence can upset people who interpret it as dumb insolence or sulking. The other is that if you use the telephone, you (a) can't hear it ringing and (b) have to take one earful out and put it down on some surface where it will be visible. As this little squashed ball is a dreadful knicker-pink colour, like something you bought in a sex shop, it can give strangers a shock, especially if little hairs or bits of fluff stick to it.

Buy soft slippers for small children. Deal with the teenage stereo-maniacs by buying them headphones for Christmas, with volume control. Better still, encourage the use of a Sony Walkman and tell them you'll buy them some roller skates so they can have music on the move (outside **your** home).

Put a foam-rubber mat on a metal draining board. This not only cuts washing-up clangs, but also slipping and chipping.

Refrigerators that vibrate like Mick Jagger can sometimes be kept quieter if stood on rubber or a cork mat.

If water pipes bang and shudder when the cold tap is turned off, the water pressure may need adjusting, but before you call in the water board, check that the pipes are close enough to the appropriate wall and that the fittings haven't worn loose. Sometimes it's possible to fit a plastic paddle device on the ball valve arm in the cold water tank. This kills vibration.

Deal with any embarrassing plumbing noises by putting an equilibrium valve in the cold water storage cistern or toilet cistern.

If the drip of a tap is getting you down, check whether it needs a new tap washer; if so, get one you can use on both hot and cold.

Squeak and rattle check

Oil anything that squeaks, from chair castors to curtain runners. Alternatively, rub Vaseline on it.

Castors If a castor isn't moving smoothly, check that dust or cotton thread hasn't become wrapped round the wheel or axle. If it has (and you can get at it), cut it away with a sharp knife. Oil the castor while working it around, then wipe surplus oil away.

If chair castors are loose, tighten the screws. If one of the screws turns maddeningly around, insert spent matchsticks to jam it. Alternatively, remove screw, insert plastic wood into the hole and wait overnight while it hardens, then re-insert the screw. If the shank of the castor is loose, remove castor from socket, wrap shank with masking tape or electrical tape and then try to re-insert it into the socket, where it should grip better. Then buy a new castor, because it won't last more than a fortnight.

Doorknobs If a doorknob is loose and rattles, there's a good chance that all you have to do is to tighten the tiny screw (it's called a grub screw) behind the handle. That's also the screw you have to turn to remove an antique brass doorknob in order to give it a real polish for the first time in a hundred years. Before unscrewing, it is vitally important to open the door wide and wedge it (with a wad of newspaper?). Otherwise, what invariably happens is that you drop the screw, the door swings shut and you find yourself grovelling for a grub screw in a locked room that no one can open.

Many knobs have vernier adjustment. When you remove grub screws behind both handles and remove handles, you will see that the doorknob shanks have more holes on one side than the other, so by varying the grub screw into different holes, you get a different adjustment. Just go on fiddling until one works.

If you tighten the grub screw and the doorknob *still* rattles uselessly, unscrew the screw again, remove the knob, pull out the spindle that goes through the hole in the door by drawing out the knob on the other side of the door, then replace the spindle (and knobs, if you want) with a new one from the DIY shop. If this doesn't work, reach for the *Yellow Pages* and a workman because you'll probably need a smaller hole in the door.

Floorboards Squeaking floorboards should be nailed down. Drive the nails in at an angle, and use a nail punch to bury their heads, filling the holes with plastic wood filler. If this doesn't work, call a carpenter, as the boards may need replacing.

WHERE TO GO FOR MORE HELP AND ADVICE

If you can, get two free booklets on the merits and method of do-it-yourself double glazing from Pilkington Glass Ltd, Prescot Road, St Helens, Lancashire WA10 3TT (tel: 0744-28882).

To repeat, if you should decide *not* to do it yourself, it's vital to get a reputable firm to do the job. The Glass and Glazing Association (44–48 Borough High Street, London SE1 1XB, tel: 071-403-

7177) will send you a leaflet on their pet subject and also a list of members in your area. They have also published, with Collins, a booklet called *Glaze It*, a cheap practical guide to using glass, repairing windows and double glazing. The British Plastics Window Group (5 Belgrave Square, London SW1X 8PD, tel: 071-235-9483) will also send you technical information and a list of installers and manufacturers who use their code of practice. The Heating and Ventilating Contractors Association (ESCA House, 34 Palace Court, London W2 4JD, tel: 071-229-2488) will send you a list of members for your area. They also produce *free* explanatory leaflets on heating and air-conditioning.

Unless otherwise mentioned, nearly all the items mentioned can be obtained from Selfridges, Oxford Street, London, W1A 1AB, or from good do-it-yourself shops or builders' merchants all round the country.

When applying for any free literature recommended here, please enclose a stamp, *not* an envelope, which may be the wrong shape or too small.

HOW TO STICK ALMOST ANYTHING

In my experience, there is no such thing as an all-purpose adhesive, any more than there is an all-purpose book or all-purpose food or all-purpose shoe. A home needs more than one adhesive to hold it together, because the secret of sticking is to select the most suitable adhesive for the job.

How to go about it

Start sticking by making sure, if possible, that you're fixing whatever it is on something that can be thrown away, such as old newspapers. Wear an overall (not an apron), even if you never do, even if you

What to stick with what

Main grouping	Trade name	Solvent	Use
Natural rubber	COW GUM	When wet, you can rub it off with your fingers if it gets in the wrong place. When dry, use dry-cleaning fluid such as BEAUCAIRE	Paper to paper, photographs, artwork, scrapbooks
Natural rubber	DUNLOP'S WALL-TILE ADHESIVE, WATER RE-SISTANT & BOSTIK NO. 4	Dry-cleaning fluid	For sticking ceramic wall tiles to all interior surfaces
Nitrile (synthetic rubber)	DUNLOP'S CLEAR HOUSE-HOLD ADHESIVE DUNLOP'S THIXOFIX	Remove with ace-tone or clear (*not* oily) nail-varnish remover DUNLOP'S CLEAN-UP	All-purpose glue for most materials, including flexible PVC. Ideal for handbags, belts, satchels, suitcases, canvas, carcovers, braid, lamp shades, picture frames, book binding, and for patching paddling pools, beach gear and mackintoshes
Neoprene (synthetic rubber)	EVO-STIK (liquid) or DUNLOP'S THIXOFIX (spreads easily like butter) BOSTIK 3 CONTACT DUNLOP'S POWERFIX or DUNLOP'S ULTRAFIX LIQUID CONTACT	Dry-cleaning fluid No solvent – be careful	For laminated plastics and general purpose do-it-yourself, such as rubber to wood, felt to wood. *Not suitable* for flexible plastics such as PVC or foam polystyrene
Synthetic rubber	BOSTIK'S BLU-TACK	Dry-cleaning fluid	Posters to walls
Epoxy resin adhesives (which give the highest bond for the smallest area)	ARALDITE or EVO-STIK HARD & FAST	Remove when wet with hot water and soap. *Warning:* it can set in 10–13 minutes	China, glass, metal, wood, brick, stone, concrete, sticking spectacle frames and shoes, chair legs, teacup handles
Polyurethane	BOSTIK 7 QUICK-SET ADHESIVE	No practical solvent	The recent addition to epoxys for above items
Latex	COPYDEX	Remove when wet with cold water	Paper, card, upholstery and carpet, fabrics. It dries fast and repairs almost invisibly
Latex	DUNLOP'S FLOORING ADHESIVE BOSTIK 10 (glazed wall tiles) BOSTIK 11 (floor tiles) BOSTIK 12 (ceiling tiles)	Cold water, when wet. Try dry-clean-ing solvent when dry, or acetone	For sticking PVC, cork tiles, felt or hessian materials to floor surfaces
PVA (poly-vinylacetate)	DUNLOP'S WOODWORKER BOSTIK 8	Remove when wet with cold water. Can dry in 10 minutes! When dry remove with acetone	A woodworking adhesive. Good for most porous materials, including hard-board

Main grouping	Trade name	Solvent	Use
PVA (poly-vinylacetate)	DUNLOP'S CEILING TILE ADHESIVE	No solvent – be careful	For foam polystyrene ceiling tiles
Ceramic wall tiles	DUNLOP'S WATERPROOF CERAMIC TILE ADHESIVE	No solvent – be careful	Already mixed, ready for use
Ceramic floor tiles	DUNLOP'S WATERPROOF FLOOR AND WALL ADHESIVE	No solvent – be careful	Recommended here only for floors

haven't got one. Borrow one from your local midwife or grocer, or whoever you've noticed has one.

Take the telephone off the hook and do not answer the front doorbell. Try not to scratch ears, nose or rub eyes, however harassed or itchy you become.

How to come unstuck (if you've spilt the adhesive)

Plan pessimistically. Discover, before you start to unscrew, how to get the sticky stuff off. I can't think why They don't print the correct solvent on all containers, but as they don't, I give main groupings with their solvents. Treat the disaster areas as soon as possible. Some say you should keep an old sheet or tea-towel to mop up any mess. As you won't have an old sheet, use newspapers.

If you have no idea of the chemical content of the mess you've just made, first mop it up, then try to remove with cold water, then warm water, then dry-cleaning fluid.

When spilling latex, epoxy or PVA adhesives, remember that once it's dry you'll probably never be able to remove it. You *may* be able to remove a *small* dried drop of it from, say, a carpet, by softening it with dry-cleaning fluid and then picking it off with a comb or your finger, but it takes patience!

HOW TO KEEP A HAPPY CAR

Most women feel that a car should ap-

preciate in value and give as little trouble as emeralds; but a car depreciates, like a fur coat, so look after it as you would a beloved pet. All you need to know is how and why.

'You can always find a woman who doesn't know how to care for a car,' I was told by the Automobile Association, 'but for every woman, you will also find a man.' Sweet of them.

The main reason for joining a motoring organization is for its emergency services: no matter at what hour of day or night the thing packs up, all you have to do is get to the nearest telephone box and ring the AA Emergency Service: help should be with you quickly. When joining, you receive a free handbook with map and a key to the AA telephone boxes (but *any* telephone will suffice).

Sudden paralysis apart, if you do not look after it carefully, sooner or later your car will fall to bits and, before the final death throes, you will probably have lots of expensive trouble. Although you don't grease it for quite the same reasons, you should care for your car as you do for your face and have it serviced according to the manufacturer's instructions. As in love, major problems often stem from minor initial causes, so immediately check any trivial fault; you may avoid a more serious one. Do not close your ears to that little clicking noise in the hope that it will go away.

Keep a record of any repair bills and the dates of service (what was done and when), useful proof of careful ownership when you want to sell it.

Supposedly *every week* but definitely *before a long drive*, check distilled water in battery, water in radiator, oil level and tyre pressure.

Battery

Check the water level and top up to 6 mm (¼ in) over the plates with distilled water. Any garage should provide this. Top it up, but do not overfill. If fluid seeps out at the top, it may corrode the case.

Make sure that the terminals – the knobs where the thick wires join the battery – are free from dirt and corrosion. Clean them with a little wire suede brush or even with a toothbrush (though onlookers may think you mad) and lightly grease.

Warning! If you use ordinary water you may reduce the efficiency of the battery, which is the engine room of your engine: everything depends on your battery.

Plugs

Check that the terminal leads to the battery are in good condition and secure, otherwise your engine won't work properly. Replace spark plugs every 16,000 km (10,000 miles). Plugs in good condition will cut your fuel consumption. Plugs in bad condition make you very prone to breakdowns.

Radiator

Check water level (unnecessary with sealed radiator systems). Put antifreeze in your radiator to prevent the water in the radiator from freezing overnight and cracking the cylinder block. Possibly the best thing is a dual-purpose antifreeze, which also helps to prevent corrosion in the summer.

Warning! The fragrant smell of burning hot cross buns sniffed while the car is running may mean that there is no water in your radiator. If there is no water in your radiator, your engine will overheat immediately. At the least you will be unable to restart the car for some time, and at the most you will need a new engine.

Warning! If your radiator steams, the top cap will be boiling hot and the water may be a scalding jet. Wait ten minutes, then use a glove or cloth to ease the cap off, bit by bit. Remember James Watt and the kettle. If you unscrew it right off while it's still hot, it will probably blow off and scald your hands, if not your face. Let it cool down for fifteen minutes before refilling.

Oil

Check the level of the oil with the dipstick. Keep oil to the correct level and change it at the intervals recommended by the manufacturers.

Warning! If there are tiny specks of white metal on the dipstick, have it investigated: it may mean that an engine bearing is wearing badly and needs immediate attention. Worn engine bearings lead to a gradual wearing down of the engine.

Replacements

Just as some things, like shoes, men or scrubbing brushes, need renewing from time to time, a car needs the occasional replacement.

Replace **tyres** before they reach the minimum legal requirement of 1 mm of tread all round, which is as worn as it sounds.

Treat yourself to a new pair of **windscreen wipers** before each winter. Not only do you risk developing crow's feet as you peer ahead, but it is dangerous to drive with a dirty windscreen because you ought to be able to see where you are going.

Cleaning

You're supposed to keep your car exterior in good condition by cleaning it or getting it cleaned once a week. One way is to drive through a car cleaner. The bliss of yielding self and car to be soaped, washed and brushed by those trembly machines is equalled only by the luxury of having a nanny to wash between your toes.

If doing it yourself, clean the car from the top, preferably with a hose and with warm water. A relatively easy way to swab the whole thing down is with a softish brush attached to a hose. Cover every bit of the car with the brush or it will look splodgy when dry. With an ordinary bucket and sponge you risk putting back the grit you have just washed off, so make sure you rinse the sponge carefully – and it's quicker if you use a large sponge.

If you get a dollop of bird dropping on your car, sponge it off as fast as possible, or it eats the paintwork. There's a dull patch on the gleaming black bonnet of my car because I didn't do this. Eventually I took it to a Rolls-Royce garage, but even they were unable to remove the splodge.

Clean windows with a chamois leather. It doesn't leave scratches on the glass, which is why window cleaners use it.

You are also supposed to *polish* your car three or four times a year. Get the car really clean and dry before you wax it, otherwise it will be twice as hard next time.

There are masses of car-cleaning products available, with not much to choose between them. If your car is really filthy with pore-deep dirt a particularly powerful cleaner is Jove, which removes grease, wax and road dirt. For polishing you might use Turtle Wax.

Clean chrome with Solvol Autosol. You rub a little on like toothpaste.

Warning! Once chrome is deeply rusted, nothing simple can be done to eliminate it. You have to have it rechromed or buy a new bumper or whatever.

Corrosion

You are unlikely to get salt under your car in summer unless you race along the beach, blonde on your bonnet, like a cigarette ad. You are far more likely to get plastered with municipal salt sprinkled on winter roads, so get a garage to hose underneath the car in winter if you use the car a lot.

If you think this is unnecessary, try soaking an ordinary pair of steel scissors in salt water for a couple of hours, whereupon they will start to rust, whereupon they won't work so well.

What to keep and what not to keep in the car

In the glove compartment keep instruction handbook, maps, torch, boiled sweets (chocolate melts), sun-glasses (a genuine safety precaution) and your motoring organization membership card and call-box key. Heaven knows where you will keep your gloves.

In the back of the car keep an empty plastic shopping bag to use as a wastepaper basket and another one to contain two sponges, two towels, two dusters and a can of windscreen de-icer and demister.

Keep a spare car key in your jewel box.

Cars over three years old must be MOT-tested annually by a garage. Keep the test certificate, the log book and the insurance certificate at home in a safe place, in case the car is stolen. Keep your driving licence on you.

Tool-kit Check you have a jack, set of

DOWN WITH SUPERWOMAN!

spanners (or one adjustable spanner), screwdrivers (large and small), spare fan belt, wheel brace (for fitting nuts on wheel), hammer, oil.

Dramas

If your car won't start ... Have you switched the ignition on? Is there any petrol? Does your battery need recharging (check by switching on the headlights)? Now you can go for help without feeling a real idiot.

Before you skip merrily on to the next page, pause ... now imagine a lonely road. Night is falling, it is raining. Your tyre has just burst. There is no AA box in sight. Somebody will have to do something and *there is only you*. Now read on.

Changing a wheel Tyres burst in calamitous conditions, so practise changing a wheel somewhere near your local garage. How that friendly mechanic will chuckle if he has to rescue you! When you are faced with the real thing:

1 Get the car off the road as fast as possible. Never change a wheel near a drain or the bolts jump down it.
2 Put the brake on and leave the car in gear so it won't slip and run over your hand. Put a block against at least one wheel – a stone or a brick or *something* to stop it moving.
3 Remove hub cap with the handle (the pointed end) of the jack.
4 Loosen nuts with spanner, but DON'T take them off yet.
5 Jack up car (look in your handbook for correct position) until the wheel is clear of the ground.
6 Remove nuts and put somewhere safe, such as the driver's seat or inside the hub cap.
7 Heave wheel off.
8 Put on spare wheel.
9 Replace nuts and bolts, then tighten.
10 Lower car, until wheel just touches ground.
11 Tighten nuts again.
12 *Check* you've tightened them all.
13 Remove jack.
14 Replace hub cap.
15 Remove block against wheel.
16 Drive off and double-check fit, plus tyre pressure at the nearest garage.
17 Have punctured wheel repaired as fast as possible.

Maintain yourself in good condition – then you will find it easier to stop a lorry driver than change a wheel.

SELF PRESERVATION

FAST FIRST AID

In a medical emergency, keep calm. If you can't keep calm, you won't think sensibly. *Force yourself to think.* Don't move the victim because he might already be badly injured. Keep back crowds if necessary. Call a doctor or ambulance as soon as possible. *Your* main job then is to soothe and reassure.

The short first-aid course

* Most people who die from accidents do so in the first seven minutes, so move fast.
* Avoid further injury. Turn off power in cases of electric shock. Don't touch patient.
* If no breathing is apparent, give the kiss of life (see p.190).
* Control bleeding by pressing hard on wound. Apply bandage firmly and raise the bleeding limb.

* Turn an unconscious breathing victim into the *coma position*, on his side, with top leg flexed at the knee, pelvis tilted forward, lower arm behind, top arm extended in front of victim to help prop him up (see drawing, p. 190).

Shock Every injury or accident brings with it a certain degree of *shock* (sometimes even to onlookers who are otherwise unharmed), which leaves the victim shaken, giddy, very pale, with blurred vision, shallow breathing and sometimes loss of consciousness.

Reassure victim. Lay him flat on his stomach, loosen constricting clothing, cover him up to keep warm. Turn head sideways so that if there is any vomiting, it doesn't choke and suffocate him.

Give nothing by mouth, *especially not alcohol*. Don't apply hot-water bottles. Remember that shivering is nature's way

189

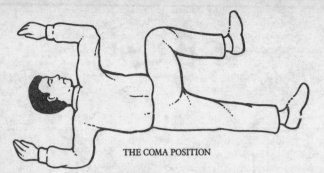

THE COMA POSITION

of keeping the metabolism going. If the injury is severe, don't let him drink anything, as he may require a general anaesthetic later and this must be given on an empty stomach.

Severe injuries, which may be internal and not immediately obvious, induce a more severe form of shock in which the casualty collapses and becomes deathly pale – a very serious condition.

Kiss of life If you think the victim may have stopped breathing, apply the kiss of life as follows:

Lay person on his back, open his mouth and press down tongue to check there's nothing blocking the air passage; tilt head backwards with your hand under his neck. Lie, chest downwards, by his side and expand his chest by slowly blowing hard into his mouth (about ten times a minute for an adult) while you *pinch his nostrils shut so that air goes into his lungs, not out of his nose.* Keep it up until a doctor arrives. First aid is to be given while awaiting medical help, *not* instead of it.

Choking In polite, Emily Post society, if you choked at table you could turn the colour of a turkey and be speechless, yet the people either side would consider it polite to ignore you. *Any choking can be fatal and should be dealt with immediately.*

Try to remove obstruction. Strike patient hard between lower shoulder blades. Turn a child upside down over your knee to do so. If that doesn't work, the newest treatment is to stand behind the patient, put your arms around the patient's waist and grip your left wrist with your right hand. Squeeze, suddenly, firmly INWARDS AND UPWARDS. It's very effective.

If patient turns blue, call an ambulance fast, otherwise give glass of water when choking has subsided.

How to deliver a baby Even if you're not a policeman or a taxi driver, it's something that you might need to know someday. (I nearly needed it when my younger son was born.)

* Get the mother to lie down on her back with her knees bent back to her chest. Reassure, encourage and soothe her; sound firm, calm and optimistic.
* DON'T try to pull the baby out.
* As the baby starts to appear, support him with your cupped hands and then forearms, so that he doesn't flop around or fall into the blood or gunge.
* DON'T pull or cut the umbilical cord.
* Immediately the baby is free from the mother, make sure he's breathing. Drain off any fluid in the baby's throat or nose by wrapping a towel round him, then holding the baby by his ankles, upside down. Do not pull on the cord. As the fluid runs out, the baby should start crying and breathing.

* Give mouth-to-mouth resuscitation if the baby doesn't breathe or cry quickly. Lay the baby flat on his back, cover his nose and mouth with your mouth, and gently breathe short puffs into his mouth, about every five seconds. Stop as soon as the baby starts to breathe on his own.

* Wrap the baby in a towel, blanket or newspaper, then lay him on his side across the mother's stomach with his head facing the mother's face.

* The pancake-sized placenta (after-birth) is expelled from the mother's womb about twenty to thirty minutes after the birth. It will still be attached to the baby by the cord. Don't cut the cord. Wrap the afterbirth in a bit of cloth or plastic, but leave the cord to hang slackly from the baby. Put the wrapped afterbirth next to the baby and then wrap them securely together in a towel or blanket. This will stop the placenta from falling and pulling on the cord.

IN THE FIRST-AID BOX

A first-aid kit should be kept out of reach of children, but NOT in a locked cupboard and not in the bathroom where a child might lock itself in and gorge on aspirin.

I once used the tourniquet on my car, to clamp the broken battery key to the battery. If you raid your first-aid box thus, remember to replace the item.

HELP!

Animal bites Wash the wound with clear cold water, being careful not to disturb any blood clots. Pat dry and cover with bandage. Go to the doctor or nearest hospital.

Burns are caused by dry heat or hot fat or oil. A *scald* is caused by moist heat, as from a kettle. Hold small household burns under running cold water and then

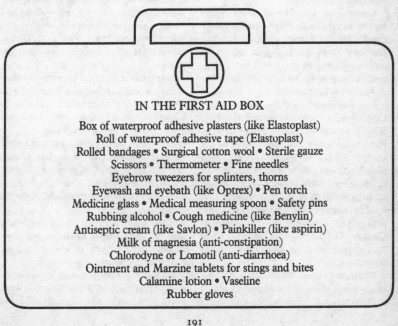

IN THE FIRST AID BOX

Box of waterproof adhesive plasters (like Elastoplast)
Roll of waterproof adhesive tape (Elastoplast)
Rolled bandages • Surgical cotton wool • Sterile gauze
Scissors • Thermometer • Fine needles
Eyebrow tweezers for splinters, thorns
Eyewash and eyebath (like Optrex) • Pen torch
Medicine glass • Medical measuring spoon • Safety pins
Rubbing alcohol • Cough medicine (like Benylin)
Antiseptic cream (like Savlon) • Painkiller (like aspirin)
Milk of magnesia (anti-constipation)
Chlorodyne or Lomotil (anti-diarrhoea)
Ointment and Marzine tablets for stings and bites
Calamine lotion • Vaseline
Rubber gloves

apply antiseptic cream, such as Johnson's.

A burn or scald is automatically a sterile area, which is a great help in healing the wound. Wash your hands, bathe burnt area with cold water, then cover the burn or scald with a dry sterile dressing or a piece of freshly laundered linen. DO NOT APPLY ANYTHING – ANY LOTION OR DRESSING WHATSOEVER – TO A MAJOR BURN. Bandage the dressing lightly if the skin is blistering, firmly if no blisters are present. Treat for shock.

If a person is badly burned, either call an ambulance or wrap him in a sheet and take him to hospital. Don't use any ointments.

Concussion A blow to the head can result in loss of consciousness – stunning. Place patient in coma position (see p. 190) and keep him warm. Watch to see breathing continues. If it doesn't, apply kiss of life (see p.190). Always call the doctor, even if patient seems to have recovered.

Cuts Clean wound with warm water and antiseptic, and cover with a dressing. Press edges of wound together and put pressure (rub hard, repeatedly with finger) on a wound that won't stop bleeding, so long as there is no foreign body in it, such as a glass splinter.

For a really ghastly hole, don't waste time trying to clean the wound: the body is built to cope with quite a lot of dirt, so just concentrate on covering up the wound so that no more dirt gets in or blood gets out. Make a king-size wedge of some absorbent material (e.g., gauze, clean towelling or handkerchiefs) and hold or bandage over hole with firm pressure. The doctors in the hospital Casualty Department can clean up when they do the stitching and give the anti-tetanus jab.

Diabetic coma Two lumps of sugar or a piece of chocolate. Call the doctor.

Drowning If possible (certainly if it's a child), turn patient upside down to drain water from lungs. Give kiss of life (p. 190). Call for ambulance.

Electric shock DON'T TOUCH THE PATIENT before switching electric current off and then pulling out plug from water, unless you wear rubber gloves, or *you* risk getting a shock. Pull patient away. Apply artificial respiration. Treat for burns if necessary and then for shock. Call ambulance.

Fainting Loosen neck clothing and put patient's head between his knees. If a *heart attack* is suspected, prop up patient and on no account move him until an ambulance arrives.

Fractures and sprains are generally caused by a fall. *Do not move a suspected fracture.* Symptoms are pain, tenderness, swelling, deformity of the limb, loss of movement and function of limb, and ghastly bone-on-bone grating sounds. DO NOT MOVE THE CASUALTY OR ATTEMPT TO SET THE BONE STRAIGHT. Be very gentle and do not bandage over the suspected fracture. Stop any bleeding and treat for shock. Call ambulance.

Firmly bandage a **sprain** and, if possible, immerse in cold water. Treat for shock.

Hysteria If a person becomes hysterical, it is usually because he or she is making a bid for attention. Give it to him, soothe him, but don't catch his hysteria (it's very catching). If he calms down, other people will not panic. In a crowd, get the hysterical person out to a quiet place as soon as possible. Sit him down, give him a hot (non-alcoholic) drink and continue to soothe him.

Nose bleed Don't hold the head back so that the patient swallows his own blood. Make patient sit and calm him. Don't let him blow his nose.

Poisoning Call the doctor immediately, telling him – if you know – what poison the victim has taken. If a person is found with an empty bottle of tablets, call an ambulance (not doctor) and keep the bottle for the attendant. Make every attempt to keep the patient awake, such as keeping him on his feet. If he's asleep, do your best to wake him.

If the poison taken is *corrosive*, the lips and mouth may be burned (corrosive poisons are disinfectants, cleaning fluid, petrol, etc.). If the patient has taken one of these or has burned lips, do *not* make him vomit, just make him drink lots of water to dilute the poison. If the patient is unconscious, place in coma position (p. 190). If breathing stops, give kiss of life (p. 190).

Non-corrosive poisons include tranquillizers, sleeping tablets, aspirin overdose, lead-based paint and poisonous plants; they should be vomited. Start by sticking two fingers down the patient's throat. If possible, make him *repeatedly* swallow a glass of warm water with two heaped tablespoons of salt, and *repeatedly* vomit. If the casualty is unconscious, place him face down with his head turned to one side in the coma position (p.190), so he can breathe easily. If breathing becomes very slow and feeble, apply artificial respiration.

Gas and exhaust fume poisoning Get patient to fresh air and give artificial respiration.

Something in the eye Don't rub the eye. Bathe it with an eyewash, preferably with a weak solution of boric acid. Look under eyelid if necessary. If object can be seen (hair or grit), try to remove it with a tissue or corner of a clean handkerchief. Never use anything hard to remove something from the eye. If you can't see anything, get patient to the Casualty Department of a hospital.

Stings and bites

Bee stings The bee leaves the actual sting behind in the flesh, so extract this first with clean tweezers. Apply a solution of water and ammonia or bicarbonate of soda.

Wasp stings Apply vinegar or lemon juice.

Jellyfish stings The acid left on the skin should be removed with oil as soon as possible.

Mosquito bites Apply water and ammonia or bicarbonate of soda.

Suffocation Remove obstructions such as plastic bag, baby-bonnet ribbons or cord. Apply kiss of life (p.190) immediately. Call ambulance if necessary.

HOME HAZARDS

The most dangerous game

Do you tempt fate? Why should the gods be especially kind to you and not let your old mum break her neck on your loose stair carpet, or your 2-year-old catch her nightgown alight? (Fifteen seconds is all it takes for a child to burn to death.)

Here is a check-list of the most frequent home accidents. Award yourself one mark for each of the following items that apply to your home. If you score more than ten points, you may be living in a death-trap and should do something about it.

Making your home less dangerous than a motorway on a foggy Bank Holiday isn't difficult – it merely involves checking this list, which can be done on any wet weekend and dealt with on subsequent ones.

★ Loose stair carpet.
★ Frayed or worn patch of carpet.
★ Missing floor tile, or loose brick on outdoor steps.
★ Faulty or wobbly stepladder.
★ Slippery floor or mats.
★ Chair or stool used instead of a properly balanced stepladder (especially swivel chairs).
★ Spills that are not wiped up.
★ Cleaning equipment, such as brooms or a bucket, left in unexpected places, like just round the bend in the stairs.

DOWN WITH SUPERWOMAN!

* Poor lighting in corridors and on stairs, especially with pets.
* Trailing electric flexes.
* A step in an unusual place – which the family know well but may forget to warn a visitor about.
* No grab-bars on the bath or shower wall, particularly for the very young, the very old, the very pregnant, or for those who are apt to feel dizzy after a too-hot bath or after getting up suddenly.

Slipping in the shower or bath is one of the commonest causes of accidents, so if possible put in solidly mounted grips or grab-rails (*not* towel rails). Also fit non-slip, rubber suction-cup mats or permanent non-slip strips.

Manhole covers

Check that they are safe – I once nearly broke my leg in the dark on a missing manhole cover in the pavement: beneath it was a coal cellar. The woman to whom this death-trap belonged had the sauce to say that it wasn't her responsibility: in law, it is.

Burning issues

* Unguarded, unscreened fires of all types.
* Cigarette butts that aren't stubbed out, especially in bedrooms.
* Clothes left to dry in front of an open fire or an electric heater.
* Newspapers or books left in front of an open fire.
* A switched-on electric iron left on a work surface or standing on top of its cord.
* Faulty electric equipment, particularly frayed extension cords and make-do plugs and sockets.
* Containers of scalding liquids, left where children can reach them.
* Saucepan handles sticking out from the cooker.

* Grease-filled frying pans left unattended over a burner.

Spilling blood

* Razor blades left lying around.
* Broken glass left unswept.
* Sharp knives left in a kitchen sink full of murky water.
* Sharp knives in a drawer (keep them in a jar, blades upwards (so that they don't bend and break), out of children's reach or in a wall holder).
* Walking barefoot or kneeling on the grass without protection.

Kitchen risks

Most common cleansers are POISONOUS (and sometimes inflammable) and must be kept out of reach of young children. If it is not possible for you to have a lock on your cleaning cupboard, avoid storing the cleaning materials under the sink. I was once poisoned by my host, who poured a drink from a bottle labelled 'sherry' that contained washing-up fluid. Ideally, keep cleaning materials on a high pull-out shelf where they can be properly organized and selected. If you haven't got one, then use a washing-up bowl or cat-litter tray and stand your cleaners in that.

Don't leave a chip pan unattended.

Are your children at risk?

In France on the birth of your child you get a health notebook for it, in which everything related to the child's health is logged – blood group, rubella immunization, vaccinations, allergies, growth, weight, hospitalizations, illnesses, etc.

The mother keeps the child's medical history handy and always gives it to the babysitter, so if anything happens to the child while the mother is at work or out for the evening, the babysitter has all relevant details concerning the child's health. Why not start one now?

A baby should not be given a pillow until after his first birthday, as he might roll over and smother. Don't give a baby any lumpy food until he's old enough to chew. Never leave a young child while he is eating. Always stay with him.

Don't leave a young child alone in the bath. Never leave sharp objects where a child can reach them. That includes knives, pins, needles, nails, saws, scissors, axes and meat-grinder blades. Replace the hard glass eyes of stuffed toys with embroidered wool optics that can't be pulled off.

Children need protecting from their own passion for picking up, sticking fingers into, disassembling or eating anything within reach of their tiny starfish hands. All electric outlets should ideally be of the shuttered type.

All breakables and medicines should be kept out of children's reach. Pills should always be bought in containers with child-proof tops. (Some also find them adult-proof.)

Don't leave plastic bags within reach of children. If a child puts one over his head, he might suffocate.

Senior citizen risks

Older people are in constant danger of falling and breaking their brittle bones. Non-skid bath mats are essential, as are bathtub grab-bars and a handgrip next to the lavatory. Use a slip-retardant polish on floors. Small rugs should have non-skid rubber backing. Make sure banister rails are firm. Don't leave toys, shopping baskets or other obstructions in hallways or on a staircase (which should be well lit).

Electric shocks

ALWAYS SWITCH EVERYTHING OFF BEFORE INVESTIGATING TROUBLE (I lost a good electrician because he didn't do this and killed himself in my bedroom). *And* wear rubber gloves.

Check for a loose connection, frayed wire, frayed extension cords and possible electrical overloads (like you, there's only so much a circuit can bear). Never put electrical appliances into water. James Bond killed one villain by throwing a connected electric fire into the villain's bath: as water conducts electricity, the villain was killed instantly.

Don't lace your space with wreaths of extension cord – you'll trip over them. Staple or tape the wires to the skirting board, off the floor, or wind the excess cord around a cheap plastic stool. Alternatively, wind the flex round your hand like knitting wool, then secure it round the middle with a rubber band.

Have loose sockets or cracked plugs mended immediately. If a plug feels warm or smells of fish, or if an appliance fizzles or crackles, TURN IT OFF.

Never clean an electric cooker until you've disconnected it at the mains. Never fill an electric kettle when it's plugged in. Never use a portable electric appliance near a water source without extra caution. This particularly applies to plug-in heaters and radios in the bathroom. Never touch a switch with a wet hand or a damp cloth. Always plug in the electric lead to the appliance *before* you connect it to the wall socket.

Gas hazards

Never look for a gas leak with a naked flame or *pfffttt!*. Get a torch.

Always light the oven as soon as the gas is turned on. Never leave gas burners on when you've finished cooking. If a gas jet is not working efficiently, get it fixed. British Gas should swiftly cope with it.

Get your gas appliances serviced regularly. Just ask your local British Gas showroom to send someone every January or whenever.

DOWN WITH SUPERWOMAN!

If you smell gas – or even if you *think* you do – open all the windows and doors, turn off gas at the mains and phone the gas board for their emergency service. If gas leaks for any reason, make sure all outlets are turned off. If you have a slot meter, turn the gas tap off before you put the coins in. When the gas comes on, rekindle any pilot lights.

FIRE GUARD

It's highly unlikely that you will rise from this chapter and rush round like a fireman's fiancée, making your house entirely safe from flames. However, here's a list of *fire dangers*. Spend ten minutes checking the more obvious ones to keep yourself out of the obituary columns.

Remember that, if you need it, the Fire Brigade is a free service. Just dial 999.

★ DON'T overload any domestic appliances. If your washing machine is designed to cope with 3.5 kg (8 lbs) of laundry, never feed it more than this amount. Otherwise the motor could burn out and start a fire.

★ DON'T hesitate to repair any electrical equipment that shows scorch marks or emits burning smells.

★ DON'T run an iron or any other appliance off a light-bulb socket.

★ DON'T allow the flex from an electric kettle or other appliance to drag over the cooker, where it might burn.

★ If an extension cord is not long enough, get a longer one. Make a join only with proper connectors.

★ A lot of appliances wired to one socket outlet can overload the circuit and blow a fuse or overheat and start a fire. The safest rule: one appliance to one socket.

★ NEVER run an electrical cord under a carpet unless you check it at least every three months.

★ DON'T use an electric under-blanket over you, or an overblanket under you. An underblanket (unless of the low-voltage type) must be switched off before you get into bed.

★ NEVER keep matches within reach of children.

★ NEVER leave burning candles unattended.

★ DON'T dim a lamp by covering it; the cover might get hot enough to ignite. I know a girl who wanted a romantic atmosphere in her bedroom and so threw her pink knickers over the bedside lamp. She started a *real* fire. She should have bought a low-watt pink bulb.

★ Gas and air form an explosive mixture. Be ready to light gas appliances before you turn on the gas, especially when lighting the oven. If the pilot light doesn't ignite the burner at once, turn it off and check that the pilot is alight.

★ DON'T leave tea-cloths or washing over the cooker to dry.

★ If you use smokeless fuel, your chimney should be swept at least once a year, more often if non-smokeless fuel is used. Keep the hearth and surround clean.

★ DON'T hang a mirror over the fireplace – it invites people to peer at themselves, get too near the fire and risk getting burned. (I singed a good coat this way.)

★ DON'T put anything on the mantelpiece that a child might try to grab.

★ DON'T put furnishings or clothing close to a lighted fire.

★ DON'T leave a room without putting a guard in front of an open fire. Don't bank the fire up too high – the chimney might catch fire, or burning logs or coal could fall out.

★ DON'T use petrol, paraffin, etc., to light a fire – you might set fire to the room. Use fire-lighters.

* An oil stove should be refuelled out of doors, if possible. Don't overfill it. Keep fuel in a safe, cool place, preferably out of doors.
* DON'T move or refuel an oil heater when it's alight. Keep it clean and well maintained.
* DON'T leave cleaning or lighter fluids lying about.
* DON'T smoke in bed – it causes about 1,000 fires a year in Britain, many with fatal results. Have your last cigarette of the evening downstairs – and make sure it's stubbed out!
* NEVER burn or puncture aerosol containers. Keep them away from heat.
* DON'T leave a lighted cigarette on an ashtray, where it can fall off and so start a fire. Never empty ashtrays or throw matches into a waste-paper basket or a plastic bin. I once saw a fire started this way in the office of a national newspaper.
* When buying children's nightwear, check that the garment is 'flameproof'. I can't repeat often enough that a child can burn to death in *fifteen seconds*. When flame-resistant garments are washed in soap or nonphosphate detergents, they lose their resistance.

How to handle a fire

QUICK ACTION IS ESSENTIAL WHEN SOMETHING CATCHES FIRE. YOUR REACTION SHOULD BE AUTOMATIC, SO IT REALLY IS WORTH CAREFULLY READING THE NEXT SECTION.

If a person catches fire, stop the victim from running. Don't strip his clothes off. Never throw water at him, as the extra shock can be more dangerous than the flames, and even fatal. Smother the flames by rolling the victim on the floor in a coat, rug, etc. Make sure that no part of the clothing is still smouldering. Phone an ambulance (999).

Check your fire escape method and fire extinguishers. Make sure that means of escape from second- and third-storey rooms have been provided (one of those folding ladders or a rope ladder). Make sure that all the family can climb the thing.

Make sure that fire extinguishers are checked annually and refill them, if necessary, according to the manufacturer's instructions. Every household should have at least two fire extinguishers and everyone in the home should know where they are kept and how to work them. Check the gauges every three months and refill them when necessary.

Make sure that each family member knows what to do in case of fire. Have fire drill twice a year. My father used to enjoy drilling his six children; *we* all enjoyed throwing plant-pot earth over the carpet, aiming soda siphons at the armchairs and being awarded chocolate biscuits for the fastest times with the extinguisher (Mother didn't enjoy fire drill nearly so much).

Small fires A cup of water, a package of baking soda, salt, sand or even earth thrown from a plant pot may be enough to stop a small fire. Or you may be able to suffocate it with cloth, rug, drape, fire blanket or coat. Shut doors and windows to prevent it blazing up again.

Extinguish a fire in a **waste-paper basket** by covering it with a tin tray or a drawer or a telephone directory or another waste-paper basket.

When fighting a small oil, paint or petrol fire or flaming grease, never use water or the liquid will probably splash and the fire will spread. Use an extinguisher.

If a **frying pan** catches fire, turn off the heat. Smother the flames by throwing a door mat or rug over it. Don't throw water over flaming oil because it spreads out.

DOWN WITH SUPERWOMAN!

If the fat in a **deep-frying pan** over-heats, turn off the heat, but DO NOT MOVE IT, because movement of air against overheated oil can cause it to burst into flames.

If an **electric appliance** catches fire, DON'T POUR WATER ON IT. Use a fire extinguisher. Unplug the appliance or turn off the main switch.

If a **chimney** catches fire, close all windows and doors. If possible, close the damper to shut off air. Call the fire brigade and get out of the building.

Lots of salt and sand will put out a fire in the grate. After the fire is out, make sure no woodwork in or around the chimney is smouldering.

If **curtains** catch fire, pull them down before attempting to quench the flames.

There should always be a pail of water or sand handy at a **barbecue** in dry weather.

If a **television** catches fire, throw a blanket, rug or thick coat over it and unplug the set.

Big fires If you can't immediately extinguish a fire, get everybody out of the building in whatever they're wearing, no matter how little. Call the fire brigade at once from the nearest outside phone. Don't assume someone has already done so; two calls are better than none. Never stop to dress or rescue valuables. NEVER GO BACK INTO THE BUILDING, NOT FOR THE FAMILY JEWELS OR PETS OR DOCUMENTS.

Never take a lift to escape a fire. The power may fail, the lift may stop between floors and you'll be trapped; *use the stairs or fire escape.*

If cut off by fire, close the door of the room and any other opening, and block up any cracks with bedding, towels, rugs, clothes, etc.

If you're trapped in a building, try to attract attention from the windows. If the room fills with smoke, lean out of the window. If you cannot do this, lie close to the floor, where the air is clearer and take short breaths until you hear the fire brigade.

If you have to escape before help arrives, make a rope by knotting together sheets or similar material and tie it to a bed or other heavy piece of furniture. If you cannot make a rope and the situation becomes intolerable, drop cushions or bedding from the window to break your fall. But don't jump from any height above the second floor unless firemen are there to catch you.

If you have to jump, wait until the very last moment, and then lower yourself out, feet first. Hang by your arms from the window-sill, then try to go limp as you fall.

Which fire extinguisher to choose?

Water and sand are the oldest, simplest fire-fighting tools, especially when in a pail. But you'll also need a more modern alternative and there is a bewildering array.

There are *three* basic types of fire in the home. Type A fires involve combustible solids, such as woods, textiles, paper and rubbish. Type B fires involve flammable liquids such as paint, grease, oil, petrol, etc. Type C fires are started by faulty electrical wiring or appliances.

There are *five* different types of fire extinguisher, ranging from the old-fashioned water type, which can be used only to fight Type A fires, to the foam variety, which is effective against Types A and B but can cause electrical shock if used against Type C.

So, instead of getting five different types of extinguisher, get one multi-purpose type, specifically labelled with the types of fire it extinguishes. Look for a dry chemical 2-kg (5-lb) all-purpose rechargeable unit. It should come with precise directions – not only for use but also for refilling.

You should have a fire extinguisher in

the kitchen and on every upstairs landing, where everyone can see it.

Warning! Avoid those small extinguishers in aerosol cans, which are inadequate and unreliable.

IN CASE OF EMERGENCY

Until a real disaster strikes, people tend to think optimistically that it-can't-happen-to-them. Because people are unprepared, natural disasters or even simple power strikes may cause unnecessary casualties each year. Here's a simple survival check-list.

* Have an alternative source of energy (light, heat, cooking source): a butane camp-fire cooker or solid-fuel stove, oil lamps, candles, a torch.
* Check that you have a bottle opener and a can opener. Always have a store of drinking water and canned or dried food in good condition. (You can't count on a freezer in case of prolonged power failure.)
* If any emergency threatens, run the bath full of cold water. Also fill any buckets.
* Keep a spare radio (especially if you live in the country) with fresh batteries in some accessible place.
* Get a first-aid kit and a first-aid manual, if you don't already have them. In addition to the standard first-aid items (see 'In the first-aid box', p. 191) get an anti-diarrhoea preparation like Kaopectate.
* If you get a **flood warning** and are advised to evacuate your home, turn off the electrical supply at the mains. If you have time and it's feasible, move electrical appliances, mattresses and valuables to the top of the house and then lock up. If the warning period is short, don't wait; valuables can be replaced – you can't.
* When **severe storm warnings** are broadcast, close all your windows

and shutters, batten down or bring inside everything that might blow away, such as garden furniture, garden tools, awnings, rubbish bins – large flying objects can be lethal. Try to put your car in a garage.

After a disaster, contact your insurance agent as soon as possible.

BEATING BURGLARS

The best way to foil burglars is not to have any valuables – or so says the judge who lived next door to me. But many people never realize that they own anything of value until they have to replace it. You only need to have an electronic machine stolen by a casual caller or to be really burgled *once* to know that what is upsetting is not just that your possessions are missing, but the fact that an aggressor has been in your home. The trauma can upset you for months afterwards. And you're lucky if your home isn't ransacked and vandalized. Mine was stripped clean in twenty minutes one Christmas day; the only thing they left in my jewel box was the plug to the plastic paddling pool.

What it's like to be burgled

The likeliest scenario for a burglary, which can take under two minutes, is between 2 and 6 p.m. A burglar rings your doorbell and, if there's no answer, he opens the door with a small strip of plastic, like a credit card. If it's a house, he then goes straight to the back door (if in a block of flats, any window on to the fire escape), which he opens as an escape route. He nips into the main bedroom, spreads out a sheet, empties the drawers upside down on the floor, checks under bed and mattress and in wardrobe, takes jewellery, valuables and cash box. Any valuable clothes or furs are stuffed into one of your suitcases. He then takes the bundle to the living room. He checks the

DOWN WITH SUPERWOMAN!

desk (more drawers upturned) and picks out the goodies of his choice. Allow one extra minute to check for secret drawers – he knows all about them.

Most thieves are frightened and in a hurry. Often, if it takes too much time to gain admittance, a smart burglar will give up and pass on to the next door.

A simple latch lock is no deterrent. What you need – provided your door is thick enough – is *an automatic deadlock*. With this, part of the latch remains rigid if a bit of plastic is pushed through. And there should be *a second, mortice lock* with a hardened steel insert. Ideally, you're supposed to have the lock fitted at knee level, so that the burglar can't put his full weight behind his knee and *heave* the door open. However, you then risk slipping a disc or dropping your shopping every time you bend to unlock it.

There's only one way in which you can definitely protect yourself – by fitting the right locks (see 'Sex maniacs', p. 235).

Internal handles should be out of reach of a wrench or wire coathook that a burglar could lower through the letter-box from outside.

Even though a burglar can get through a 23-cm (9-in) square window opening, all windows should be closed if your house is empty.

Violence attracts violence. Unless you're trained to do so, never try to grapple with a burglar. A frightened man will hit hard. Let him escape, having remembered enough of his looks to give the police a good description. Don't do *any* tidying up until the police have completed their checking for fingerprints, etc.

One home in thirty is burgled every year in Britain – and, according to police, nearly half of the burglaries could be prevented if people didn't make it so easy for the criminals. So:

★ DON'T advertise your absence.
★ DON'T leave tempting smallish articles, like the stereo or typewriter,

lying around in full view of a downstairs window.

★ DO fit a magnifying peephole and chain to the front door (and back door if you have one) *and use them*.

★ DON'T open the front door when you're alone, unless it's on the chain.

★ DON'T let strangers into your home, however plausible their excuse, without checking their credentials. Any genuine charity fund collector, social worker or meter reader should automatically present credentials.

★ DON'T nip out for five minutes and shut the front door while leaving the back door and windows open.

★ DON'T sit in the back garden or on an upstairs terrace with the front door unlocked or the front window open.

★ DON'T leave a garage or tool-shed open. It offers the burglar a beautiful choice of break-in tools.

★ DO turn on a light upstairs when you are out after dark. Draw the bedroom curtains, but not too closely. If you're going to be away for several nights, fit a time switch to a lamp that will turn it on every evening and switch it off every morning at 2 a.m.

★ DON'T leave just the hall light on. Burglars are not idiots. They're fast, sharp, nasty, clever villains just like the ones on TV.

★ DON'T keep the TV turned up downstairs at night when the upstairs windows are open.

★ DON'T take so many burglary precautions that you make your life a misery. As well as burglars, you are also prey for the expensive burglary preventers. I once spent a great deal of money having special keys put on each window and internal door and installing diamond-shaped grilles like those they put on shops at night. All that happened was that we quickly lost the keys – and so for two years we never went into the garden and hardly opened a window because it was too

much trouble. Then we all locked ourselves out one night and my 12-year-
old son climbed up a drain-pipe, broke
a pane of glass and was inside in three
minutes.

★ DO take a snapshot of any irreplace-
able valuables and make a list of paintings, *objets d'art*, silver, jewellery,
cameras, TVs, radios or other valuables. The police say you should also
make a note of all the serial numbers
on your machines. Have your name
stencilled on any valuable machines.
This makes it harder to get rid of the
goods (also see 'Asset register', p.
285).

★ DON'T leave the TV on view if you
go away. Hide it. And any other valuables.

★ DO check whether any hired or
borrowed appliance you may have is
the responsibility of the owner and, if
it is not, check that it is insured under
your household policy.

★ DON'T keep cash in the house. Don't
think you can fool a burglar by taping
an envelope of cash under the wardrobe or to the underside of a bed.
When you're burgled, everything possible is turned upside down and anything locked is smashed, including interior doors, wardrobes, jewel cases
and strong-boxes.

Before going away for the weekend or on holiday

★ DO stop newspapers and any other
tell-tale regular deliveries, such as milk.

★ DO lock all windows and doors.
Leave a key with a neighbour and ask
him to drop in regularly to check that
all's well; offer to do the same for him.

★ DO turn off the water and drain the
pipes if you're going away in winter.
Burst pipes can be an expensive
proposition – especially if they also
reassure an intruder that you're not just
around the corner.

★ DON'T leave a message on your
answering machine saying that you are
away.

★ DO tell the police that you're going
away if you live in a small town or
suburb where the police know you and
regularly patrol the neighbourhood.
Don't tell the police about your
coming holiday if you live in a big
city; news will get around.

How your local police station can help you

★ Ask the Crime Prevention Officer to
inspect your home, and particularly
advise on locks.

★ Ask if there is a Neighbourhood
Watch scheme in your area, so that
your neighbours automatically keep an
eye on your home and telephone the
police if something odd occurs.

★ If there isn't a Neighbourhood
Watch scheme, ask the police to tell
you how to start one.

★ Ask them to tell you which specialist
firms can burglar-proof your home
(don't get anything too exotic, we had
infra-red alarms on the doors and kept
setting them off ourselves).

★ Don't have a house alarm, because
they go off in the night, wake the neighbours and the police refuse to come
after they've been called out unnecessarily for the third time.

★ Expensive but reliable is a hidden
panic button at your bedside that rings
at the police station. You'll need an
extra telephone for this and you also
have to pay a yearly charge to the firm
that installs it.

Insurance

The visit from the insurance adjustor can
also be upsetting. He is employed by the
insurance company to look after *its* interests. I always have new-for-old policies,
clothing and household linen excepted.

DOWN WITH SUPERWOMAN!

So keep all original receipts, check your insurance policy carefully and if you have any valuables, get them valued by an expert (not by you) on a regular basis; the valuation should be on official letterhead.

Sotheby's and Christie's have offices all over the country: check your local telephone book. (For further insurance information, see 'Asset register', p. 285, and 'The professionals: insurance agent', p. 338.)

MONEY MONEY MONEY

HOW TO SPEND MONEY

Mr Micawber's crisp advice on budgeting hasn't been improved on in the past hundred years: 'Annual income twenty pounds, annual expenditure nineteen, nineteen and six, result happiness. Annual income twenty pounds, annual expenditure twenty pounds, ought and six, result misery.'

If there's trouble in a home, it isn't always in the bedroom – it's quite often in the budget. I wouldn't be surprised to hear that more families fight over money than over sex and mothers-in-law combined, usually because they've built the battleground into their lives by planning their money badly or not planning it at all. (In fact, Relate, formerly the Marriage Guidance Council, says they find that sex is the main contributor to marriage difficulties, with money in second place.)

The first financial fact that a couple should discover is *what system can be operated by both of them*. One couple might happily operate a system based on a piggybank on the mantelpiece and a two-sided purse. Another couple might positively enjoy running six bank accounts plus an accountant. But woe betide the togetherness when *she* operates the piggybank and *he* divides the laundry bill into his, hers and theirs with the aid of one of those push-button desk calculators.

According to certain marriage experts, a good test of a relationship is supposed to be whether you can happily operate a joint account. You might feel it would be safer to try going over Niagara in a barrel than to check in this particular way whether either of you is losing out on the domination/submission pattern. All I can tell you is that *no* system will be any good unless you *both* understand and agree to it.

An annual budget is basically two

simple lists. One list is of money coming in from different sources over the year, the other list is of money being spent on different items over that time.

Divide the second list by twelve to get the monthly amount you plan to spend (or divide by thirteen if you want four-week periods), or divide it by fifty-two if you want to budget weekly. If you get paid weekly, it's sensible to work out a weekly budget. If you are paid monthly, do a monthly one.

Experts say that you should be precise in your accounting – no rounding out sums to the nearest pound. State the actual amount down to the last penny.

The point of a home budget is knowing what you want to do with your money, keeping track of where the money actually goes (theoretically, these two figures should be the same, but life isn't like that) and making sure that you don't overspend and get into debt without realizing it.

In working out the budget everyone should be absolutely clear where even the smallest expenses fit in and make sure that everything fits in somewhere. For example, cigarettes. Are they a necessity, to be bought regularly and paid for on the weekly supermarket bill? Or are they luxuries to come out of individual personal allowances?

'Mistakes and contingencies' is the disaster fund (unpredictable, act-of-God stuff). Leave a really pessimistic amount of the budget to go into the disaster fund. After all, if you don't use it, you can divert the money into savings or a spree at the end of the year. But you will use it. The budget for saving should *not* be lumped with the disaster fund, or your savings will just melt.

Save what you can in a deposit account or building society, or by purchasing investments, or cream part of the savings off into mortgage repayments (since bricks and mortar are also an invest-

ment), or buy potential old masters, silver or similar items.

If you can't seem to save, you could make yourself save by taking on savings commitments and having your bank enforce them by banker's order, or you might firmly commit your money in a direction other than a piggybank. HP can be a great way to force yourself to save up for things, but *only* if you don't allow it to exceed 10 per cent of your annual income. I know a girl who bought a diamond tiara this way. It's the smallest tiara in captivity and she's never worn the thing because it's always in the bank guaranteeing something. But it certainly was a glamorous way to save and the value increased six times in ten years.

If you are self-employed, allow for tax and national insurance stamps when budgeting. Work out what your tax should be and deposit this money in a savings account, where it will earn you interest until the tax-man needs it, as he eventually will.

Working out the budget

Separate out your housekeeping money, your personal spending money and money relating to any personal business project.

* **Charities** Church, other.
* **Children** Pocket money.
* **Christmas** Food, drink, presents, parties.
* **Clothes** New clothes, shoes, repairs, dry cleaning.
* **Domestic** Cleaning help, babysitter, other help.
* **Education** Tuition for children or self, school-books and supplies.
* **Entertainment** Cinema, theatre, concerts, hobbies, holidays, books, newspapers, magazines.
* **Food** Groceries, eating out (including lunch at work).
* **Gifts** Family, friends.

	Percentage of income
Rent, mortage repayment, taxes, maintenance, insurance, fares to work, etc.	30
Household expenses (including food, fuel, laundry, telephone, cleaning)	45
Clothes	10
Amusements and holidays	5
Savings and insurance	5
Incidental expenses (including licences, periodicals, subscriptions, pocket money)	5

* **Health** Medical, dentist, optician.
* **Home** Mortgage payments or rent, local tax, gas, electricity, water, telephone, heating, repairs, maintenance.
* **Insurance** Property, life, health (may be covered in part by employer's insurance plan), car.
* **Interest charges** Hire purchase, card charges, bank interest, other bank charges.
* **Mistakes and contingencies** Allow 5 per cent of your income for unforeseeable bad luck and mistakes.
* **Personal** Hairdresser, petty cash.
* **Pets** Food, vet bills, equipment, other.
* **Savings** Savings account, pension plan, other.
* **Subscriptions** Unions, clubs.
* **Transport** Car payments, car upkeep (insurance, fuel, MOT test, subscription to AA/RAC), commuting transport (bus, Tube, etc.), other.

How much to spend on what

I think that on the whole it's unrealistic for anyone to tell anyone else what percentage of their income they should spend on rent or savings. Everybody has different priorities. However, as a vague guide, the table above shows the allocation of income suggested by one of the country's leading home economists.

Sorting out the income

If there is more than one contributor, either sort out separate responsibilities or pool the family income, whatever its source – family allowances, dividends, earnings, legacies or whatever – and add it up. Then try redistributing it under headings such as I've suggested.

Some think it is important that the chief earners should not allow themselves to think that because they bring in the money they have a greater right than the rest of the family to determine how it should be spent. A husband might work and get paid and a wife may work full-time in the home and not get paid. He is the breadwinner for the family, but she is not just a bread-consumer. Some wives feel that he gets paid (to a greater or lesser degree) for both their work. That's certainly the main reason given by men for unequal pay. But the days are gone when you could get a woman to work for a week merely for full board and a roof over her head.

Where a young husband and wife both work, they often feel it is better to learn not to rely on the wife's pay in case she has children or stops working for any other reason, so that there would not have to be a painful adjustment to a lower standard of living. Provided there is some compensatory form of security for the wife, such as a joint mortgage or having a chunk of the family assets in her name, it seems reasonable that the extra money that comes into the kitty because of her work should be earmarked for major but slashable items, such as central heating and household appliances.

Separate bank accounts

You cannot afford to be sentimental

DOWN WITH SUPERWOMAN!

about money. If you and your husband are madly in love, well that's wonderful, but statistically you have a good chance of falling out of love and divorcing. So without being offensively self-protective, avoid entwining your money or goods (assuming that you have any) with those of your husband (or any other member of the household). Not to be mean – just to keep things clear.

I consider that only one joint account for two people puts the budget at risk as well as the relationship, and so does the judge who lives next door. His non-working wife has a personal account and a housekeeping account.

If you have a separate income, which will be assessed separately, run the housekeeping on a third joint household account.

Always consult your accountant or tax adviser before assuming that anything is 'off tax'. Remember that if an item is tax-deductible as a genuine business expense, that doesn't mean it's free. *You still have to pay for it*.

If your housekeeping money is paid into a joint bank account in this way you might like part of it in a cash sum sent to you weekly or monthly *on standing order*. This means you have only once to tell the bank what to do and then it just keeps coming. This helps to keep some control over your cash spending.

If more than two earners are sharing a home (husband and wife, mother and son, two or three friends), each might pay an agreed sum regularly (every week, month or quarter) into the joint household account for the purpose of running the home.

Keep your own private money apart from the housekeeping money It could be by having two purses, or a purse with two pockets, or two separate bank accounts and cheque-books.

In fact, for me the secret of keeping track of home budgeting was to reduce as many outgoings as possible to a regular basis, and for this I opened a number 2 housekeeping account.

First, add up all your regular payments for *everything*, from the milkman to the TV licence. Estimate what fuel and telephone bills will be by looking up last year's costs. Take a deep breath and don't panic at this point, because the total amount will be truly staggering. Divide it by twelve, prune, then arrange to have the resultant sum paid monthly into a *number 2 budget account*, preferably an interest-bearing one (try Nat West). All *regular* bills were paid from this account, so I didn't feel faint at the *thought* of opening the electricity bill. If I was overdrawn one month, it should theoretically have balanced out in following months. Food and unexpected or unbudgeted expenses were paid from the number 1 account. This meant I had three bank accounts in all: a personal account, a housekeeping account mainly for food and fares and a second housekeeping account for regular payments. It was slightly more expensive but I preferred to pay for clarity than having to keep doing little sums to find out whether I could afford to buy a window-box.

Bookkeeping

I do as little as I can get away with and so might you. Stop reading if you wouldn't dream of organizing your money. Come back to this page again if you start raising Corgis or cucumbers or get in a money muddle.

The easiest form of housekeeping or business bookkeeping is to get a *cash book* because this has lines and columns conveniently ruled for you. Fill in the date of entry, money that comes in and money that goes out. I don't mean the cost of every lettuce ... I just fill in 'food' as such. This book not only calms

Your housekeeping budget

Item	Cost		Cost per week		Cost per year	
	£	p	£	p	£	p

you when you wonder where on earth the money went or when someone sends you a second bill for something you've already paid for or when you want to check how many times the vacuum cleaner has been repaired since you bought it, but it is also a good indicator of where you can economize.

It is a good idea to make a point of entering cheques in the book *before* filling them in, otherwise you tend to forget to enter them at all. To pay bills, sort them out alphabetically, enter them in your accounts book, fill in the cheque stubs, then nerve yourself to make out the cheques.

For the advanced muddler If you want to know exactly where you are financially, you can do a satisfying little sum, that grandly calls itself a cash reconciliation. An average 13-year-old child who is weak on maths could do one. First telephone the bank and find exactly what is in each of your accounts, then write them down on a line (see below).

Business bookkeeping If you have your own little cottage industry steaming along nicely (embroidering blouses, making cushions or cakes or fibreglass sculpture or breeding Burmese cats), then keep separate accounts of what you spend exactly as above.

In a second, separate cash book on the left-hand page keep a dated list of the invoices you send out (how else will the accountants of other firms know that they owe you money?). Enter the date on the right-hand page when payment is made. Anything undated on the right-hand page is unpaid.

When you send someone an invoice, which is an exact account of what they owe you money for, you should send a short summary, or statement, of it at the end of the month. You can normally expect payment at the end of the month following that, i.e., in five weeks at the earliest after delivery of goods and eight weeks at the latest. You may have sensibly made arrangements that the goods should be paid for *before* delivery, in which case you send a *pro forma invoice*, which is just the same as an invoice. It means 'cash in advance, please!'

It is inadvisable to sell goods on a sale-or-return basis. Your goods are gone and the shop hasn't invested in them, so it might be less keen on selling them than some other product in which the shop's money is tied up, and the position about possible dirt or damage is unsatisfactory.

I mention these points because though they are simple I have seen many housewives, who have never been in business,

Cash reconciliation

Date: _____	Me	1st housekeeping account (food and petty cash)	2nd housekeeping account (regular bills)
State of play today	+ £2	+ £20	+ £200
Deduct bills to pay	0	− 17	− 120
Deduct cheques not yet presented	− 1	− 0	− 32
SUB TOTAL	+ 1	+ 3	+ 48
Add cheques not yet paid in	+ 13	+ 10	0
FACTUAL TOTAL	+ 14	+ 13	+ 48
Add, tentatively, money due in	+ 25	0	0
THEORETICAL TOTAL	£39	£13	£48

muddle a good start by not understanding the procedure.

FAMILY FUNDS

Involving the family

Some families have regular conferences about money – once every three months, say. Get the children in on these as early as possible, even though they may be bored, and treat their contributions with respect. After discussing the budget, analyse disasters to find out why they happened and how to prevent them, suggesting amendments to the budget (more pocket money may mean a less expensive holiday) and take account of future changes, such as rising prices. After this the family should all go out to dinner – even if it's only fish and chips – to cheer themselves up again.

This may sound horrendous, but my pretty cousin Corinne, when a new bride, said she was eternally grateful to her father for doing this. Not only did she, as a little girl, see the point of switching lights off (more money for holidays), but she sailed into marriage able to run a budget without ever realizing she had been taught to do so.

Major expenditure in the house should, ideally, be discussed and approved by all the family. If he wants a scarlet sports car, if you want a dishwasher, if your eldest son wants to spend a year travelling before settling down, it's a matter that all the family should know about if paying for it will affect the finances of the whole household. This is what the quarterly conference is for.

If one adult member of the family tries to explain a major change that the rest can't see the sense in (i.e., how the aforementioned sports car will actually *save* money), get him/her to explain it in front of the family bank manager, who can then act as an impartial adviser, poor soul.

WHAT TO DO IF YOU'RE A CASHAHOLIC

A cashaholic is someone who's hopeless with money. Psychologists say that hopeless extravagance is inculcated in children by parents who don't give their children a proper allowance and make them responsible for their own expenditure, but who give pocket money only for treats and presents. The result of this is that the child, when grown up, thinks of cash as meaning treats and money for personal pleasure and never for dreary things such as maintenance and electricity bills.

I've never really found a cure for this condition, but you can survive solvently as a cashaholic by treating yourself as an alcoholic and hiding the bottle – i.e., don't own a cheque-book, certainly don't own a credit or charge card, deal only in cash and when your purse is empty, stop spending. Form a Cashaholics Anonymous with a similarly minded friend and telephone her when you get the urge to spend – she will then reel off a litany of bills and responsibilities and, in theory, deter you. Don't go out of the home, stick to your shopping list and don't add one extra item. If you can't do this, shop by telephone to avoid temptation. Yes, it's a bit more expensive, but you're avoiding larger areas of temptation.

Finally, commit your money firmly in other directions.

How to bring up more sensible children You won't raise a second generation of cashaholics if you teach your children how to handle money as soon as they can buy their own ice creams.

Involve them in the family affairs as soon as possible, as I have suggested, and give each child an allowance – yearly or monthly – to cover all he or she spends; older children can have clothes on their own budgets, plus hobbies, sports, travelling, school expenses, going out to the cinema, sweets and ice creams.

DOWN WITH SUPERWOMAN!

Expect drama in the first six months, when they learn that early over-purchasing of ice cream leads to later lack of model-making glue. *Be firm at this point.* Kindness will not equip your offspring to stand on their own feet in later life.

As soon as possible put the allowance in the form of a post-office savings book or bank account and arrange with your bank manager to make the most almighty fuss if there's an overdraft, accompanied by extremely stiff letters from the bank.

My children have had bank accounts since they were 8. I pay their allowance on standing order and they sort out everything for themselves, including mistakes and contingencies. Although I advise them, I never bail them out. Incidentally, this seems a good method for parents and children alike, once the children have recovered from discovering the hidden disadvantages of a cheque-book.

HOW TO CUT THE COST OF LIVING

No matter how tight your budget, there is room for economy.

If, like me, you have been married to a self-made multimillionaire, people tend to think that you have lots of money and are used to lots of money. But how do they think he acquired it in the first place? By living on a permanent, lunatic, public-prosperity/private-poverty breadline in order that every available penny could be used for Our Big Scheme.

So if you've been married to a multimillionaire, you *really* know how to make every penny do the work of two.

I also learned a lot from living in a farmhouse in France. All the rich farmer neighbours never threw a thing away, not a bottle, not even a jam jar, and they hoarded bits of string. I turned up my nose at this parsimony until . . . I needed jam jars for my jam and empty bottles for my elderberry wine and seemed to be

in permanent need of string, all of which my neighbours cheerfully provided. My 16-year-old son then bought a notebook. He said, as we watched them using wood fires to boil cauldrons of water as well as the evening soup, 'They've been living this way for 300 years, and none of our rich friends lives nearly so well, so I'm taking notes.'

By learning to get along with less, you will not only save money but also help to preserve the Earth's resources.

Cut down on big things

If major financial troubles are likely to be temporary, you can attack the problem by looking at your budget. Remember all those figures you were keeping in your household budget? Now's the time to take a fresh look at them.

After you have examined those figures, put the fixed ones to one side. Without a drastic overhaul you obviously can't make cuts in the fixed expenses – rent or mortgage, car payments, instalment payments, insurance. But the flexible ones could be subject to reduction. Will your strain be relieved if you cut 10 per cent out of your food costs? Ten per cent out of clothes and upkeep? (Discount stores help a lot here.) If so, here's where you should start.

Don't economize on things that will save hardly more than a few pence – margarine instead of butter, for example, or cutting out the newspapers. This will not be much of an economy and will make everyone feel pinched.

And never cut down on what makes your life worth living: if you have chocolate cake for Sunday tea, don't switch to buns; if your one joy is playing squash, don't hang up your racquets. The trick is to economize in a big way on something boring, and get the co-operation of the whole family to do it. Don't bring down the family by being miserly and making yourself miserable.

If your plight is more serious, then the fixed expenses must be tackled. Will moving to a smaller home help? Can you rent a room to bring in some more money? Can you trade in your car for a smaller model that would be more economical to run and insure, or put the family on bicycles – which is anyway more sensible in cities.

During one lean period I sold my car and bought one of those funny French mopeds. You can bicycle it with your feet (my thighs dwindled!), then flip on the engine when you get tired. And as it does over 300 kmpg (200 mpg) I felt virtuously patriotic as I sailed along with the shopping at 50 kmph (30 mph).

Don't be sentimental or afraid of what the neighbours will think if you have to move for money reasons. You won't be around to hear them. On the other hand, do go into your economies carefully before you make them – moving to the country may save money in some ways, but with the dearth of big supermarkets and the increase in travelling costs it entails it may not help you at all. And moving itself is a great expense.

It isn't easy. When Doomsday hit me I moved home five times in eighteen months. Oddly enough, I was cheered by my solicitor telling me how difficult *everybody* always found it, not just me. 'One of the most difficult things you can do,' he said, 'is to cut your budget drastically, because nobody ever thinks that he is personally being "extravagant", or he wouldn't live that way.'

I was also cheered and urged on by another lovely man who said, 'Come on, Shirley, see it as a challenge. I mean, you could have the most marvellous garage in London, if only you put your mind to it.' From then on I upset my mother dreadfully by drawing garage conversion designs on the backs of envelopes and working out how three of us could live in an area 3.6 × 4 m (12 × 14 ft). But the point had been hammered home. Every-

thing is easier once you face it and get interested in the situation, as opposed to being appalled by it.

HOW TO AVOID PAYING A BILL *OR* WHAT TO DO ON DOOMSDAY

Doomsday happens in every family sometimes – the day when Father is made redundant, Mother's secret extravagance comes home to roost, the accountants turn out to have been crooks, or whatever. The essential feature of the situation is that the money just won't go round, there are too many bills and not enough money to pay them.

When Doomsday comes to your family, you *can* cope with it if you remember two basic facts. Firstly, all the people you owe money to are chiefly interested in getting their money, not in suing you, which will only cost them more money. Secondly, as these disasters happen to everyone, it's nothing to be ashamed of, but something to be calmly explained in your dealings with your creditors as soon as possible.

Make a list of all your major creditors – building societies, service industries, HP companies, tradesmen and so on – and how much you owe each of them. Then work out how much you can afford to pay each of them – thinking in terms of paying off what you owe in instalments. This is called 'keeping your credit good' and it ensures that you don't get blacklisted by credit investigators, which might mean no more HP or mortgages.

Then write each creditor a letter, addressed to the chief accountant, explaining that your family is in a financial crisis (no need to go into details) and it would help you enormously if they would accept payment by instalments, quoting the sum you have decided you can afford. Almost all firms will accept this offer, and then it's simply a question of slog

DOWN WITH SUPERWOMAN!

and cutting down expenses until all your debts are paid off. Two things to remember are:

1 Always get your letter off *before* the creditors start demanding money.
2 Don't overestimate your income or underestimate the cost of living when working out what you can afford to pay off. Offer less rather than offering more and risking not being able to live up to your promises.

NEVER, NEVER, borrow money to pay off debts unless you borrow from your bank.

But never ever run up an overdraft without asking permission from your bank manager. Apart from anything else, it's only polite to ask before you help yourself to his money. Don't think that it might pass unnoticed. And you don't want to jeopardize your credit rating on that little pink card they keep with your name on it, on which they note every letter or telephone call you make to them.

Although financial matters can never be straightforward, it's useful to have a simple guide for money matters. *The Family Money Book* by Douglas Moffitt (published by J. M. Dent & Sons) ranges from savings, budgeting and cash flow, life assurance, buying a home and shares to planning for retirement and the financial complications attending divorce and widowhood.

CREDIT CARDS

Not so long ago, only people like the Queen or a Mafia godfather dared go shopping without a penny in their pocket. Today we still need petty cash but the world economy and our part of it runs on *paper* (cheques) and *plastic* (credit cards): we live in a signature society. The new French banking card is, in itself, a computer that automatically

deducts any amount paid by your card from your bank balance and we may yet see thumbprint cards.

Credit cards and charge cards are basically a crafty form of banking, where the shopkeeper, instead of the customer, writes the cheque.

There is a difference between a charge card and a credit card.

A charge card (such as American Express or Diners Club) entitles you to make purchases on that card up to a sum pre-arranged with the card issuer (even if that sum is 'unlimited') and **you are obliged to pay the complete debt as it is invoiced to you at the end of each month**. You are not allowed any further credit and are charged *high* interest on the money you owe if you do not pay the complete debt when due.

The basic principle of a **credit card** (such as Visa or Access) is similar to that of a pre-agreed amount of bank overdraft. So long as you don't exceed your credit limit, you spend the money, then pay it off pretty well as you wish. If you don't pay your entire bill when invoiced, you pay interest (often high) on any borrowing.

Card protection

1 Make sure all redundant, expired cards are completely cut in half *across the signature*.
2 Sign all new credit and charge cards immediately.
3 When applying for a new credit-card/charge-card facility, keep a note of the *application date*. If the card or acknowledgement of your application does not arrive within a reasonable time, telephone the credit company to ensure the card has not been intercepted in the post.
4 Keep a note of the card *expiry date*. Replacement cards are usually posted automatically one to two weeks before the expiry date. If the new card does

not arrive seven days before the month-end, telephone the credit company immediately.

5 On discovery of the loss or theft of a card, *immediately* telephone the company to cancel your card and *keep proof of the cancellation*. Record the time of the telephone conversation, the name of the person you spoke to, ask that person to write to you immediately or fax your hotel if you are away from home, giving confirmation that the card has been cancelled.

6 Check all conditions of all cards you use, which should be clearly stated in the Cardmember Agreement.

7 What happens if you lose a credit or charge card? American Express say 'provided a Cardmember has acted in good faith and has not been negligent, liability is limited to £20 up to the time that the loss, theft or non-arrival of the card is reported to us.'

The dictionary definition of negligence is 'carelessness, neglecting responsibility, lacking attention, care or concern'. 'Acting in good faith' means not trying to con American Express, who have ways of finding out should you do so. Barclaycard and Access have a similar proviso.

Other card companies insist that you are liable to pay for any purchases on a lost or stolen card up until the moment that you notify the card company.

Where to ring when your cards are stolen or lost

American Express 9 a.m. to 5 p.m.: 0273-696933. After 5 p.m. and at weekends: 071-222-9633
Access 0702-352255
Diners Club 0252-516261
Barclaycard/Visa 0604-230230/252139

8 American Express offer a further useful service for a very small annual subscription. *They will arrange to cancel all your other credit and charge cards should you lose them.* So one telephone call from Timbuctoo (or wherever you happen to be when you lose your cards) covers all the laborious work of cancelling each one. For this service call the Card Registry Service at American Express (tel: 071-834-5555). Some other agencies that offer a similar service will include insurance against fraudulent use resulting from the loss of your cards.

9 Do not give your card or card account number to *any* third party (including employees) to be used on your behalf. Give your card account number only to people *you* call, and keep details of what you ordered.

10 To get cash from a cashpoint dispenser, you will be given a Personal Identification Number (PIN). Never keep a written record of it – but if you do, just scribble the number, don't identify it and keep it separately from your credit-card wallet.

11 **Points to consider when deciding which card company you will join**

Each card company has different strengths, some of which *may* be important to you. Before deciding which card to use, compare what each company offers you.

★ **Acceptability.** This consideration is more important to me than anything else. A card company that no store has ever heard of won't get you much credit. I use American Express in America and Barclaycard in Europe.

★ **Any annual charge.**

★ **Any extra goodies offered.** For instance:
Some companies automatically insure you when you travel; if you buy your tickets with the card.
Some companies will reimburse you if you buy goods that later prove faulty.

DOWN WITH SUPERWOMAN!

Extra goodies tend to be impossible to compare – one company offers higher insurance cover, another offers more credit.

* As in all things a personal recommendation from someone who has used a card for several years is worth more than flashy advertising.

12 Points to remember when you are making a purchase

Make sure that:

* You don't use a credit card if you've used up your legal limit.
* The card is returned to you after each transaction – and check that you haven't been handed someone else's card.
* The 'total' box has been filled in on the bill.
* Any incorrect imprints of the card are torn up in front of you.
* All carbon papers (which were between the various copies of the bill) are destroyed, to prevent unscrupulous people getting your card details.

Doomsday doesn't fool around if you haven't paid your credit cards by the date due; the computers are already preparing your next bill and a month's interest is added to your unpaid balance on top of the original charge. You will have to pay interest on the interest. As months go by, this can spiral. The interest on these accounts is like a taxi meter – it never stops running. After you write your cheque settling the whole bill, you'll get another bill for some small amount – interest that accumulated while you were writing your cheque to pay off the borrowed amount.

So, except for your power and telephone bills (you don't want these cut off), pay your credit-card bills before all other short-term obligations.

What happens if the credit-card company sends you an inaccurate bill? Chaos, in my experience. If the card companies send you someone else's bills, or send you the same bill twice, they then start billing you for the interest on these items that you haven't had, while you are still querying them – then you have to argue about the interest.

So I don't leave it to the card companies to bill me. I keep track of my expenses and I pay for them all at the end of the month – before I am invoiced. I've been using this hassle-free system for three years.

I cut my cards to the minimum and in my card case I keep a bit of lined paper ruled into four columns. On this I note the date, name of shopkeeper and amount paid, just as I do on a cheque stub. At the end of the month I can see the total amount I owe to each card company. I then know exactly where I stand – incurring no interest. I photostat my bit of paper and send it with my cheque in full payment to the relevant card companies. When the credit-card statement arrives, I then check off the items on the statement against my own record, to ensure that I have not been billed twice.

HOW TO CHOOSE A BANK

Thanks to competition for our money, more and more banks are begging for our funds and dropping those nasty little charges – 50p a cheque or penalties if a minimum deposit (something like £500) falls below the specified sum for free banking. They need our money because *our* deposits add up to a massive lending pool for banks: it's *our* money loaned out to others that brings them the interest that becomes their profits. Banks hire out money like Avis hire out cars.

There are four sorts of basic bank account, all with advantages and disadvantages:

1 **A current account**, into which you pay money you want to use for expenditure.

2 **A loan account,** where the bank loans you a sizeable amount (generally over £1,000) and charges you interest for that amount.

3 **A deposit account,** into which you pay money and don't withdraw it except by pre-arranged notice (seven days, thirty days, three months, etc.). The bank pays *you* interest on this. Some banks don't need notice of any withdrawal and no longer charge a penalty for this.

4 The majority of British banks now offer an **interest-bearing current account,** and pay you interest on any money in the account. On a high-interest-bearing current account, it is probably stipulated that you write no small cheques. Keep any capital sum in this account. There are also interest-bearing current accounts that pay a lower rate of interest but allow you to write cheques of any size.

To comparative-shop, on the same day telephone your local branch of the top banks (Barclays, National Westminster, Midland Bank, Lloyds and the Bank of Scotland) and see who is paying the highest interest on money you lend them and the lowest interest on money you borrow. Ask 'What is the highest rate current account you offer?'

Base rate is the interest rate at which banks lend money to each other. They will borrow it from Mr A at 3 per cent *under* base rate and lend it to Mr B at, say, 3 per cent *over* base rate. The difference in interest is the bank's gross profit.

Always let your *bank manager* know your plans. Explain them precisely. This is a very useful exercise, because you have to clarify your ideas in order to explain them to someone else. He's a good person to bounce ideas off, but don't expect him to have creative ideas. If he did, he wouldn't be where he is. Keep these plans as short and accurate as possible. Say, 'I plan to do £X turnover

this year: I have the following firm orders in hand and I expect the following orders that have not yet been confirmed. I need to borrow Y in order to buy new materials and pay workers. Here is my cash-flow forecast and my accountant has drawn up this repayment plan that I'd like you to comment on.' Should you need to borrow money from the bank, you may wish to ask for an overdraft or a bank loan.

Bank statements

When you receive these monthly accounts of deposits and withdrawals, *immediately check your bank statement.* They are not always correct. During a two-year period my bank paid £1,800 and £3,000 of my money into a stranger's account without being asked to do so. (Never the reverse, I noticed.) Always check all your bank statements as carefully as you check your bills. I *collect* bank statement errors. Every year I 'save' a lot of money by checking every single statement.

BORROWING MONEY

Overdraft

An overdraft is an informal loan. A good rule with banks is to *arrange to borrow 10 per cent more than you think you need.* (Make sure that you needn't borrow it if you don't need it.) It may also be prudent to arrange repayment 10 per cent slower than you think you can. Honest people are generally anxious to repay and therefore overestimate their ability to do so.

Bank loan

A bank loan is a formal loan of a specific amount for a specific period. If you want to raise a loan, *on no account* go to a

DOWN WITH SUPERWOMAN!

bucket-shop loan company: do business only with a reputable bank. Tot up your assets (if any) before discussing a loan with the manager and decide what collateral you can offer to secure your loan, and how you're going to pay that inexorable interest. You won't be able to get a loan without any collateral.

You may find that a British woman starting a new business has very little credibility. Everyone is polite but they don't altogether take you seriously and there is good reason for this. Too many women have started a business frivolously, for pin money. They started it on a whim and they dropped it on a whim when they got bored or when the going became difficult or they realized that they would have to forgo their holiday in order to look after the warehouse.

Be tolerant of this masculine attitude: it is not based on sexism but experience. It's up to you not to whine that it's not fair, but to *show* them that you are to be taken seriously.

Never, never borrow money from loan agencies to pay off your debts. It's far cheaper to borrow from your bank, which can be a tidy way to consolidate your debts into one lump sum, thus enabling you to clear the debts and then repay the bank debt on an instalment plan. This may spare you heavy interest payments to some *usurious loan agency*. Next time you hear an easy and persuasive voice on the radio suggesting that you 'just pick up the phone for immediate relief', remember that in exchange for immediate relief, he is offering you long-term misery.

A Mother's Place... ...is in the wrong!

A Mother's Place...is in the wrong!

AN A–Z GUIDE TO GOOD BEHAVIOUR FOR MODERN MOTHERS

They're always saying that you never listen to them, so I asked some teenagers to help with this section. The panel was aged 13 to 17 – young enough to remember what it was like to be a child, but old enough still to give trouble.

If you disagree with my panel's guidelines, why not discuss them with your children and draw up your own?

Authority (yours) Child psychiatrists stress the importance of laying down guidelines for children from birth because this gives security; the most frequent problems, they say, are too much and too little control. Children like clear behaviour guidelines. They want to know where the boundaries are. If they help to decide the rules, they are more likely to stick to them.

Books Which to ban? None. Be grateful, whatever they read.

Bribery (yours) If you try to bribe them not to touch alcohol or smoke or try drugs until they are 21, they will smoke, drink, do drugs and also lie about it. And you will lose your bribe money.

Broken homes, missing fathers and similar deprivations If a father isn't there, he isn't there. If you have to go out to work, you have to go out to work. This involves perpetual guilt feelings on your part, but doesn't worry them unless they realize how much it worries *you*. They then have a wonderful weapon.

If you are a one-parent mother, you can't use the weak threat, 'Wait till your father gets home', which is not dealing with a situation but dodging it.

Bullying Children often suffer in silence rather than tell an adult that they are being bullied. Danger signs are: bedwetting, nightmares, reluctance to go to

DOWN WITH SUPERWOMAN!

school, truancy, dropping standards of schoolwork, vomiting, sickness, feigned sickness, missing money, torn clothes, bruises, scratches, a strained white face. Discuss the matter with his teacher at the earliest opportunity. If the teacher isn't co-operative, both parents should see the head teacher together, by appointment.

Callousness Most children are callous. They quite like hurting you; it proves their power over you.

Childhood is a preparation for adult life. A sheltered childhood results in an unprepared adult.

Panel comment: *'If she's bringing you up sensibly, she doesn't protect you, she prepares you for the worst, "for real life".'*

Clothes (theirs) A boy who finds it impossible to keep his shirt-tails tucked in generally can't manage to keep his flies zipped up either. Face the fact that boys will never look tidy and try to keep them clean. If you buy them clothes they like, however mad they look, they'll keep cleaner longer.

Clothes (yours) You never know when they're going to want you to melt into the background like a chameleon or stick out like a film star. They express total lack of confidence in a mother's sartorial sense. ('You can see *right through* that thing you're wearing, you can see your *knickers* and you can see through them too.')

Coaching If your child needs extra coaching in some subject, don't just leave it to the coach. Clearly extra effort is needed on your part in this area. After my 11-year-old son failed his maths exam, during the summer holidays he went to the coach in the morning, did his homework in the afternoon and had to teach it all to me when I got home from the office in the evening. ('Oh, why did you do such a *stupid* thing, Ma, you *know* the square root of . . .') Teaching me restored his self-confidence and he eventually took maths as his main A-level subject.

Communications, verbal (yours) You hold mad dual conversations that only other mothers can tolerate, your normal feminine tone interrupting itself with gym-mistress barks, 'PUT THAT DOWN!' 'TAKE YOUR FINGER OUT OF THAT BOWL!' Your voice rises at least ten decibels when your first child is aged 1, then deepens via 'I-really-mean-it-this-time-dammit', until your voice eventually breaks when your son's does.

Communication (yours with them) They're the only people in the world who pay not the slightest attention to whatever you say and you're stuck with them.

However, children are very good at receiving messages – the ones that they're not supposed to: they quickly pick up body language and the sub-text of conversations.

Correction Save your strength for what you think is really important. I corrected my children only on the points that were important to me. They mimicked me ('What *exactly* do you mean by that?'), but they grew up articulate.

Let them know that what is important to you and what is going to help them get along with other people are not necessarily the same.

Crimes (yours) The worst seems to be kissing in public and not kissing in private, but generally a mother's place is in the wrong, as James Thurber should have said.

Criticism (theirs of you) They tend idly to enjoy it when there's nothing better to do. Normally, they tread on a mother for the same reason as Mallory gave when he was asked why he climbed Mount Everest, because she's there – a constant background and their personal provider to ignore.

Definition of a good mother Panel comments: *'Someone who understands.'*
'If you got into trouble with the police or

smashed a window, she'd stick up on your side and not even listen to the man before she'd heard your story.'

Definition of a bad mother Panel comments: '*I can't stand mothers that always yack at you and keep you clean and don't allow you out when it's raining unless you're wearing a hundred pullovers.*'

'*I can't stand ones that force you to finish your supper and send you to bed before you want to go or ones that come in and switch over right in the middle of a TV programme and say "This is rubbish" and then turn to something you think is rubbish.*'

Dental visits should be rewarded but not with sweets.

The Difficult Age All ages are difficult. My mother warned me that the period when a child starts to give you *serious* anxiety is from 17 onwards. I think the most difficult age is between 1 year and 2½ years old, when a child is old enough to have a mind and will of its own, but can't communicate with you and yet has to obey you. He finds this as frustrating as you would, hence bad behaviour.

Dirt Leave it to time. Boys attract filth. Girls tend to sluttish habits.

Panel comment: '*She mustn't nag: going on and on about behind your ears; people just don't go around looking behind your ears.*'

Discipline (theirs) The fewer the rules, the fewer the rows and the fewer the punishments you'll eventually never administer anyway.

Discipline (yours) More necessary than theirs. If you ask them to shut the door after they've left it open three times, you'll wish you'd never asked them, after they've kicked it shut for the tenth time.

Discussion Encourage your children to talk. Ask their opinion. Listen with respect to what they say. Try to take their advice, if possible. This makes them feel responsible.

Like a child, a mother should be en-

couraged to say what she means and express herself clearly. No use her saying, 'You *know* why I'm cross'; she should say *why* she is cross.

Have *family discussions* with them in a fairly formal way. Go out for a meal. In the local hamburger joint they're less likely to scream and shout and run out of a room.

What children dread is a mother who is absent, late, ill or neurotic.

Drinking seems to start younger. Beer, cider and wine are being drunk by 10-year-olds, the theory being that they had better get used to it as early as possible. A horrific view.

Panel comments: '*She's sensible about drink. She doesn't let you get drunk. She doesn't give it to you, but she doesn't stop you having it. She brings you up to know your capacity, otherwise BOING! the first time at a party.*'

'*When kids are drunk is when the pushers pounce.*'

Drug addiction The teen years are a time of stress and anxiety, as a teenager gropes his way towards individuality and independence. It's relatively easy to hook a teenager who is uncertain of himself on to drugs. Don't think that drug pushers are sinister-looking men in night-clubs. They are often attractive, well-mannered, charming teenagers and they do it for money or free drugs. They use peer pressure ('everyone else does'), persuasion ('one won't hurt you') and sympathy ('never mind, here try this'). One more alcoholic drink than he is used to, one pep pill offered by a pretty girl, one downer to ease the next morning's hangover and the teenager may well be heading for addiction. At any sign of odd or unusual behaviour discuss the matter with his teacher, who may have noticed similar changes. Most schools are well informed on this problem and can advise where to seek help on teenage addictions.

Electronic machinery Except for

DOWN WITH SUPERWOMAN!

the TV, children shouldn't operate machinery. Unfortunately, children are often the only people who can work the video.

Exasperation (theirs with you) Inevitable. One 11-year-old summed up the situation by drawing a birthday card for his mother. It was a portrait of the artist shooting his mother through the stomach with a gun that shot heart-shaped bullets. 'I love you' was embroidered on the unfortunate woman's sweater. The caption read: 'At times I feel I could shoot you.'

Experience (yours) They will never learn from it. Don't ever relate your childhood to theirs; it only makes you seem older and dimmer.

Food Panel comments: *'She's got to have plenty of food available.'*

'She doesn't insist on you eating what you don't want.'

'She's got to be a good cook, capable of cooking basic English food without burning it . . . risotto, pizza . . . that sort of thing.'

'She tries to encourage you to be able to cook because otherwise you have to get married when you leave school.'

They'll eat when they're hungry. Don't forcibly feed them, just don't provide any alternative items. Read *Feeding Your Family: a guide to healthy and delicious food* by Dr Miriam Stoppard (published by Penguin Books).

Free time (theirs) This should be made clear. You should not interfere in their free time or tell them that they're wasting it.

Free time (yours) A couple of pauses between interruptions.

Friends (their attitude to yours) A source of profit. When your eldest shows signs of becoming a card-sharp, con man or two-arm bandit and fleeces your guests of pound notes with the three-card trick, console yourself by thinking that maybe it's not so important that he hasn't passed his exams.

Friends (your attitude to theirs) Total acceptance. A friend can change overnight into a wet, who is ignored; you are supposed to know when a friend has metamorphosed into a wet.

Getting up in the morning and going to bed at night If you never set a time for your children to go to bed, but insist that they are *out of bed* and standing in front of you at 7 a.m. (or whenever) they adapt to going to bed at a reasonable time.

Godparents Who can they talk to about their problems when their parents are their problems? A godparent should be someone they can run away to for the next eighteen years. The ideal godparent is someone the child feels will respect his confidence and won't tell his parents.

A godparent's traditional duty is to see that the child is instructed in religion when he is old enough: some godparents interpret this as 'not before 16'.

Gran Has the experience but not the responsibility. A bit of spoiling doesn't hurt.

Great expectations (yours) You are their good example. A child's role models are his parents. Your children are going to do what you do, not what you say. My children never listened to a thing I said. But I noticed that they copied what I did.

Are you prepared to be as angelic as you want them to be? It's surprising how noisy, undisciplined, unreasonable, thoughtless, careless and badly behaved some parents can be.

Incidentally, quiet, obedient, well-behaved children can grow up into wimps. High-spirited, adventurous, curious, questing children are naughty when young (and possibly naughty when old), but are likely to grow into interesting and independent adults.

Great expectations (yours and theirs) Why do they appear to regard you as a paragon of perfection and yet criticize you constantly? Make it clear that you aren't Mary Poppins. You are doing the best you can and no one can do better than that.

A mother should be herself. Don't try to be what you think they want.

Panel comment: *'When you're young, you tend to think that your parents are perfect because they say they are. They say your father's always right. It's nicer if she makes it quite clear that they're not perfect because nobody is. So she mustn't expect you to be perfect.'*

Home Beg them to treat the home like a hotel; they treat hotels much better.

In his home there should be some space that belongs only to the child. Ideally, it's his own bedroom, to decorate as he wishes. Whether it's a cupboard or merely the space under his bed, it is *his* territory and should be respected (and after he's 8 not tidied by you).

Homework If this is being done late at night or not at all, try laying a tea-tray on the table for homework. The child goes straight from the front door to the table, which he doesn't leave until homework is finished.

Getting him up early the next day is impractical and does not work nearly so well.

If homework is supposed to take a certain time (ask his teacher what time is allowed), carry a kitchen timer in your pocket and take away the work when time is up – even if he is in mid-sentence. Both he and the school will then know his true work capacity. He will eventually enjoy freedom after homework, instead of having it hang over him all evening.

Housework If you want a good man, grow your own. Who is responsible for men behaving as if housework is not their concern? The person who brought them up, that's who. Raise your sons to do it and your daughters to expect men to share equally the work of running a home.

Ideas Always try to adopt a child's ideas (unaltered) whenever practical. It encourages them to have more and better ideas.

Independence As with sparrows, a parent's aim is to rear an independent child. Gently edge it out of the nest when the time comes. Don't complain or obstruct if it leaves earlier of its own accord without a second thought or backward glance at you.

Jealousy It hits them at times, like it hits you, and they have to sort out the green spikes by themselves, like you do.

Karma and other esoteric words. Do not ask what they mean. You're not *supposed* to know.

Labour Don't use your children as unpaid casual labour, to run errands or do small jobs, simply because they are *there*. I was cured of this when my 12-year-old son gave me six handpainted vouchers for Christmas, each entitling me to one free job. I hoarded these vouchers for really vile jobs rather than waste them on small jobs, like running to the corner grocer. I found that, magically, these small jobs disappeared.

Lies (theirs) You can't stop them or even recognize them, any more than your mother could. Don't worry. Incidentally, don't lie about his age to hide your own.

Lies (yours) Panel comment: *'She must tell the truth. She mustn't say if you pick your nose your hair will go green, I mean, that's straight lies.'*

Love Nothing material matters – what they eat, what they wear or whether they're clean – if children feel secure and loved.

What makes them love you? When, without a word, you give them your jacket after they've refused to wear theirs to the match and it rains, like you said it would.

Manners Panel comments: *'She must treat you like a grown-up if she wants you to behave like a grown-up.'*

'Nowadays, she can kiss you in public but not as if she wanted to.'

'She doesn't argue with your father. They shouldn't really throw things. Not wine glasses, eggs or anything. Violence breeds violence, you know. Real pacifist parents mean you'll grow up peaceful.'

DOWN WITH SUPERWOMAN!

Money Panel comments: *'A good mother is sensible about money. She isn't mean but she doesn't give you money whenever you want it. But she should give you pocket money as soon as you're old enough to go into a shop.'*

'She doesn't spoil you, doesn't give you things except at Christmas and birthday. If you tell her you want something, she waits until Christmas to give it to you. She wouldn't faint if you wanted a bike.'

Motto (yours) is DO AS YOU WOULD BE DONE BY. Ideally, they should have the same motto, but it generally takes a child a long time to learn why.

Music in a child's bedroom. Of course you have to allow it, but only within certain times (not before 7 a.m. or after 10 p.m.) and not loud enough to upset the neighbours.

Naughtiness Lively children can be a nuisance, but every teacher knows that the high spirits, dash and daring that lead a child into escapades are often signs of individuality that will prove him an interesting get-up-and-goer when he leaves school. Children that are easily led by others grow up into followers, not leaders.

However, if your child is considered *bad*, and his teacher thinks that his behaviour is likely to lead to a serious social problem, ask for guidance from the school's counsellor, if there is one. If there isn't one, the school can put you in contact with the Child Guidance Clinic.

Neglect A certain neglect is healthy. When the litter in his room is waist-high and you can't open the door he'll ask your advice on which shirt to wear, praise your cooking and say you're a wonderful mother.

Nudity is seen as a natural part of life; it's only the wets with *'good'* mothers who make furtive, feeble jokes. But this enlightened attitude prompts questions – they prod your breasts with a small frown as if you were a bit of meat, and say

'Why do they go flat as a pancake when you're lying down and then float to the top in the bath?' And of course you don't know.

Opinions (theirs) might well be worth listening to.

Opinions (yours) Panel comment: *'She must state her opinions clearly and reasonably. Like, if she doesn't want you to have a bike, she says so QUIETLY, then shuts up.'*

Personal appearance (theirs) Panel comments: *'In clothes, she's got to guide you, but she shouldn't make remarks about your choice.'*

'She should get you into jeans at an early age. (Burst of agreement then pause, while they all looked dreamily reminiscent.) That first pair of jeans, what a thrill.'

Personal appearance (yours) Panel comments: *'She's got to be quite young, really, but not blonde, unless she's really that colour. Otherwise they look like wars; well wars is how they spell them. With a nice motherly figger, not some sex symbol.'*

'She is well groomed. She has her hair done before coming to your school. Her hair should look nice, like she says yours should. She doesn't say anything at all about your hair-style so long as it's clean.'

'For school occasions, she should wear something ordinary and no hat. Joe's mother turned up wearing a young-type see-through pink lace outfit. When he told her ... truthfully, mind you, exactly what she looked like, well, that was the end of Sports Day.'

Playing alone in the street is not a good idea in town for children under 12. Street life has recently become far more vicious. Children aren't streetwise and you don't want yours to hit the headlines. There's nothing wrong with a group in a neighbour's enclosed back garden (away from the road) so long as you know where your child is and which adult is looking after him.

See children on to the bus and see that they sit downstairs. Try to avoid the city Tube.

Pocket money, if given regularly, teaches a child to budget and plan, even if it's only to buy marbles. If you don't give pocket money, they steal from your purse.

Their pocket money is theirs to spend when and on what they like, whether they spend it on bull's-eyes or cricket bats. The amount depends on what it has to cover. If it's entirely for frivolity (a bad idea), then the cost of two comics and two pounds of apples. I prefer an *earned*, regular payment for regular tasks. Don't be conned into giving them more by what they tell you other children get.

Be polite to children – your own as well as those of other people. If you treat your child with respect, eventually he will treat you with respect and he will grow up to have a clear sense of self-worth.

Possessions What's theirs is theirs and yours is not to wonder why, throw away or even disturb.

Power is what everyone wants. (It's called getting your own way.) Power is what you have, as Queen of the Hearth. Give a child some power. Allow *him* to make the rules within his territory, time, money and decisions.

Privacy Children want it for the same reasons as you. If you respect their privacy, they are more likely to respect yours.

Panel comments: *'She shouldn't go into your bedroom. She doesn't knock and walk in, she knocks and WAITS.'*

'She doesn't use your bed for her visitors. That makes you pretty angry. She wouldn't like it if, without asking mind you, she found that you had had your friends in her bed.'

Punishment How strict should it be? They'll scorn you and will never have any respect for you or learn discipline unless you punish when you say you will. Don't weaken.

Never strike a child in cold blood and if he strikes you, dodge.

Establish rules, with pre-arranged punishments when they are broken. Let them decide these with you, then they know what risk they run.

These punishments shouldn't be a deprivation of the child's power (money/time/territory). What is left, you may wonder?

Quarrels Don't take anyone's side in a quarrel. Let them bicker – they enjoy it – until the noise gets to window-rattling pitch. (*'Why should I be punished? We were quarrelling perfectly happily,'* an aggrieved 12-year-old once said to me.)

Big, noisy quarrels are not so irritating or exasperating as a constant background of bickering and whining, the ancillary tale-telling and unctuous pleas for sympathy: 'Did you *see* that, Mummy? He *hit* me! AAAAaaagh!' This is what erodes a mother's patience. (What does she want for her birthday? Ear-plugs of course.)

A mother should be **reasonable**, she should act and speak with reason. 'Because I say so', is not reasonable, even if you've just walked under a flour bomb.

Panel comment: *'She's got to stick to reason when she tells you to do something. It's irritating to always go on about sitting with your back straight but you UNDERSTAND if she explains that otherwise you'll end up a hunchback like your father.'*

Recreation (theirs) Panel comments: *'She should encourage you to be creative. You get these Philistines because their parents never showed them how to make things.'*

'She encourages you in your hobbies. About paying for the equipment for your hobbies, it's fair if she pays half and you pay half, then you're not likely to be so wasteful with it and you learn the value of money. Of course she has to give you enough pocket money to pay for your half and of course the trick is getting everything called equipment.'

'She should show interest in your hobby and THINK about it. You can see when

she says "Yes, it's a lovely model" without really thinking about the tank.'

Recreation (yours) Panel comment: *'She should have a hobby, that's essential. Otherwise she disintegrates when you leave home and you get guilt.'*

Respect (yours for them) A child likes to be treated as if he is a person and not a disobedient pet. When children are treated with respect – listened to and disagreed with as carefully and respectfully as you would if contradicting the Vicar – when they see that their opinion counts because it has just changed a decision, a child feels wanted and valued.

If you don't want your daughters to grow up to feel unsure, inadequate, anxious, placatory and with no self-confidence, treat them with respect.

Rewards, praise and positive encouragement give better results than punishment, psychologists say.

Rules Three is the most that a mother can enforce at any one time without going out of her mind. For example:

1 Anything you put on the floor you must expect to see trodden on by clumsy grown-ups.
2 Life is unfair. (I didn't like it when they quoted this back to me.) This cuts out the whole business of 'It's not fair' by making it clear that that's the way life is.
3 A joke is funny only once. Vital when you start to feel you couldn't bear to hear the one about the parrot and the sealing wax again, especially after you've heard his father tell it for the last ten years.

School reports Panel comments: *'She doesn't say something is great if it isn't, she doesn't say anything if your report is bad, she says carry on and do better.'*

'She must realize that reports don't always tell the truth. Basically they are right but not in all aspects. When it says "Not too good" or "Slightly weak", she

must realize that it's silly to let one report ruin the whole holiday.'

'If a report is good, she should say "Good" and NOTHING ELSE. If it's bad, she should blow you up and then forget it, unless you're clever but haven't been working. Then she should use straight threats: supervised work during the holiday, that sort of thing. The point is, she doesn't drag it on too long.'

Sex deviations Prepare them casually and tell them to watch out. My eldest, when 12, once cried, 'Guess what, today I met my first sex maniac and, Mummy, he was just like you said, all rabbity-faced with spectacles and a raincoat with the collar turned up.'

Panel comments: *'What about homosexuality? Well, what about it? There's nothing you can do really, is there?'*

Sex instruction Answer *all* their questions in a laconic, matter-of-fact voice. Sound casual, not earnest.

Panel comments: *'She should see you know the proper facts and how to do it. She shouldn't just leave a book in the sitting room about how goldfish do it.'*

'She should have lots of sex books just lying around as if by accident.'

'She should never be embarrassed. She should be frank about sex and she should never tell you lies like babies are brought by the stork.'

'She shouldn't tease you.' (The only thing the panel constantly repeated was 'She shouldn't tease you.')

Sexual diseases: Warn them clearly until *they* can explain to you *how* sexual diseases are transferred. Do this before they're old enough to catch them.

Shopping Always unbelievably nerve-shattering, whether it's for hooded rats or regulation grey flannel.

Let a **sneak** (even a tiny golden-haired one) see that you have no time for it.

Step-parents shouldn't try to step into somebody else's shoes, but slowly build a *different* relationship. My sons love their stepmother. When I asked her how she had avoided the pitfalls of step-parentdom, she said she had tried never to treat them like sons, but like people.

Expect a conflict of loyalties from step-children who are loyal to their parents, however undeserving. It can be as bewildering and destructive to a child as a Stalinist purge to be told (directly or by insinuation) to do a mental somersault and erase his father from his memory, to be told that the official line on his Dad now is that he is a traitor to the family and so is mentally being sent to Siberia, to be replaced by another man chosen by Mum to whom the child will now instantly transfer his loyalty and love.

Always **support** a child as much as possible in whatever it is trying to do.

Swearing is no longer chic among the young, so you shouldn't have a problem.

The systems support work Panel comments: '*She's got to be tough right at the beginning and teach you housework as soon as you're old enough to make a bed.*'

'*She should make your bed if you haven't made it very well.*'

'*She mustn't be a sort of slave to you. Mothers can easily slip into the role of being the family servant, you know. She ought to make you all help.*'

Table manners Discourage throwing, dropping or spitting food, gobbling food, starting to eat before everyone has arrived at the table or leaving before everyone has finished eating. Make it clear you expect them to sit up straight, keep their elbows off the table and offer dishes to the people on either side before helping themselves.

Tantrums (theirs) Ignore them. Once a child discovers that tantrums *work* as an attention-getting device, you will obviously get more tantrums. Go to a different room or put the screamer somewhere else. When the child has calmed down, always discuss the reason for his tantrum. If you always do this, he'll eventually realize that tantrums are a waste of time.

Temper (yours) Panel comment: '*She must have a very cool temper. She mustn't get het up over petty things. Like the way you pack or catching trains.*'

How to get a child to clean its **teeth** properly: I don't know why this works, but it did for me and other mothers have reported similar success. One morning, tired of sitting opposite two pairs of green fangs at breakfast, I asked my sons 'If I bought you an expensive bit of equipment, say a *really good* stereo, would you look after it properly?'

'Yes, yes,' they said eagerly.

'Teeth are expensive equipment,' I said.

Travelling games If you want to keep the peace and can afford it, get a Sony Walkman as soon as a child is old enough to listen to it (6 or 7).

Otherwise, children are more likely to be good if encouraged to make a noise (singing in a car, for instance). However, there are just so many times a mother can listen to 'Ten Green Bottles' bawled off-key by three pairs of lungs.

Children bicker when they're bored on long journeys, so suggest a few games – old favourites seem to be best. Family favourites are: THE MOST (who can spot the most shops, or red cars, or boats within a time limit of, say, ten minutes); I SPY (choose objects from inside or outside the car and give the first letter of the word it starts with); WHAT TO TAKE ON A DESERT ISLAND (name six favourite foods/drinks/animals/books/people).

Take a bag of little prizes (nothing to eat in case they are sick). Stock up at Christmas when there are plenty of cheap rubbishy stocking fillers around.

Umpire Whoever the child trusts. Never Dad. Grans are often good. Possibly an older child, an uncle, a teacher or a godparent.

Vices (such as cheating, stealing, lying, prevarication) These are regarded as vile crimes by schools, so hopefully they will be dealt with at school. If your child persists, discuss it with his teacher.

Worry The invisible umbilical cord that will always join you to your child.

DOES THE SCHOOL PASS YOUR EXAM?

It's your responsibility, *not* that of the school, to see that your children get the best possible education, and I think that is all you owe them in life. This need not necessarily cost you money, but it will cost you time and attention.

How can parents help their children?

Be interested in the child's work (which is as real as a parent's job) and in all school activities (fathers as well as mothers), even those that do not seem to concern your child.

Keep in touch with your child's teachers. Children are now assessed all the time and your teacher should be up to date in all areas of your child's work.

Make sure that a child understands that all work done in the classroom as well as work done on his own counts towards his GCSE grades. Far more importance is laid on understanding the subject rather than giving pat answers to set questions because GCSE shows better than exam results whether a child has been well taught.

Make sure that any homework is done in pre-agreed hours at home, so that it doesn't loom over all a child's free time.

Do your homework first

If you are new to a district, phone the Local Education Authority for a list of state and independent schools. They usually offer quite a good synopsis of each. Phone for prospectuses from other schools. Peruse them all carefully and make a short-list.

Before choosing a school, carefully consider the journey. Girls, especially, miss out on after-school activities because parents fear hazards of travel after dark.

Heads are overworked and harassed people, who will not thank you for asking questions that you can easily answer for yourself.

Phone the schools and find out the open days, when parents can see around the school, watch lessons, interview staff, etc. Try to speak to the pupils – usually Sixth Formers show you round and are less wary than staff.

Try to drop in to an event not intended for prospective parents, such as a carol concert, play, sports day, fête. This will not be put on just to impress and you will see the staff and pupils being themselves.

All schools produce a school magazine. Borrow or buy one. It will give you a fair indication of all activities, the standard of writing and art, exam results (though these can always be doctored and are never reliable).

Ask the School Secretary to show you the last Prize-Giving programme, which will give you the list of exam results. (Ask the Head how many actually sat the exams.)

If you can, talk to other parents and present pupils about their schools; children will be devastatingly honest if they trust you and will probably surprise their parents with their answers.

Even if you like the school, if you don't like the Head, forget it.

How to interview the Head

Start off with *the right attitude*. Don't be anxious, obsequious or unnaturally reticent. *You* are the one who is conducting this examination. A headteacher told me that nowadays the Head is far more frightened of a parent than a parent of the

Head. The Head wants to keep his job; he knows he is being watched critically by the school governors, the Local Education Authority (LEA) and also by the parents (state schools now have parents on the Board).

Wear casual, very clean clothes (brush your shoulders). Nothing polyester. Sports jacket and skirt or trousers is acceptable. No jeans. Nothing sexy.

If both parents can't be present at the meeting, take a pocket tape recorder and at the interview ask permission to use it, so that the recorder is seen not as a threat but as a simple way of ensuring that your unavoidably absent but *deeply concerned* mate knows what went on. Otherwise, make notes of what was said as quickly as possible.

Some of your exam questions

Don't think your questions may be misconstrued as aggressive and that, as a result, your child may suffer. What a good Head wants is *concerned parents*.

What is the pupil to teacher ratio? If it's over one teacher to ten pupils, classes may suffer as a result of lack of individual attention and rowdiness from lack of discipline. Classes should not have more than twenty pupils.

Does the Head think that the pupil to teacher ratio is a good balance? Why?

What is the school attitude to discipline and how is it enforced? (Does this seem reasonable to you?) Is corporal punishment used? (Corporal punishment is now banned in state schools, of course.)

What is the school attitude to drinking, smoking, sex and drugs among its pupils and among its teachers? Does this tricky area seem reasonable to you?

How does the school stress that academic school subjects and technical subjects are of equal importance in today's world?

How does the school stress the importance of working with your hands?

What art subjects are encouraged? Paint-

ing? Sculpture? Design? History of art? Photography? Drama?

What crafts are encouraged? Metalwork? Pottery? Weaving? Printing? Dress design? Carpentry? (Even more necessary for girls than for boys?) Cookery for both sexes?

What combined design and technology courses are there? (Such as Craft, Design, Technology GCSE course.)

Music – what instruments are taught? How many specialist teachers are there? What choirs, what orchestras, what outside engagements, what concerts are offered?

Make sure that the school curriculum is diverse but not too all-embracing. A school that offers too many subjects may not be able to teach them all thoroughly. If the school offers them, they will probably teach them thoroughly, but too many schools, particularly independent ones, force pupils to take ten to twelve GCSE subjects so they can't cope with arts activities.

How much homework is there? Do the teachers take time into account when deciding how much homework a child can produce during a week? This is a running battle between parents, teachers, departments and pupils; there has to be give and take.

Apart from exams, how does the school evaluate its pupils? By profiling? All schools have to keep academic, behaviour and social profiles on every pupil available to teachers, parents and pupils.

Are the extra-curricular activities held after school, and if so, does this leave enough time for homework? Extra-curricular subjects bring out a child's self-confidence and individual talents.

What extra-curricular subjects does the school offer? Cookery? Sewing? First aid? Drama, music, singing, public speaking, film club, theatre visits, school magazine, puppetry?

Is there a debating society? This is particularly important as it teaches a child to think fast on his feet, be articulate, stand up for his views and be prepared to see the other person's viewpoint. Does the debating society compete in competitions, such as local public speaking or inter-schools contests?

Are there any lectures given by outside speakers – for example, old pupils, parents and local interesting speakers such as the MP or the chief of the fire brigade?

What are the school clubs? Photography? Stamp collecting? Sketching? Swimming? Chess? Computers? Films? History? Science? Drama?

What are the school-organized holiday projects? A visit to a French sister-school? Other foreign exchange visits to Russia, Greece, Italy, Germany? Camping trips?

What are the school communal responsibility projects? As a child grows older, he should acquire responsibilities: he is not only part of a family and a school, he is part of a community, a country and a planet.

What are the community work projects? Visiting the elderly? Shopping for the sick? Collecting money for charity or working for the Third World with sponsored walks or swims.

Bob Geldof's Ethiopia famine appeal showed children that one young(ish), unknown person *could* make a difference to the world. He organized and united the ordinary people of the world, not to make war but to help the unfortunate.

What is the religious attitude of the school? Is Religious Instruction (often known as RI or Humanities) denominational (a specific religion such as Roman Catholic) or ecumenical (concerning the United Christian Church throughout the world except for Roman Catholics)?

Confirm that the school teaching covers a description of all major religions of the world, as well as arguments for being agnostic (usual today to meet multi-ethnic admissions).

What sex education does a school offer, how is sex taught and at what age? (Most primary schools teach sex at 10–11 years.)

What is the school's attitude to games? Not too obsessional, you may hope. On the other hand, you want them to be able to spot and encourage your potential Olympic champion.

Does the school offer some alternative to competitive sports? Such as swimming, walking, running, aerobics, gym, dancing, golf, skating, squash, badminton, riding or dry skiing?

How are students prepared for the real world? Young Enterprise Schemes are countrywide: Sixth Formers run their own businesses, make products, sell shares. What does this school do?

YOUR ATTITUDE TO EXAMS

I like to think that exams aren't only a test of the child, but also of the teachers. Don't pay too much attention to exam results: naturally exams are important, but they are not all-important. Exams are only all-important until they have been passed. How long is it since somebody asked you what A levels you got? If a child doesn't pass an exam, well, that's that, but it isn't the end of the world. You don't want a child to be terrified of failure. Failure is part of life and children should learn how to handle it.

You can't control whether or not your child gets good exam results, but you can encourage an eager attitude to exams. A friend of mine always behaved as if exams were the most exciting thing in the world. Her children had special breakfasts before exams and special teas afterwards, and she listened to the child's account of the exams as though it were as exciting as a Grand Prix. My daughter-in-law's parents bought bicycles for their children *before* taking O levels as a reward for five years' hard work.

Exams are stressful, but they develop determination, tenacity and fortitude – all valuable characteristics in the world beyond school. Exams encourage championship behaviour, which is simply being always able to produce your best performance at will.

When commenting on exam (or school) results, accentuate the positive and play down the negative. The child that is frightened of exams and reports is a child that won't grow up to enjoy the process of learning by himself – and that should be the ultimate aim of an education.

HOW DO YOU CHOOSE A STATE SCHOOL FOR YOUR CHILD?

Or change his present school if you are not satisfied? Where do you get correct and comprehensive information about state schools? What are your rights if fighting the authorities?

A parent has three basic rights: the right to choose a child's school, the right to information that will enable the parent to choose the most appropriate school for the child and the right to appeal if the child doesn't get a place at the chosen school, when there is no reason why he shouldn't. Thirty per cent of appeals are successful.

If you decide to change your child's school, you have all the rights that you had on your previous choice. You are legally entitled to request a place at a school outside your county or Local Education Authority (LEA), if you have good reason.

Each state school has distinctive strengths and weaknesses. Each state school is legally obliged to provide an easily obtainable prospectus giving details about its educational, social and religious attitudes; secondary schools also have to publish full details of all their examination results. Each LEA is obliged to provide easily obtainable information for parents about the schools in its area.

Choosing the best school for your child – primary, secondary, state or private – can be a study in itself. A concerned parent's A-level textbook is *Choosing a State School – How to find the best education for your child* (published in paperback by Hutchinson). With a zero-level fog index, it is well laid out and clearly written by Caroline Cox, Robert Balchin and John Marks, all of whom have good qualifications and whose children have attended state schools.

Their message is clear. If you want a child to get the best possible education at a state school, the parents have to put a lot of effort into checking the schools and choosing the school, then monitoring the school and taking part in as many school activities as possible.

If you are one of those parents who doesn't know where to start, what to look for or what questions to ask, this book shows how to compare different state schools in your area (compare the exam results of each school and then compare them with the national average; the book provides an easy system to do so).

It also includes check-lists of suggested questions. A query specifically for a primary school is: '*Do there appear to be any disruptive pupils?*' The presence of just a few disruptive children in a school can cause problems out of all proportion to their number. All schools have one or two difficult pupils. How are they dealt with so that they do not disturb the education of the majority? What punishments does the school use? What back-up from LEA and the governors does the Head receive if he or she wishes to suspend a pupil?

When reading a secondary school prospectus, the book suggests questions that include: What different subjects are available for GCSE? Does the school have a Sixth Form? How many pupils go on to higher or further education? How many school-leavers get jobs fairly quickly?

The book also gives information on

DOWN WITH SUPERWOMAN!

children with special needs. For instance, you may be entitled to free transport if your child has to travel more than two miles to a primary school or three miles to a secondary school; your child may be suitable for one of the 5,500 assisted places that are available each year at independent schools. About 6 per cent of the children in the UK are educated at independent schools, but these obtain about 50 per cent of all A grades awarded.

SCHOOL HOLIDAYS

The original reason for the long summer holiday was so that the children could help get the harvest in. This no longer applies.

I think it is bad for children to have such a long, undisciplined break in which they forget what they have learned and get out of the habit of learning.

In addition, the mid-term break, which used to be an extra day on a weekend, is now often a full week: this is not for the convenience of the child but for that of the teachers. These insidiously stretching mid-term holidays are an organizational nightmare for working mothers. Mid-term holidays should be put back to one extra day on the weekend (which a mother can always take off as a holiday) and four weeks maximum in the summer.

A headteacher's views of school holidays

'In a hundred years' time British teach-ing methods will be viewed in the same way as we view chimney boys. I think the whole process of school education is unnatural and, for some, barbaric, and the holidays are the only time when many children feel normal and free.

'Children need at least three months holiday a year just to *be* children. They need it for health reasons – to sleep, swim, cycle, walk, etc. They need it to develop the skills and interests which may be force-fed into them at school but where they have little time to enjoy reading, painting, cooking, writing and music or visiting museums, historic houses, libraries or the zoo.

'A week's half-term holiday is essential for many reasons. Pupils need the Whit-week half-term to revise for GCSE, A levels and school exams. Teachers have to catch up with work during this week (I set and type school exams). Many adults now get six weeks' holiday a year and want to go away out of season, and many now go on skiing holidays. Many schools use half-term holidays to take pupils on special trips abroad. You do not get student rates at peak holiday times.

'Teachers are badly paid: they regard the long holidays as a period in which they can earn extra money by marking exams or coaching, can prepare and read for the following term, can accompany a group of children on a school trip or develop their own interests – a major perk of a badly paid job.'

SEX
MANIACS

○ RAPE CRISIS
CENTRES
○ London :-
(enquiries) 071-278-3956
(counselling) 071-837-1600
(24 hr line)

Edinburgh - 031-556-9437

○ Belfast - 0232-249696
○

Sexual aggression from a stranger may take the form of:

1 Obscene telephone calls.
2 Frottism (such as being rubbed up against in a crowded train or bus).
3 Indecent exposure (such as showing genitals to little girls in a park).
4 Letter threats to rape, maim or kill.
5 Odd burglaries involving violation (such as urinating on the bed) or the theft of fetish objects such as frilly knickers or black suspender belts.
6 Peeping Toms.
7 Unintentional rape (sometimes called 'going too far').
8 Attempted rape.
9 Rape.
10 Child molestation.

A man, or any woman who has not experienced any of these forms of sexual aggression, might find it difficult to comprehend why minor cases are so frightening and why women are so 'unreasonable' about them. About telephone calls, one woman said: 'I found the unreality, the nightmare lunacy aspect, the most difficult because the police didn't seem to understand *why* I was frightened, because nothing had happened.' A strapping, normally self-assured 6-foot blonde said: 'What I most hated was being instantly turned into a gibbering idiot by some cowardly twit on the end of a telephone.'

Other comments were: 'It's the unprotected feeling. You feel stark naked and vulnerable. It might happen any time of the day or night. You're powerless to stop it and you're at his mercy. You're helpless.' 'The police don't seem to think that threatened sexual assault is important. Assault doesn't seem to be an important crime unless it's on a policeman. Motoring offences and smoking dope, that's the sort of thing they seem to take seriously.'

What a woman wants when she is

231

being sexually threatened by a stranger is PROTECTION. She also wants sympathy and understanding. Often it is not possible for the police to give her any of these things to the degree that will allay her fright.

A senior CID officer commented: 'If a person has been offended against, no matter in how minor a way, that person feels aggrieved; therefore, as far as the police are concerned, it is an offence and the duty of the policeman to investigate and assist the aggrieved person inasmuch as he is able.' '... inasmuch as he is able.' That's the crunch.

Policewomen may, but policemen in general can have no conception of *why* a woman is frightened by a mystery prowler or heavy breathing down the telephone. This is because they are the wrong sex: they are not frightened of a man because they *are* men. This attitude is apparent in some of the things they say, some of which are hurtful. DO NOT LET THESE PHRASES UPSET YOU.

'Is he a friend of yours?' (Thirty-one per cent of rape convictions involve casual acquaintances, such as a neighbour who enters a single woman's home on some pretext.)

'Have you broken up with a boyfriend lately?'

'What makes you think this man is threatening you?'

'Are you sure you weren't encouraging him?'

'Well, you must have been doing *something*.'

'We'll keep an eye on the place' (i.e., drive past now and then).

'We'll have a squad car over right away' (twenty-three minutes later at the earliest, with enough flashing lights to announce a royal wedding procession).

'Don't you worry now.'

'You're perfectly safe inside.'

The police certainly get plenty of frivolous complaints or complaints made by women who are unnaturally nervous or mentally disturbed and which, when investigated, prove groundless. For instance, steady footsteps behind you at night across the darkened common might not necessarily mean that a man is following you. His route from the bus stop might be the same as yours.

To expect automatic protection in every case is impractical. Be sensible. The police haven't got the men or the money. They can't give twenty-four-hour protection to the recipient of every obscene telephone call or it would cost at least three policemen's salaries per year per protégée. Sympathy you may get, but not always protection or understanding.

So what should you do if you or one of your family is frightened by sexual aggression from a stranger? A senior CID officer, Barbara Kelly, helped me to compile the following answers.

Try to deal with *obscene telephone calls* by putting the phone down *at once*. Then he's lost his money and got no satisfaction.

'The call may be to assist masturbation,' explained Miss Kelly, 'and that's one good reason to slam the phone down. Of course he may ring again. The essential thing is: *don't reply to him*. Leave the receiver off the hook and cover it with a cushion or a rug.' As soon as you reply you are becoming involved and could even be inveigled into connivance.

The main reason for slamming down the phone is to avoid giving the pervert at the other end the satisfaction he achieves by frightening and flummoxing you. Such people are often sexually inadequate and do not feel they are 'men'. They feel they lack power and potency. So the more distressed you get, the happier they are to be proving to themselves that they *do* have a sort of sexual power over you – the power to upset you. So replace your receiver immediately.

Telephone or call at your local police

station and ask to speak to the duty officer to report what has happened. It is then up to the police to decide objectively on the gravity of the situation and what they can legally do. Remember that, for good reasons, the police are trained to keep calm, keep a poker face and proceed methodically. They should be unbiased towards one side or the other. They can't do much about a frightened woman, but they understand that in these cases a woman can't always control her emotions.

Understandably, Scotland Yard have asked me not to reveal their methods of dealing with obscene telephone calls, but if a pattern starts to emerge, then action is taken. One of the obvious things that the police can do is get your telephone number changed fast and kept secret. Inconvenient, but generally effective.

If you receive *obscene, anonymous letters* try not to talk about them. Take them straight to the police.

Obviously you would contact the police as soon as possible after a burglary, so they would quickly learn of any details other than theft, such as messing the carpet. Burglary can feel like a minor sort of rape. It results in the same sort of shock of uncleanness, of being violated, of sudden, unexpected violence.

The best way to treat *indecent exposure* is to ignore it and walk on. Try to move away from the man who is pressing against you in a train, bus or lift.

The way to deal with *peeping Toms* is to cover yourself up and inform the police. If you haven't any curtains to draw, pin a sheet over the window until you can make curtains.

Stealing knickers is a well recognized minor fetish, so the police advise you never to leave any underwear on the washing line. It's asking for trouble, they say.

If you feel a *groping hand* in a darkened cinema or other closed space you could say loudly and clearly, 'KINDLY TAKE YOUR HAND OFF MY KNEE,' whereupon

he will skid off. Alternatively, change seats *at once*, keeping an eye on the man. 'If he thinks you've merely moved and aren't going to report him, he'll probably stay in the cinema,' says Miss Kelly. '*Then* slip off and ask the usherette for the manager, go back and point him out.'

Miss Kelly also advises: 'If a woman can see that she's going to be left alone in a train carriage with a man, she would be wise to move before the train leaves or at any rate at the next station. Similarly, if a man gets into a carriage with a lone woman, he might think of moving: there are unbalanced *women* as well as unbalanced men you know.'

RAPE

What is the likelihood of your being raped? At time of writing rape is one of the fastest growing crimes in Britain. The figures for England and Wales during the past ten years show an 85 per cent increase, even though it is estimated that 44 per cent of attacks are not reported to the police.

Avoidance is best

Easily the best method of dealing with rape, say the police, is avoidance. Particularly after dark, avoid lonely places such as commons, churchyards, alleys and waste land. On the street, especially at night and in unfamiliar surroundings, be alert at all times. If a bad or potentially bad situation starts developing, the safest thing to do is run. Head for a shop building or lighted area where people are likely to be. Yell 'HELP!', go to a nearby house, knock on the door and ask to telephone the police. Don't feel silly.

Hitch-hiking can be a serious hazard for a lone woman. A girl who's a passenger may have no means of escape other than jumping out, maybe while the car is travelling at speed. A car can be a moving

DOWN WITH SUPERWOMAN!

prison, cut off from help from the public. Beware particularly of the male driver who slows down and offers you a lift when you haven't even raised a thumb. If you suspect that a car is following your car for no good reason, *don't* drive home – an attacker may get you as you run for the door – but instead head for the nearest service station or police station, and tell them your suspicion. They will take you seriously.

After four French students that I'd given a lift forced me to take them miles out of my way, I decided that never again would I give a man a lift, not even a student. You shouldn't casually invite a stranger into your house, and you certainly shouldn't invite a man into a car, where you are more vulnerable, and trapped.

Also, be wary of the casual pick-up who may seem decent enough at the art gallery, lunch bar or party (and not really a pick-up), but who turns out *not* to be when you've invited him back home for a cup of coffee. Many situations of possible attempted rape are with pick-ups who don't seem pick-ups to the woman. It can be hard to convince police that you have been forcibly raped if you have to admit that you invited a strange man into your home.

Other streetwise tips

Don't think it's stupid to take these precautions. I learned them in New York, where every street holds potential danger – and every woman knows it.

1 Look confident and as though you know where you are going – even if you don't. Avoid eye contact, but don't look down.
2 If you suspect you are being followed, cross the road to check whether you really are being followed. If you turn around to face the person who is following you, he or she may well walk right past you.

3 Use the street-side edge of the pavement to avoid concealed doorways and bushes. Don't turn sharply around corners – give yourself time to see what's ahead.
4 Always wait for friends under a street lamp or other light. Keep among a crowd.
5 Don't enter a Tube or railway carriage unless it has at least two people in it who are not together. Sit near the door. If the carriage empties, move to another one.
6 Drive with doors locked and windows shut in city centres or unfamiliar neighbourhoods, particularly at red lights.
7 Take radio cabs or black taxis at night if you can afford it. Beware of mini-cabs that approach you (how do you *know* he's a mini-cab driver, not a rapist?) and use only firms that have been recommended to you.
8 Joggers and cyclists should keep to well-lit and populated routes.
9 Walk facing oncoming traffic, and carry a torch if you are out regularly at night.
10 It's worth carrying a personal alarm but only if it's accessible for immediate use, not at the bottom of your handbag.
11 When you enter your front door, make sure you are not followed. Otherwise you risk this scene: *you* stagger in with two shopping bags; while you are putting them down in the hall, *he* whips inside behind you and slams the door shut.

Be wary of, not sympathetic to, any stranger who says that he is lonely: there may be a good reason for this sad state. 'A woman who goes anywhere alone, to a garage, a flat or any closed place, at the invitation of an unknown man or casual acquaintance, is *putting herself at risk*. In fact, unless a woman knows a man very well, she must remember that many cases

234

of complaint have been lured somewhere on a simple and innocent pretext.'

Home security

Try to make your home as secure as you can. 'If it's terribly difficult to get into a place and a sexual marauder has to make a noise, he's less likely to persist.' A burglar opportunist is a minimum risk.

Fit proper locks on doors and windows – this shouldn't be too expensive. Fit security deadlocks on all external doors, either mortice deadlocks that fit into the door itself or rim deadlocks that fit on the back of the door. When you are at home, never leave any doors open and draw the curtains at night.

A telephone extension in your bedroom is a good idea. Practise ringing 999 or the number of your local police station in the dark.

Fit a bright light outside your front door to deter attackers from waiting in the darkness of your doorway. Make sure that there are no bushes or other objects near the front door that could conceal a prowler.

What to do about strange callers? Fit a door chain and viewer, and *use them every time someone calls*. Never let anyone into the house if he claims to represent a public service or company unless he shows you his identity card. All public-service employees carry identity cards and are required to show them. Inspect the card *carefully*. If you are at all suspicious, don't let the man in. You can always ask him to come back later, then arrange for a friend or neighbour to be there with you.

If you live in a building containing several flats, don't give away the fact that you are a single woman on your name-plate or in telephone directories. Just give your initials and surname.

If you are selling your home, don't show people around it on your own. Either arrange for someone you know to be with you or ask the estate agent to send one of its employees with the prospective buyer.

What if you're attacked on the street?

Predictably Miss Kelly said, 'I can't tell women whether or not to defend themselves: all situations are different. So is the timing, the woman's ability and strength, and her level-headedness.

'To introduce more violence into the situation may be disastrous. If you yell, whether it's a scream for help or a blood-curdling battle cry, he may put his hands round your throat to stop you and squeeze too hard and too long.

'However, should you wish to defend yourself, don't be afraid to hurt someone who's hurting you. If you're caught by surprise and don't think you can run away or have nowhere to run to, you might use something you're wearing as a weapon. Probably the best thing is the heel of your shoe (holding the shoe by the sole) or maybe your belt buckle, umbrella or handbag. If your arms are free you might try to stick your fingers in his eyes and if you scratch him hard the marks will be unmistakable as a later possible means of identification.'

If you're grabbed from behind, don't try to flick him over your left shoulder unless you really know what you're doing. Try to stick your elbows backwards and upwards into the top of his solar plexus, just under the centre of the rib-cage. Try it on yourself with your left fist and you'll see that just a little thump leaves you gasping.

What if you're attacked at home?

Should you invest in knives or airguns?

'I can only tell you the law,' said Miss Kelly, looking a trifle uneasy. 'If someone's *trying to enter your house by force*, you can eject him by force or stop

DOWN WITH SUPERWOMAN!

them entering by force. There are certain cases where it is justifiable homicide, and one is if it's the only way to stop a really outrageous crime, such as an attempt to murder or rape, when a woman uses whatever she has to hand, such as an umbrella. Anyone else who comes upon the scene can do likewise.'

I personally think that knives, guns, fake guns and bedside empty milk bottles are dangerous to use against somebody stronger than you since they can be turned against you. It's introducing violence into a situation that *might* have become violent and uncontrollable, and now *certainly* will.

Where to go for help

If you are raped, you are supposed to report it to the police *as soon as possible.*

If you can't face going to the police immediately or talking to a close friend or relative, then contact the nearest Rape Crisis Centre. The service is free. There are centres throughout England, Scotland, Wales and Ireland. To find out where your nearest centre is, look in the phone book or contact one of these centres:

The London Rape Crisis Centre, PO Box 69, London WC1 tel: 071-278 3956 (inquiries – open Mon and Fri only from 10 a.m. to 12.30 and from 2.30 p.m. to 6 p.m.); tel: 071-837-1600 (counselling only – nights and weekends. A recorded message will give the tel. no. of the woman on duty)

Edinburgh Centre, PO Box 120, Edinburgh, EH7 5XX tel: 031-556-9437

Belfast Centre, PO Box 46, Belfast BT2 7AR tel: 0232-249696 (open 10 a.m.– 6 p.m. weekdays, and 11 a.m.–5 p.m. weekends).

The centres will talk to any woman who has been raped and sexually assaul-ted, and will offer sympathetic and practical advice. They feel that women who have been raped need to talk to someone who understands the nature of rape, someone who is not going to disapprove or think less of the victim because of what has happened. The Rape Crisis Centre will provide emergency care. Someone from the centre will accompany you to the police (if you decide to report the crime), VD clinic, doctor or court. The centre will also explain the police and medical procedures that will take place.

IF you have been raped:

1 Tell someone what has happened as soon as possible – it helps to have a witness to your distress. Call a friend or the Rape Crisis Centre.
2 Don't shower, wash or change your clothes – you may be destroying vital evidence.
3 Don't drink alcohol or take any tranquillizers or other drugs. You need a clear head to give a clear account to the police.
4 Take a change of clothes with you; the police may need to keep your original clothing for evidence.
5 Try to remember as much as you can about your attacker; the important things are the sequence of events, details and what was said. Make notes if you can, as soon as you can.
6 Above all, remember that you are the victim of a terrifying attack and should not feel ashamed or guilty.

Going to the police

You will probably be at the police station for several hours. You should be prepared to recount the horror because, as soon as you feel able to talk coherently, the police will want every detail of what happened, where he touched you, etc. This may be humiliating, but it is necessary if they are going to try to trace a man (who has perhaps raped before) and then prosecute him before a judge and jury. You can ask to make your statement to a woman police officer.

Don't expect tea and sympathy from the police. It's not their job to provide it. It's their job to get your statement, get evidence and get after the villain as fast as possible.

A police station is not a hospital. If it's four o'clock in the morning, don't expect them to have hot milk at the ready, or a spare greatcoat or a spare police doctor waiting to examine you. They may need your clothing for scientific examination for blood, seminal and other stains, tearing or other similar evidence for possible use in court. They might have a blanket.

You can be medically examined to support your statement only with your consent. Rape is very difficult to prove medically. What does a doctor look for? Evidence of semen in the vagina and on clothes as well as evidence of internal and external trauma, such as lacerations. You can ask for your own GP or a woman doctor to do the examination. You can telephone a friend or relative from the police station, and normally they will be allowed to telephone you back.

See a doctor

After you have informed the police go, or get someone to take you, to a hospital or doctor.

You have three worries:

1 Disease. A hospital may give rape victims preventative penicillin for VD.

2 You can wait until six weeks after your last period, get a pregnancy test and possibly arrange for an abortion if necessary. In case of extreme anxiety the 'morning after' pill can be taken. This is oestrogen, which is available only on a doctor's prescription. If taken within twenty-four hours of intercourse, this should prevent implantation of a fertilized egg. The oestrogen drug can make some people nauseated and violently ill for the five days it is taken. These factors have to be weighed against the dangers and anxiety of pregnancy. It's preferable to wait and see whether pregnancy has occurred.

3 If you are bruised, cut or even just generally shaken, you may want to get a medical check-up.

If you want a man convicted, possibly deterred from raping others, you have to be prepared to go to court. Your anonymity will be protected, since nothing that might identify you can be reported by the press.

In the 1970s Mr Justice Melford Stevenson was reported in *The Times* to have summed up one rape case saying, 'It was, as rape goes, a pretty anaemic affair,' as he awarded the guilty party a two-year suspended sentence.

This still appears to be a prevalent male attitude and is not confined to judges. If a man's home has ever been vandalized by a burglar, you can tell him that is a tiny little bit like the shock of rape. This is compounded of surprise, then fear, with growing horror, followed by terror, pain, exhaustion, disorientation and fear of possible disease or actual disease and/or pregnancy. It's an unclean feeling that you perhaps can't wash out of your head for weeks or months and which may cause grave psychological damage.

Mud sticks. Rape myths abound. 'No decent girl ever gets raped.' 'Every woman really wants to be raped.' 'A girl gets raped only if she wants to be.' (But how would an 8-stone boxer fare against a 14-stone boxer?)

So if you're raped, that's sad. But what follows when you report it to the police could make you feel worse, unless you

DOWN WITH SUPERWOMAN!

are prepared for it. I know it may be considered antisocial, but I feel that a raped woman may suffer less in the long run if she does not go to the police first, but gets to a doctor or casualty ward as fast as possible and then informs the police.

DANGER AT WORK

During the summer of 1986 a young woman estate agent in Fulham, in south-west London, disappeared after showing a client around a house just before her lunch-time break. Her name was Suzy Lamplugh and no trace of her has ever been found. Her case highlighted the dangers that many women face during work, especially those who spend a lot of time outside their office or work-place or who work unsocial hours.

Estate agents, social workers, chartered surveyors and factory shift workers travelling alone at night are particularly at risk. Once a door has been closed behind you, there is not much you can do to escape if a client reveals himself as a predator. Remember that even a fairly weak man can overpower a strongish woman.

If you are exposed to such situations, please read this chapter again, and take the precautions listed below. None of what follows is a substitute for being AWARE at all times. That means being conscious of your surroundings, of who is around you and where you could run for help if necessary.

If you feel uneasy, make an excuse and leave. Trust your subconscious to spot that something is wrong before you can consciously work out what it is. Get away fast. Any excuse will do. (You think you hear your boss's car. You feel faint. It's time you took your medicine, which is in the car outside.) Work out *now* an excuse that you could plausibly use. In addition:

1 Always take a male client's name, address and telephone number when making an appointment to meet him. Ring him later in the day at that number to confirm the appointment and to say that your boss might come along. Really you are checking that the client can normally be contacted at that number. Write his details down in your office appointment book, the one that you *leave in the office all the time*.

2 If possible, arrange for the client to meet you in the office rather than at a house or site elsewhere. Introduce him to a colleague before leaving.

3 Tell a colleague where you are going and at what time you expect to return.

4 Carry a personal attack alarm and hold it in your hand – an alarm at the bottom of a handbag is useless. These alarms are cheap to buy and are available from DIY shops, department stores, office stationers and hardware stores. It is a good idea to get one that continues to emit piercing screams after it has been dropped. You can also get alarms that fit on to your briefcase.

Sexual harassment at work

Sexual harassment at work is at last being taken seriously. It is any unwanted sexual attention that is pressed on an unwilling person and may threaten that person's job security or create a stressful or intimidating environment.

Sexual harassment takes many forms: unnecessary touching, suggestive remarks, jokes or verbal abuse, demands for sexual favours, leering at someone's body, offering compromising invitations, physical assault, displaying pin-ups and other offensive material.

If you are subject to any of this at work, don't ignore it in the hope that it will go away – it probably won't. Make your attitude clear by writing a note to whoever is causing you distress and explaining how you feel about it. Date the note and keep a copy.

If this doesn't work, start keeping a diary of events, including dates, times and locations; note witnesses. Find out from other women with whom you work whether they have had similar problems; ask them to help you keep your record. If you are eventually going to accuse someone formally of harassment, you must be able to produce the facts of the case. Also take steps to ensure that your colleagues know that your work performance is at least adequate in order to counteract possible later attempts at victimization.

When you have assembled your evidence, go to your boss (if the trouble is being caused by a workmate) or to the appropriate person in management or personnel. Also ask for an appointment with your shop steward or the women's officer of your trade union. Be formal and calm. Explain the situation. Make it clear that you want the harassment to stop. It is then the responsibility of the union or management to sort out your problem.

If this doesn't happen, or if you find it difficult to speak to the appropriate person at work, go to your local law centre or Citizens' Advice Bureau to ascertain your legal rights and for practical advice. You can also contact Women Against Sexual Harassment (WASH), a charity based in London who offer legal and practical advice, with counselling sessions on Thursday evenings by appointment. They can refer you to help in other parts of the country. You can write or telephone to WASH, 242 Pentonville Road, London N1 9UN, tel: 071-833-0222.

Unfortunately, in the case of persistent advances, a woman may have no choice but to hand in her notice. Recent industrial tribunes have accepted that if this is the case, then she has, in effect, been unfairly dismissed and have awarded the woman compensation. The same situation would apply if a woman were fired after complaining of sexual harassment at work.

WHAT SHOULD YOU TELL THE CHILDREN?

The single girl bothered by sexual perverts can sometimes be very young indeed. What can you tell children to protect them without frightening them about any possible child molester?

It's best to be as short, clear and factual as possible in order that there may be no misunderstanding and no mystery. Don't beat about the bush no matter how embarrassed you are. Come out and say it calmly and firmly in a matter-of-fact voice.

Don't merely inform. Try to set up a dialogue so that the child knows that it can ask you or tell you about such things. (If one thing leads to another, two good sex-education books for older children are *Boys and Sex* and *Girls and Sex* by W. B. Pomeroy, published by Penguin Books.)

Exhibitionists and child molesters, commonly called 'dirty old men', are not always dirty and old. Although they can be frightening, they are rarely dangerous and generally act the way they do because they are sad, lonely, depressed, frustrated and immature. A child who comes across one should be told not to panic but to immediately tell a grown-up person whom she trusts, even if she would rather not tell a parent. But a child may not be sure. If in doubt, TELL.

Children who are old enough to travel to school on their own should be taught never to be alone in a lonely sort of place, if possible, and to report as soon as possible anything nasty, silly or upsetting to the nearest grown-up in charge, such as the bus conductor. They should also be told:

DOWN WITH SUPERWOMAN!

1 Never talk to a stranger *who approaches you*. (If a child is lost and asks someone the way, that's different.)
2 Never take sweets or presents from any strange men or women.
3 Never let a stranger touch you anywhere. Not lay a finger on any part of you. If anyone tries, get home as fast as you can or find a policeman.
4 Never get in a strange car or go to a strange place unless it's with someone you know well.
5 Usually, adults have the bottoms of their bodies covered. If you see an adult unzip his trousers, move away fast and tell a grown-up. Always immediately report any 'rude behaviour' to the nearest person in authority, whether it be a schoolmaster or policeman. In fact, anyone in uniform will do, or even a taxi driver.
6 What if it isn't a stranger, but a schoolmaster or uncle who is behaving in an undesirable fashion? Tell your mother as soon as possible. It can be most difficult for a child to inform on someone she knows, so this must be emphasized.

The police add that a child should be taught that whenever he or she is in trouble, lost, without any money or upset in some way, always ask a policeman. If you can't see a policeman, ask someone where a police station is. As soon as possible teach a child to dial 999 and be able to read out the telephone number from which he or she is speaking.

YOUR REF:
OUR REF:

How to be a Working Wife and Mother

WHAT A WORKING MOTHER NEEDS

I've read a lot about women who serenely cope with the three roles of full-time working woman, wife and mother. However, I've never actually met one. All the ones that I know feel inadequate.

Going back to work after having children is a practical and emotional problem and the two aspects are interdependent. You risk worrying about children when you're at work and about work when you're at home, and end up being happy in neither situation.

Two requisites for a working mother are stamina and an understanding family. Sympathetic they may be, until it comes to your interests versus theirs: they still want their evening meal on time and they don't want to hear about the bus queue that made you late.

What a mother risks if she goes out to work is her health. She needs to be an exceptionally well-organized person to survive and even if she manages the mechanics, she will probably have emotional problems. Her biggest unrecognized problem will probably be to get a certain amount of private time to herself every day.

Apart from that, what a working woman needs is the tangible support of a family that shares out the household tasks and takes as much pride in her achievements as she does in theirs.

PORTRAIT OF A WORKING WOMAN

It has been said that some women prefer *not* to work. Some women discover that the lure of a career is less enticing than they expected, because remarkably few women obtain top jobs. However, many women do not work to obtain a career, but to survive. Only since 1970, when

DOWN WITH SUPERWOMAN!

social attitudes began to change to work and divorce, has it been assumed that a woman (like a man) has a right to both a family and a job. A woman who no longer has a mate or who feels oppressed, victimized or bullied by her mate now has the chance to break away, either to be rescued by another man – or by her own ability to earn her living.

Women tend to enjoy their work more than men do. A careers officer told me. 'They don't have the unmaskable arrogance of many men, who still assume that the skills acquired in their early 20s will earn them their living in their 50s. Men expect a full-time job, a life-long career. Women are used to the idea of career breaks, retraining and flexible hours.'

Since 1967 the number of men in the workforce has fallen at pretty much the same rate as the number of working women has increased. *But they are doing different sorts of work.* Jobs traditionally held by men have declined during this period while women have been going into the service jobs (public and private). Men often disdain this sort of job, such as part-time work in schools, hospitals, catering, shops and local government and other welfare areas. This has been a world-wide trend, according to one study.

Roughly one woman in two now goes out to work and the increase has been especially drastic among the over-45s. More jobs are now open to women. There's more social approval of working mothers. Families are now smaller.

Part-time workers

Ninety per cent of part-time British workers are women, especially in the growing services area. Many women are now *paid* for – guess what – cooking, cleaning, nursing and child-care.

It is official government policy (because women are needed for work) to offer retraining schemes, refresher courses, career guidance and even confidence-building courses in order to encourage women to return to work.

We've come a long way since the Sixties, when most women graduates became *teachers*. In the Seventies they branched out into *banking*, *medicine* (47 per cent of medical graduates are now female), the *law* and *insurance*; in the last ten years, the number of female *solicitors* has tripled and female *insurers* has quadrupled. Women are also doing well in the *information industry* (which includes public relations, journalism and computer services), *design* and the *travel industry*.

The Nineties are going to see many British women emerge as *employers*, *bankers*, *politicians* and *entrepreneurs*. Women now own 20 per cent of French small businesses, 25 per cent of American small businesses and 39 per cent of Canadian businesses. British women are about to do likewise.

A FEW NEW FACTS OF LIFE

Your life

The average female life is now 75 years. The trend is towards early marriage. Your child-care years could be over at 35. That leaves forty years ahead for Ms Average.

The average woman works (sometimes part time) for *all but seven years* of the time between leaving full-time education and retirement.

What sort of women work?

- ★ Over 40 per cent of the British labour force is female (9.3 million women).
- ★ Sixty-four per cent of working women are married.
- ★ Forty per cent of women with children aged under 2 are working.
- ★ One in four women with children

aged under 5 work outside the home full or part time.

* Two million British women with children aged under 16 work full time. Three and a half million British women with children aged under 16 work part time.

The state of divorce

* Marriages last on average 9.4 years.
* One in three of first marriages ends in divorce.
* Of this year's teenage brides, one in three will divorce.

Breadwinners

* One in five heads of British households are women (breadwinners not always from choice).
* In Britain there are 830,000 single-parent families headed by a woman.

YOUR ATTITUDE

Today everybody knows that a woman's place is not necessarily in the home. Sometimes home is where the harpy is, and sometimes she has good cause to be bitchy.

Nagging is often a symptom of frustration that disappears when a woman feels happy and interested in her work.

Work outside the home can be a means of forgetting troubles, despair, loneliness. A growing number of women who feel that they're taken for granted, unappreciated or neglected in the home are starting to find that in a job you enjoy, where you're paid, needed and welcome, be it ever so hectic, there's no place like work. Work can be the basis of self-esteem and fulfilment. What also makes a job worthwhile for the person that does it is the enthusiasm it generates, the job

satisfaction, the sense of achievement and the MONEY.

Your home need *not* suffer if you work, provided you're sensible and drop unnecessarily high standards. A recent German study of Common Market housewives proves that we don't save time with our labour-saving gadgets – we raise our standards unnecessarily high and work harder and longer. But if you organize your life so that you haven't got much time to spend on housework, then the housework magically diminishes.

It seems to me that the homes of non-working mothers are seldom any more neat or clean than those of working mothers. It is possible for non-working housewives to be lazy or not at home – they may be out socializing, playing tennis, having coffee mornings or playing ideal home (matching the candleholders to the curtains, combing the town for the right-sized pine cones for the fireplace, etc.), popping tranquillizers or drinking (there are now over a quarter of a million female British alcoholics, according to Alcoholics Anonymous).

The two dangers of going out to work, both of which can be avoided, are exhaustion and guilt, and they are linked.

By exhaustion, I don't mean physical fatigue, which is remedied by a long night's sleep, a day spent alone and doing nothing, or a weekend with friends. I mean a bone-deep, draggy, never-*not*-tired feeling.

The more guilty you feel because you are working, the more you rush around polishing doorknobs, taking the children to the zoo and slaving over a cold deep-freeze – so the more exhausted you become. *Then* you feel guilty about feeling exhausted. At this point you can't think how to cope and you're too tired to work out what's gone wrong and who's to blame. You feel inadequate and near to tears. That's when you start to feel resentful. But you feel that you're not allowed to show it – because you suspect that everyone will triumphantly ask, *'Whose idea was it to go out to work in the first place?'*

Mothers have been conditioned to feel guilty about taking a job outside the home, especially if they *enjoy* it; recognizing this and accepting it will considerably diminish the problem, as any psychologist will tell you. The generation that *won't* feel guilty is, we hope, the one that we're bringing up now. Develop a positive attitude to your job and stop trying to compensate for it. Your family is benefiting and so are you, and never let them forget it.

Avoid this vicious exhaustion/guilt circle by making sure it never starts. I'll tell you a secret. Even if household tasks are shared, it is generally the woman partner who bears the responsibility for organizing the domestic three-ring circus. This is the exhausting part, not the work. So try to share the responsibility, not only the tasks (see 'How to get help in the home', p. 262).

Incidentally, don't think that only mothers with jobs feel inadequate and exhausted. Instead of the working mother's anxiety as to whether she can juggle the whole lot simultaneously, many non-job mothers have a restless feeling that they should *want* to do more, that they are wasting the best years of their life, with only a clean kitchen floor to show for it.

However, if a job feels too much for you, discuss it with your boss. Can you work fewer hours for less money? Can he offer you a different job that is less demanding and exhausting? Or can you get a job nearer home that cuts out travelling time?

YOUR CHILDREN'S ATTITUDE

Your children will probably never regard your work as anything but tiresome. It is important that you shouldn't feel guilty about working – and this is impossible. *You have been conditioned to feel guilty. Accept it.* Children instinctively know when your guilt about your work is your Achilles heel and they will use this knowledge when they are bored, cross or want to take a crack at you. 'Why don't you ever make *cakes*, like *other* mothers?' once nagged my son, who hates cakes.

When a child complains, point out what he is getting instead of cakes, whether this is a video, holidays or simply three meals a day.

A doctor once told me to do as much as you can for your children, but never make gargantuan sacrifices for them because they will resent it.

Women who martyr themselves harm not only themselves but possibly their families as well if the children are left with the uneasy feeling that mother has sacrificed herself for them, which may be 95 per cent untrue. Mother has probably done exactly what she wanted to do, no matter what she says.

The sort of woman who *really* has to make sacrifices for her children and is *really* prepared to do that makes sure that her children never know.

The doctor also told me that children have a very good basic set of priorities. They don't care about mess or dust so long as they feel they are loved, and if they feel secure in this, then it doesn't matter much what else you do, because that's the only thing that really matters. This seems so obvious that you are left wondering what you've been so worried about all this time. However, it's a good thing to remind your eldest of it when, raising an eyebrow, he runs his forefinger along a window ledge like a music hall mother-in-law (hand him a duster).

There are obvious advantages to a child in having a working mother. Children with working mothers don't suffer smother-love or over-fussing or nagging (no time). They learn to be realistic, independent, responsible for their words and deeds and sometimes even stoical – no mean preparation for the toughness of life.

Children of working mothers don't have a permanent, in-house punching bag and prayer rail, but they do have a mother who is likely to have a younger outlook, who is more likely to be tolerant and open to new ideas.

A working woman is not so likely to cling to her children when it's their turn to leave the nest. A working mother has her own interests. She won't feel useless, left-over and ignorantly timid when her children grow up and leave home, although, of course, she will always miss them.

A working mother develops self-control and discipline, useful qualities that form a strong base of self-esteem, fulfilment and contentment. These qualities will act as an example to her children; children don't take the advice of their parents, but they copy them.

A working mother may turn out to be a more respected and valuable adviser to her children in later life; you have to rely on reason, not authority, if you hold down a job.

Your child's teacher is tremendously important to you because he or she has a balanced, objective view of your offspring and his problems. (My son's teacher once offered to sew name-tapes on their clothes, but she was rare.) Ask the teacher's advice if your children develop any antisocial habit, such as bullying, or it they seem to be doing badly at school, or if any misfortune occurs (such as divorce), which will affect your children.

YOUR MAN'S ATTITUDE

If you work outside your home, what problems might you have with your mate?

There are three types of husbands:

Type 1 Liberated.

Type 2 Unliberated.

Type 3 Reluctant Husband; this is the man who thinks he's liberated but is unconsciously resentful of any of his mate's interests if they interfere with his life as he would like it led.

Nowadays husbands are less likely to prevent their wives from taking a job; some men almost weep with relief at the idea of help with the inexorable mortgage and the household bills. Increasingly, men realize that a mate with a good job brings more money, more friends, more interests and the financial insurance of a second income.

It is also reassuring for a man to know that his wife could support herself and their children and even *him* should disaster strike. Men in our society have always tended to die earlier than women. For a family, a wife's job-training can be better insurance than insurance if a man dies, is disabled, divorces or simply disappears.

The Reluctant Husband

The Reluctant Husband's attitude seems to encompass only marriage. If a woman is living with a man and she has her own job and income, then the man knows (and this is recognized among men) that he has to be courteous, careful and respectful: if he isn't, she can pack her bags and leave at any time – she's free to do so. This live-with situation is a relationship that is clearly understood *on both sides* and encourages straightforward one-to-one communication, which allows for reasoned adult debate on major issues.

However, there are still a few deeprooted masculine fears about a working wife, as a result of which she may, *without realizing it*, have problems with her husband if he is emotional, unreasonable and selfish about his wife's job – openly or otherwise: this attitude might result in a lot of unfocused hostility.

There are three types of Reluctant Husband and each of them presents a serious sabotage-threat to his wife.

* Type A is a male chauvinist pig and proud of it.
* Type B knows that he is a Reluctant Husband but keeps his ambivalent feelings secret, except when with fellow sufferers at pub or club. At other times, he says what he knows he *should* say – what is socially acceptable.
* Type C is the man who doesn't realize that he is a Reluctant Husband: it is therefore very difficult to discuss this problem with him, because, so far as he is concerned, it doesn't exist.

It's important that the wife of a Type C Reluctant Husband *shouldn't* get resentful or indignant. She must realize that *he doesn't realize* that he is being selfish, emotional and unreasonable. It is unreasonable to expect an unreasonable man to be reasonable.

However tolerant and understanding a man is about his wife's job, there's almost bound to be *some* area of resentment – a result of early indoctrination – for men born before 1955, which means that they were over 13 years old in 1968, when the Women's Movement got under way.

There are several reasons for the Reluctant Husband's resentment: some husbands fear *the threat to male authority and power* as the one-and-only King of the Castle, Benevolent Provider and Resident Tarzan. Some husbands fear that women are going to grab men's jobs at cheaper rates, and many a dominant and controlling husband *consciously* resents giving up any of his traditional rights in order to allow his wife a separate identity: he's afraid he'll get less status, less attention, less support, less sex, more household jobs – and rivalry, if she is more successful at her job than he is at his.

For these same reasons, a passive and dependent husband who has subconsciously chosen a competent, efficient and organizing partner to complement himself may then do his best to undermine her ability.

Many a husband, *even* if he says that his wife has the right to work, *even* if he enjoys a two-salary life-style, *even* if he's proud of her, would nevertheless prefer that she *didn't* work. A husband likes to come first. (*Anyone* likes to come first.) He wants to have his cake and eat it.

The Reluctant Husband has three main fears about the extra money his wife brings in, even if they *both* agree that they need the extra money.

1 If she works to provide luxury extras, a husband may feel alarm and anxiety at the idea of getting used to living beyond *his* income. This is understandable and due to a sense of unworthiness, but it is illogical.
2 Although he likes the idea of more money coming in, what the Reluctant Husband doesn't like is that as a result of this, his wife and fellow-earner is now going to expect to decide jointly how they spend *their entire income*.
3 If his wife earns *more* than he does, the Reluctant Husband will feel that she has more power than he does. He feels that the one who has the money has the power; he knows that money power leads to other powers; he doesn't want to be Under Dog, he wants to be Top Dog in *his* home. *She* doesn't understand what is worrying him. She doesn't realize that, in cultural terms, she is escaping from her domestic overlord. But *he* does, subconsciously.

So if your husband starts to act in a bewildering, contradictory manner after you've had a salary increase or some public praise, DON'T LISTEN TO WHAT HE SAYS, WATCH WHAT HE DOES. His actions will show whether or not he is a Reluctant Husband.

Some Reluctant Husbands also feel a threat to their sex life. Statistically, when a woman works outside the home, she is twice as likely to have a love affair than is the stay-at-home wife. Any man who works in an office, or who travels, knows this without statistics.

Some Reluctant Husbands take out their resentment in their sex life (absence of). This husband does not want a wife whom he sees as competition in the masculine world. Most men are fiercely competitive and don't want to sleep (on a long-term basis) with someone who's got a better job, a better salary and more success, recognition and responsibility than they have.

For example, male potency depends on being Top Dog, and a Reluctant Husband may have problems getting an erection if he feels his wife is Top Dog.

He may also resent his wife travelling on business and her working hours that don't coincide with his. He may feel that he is unfairly expected to compete with potential rivals from her world; sexual failures on his part will serve to disappoint and punish her.

The Reluctant Husband may demonstrate that intellectual agreement of equality is not emotional acceptance of it by carefully sabotaging his share of the household chores. Although he is an intelligent man and not clumsy in other areas, he will burn meals, break dishes, drop loaded trays and his cleaning will be sloppy, inefficient and exasperating. Scientists can be particularly ham-fisted. There they are, mixing a milligram of this with a microgram of that in a delicate little test-tube all morning, splitting the atom all afternoon, but forgetting how to use their hands by evening.

An insecure man in a low-earning job may feel that it is humiliating to his God-given status as Head of the Family to be seen wearing an apron or going shopping. Openly or otherwise, men often resent 'menial' household tasks on principle (except that they're not menial when wives do them, then they are tangible proof of love, unmentioned though it may be). Some men regard domestic jobs as time-wasting when *they* do it, and resent it accordingly. Although not all men resent looking after their own children, they may well be amazed by the time, energy and patience that they find it requires.

Another secret male fear is supposed to be that one day she will no longer need him and he will be redundant. But the theory that a modern woman needs a man only as a crutch is as weak as the old-fashioned woman's reasoning 'If I'm fragile and dependent, then he will be strong and I can depend on him.' (This lunatic logic is a gamble that can leave her helpless and stranded if it doesn't work and he leaves.)

What does it mean if a husband *doesn't* want his wife to be successful at her job and *does* want her to be dependent on him? It means that he is himself dependent and is happier in a role-reversal situation because he lacks self-confidence. A man who lacks self-confidence may easily try to undermine his wife's success so that she again becomes dependent on him. He also becomes jealous, resentful, self-pitying – and avenging.

This may be because he fears domination. He may have been dominated by an overbearing mother using emotional blackmail ('How could you treat your *own mother* like that?', 'How can you think of doing that, when you know it will *hurt me*?')

Expect such a man to justify his resentment with pseudo-logic. Keep alert for well-worn phrases often heard and picked up in his childhood, such as 'sheer selfishness', 'lack of responsibility', 'your duty' and 'neglect'.

The wife of a Reluctant Husband might have a serious problem because if challenged, her man will probably deny it, so the situation will be difficult to discuss. But she won't resolve the problem *without* discussing it.

The wife's difficulty also is that she can't tackle the problem logically – because it isn't a logical problem, it's an emotional problem. In adult life dependency and hostility go together. If the Reluctant Husband's mother had encouraged him in every way to be independent, then her son would have moved on to become a balanced adult. If she didn't, then the man still feels that his mother owes him the care that he should have had as a child, which would have led to his independence. His mother is still the person that he subconsciously resents and wants to stand up to: he takes this out on his wife but he won't admit it.

If this wife continues to work, her Reluctant Husband is going to continue to resent it, but if she stops work, there's a good chance that *she* will resent it.

If a man wants his wife to leave her job (or she thinks he does) because 'it isn't working out', she should ask her family doctor for advice and get him to see her husband on any pretext, such as her health. The average husband won't want to look anything less than a saint to the doctor, he won't want to appear to be the guilty party, he will want to look a concerned reasonable man.

The doctor may well suggest that the couple both consult Relate (previously known as the Marriage Guidance Council), who are used to dealing with this problem. (Check local telephone directory for address and telephone number.)

THE HIGH COST OF WORK

There's nothing more satisfying than doing the work you love. Work is a wonderful antidote to misery and grief, and it can be a constant stretching of your mind and capabilities.

But are you sure that you can afford to work? In terms of money, that is. Working can be expensive. Add up the weekly costs of doing your job, then multiply it by fifty-two to get the rough, real annual cost. Include tax, fares, lunches, union dues and contributions, hairdresser, extra laundry, make-up and clothes (although you wear *something* wherever you are, you undoubtedly spend more on your appearance if you go out to work) and food costs. This last is also a difficult figure to calculate, but convenience foods, weekend shopping or late-night supermarkets can certainly add up to 15 per cent extra to food bills and in addition you have to accept the fact that some food is bound to be wasted.

The cost of home help and/or childcare can be high, especially if you have living-in help. Home help is very expensive when you do a proper accountant's costing of it and include wages, insurance, room, light and heat, food and general extravagance, such as not switching off the electricity because she isn't paying the bills. *And* you have to deal with her neuroses when you've just got back from the office and want to nurse your own.

Although you may not be working primarily for money, how many weeks of the year do you have to work before you start to show a profit? And when you've actually made some money, do you have time to spend it carefully?

TAKING A BABY BREAK

There is no ideal time to have children in terms of your career; trying to decide whether you should and, if so, when to take a break and for how long can be very difficult. Having children can be an enormous disadvantage in most jobs to a woman who wants to get to the top. But having made up your mind that's what you want, be aware of your rights.

The regulations covering maternity payments and rights at work are many and very complicated, so don't lose out by not being fully informed.

Planning to return to work

You cannot be sacked from your job because of your pregnancy if (a) your employer employs five or more people, (b) you have been working for your employer for at least two years full time (sixteen hours a week or more) or five years part time (less than sixteen hours a week) up to the eleventh week before your baby is due.

You are entitled to return to your job after taking a break and to receive all the normal benefits (such as pay rises, holiday pay) that may have become due to you in your absence.

However, you must send a written confirmation of your intention to return to work at least twenty-one days before doing so and reply to that effect within two weeks to any letter your employer sends you asking for this confirmation.

If you are employed, discuss your plans with your boss as soon as your pregnancy is established. You may be lucky enough to be able to arrange new working hours when you return to work, but these things usually take plenty of time to arrange. If you decide after the birth of your baby that you don't want to, or can't, return to work, it won't affect any of the maternity pay you have received. But in this case tell your employer as soon as possible that this is what you have decided. It will make his or her life easier and other female employees who decide to take a baby break will thank you for it.

Antenatal visits

Every pregnant woman is entitled to take time off work to attend antenatal clinics.

Maternity pay

If you have worked for your current employer for at least twenty-six weeks at the fourteenth week before your baby is due and your average earnings for the last eight weeks of those weeks are at least £39 (the amount where you have to start paying NI contributions), you are entitled to statutory maternity pay. You can be paid for up to eighteen weeks, starting any time from the eleventh to the sixth week before the baby is due. There are two rates of pay. If you have been working for your current employer for at least two years full time (sixteen hours a week or more) or five years part time (at least eight hours a week), you can get 90 per cent of your salary for the first six weeks and a flat rate per week thereafter. If you haven't worked for your employer for this qualifying period, you will receive the flat rate for the entire period.

In order to claim maternity pay you must also supply a certificate of maternity from your doctor or midwife and, three weeks before you intend to stop work, tell your employer in writing that you will be stopping work, which week the baby is due and if you intend to return to work.

If you are not entitled to maternity pay from your employer, if you are self-employed or unemployed, you may still be able to claim a maternity allowance from the Department of Social Security. In order to qualify for this, you need to have paid standard rate NI contributions for at least twenty-six of the fifty-two weeks up to the fourteenth week before the baby is due.

The payment period for maternity allowance starts eleven weeks before the baby is due. But if you are still working at that time, your allowance may start later. Payment will normally be made for a core period of thirteen weeks, beginning six weeks before the baby is due, but you decide when you take the remaining five weeks. (You can take some before and some after, or all before or all after.) As with statutory maternity pay from your employer, you cannot get the allowance for any week in which you have worked.

In order to claim your maternity allowance, you must fill in a form, MA 1, which you can get from your local social security office or from an antenatal clinic. Send it off after you are twenty-six weeks pregnant.

If you are self-employed or unemployed, obtain a leaflet called *Babies and Benefits* from your local social security office, clinic or library.

For further information, read *Working Mother: A Practical Handbook* by Sarah Litvinoff and Marianne Velmans (published by Corgi Books), which takes you through the jungle of legislation covering this subject quite painlessly.

WHAT TO DO WITH THE CHILDREN (a quick guide to the under-5s care system *(if you can call it a system)*

It's hard to find your way around the British pre-school care system for under-5s. This is not because your brain isn't big enough to cope with it. It is because it is an inefficient, confused system, born of inadequate and confused policies. But, as you'll have to find your way around it, there's a guide on pp. 251–2.

YOUR STAND-IN AT HOME

The lack of enough affordable day nurseries, day schools and child-care arrangements is what prevents most mothers who would like to do so from returning to work.

Looking after a family and taking care of children is obviously the most important job in the world. Unfortunately, in Britain, society pays only lip service to this. It doesn't pay us for doing it and it is not particularly interested in seeing that it gets done: otherwise day-care centres would be every city's priority. Many mothers have no choice as to whether or not to work. But, whatever the Government says, the Government's motto seems to be 'Women and children last'.

It may come as a shock to a lot of mothers to learn that the problems of holding down a job when they have small children only increase when they reach school age. School hours are school hours and they don't correspond to normal working hours. And then there are the school holidays. The only working mothers of schoolchildren who seemingly don't have problems in the yearly fifteen weeks of school holidays are school-teachers. Other working women with no home help have to rely on family, friends and neighbours. You might pay a non-working neighbourhood mother to cope with your children as well as her own for a few hours at the end of the day. A granny or aunt might be persuaded to help, but nowadays there's a good chance that granny is running her own boutique and aunty is a trainee computer programmer. A lot of women who have managed to cope quite well with nursery facilities now find that they are forced to give up work if they can't either get home early enough to pick up small children from school or make suitable alternative arrangements. And then there are the never-ending school holidays!

The only way out may be to hire a home help, a nanny, au pair or mother's help.

If you have several children and if you can afford it, I think the best home help is to get a daily mother's help rather than a resident nanny, because children, no matter how young, shouldn't get used to a lot of attention all the time. And you're far more likely to be lucky with people

Guide to child care

Name	Description	Category	Further information (how to find/get into) from
The Department of Education and Science (DES) and the local education authority are responsible only for the following:			
Nursery schools	For 3- to 5-year-olds. The children are taught lessons (full or part time). Open *only* during school hours and school term. Free.	Public	Local education office (ask at town hall or local library)
	Parents pay fees. Expect long waiting lists.	Private	Local social services, with whom they have to register.
Nursery classes	For 3- to 5-year-olds in primary school, full or part time.	Public	Local education office
The Department of Social Security and the local social services department are responsible for the following:			
Local authority day nurseries	For children up to 5 years in difficult family situations. Most don't take children until they are 2. *More* than full time. Open 8 a.m. to 6 p.m. all year round except public holidays. Staffed by nursery nurses, not teachers. Almost always overbooked and difficult to get into.	Public	Local social services department (find whereabouts from your doctor, Citizens' Advice Bureau, town hall or local library).
Day nurseries and day-care centres.	Usually for 2- to 5-year-olds, usually expensive. Hours to suit working mothers. Staff training standards vary, so watch out. Some have long waiting lists.	Private	Local social services department, with whom they have to register. See *Yellow Pages* under 'Nurseries'.
Crèches	Usually for children of 6 months to 3 years (often attached to factories and private companies that depend on female workforce). Sometimes they have spare places to fill, so worth inquiring about even if you don't work for the place concerned.	Private	Local employment office or Job Centre. Contact the Workplaces Nurseries Ltd, 77 Holloway Road, London N7 8JZ (tel: 071-700-0281) for information about establishing new crèches. Some crèches have gone 'underground' since they have been rated as a taxable perk.
Playgroups	Originally started by parents on a voluntary part-time basis while the nation-wide network of nursery schools and day nurseries was being organized (ho hum!). This is really supervised play. Children are supervised by voluntary part-time minders, including mothers or fathers, who take it in turns. Nominal fees.	Private	Local social services.

DOWN WITH SUPERWOMAN!

Name	Description	Category	Further information (how to find/get into) from
Child-minders	Look after children in their own homes. If they are not registered with the local social services department, they may be cheaper but also dangerously unfitted to look after children.	Private	Local social services, with whom registered ones are registered. Anyone who isn't registered (and there are thousands of them) is operating illegally. Local child-minding organizations (look in the telephone directory) are more likely to have up-to-date lists of minders. Also contact NCMA (National Child-minding Association), 8 Mason's Hill, Bromley, Kent BR2 9EY (tel: 081-464-6164)
Supervised holiday play schemes	These are not often for the under-5s, but sometimes you may be lucky.	Public	Local Citizens' Advice Bureau.
Nannies and other helps		Private	Local Job Centre, advertisements in local newspapers. The best place to advertise for a mother's help seems to be *Nursery World*. For any other sort of living-in help the best place seems to be *The Lady*. There are many specialist nanny and au pair agencies – look in the *Yellow Pages*. Get NNEB (National Nursery Examination Board) graduates straight from state or private college. Write to the principal six months before the course ends. Locate your nearest NNEB college via your local librarian.

who don't live in, because your setting is then just part of their life; they're not subconsciously fighting with you for centre-stage.

Home helps and au pairs

Alternatively, it seems easier to live happily with young foreign girls who know that they're going home within a year and who are here for a reason (to learn the language from your children). There are drawbacks. They don't know how to do any housework or cookery: back home, that was all done by *Mutter* or the servants. They are unlikely to be responsible, and likely to need supervision. Remember what you felt like at that age? Indifferent to everything (especially children) except make-up, hair and boys. Why should you suppose that, deep down, Helga feels any different?

Most workers have the weekends and the evenings off, and one way to keep Helga happy is to let her have this time off. If you get someone whom your children like and who just covers you for your full-time office hours, then you're either lucky or clever and probably a combination of both.

Don't push your luck. *Never stop checking on your stand-in*. It isn't sneaky. It's only fair to your children. It isn't unfair to your stand-in. There is no need to trust her until she is proven trustworthy. If you can't hop home unexpectedly at lunch-time, get someone else to do so on a pretext of picking up a book or a letter. This sounds nasty, but they're *your* children, and you have a duty to them and you can't afford to take risks.

As in all contracts, what has been arranged should be clearly understood. You should both have a written copy of your agreement, dated and signed by both of you. Any later variations should be similarly noted, so that there's proof of what has been agreed.

I have found only one system of remote control that works faultlessly: lists behind the kitchen door. A list of emergency telephone numbers and addresses. A timetable for the children. A timetable for your stand-in with time off (*and* time on) clearly marked down in black and white. *You* need to know what *she* has agreed and what *you* have let yourself in for. You can also point this out to your friends who say that the lists remind them of Eton/prison/Auschwitz/the Navy.

Have a few trial runs with your emergency list: the house is now on fire, the children haven't returned from the park, the baby has fallen downstairs, the cat is eating the lunch – what is Helga going to do about it?

The simpler the children's meals, the more likely they are to get them as you planned. Fruit, cheese, salads and hot vegetable soups are nutritious and undemanding, and easy to organize. How did author Elizabeth Pakenham manage to raise eight children and write books? 'Baked potatoes and fruit for pudding,' she said.

If she is supposed to do any housework, your stand-in should clearly understand that the children come before the home, and you just have to accept that this is a golden excuse not to do housework. There should, however, be good evidence that the time has been 'spent' with the children and not watching the television or doing homework (hers, not theirs). Check by simply asking your children (if they're old enough to tell you), 'What did you do today?/ What did you make today?/Where did you go today?'

You have to decide whether you want an au pair or a full-time home help. An *au pair* is a part-time helper who will do thirty hours' work a week (that means she's on duty for only thirty hours a week, including evening baby-sitting; the Home Office say she should do a maximum of five hours a day and have one full day off per week, when she's not at school). She is supposed to be treated as a daughter of the house, not given heavy work, not paid much (comparatively) and you don't have to pay National Insurance contributions for her.

Employing a nanny

A nanny can work full or part time, live in or come in daily and can even be shared with another household. She may have a formal qualification, such as the NNEB (National Nursery Examination Board) earned after a two-year course, but may be unqualified, in which case she should have at least two years' experience of looking after young children or an extremely strong recommendation.

Unfortunately Nanny will be expensive. In addition, a trained nanny is a professional and will expect to be treated as such, not as a domestic slave. A nanny who lives out may cost you anything between £100 and £150 a week, and a live-in nanny slightly less. On top of these wages you will have to pay her tax and National Insurance contributions as well as NI contributions as her employer.

What you will get for this should be a professional who works forty hours a week, expects a room of her own with a TV (if she is living in), all her food and

DOWN WITH SUPERWOMAN!

no bills to pay. Whether living in or out, a nanny would expect to have reasonably regular working hours, which won't always cover you if you frequently arrive late from work, and (unless you have negotiated regular baby-sitting at the beginning) evening duties to be paid for as extra. Make arrangements about use of telephone (in and out calls) and show her previous, pre-nanny bills.

You shouldn't expect a nanny to do any housework that isn't related to looking after children. Most nannies will wash and care for children's clothes, do light shopping, tidy children's rooms and play areas, cook meals for themselves and the children. However, you are hoping for much more than this. You hope that she'll be lively, loving and interested in the children. You hope she will read and play with them, organize activities, make friends with other small children and their mums or minders. You hope she will be tactful, patient and easy to get on with.

Obviously, this Mary Poppins paragon is not going to be easy to find. Allow yourself plenty of time for the search – at least two months. The best places to advertise are still *The Lady* and *Nursery World*; buy a copy of each and study the style and content of the ads before placing your own. The golden rule at this stage and later on when interviewing is to be frank, clear and firm about what you want from your nanny. How much baby-sitting do you expect? Will Nanny eat with the family? And with guests? Will she do the shopping? Work flexible hours? Entertain her friends at your house? Smoke? Drink your gin?

Then establish what she expects from you.

Write her a letter confirming both sets of expectations and agreements.

There are many nanny agencies (look in the *Yellow Pages*) but introduction fees can be high – you may lose a lot of money if Nanny leaves you after only two months. You may also be bullied by an agency into accepting a candidate who is not ideal for you. This is less likely to happen if you pick a good agency that has been personally recommended.

Whatever kind of home help you get, remember that untrained or inexperienced people are often more demanding and neurotic. If you pay more than the going rate, you will not be popular with your neighbouring working mothers but you will generally find someone who is that bit more responsible. A bonus system can be a good idea, provided you don't pay the bonus before Christmas, when extra-to-contract money is regarded as a Right, or before Nanny visits her own folk or goes on holiday, when the temptation to stay with them or continue to sit at the sea-shore is often too great. Pick your own bonus system, related to achievement. I know someone who employed her evening baby-sitter on a yearly basis, with an end-of-the-year bonus paid after Easter. She had reliability and the children always got the same person. A good idea.

Be businesslike with your nanny. Don't let Nanny get the upper hand. Nobody should have the upper hand. She is supposed to help you do your job, so that you can pay her wages; if she makes work for you, or she turns out to be an added anxiety, telephone her agency, then talk to Nanny quietly, with someone else present (and silent). It's often easier thus to clarify what is unreasonable behaviour on the part of you or the nanny. Don't allow Nanny to red-herring you. State your problem. Ask for her comments. Listen carefully to any complaints she has. Say you'd like to think about the situation for a couple of days. (Try to say this on a Wednesday. Then, if on Friday, you decide it's best to part, you have the weekend to make any alternative arrangements, especially if Nanny walks out.)

Recommended reading

Even when I could afford it, I couldn't

stand the horrors for both sides of live-in help (no privacy, forced jollity), but if you are thinking of having a live-in nanny, au pair or mother's help, *The Good Nanny Guide* (by Charlotte Breese and Hilaire Gomer, published by Century) is comprehensive, entertaining and instructive. It is written by two working mothers who met in hospital while having babies; they have since interviewed 100 nannies and 100 mothers on all aspects of living-in help for children.

The book covers training, job description, sackable offences, time off, holiday, perks, the interview, daily routine, possible causes of friction, stress and conflict. There are plenty of fascinating horror stories that may put you off the whole idea, but, if not, the authors set out the rules to establish a good working relationship for all parties. By disagreeing with them, you may evolve your own guidelines.

WHICH WORK PATTERN IS EASIEST?

Should you work part time or full time? It depends on your needs. When I had my first baby I did part-time design work at home. Then I worked full time from an office and had a home help. Then I worked full time at home with no home help. Then I worked at home as a freelance writer, working full time during the term and theoretically not at all during school holidays.

I found it easiest (but not always possible) to go out to work full time and pay for adequate home help. For me, working part time seemed to involve twice the work for half the money with none of the office perks and protection.

I am not the only woman to have found that part-time work from home is ten times more difficult than it sounds: this is because you are trying to do at least two jobs at once. Of course the children interrupt you, and so does the milkman, whether you're trying to start a business or write a short story in your own kitchen. Of course you answer the telephone, the door, take in your neighbour's laundry and stave off a Jehovah's Witness.

It's certainly easier to work part time if you leave home to do it. I know a Cambridge professor's wife who writes detective stories: she leaves her house every day at 11 a.m., catches a bus to a room she has hired and works until 2 p.m. If you can't afford to rent a room for your work, try swapping homes with a friend who also wants to work. (You'll have less difficulty in not dealing with *her* home life.) Or advertise locally.

After I established myself as a freelance working from home, I was able to afford a secretary for one day a week and *knowing* that I was going to have Nicola's help on Monday acted as a good discipline to get all my office work ready in time for that day – no matter how early I had to get up – when it got polished off in one go.

Job sharing

National Westminster Bank are pioneers in this field, where two people share one job (such as cashier) and do a full-time fortnight each. They share the pay, holidays and benefits. Other schemes may divide the week into two and a half days each, or alternate weeks. Even senior jobs can be shared in this way. Get your twin before approaching an employer, appear together at the interview and explain how you will tackle the drawbacks. Don't both talk at once.

New Ways to Work (Job Sharing Project), 309 Upper Wimpole Street, London N1 2TY, tel: 071-226-4026, keep job-sharing registers in certain professions and will send you information on your local job-sharing groups or contacts.

DOWN WITH SUPERWOMAN!

ADVICE FROM TOP MOTHERS

Penny Perrick, literary editor of the *Sunday Times*, liked a once-a-week preparation time for food and found that the best day to do the bulk of the shopping and a good bit of housework was Saturday.

'Any meals that had to be prepared on Saturday had to be fitted in between painting the ceiling and washing the dog. I reserved Sunday morning for fixing casseroles and baking pies and all the other things that resulted in stacks of dirty dishes. Then I tackled this chore in one fell swoop.'

Writer Anne Scott-James once told me that her organizational secret was never to take her coat off until she had laid the table and the evening meal was well under way. Otherwise she would have flopped into an armchair with a drink and the meal would have been extremely late, if indeed it appeared at all.

Architect Margaret Casson told me that she never entertains; never, ever. She sends flowers, notes and gifts to her hostesses, but she never asks them home, and eventually this has been accepted by all the friends she has left.

Elinor Guggenheimer, consumer expert and grandmother, told me, 'Where a mate is involved, there is still some predetermined code of Gracious Living to live up to and a whole lot of guilt if you don't.

'We eat simple dishes that can be put together quickly. When my husband and I are alone together we eat in the kitchen from paper plates. I have moved very far away from Gracious Living because, for me, Gracious Living has nothing to do with whether you eat from a paper plate. It has to do with the feeling of fulfilment, of time for yourself, work for yourself, leisure for yourself.

'Nobody gets *everything* they want in life; you must decide what you want *most*. I have cut out a lot of our social life.

'You need some time of the day exclusively to yourself: you really need it. It's more difficult to get if you have small children, but then it's more necessary that you get it. For me, when I come home tired, thirty minutes is spent in the bath.'

HOW TO RUN A HOME AND A JOB

When you become a working mother, you will with any luck get twice as much out of life, but you can't run your home as if you weren't working. A working mother has to work faster and more efficiently in the home and she has to be *twice* as reliable outside it, because people expect her not to be.

I evolved my own set of guideline rules for housework, which I slowly slipped away from, but it pulled me back to reality at regular intervals and Heaven knows what I would have been like without it. Here it is.

Conserve your energy

Realize that you can't do everything.

Know your limitations Allow for the fact that you can't get a quart out of your pint pot. Plan around your own capacity, your own strengths and weaknesses, and any situation will become easier to deal with.

Know your priorities The secret of getting things done is to know what to leave undone and the secret of that is learning to sort out your priorities clearly and fast.

So decide your basic priorities. I decided that my children came first and apart from that nothing came before my job, which was a responsible one, working to national newspaper deadlines.

1 **Disregard what you're SUP-POSED to do.**

2 **Do only what you can't avoid doing.**

3 **Decide what you CAN avoid doing.** For instance, daily cleaning, drying up, most of the ironing and producing two hot meals a day. Remember, however, that evening candlelight or soft lamplight may be kind to your face and your standards of housework, but it can't disguise canned spaghetti *ad nauseam*.

4 **Eliminate THINGS as well as tasks.** The less you have, the less you have to take care of.

5 **Do everything you dread doing STRAIGHTAWAY**, then things seem immediately much better.

6 **Never leave anything until the last minute.** This is a straight gamble with fate and time, and the dice are NEVER weighted in your favour.

7 **Apply determination.** It's simply that nothing else works. Winston Churchill's speech to his old school consisted *only* of saying, 'Never give up – never. Never. Never. Never.' This is enough to live by.

8 **We all get tired.** *Life* is tiring. Try going to bed really early once a week.

9 **Your lunch hour is for lunch and relaxation.** Try to keep shopping out of it. Try to relax and do nothing but count your blessings for ten minutes around lunch-time. I find this easiest if I take off my shoes and lie on the floor, if possible. Just shut your eyes and stop thinking, if not at lunch-time, then at some other time during the day. I seem to collapse around 6.30 p.m. and I've now learned to combine this with a bath and a rest. If I stubbornly totter on, then I won't recover my strength all evening.

10 **Making more time.** The choice is to get up early or to go to bed late.

You are either a lark or an owl. Owls can't open their eyes in the morning but they can cheerfully perform amazing feats such as painting the spare room at 1 a.m.; larks can't stay awake for the late show but are happy to be laying breakfast at dawn. If you are not a lark, you might have to invest money in getting up: try a costly telephone alarm call or one of those radio-alarm clocks that keep coming on again however many times you shut them up. If you can't summon up enough energy to get up early then you can go to bed later, a regular 2 a.m. owl.

If you do neither, then you don't really want to be a poet or study Mandarin or whatever. Bernard Levin told me this and I was furious with him for months because he was right.

HOW TO GET BACK TO WORK

If a person wants to get back to work after a baby break, she may have two problems. One is an understandable lack of self-confidence. The other problem for women who *say* they want to get back to work is unrealistic expectations. Someone who has been Queen of the Hearth for a few years may not be prepared to make a *real* effort, to take a risk or even to use her clearly established gifts ('No, I want something different.').

What this unrealistic, over-romantic woman wants is simply a glamorous £30,000-a-year job (no experience needed) where she can meet people and express the 'real me' during working hours of 10 a.m. to 4 p.m., with all school holidays off. And she doesn't want to apply for the job; she wants it *offered* to her by some Fairy Prince of Industry.

I have never come across such a job (if I had, I'd have taken it) and it is vital to

DOWN WITH SUPERWOMAN!

understand that this sort of job doesn't exist.

Going back to work can be as alarming as the first time you went to school. Careers Advisory Officers all made surprisingly similar comments on the problems of a woman who wants to go back to work. 'Lack of self-confidence. The majority of women returners I see underestimate their competence and abilities.' I was told, 'A woman needs to make a conscious effort to be positive: she mustn't cop out by saying that she's shy or hasn't any self-confidence. Everyone's shy and nobody has. Her family attitude can make or break a woman in this frame of mind: a condescending or tolerantly amused attitude can be crushing.'

Self-confidence can fall suddenly, like a soufflé, for minor reasons, major reasons or none at all that you can see. It's only human to sometimes lack confidence for short or long periods. You may have reason to do so, but you're far more likely to exaggerate the reasons. When you lose confidence, your judgement goes as well. You can't tell the mountains from the molehills.

If you lack confidence, it's important to realize that you *can* gain or regain it. It's also important to know how to (see 'Self-confidence', p. 388).

'Of course someone who has run a home has job qualifications,' said one Careers Advisory Officer. He added that a woman should never underestimate her home job, for job it is, albeit unpaid, and never *ever* describe herself as 'just a housewife'. That 'just' is bad for her confidence.

Running a home, like running a factory, involves principles of management, judgement and decision-making as well as other practical skills: you're not only the managing director, you're probably also all the workers, the personnel officer, the canteen staff and the all-important office cleaner. But after two to twenty years of looking after a home and being her own boss, a woman often doubts her advantages, loses some of her self-confidence and thinks that she's incapable of doing anything else. How wrong she is.

If you have survived motherhood, you have coped with many more pressures, problems and tensions than are met in an office. If you have dealt with difficult relations (all relations are difficult), this may have led you to develop the sort of tolerance and adaptability that no young woman fresh from school or college has had the time to acquire; no one can go to college to learn this. You have served a long and hard apprenticeship and have acquired many skills that you didn't have when you walked down the aisle. And that's what qualifications are – proof of skills and experience. All you have to do with yours is realize this and sort them out to your best advantage.

Sometimes your experience is positively preferable to five O and two A levels. For instance, reliable people with a family background are badly needed in the social services, especially if they have had experience with children. You are qualified for special social work training courses without having the Os and As that are necessary for the young. Some of these courses are especially for non-graduates and geared to women with family responsibilities.

However efficient you are, expect to be rusty. One Careers Advisory Officer commented, 'When a woman starts work again, she tends to underestimate how much time it takes to run her home in the way that she's been doing it. It's often a good idea to have a dummy run for a week or two before you start the job.'

Another explained, 'She's so used to being on her own and not working to a set routine that she finds it hard to accept a timetable and stick to it ... I have found that anyone who has been to any kind of afternoon or evening classes always has more realistic ideas about herself when she starts looking for a new career . . . I always suggest that a woman go to a class before going back to work: something that she will enjoy. It's not so much what she learns. It's the regular commitment to do something, being with other people, exchanging ideas, having to do set reading and writing in an orderly way that is invaluable.'

What is often most difficult for a woman is *not* acquiring the training, or finding the opening, or reorganizing her home life in order to let her get away from it for a bit – but facing her own ambivalent attitude. She wants to go out into the world she's missing, but deep down she doesn't want to leave her protective shell, so she finds masses of excuses not to do so. This can result in an understandable lethargy that she wants to escape from, but actually *prevents* her from escaping.

This problem is common, and most of us have it at some time. The way to deal with it is by admitting it, facing it and stamping on it. What is difficult, but essential, is to stop making excuses to yourself (and to anyone else who will listen to you), then to decide coldly that you'll just have to live with whatever it is you might fear – embarrassment or shyness, rejection or ridicule. (Remember that these things probably exist only in your head.) Mumble to yourself the-only-thing-we-have-to-fear-is-fear-itself and get up, go out and DO IT. The most important step towards getting back to work is also the most difficult step – the step outside your own front door.

Lots of people already know exactly what they can do and what they want to do and they trot out and do it. Well, that's wonderful, but if you're not like that, join the club (I had no idea I was going to be a writer). As a matter of fact, such clever know-alls might be missing *better* opportunities that they don't know about. Not being too sure of what you

want is not a bad position to be in these days; there are so many good schemes to give you advice, practical help, training courses – and sometimes even money while you train.

You might sign up for one of the many courses that prepare women to return to work. Some are run by your local adult education authority, some by the Manpower Services Commission. Inquire at your local library to see whether something like the admirable 'Women's Taster Course' is available in your area. It is designed to help build your confidence and increase your self-esteem with assertion training. You learn how to look for jobs, how to apply for jobs, how to present yourself by letter and at an interview. It teaches you basic skills in bookkeeping and budgeting, computers and word processors, video-making, starting a business, and working co-operatively. There's also advice on other educational and training opportunities as well as individual counselling. The course runs for twenty weeks, five hours a week. Many adult institutes all over the country will offer something similar.

The Manpower Services Commission runs WOW courses (Wider Opportunities for Women), which are longer and go into more detail. Lasting six weeks full time or twelve weeks part time, they are aimed at unskilled or unqualified women and unemployed women who have been out of work for at least two years or who have never worked. Contact your local Job Centre for information about their next courses.

CAREERS FOR MOTHERS

If you have had some job training or professional qualifications, you can probably find job opportunities through your professional organization. Otherwise, check the advertisements in the classified pages of a newspaper or your trade

DOWN WITH SUPERWOMAN!

journal. If you have a managerial, professional or technical background and want advice on how to take up your career again, there is a specialist government employment agency, Professional and Executive Recruitment (PER). You don't have to be unemployed to register with them. They run free courses on self-presentation, career development and training opportunities, as well as acting as a regular recruitment agency. You'll find them in the telephone book under Manpower Services Commission.

If you had no training prior to marriage, what job is available for you? There are plenty of suitable training courses for 'mature' students (the official description of any woman over 23).

First, sort out in your own mind:

1 The kind of job you want.
2 What training may be necessary for it.
3 What you have to offer. This might be organizational ability, patience and stamina as well as skills such as driving, gardening, cooking and budgeting.
4 Decide the restrictions within which you have to work; for example, school hours, no help during the school holidays, lack of transport and a dachshund to look after.
5 When you apply for a job, ask if you can take occasional days off your holiday time to care for unexpected child ailments and any special occasion involving your child at school.

Having completed this self-examination, go to one of the following for careers advice.

Your local library The reference section will have a selection of books and leaflets on careers opportunities. One publication to look out for is *Equal Opportunities, a Careers Guide* by Ruth Miller, published by Penguin Books. This splendid book lists practically every job you can think of plus training courses and contact addresses, as well as describing the possibilities of career breaks and late starts in each.

Your local authority careers officer Although their services are used mostly by school-leavers, some careers officers are sympathetic and helpful to older people looking for a change of career or a late start. They know about local opportunities and training facilities.

Your local Job Centre Ask to speak to the employment adviser. After discussing your situation, you may be referred to the Job Training Scheme, which has replaced the old TOPS scheme. More on this later.

A private careers counsellor Private careers counsellors are sometimes investigated by journalists wearing a false beard or some more plausible disguise: these people are always advised to become journalists, which shows the career counsellors are good at their jobs.

If you are prepared to spend a few pounds (telephone first to check the current price) and can get to London, you can make an appointment for a consultation with the National Advisory Centre on Careers for Women (NACCW) at Drayton House, 30 Gordon Street, London WC1H 0AX, tel: 071-380-0177. They will also give information by letter on request. They specialize in returners, and advise on both training and careers. However, they are *not* an employment agency, although they will put you in touch with one.

Another place to contact for a private consultation is Career Development for Women, 97 Mallard Place, Twickenham, Middlesex TW1 4SW, tel: 081-892-3806.

Specialist training

Having decided what job you would like to do, you need to know what training you need and where to get it. If there is a professional association or other body in your field (there almost always is), they will tell you what specific training and qualifications you need and where to study.

Warning! Lots of women spend time and money on correspondence courses that lead to certificates that *count for nothing* as a qualification for employment. It's infuriating to find that you have carefully learnt out-of-date methods of computer programming or accountancy.

The training officer at your local Job Centre will tell you whether you are eligible for a place in the Job Training Scheme. The scheme now operates more tightly than did the old TOPS courses. Courses vary from place to place, according to the employment requirements of a particular area; they last from one month to a year. In order to qualify, you have to be unemployed and have been out of full-time education for at least two years. You receive an allowance while training, plus meal allowances and travel to and from the course. Get the leaflet called *Thinking about Training* from your Job Centre.

Courses run by your local adult education institute may not lead to specific qualifications but can give a good grounding in areas such as word processing, shorthand and craft skills, such as upholstery and dressmaking. Some institutes offer professional courses, such as the RSA Stage 1 examination course in bookkeeping.

WHERE TO FIND A JOB

* At your local Job Centre or PER office.
* In advertisements in local, national or trade newspapers and journals. Your local library will have most of these.
* At private employment agencies.
* Ask advice from someone who is already well established in the field you wish to enter.

* Use contacts. If you haven't any contacts, plan a campaign to get *one*. Stalk him or her through friends. Make a research project of reaching a contact in, say, window-box gardening. Your first contact will lead you to other contacts.
* Apply 'cold' to companies, even if they haven't advertised a vacancy. Write to the personnel manager or head of the department that you're interested in – find out his or her name by ringing up the switchboard. Find out as much as possible about the company before doing this, then write a convincing letter to the name, saying *briefly* why you want to work for that particular company. This is a long shot, but if your letter and CV (personal details and previous experience), are interesting enough and clean and neat, they may well be placed on file for the next vacancy.

Some employment agencies specialize in part-time work; others in particular fields, such as publishing; many handle secretarial work, some specialize in graduate placings.

However, don't expect someone else to look after you – that's another version of expecting Prince Charming to offer you a job. Even if an agency is advising you, pursue your own line of research, because they are dealing with hundreds of people; *you* are more interested in you than anyone else is likely or able to be. (Nevertheless, check regularly with the agency.)

Don't pursue one job at a time. *Pursue them all, all the time.* This is the lucky dip approach and the one I always follow.

Don't mind taking a low wage to get some fast experience or to get your foot in the door. Once you've discovered how your job is done, you might improve on it and get a promotion, switch to a competitor for a higher wage or even eventually start your own business (see 'Starting your own business', p. 360).

How To Get Help In The Home

GRAND FAMILY PLAN

Easy enough for an 8-year old!

EVERYDAY TIDYING!

Special Jobs!

> I sit at my typewriter remembering my grandmother
> and all my mothers,
> and the minutes they lost
> loving houses better than themselves
> and the man I love cleans up the kitchen
> grumbling only a little because he knows
> that after all these centuries
> it is easier for him
> than for me.
>
> *Women Enough,* Erica Jong

HOW DOES A WORKING MOTHER GET THE FAMILY TO HELP IN THE HOME?

Many working mothers today are doing three jobs while their man is doing only one job. Even if he helps in the home, what he does is unlikely to be a fair share of the complicated, time-consuming job of running a home and keeping it clean.

Naturally, a man expects to be able to recharge his batteries at home after a hard day's work. Perhaps a woman should expect the same thing. Instead, she returns home at night to *more* work and the job of recharging the family batteries, while her own battery flattens. She may then hear complaints that she isn't the lively, sparkling companion that she once was.

Today 60 per cent of women work

outside their homes. If working mothers continue to be totally responsible for running their home unaided, the stress will be dangerous to their health, because it isn't the salaried job that's stressful – it's the unpaid, *never-ending* job at home.

So what can a woman do to lighten her load?

Brainwash herself for a start. Get a refreshing drink, head for the sofa, put your feet up and prepare to wipe from your memory banks the conditioning of centuries. It is *not* the natural duty of a woman to give most of her time, strength and intelligence to others, especially her family, and you should not make yourself immediately and at all times available to them or else feel overwhelming guilt. This is not the way to make yourself an interesting person. This is the way to make yourself a drudge who is taken for granted.

Other people can collude to make you feel guilty: not only your loved ones – who complain if their football shirts aren't clean or a hot dinner isn't on the table when they come home – but also every serviceman who knocks on your door. They all wear the same surprised expression if a woman complains that the plumber didn't keep his appointment and didn't warn her of this. No, they just *expect* her to be there, uncomplaining and available, three hours after the agreed time.

Now answer the following questions.

What are your most precious possessions? Perhaps your brain, your time and your creativity.

What do you like doing most?

How many hours of your week are spent on your own pleasure *when* you are feeling your best and your mind isn't busy working out the next school run?

How many hours of your week are spent doing housework?

Why do you spend more time on housework than pleasure? Of course somebody has to do it, but why should it

be *just* you? Even if you enjoy ironing, I'm sure there are things you like *more* than ironing. What you perhaps mean is that you'd rather do the ironing than clean the oven?

Nobody with any sense enjoys housework when they could be doing something else. I have never seen housework as anything other than a waste of time and if I can avoid it, I will.

Of course, the people who know this already and avoid it already are men.

Most men have a much more healthy and logical attitude to housework than most women. A man sees housework as a tedious necessity to be dispensed with as fast as possible by any means or person at his disposal.

A man has no anxiety or guilt about getting the place clean prior to doing something more interesting. I have yet to meet the man who insists that he *loves* ironing, that he wouldn't have an identity without it and his family might love him less if he didn't do it. A man doesn't feel guilty if he isn't available to his family every minute of the day. A man won't feel guilty if he's caught with his feet up on the sofa because any sensible executive knows that planning proper leisure is part of his job.

SOME WAYS TO START HIM DOING HOUSEWORK

If he already helps a bit

A household management study by the International Labour Organization showed that full-time housewives spend an outrageous average of fifty-five hours a week on household jobs while women who work outside the home spend roughly thirty hours on housework. This may mean that the employed women work faster, or it may mean that they do less work – either possibility is to be recommended.

How much does your man think he helps in the home?

Him	Mon	Tue	Wed	Thu	Fri	Sat	Sun	Total hours
Washing & ironing								
Preparing meals								
Cleaning								
Shopping								
Washing-up								
Organizing money & bills, etc.								
Repairing household equipment								
Looking after children								
GRAND TOTAL								

The reality of the give-and-take in marriage *still* seems to be that the woman gives and the man takes. In a recent survey, only one in seven marriages showed a husband and wife *equally sharing* the housework. Relate (formerly the Marriage Guidance Council) believe that most men are well intentioned but they *simply don't realize how long it all takes*.

So let him know. Next week, check how many hours you work in the home – and include child-care; then check how many hours he works in the home (see check-list above). Then ask him if he thinks he's helped and, if so, how many hours he reckons he spent working. Don't argue with his estimate, accept it. Ask him if he'll give you those hours next Saturday morning. Hard to say no.

When proportioning equal shares of housework, always relate to hours not to tasks. Otherwise you may argue whether mending the vacuum cleaner is equiva-

lent to getting breakfast. You can't really share any other way – except with money, when paying someone else to do it.

White-collar workers think they help their wives more than they actually do. Macho blue-collar workers help more in the home than they are prepared to admit.

If he doesn't help at all

Ask him how many hours he thinks your housework takes (on no account disagree with his assessment) and next week you work to those hours.

At the end of the week, ask him if he's happy about the state of the place. If he says yes, ask him to do half your hours. If he says no, ask him to do the same hours as you, at the same time as you. Work only *at the same time* as he does. After all, you'll both be working outside your salaried hours. There is then no

How much does your man really help in the home?

You	Mon	Tue	Wed	Thu	Fri	Sat	Sun	Total hours
Washing & ironing								
Preparing meals								
Cleaning								
Shopping								
Washing-up								
Organizing money & bills, etc.								
Repairing household equipment								
Looking after children								
GRAND TOTAL								

argument about how long a job *should* take or has taken. By the end of the week, at least, he will face the fact that housework is a complex, demanding and exhausting job.

If he clearly doesn't want to help you

Don't force him or you may find yourself with a clever saboteur who doesn't even realize how destructive his resentment is to your relationship (see ' The reluctant husband', p. 245).

A recent survey revealed that 20 per cent of arguments in the home are about men not helping enough in the home (I'm surprised that the figure isn't higher). However, if there's an argument about his unwillingness to help, clarify the situation. First go to the doctor and complain of stress. Explain that you are working outside the home because your family needs your salary. If the doctor advises you to do less work, ask your mate to decide which job you give up.

If you have to give up something

Unfortunately, if you give up the paid salary, he may resent not having your money, and if you give up work in the home, he may subsequently resent the discomfort. If you've got the sort of mate who seems to think he deserves a slave, ask him if he wants you to get a part-time instead of a full-time job and lower the housekeeping standards accordingly. (He won't like that, of course, any more than Women's Lib will, but it *is* another alternative.)

Subcontract the housework

A happy relationship is one that offers equal value to both partners, so if *he*

DOWN WITH SUPERWOMAN!

doesn't want to help you with the housework, suggest paying someone else to do it.

I don't know about your principles, but so long as people want cleaning work, I don't see why there shouldn't be cleaners. I prefer to employ strong, male cleaners to do the manual work.

Both of you might pay the same percentage of your salary towards the total cost. Where a woman's health and happiness are at risk, affording outside help is a top priority.

SOME MISTAKES THAT WOMEN MAKE

1 **She doesn't get her mate to clarify his priorities to himself.** Many men don't value housework; what they value in their mate is an attractive status sex symbol, not someone who dusts the bookshelf very carefully. If you haven't enough time or energy to cope with housework as well as passion, ask your mate to state his priorities. Does he want to find you waiting for him in a sheer black nightdress and jackboots, with the breakfast dishes still dirty? Or does he want to inspect the bookshelf? Explain that one of the reasons you want him to share the housework is so that you aren't too tired. (Of course, he may then be. This makes an interesting change.)

2 **She thanks him for his work.** Once he's started doing housework, don't thank him (unless he thanks you every time you wash-up), otherwise he may expect some reward.

3 **She is impatient and unwilling to let him make mistakes while he is learning.** When you're getting someone else to help, it's important to realize that however agonizingly slow, clumsy and incompetent he is at whatever he's doing, he is also learning to do several very important things:

a Help you.
b Clean up after himself.
c Acquire standards that relate to the time available.

4 **She resents doing the housework but doesn't say anything about it.** Instead she allows her resentment to mushroom until her temper snaps: she either pretends that this is about something else or shrilly accuses her surprised mate of never helping, in an aggressive way that is asking for an aggressive reaction from him.

5 **She feels resentful if her man doesn't help in the home but is not prepared to do anything about it,** such as insisting on the man doing his fair share (naturally, fair = half, if both work outside the home).

6 **She's already written him off as a dead loss without asking him to help.** 'No, that's all very well as a theory in a book, but my Bill would *never* ... no ... no ... no ... no ..., it's useless, I'm not going to *try* to get him to help.'

Is Bill at fault?

SO WHAT CAN A MAN DO TO HELP YOU?

Remember that giving birth is the *only* woman's job that a man can't do if he puts his mind to it.

Child-care

Child-care should be carefully and equally shared by both parents, especially when it means sitting up at night with a teething child.

Organization

Have you ever heard a man tell you that you think like a man – clearly meaning this as a compliment? Many men think that they are better disciplined thinkers than women and, therefore, better at organization – so let your man organize the housekeeping. Organizing a family today requires the judgement, concentration and the patience of an air-traffic controller; the grander his job, the more capable he should be at running his home. If he can organize an office, or a union, then he can organize an itsy bitsy little home.

It's the organization side of running a home that's the killer – getting child to dentist, getting cat to vet, getting overcoat to dry cleaner. You don't wake up in the middle of the night thinking 'Aaagh! I forgot to clean the oven.' No, in the small hours you suddenly remember appointments that you didn't keep and arrangements that you didn't make.

Home organization (which used to be called household management) is a skilled job because you're generally dealing with voluntary, unpaid labour (your family) who never listen to a word you say, don't take you seriously and may, from time to time, be unhelpful if not downright subversive.

Managing the home *doesn't count* in the minds of most men as a job, so if you can get him to take this on, I strongly recommend it. Pause for a minute to daydream. Imagine yourself saying 'Isn't my overcoat back from the cleaners *yet*?' . . . 'Toothache, I thought you were going to take her to the dentist last week?' . . . 'That's terrible, but I thought you had her spayed.'

Home organization also involves social life, kids' parties, meeting the in-laws, arranging Christmas, birthdays and remembering anniversaries.

Shopping

I don't know who started the myth that women enjoy shopping, but I'm sure he didn't have to queue up for lamb chops in his lunch hour and then lug them home. However, if a woman can shop in her lunch hour, so can a man.

Men shop better than women because they don't impulse-buy, so another sneaky job to delegate is the shopping, which needs manly strength to carry it home. Pause for a minute and imagine the pleasure of saying, 'But *why* do we need a bottle of *crème de cacao* and artichoke hearts in syrup?'

Cooking

We must remember that men have to counter centuries of conditioning before they pick up a wooden spoon. It is therefore *our duty* to encourage and help our underprivileged menfolk to cook for us, to realize how glamorous and exciting this pastime is and that it is not just women's work.

We are always being told that men are better chefs than women, so don't stand in his way. Cooking is creative and most males are as creative as most females. (More so, if you pay attention to people who draw up huge lists of male composers/writers/artists.)

Weekends are the ideal time to start putting your husband and sons in charge of the kitchen.

If, in however small a way, you can involve the people you cook for in the actual preparation of the meals (fetching and carrying if not cooking), you will be amazed at the swiftness by which their standards of expectation fall.

Vary your methods according to the man, but before he starts always make it clear that a good cook always cleans up after himself, or the whole performance will turn into a charade as far as saving work for *you* is concerned. And get some manly apron for him, such as a navy blue butcher's apron.

Praise every single burnt offering he produces. Don't tell lies, just notice the good bits, as you wish he did for you.

DOWN WITH SUPERWOMAN!

Remember, it is easier to praise than to cook.

Next, plan some exotic dish that is *assembled* rather than cooked. Ask him to help you, and praise, praise, praise. The following week, ask him to make it while you do some nasty essential job (so you can't be asked to help). Cleaning a lavatory is a good alternative job.

Use Positive Encouragement for your man's Sunday barbecue effort, or whatever his speciality develops into, and tell all his friends about it. Get it *firmly labelled* as his speciality. Buy him the special equipment needed for making this dish.

Then, gently suggest that as he is so marvellous at barbecues, or whatever, would he like to try ... (you name it – something dramatic that he loves to eat). You buy the ingredients, you lay them out, you lead him to them, then head back to the sofa.

The one-parent cook

I personally can never, never understand anyone who sees cooking as a refreshing hobby. I wish I could. I see it as something that keeps on coming at you three times a day, relentlessly, a thousand meals a year for years and years.

Cooking for a family is the most time-consuming chore in the whole home routine, and one of the advantages of *not* having a mate around the house is that, suddenly, it *isn't*. You cook for the kids and they're easily satisfied; you're satisfied even more easily.

A one-parent cook has a much easier job than cooking for a family, because once your mate isn't around, you behave much more logically about food.

When I stopped doing a full-time job (so stopped being able to afford home help), what I found most irksome was that my children were invariably late to the midday meal. But, as they pointed out, I had always said that if they were

doing something productive (such as finishing a puppet, *not* such as watching television), then they shouldn't drop everything to focus on their stomach.

We reorganized meals to really suit ourselves, not what we were supposed to want. I cooked a hot breakfast early in the morning and they were expected to be on time.

I saw that there was always plenty of fresh fruit, cheese, salads and home-baked bread (and home-made soup in winter). When my sons decided it was mealtime, they helped themselves. They didn't snack, a habit that they knew led to incessant eating and thick waistlines.

I still did the cooking and when they wanted a traditional evening meal, I prepared a menu on a bit of thick card, like a restaurant. They ordered a meal from me, as if they were in a restaurant, booking it in advance and sometimes inviting friends. They felt deliriously grand placing their orders with me, and I got away with very little cooking. I could check that they were eating properly at lunch-time simply by checking my shopping list against what remained in the refrigerator. (At first, they immediately ate all the fruit, so we didn't have any until next shopping day.)

Eventually, without much effort on my part, my cooking was cut down to about four meals a week, which I quite enjoyed, because I then cooked without resentment and was greatly praised for it.

Encouraging the kids to cook If a child can do it, let it. My system worked well with my two sons. Lead your own down the path that *they* want to tread.

The extension of teaching my sons to cook for themselves was to teach them to cook for me. My youngest, unaided and unsupervised, began doing the marketing, cooking and cleaning for my business lunches (at home) when he was 12. I paid him and we were both pleased with the system. I kept the meals simple, with dishes that I knew he could put together correctly. All my guests were fascinated.

This also had a hidden benefit: it stopped the finicky habits he and his brother had before the pay-as-you-cook system was put into operation. Before that, one son wouldn't eat meat, the other refused to eat eggs, and they both refused to touch fish: I used to live from one cauliflower cheese to the next, because neither of them complained about *that*.

Cleaning

I've never understood why women were supposedly created by God to do housework. Housework is exhausting physical labour and therefore men were created bigger, stronger and better equipped than women to, say, scrub floors. Clearly, God intended men to do the heavy work – because he gave them muscles.

Vacuum-cleaning is a job that many men actually enjoy (because it is working with a machine?). And it looks easy – until you start heaving sofas to one side. Vacuuming is also *the longest cleaning job in the home*, if it is done properly. Naturally, you keep quiet about both these drawbacks and if he offers to vacuum, say yes very fast.

The one-parent cleaner A single woman with a family not only has to do all the work herself but may find it punctuated by constant interruptions. If you are in this position, pair with a woman in a similar position and share chores. For instance, one woman can shop for both of them while the other baby-sits. One woman baby-sits for both while the other cleans.

THE GRAND FAMILY PLAN (Sneaky ways to get your family to clean)

The people who should do the housework are the people who live in the house and make the work in the first place: when they do, somehow this immediately and magically cuts down the work.

However, you have to coax them to do it, and there's no use getting away from this. So try to make it fun for them, just as you try to coax a baby to eat its egg by cutting the bread and butter into soldiers.

Your initial aims should be:

1 Get the rest of the family to help you, in the way that they accept, or it won't work (see below).
2 Get the rest of the family tidy, which they will accept only once they are sharing the responsibilities of the housework (see below).

Women raise their sons, then complain that men don't work in the home. I managed to get my two sons tidy and persuaded them to help me do the housework between 9 and 11 on Saturday mornings. Should you try this, it would be training your sons to be helpful husbands and your daughters to *expect* helpful husbands.

I am proud of my sons because they can clean a room, cook a meal and expect to share the housework wherever they are. If you want the perfect man, then grow your own.

One of the best ideas I brought back from a world tour was ... try *making it competitive*. (In fact, try this even if you're alone.)

I was introduced to this idea by a Canadian disc jockey who had turned his weekly cleaning routine into a personal mini-Olympic marathon. His system for cleaning his two-bedroom flat every Saturday morning was to set the kitchen timer and try to beat his own Olympic record, which was 45 minutes and 32 seconds, when last we spoke.

Mentally divide all work into three parts, preferably with each person handling one part: 1 kitchen; 2 bathroom; 3 tidy/dust/vacuum/spot clean items.

DOWN WITH SUPERWOMAN!

Think: BEAT THE CLOCK!

Note: Don't try this idea on any hired help or they won't stay long. This routine is strictly to get volunteers to finish the work as fast as possible.

How to get them tidy

You can't expect other people to be tidy unless you make it easy for them. Put all your drawers, cupboards and shelves in order – and then keep them that way. Have a place for everything, then everyone knows its place. This is why my kitchen has no china cupboards – only wide shelves over the double sink unit – so anyone who is washing-up can see where everything goes.

Establish order, not chaos, in your kitchen cupboards. If you don't keep things in order, then *they* won't know where to find them – or put them away. (You can always tell if someone is careless, lazy, dirty and untidy by looking in the cupboard under the kitchen sink.)

In spite of every temptation, stick to the order you plan. If you wander away from this, *you* will forget where you've put things; it's restful to know that the string is *always* in the string place and the bin liners are *always* in the bin liner place.

If you really have trouble getting your family to be tidy, try *paying* another person in the family to tidy up for a week. Pay him outrageously well to do this. Make it clear that everyone else is *supposed* to tidy up after themselves to help him. The tidier will complain (justifiably) about everyone else (including Dad). Do not tidy up yourself during this period.

Let everyone in the family have a turn at being the money-making tidier. This plan takes time to work and it won't work until everyone has had a go at being the tidier. It's quite amusing to watch the predictable reactions as an untidy person changes to the tidier. As soon as a child has to tidy a room, it becomes aggressively tidy: '*Why* did you leave that *there*? *Now* I'll have to pick it up next Saturday.'

Training your family to be tidy is far easier and far more important than it sounds. It will add to your comfort and save aggro and harassment because you'll know where to find things.

How much can children help to do the actual work?

Be careful not to ask too much too early from children – otherwise you may double the work for Mum and harass both of you. When my sons were small, I found it difficult to slow down my working pace to a child's pace. I found it easier not to expect any help from my children when small. I find that small children are *no use* in an effective domestic routine. They are slow and messy and they break things.

Children over 8 *can* be expected to provide a certain amount of self-help. They can make their own beds and tidy their rooms. When over 10, they can wash-up – but not before; it's not worth the effort to get them to do it and then have to check it, and then get them to re-do it.

After my youngest was 10, we *all* did all the work on a Saturday morning, from 9 to 11, at which moment we *all* smartly stopped work. From the age of 8 they bought and looked after their own clothes (except for overcoats). Instead of dirtying two shirts a day, my eldest wore the first shirt he bought – smothered in purple flowers – for a week and would not be parted from it.

Introducing the Grand Family Plan

The aim of the Grand Family Plan is to get the entire family happily doing the housework with you. No one is suggesting that you start to run the place like a concentration camp, but merely to clarify who is willing to help you keep the place clean, which is only a part of running a happy home.

Only ever discuss the Grand Family Plan when the family is together (over a festive meal is easiest) because unless they *all* hear what's going on, they won't understand what's going on. And if they don't understand, you won't get their co-operation. Don't call it housework, call it system-support work (space rocket jargon), which sounds more fun to men.

1 Establish clearly whether or not they are willing to help with the system-support work and, if so, how many hours or how many job areas they will do. (Refer back to the check-list when discussing help from your man.) If children are helping, train your team to be self-sufficient (another acceptable manly phrase).
2 Decide how much work *you* personally are going to do and at what times, and stick to these times or this plan won't work. *Casually* tell your family what your new working hours are. Ask them to decide what they want *you* to do in your system-support time.
3 Don't force any job on an unwilling worker. Just don't do it yourself in future.

Now divide the system-support work into four sorts of jobs:

1 **Easy enough for an 8-year-old** and aimed at getting him to clear up after himself by making his own sleeping bag, emptying his own waste bin and clearing away *completely* after play.
2 **Everyday tidying and cleaning.**
3 **Entertaining** Christmas/Easter/birthday celebrations/dinner parties.
4 **Special jobs** such as gardening, looking after pets and leisure equipment.

After the festive meal, get family agreement on the No. 1 jobs. Don't try any-

thing else for the **first month**. At times this may seem like more work for you, not less, but remember that you are training people, which takes time and patience.

At the second month give another festive meal and suggest that each family member is responsible in turn for a week at keeping the place tidy during the second month. Don't lift a finger to tidy yourself, except during your week.

At the third month repeat the festive meal and ask your family to agree to do the housework all at the same time once a week. Choose a time when everyone can be present: the earlier in the day, the easier this will be.

Ask them if they would like to try the BEAT THE CLOCK routine.

At the fourth month ask for volunteers for the No. 4 jobs. Discuss whether it is possible to cut down on gardening. Should you keep the pets (howls of rage)? If so, who will look after them?

After the fourth month, when a No. 3 job looms ahead, discuss how you can all divide up the work. Give them another delicious meal, after which you produce a list of the work involved and ask for volunteers. (No volunteers is a wonderful excuse for cutting down on Christmas.)

Naturally, the Grand Family Plan won't proceed smoothly, but remember that *you are training your family*. You are breaking the conditioning of centuries. You won't succeed overnight, but what you are doing is very important: you're teaching your children to do work and accept responsibility, and to delegate both.

Ask your family for their suggestions and try hard to get their suggestions to work. Your co-operation will encourage their co-operation. Ignore sarcastic remarks.

Don't let your family manipulate you

into losing your temper, because you will make no progress. Remember that anything that isn't done as agreed *stays undone*. Remember your antenatal breathing exercises and try to distance yourself from the stormy situations that are bound to happen.

In a showdown, ask your family in what priority they see the No. 1/2/3/4 category jobs. You will then see how much they value a smooth-running, clean home – and how much they value *you*. You may decide to lower your unappreciated high standards.

Our motto: A home that runs on oiled wheels is a caravan.

HOW ORGANIZED DO YOU WANT TO BE?

A tycoon millionairess once told me that she found a business easier to run than a home. I'm sure she's right. I've never yet been able to make the housekeeping show a profit, but my system is to run it in the same way as I run an office, with a planned budget, purchasing and filing department (all me). This is not nearly as clever or complicated as it sounds. Any sane woman in a perfect world wouldn't bother, but if like me you've lost two vacuum cleaners and £140 worth of laundry in one year you'll know it's worthwhile.

The equipment

All you need to get organized is a writing surface, a chair, a kitchen drawer (or a tote bag or a concertina file), a large cardboard box or a bit of shelf space on which to store three wire office trays or shopping bags (IN, OUT and PEND), eight double-sided envelope files with which to start a filing system, a duplicate book, two notebooks, envelopes and writing paper, a handbag diary and notebook, an address book – and some pretty postcards.

Throw anything that isn't urgent into the PEND tray. Mysteriously, you will be able to throw most of it away at the end of the month.

DOWN WITH SUPERWOMAN!

Shopping lists

Using Magictape, stick a shopping check-list of food and household items you often buy in the back of your address book.

Expect – or rather, exact – no co-operation from your family; it will result in a restful state of non-expectancy and consequent non-nagging, non-resentfulness for everyone. The only family rule is: everyone must write in the shopping list notebook what is *about* to run out. This works, because the family doesn't see it as a chore but a sensible necessity. They know if they don't do it, there will be no peanut butter or whatever they're about to scoff.

Keys

Keep a spare set of all your door and car keys. If you haven't got a spare set, have another set made by a locksmith – find him in the *Yellow Pages*.

Telephone

A telephonaholic cannot resist the ring; she sits there twitching and wondering what important or wonderful thing she is missing (on the some-day-my-prince-will-phone theory). If you are a telephonaholic, while you are doing a job that you don't want interrupted – whether it's making love or pastry – pull out the plug or take the phone off the hook.

Bernard Shaw didn't answer the telephone because he said if the reason was important enough, the ringer would write, and if it wasn't, then it didn't matter.

If you are a slave to the telephone (that is, if you always pick it up obediently when it rings for you) and you want to learn *not* to answer it, remember that you are not one of Pavlov's dogs. Regard the telephone as an intruder, an interruptor. When it rings, ignore it.

Decide to be the one who *makes* the telephone calls rather than the one who answers them. Of course, this is more expensive, but it saves your time.

The mail

When I worked from home, I used to throw incoming mail in a wicker basket on top of the refrigerator and outgoing mail in a string bag hanging by the kitchen door. I opened the mail immediately after breakfast and dealt with small items by postcard.

It's easier to write a line than a letter. Try to write thank-yous on pretty postcards as soon as you get home, while you're still feeling grateful. Also use postcards for Christmas thank-yous: last year's list was polished off in half an hour. I know a barrister who keeps her postcards *already stamped* in an elegant basket by her bed.

Weightier things such as bank statements were thrown into the IN tray for Wednesday morning, when I did all my office work, tardy thank-yous and general organization. Anything that didn't get done on Wednesday didn't get done. There is always another Wednesday.

Bills

Always save business letters, bills and *receipts* (otherwise what proof have you that you paid cash to the man who mended the sink, when his firm sends you an invoice for it six months later?). This is especially necessary in this unnerving age of automation: computers *do* go wrong, and people with (or without) computers *can* be even more inefficient than you.

I may be paranoid but I've noticed that computers never go wrong in my favour. And, when you've been invoiced for £200 for a real pigskin bidet, which you haven't dreamed of, let alone bought, remember that it can take six weeks for a computer to answer the simple question: 'What proof have you that this was ordered?' Keep a duplicate book in your bill file for letters about bills-in-query. Don't send them the receipt that proves you've paid; if you do, you may lose your proof. Trace the signature, send a photocopy or quote the reference.

Work lists

My work notebook is just a list of non-food work to do and reads 'buy name-tapes', 'order lampshade', 'get new sink stopper', etc. I never promise to do anything unless I have scribbled it down in a handbag notebook or work book.

I went through these every Wednesday morning, ticking off a job when I had done something about it, and crossing it out when it was completed. I wrote work lists on right-hand pages only and made any notes about the job on the left-hand side of the page. So when the laundry promised it would return the purple towel, I ticked the note, but not until the towel had been welcomed home did I cross it off completely.

Supposing the right-hand page says 'Query telephone bill'; on the left-hand page jot the date and name of the person you have discussed it with. If the argument goes on for weeks, you can *always* flip back to that left-hand page and make dated notes of the continuing saga (it helps to have a wristwatch with a day and date calendar).

I used to go through six notebooks a year and I kept them (they take up little room in a grocery box under the sofa, and it's amazing how useful they are).

Always check everything in and out of your house, getting someone to sign in your work notebook for anything they remove. Date it. As service gets worse, people get more harassed and work is skimped or rushed. The busier you are, the more you should make it a rule always to keep check of who has what and where.

When signing for any parcel, always add 'not inspected' or 'not tested', whichever applies.

Jeer if you must, but this sort of efficiency takes no time, only care, and can save a lot of trauma.

The only New Year's resolution I keep is to look at my yearly list – things to do on 1 January. Sometimes you may feel too frail to cope with things on 1 January, in which case do them as soon as convenient. The list may look dreadful, but I found that mine (reproduced here for your inspiration) took only two hours to sort out last year. On 1 January? No, on 14 February.

New Year check-list

* Apply for car licence with MOT certificate, registration book and insurance certificate.
* Insurance, personal, house, etc.
* Check national insurance payments are up to date. (If you're running a business, even the smallest business, consider sending accountant one year's stamp money in advance after April, when the yearly amount is fixed.)
* AA membership renewal.
* Check bank standing orders.
* Check passports up to date.
* TV licence.
* Service central heating and Ascot, also all electrical appliances, such as dishwashers and washing machine.
* Check roof and gutters, chimneys.
* Service car.

Fill in your check-list on p. 277.

Income tax

If you use an accountant (perhaps you work at a part-time business), at the end of your financial year the minimum you should prepare for him is the following:

1 Cheque-books, up to date, with stubs

properly filled in and list of entries from current cheque-books (or, if you haven't finished your current cheque-books, send them off and start new ones).

2 Bank paying-in book.
3 Other bank correspondence.
4 Order books.
5 Invoices for work.
6 Receipts in date order. (If you've got a lot of receipts, subdivide them into twelve clear plastic folders, each labelled with the appropriate month. The more of the accountant's work you can do yourself, the less it costs you for expert time.)
7 Diary.
8 Cash-flow position at end of year.
9 Other items as follows:

If you haven't an accountant, deal with any income tax work.

New diary

In my new diary I jot down all seasonal items, transferring them from year to year. (Sow 8 kg (18 lb) coarse shade grass seed every March, rake up lawn, ignore existing grass, which will look messy for a few days then spring to life. Hose well immediately after.) I also jot odd notes in the back of the diary, knowing that I won't read them until the year's end: a Christmas present list, a list of the current medicines the family is dosing itself with, the collar sizes of my favourite men and the overall size of my mother-in-law.

Writer Katharine Whitehorn wants me to recommend her one and only organized habit. Write your name and address and 'Please, please return' in front of every single notebook, diary or address book you ever use. These have frequently been returned to her by bus conductors, taxi drivers, friends and strangers.

THE DRAWER WITH THE ANSWER TO EVERYTHING
and what to put in it

Filing is a word that makes most women look mutinous, but it's not only a good idea – in home emergencies it's absolutely essential. Don't be frightened by the idea of filing. The verb only means putting things in a sensible place where you can find them quickly and easily.

Know your limitations and don't plan a filing system that is better than you are, as you won't stick to it and you *will* find that even more depressing than doing it.

What follows sounds amazingly neat and tidy, but it isn't. Most of my key work seems to be on the front of old envelopes (backs already used for key work). If I stopped to type or write them out, they would never get done; it's easier to shove any old scrap of paper into its correct place in the system than to have it lying around.

The simplest filing system

This might just be an alphabetically indexed cardboard document wallet. 'Do

NEW YEAR CHECK-LIST

_____
_____
_____
_____
_____
_____
_____
_____
_____
_____
_____
_____
_____
_____
_____
_____
_____
_____
_____
_____
_____
_____
_____
_____
_____
_____
_____
_____
_____
_____
_____
_____
_____

DOWN WITH SUPERWOMAN!

tell teenagers to buy one of these and use the front section as an IN tray,' urged a 22-year-old musician. 'I got one six months ago and it has revolutionized my life. At last, instead of wondering if it's under my bed or behind the bookcase, I *know* that my bank statement's in the file, and so are my CVs, exam certificates, school reports and insurance certificates.' Alternatively, a Twinlock personal file suitcase is more expensive but durable.

My humble system started with two cardboard mushroom boxes labelled IN and OUT, and one kitchen drawer that deserves its peeling label: The drawer with the answer to everything. It contained eight standard office cardboard files with two pockets each, providing sixteen compartments, which should be enough for any fun-loving, file-hating, harassed housewife.

What to put in your files

Everyone's individual filing system is a different sort of organized chaos. Once you've started it, the only thing you will have to remember is that this repository, whatever its size or situation, is from now on the *one and only safe place in the house*. Any scrap of valuable paper (except money) should be in it, even if it's just saved in the huge envelope labelled 'For sorting out sometime'.

File roughly as follows, according to your circumstances and tidiness potential, in the eight double pocket files you have bought.

File 1 (A) **Guarantees.**
(B) **Instruction leaflets.**
File 2 (A) **Health** A little notebook listing children's illnesses with dates, health certificates, family National Health cards.
(B) **Licences** for yearly renewal, e.g. television licences.
File 3 **Household** (A) Hopeless garden-

ing schedule, with plan of garden, so when next spring's tulips fail to appear, you can check that you were at least looking for them in the right place.
(B) Linen, cutlery and china list, if you care about these things. I do. I like to know how much disappears each year. Also a list of the different strength light bulbs used in the house.
File 4 **Personal** (A) Recipes and diets and all their magic appurtenances, like the note you wrote to yourself saying 'One slice of bread a day equals 365 slices a year, which equals huge hips.'
(B) Useful things torn out of magazines, such as how to clean your jewellery, and how to get to Hong Kong for £50, what revives a cyclamen and a list of all-night rave places in Paris. This file is never used, but I find it a comfort.
File 5 (A) **Important documents** What's important is a highly personal decision. When I was bringing up a family, my file contained passports, children's post-office savings books, premium bonds (we had one), marriage and birth certificates, insurance certificates, tax coding notices and similar potential drama, along with the first (and only) love letter my first husband wrote to me. Ah well, on with the filing.
(B) Overspill from 5 (A).
File 6 (A) **Money** file. Stick bills in one pocket, leaving the other side for bank statements, used and unused chequebooks, and paying-in books. As my official paying-in book meant entering everything twice, I now use a stationer's little duplicate book with numbered pages and carbon paper. So far it hasn't jammed the bank's computer.
(B) **Expenses** This is essential if you are running a business, however small. You *must* keep all expense records, however trivial, for income tax purposes. Your accountant can't win the battle without the maximum ammunition.
File 7 (A) and (B) **Receipts** Just put them in and sort out only when

someone's accusing you of not paying the parking fine for which you bitterly remember writing a cheque. (No one ever puts that seven-figure reference number on a cheque stub; partly because there isn't room for it and partly because you're so cross at the time.)

File 8 (A) **Household addresses** This file contains a sheet of paper with a list of names, addresses and telephone numbers that are important to you and anyone who is temporarily in charge. For example: doctor; dentist; vet; garage; AA or RAC emergency numbers; taxis; police; hospital; child welfare/antenatal/family planning clinics; telephone engineer, directory inquiries and telegrams; drain cleaner; plumber; builder; local town hall (for complaining about non-removal of dustbins or eccentric reshaping of same); local fuel sources (i.e., coal or oil supplier); British Gas; Electricity Board; electrical repair shops (incidentally, I vaguely believe in buying all electrical appliances from one firm, if possible (depending on what *Which?* recommends) as you can then establish a friendly first-names relationship with *one* complaints department instead of several); TV repair men; window cleaner; local shops; laundry; railway station, coach station, airport; nearest all-night chemist, if you're lucky enough to have one; local cinema and theatres, ditto; odd-job man. And so on, according to your own idiosyncrasies and odd-job men. (See 'How to get hold of the VIPs in your life', p. 418.)

(B) **Photographs** of any good silver or other portable valuables and antiques. With crime on the increase and insurance premiums soaring at rates that defy gravity, the prompt supply of these details to the police can often lead to their recovery. Could you describe such things from memory at this agitated moment, including the brand name of radios and watches?

In fact, you might, given the strength, time, patience and a rainy Sunday afternoon, draw up a list of your **family numbers**, so you won't have to remember to fill them in the beginning of your diary every year. These range from National Health numbers, National Insurance numbers, passport numbers, driving licence numbers, insurance policy numbers, radios, cassettes, stereos, TV, video recorder, answer machine, cameras, watches, bicycles, slide and cinema projectors, cars: almost anything mechanical and stealable has a serial number somewhere on the case. Note these numbers with a description of the object. Also include any car or scooter numbers. For some reason the police think you need slapping straight into a straitjacket if you can't remember your car number – but some brains are pondering mightier things, such as whether to file love letters under X for kisses and did you remember to put the plastic losable key to the washing machine in your jewel box, where the baby can't grab it to teethe on?

It's a good idea to add a list of the items that you keep in your handbag, together with their *serial numbers*: credit cards, Barclaycard, Access card, £50 cheque card, cheque-books, union card, library card, driving licence, car insurance certificate, National Trust life membership card. In case of theft you can quickly inform the police, credit card companies and bank, and cancel or replace these items.

If there is still room in your drawer, keep an envelope or plastic bag full of assorted sticky labels, for files, jam jars, etc., and if you can bear it, wander round your home with string and labels and remove unused keys from furniture and suitcases, labelling the keys as you go and putting them in a plastic bag. This saves time when you are trying to keep, find and/or identify keys that are rarely used. I also note in my receipt book anyone who has a front door key, however temporarily. Burglaries are most upsetting and unsettling.

DOWN WITH SUPERWOMAN!

That is the minimum efficiency method. Read on if you feel you can take something slightly more grandiose; if, for example, you have complicated home help or do stalwart voluntary work or are running a cottage industry (I know a girl who started a thriving lunch business by selling pizzas out of her kitchen window to the office workers in the factory opposite).

More advanced filing

The advanced filer uses a proper filing cabinet. You might – as I did – use an old orange box or a wire crate, until I bought a second-hand filing cabinet and resprayed it scarlet. Now if anyone asked me what I would save in a fire, I would say that cabinet.

I was encouraged to buy that filing cabinet by the beautiful historian Lady Antonia Pinter. She said that it took her two years to get around to buying one and another year to summon up the energy to fill it, but that it really does work and she can find something like the television licence in a minute. But only *she* can find it, because Lady Antonia believes in surrounding herself with a certain amount of uncertainty, if not mystery. So, she has a secret system which only she understands: bills, for instance, are not filed under B but under U for unpleasant.

My filing cabinet is a four-drawer clanger. The top drawer is for boring business and the files are in alphabetical order A–Z, then Insurance, Accountant, Receipts, Bills; the second drawer is for my writing work; the third drawer has personal files labelled Art, Skiing, Swimming and Voluntary Work; the fourth drawer holds family things such as birth certificates, photographs and letters.

You think that's going too far? American matriarch Rose Kennedy kept a card index on *each* of her eight children.

Your filing system

Ruthlessly cut down on filing. One way of doing this is to do it yourself even when you can afford not to.

The basic theory of a filing system is that of drawing up a family tree. Starting from the trunk, everything from the tree branches outwards until you get to the twigs, which are subdivisions of the smallest branches. Similarly, everything in your filing system stems from a group of ideas that become increasingly refined. There's the main subject, then subsidiary branches, then perhaps twigs on each branch.

The front pocket of your filing system should contain a guide to the system, in case you forget it.

Don't leave paper-clips in filing, because they come apart; instead use staples. Always file in date order, with the most recent paper in front. Always file *behind* the file reference (people whose names start with A are filed *behind* A – not in front of it – in an alphabetical file index).

Your main subjects might be:

Accountant, general correspondence
Accountant, paperwork for
Accountant, notes for
Agents
Bills
Correspondence, specific, for people and firms with whom you regularly deal (keep in alphabetical order)
Design, ideas
Design, job costings
Design, orders
Design, correspondence
Export, orders
Export, correspondence
Insurance, policies
Insurance, correspondence
Invoices, yours to other people
Lawyer
Miscellaneous correspondence (date order)
Money, bank statement

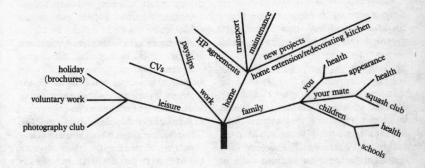

Labels in diagram:
holiday (brochures) · CVs · payslips · HP agreements · transport · maintenance · new projects · home extension/redecorating · kitchen · health · you · appearance · health · voluntary work · leisure · work · home · family · your mate · squash club · photography club · children · health · schools

Money, bank correspondence
Money, bookkeeping books A, B, C, D, E, F
Office administration
Orders from you, order book A
Orders to you (never accept an order, unless it's written on official letterhead, dated, numbered and signed)
Invoice books
Petty-cash vouchers

It doesn't matter how simple and scruffy your system is, so long as you bother to invest a couple of hours in setting it up. You don't even need a filing cabinet: use a couple of grocer's cardboard boxes.

THE SHORTEST SECRETARIAL COURSE IN THE WORLD

If at my christening a fairy godmother had offered me the choice of beauty, brains or brilliant opportunities in life, I'd have sat up in my cradle and said, 'What's the long-term use of those in today's world without a secretarial training?' If, like me, you haven't had one, here are a few tips to make the family admin as fast and as easy as possible.

Forget shorthand and typing. As a journalist, I never felt the loss of shorthand because I learned to write fast and shorten words: biz admin isnt dif.* I have worked with different people all around the world with a communication system that consisted only of a telephone, a duplicate book and a ballpoint pen. Nobody complained; a few people started to use the same method.

What you *may* need to know about is *basic bookkeeping and filing.* Learning how to do both efficiently shouldn't take you more than two hours (for bookkeeping, see 'Starting your own business', p. 365). The reason that I had to learn both these things was not only to earn my living, but also in order to run a home in minimal time.

I asked Kathy (who used to work with me and now runs a button-dyeing business) what were the most useful things she had learned from me. She said, 'You taught me to run a home efficiently, so when I went into business, I just ran it like a home! It's all a matter of common sense and it's no trouble, once you buy a few notebooks and start *doing it.*'

* Business administration isn't difficult.

DOWN WITH SUPERWOMAN!

When I had no help in my home I used to imagine that I was looked after by the entire cast of *Upstairs, Downstairs*. 'Thank you, Rose,' I would say on Sunday morning as I looked at the pretty breakfast-in-bed-tray that I had just prepared for myself. The most useful person on my invisible staff was Sally, my invisible secretary, who did all my secretarial work on Wednesday morning (Monday morning was spent cleaning up after the weekend, Tuesday morning was washday). Problems that arrived after Wednesday morning were saved for the following Wednesday. This is how Sally operated; perhaps you can use some of her methods.

Setting up as your own secretary will cost you a few pounds and a few hours, but it may be the best investment you have ever made. For the cost of a cotton dress, your home should run smoothly and efficiently, in minimal time. Don't start using all the suggested systems simultaneously: wait until you are comfortable with one system before moving on to the next.

Sally the secretary's shopping list

Everything is available from Ryman's stationers unless otherwise mentioned.

* **A twenty-four page book with plastic pockets** measuring 23.5 × 31 cm (9¼ × 12¼ in) (Ryman's display book, black, 24-pocket, ref. A4-93270) to use as a stationery dispenser. Alternatively, use an old magazine.
* **A box of big paper-clips**, as small paper-clips don't grip a lot of papers. Keep them handy in an ashtray.
* **Six big bulldog clips**, approx. 8 cm (3 in) long. Small bulldogs don't grip a lot of papers.
* **Stainless steel shears** with 15-cm (6-in) cutting edge.

* **Tippex** A fast-drying white liquid for painting out your secretarial mistakes. Always buy white writing paper, otherwise white Tippex will not be invisible: coloured Tippex complicates life.
* **A proper office stapler** A small one doesn't grip a lot of papers. Also useful as a paperweight.
* **Magic tape**, for sticking paper together. Magic tape is the only sort you can write on in ballpoint pen.
* **A proper heavy desk dispenser for the Magic tape,** which you can manipulate with one hand.
* **Three HB pencils with rubber on top/three black ballpoint pens/three red ballpoint pens/three coloured highlighters** Highlighting makes things easier to take in at a glance, when you refer to them for a second time. For instance, on an electricity bill, highlight the amount payable, the reference number and date of the bill.
* **A big loose-leaf address book** measuring 22 × 17 cm (8½ × 6¾ in), with an easy-clean plastic cover (ref. Concorde CD6/P).
* **A big desk diary with yearly planner** measuring 21 × 14 cm (8¼ × 5½ in) (Langham Diary, A4 size, ref. LA53). Provides a week at a glance.
* **Some small, lined, coloured index cards**, approx. 10 × 13 cm (4 × 5 in).
* **A large duplicate book** with a piece of carbon paper in it – this is what I took round the world (Challenge duplicate book, 19 × 25 cm (7½ × 9¾ in), ref. 6 6617 3). Use it for writing letters when you want to keep a copy, for confirming telephone conversations or notes at a two-person meeting. Tear off the top copy, hand it to the other person and you both have a record of what was agreed.

* **A small duplicate book for receipts,** approx. 9 × 13 cm (3½ × 5 in) (ref. Challenge).
* **Coloured notepads,** approx. 9 × 9 cm (3½ × 3½ in) to keep by telephone, bed or on desk. If you make notes on these, it's very easy to shuffle them, like a pack of cards, into logical order.
* **Two exercise books with different coloured covers** (so you can tell them apart) A4 size, 21 × 14 cm (8¼ × 5½ in).
* **A yellow legal pad,** approx. 20 × 30 cm (7⅞ × 11¾ in). Get the sort with a margin and a serrated tear-off top.
* If you haven't a desk, you'll need a stiff **clipboard,** so that your writing pad doesn't bend beneath your pen.
* **Yellow Post-it notes,** approx. 7 × 7 cm (2¾ × 2¾ in) (see 'Monitor a project', p. 285).
* **Six clear plastic files,** approx. 23 × 32 cm (9 × 12½ in). Keep them in a box file or a tote bag.
* **Two red plastic files,** approx. 23 cm × 32 cm (9 × 12½ in), for top priority work.
* **Sticky labels** for labelling the above files. Once you've finished one job, stick a fresh label over the previous label. The *only* label size to get is 4.5 × 2.5 cm (1¾ × 1 in): bigger labels are too difficult to handle neatly in a hurry, smaller ones have insufficient room to write.
* **A book that teaches you how to find out anything you want to know:** *Research: A Handbook for Writers and Journalists* (published by A. & C. Black). How I wish I had read this slim book before I worked in Fleet Street, where I spent years discovering what it contains. Whether you want to trace your family tree or research your first novel, read it. I have never met author Ann Hoffman, but I think of her as a valued friend because of the

charm, usefulness and enthusiasm of her book.

Optional purchases

* **A five-tier stationery dispenser (in/pend/out/file/paper dispenser)** This leaves working space on your table top.
* **An A4 lever-arch file** (see 'Project files', p. 286).
* **A set of coloured file dividers**
* **A hole puncher,** if you're buying a lever-arch file.
* You don't need a room to work in if you get a **trolley;** a household trolley or a vegetable rack on wheels (from John Lewis) will do. You can then wheel it up to any table and SHAZAM!, you have a desk. Alternatively, Habitat have a chest on wheels, which contains 2 drawers and a filing system – your portable office.

Have nothing on your desk or tabletop except the project you are working on and at the end of the day sweep that on to the trolley or into a basket or drawer.

* I have **two stacking wire baskets,** which are easier to shove things into than a drawer.
* Have a **large waste-paper bin,** not a small one that constantly needs emptying. I have used a wicker log basket, a swingtop plastic dustbin and a laundry basket as a waste-paper basket. The plastic dustbin suits me best.

How to use your equipment

Address book Never throw away an old address book. Keep it in the filing. If you use the following system, you'll never need another address book.

Get a ring-binder address book, so that you can add extra pages. Make a plastic pocket in the front and back of the cover by cutting two plastic folders a bit smaller than the size of the cover. Using Sellotape, strap one plastic folder to each inside cover, with the open part pointing towards the ring binder (otherwise everything will fall out).

In the back envelope put directions to get to people's homes or offices; use the front envelope to keep visiting cards and notes of people's addresses until you've got time to write them in your address book.

Write only in capital letters. Write only with a pencil, which you keep in the front plastic pocket. As it has a rubber on top, you can easily amend the entry if someone changes his telephone number.

At the back of the book I keep extra blank pink pages for insertions. Some addresses are lodged, not under names, but under occupations: D for Doctors, H for Household (you'll never remember the name of the drain expert), O for Office contacts, B for Birthdays, N for Numbers (I've put down everything from NI number to car number). In the front of the book I have A for Amnesia – for people with forgettable names who I want to remember for a reason, such as an expert on bats.

The desk diary has a yearly planner up front. Use your highlighter to fill in holidays, school holidays, any other blocks of time that you want to remember when making other plans.

My diary plan The left part of the page is for appointments, the right part of the page is for things I have to do and people I have to telephone. Anything I don't manage to do, I highlight in yellow and these items are then my priority for the following day. I always try to fill in tomorrow's activities the night before.

It took a couple of weeks for me to get this system working. At the end of the week I could instantly see which jobs I somehow never got around to doing. There they were – highlighted and carried forward from day to day. I either do it first thing on Wednesday morning or forget it for ever.

Incidentally, this size diary is a good one to use as a bedside journal: as there isn't much space to fill, you might get beyond January.

If I go out for the day, I take a **small coloured index card** upon which I write the day's appointments, addresses and things to buy or do. This is a system that other people notice and start copying; suddenly, you have no cards left.

Never let anyone have your business papers without a detailed *receipt*, not the Duke of Edinburgh or the Archbishop of Canterbury or your sister or your lawyer. I keep my receipt book near the front door ever since my accountant friend, Brian, told me that when handing over anything to anyone (especially if it's any sort of a document) I should *get a receipt*. Brian also carries a small duplicate book to *all* meetings; any agreement can be scribbled down and signed and as the book is in date order, he can check back in it by comparing it to his diary. He never tears anything out of this book but, instead, photostats it.

The yellow legal pad Everyone I know who gets things done has some sort of personal organization system. It may be a simple list of things to do. It may be a notebook in the handbag plus a pocket calendar; it may be a diary; it may be a legal pad. What they all have in common is *they write down what they have to do and thus get it out of their mind*. They always know where their system is: in handbag, in kitchen drawer, in hall drawer or in desk.

On secretary day I sort out the jumble in my wire basket in-tray and make a list on one page of the legal pad – things to do and to buy, people to telephone or to see. Every day I choose a few tasks from this page and jot them in my diary.

I use an **exercise book** to list any repair done, how much it cost and when. You then have your facts to hand if the washing machine breaks down three times in a month. I also keep this book in the hall drawer.

NO MORE MUDDLE

Another exercise book is grandly labelled **Asset register**. Everything I buy of any value is photographed (with Instamatic camera) and stuck in this book, with the bill and a note of when I bought it, for how much and from whom.

This book is invaluable if ever you make an insurance claim. Do you think you haven't anything worth stealing? Do you have a TV? A video? A stereo? A car? A bicycle?

Here is a proper asset-register entry:

Item
Location
Relevant documents
  (such as bill or valuation)
Guarantee
Purchased from
Purchase date
Cost

Last valuation date
Estimated value
Valuer

Insurance policy number
Insurance agent
Date first insured
Renewal date
Sum insured for
Insurance premium

PLAN A PROJECT

If I am working on a special project, I sort out the action list of things to do for that project on a yellow page. I always date an action list, then I can see how long it has taken me *not* to get something done. On the right, I list what has to be done, on the left I list who has to do it and in the margin I jot down when. (See p. 286.)

Use the **yellow Post-it notes** to stick on the right-hand side of your action list. 'Telephone Jack at 4.50 p.m. to make new date to install oven.'

Naturally, what happens is that the plumber cancels at the last minute and you either have to get an emergency plumber (at rates slightly higher than those of a brain surgeon) or else reorganize everyone else, all of whom have lots of other work apart from yours.

When I have made an arrangement (say, with the electrician), I make a vertical line in the left-hand margin. *When the job has been completed and I have proof of this*, I make a central vertical line through the job description. It is then easy to see, at a glance, what has been done, what remains to be done and whether the job is on schedule. I never cross out horizontally, because it is confusing.

If something has to be done fast, I make an asterisk (*) on the right-hand side of the page: this side is reserved for action by me. Two asterisks mean 'do this as fast as possible'.

MONITOR A PROJECT

To achieve anything you have to plan to make things happen, and then you have to make sure that they happen when they are supposed to happen.

Check

If a builder says your kitchen will be finished in six weeks' time, don't take his word for it. Ask him *exactly* how he has planned to do this, day by day. He must have some idea or he couldn't have told you it would be ready in six weeks' time. If you find out that he simply plucked the date of six weeks out of the air, your question will force him to reconsider his schedule.

Chase

Find out why something that was arranged to happen hasn't been done and make new arrangements to do it.

Action list for the kitchen redecoration

When	Who	What
Mon 11th 4 p.m.	Plumber	Sink blocked. Leaking cold water tap.
Tue 12th 8 a.m.	Electrician	Mend faulty socket. Check overhead light.
Before Wed 13th	Self	Buy black floor tiles for area 3 × 4 m.
Wed 13th/Thu 14th/ Fri 15th	Self	Remove old floor tiles. Lay new ones.
Mon 18th 9 a.m.	Carpenter	Remove upper cabinets. Mend base of one unit.
Before Tue 19th	Self	Buy paint – 3 litres white undercoat, 2 litres white, 4 litres pink emulsion, small tin black gloss. 3 brushes, 2 litres turps.
Tue 19th 8 a.m.	Painter	Ceiling white. Walls Dulux 'bathroom pink'. Touch up mended cabinet base with black paint.

Monitor a job by keeping track of all the happenings before the date each is due to start. This sounds like a lot of trouble, but it always saves trouble.

First telephone call Well before the date on which the work is due to start, you confirm that the job will start on time. **Second telephone call** is on the day before the job is to be done. **Third telephone call** is made if the workers don't arrive on the day they are supposed to.

If you are not present, the **fourth telephone call** is to check that the work has been done. At this point, don't accept anyone's word, only *proof*, that the job has been done (photos, receipts, whatever is suitable).

You won't be popular if you monitor, but you will be respected. There's no reason for other people to sound irritated when you telephone – unless, of course, they haven't done what they were supposed to do.

If you leave a message, always take the name of the person you've left it with, otherwise you can never refer back. I always assume that a message left by me will not be given to the person for whom it is intended. Instead, I ask when it would be convenient for me to phone again and try to make a telephone *appointment* at a stated time on a certain day.

PROJECT FILES

A clear plastic file is used to keep track of a job. If you're giving the kitchen a face-lift, shove every bit of paper in date order in this file (quotations, messages, excuses, etc.) with your action list on top. If you want to review the file, take the whole heap out, turn it upside down, start reading and reassemble the file in date order.

If your job grows, triffid-like, then use different plastic files for different parts of the job (plumbing, electricity, carpentry, etc.). Label each file with a sticky label.

Use red files only for priority work: you then know that anything in a red file has to be done as soon as possible.

Whatever your project – voluntary work, adding a house extension or emigrating to Australia – once your plastic files start to bulge, transfer the project to a lever-arch file. Get only a lever-arch file, not a ring binder, because it is bigger, sturdier and easier to open.

Keep the same file divisions (plumber, carpenter, etc.). Use coloured file dividers to separate them and number the dividers. Always pencil the index of numbers; use as few numbers as possible with the simplest description. Insert the action list right behind the index (1 = plumber, 2 = carpenter, etc.).

I make a plastic pouch and stick it inside the left-hand cover of the lever-arch file. Into this I shove anything that relates to the job until I have time to file it in the right place.

Extra notes In 1976 I asked an oil man from Texas what was the most important bit of business advice he'd ever been given. He instantly said, 'Always date the top right-hand corner of letters and notes, and always make notes of business conversations, whether in person or on the telephone.' At the time I was mystified, but I can't tell you how much trouble and expense this tip has saved me. To his advice I would add: only ever write on one side of a piece of paper.

HOW TO RUN AN EFFECTIVE COMMITTEE: A BRIEF GUIDE

Whatever the reason for forming a group (organizing an outing to the zoo or protesting about a proposed motorway), what all groups have in common is *motivation* – an aim, a goal. A good, effective group is one that achieves its goal with minimal effort, cost and internal disagreement. Here's how.

The best way to channel the energy of a group is to form a **committee** to carry out the wishes of the group. A good committee is a group that can work together without loss of energy to achieve its objective. A bad committee is the reverse.

For me, the minimum number of people on a committee should be three and the maximum number twelve. I like to invite committee members to contribute a specific amount of time, such as a total of twenty hours over two months. Often, someone will agree to a specified involvement rather than a vague one. Ideally, a committee has among its members all the skills and knowledge necessary to get the required result.

A committee will often have at least one charismatic member – the person who everyone wants to know and work with. Equally important are the quiet, reliable members who will tie up *all* the ends of their job.

A good **committee member** produces ideas and helps develop other people's ideas. He or she recognizes the authority of the Chair and addresses it at all times. ('Chair, I would like to comment on what Michelle has just suggested', not 'Frankly, I think Michelle's idea is terrible.') Listen carefully to the meeting and don't interrupt, but make a pencilled note and ask the Chair about it after the speaker has finished. If necessary, ask the Chair for clarification of a point or summary of what the meeting has achieved so far.

A good committee member is polite, speaks briefly and clearly and sticks to the point. He listens to other people's arguments with an open mind, prepared to change his mind as a result. He doesn't indulge in tantrums or ego displays and never shakes his rattle. (If other people scream and shake their rattles, he ignores such bad behaviour.) He always acknowledges someone else's idea before suggesting his own (possibly better) idea. A suitable phrase is: 'That's a good idea and it might work even better if . . .'

When reporting to the committee, a member reads from brief notes. (Don't bother to make a report, because by the time the meeting gets around to you, the situation may have altered.)

A committee member does what he

said he'd do when he said he'd do it. If this is impossible, he lets the organizer know in good time in order not to upset the specific jobs of other committee members.

Once a committee has been formed, its members should elect a **Chair** and a **secretary**.

A good Chair should not be bossy; he should be friendly but firm. The main problem of running a voluntary committee is that the Chair has no real power. He can't fire a member who is selfishly unreliable.

The Chair's first job is to state clearly the aims of the group and hitch the aims to a date. 'We are meeting to overthrow the Prime Minister by . . .' or 'We are meeting to organize an outing for the handicapped children of St Agnes to go to the zoo in the Easter holiday.'

The success of the group depends on a firm, courteous Chair, an accurate, reliable secretary who takes the minutes efficiently and sees that everybody does what they have agreed to do by the time they agreed to do it, and members who know what their job is, are prepared to do it responsibly and will not interfere in somebody else's job.

Committee members may work because they want to meet people, they want to feel needed, they want an interest in life or they want some FUN. A good Chair always remembers this. The Chair must also know how to deal with a selfishly unreliable or disruptive committee member, who will be destructive to the group. If he is consistently unreliable, the Chair should politely take responsibility away from him ('If you can't manage Saturday, Brian, Ruth has kindly offered to take your place').

The glue that holds the group together is the simple but formal etiquette described here. If you are organizing a group for the first time, stick to the etiquette. It has evolved because it works.

The Chair establishes responsibilities.

Everyone is responsible for getting his own job done as best he can in the time available. Two busy people can 'pair' to be responsible for one job.

Anyone who can't get his job done on time should immediately report back to Central Organization: in practice this often means reporting back to the Chair. Draw up a **critical path** (see 'How to run your own building site', p. 109). This is an action plan, naming the person responsible for each action and the date by which it should be done. A critical path should be drawn up and *agreed by all the committee* as fast as possible to make sure all jobs are done on time. A critical path shows each committee member that his action is not an isolated task but an important link in the chain that will lead to the ultimate goal, and that the *whole* plan depends on each person's punctuality and reliability.

Once the critical path is drawn up, a Chair checks whether further expertise is required and, if so, may ask for more committee members or form a **subcommittee**. The job of the subcommittee is to report back to the committee with its findings and conclusions – in time for them to be useful.

One of the tools of a **meeting** is a sixty-minute kitchen pinger (so that everyone hears it ping). If the meeting is held around a table, each place should be provided with a pencil, pad of paper and glass of water. The agenda and minutes of the previous meeting should be on the table: this gives a brisk, purposeful look to the table.

An **agenda** is a list of things you want to discuss, put in logical order of discussion. If you don't have an agenda, your meeting may be chaotic. Keep the agenda as short as possible and allocate a specific time for discussing each item ('Fund-raising for trip to zoo – 30 mins').

The secretary should distribute any relevant information with the agenda, and it should be labelled: 'Choice of coach – 20 mins. See appendix A – coach brochures.' Try to keep appendices to the minimum and off the table. A paper-covered committee table can quickly reduce a meeting to chaos, as everyone burrows for the relevant bit of paper.

The first item on the agenda is: 'Arrange the time and date of the next meeting'.

The secretary records the minutes on a tape recorder or by hand on paper. Only decisions are recorded, not the reasons for and against them. For instance, 'It was agreed to go to the zoo on Easter Monday, 16th April.'

If, as the meeting progresses, any agreed future action is noted in the left-hand margin, a critical path is formed.

Good ideas and decisions are useless unless they are put into practice and completed. They therefore need to be monitored (see 'Monitor a project', p. 285). The minutes should be prepared by the secretary, approved by the Chair (as being what he understood to have been agreed) and distributed as fast as possible before the next meeting.

The second item on the agenda is to agree the minutes of the previous meeting.

He who writes the minutes holds the power. It is always necessary to approve the minutes in case something has been left out, either deliberately or by accident. The minutes are *never* supposed to be rewritten after a meeting; this is a serious crime and I have resigned from committees where this has been done.

I always take my own notes of meetings; then I listen more effectively (because I am more attentive) and I am sure to note all the points that are inportant to me, so that they won't 'accidentally' be left out of the minutes.

At any time during the meeting a committee member may ask the Chair to summarize what has happened to date. The Chair may then ask the secretary to read the minutes that have been taken.

The last item on the agenda is the Chair's summary, which should be as short as possible. It summarizes progress made to date, unresolved problems, untackled problems and future action required. In order to do this, the Chair makes his own short notes as the meeting progresses.

The Chair's job is also to control the meetings. He has three principal responsibilities:

1 To achieve the required results, according to the agenda;
2 To keep order;
3 To keep everyone happy.

The Chair shouldn't take part in the discussions or state his own point of view; should he wish to do so, he says 'I should now like to leave the Chair,' says what he has to say and concludes, 'I will now take the Chair again.'

The Chair can rearrange the agenda if this looks necessary at some point. ('As Michelle brought the wrong coach brochures, I suggest we reposition "choice of coach" to last item on the agenda.')

It is the Chair's job to make sure everyone present feels a part of the group and is allowed their turn to speak, and that shy members are encouraged to do so. ('What do you feel, Isabel?') To do this, the Chair can work his way clockwise round the table at one meeting and then counter-clockwise at the next meeting.

The Chair stops someone who has been talking too long by saying mildly, 'Michelle, could you please make your point quickly, as it is time we moved to the next item on the agenda.'

The Chair's job is also to get agreement ('Do you agree, Jean? Good. Now we are all agreed . . .').

The Chair always thanks the previous speaker and specifically acknowledges at a meeting *all* work done by *all* members of the committee.

Occasionally, a committee can behave like a group of spoilt brats in a nursery.

DOWN WITH SUPERWOMAN!

The Chair will get nowhere if he behaves like a nanny: the Chair has to treat the spoilt brats with the politeness and firmness that he would reserve for a rich aunt about to make her will for the umpteenth time. If they *all* walk out, there'll be no committee, and if anyone resigns, it will mean more recruitment work. Whenever possible, he suggests dealing with the disruptive matter after the meeting.

So the Chair must be prepared to deal swiftly with complaints, criticism, disagreement, clashes of personality, grievances, letting off steam, resentment, hostility, boredom, jealousy, red-herring ideas and other treacherous undercurrents that threaten the group as a whole. He does this with formal politeness, tact, respect and firmness.

Complaints are dealt with formally. ('Jean has very reasonably pointed out that after the last three meetings she was left alone to clear up the room. Might I now have volunteers for that job today?')

It's worth repeating that **criticism** or **disagreement** is best sandwiched between two layers of praise: the Chair makes it clear that he is criticizing only an incident, not the person who was involved in that incident. ('It's clear that Michelle telephoned the zoo, but nevertheless the opening times she gave us are not accurate.')

Clashes of personality are firmly dealt with by the Chair. ('Personal criticism is not the business of this meeting, although it *is* unfortunate that Michelle forgot to bring the envelopes. When *are* we going to get the envelopes, Michelle?')

Deal with **grievances** and **indignant people who want to let off steam** by asking if the person concerned would like to discuss the matter with the Chair after the meeting. After the meeting the Chair *listens* . . . then he seeks to clarify the grievances with why/where/when/

what/how questions. He asks questions that will guide the person with the grievance rather than suggesting solutions to the situation. 'Why do you feel that Michelle is counter-productive?', 'How do you feel we could harness Michelle's clear enthusiasm?', etc., etc.

Resentment and **hostility** are dealt with firmly. ('I'm sure that none of us feels that this meeting is the right place to have arguments that may verge on the personal.')

Jealousy is difficult. Make sure that the jealous person has his share (but no more) of the spotlight. ('And I think we'd all like to hear a word from Henry after his magnificent achievement in selling 250 tickets.')

Red-herring ideas are pended until after the meeting. ('Perhaps Michelle and I could discuss the idea about borrowing a helicopter from the Queen afterwards and incorporate it in the next agenda.')

Boredom is dispelled when the Chair makes quick summary of what has been achieved up to now and rounds up the meeting with the time allocated to each subject. 'We have only seven minutes to resolve this' adds a note of urgency.

Whatever *his* views, the Chair should at all times show his interest and concern and be comforting and supportive. He should talk as little as possible.

If a meeting is held mid-week and it is clear that people will be travelling to the meeting straight from their work, allow time for the journey plus twenty minutes to unwind, chat and lobby before the meeting starts. ('Lobbying' is asking someone to support your idea before the start of the meeting.)

Small committees may start with a welcoming cup of tea on a cold evening or a cold drink on a warm evening and perhaps biscuits, cheese or fruit. Never serve alcohol before a meeting.

Briefly, this is the way big business conferences are run.

What to do with the time you've SAVED

First, take a good look at yourself (body, soul and inside skull). Decide what areas could stand a little pleasant improvement. Decide what your life lacks.

New friends?

Less weight?

More fun?

Once you've decided what you want, stand up, take a deep breath and START.

WHAT YOU CAN DO INSIDE YOUR HOME

Make yourself more beautiful

This is basically taking better care of yourself, encouraging healthy narcissism, learning to love and take care of your body, condition your skin and hair.

Learn to relax. Take care of your clothes. (See 'Bodywork', p. 295.)

Make yourself healthier

Do exercises every day – find the sort that work best for you. Grope your way out of bed and *do* them straightaway. (See 'Bodywork', p. 295.)

Get better educated

Home can be the best place to study.

Do you want to know more about anything? Did you get enough O and A levels?

Do you need a degree in order to get out there and work at something that is fun and lucrative?

Write to the Open University, Walton Hall, Milton Keynes, Bucks.

DOWN WITH SUPERWOMAN!

WHAT YOU CAN DO OUTSIDE YOUR HOME

Get a job

See 'Careers for mothers', p. 259.

Go to evening classes or daytime classes

Do you realize just what you can learn in the evenings? Wouldn't you like to know just a bit more about at least one of the following? Antiques, art, astronomy, beauty culture, boat-building, chamber music, chess, citizens' rights, cookery on a shoestring, drama, dressmaking, French, Russian, German, Greek or Italian, guitar-making, jewellery, model engineering, photography, pigeons, psychology, toy-making, wine-making or woodwork.

If you can spare a *lot* of time you could sign on for a full-time course in something you like and/or something useful; you may even be eligible for a grant to help you study. You can also sign on for plain recreational courses of lectures on the arts, archaeology, music or whatever; ask at the town hall or library for full details.

Choose a physical activity

By which I don't necessarily mean play netball, unless you really like netball.

Visit your local library or town hall to find out what's on. When I lived in a city, there was a local council-sponsored choice of eleven sports, including judo, golf and fencing to Olympic standard.

If you were always hopeless at games at school, don't allow yourself to continue your career as a physical wreck.

Go in for something gentle and un-

competitive like yoga or dancing. Your local council might easily offer classical ballet, modern ballet, ballroom, Latin American or 'Old Time' dancing, so check on it.

Half the battle is forcing yourself to organize it. If you want to, do it now. Try to do it with a friend as a check against dropping out.

Help somebody who needs you

All charities are gasping for your help. Working for others can be the most fulfilling of all out-of-home activities – it can also be the most demanding. Most good causes are well advertised and all you have to do is turn up or telephone and offer your services. If you would like to do charitable work and really don't know where to offer, ask your local vicar for advice. You needn't be a church-goer.

Meet men

If this is your specific aim in your free time, just go about it methodically and intelligently, like any other project. Lady Docker, who was once a salesgirl at Debenham and Freebody, said that she married millionaires because she mixed with them. (This just goes to show where a lingerie salesgirl can end up.) Go where the men are: to work first and foremost; to educational courses in man-filled areas such as accountancy, science, maths or engineering; to two-sex sports that men prefer, such as skin-diving or fencing. Do not allow yourself to be conned into amateur dramatics, tennis clubs, charity work or artistic evening classes for the purpose of meeting men – all these areas are full of beady-eyed man-chasers (not like you, of course) and weedy un-chaseworthy men.

How to Survive LIFE

Do you give yourself enough credit for having survived life to date? Life is a game of snakes-and-ladders – not just ladders – and nobody wins the game; they get to the end. Generally, you hear about other people's ladders but not about their snakes: this can make you feel inadequate when you peer into your own snake-pit.

Being in charge of your own life (as opposed to being thrown into other people's snake-pits) is a matter of knowing six things:

1 Know what MUST be done and do it. (You must feed your baby or it will die.)
2 Know what you're good at and do it.
3 Know what you're not good at and avoid it.
4 Know what you WANT to do and make every effort to do it.
5 Know what you *don't want* to do and make this clear to everyone concerned.

6 The SHOULD and the OUGHT are generally things that somebody else wants you to do, because it's on their WANT list. That somebody might be a mate, a parent, a teacher or a body, such as a church or a government. But you don't always have to do what someone else (selfishly) wants you to do. Forget the SHOULD and the OUGHT if they are not on your MUST or WANT list.

It's also important to realize that you are not living in the land of OUGHT-TO-BE; you are living in the real world and the real world is a mess. Things aren't always the way they appear and the pronouncements of experts should be viewed sceptically, as they often change with the experts. Experts have been wrong about the flatness of the Earth, the circulation of the blood and the superiority of a white skin to a black skin.

DOWN WITH SUPERWOMAN!

As you don't live in the land of OUGHT-TO-BE, allow for the weakness of human nature. Don't automatically expect honesty, loyalty and truthfulness in others. Be wary, be cautious. Keep alert. Don't trust people until you have known them long enough to be sure that you can, and you have proved to them that they can trust you. The world outside the nursery has always been tough. The Scouts' motto is a good one: BE PREPARED. To be prepared, you need to know your strengths and weaknesses.

BODYWORK

THE HIGH COST OF BEAUTY (AND THE HARM IT CAN DO TO YOU AS WELL AS YOUR PURSE)

You are unlikely to find this chapter or the information it contains reproduced in any magazine or newspaper, lest the powerful beauty manufacturers withdraw their advertising.

Do you spend a fortune on witchcraft? Enough women do so to make fortunes for the cosmetic industry from their creams, potions and lotions. The number of beauty products offered and the seductive-sell poetry that is used to seduce you are not only beguiling but bewildering. Here are a few sales pitches:

* **The traditional luxury pitch:** ingredients – rose petals and jasmin.
* **The back-to-nature pitch:** rosemary, camomile and nettles.
* **The organic pitch:** synthetic peach extract.

* **The scientific pitch:** with added vitamin E, they say, not mentioning that this cannot penetrate the skin.
* **The esoteric ingredient pitch:** extract of jelly from the knees of selected queen bees or the more intimate bits of whales.

Which do *you* fall for? If you don't fall for *all* of them, perhaps you fall for *some* of them.

If you don't understand what your skin needs and why, you may be lured into buying beauty products that are unsuitable for your skin. You can *create* skin problems with beauty products, which you then buy *more* beauty products to treat and conceal.

In some countries, such as America, you can examine the contents on a beauty-product container. The manufacturer is legally obliged to state the ingredient with the maximum weight first and the minimum weight ingredient last. So your vitamin-E-enriched queen-bee's-

DOWN WITH SUPERWOMAN!

knees-extract face cream contents may reveal that the maximum ingredient is water and the minimum ingredient is a microscopic amount of the magic stuff that they are using as a sales pitch to flog their product to you.

Never believe the label; don't trust the advice on it; instead trust the reactions of your own skin. If a product is harming your skin, you can *feel* it fairly quickly. If your skin feels taut, it means the product is too drying for you. You can tell by the oily feel and the shine on your face if a product is too oily for you. If your skin itches or reddens, then you are allergic to something in the product, so stop using it.

Product description	Major ingredients
cold cream and vanishing cream	mineral oil, wax, borax
night cream	lanolin, soap, water, wax
thick day creams	lanolin, soap, water, wax
creamy day lotion	lanolin, wax, more water and less soap than a thick day cream
moisturizers (to be worn under make-up)	oil, soap, water, wax (more water, less soap than thick day creams)
all-purpose body lotion	lanolin, water, wax, glycerine
soap	animal or vegetable oil (from peanut, coconut or olive), alkaline cleansing chemicals such as potassium hydroxide
skin freshener	ethyl alcohol, menthol or peppermint
astringent	less alcohol than a skin freshener, glycerine, aluminium

Whether their job is to clean or moisturize the skin, most creams, from a milky emulsion to a stiff night cream, are a mixture of wax and water, glycerine or oil. Wax is used for moulding the solid and liquid components so that the result is a smooth cream or lotion. Glycerine is used to slow the drying-up of the cream or lotion. Alcohols (ethyl or methyl) are solvents, used to mix the ingredients and stop them separating. Often, the differ-

ence between a thick cream and a thin, milky cream is only added water.

What cleans the skin in a cleanser is the oil. What moisturizes the skin in a moisturizer is also the oil, which acts as a barrier that delays the evaporation of the natural water in the skin.

Three sorts of oil are used in skin products: **mineral oils** derived from petroleum, **vegetable oils** from olives, nuts, etc. and **animal oils**, such as lanolin. Animal oils are best for human skin as they most resemble natural human skin oil and do not interfere with the skin's excretory activities, such as sweating.

The cost of the same product from one factory can vary in a shop by a factor of at least five, depending on the sales pitch. The same face cream can cost £1 packaged under one name and £5 packaged under another name – so why not try the cheaper ones?

I've noticed that the beauty queens I know (businesswomen who dominate the beauty industry) seem to have in their own bathroom a lot of jars labelled Nivea, Johnson's and Pond's.

Often it is the elegant and expensive packaging that hooks you on the product. In which case keep the empty jars and fill them with the inexpensive beauty products listed here, which are packaged in cheap but non aesthetically acceptable containers. Keep these supply packs in a tote bag out of sight and decant them into your expensive little bottles. The Body Shop sells simple plastic bottles.

SKIN STRUCTURE

If you want a better complexion and a smaller cosmetics bill, you need to understand the structure of the skin and how to care for it.

The skin is an excretory organ: you can't shove things back into it, any more than you can into any of your other excretory organs.

Purpose	Suggested brand
To clean the face Instead of vanishing cream, cold cream or milky cleanser	Try Johnson's Baby Oil
To soften the surface of the skin – on the face Instead of night cream, thick day cream or creamy day lotion	Try Johnson's baby moisturizer cream Try Pond's Skin Food
As a moisturizer	Try a Pond's face cream that suits your skin type Try Johnson's baby moisturizer cream Pond's No-Shine Moisturizing Cream
To remove the residue of cleaner from the face	Try Nivea Skin Freshener
Mask	
Shampoo Unless you have really greasy hair	Try Johnson's Baby Shampoo
Face powder on a coloured foundation Pat it on, then gently wipe off with cotton wool so that only the 'bloom' remains, not a clown-like layer of white flour.	Try Johnson's Baby Powder

If the products I recommend don't feel good on your skin or hair, simply stop using them.

All types of skin work the same way. The skin has a natural acid mantle that protects it from bacterial infection. Skin products should therefore be neutral or slightly acidic, not alkaline. The mysterious PH factor (used to sell so many products) is merely the correct acid/alkaline balance of the product.

The fine outer layer of the skin (the epidermis) protects what lies beneath it and it is the epidermis that gets the rough treatment. This outer layer consists of invisible old dried cells and the waste products of the skin – particularly old sweat and stale oil that lie on the surface of the skin. This dead outer layer of skin needs to be regularly removed in order to stimulate cell growth in the skin layer beneath. If it is not removed, the waste products block the pores and cause acne – whiteheads, blackheads, blind boils, cysts and other eyesores.

The underlayer of skin (the dermis) contains the oil glands, sweat glands, blood vessels and hair follicles.

Between the two skin layers is a barrier, which contains natural moisturizing compounds that maintain the natural water level in the skin.

It is not the oil in the skin, but this water that keeps the skin soft and smooth. A fine layer of natural oil – nature's own moisturizer – retains this natural water in the skin. A dry skin produces too little oil to act as an efficient barrier. An oily skin produces too much of nature's own moisturizer, which *also* helps to clog the pores and thus produces acne.

The two main enemies of the skin are sun and soap. Central heating also dries the skin.

SKIN CARE

Why is soap bad for the skin of the face? Soap is drying to the skin and soap is a detergent. When you wash your face, the warm water softens the skin and opens the pores; the soap loosens the dirt, and if it isn't rinsed off thoroughly, the soap may clog the pores. Soap dissolves the protective natural surface oils, temporarily leaving the skin with no protective film against evaporation.

Dry skin is due not to lack of oil, but to loss of water from the cells of the skin by evaporation, which occurs more quickly in a dry climate than in a damp one. A dry, cold climate reduces sweat, increasing the dryness of the skin.

Dry skin results in a lot of dead cells on the surface of the skin. If you have dry skin, use moisturizer lavishly on face and neck. Stop using any astringent that leaves your face feeling taut, as it is too strong for you.

DOWN WITH SUPERWOMAN!

Oily skin is the most difficult to clean because the oil sticks the dead skin cells together, which plasters down the gunge beneath. A 'muddy' skin may be due to inadequate removal of these dead cells. To remove them, regularly steam and use a face mask (see later). An oily face should not be soaped because the invisible sticky soap residue may further clog the pores. Oily skins do not need creams, lotions or moisturizers because too much of nature's natural moisturizer is already present. (One expert told me that a main factor of adult acne is unnecessary creams, oils and moisturizers.)

A face with **combination skin** has dry taut skin everywhere except the nose and chin area, where there are blackheads.

Sensitive skin is easily irritated. Every type of skin can be sensitive. The irritated areas redden as a result of an allergy: this is the over-reaction of the skin to certain substances in cosmetics.

There are two ways of getting dermatitis:

1 As the result of using a *primary irritant*, when a bad reaction is immediate (some people are allergic to soap).
2 *As a result of using a sensitizer*, the reaction to which may not be immediate. Only some people are allergic to some sensitizers (which are often perfume ingredients) and it is not known why or how: it can hit you suddenly after you've been using the thing for years without a problem. The treatment for such a problem is to locate it (by allergy testing) and stop using the product.

The fragrances used in cosmetics are most likely to be the allergy-causing substances. Hypo-allergenic cosmetics (such as those produced by Almay) are generally without fragrance, and *different* raw materials are substituted for those that are known to cause reactions in some people.

'Natural' cosmetics are not neces-sarily beneficial to sensitive skin, because vegetable, fruit and herb extracts may all produce allergies.

Sensitive skins should avoid rough or extreme treatment – very hot or very cold water, rough cleansing grains, abrasive buffing puffs, very rough face flannels or very thick creams. Don't steam the face, avoid saunas, have no face massage (because you risk breaking tiny blood vessels) and keep your hands and hair off your face.

Cleaning the facial skin involves removing from the outer skin layer invisible dead cells, stale oil, stale perspiration and dirt from the atmosphere.

When cleaning, first remove make-up (use water to remove water-based make-up and oil to remove oil-based make-up) and *then* start to clean the skin. Don't think you are cleaning the skin when you are merely removing the make-up.

To clean Oil your face. Remove the oil, using a tissue in both hands (as professional make-up artists do, using a different bit of tissue for each wipe). Working outwards, wipe jaw, cheeks, forehead, nose. Then working inwards towards the nose, swab above and below eyes.

Wipe off residue oil with two cotton-wool pads (one in either hand) soaked in skin freshener. Be extravagant with cotton-wool pads and tissues with money you have saved on the beauty products. The secret of good skin is cleaning it morning and evening and using *clean* cloths and tissues.

I use the dry-skin routine on the 'Simple skin-care plan' on p. 300 and I use a clean face-cloth every day: seven face-cloths isn't much more to wash than one towel.

Quick summary of skin care

Forget the phrase 'cleanse, tone and nourish'. 'Tone' and 'nourish' are meaningless in this context. 'Cleanse' means 'clean'. You don't say, 'I must cleanse the car.'

1 Clean.
2 Remove final traces of cleaner. Don't leave an astringent or a skin freshener on your skin – always rinse it off with cool water.
3 Apply moisturizer. A moisturizer does not add moisture to your skin. However milky it may look, it provides a thin film of *oil* that prevents the natural water within your skin from evaporating.

Always use moisturizer before applying foundation. Otherwise when you rub coloured foundation into your skin, you rub in coloured dirt.
4 Because your skin needs to excrete, don't put anything on it at night, unless you need to dry out spots. If you have a very oily skin, try wearing a mask of calamine lotion once a week at night. Wash it off with warm water. Don't buy calamine lotion with glycerine in it.

If any part of your skin feels taut (hands, feet, elbows, nail cuticles), soften it by massaging in a cream, such as Pond's skin food, then blot off the surplus with a tissue; splash with cold water and then blot dry. (However, if you are allergic to lanoline don't use a lanoline-based cream.) This is best done first thing in the morning or just before a bath, after cleaning the skin.

Regularly, perhaps once a week (perhaps more or less often, depending how your skin feels), clean your face thoroughly.

What a salon skin treatment or facial does is thoroughly clean the skin; you can do this yourself at home. Forget facial massage; it's an outdated idea that massage prevents wrinkles – and it might irritate a sensitive skin.

A facial routine Steam the skin, clean the skin, apply a mask to tighten the pores and lie on your back for twenty minutes while it sets.

Steaming generates moist heat, which melts stale oil and loosens the debris sticking to the skin surface so that it can be removed more easily by a mask.

Fill a bowl with hot, but not scalding, water, add a drop of peppermint essence, drape a towel to form a tent over your head and the bowl of water, and bend over the bowl, keeping your face at least 46 cm (18 in) from the water. Stay there for five minutes. Best to do this in a locked room, so that no one can bang into you and upset the hot water.

Scrubbing grains act as a very mild abrasive that, when rubbed on the skin, removes dead cells from the skin. Oatmeal was used as an early cosmetic abrasive but I use Body Shop's Japanese Washing Grains, which smell deliciously fresh. After you have rinsed off the abrasive, apply a mask.

Masks are either clay- or gel-based. Use a clay-based, drying mask for oily skin and a moisturizing mask for a dry skin. Use a mask only after steaming. Spread the moist mask over the face and allow it to dry; as it does so, it absorbs excessive oil, dry cells and dirt from the surface of the skin. Use a mask when your skin looks dingy or to remove a peeling tan. Elizabeth Arden make a good clay mask, called Velva Cream. Body Shop sell a number of useful masks: Rose Refining mask for dry skin, Aloe peel-off mask for sensitive skin (also great fun if you like picking at your skin) and Honey and Oat Scrub mask for all skin types (it's very mild).

Never put a mask around the area surrounding your eyes and never rub this area, because it will encourage the skin to sag.

Night creams sell to the anxious, who often believe that the more they pay, the better the result will be. These creams cannot prevent lines or wrinkles or rejuvenate the skin; the outer skin will renew itself regularly without any help.

Don't wear any creams at night, when the skin should be allowed to excrete.

Simple skin-care plan

Clean your skin morning and evening

	Dry skin	Normal skin	Oily skin	Sensitive skin	Combination skin
Never use	soap	soap	soap, moisturizer	soap	Treat as dry, normal or sensitive skin, whichever is applicable. Clean the oily parts of your skin with skin freshener on cotton wool when you wake, at midday and before you sleep
Remove water-based make-up with	sponge and warm water	sponge and warm water	sponge and warm water, then Johnson's Baby Oil	sponge and warm water	
Remove oil-based make-up with Clean skin with	Johnson's Baby Oil Johnson's Baby Oil	Johnson's Baby Oil Johnson's Baby Oil	Johnson's Baby Oil Johnson's Baby Oil	Johnson's Baby Oil Johnson's Baby Oil	
Remove residue of cleaner with	home-made astringent for dry skin, recipe p. 303	home-made astringent for normal skin, recipe p. 303	skin freshener	rosewater	
Day care, moisturize with	see chart p. 297 for recommended moisturizer	see chart p. 297 for recommended moisturizer	use no moisturizer; your skin naturally produces too much oil; when skin is shiny, wipe with skin freshener on a cotton pad.	Almay moisturizer	after applying moisturizer, wipe oily part with skin freshener on cotton pad
Night care	none	none	calamine lotion dabbed on spots; calamine mask regularly (try weekly)	none	none
Special treatments	Weekly: steam for 5 mins; slough off dead skin with Body Shop Japanese Washing Grains; wear face mask for 10 mins. If skin feels taut after exposure to rough winds or central heating, then after a bath, when pores are open, massage in a lanolin-based cream.	as for dry skin		as for dry skin	as for dry skin

Never use *any* beauty products at night, except calamine lotion dabbed on spots to dry them. In particular, don't put heavy cream on your face at night because you will wake up with puffy eyes.

What can be done about wrinkles? Don't waste money on anti-wrinkle products in shops. The main cause of wrinkles is the sun – keep out of it. Collagen injected into the wrinkled furrows will fill them up so that the skin is left smooth: this treatment has to be repeated every nine months by a *qualified* plastic surgeon and it is not cheap.

Retin-A is a vitamin A derivative that has a similar effect to collagen. Nobody knows how it works. It is used for crow's-feet around the eyes, costs £7 a tube (1989 price) and is available in the UK only on prescription. Some people are allergic to it and it reddens and irritates their skin.

The sun is the skin's worst enemy, because it dries the skin. If you sunbathe, use the correct sunscreen. Check the sun protection factor (SPF) marked on the label. SPF is graded from 1 to 30. A sensitive skin that burns easily needs at least an SPF-15 rating. A fair skin needs an SPF-8 rating. Don't bother to buy anything rated under SPF-5. Always slather on moisturizer after sun exposure.

Acne

Plagued by acne for twenty years, after unsuccessful treatment by many dermatologists, I visited Georgette Klinger, a renowned New York beautician. I have a dry, sensitive skin with a central oily patch. The beautician told me to wear no night creams, no foundation make-up and use no soap to clean my face. 'Oh, I couldn't possibly go without *soap*,' I said, 'I wouldn't feel *clean*.' She shrugged her shoulders, 'Then I can't help you.'

So I stopped using soap and night cream, and I did what she told me and within a month my skin was free of spots.

Within two months there was not a blackhead to be seen. So I permanently stopped using foundation, blusher and powder, which left me with a basic kit of lipsticks, eyeshadow, mascara and a bottle of Johnson's Baby Oil and Vaseline. (Don't use baby oil to remove eye make-up because it might run in your eyes; try Vaseline.)

Within a year I was being told what a wonderful English complexion I had. (At first I thought they were joking.) What was more important to me was that I could look at myself first thing in the morning without feeling depressed and thinking, 'I could put up with *anything* if only I didn't have spots.'

Acne can happen at any age (it hit me at 30). Acne occurs in a skin with overactive oil glands when the surplus oil is not removed from the skin and clogs the pores.

Every pore is the surface opening of a tunnel called a follicle. A **blackhead** isn't a lump of dirt. It is a plug of excess solidified oil that blocks the exit of a follicle and turns black when it contacts the oxygen in the air.

Whiteheads occur in an oily or dry skin. They are caused by too much cream or moisturizer and dead cells. The new flow of oil cannot reach the surface, because the follicle exit is blocked by dead cells. So a white lump forms beneath the skin's surface and the longer the pore is blocked, the bigger it gets. Visit a beauty salon for professional removal.

A **pimple**. In a blocked follicle, the oil can't reach the skin surface because of a blackhead or whitehead. So bacteria form around the trapped oils below the surface, irritate the lower layer of skin and an inflammation develops, which turns the skin red. White blood cells (pus) rush to the spot to counteract the inflammation.

What you should not do at this point is interrupt the action of the friendly white blood cells by squeezing out the pus and pale watery blood – but you know what might happen if it's party time and you have a spot on your nose.

If the follicle gives way near the skin's surface, the spot should soon go away and should not leave a scar. If you squeeze, the spot will take longer to heal and you might have a scar.

If the follicle gives way far below the skin's surface, the spot will be a bigger problem and may turn into a painful red lump with no tip to squeeze. A **cyst** is when a wall forms around this lump, which is unlikely to disappear without medical treatment.

To avoid acne, keep your face scrupulously clean, so that the new flow of oil can reach the skin surface without obstruction. Otherwise the fresh oil has nowhere to go, except backwards, when inflammation and infection will easily occur.

Avoid creams, make-up and oil – anything that blocks the free flow of natural oil to the surface of the skin. Don't use *medicated cosmetics* (which are produced mainly for acne skins). They are fragrance-free and contain a smidgen of antiseptic – which is unfortunately counteracted by the oil and cream in the product. It is best for your skin that you wear no cosmetics, keep your skin clean and, if you are self-conscious without make-up, wear dark glasses for a month.

Instead of squeezing them, dry out the spots (not such fun, I'm afraid) by dabbing them with a cotton bud doused in wych-hazel during the day, and a cotton bud doused with calamine lotion at night. Be careful not to dab more than one spot with the cotton bud or you will transfer infection from one place to another.

Beard-area infections are avoided by using the following:

* **Razor** A Braun up-and-down (not circular) electric razor is the only one used and recommended by my Harley Street dermatologist.

* **Shaving cream** The purpose of shaving cream is to soften the skin prior to shaving with a razor blade. If you use an electric razor, don't use a cream beforehand or anything else afterwards. If you use a brush, use Palmolive or Ingram's shaving cream. If you use a razor but not a brush, the recommended brushless creams are Erasmic (aerosol) and Palmolive (tube).

Aftershave is good only for the profits of cosmetic companies.

Infection of the beard area of a man's face may be due to faulty shaving methods (dirty razor blades) or a latent infection in the nose or ears: when the nose is blown or picked, when a finger rubs or scratches the ear, the infection can be spread by the finger over the lower face.

Another problem (once known as 'barber's rash') can occur from a small area of infection that is spread continuously from one pore to another while a man shaves. All beard infections should be treated by a dermatologist, as should any other skin problems that are not due to faulty cleaning or the application of so-called beauty products.

The cheapest way to deal with any skin infection is to ask your doctor to recommend a dermatologist.

If you consult a dermatologist, have a facial beforehand at a reputable beauty salon. Your dermatologist won't be able to provide that and he'll be able to examine your skin better once you've done this.

How do you know if a beauty salon is good? A good beautician will tell *you* what you know your skin to be like. Never let a beauty specialist touch your face unless she has a licence to do so and that licence is hanging on a wall where you can see it, and not if the licence was issued only last month.

MIX YOUR OWN BEAUTY KIT

Get the ingredients for the following recipes from a dispensing chemist.

All-purpose astringent Add 4 per cent acetone to rosewater. For example, 1 tablespoon acetone to 25 tablespoons rosewater.

Astringent for dry skin Mix 227 ml (8 fl oz) of distilled water with half a teaspoon of alum.

Astringent for normal skin Try three parts rosewater and one part wych-hazel. If it's too strong, use less wych-hazel.

Skin freshener for oily skin Mix ½ cup of wych-hazel, ½ cup of distilled water and ½ teaspoon of alum.

Clay mask 1 tablespoon of fuller's earth, 1 tablespoon of water and (optional) 1 drop of peppermint essence. Mix to a paste, spread on face and allow to dry for twenty minutes. Wash off with lukewarm water, then splash face with cool water. (For an *oily skin*, substitute astringent for water. For a *dry skin*, substitute an egg yolk for water.)

Note: If your shop-bought clay mask dries out, put it in a bowl, add a couple of teaspoons of flat mineral water and remix it to a smooth paste.

Oatmeal face-mask Mix 2 tablespoons of oatmeal to a paste with astringent or rosewater and spread paste on your face (avoiding eye sockets). Remove twenty minutes *after* it dries, by rubbing off gently, as if you were erasing with a rubber. Finally rinse off with lukewarm water – and feel your skin!

Water-based foundation This is a good way of using up the left-over pressed powder around the edge of your compact. Gouge it out with the wrong end of your eyebrow tweezers. However, it's better to buy face powder (dark for summer, light for winter). You can then, by adding dark or light powder, change the colour of your foundation to match your face as the seasons change.

In a cup, with a toothbrush end or a teaspoon, mix 1 tablespoon of face powder with rosewater or your toning lotion until it is liquid (you can make it thin or thick, whatever suits you). Pour the mixture through a funnel into a small bottle. Shake well before applying to your face with a cosmetic sponge as you bend over a wash basin (it may drip). Allow to dry, then again stroke with make-up sponge to get an even cover. Always apply over moisturizer.

Lotion to dry spots This lotion can be used for three purposes:

1 To hide spots during the day.
2 At night, to dry out spots.
3 As a night lotion for a very spotty skin.

Buy 500 g (1 lb) of calamine powder (which costs very little) from a dispensing chemist. It's important not to buy ready-mixed calamine lotion from the chemist, because you will be sold a lotion that contains glycerine and this will not work.

Get a cup, a tablespoon, two small bottles and some dark-brown face powder.

Measuring with a tablespoon, mix equal quantities of water and calamine powder in the cup, until you have a smooth pale-pink lotion. Fill the first bottle with half this lotion.

To the remaining lotion in your cup, stir in dark-brown face powder to taste. Fill the remaining bottle with this brown liquid. You now have a pale liquid and a dark liquid. Mix a dab of each on the back of your left hand, matching the colour of your skin. Dab mixture on spots. Use this spot cover for special occasions only.

At night, dab the pale lotion on spots to dry them.

For a very spotty skin, use the pale lotion over your entire face overnight. Try this once or twice a week. When you do this, use nothing on your skin the next day so that your skin can excrete. If in the mornings your skin feels unpleasantly taut, then stop using the lotion.

HAIR CARE

Treat your hair as if it were precious silk, not old rope. Never yank a comb or brush through it. Never use a brush if you can avoid it, because it tears your hair. Use a comb gently and slowly. Avoid plastic combs: buy an expensive one that doesn't have rough edges to the teeth.

For a quiet life and hair in the best possible condition, do as little to it as possible and learn to love the natural state of your hair. If it's curly, don't long for straight hair. If your hair breaks easily, have a short or layered cut.

Invest in a good haircut regularly. A good haircut is easy to maintain and makes your hair more obedient.

Use minimal heat on your hair because heat makes hair brittle and brittle hair breaks easily. Minimize the use of heated rollers. Tame your hair with minimal use of a Braun butane-gas-powered, carry-anywhere curler; use it to bubble-curl short hair, to straighten kinky hair, to curl the edges of long hair under or over. To avoid burning your fingers, wear cotton gloves while you use it.

To shine and smooth 'fuzzy' hair, instead of something more expensive, rub *one drop* of baby oil on the palm of your hands, rub palms together, smooth palms over hair, then gently brush out.

Wash your hair only when necessary. At one time I used to go to the hairdresser twice a week until he whispered that I wasn't doing my fine hair a favour, so I went back to washing it once a week in the bath and rinsing well under the shower.

Remember that you are cleaning your scalp as well as your hair, so use your finger-tips to massage the scalp.

One of my beauty queens told me, 'Everyone in the industry knows that **shampoos** are detergent – a "mild" shampoo is just a *weak* solution. Unless you have really greasy hair, you can't do better than Johnson's Baby Shampoo followed by a tablespoon of vinegar in the rinsing water to leave your hair silky.'

Manufacturers tell you to use much more shampoo than you need (so they make more money). Dilute 1 teaspoonful of shampoo in $\frac{1}{2}$ cup of water (2 teaspoonsful for long hair). You don't need more than that and excessive shampoo strips too much oil from your hair.

Most shampoos are alkaline and make the hair feel stiff and lifeless, like candy floss. One tablespoon of acid – lemon juice or vinegar – in the final rinsing water should counteract the alkaline effect of the shampoo and soften the hair.

For normal, dry and processed hair, use balanced PH shampoo (which balances the acid and alkaline content of the shampoo).

There is no hair product that makes hair thicker. **Protein conditioner** doesn't improve dry, normal or oily hair. A conditioner *coats* the hair to make thin hair *appear* thicker. It is useful for processed, split, broken or otherwise damaged hair because the conditioner forms a protein coating (derived from animal cartilage) on the outside of the hair shaft, which sticks down all frayed ends. But it *cannot* repair the hair shaft (see diagram).

Cream hair conditioner isn't as effective as a protein hair conditioner.

Don't put hair conditioner directly on your scalp because it can cause itching and flakiness. Apply conditioner only to the ends of your hair from the ears downwards. (If you haven't any conditioner, use an egg yolk – but be careful to rinse off all of it. Always rinse off *all* the conditioner.)

Diagram of a hair, magnified 842,701 times (or thereabouts)

Before conditioner   *After conditioner*

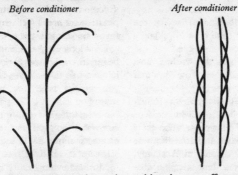

The conditioner glues the broken ends together and has the same effect on a hair as licking a paintbrush does – it plasters it down.

Avoid **hairspray**: it coats your hair, might dry your hair and attracts dust.

To set fine hair, use beer as a setting lotion. It stiffens the hair and the smell of hops fades within minutes.

Hair treatment

Olive oil is the best conditioner for damaged hair (broken, permed, tinted, streaked).

1 Heat olive oil until warm but not hot.
2 With a comb, part the hair at 1.25 cm (½ in) intervals, apply oil to partings with a stiff paintbrush or your fingers.
3 Comb hair with a big wide-toothed comb to distribute oil from scalp along hairs.
4 Heat helps oil penetration. Cover head with bath cap or kitchen cling-film and around it all, wrap a towel that has been saturated in hot water and then wrung out. Another idea is to forget the towel and instead cover the scalp with aluminium foil.
5 Leave for fifteen minutes.
6 Remove oil by shampooing the hair, rubbing really well. Lather twice. Rinse well.

Just like the rest of your body, the scalp sloughs off invisible flakes of dead skin. On an oily scalp the discarded flakes of skin stick together and so form bigger, visible flakes. This is called *dandruff*. Get the strongest sulphur shampoo to counteract the oil in the scalp.

NAILS

Water breaks nails and weakens them, so wear rubber gloves to wash-up or do the laundry. Many nail-polish removers contain acetone, which is a drying agent that can split nails.

I know of no nail strengthener and neither does the specialist doctor that I consulted; he asked me to let him know if I found one.

To protect your hands when doing dirty jobs, wear gloves. Use old cotton gloves or surgeon's plastic gloves that fit like a second skin and are sold in a dispenser box by the chemist. For washing-up, don't buy rubber gloves that fit your hands correctly; instead, buy huge rubber gloves that are lined: they are then easy to pull on and off.

Get ingrained dirt off your hands by coating them with Vaseline, then tissue off. (Incidentally, Vaseline can also be used for lip gloss, eyebrow gloss, eyelid gloss and to remove eye make-up.)

DOWN WITH SUPERWOMAN!

YOUR PUBLIC IMAGE

Recipe for tired eyes: lie flat for ten minutes with your head on a towel and a wet, used tea-bag over each eye.

Treat your teeth as the world's most expensive and fragile substitute for a pair of pliers. Do nothing but eat with them.

If you need cosmetic dentistry, *don't* go to your normal dentist. Cosmetic dentistry is an art. You wouldn't expect a house painter to paint a picture that was going to hang in the Royal Academy, would you? Allow a dentist to do cosmetic work only if you have seen examples of his work, no matter what your normal dentist says. Personal recommendations are always preferable.

Floss your teeth, if only once a week. Smell the floss and you'll see why. If old people smell, it's often because they don't floss their teeth.

Where it's better to spend than to economize

With **perfume**, you get what you pay for. The best perfumes are French. Good perfume requires expensive ingredients. Cheap perfume makes you smell cheap. If you want to feel lavish, buy expensive eau-de-toilette, which has more alcohol than perfume, but less than eau-de-Cologne.

I invest in good eau-de-Cologne because it isn't sticky and doesn't smell cheap. I use Roger et Gallet, who also sell a good matching stick deodorant.

Perfumed bath oil I use a few drops of eau-de-toilette plus a dessertspoon of Johnson's Baby Oil. Your skin may need less oil than mine. Clean the bath by putting a capful of washing-up liquid in the water after you've stepped out of it.

Make-up

Grooming means keeping clean and *looking* it. (Think of the impeccable gloss of a show horse that has been well groomed.) American women have a reputation for being well groomed because, for them, this has *become a daily habit*.

How long do you spend on your daily beauty routine? Are there days when you haven't had time to do your make-up, so you wear a bare face and other days when you look like Cleopatra but are late for everything? If you 'put on' an elaborate face, do you feel embarrassed if caught without it? If so, the plunge in self-esteem is bad for your morale.

Minimize your beauty routine. Decide how much time you can (and are prepared to) devote to your appearance *on a daily and a weekly basis*. Better a short routine that you can stick to than a more ambitious one that you can't.

Estée Lauder claimed that if your make-up takes longer than three minutes, then you're doing something wrong. I allow myself five minutes a day plus an hour once a week for a cleaning overhaul, and a visit to the hairdresser four times a year. On special occasions I allow myself ten minutes extra to do my hair in a more elegant manner than just sticking it behind a headband. Like film stars, I use a hair-piece for gala occasions – because it saves time and I can rely on it.

My one-hour Sunday overhaul routine, written on an index card, is: hair, face, teeth, hands, legs, feet, check grooming and vitamin supplies, put out next week's clothes and underwear.

My attitude is: I *could* look a lot better – but I could look a lot worse.

'Only young girls should wear heavy make-up,' once said my 12-year-old son, looking at me carefully. The older you get, the less make-up you should use because it sinks into what are laughingly called your 'laughter lines' – and stays there. Older women who don't want to look even older might stick to natural facial colours – no maroon lipstick or black eyeliner – except for one area: nowadays grannies no longer go grey, they go blonde.

Good tip To avoid queues outside the bathroom door, try hanging a mirror near the kitchen sink and keep make-up near it in bag or knife-box.

The slut rating

How much time and money are you prepared to spend on your appearance?

You can save a lot of money on your clothes if you're prepared to spend a bit more predetermined time on upkeep. Part of looking good is feeling good and if the most important part of your outfit is a safety pin, this could literally prick your self-confidence.

Do you ever have:

* Safety pins anywhere?
* Dirty bra straps?
* Scuffed or down-at-heel shoes?
* Chipped nail varnish?
* Laddered tights?
* Stained armpits?
* Holes in clothes, whether or not visible?
* Crumpled clothes?
* Moulted hair on your shoulders and back?
* Clothes that smell of cigarette smoke or stale perfume?

If your answer is 'never', to all these items, you can award yourself a zero slut rating. If your score is over 4, try putting aside one hour a week (or a month) for being your own ladies' maid. Keep anything that needs attention at one end of your wardrobe. As your wardrobe is checked regularly, you are then not in a permanent state of anxiety and running repairs. This is the simplest, cheapest thing you can do to improve your appearance. Here are a few more:

To get that Royal Family, just-brushed-by-my-valet look, lavishly use a sticky-roller clothes-brush. Buy the lavatory-paper-shaped refills a dozen at a time.

Before going to bed, nurses are trained to lay out the clothes that they will wear the following morning. I tried to do this, but I was always too tired at night. So now on Sunday morning I hang seven sets of clothes at one end of my wardrobe and then wear one outfit a day. This is not as grand as it sounds: yesterday I selected two pleated skirts and seven jogging tops plus changes of underwear.

Unless she's wearing white, Audrey Hepburn only ever wears black shoes because she doesn't have to bother about matching them to her accessories. Writer Antonia Fraser keeps a bottle of Mary Quant black nail varnish for dealing with scuffs on her black heels.

Keep shoe-cleaning equipment in a bag, near where the shoes are cleaned, which is by the sink. Keep a towel in the bag for spreading out on the counter before cleaning.

Never wear the same pair of shoes two days running or they don't have time to recover their shape. Buy a pair of plastic shoe trees, as they really keep shoes looking shop-shape.

MAKING THE MOST OF YOUR WARDROBE

So that it doesn't get grubby looking and so that the clothes look more dramatic against it, I paint the inside of the wardrobe a dark but dramatic colour – it has been plum, cigar and navy.

Try hanging your clothes not in *logical* order – all skirts, all blouses – but in the enticing, inviting way in which they're displayed in some shops: in *colour* order. It's just as easy to remember that you want the *pink* blouse as to remember that you want the blouse.

To keep my drawers neat and garments accessible, I file all my underwear in clear plastic bags in two sizes – big ones and little sandwich baggies.

If you have very little wardrobe space, make sure you don't waste any of it. Use hang-up shoe holders, not for shoes but for fiddly accessories. Use plastic trays, cat-litter trays, shoe boxes and stacking wicker baskets to keep belts and other small items on one deep shelf. Habitat sell some good storage boxes (like shoe boxes, only bigger) that make good use of the space on the top shelf of the wardrobe – the one that you can never get at.

I use a miniature office chest of drawers as a jewel box – Marie Antoinette wouldn't approve but she didn't have as much junk jewellery as I do. (Available in black, white or red from Rymans.)

How to give your clothes a rest

Twice a year I file my clothes into two piles. I ruthlessly sort out:

1 Clothes that I never really felt comfortable in after leaving the shop.
2 Last year's cheap, passing fashion fads.
3 Anything that's too small.
4 Anything bought in a sale and never worn (*never buy at sales unless you'd planned to buy it anyway*).
These disappear to charity or thrift shops.
Next, I sort out a second pile of clothes.
5 Things I once loved dearly but haven't worn for a year.
6 Any fashion that has *just* passed (which is when it looks its worst).
7 Anything that you feel that everyone has seen you in too often.

Do not sell these, give them away or throw them away; instead, give them a rest. Pack them away in suitcases (kept under the bed?). You do not then immediately regret your commendably ruthless weeding the week after – if not the day after – disposing of them.

Next year, what joy to see once again that classic navy and white striped silk

scarf that you'd forgotten about, that low-cut black number that makes you look at least one size smaller and that high-necked angora dress that looks quite different now you've had your hair cut short. And they *all* fit you!

All clothes should be cleaned before packing, although not pressed.

Staying slim is the biggest economy you can make: almost anyone can look good in almost anything if they put their mind to it and aren't overweight. Nevertheless, I keep a few clothes for when I'm larger. I hang them at the far end of the closet so that when there is more of me to love, the extra is not visible through bursting seams.

I also store old make-up. I never throw out anything I've stopped using, but keep it all sorted out in different deep-freeze bags in a big cardboard box. It takes up hardly any room and on those days when I feel that I badly need a new face, I don't rush out and spend a fortune. I have a happy dip in my make-up box, experiment with products I'd forgotten about (all of which, amazingly, are in the correct colour range for me) and emerge with several products that *feel* new to me. If some of the creams separate, I mix them up again with my finger; if some of the water-based products dry, I add a little water or skin freshener.

THE ART OF PACKING

I once met a travel agent who toured the world for three weeks at a time carrying a minimal wardrobe in hand luggage *alone*. Her handbag was a shoulder satchel, which also held make-up and washbag. She carried a heavy navy coat, wore walking shoes and a navy suit. Her hand luggage contained a pair of navy slacks, jeans, two T-shirts, two silk blouses, two sweaters, two silk dresses, underwear and a bikini.

This woman didn't allow her holiday

anticipation to be spoilt by *the trauma of packing*.

Because I travel a lot on business, much of it at short notice, I use the back of the wardrobe to stick up my current *check-list of travelling clothes* (see later) and can in ten minutes pick out what's necessary and pack to travel half-way around the world.

Here are other tips I've learned.

Airport thieves choose expensive luggage. So buy inexpensive, light, strong suitcases with wheels. Always pack a spare folding canvas suitcase for the extra garbage that you mysteriously acquire on any trip – even if you don't buy anything.

Think of your hand luggage as being what you'll be left with when they lose your suitcases (I always carry a spare bra in my hand luggage). Pack nothing in your luggage that you would mind losing (such as a passport or jewellery).

Shirley Lord, beauty editor of American *Vogue*, keeps a separate make-up case for travelling. Even if you aren't (as she then was) married to a millionaire, you can make your own instant travel kit by saving up little empty bottles and decanting a little of your everyday make-up into them. And try not *quite* finishing your blusher or eyeshadow, then putting the old one into your travel bag when you buy a new one.

Never carry glass bottles in case they break; decant them into plastic bottles. Always carry plastic bottles in your hand luggage and double-check that the screwtops *are* screwed on as you actually shove them in: this way you don't end up with a heap of clothes reeking of Ambre Solaire.

I carry an emergency first-aid kit in a small plastic bag, because a plaster in time can save trotting out to hunt for a chemist in a foreign place.

If you regularly take any medicine, get a spare prescription beforehand and if you depend on any equipment, such as a pair of spectacles, then travel with a spare pair.

Always travel with a bathing suit (it's hard enough to find one you look good in when you're shopping for one and you may rarely look better than awful in a borrowed one).

If you travel with duffel bags only, the way to minimize creasing is to make a huge roll of everything you're taking with sweaters on the outside, T-shirts and underwear in the middle, then stuff this in the bag.

If you're taking two suitcases, use one only for 'hard items' (such as shoes, boots and bags) and the other for clothes.

Use kitchen plastic baggies to pack things like swimsuits and underwear, and leave them in the bags at the other end of your journey. Take the plastic baggie roll with you to bring home damp swimsuits and dirty laundry.

If you're filling a suitcase, pack clothes on wire dry-cleaners' hangers, then simply hang them up at the other end (hotels never have enough hangers). If a garment has just come from the cleaner and has a plastic cover, leave this on, fold the garment in your suitcase and it may not need ironing at the other end.

When folding clothes, do up as few buttons as possible and fold the garments, face-upwards, *into* the suitcase, rather than folding them on the bed and transferring them to the suitcase, which they then don't fit.

Pack in this order:

* *Trousers*, folded over at the crotch, not halfway down the leg.
* *Skirts*, folded at the hips.
* *Jackets*, buttoned and placed face-upwards.
* *Sweaters*, laid flat, sleeves in a V, and folded over.
* *Shirts*, collars fastened, arms folded in at the shoulder.
* Now add everything else: T-shirts, scarves, nightwear, woollen stole for evenings.

DOWN WITH SUPERWOMAN!

Push your plastic bags of underwear and shoes in the pockets or odd space around the edges of the suitcase. Tuck belts around the sides without folding them.

Man-made fibre enthusiasts won't have a crease problem because all garments can be dipped in the hotel washbasin and drip-dried afterwards on plastic hangers over the bath. If you are not, you might want to buy a Braun iron and hair-dryer combined, plus an adaptor for foreign voltage (available at major airports).

If you travel with a hair-dryer, you can also use it to blow-dry your clothes into shape. Hang up the outfit, damp the creases with your face-cloth and point the hair-dryer at it.

Alternatively, hang all clothes in the bathroom and run a very hot bath – aim for sauna steam – which dewrinkles clothes. Keep the door shut.

My packing check-list

1 **Luggage** All black suitcases: spare folding suitcase, handbag (always on a shoulder strap), chic black tote bag, suit bag for carry-on crushable clothes.
2 **Handbag** contains two compartments. *Left side* for business: passports and other documents, money, chequebook, tickets, keys, foreign-address book, diary, reservations confirmation. *Right side* for personal: paperback, make-up bag, scent, spare specs, sunglasses, brush, comb, hand mirror, scissors, scarf, and normal contents of handbag.
3 **Tote bag** contains: roll of plastic baggies, washbag, tissues, cotton wool, clothes-brush, odourless shoe polish, sun cream, anti-midge jelly and similar toiletries, elastic bands, safety pins, hair-grips, sewing kit, hair-pieces and hair ornaments, work equipment (such as stationery and writing pads), jewel-

lery (never real, even if you have any; it's too much trouble checking it in and out of the hotel safe and even more trouble if it gets stolen).
4 **Suitcase contents** Clothes: underwear; nightclothes; evening clothes, long and short; trousers and sportswear; daywear (suits, dresses, blouses, sweaters, skirts); *possibly in second suitcase*: bags, belts, shoes, boots.

THE BODY INSIDE THE CLOTHES

Modern man is no longer at the mercy of enemies such as the sabre-toothed tiger, but we fight a constant battle for our health. Trapped in the fumes, noise and stress of the urban jungle, we don't exercise properly and we eat food that has been treated with chemicals. These stressful factors diminish the energy reserves that are needed to fight off illness – which we treat with more chemicals, some with bad side effects.

Helena Rubinstein once asked me how many things were wrong with my body. 'Nineteen,' I said immediately.

Madame Rubinstein said, 'Then there are 181 things right about your body,' and she started to list them, right down to my perfect elbows.

You also probably know what's wrong with your appearance. You probably worry about it too much. Instead, start concentrating on what is *right* – emphasize your assets and camouflage (or ignore) everything else.

Never wear a colour that doesn't suit you or a style that doesn't suit your shape – no matter if every other woman in sight has one in her wardrobe. There is *always* something in fashion to suit your shape, your size and your style.

Always look at yourself backview before you buy anything – especially if the salesgirl assures you that you don't need to. Take a pocket mirror when shopping, because shops rarely have them (they don't *want* you to see your back-view).

What you do about your age is ignore it. It isn't the number of years that count, but the number on the weighing machine. However, don't worry unduly about that. When for two years I kept myself grimly at size ten, I had no life or energy, achieved nothing and was a drag. So ignore the fashion browbeaters and stick to the size at which you feel best. I'm not saying that you shouldn't watch your figure; I'm saying that you shouldn't get it out of proportion in your head.

If your weight yo-yos or you swell up before your period, gradually accumulate a set of clothes for these times.

You can tell if you're out of condition and overweight by lying naked on a towel on the floor and putting a ruler across your pelvic bones. If you can't feel your pelvic bones or if the ruler touches any flesh between them, you need to diet and exercise until it doesn't.

If you're dieting, pay extra attention to your face and clothes. You're probably fairly depressed by your appearance or you wouldn't be dieting, so compensate by trying to look better than usual. Don't go into sackcloth and ashes; wear pretty clothes – you need to cheer yourself up.

Before you go on a diet, get yourself into mental shape for it.

I don't feel hungry at breakfast but I can see the energy difference in reduced output if I don't eat it. Always eat breakfast and lunch, *especially* if you're dieting. If God had intended you to eat only once a day, he would have given you a huge digestion system like a Rolls-Royce petrol tank, not a neat small efficient system like a Mini petrol tank, which needs topping up three times a day.

Drink lots of water (at least 560 ml (1 pt) a day).

Every day drink 285 ml (½ pt) of skimmed or powdered milk (serve this on the table in a bowl, like sugar). If you don't have time for a meal, drink a glass of skimmed milk. If you can't sleep, drink a cup of hot skimmed milk with a teaspoon of honey.

Avoid white flour, sugar, anything fried, mayonnaise, cheese, salt, coffee and strong tea.

If this is your umpteenth diet and you keep taking off the same 7 kg (15 lb) and then putting it back, consider what you might look like had you *never* been on a diet. I look at the photos of my ancestors (all shaped like bolsters) and I think 'things could be a lot worse'.

The 24-word, 24-day diet

I accidentally discovered the diet that works best for me when I had a gall-bladder problem. I stuck up a card on the refrigerator that said, 'No alcohol, sugar, nuts, fat, eggs, dairy products. Eat sparingly raw fruit, raw vegetables, salad, white fish, skinned chicken. Never go hungry – nibble carrots.'

The weight fell off my stomach, hips and thighs, but *not* from my bosom. When I read Rosemary Conley's *Hip and Thigh Diet*, I recognized her thorough approach to a no-fat diet. If jodhpur thighs are your problem, buy this book.

The catch in all diets comes at the end, when you are told to 'correct your eating habits'. Try doing this *before* dieting, because by the time you fall off a diet, your will-power may be too low to reform your eating habits.

On pp. 312–13 you will find an 800-calorie diet. Most people will lose weight on this diet. People (like me) with a low metabolic rate can use it as a maintenance diet. It was given to me by HM the Queen's doctor.

Eat as little as possible of what is allowed. Be sensible. Anything I've forgotten to tell you about is forbidden.

Highlight your danger areas (mine are grapes and mayonnaise). At parties,

The National Heart and Chest Hospital's diet

REDUCING DIET 800 calories (approx.)

Early morning
Tea with separated milk (no sugar).

Breakfast
Tea or coffee with separated milk (no sugar).
1 portion fresh fruit, e.g., grapefruit, or unsweetened grapefruit juice.
1 egg, portion of fish, lean grilled bacon, lean ham, cold tongue or jellied veal.
Tomatoes or mushrooms.
19 g (¾ oz) bread (white or brown).
Butter thinly spread.

Mid-morning
Tea or coffee with separated milk (no sugar)
or Bovril or Marmite.

Lunch
A small helping of lean meat, offal, rabbit, chicken, cheese or fish (grilled, steamed or baked).
Cabbage, greens, Brussels sprouts, cauliflower, marrow, mushrooms,
spinach, French and runner beans, carrots, swedes, turnips, onions, ⎱ or salad
leeks or tomatoes.
Fruit – raw or stewed (without sugar).

Tea
Tea with separated milk (no sugar).
19 g (¾ oz) bread (white or brown).
Butter thinly spread.
Salad, Marmite.

Supper
A small helping of lean meat, chicken, cheese, egg or fish.
Vegetables or salad (as at lunch).
Fruit – raw or stewed (without sugar).
19 g (¾ oz) bread (white or brown).
Tea or coffee with separated milk (no sugar).

Bedtime
Remainder of separated milk allowance in tea or coffee (no sugar).

DAILY ALLOWANCES

Butter 15 g (½ oz). Separated milk 285 ml (½ pt).
A small helping of various foods as indicated below.
Meat 43 g (1½ oz).
Fish 85 g (3 oz).
or Cheese (Cheddar) 21 g (¾ oz) *or* 43 g (1½ oz) cottage cheese (fat-free).
Egg 1.
Bread (wholegrain) 55 g (2 oz).

(A) FOODS ALLOWED

Condiments.
Salad (without oil or dressing).
Cooked vegetables (except those mentioned in section B).
Unthickened vegetable soup, Bovril, Marmite, lemon juice, tomato juice.
Worcestershire sauce.
Saccharin, Saxin, Sweetex or Hermasetas.
Dietetic fruit squashes, water, soda water, pure lemon juice (PLJ), slim-line drinks.
Gelatine for making jellies.

(B) FOODS NOT ALLOWED

Sugary foods
Sugar, glucose, sweets, chocolate, jam, marmalade, syrup, honey. Diabetic jams and chocolate, packet jellies, ice cream. Dates, dried and canned fruit, bananas, grapes. Beetroot and sweet chutney.

Starchy foods
Cakes, pastry, puddings, sweet biscuits, breakfast cereals, pudding cereals, e.g., rice, spaghetti, etc.
Sauces, thick gravies and soups, flour, cornflour, etc., Bisto.
Potatoes, beans (baked, broad, butter and haricot), lentils, parsnips, peas (all kinds), sweet-corn.
Bread – except as shown on diet sheet.

Fatty foods
Fat on meat, ham, etc. Fried foods.
Cream, margarine, dripping, lard, suet.
Mayonnaise, olive oil, cream cheese, pork, sardines, sausages.
Butter – except as shown on diet sheet.

Drinks
Beers, stout, cider, sweet wines, spirits, sweetened fruit drinks and sweet mineral waters.
Lucozade, Ribena, Horlicks, Ovaltine, cocoa, sweetened condensed milk.

---

drink neat or diluted lemon juice, mineral water or soda water with a dash of Angostura bitters.

Allow yourself 500 calories a week for the occasional madness – a glass of dry wine or scoop of chocolate ice cream.

If you're hungry, drink a glass of water, make a cup of weak tea or weak Bovril.

I can lose weight only when eating under 500 calories a day. My doctor prescribed a skimmed-milk plus vitamin diet: there are many of these powder diets on the market. After personally testing others, I use only the Cambridge Diet because I feel so well on it. I am told that this was developed by two doctors and is used in hospitals – and, of course, I use it only under my doctor's supervision. This diet is controversial because some people believe that the calorie level is too low, but this is refuted by the scientists of Cambridge Nutrition Ltd.

Avoid people who are going to be destructive to your diet ('*You* don't need to diet', 'One won't hurt you', 'But *it's home-made*').

Your will-power will be at its lowest when you are tired. Other danger times are:

⋆ When you feel sorry for yourself and need comforting.
⋆ If you feel nervous.
⋆ When you've had a disappointment.

⋆ On the day before you start a crash diet.

Don't use food to celebrate, when you deserve a reward or when you're on holiday.

Remember that 85 per cent of people who lose weight gain it back if they don't combine their diet with an exercise programme and keep up the exercise.

Perhaps because human beings eat three times a day, almost all of Western socializing seems to centre around food and drink. Break this mould by inviting friends to *do* something – go bowling, or skating, go to a film, play, ballet or concert; do anything, but don't go out for a meal afterwards.

A lot of the reason for cravings is simply habit. If you don't bring up a child on sweetie treats, that child won't develop a 'sweet tooth' – a pretty phrase for a craving. It is a sign of love *not* to give your children sweets. Dissociate love from food or you risk a fat family. Reconnect love to love through sound nutrition.

The drawback to most diets is the temptation of cooking delicious meals for the family while *you* are on the diet. An added benefit of reforming your eating habits is that while you're doing it, you can virtuously reform your family's diet at the same time – and possibly without their noticing.

DOWN WITH SUPERWOMAN!

HOUSEWORK CAN DAMAGE YOUR HEALTH

As I always suspected, housework can be harmful to your health. Doing the washing-up, peeling vegetables, making beds, pushing prams or furniture, carrying shopping bags, vacuum cleaning, gardening, even knitting can damage your spine, unless your posture is correct.

As it's invisible to them, people tend to take their spine for granted until they have a problem, but standing, sitting, walking and lifting things the wrong way can lead to aching legs, backache, stress, fatigue, pain and strain on the spine that might lead to serious problems, such as a slipped disc. The lower back is where most disc troubles occur, because people bend the spine when stooping and lifting, rather than bending the big powerful hip and knee joints.

As in all things, the experts of one generation are flatly contradicted by those of the next. In case you had old-fashioned posture instruction, what you should *not* do is the following:

1 Hold your chin up (creates neck tension).
2 Brace your shoulders (strains neck and shoulder muscles and does nothing for round shoulders).
3 Hold your chest up (prevents you breathing easily).
4 Hold your stomach in (restricts breathing, causes strain and is unnecessary if your posture is correct).
5 Tuck your tail in (strains the lower back).
6 Press-ups (strains neck, shoulders and back).
7 Bicycle exercises lying on your back (strains your neck and can hollow your back).
8 Touch your toes with braced knees. (If you are out of condition and try this, you will feel the strain on your lower back before your fingertips are anywhere near the floor. However, if

you are fit, this is a good exercise to stretch the hamstrings.)

The best way to get a better posture is to check your posture every morning in front of a long mirror and then at odd moments for the rest of the day. Catch yourself out.

A slumped body causes strain, especially on the ligaments that hold the bones together. Slump *now* and you'll feel the strain in your back. *A contracted body* that is too braced is also a strain. Stand up *now* like a guardsman on parade and check what happens to your body. All the muscles tense, your neck stiffens, your shoulders rise and stiffen and your whole body feels rigid. What you want to achieve is *an expanded, balanced, relaxed body* position in which you feel upright but light.

How to stand

Get someone to read this aloud as you stand sideways to a mirror, wearing briefs only. Put your feet together, stand straight and easy, with shoulders down. Put too much weight on your heels (do it now) and your body will compensate by stooping slightly forward. Put too much weight on your toes (do it now) and your body will compensate by leaning backwards: you will have a hollow back and your stomach will stick out.

Instead, stand with your weight at the centre of your feet. Now, like a sailor doing the hornpipe, put the back of your left hand on your upper buttocks and your right palm on your stomach. Press both hands slightly and tilt your pelvis upwards towards your chin. Gently contract stomach muscles. Gently tighten buttocks (as if you were holding a coin between them). Lift your rib-cage (ballet dancers 'block' themselves like this, before practice). You are now standing correctly – light and poised for movement. Your pelvis is tilted forward and upward, thus providing a bowl in which to rest your innards, which will then not protrude and sag.

How to walk

Look in the mirror sideways on to check that there is a straight line between your shoulder and your ankle. Lift your rib-cage and walk round the room in this position. Don't stretch, just extend to your full height, feeling lighter and moving easily. When walking, your head should be straight, your neck muscles relaxed, your body upright but not braced. If you're walking slowly, the heel should touch the floor first, then the foot rolls towards the toe.

Walking is one of the best forms of exercise and if you're doing it in town, you can check your posture reflected in the shop windows.

How to sit

The best way to sit is in an upright chair that supports your spine just above the waist – a typist's chair is designed to do this. Gently tilt the pelvis upwards and slightly tighten stomach muscles. Your feet should be flat on the floor and slightly apart; your thighs should take the pressure off your spine. Lean forward slowly and you'll feel the strain on your back. Relax totally and you will feel your breast and stomach muscles sag.

When choosing armchairs, avoid the sort that looks like a sagging elephant into which you flop. Choose a chair that is not too low, not too deep, gives firm back support and has low arms so that your shoulders are not hunched. The chair should support you just above the waist. If it doesn't, place a small cushion in the small of the back.

Check that you're sitting in the correct posture to knit or read. If reading in an armchair, put a cushion on your lap and prop your book on top of it, so that you don't strain your neck by bending over to it.

How to sleep

Sleep on a firm mattress that holds its shape. Sleep on your back or on one side, legs bent slightly with the top leg highest, the under arm behind your back and the upper arm in front of your face. Doctors say that you should use only one pillow in the hollow of your neck.

Housework

A doctor told me that some of the worst cases of arthritis in hands that he had seen were in women who did a lot of **bed-making**. Lifting a heavy mattress to tuck in sheets and blankets every day and turning the mattress is a strain on your spine (unless you bend at the knees) and a strain on your hands. Get continental quilts.

One of the things that can most easily cause housewife's backache is a sink that is too low, so you have to stoop over it to peel vegetables or do the **washing-up**. The correct height for a sink is the height at which you can put your hands in it with palms touching the sink bottom *while you are still standing upright*. Sinks are too low because architects and builders stupidly insist on fixing them too low. If this is your problem, do your washing-up in a bowl on the work surface.

Be careful with the **vacuum cleaner** because that involves push and pull movements, both of which can be harmful.

Don't put a strain on your back when **lifting coal, logs, a basket of washing, a baby or any heavy parcel**. Using your hip and knee joints, bend down to lift the object. Don't arch your back, don't hold your breath, don't lift anything heavy by bending over with knees straight and braced.

If you're **picking up a light object**,

DOWN WITH SUPERWOMAN!

Right	Wrong

St Thomas's Hospital posture chart

place one foot slightly in front of the other, bend the knees and go down with a graceful movement, like a curtsy.

When **carrying a tray upstairs**, keep the tray close to the body and elbows to your sides.

When **lifting a heavy object from a high shelf**, don't hollow your back, because this puts a strain on your lower back.

Use a bag on wheels for **shopping**. If you carry a shopping bag, carry two, evenly balancing the weight, so that the weight of one shopping bag doesn't pull your shoulder down and your spine crooked.

Pushing a pram should be done without crouching over the handle, which puts a tiring strain on the back. Instead, lean on the handle slightly to check your upright posture.

If you're **pushing something heavy**, like an armchair, don't bend over it. Keep your back upright, bend your knees a little and push – still keeping your back

upright. Never **pull a heavy piece of furniture**, because of the strain on your spine. Push it.

Think of the old-fashioned bent and gnarled gardener and you will instantly see that *gardening* in the wrong position can be harmful. Apply these principles of bending, lifting, pushing, pulling, carrying and stretching when you're doing the gardening. In particular, bend at the knees when you heave up a full spade or you may have lower back trouble. Get a Sorbo knee-pad for **weeding** and **push a lawnmower** as you would push a pram.

WHY BOTHER TO EXERCISE?

Your body is a machine fashioned to move about and it gets rusty if not used. Inertia is bad for you. Inactive muscles weaken very fast, which is one reason why hospitals are keen to get patients on their feet and so send physiotherapists tripping round the wards.

What keeps your circulation efficient is regular exercise. Otherwise too-high blood pressure, fat and blood-sugar levels can lead to heart disease.

What sort of exercise is best?

The aerobic exercise that you most enjoy. Aerobic doesn't only mean aerobic dancing. Aerobic exercise is any exercise that increases your pulse rate and is vigorous enough to leave you panting. It should be followed by another, gentler exercise that allows your pulse rate to decrease.

Yoga is not aerobic. It will stretch you and make you supple but you need additional, aerobic exercise that does not involve intense bursts of effort, as in squash.

How much should you exercise?

Whatever exercise you choose, do it three times a week for half an hour. Swimming is the best exercise because it doesn't strain the body and is a mixture of aerobic exercise, stretching exercise and a form of weight-lifting (pushing water aside), which increases your muscular strength and stamina.

Bringing up your family to exercise regularly is as important as feeding them correctly. This is no problem for those still at school, but getting grannies, aunties and uncles to exercise is more difficult. My elder son telephoned every day for a month to nag me gently until I started, and then phoned every day for a month until I'd got into the habit.

As I sit writing hunched over a desk all day, I've trained myself to regard an hour's daily exercise (except on Sunday) as part of my job: this is the only way I don't find an excuse to avoid exercise. I do twenty minutes gym, twenty minutes yoga, cycle 1 km ($\frac{5}{8}$ mile) on a fixed machine and follow it with five minutes' relaxation and a shower.

Ignore these excuses

Exercise doesn't really make a difference. Oh yes it does. You need regular exercise for the same reason a dog does, because it keeps you alert and frisky. Exercise wards off obesity, feelings of stress, diabetes, arthritis, heart disease, hypertension and constipation. In addition, exercise will speed up your metabolism.

Exercise is boring. Certainly, unless you enjoy it you won't do it – so pick an exercise you think of as fun. *Examples*: any of the many sorts of dancing, karate, swimming, netball, football, hockey, tennis, cycling, aerobic exercise, weight-lifting, circuit-training and gymnastics.

Exercise is self-inflicted punishment. Join an exercise club where you can meet other people and expand your circle of friends. Use exercise as an excuse to be sociable.

Exercise is dangerous. Too much of anything is dangerous, including the struggle for achievement that drives a body beyond its capacity. Irregular exercise in fierce bouts, between long stretches of chairbound inactivity, is unwise.

I get enough exercise during the day. Heavy housework is not exercise, neither is standing on your feet all day or working in a factory. Gardening is not exercise and neither is golf, because they do not sufficiently raise the pulse rate.

I haven't time to exercise. If you've got time to watch TV, you have.

The Owner's Manual

For any woman who wants a longer, healthier, physical life an up-to-date paperback is *The Modern Woman's Body*, which answers questions such as:

How effective are treatments such as acupuncture or reflexology, and where do I find them?
Is there any really safe way to delay the ageing process? (The answer is yes.)

This book is compulsive reading, so don't be put off by the dreary title. I spent an entire Sunday reading it when I could have gone to the beach.

How to get your own way

HOW TO GET WHAT YOU WANT

On the whole, what women want in life is love and what men want is power – and men want power as much as women want love. Women don't understand what 'power' is: in the nursery, power is called 'getting your own way'.

Of course, first you have to know *what you want*. Then you have to let other people know what you want. This can be as simple as wanting your money back for a defective electric kettle or as complicated as moving to Australia.

Many women cannot say what they mean quickly and simply because they are timid. Many women don't think they are entitled to have an opinion, to say what they think, to speak up for themselves. So when they ask for something defensively, it is because they suspect that somebody else is going to tell them bluntly '*You can't have it.*' Often such a

woman will dither from nervousness, because she expects to have her head bitten off. This is because she doesn't want to rock the boat, she wants to avoid trouble, she wants to be loved.

So how do you ask for something effectively?

1 Write it down. Compress your wish to one sentence, asking for *one specific thing* and your main reason for wanting it. Give yourself one minute to write down your situation, then one minute to put down the reasons for your wish (use a kitchen timer). This is in order to clarify your objective to yourself.

2 Pick the right person to ask for what you want – someone who has *the power* to grant your requests. Make sure you have reached the right person, before doing anything else.

3 Pick the right moment to ask for what you want. This is the moment that best suits the other person, which is rarely first thing in the morning or after a hard day's work, or during someone's lunch hour. Sometimes you can spend hours waiting for the right moment, but if you're not patient, your answer may well be NO. (You know when your timing has been wrong in the past.)

If you plan the right sort of time, you're more likely to hit exactly the right moment. With a busy executive, start by saying, 'Can you spare me two minutes?' If he says no, then ask when he can. Then say what you have to say in two minutes. Here's how.

4 When you have reached the right person make sure he understands *what* you are talking about – the tip of the pyramid of your story – in one sentence.

Have you ever had to explain your entire story five times to different people before getting to the person who can actually do something to help you? If so, *keep your story short.*

For instance, when making a complaint say 'I would like to make a complaint about an electric kettle. Which is the right department?' When you get to the right department, say 'I would like to make a complaint about an electric kettle. Who is the right person?'

Talk pleasantly but like a telegram, with no subclauses. Stick to the point. Don't be distracted by explanations or excuses. Keep repeating your telegram of wishes. Be pleasant – you don't want to sound like a malfunctioning computer.

5 You may then develop your message. State who, what, when, where, how ('I bought a kettle last Tuesday in your electrical spring sale and I paid by cheque').

Always open and close the conversation by repeating your message ('I need an electric kettle by *next Friday*').

Keep your message clear and simple. Be firm and tenacious but never aggressive. Don't swear, don't waffle, don't use 'sort of' or 'kind of', don't red-herring ('You see, my mother-in-law is coming next Friday'), don't use ludicrous Edward-

ian slang, which sounds condescending ('simply dreadful', 'horribly upsetting', 'Could you be terribly nice' . . .).

Remember that using a little-girl voice guarantees that you will not be taken seriously.

Avoid clutterbucking – generally caused by nervousness. A clutterbuck dithers on, never comes to the point, assumes that her listener knows the entire contents of her brain and life and can therefore follow all the red-herring asides in her uninterruptible monologue. She frustrates and exasperates her listeners.

6 Get the right person to identify with you. 'Perhaps you would feel the same way if *your* new electric kettle didn't work when you got it home?' or 'How would *your* mother feel if *her* electric kettle?', etc., etc.

7 If possible, suggest how the person you are talking to can give you what you want. **Always give a deadline date.** 'I need a replacement kettle or a repaired kettle or to borrow a kettle by next Friday.'

But how do you get something that is more important than a replacement kettle? Say, a room for yourself or a job.

8 In a perfect world I wouldn't have to say this but to get what you want, you also have to *make it as easy as possible for somebody to give you what you want.* In order to get a reluctant child to eat up its spinach you may need to coax it, using charm, persuasion and gentle persistence rather than reason; these are the buttons you press to manipulate the child to do what you want. You avoid confrontation because otherwise you risk having the spinach thrown at you. You deal with the problem *from the child's point of view.*

The great big world outside your home is run by people who can make things happen, who are expert at getting grown-ups to eat their spinach. These people get to the top and get what they want by methods that can be described in socially acceptable words or socially *un*acceptable words that mean exactly the same thing.

Felicity Green, the first woman on the board of a national British newspaper, once said, 'Of course it's ridiculous that a "persuasive, tactful, considerate person who gives praise where praise is due" can also be described as a "manipulative, hypocritical, calculating flatterer". But, to be honest, everywhere I have ever worked, in order for me to do my job as well as I could, the need to be manipulative manifested itself extremely early on. That is, to say what I wanted to say in a way that people would listen to me.

'Whatever you set out to do in life, unless you are going to do it alone on a desert island, you will need to communicate with other people, whether it's in a friendship, love affair or business.

'Always be tactful and kind, without being a liar. Remember that too much truth can be hard to take, truth can be cruel and destructive and, all too often, truth is more of an opinion than a fact.

'The first, essential step to getting what you want when you want it is to be realistic. Arguments, show-downs and other confrontations can be disruptive, destructive and a waste of valuable time. Save your confrontations *only* for the issues that really matter and negotiate your way around the rest.'

I would add that when someone does something for you, whether you get the kettle or the new job, thank him and praise him. Human beings *thirst* for praise and acknowledgement; they thrive on it – men, in particular; after all, titles are praise and acknowledgement, so are medals, so are uniforms with little stars on.

You may ask for what you want by letter, on the telephone or in person. As letters can go astray (or other people can pretend that they have), I prefer to ask for something on the telephone, followed

by a confirming letter by recorded delivery. This is shorter in the long run and misunderstandings can be clarified before they escalate.

When writing, use good, clean paper (no tea stains or erasures) and always date the letter on the top right-hand side (otherwise the date can't be seen when the letter is in a file).

When asking in person, remember that the first impression really *is* what counts, so project the way you want to be treated. Don't go in to see someone looking as if you expect to be thrown out. When you enter, pause in the doorway, project confidence, *look him in the eye* and look pleasant – perhaps a little smile, but not a big grin.

If you want to be taken seriously, dress seriously. My family shorthand for this is 'Don't talk to Eskimos in Swahili.' For example, if you want your bank manager to be receptive to your request for a loan, don't dress for the interview in your leather gear with a green Mohican hairdo. Dress like a bank manager, in something neat, clean, dark and non-sexy; look like the sort of person who is competent, sensible, disciplined and reliable in matters of repaying the bank's money. Don't wear too much clanking jewellery (the less the better) and avoid overpowering perfume. Of course, if you're about to meet a rock star, *he* may feel more comfortable and relaxed if you wear your leather, chains, nose-safety-pin and green Mohican.

Choose whatever clothes are most appropriate. If you're in the spotlight, dress like a star: a bride doesn't wear a neat, dark suit. If you're making an appearance, give your audience something to look at and dress with panache.

If several people with the same skills are applying for a job, the one that gets the job is the one that projects confidence and ability and *dresses the part*.

Never wear a new outfit for the first time when you have to perform. Always wear something in which you feel comfortable and wear shoes that are easy to walk in.

Never be late or you'll be flustered and give a bad first impression. Aim to arrive half an hour early for an important appointment and wait outside until the correct time to make your entrance.

At this point hold yourself alert and ready. Don't play this scene as rehearsed in front of your mirror, rushing out your little speeches without letting the other person get a word in edgeways. Remember that conversation is a two-way process and no one else has read your script.

Refer to notes if you want to: you will look well-prepared and efficient. Before going to any interview I always scribble on a postcard the three most important things I want to say and the three most important questions I want to ask. These are my conversational stepping stones. If you don't want to be seen to read notes, produce a little notebook and during the interview jot down some pearl of his wisdom on the bottom of a page. On the top of the page are your six points – ready to jog your memory.

Someone described as 'interesting to talk to' is almost always a good listener. Every journalist knows that you learn more by listening than by talking, so learn to *really* listen, not just *look* as if you're listening until it's your turn to speak again. Don't think about something else while someone is talking, because this is always apparent and very irritating.

To show that you're listening, ask a question about what the other person has just said. When he answers, you slowly nod, then ask another question. If necessary, get the conversation back to the point by referring to one of your stepping stones. ('Would that mean I could have the full amount by the end of the month?')

During a discussion, if you're asked a question you don't want to (or can't) answer, simply pause and then say, 'I'd prefer to think about that. I'll give you a definite answer tomorrow.'

Formal person-to-person communication with bank manager types can be far easier than dealing with people you know, especially your family. A family member may be the easiest person to persuade (because you know which of his buttons to push and you can predict his reaction), but he can also be the most difficult person to persuade. If he's being deliberately exasperating and uncooperative (what the army calls 'dumb insolence') or if he's trying to wind you up to the point where you'll lose your temper (because he is pushing *your* buttons), don't lose sight of what you hope to achieve (this is, of course, his objective). Quietly repeat your message.

The best way to get the co-operation of people you know well is never to take them for granted – not even your mother – and always to be as thoughtful and tactful as you would be if you were asking for a loan from the bank manager.

Always take the trouble to think about your proposal from the other person's point of view. What has he to gain? (Be positive, put this point first.) What has he to lose?

However, the big exception to logical communication may well be your mate, especially if you are married. It is difficult to explain what you want to a husband who is deliberately turning a deaf ear to you.

Many women are distressed because their mates 'don't talk' or 'won't listen' to them. One British study of 700 marriages revealed a widespread lack of conversation among couples, yet most of the men had no problem when talking to people other than their wives. A great many men don't talk to their wives because they don't feel the need to confide and won't listen to their wives because they feel embarrassed if their wives want to discuss with them emotions such as these:

* **Depression,** which can stem from drudgery, exhaustion and a need for creative self-expression that cannot be met by making cakes.

* **Insecurity,** as expressed by the questions 'Do you still love me?' 'How much do you love me?' 'How am I supposed to know you love me when you never tell me any more?'

* **Unhappiness.** Nagging is a sign of unhappiness, which may stem from frustration at being ignored or suppressed resentment, which is really suppressed anger, which is suppressed rage.

A woman who complains that her mate 'never talks' or 'won't listen' to her often means that he provides no acknowledgement of her as a thinking person in her own right, with feelings and opinions, rather than his always-acquiescent servant and harem slave. But this sort of man wants *only* a servant and harem slave. In particular, he doesn't want to confide *his* anxieties and fears, *his* weaknesses, for fear of making himself vulnerable in a way that a 'macho' man cannot accept.

If 'macho' men have problems about work or other relationships, they don't confide in their wives, although they *might* discuss a problem with another man with a view to getting advice about it in a way that would not involve any 'macho' loss of face.

His wife then feels left out and hurt because her mate doesn't allow her into his private world. She is kept an outsider. The man retains his Inner Self; he doesn't *want* his wife to understand him. A man's normal human failings are carefully hidden in his head, because his cultural upbringing doesn't allow him *any* weakness. (Johnny must be a brave little soldier.) This is why men don't want women getting inside their head.

Because he doesn't confide in her, the wife feels that she is not an equal partner in a relationship that is supposed to be based on total, interdependent trust; she is prepared to make herself vulnerable to him, but he is not prepared to do the same for her.

What a woman hopes for from her husband is the same swift, shorthand-like, intimate communication that she has with her women friends. It can often be easy for a woman friend to see the wife's problem and to swiftly summarize it objectively (because her woman friend knows her character and situation) in a way that the wife recognizes immediately to be true and sensible. As if the wife is struggling through the jungle, her friend mentally hovers overhead in an objective helicopter and can point out where the escape route lies. This sort of female intimacy depends on very receptive listening and noticing gestures, hints and silences. What the wife gets from her woman friend is *attention* and that may be what her man will silently and insolently deny her.

Another communication problem is when a wife is puzzled by her husband's contradictory behaviour. If he says one thing and does another, *listen to what he says and compare it with what he does*. Believe what he does, not what he says. If he's too embarrassed to say he loves you but cooks supper every night, he is behaving with loving consideration. Remember that it's easy to say 'I love you' and any Latin con-man can do so while planning his next conquest.

HOW TO HANDLE A QUARREL

Some married couples enjoy having marital rows, sometimes in front of somebody else. (Bickering is a low-key, never-ending nagging row.) Some married couples hate having marital rows, especially in front of somebody else. But every married couple sometimes disagrees; sometimes you both need to let off steam – at times loudly – in order to clear the air.

But how should you handle a quarrel if you want to defuse an angry scene?

Never let an angry person rattle you. If he is angry, his feelings are controlling him. Stupidity is the operation of intelligence hampered by feelings.

If he is being deliberately provocative, ask yourself *what* is he trying to provoke? An angry reaction in you, that's probably what. Why? It doesn't matter. What matters is that you don't react, however unfairly you are attacked or however indignant you are. Don't let him press *your* buttons and manipulate *you* into providing him with the reaction that *he* wants in order to make himself feel better because he's made you feel worse.

Don't shake your rattle. Don't throw a little tantrum merely in answer to his to show how much he has upset and enraged you. Remember that while you are shaking your rattle you can't think intelligently.

Then how do you stop your blood boiling? DON'T count to ten. Concentrate on getting OUT. Make any excuse that won't aggravate the situation to remove yourself from the scene as quietly and unostentatiously but as fast as possible (if only to the bathroom) and stay away as long as possible to allow yourself and the other person to cool down.

If you can't leave the scene, **don't allow yourself to be upset by vague generalities,** as in '*Everyone* knows you are a bitch.' Ignore these hand grenades, which are meant to damage your morale. In a quarrel, such tactics are proof either that you are winning the argument or that your opponent is running out of ammunition and clutching at straws. Don't respond. Don't start defensively listing all the people who *don't* think you're a bitch.

Never have the last word. When two people are both trying to have the last word, a quarrel can be prolonged for hours. Give yourself permission *not* to have the last word.

However, **never let the person who causes a scene win an angry argument** because, as with a spoilt child, you are inviting further scenes and spinach throwing. Quietly say, 'I can't accept what you say.' This is a boring statement that presses no button. It may well stop escalation – if you don't say one more word. Later, when he has calmed down, firmly say that you would like to discuss this problem. Make sure that you really mean what you say. Aim at a situation where there are two adults discussing a problem. You don't want an atmosphere in which one person is being condescending – talking down – to the other person, because if one person behaves like a lofty parent, the other person will behave like an angry child.

Never bluff. If you really decide to do something, then do it without talking about it, and let him find out afterwards. This is far more deadly than crying wolf. And what's the point of saying you're going to leave him if you're still there in the morning?

HOW TO BREAK THE ICE

Whatever the size of the group you are meeting, whether it is a small Tupperware party or a large wedding, names are all-important.

A person's own name is the most important name in the world to him – it is shorthand for his identity. Members of the royal family know that remembering names is the secret of popularity and they all put a lot of effort into doing this. When you meet a new group of people, try to remember only two names to begin with, otherwise you may get muddled and forget them all.

When introducing people, don't intro-

DOWN WITH SUPERWOMAN!

duce a large group to someone who has just stepped inside the door. If someone doesn't know or forgets your name, you quickly say, 'I'm Shirley Conran, how do you do?' The other guest should then reply, 'I'm Mel Gibson, delighted to meet you.'

Of course, if you find yourself at a meeting with ten strangers around a committee table, you will be quickly introduced to them and equally quickly you will forget their names. Get out your little notebook, draw a diagram of the table, then ask the person on your left, 'Who is the woman opposite in red, and what does she do?' Next whisper the same question to the person on your right about the grey-suited man at the end of the table. Whenever anybody is mentioned by name, scribble down that name on your diagram. At the end of the meeting fill in any gaps by asking the chairman 'Who was the interesting woman in green on your left?'

A quick way to a woman's heart (and it's also true of a lot of men) is to ask about her children. Her face will light up and she will instantly feel at ease with you – and talk.

As soon as possible praise something about the other person. There always is something to praise. Never be insincere, merely accentuate the positive ('Where did you get those lovely earrings?').

At more formal meetings – perhaps a committee meeting – if you are asked to speak, always start by acknowledging the group, their aims and achievements, before saying what you have to say. 'I'm delighted to join you in your hard work to raise funds for Birthright and the good health of mothers and future babies.'

HOW TO AVOID COMPLAINTS

Use a little cynical forethought. Don't

assume that people whom you don't know are honest. Don't assume that people whom you *do* know will look at a situation in the way you look at it.

Possession does seem to be nine-tenths of the law, and if someone else has your money and you have their faulty goods, the dice are weighted in their favour. You may have a long, unhappy and expensive wait until the law is able to act, and then the judge may not see things from your point of view. All people who go to court do so because, presumably, they think that they are in the right. But 50 per cent of court cases are not won.

Almost every profession has a society (for instance, the Law Society, the British Medical Association, the Royal Institute of British Architects). Ask *any* professional you are about to hire what professional association he belongs to, then telephone the association to check that your professional really *is* qualified and really *is* a member. Otherwise, you will have no weapon if things go wrong.

When buying a home, *always* have a survey made by a qualified surveyor and, beforehand, ask for proof of his insurance. If his survey turns out to be incorrect, you can then sue for damages.

Always get written estimates from workmen before letting them undertake a job, and deal only with reputable firms that will stand behind the products and services they sell.

Always get a dated receipt for ANYTHING that is removed from your home.

You must always be able to prove that you paid for something, so *keep receipts and fill in your cheque stubs carefully*.

The time to start worrying about **plumbing, central heating, electrical and other home installation** complaints is *before* you sign the contract and certainly before work starts. *Assume* that you are going to have problems. You must expect what are whimsically called teething troubles from plumbing and central heating installations.

Plumbing leaks on new work are hard to spot until the system is actually in use. But what do you do about the plumber who burnt a hole in your sofa with his blow-torch? Legally, his firm is responsible for the actions of its employees while they are doing your job on behalf of the firm. So, once you have put the smelling salts aside, deal with the firm, not the employee.

Make an effort to ensure that any lone service man you use is reliable. Don't just pluck one from the *Yellow Pages*: a careless plumber can cost you thousands of pounds and when you look him up again in the *Yellow Pages*, he's vanished or gone to the Costa Brava or simply isn't very interested in returning to examine his bodge or finish it. Always hire someone whose written references you've personally checked on (preferably by telephone), who comes recommended by someone you know well or who is big enough to sue.

You are likely to get better servicing from a **manufacturer of appliances** (and you must assume that *all* the household machinery you buy will have regular stomach trouble) if you use nationally advertised products that carry some form of approval. Big names don't want bad publicity. Look for the gold square of the Gas Council or the yellow triangle of the British Electrical Appliances Board: this means that the item has been tested not only for safety but also for durability. A Design Council seal of approval is another guarantee of good looks and high standards.

The BSK (British Standard Kite) mark means that the object to which it is attached has passed the test of the British Standards Institution, which decides minimum safety regulations and other sensible criteria. Never buy a toy or any equipment for children without a BS label.

Guarantees and warranties

There are enormous problems here. Some conditions are good and some are not worth the paper they are written on and, unless you can take legal advice, you won't be able to tell which is good and which is bad. The National Consumer Council is pressing the Government to pass a law that will insist on a clear and uniform guarantee form. But meanwhile . . .

Before buying an item, ask the retailer:

1 Who pays for service?
2 Who pays for new parts?
3 Who pays for replacement of the machine, if it quickly proves to be a malfunctioning machine?

Ask the retailer to put his answers in writing (signed and dated) on his letterhead. The National Consumer Council told me that this is reasonable.

You are more likely to avoid problems about guarantees if:

1 You buy from a well-established firm, such as John Lewis or Dixons.
2 You fill in the guarantee and return it to the shopkeeper or manufacturer, whichever is stipulated on the guarantee.
3 You check on the guarantee whether you must keep all the original packing (including bits of polystyrene) in order to be able to claim under the guarantee.

THE FOG INDEX

Some writers seem to delight in longwinded, foggy prose, but nobody can deny that long sentences and long words are more difficult to read than short ones.

Making a complicated concept simple to understand calls for skilled writing –

DOWN WITH SUPERWOMAN!

and testing. The people who design and write forms and instruction leaflets don't seem to *test* them on the end users.

The Fog Index actually exists: it's an American method of measuring the number of years of education you'd need to understand specific prose. For instance, the *Reader's Digest* requires about nine years of education, so the average 14-year-old should be able to understand it. The *Sun* newspaper scores six on the Fog Index, so 11-year-olds can understand it. *The Times* newspaper scored 12 to 15. Bureaucracy scores 20 to 25 for an *average* piece of literature, so no wonder most forms are difficult to fill in and most instructions can't be followed unless you already know how the machine works.

The unimaginative fools who are responsible for incomprehensible forms and instruction leaflets should commission professional writers and designers to produce them for a tested Fog Index rating of no more than ten years.

How to fill in a form

Many forms are ill written and unnecessarily complex. A wrongly filled in form can result in confusion and complaints from both sides.

First, make sure that you have been given the *right* form. Glance through it to see if you need any additional little forms as well, then . . .

1 Photocopy the form.
2 Take the form home, sit down and read carefully through the whole form – *slowly*.
3 Fill in the photocopy in peace and in pencil.
4 Root out all necessary documents – your old driving licence, birth certificate or whatever. Get photocopies if these are allowed. If originals are

needed, try to hand-deliver your bundle and get a receipt for it. If you don't live near enough, send the bundle by registered post and monitor its return (see 'Monitor a project', p. 285).

5 If this is a form you have to complete at regular intervals repeatedly, keep the completed photocopy. Then you have the basis of your next filling-in. Keep the copy with relevant papers – for instance, your driving licence application is kept with your car papers.
6 Answer the easy questions first – name, address, etc. If you get stuck, can't understand the questions or don't know what to write, don't hesitate to ring up the originator of the form and ask for help. They'll know what they want to read.
7 If any part of the form isn't big enough for you to fit in all you want to say, *don't* write smaller; write 'see attached sheet'. Answer the question on a separate piece of paper and staple it to the form (pins get unpinned).
8 If any question on the form doesn't apply to you, write 'not applicable' or NA in the blank space.
9 Fill in the form with a ballpoint pen, using capital letters, or type your entries.

How to decipher an instruction book

1 Read the *whole* leaflet or book, using a highlighter to emphasize the important bits.
2 On a separate piece of paper rewrite the instructions as simply as possible, underlining the important bits.
3 Reconsider and simplify what you have written.
4 Test your instructions on someone else and revise your instructions if necessary.
5 If a machine (such as the dishwasher)

has many complicated programmes and I use only one, I write instructions on a small Ryman's sticky label and stick it by the handle of the machine.

If many people are likely to use a machine (such as the washing machine), always stick your instructions label on it.

6 All original instructions and guarantees go in my home-users' manual, a book with plastic pockets that I keep in the kitchen (Ryman's display book, ref A4 93270).

HOW TO COMPLAIN AND WIN!

Regardless of guarantees, the Sale of Goods Act stipulates that if the goods purchased are not up to standard, not sound and suitable for use, not as described and not fit for the purpose for which they were sold, then the *original buyer* (not the recipient of a gift) can take the goods back to the *original shop* (not any branch) from which the goods were purchased and insist on a complete refund or exchange for a new product. *This applies whether or not you have signed a guarantee.*

This applies to *goods bought in a sale* unless the item was clearly marked 'damaged goods'.

This applies to goods bought by *mail order*.

You have no legal right to exchange something because you don't like it, although some stores (Marks & Spencer) offer this service.

If a shop offers you a **credit note**, you do not have to accept it. You can insist on a full cash refund. Stick out for this.

Every time you buy an article in a British shop, you enter into a contract with the **shopkeeper**, so you should complain to him first. A retailer is responsible for the goods he sells, so it is *his* job, not

yours, to take up the matter with the manufacturer or wholesaler from whom he obtained the goods. This is provided you return the faulty goods *quickly*. At the moment the law says you can lose the right to a refund *even before* any major fault has become apparent. However, you still have a legal claim to compensation, and this may equal or exceed the full purchase price.

If your retailer takes no notice of your complaint, write to the **manufacturer** of the faulty product and address your letter to the sales manager. If you don't get a satisfactory reply, go to your Citizens' Advice Bureau or local trading standards/consumer protection department.

You can also write to the **trade associations** to which the retailer and manufacturer belong. Don't just complain – ask the trade association to advise you what to do, so that, in politeness, they are obliged to reply to your question. In both cases enclose copies of relevant estimates, bills and previous correspondence.

How to query a bill

Check bills carefully. If you don't understand an account, write and politely ask to have it explained '*to my satisfaction*'.

If, for some good reason, you decide not to pay a bill, return the bill at once with a clear, written explanation of why you are not paying it and what action on the other party's part will induce you to pay up. Send all letters by recorded delivery. Keep copies of the bill and the letter.

Every organization has a 'mistake procedure': your problems are

1 Finding out what the mistake procedure is.
2 Convincing the organization that it has made a mistake.
3 Making it follow its own mistake procedure.

DOWN WITH SUPERWOMAN!

If, instead of replying to your letter the organization threatens to cut off a service – say, gas or electricity – don't panic. You now have *two* genuine grievances. Write again, asking to speak to your area manager or the supervisor of the customer accounts department.

You must now expect to negotiate with one department while another department prepares to sue you. When you get a final demand, reply with a polite letter quoting the references of the department with whom you are negotiating. Ask for an acknowledgement of your letter and see that you receive this.

The Gas Consumers Council and the Electricity Council give advice to the public and they also *collect* complaints from the public. Ask at the local showroom for the address of the regional office.

How to argue with a computer

Computers were supposed to cut down on paperwork but, in fact, they produce *more* paper and a huge increase in filing clerks and an even bigger increase in bureaucracy.

Firms that use computers seem to suffer from a lack of co-ordination between the departments that are involved with the computer. The resulting general incompetence, lack of interest in responsibility and breakdown in communication (especially at bookkeeping level) are why some computer keeps spewing out a bill to you for something you have either already paid for or not received or never ordered.

Should you find yourself arguing with a computer that takes no notice of your letters, don't blame the computer. Computers think in a very basic way and are only as intelligent as the people who programme them – and those aren't always Einstein-level logicians. Here's **how you argue with a computer:**

Send your letter by recorded delivery

and attach a copy of your receipt for this to any follow-up letter that you write.

If you owe any money, pay something on deposit, send a résumé of your case, writing on the right-hand side of the page with a note of your proof in the left-hand column.

Your letter should say that you would like a specific reply to the specific question you have asked. (This means that your letter cannot be answered by a standard computerized letter.) For instance, write 'Would you please let me know by what date I can receive a considered answer to this letter and whether there is anything you would like me to do in the meantime.'

Ask to have your case referred to the legal department of the firm concerned.

If (as is likely) the computer takes no notice of your letter, you can ignore the computer gibberish until its owner starts to sue you. At this point you post a copy of your recorded-delivery letter with the attached copy receipt. Send this second letter by recorded delivery and keep the receipt stapled to your copy.

You have now made two requests for a human being to intercede between you and the computer.

At this point their solicitor or legal department will probably be forced to deal with your problem and you are clearly on record as having tried your best to communicate with the computer owners about your problem.

Step-by-step complaint procedure

A travel agent once told me that the secret of successful complaining is having a reasonable complaint, knowing what you want, being brief and persistent and knowing your own nuisance value.

Don't complain without knowing what you want to get as a result of your complaint: an apology, a garrotting, a replacement or financial compensation. Ask for it outright, preferably in writing. Date the letter.

When complaining you should state your situation to the correct person (that is, someone who can do something about it). So:

* State your complaint.
* State the names of your witnesses.
* State your requirements.
* *Don't state anything else.*

If the new stereo doesn't work, don't tell the whole story ('I had my husband's family round on Thursday and a friend from Birmingham – he's staying for three weeks. He said after our evening meal, "Shall we play that Mozart quartet?" . . .')

Having marshalled your facts, check they are accurate, that you have dated everything and identified everyone, including your witnesses.

If you can't call in person (a personal call is generally best, provided you remain polite), then complain by telephone as early as possible in the morning, when they're all opening their mail and organizing themselves and haven't started on the business of the day's frustrations. Never complain after 3 p.m., when everyone, including yourself, is more likely to be at exploding point.

Make sure you identify the person to whom you are complaining. This can be difficult. Ruthlessly pursue identity and when the anonymous whine on the telephone says, after a long pause, 'Why do you want to know *my* name? I'm only on the staff', you reply smoothly: 'I like to know who I'm speaking to. Have you any reason for *not* giving your name?'

If you don't get a name, ring off, telephone again immediately, ask the switchboard operator for the name of the head of department, ask to speak to *him*, because Anonymous Whine is obviously going to do nothing about your grievance or else is quietly planning to leave at the end of the week.

Don't sound angry. Don't sound as if you are whining but as if you are inquiring. You are seeking the truth. Don't be intimidated.

Try not to put the other person in the wrong, because the more you put him in the wrong the more defensive he will become.

Be careful not to admit *any* error or *liability*, because you may then screw up your legal position.

When you reach crunch point, immediately thank the person to whom you were speaking.

Your letter of complaint Even if you telephone first, always put a complaint in writing, for the record.

Write a short, neat letter that doesn't sound aggressive, aggrieved or abusive. In the first paragraph say what your complaint is and what you would like to see done about it. If you want something – a repair, replacement or refund – *say so*, courteously. Give all the facts and be precise. (It's no good complaining vaguely about someone's unpleasant manner or unhelpful attitude.)

Be prepared to prove the truth of what you say and mention this. On no account exaggerate or tell the tiniest lie.

If you have to telephone *again*, it is easier if you have a written record.

When complaining to a large organization, I find that at this point it is best *not* to go straight to the man at the top (the Managing Director), but to his secretary. Her job is to prevent trouble landing on the boss's desk and she can put the fear of the Almighty into anyone else in the firm by mentioning this possibility.

If nothing happens, the following week send *another* recorded-delivery, dated letter giving the firm with whom you are dealing seven days to do what you require, or else (you say) you will take further steps. This is 'putting them under notice' and it's what a solicitor will do, so you may as well do it in an attempt to *avoid* going to a solicitor.

At this point you might also write to the readers' service of a national newspaper.

DOWN WITH SUPERWOMAN!

Many newspapers, TV and radio stations now have hot-line departments to which an aggrieved consumer can complain – often with striking results because of the damaging publicity to the guilty retailer or other company. The *Daily Mirror* and *Daily Mail* in particular carefully guard the interests of their readers.

Battling with bureaucrazy

Do you ever have the feeling that every time you brush with Bureaucratic Big Brother, *he* wins because *you* are not sure of your rights, so, uncertain and exhausted, you back down? Do you sometimes wonder if anyone, either at the organizational end of government or at the handing-out-the-money-to-the-public end, actually has a clear idea of *who* is responsible for *what*? Do you ever feel that the inefficiency, impossible forms, unreasonable delays, unhelpful clerks and bureaucratic letters of nationalized industries are calculated to reduce the customer to a docile punch on a card?

Of course, we have all felt this helpless frustration. But if, for instance, you want to use electricity, you have no alternative to your local electricity board.

With all bureaucrats the trick is to first find out how their system works and then ask, 'What is the best way for *your* system to handle *my* problem?'

Remember you are not speaking to a person; it is the voice of a machine. The second you start thinking of it as a person, you are lost. However human its voice may sound, think of it as one of those seaside I-speak-your-weight machines. You are dealing with an institution, a system, an organization, a routine – a machine; you can't reason with it or appeal to its emotions, because it has no mind or feelings. What you have to discover is how it works.

Always quote your reference numbers,

speak in a slow, clear voice and patiently insist that the clerk explains how to deal with your problem. Take notes of what he says and read them back to him to confirm that this is indeed his advice (even if he says 'I can't help you'). Jot down the name of the clerk (if you can get it out of him), the name of the department, the number of the telephone extension and *the time that you call or telephone*. The insistently anonymous clerk will know that he can be traced by this, which is why you check these details with him ('Now, let me see, it's 11.30 a.m. and you work for the Customer Accounts department on extension 453'). Then the next time you telephone, you are less likely to be shoved back to square one to start again with another anonymous clerk. If this *does* happen . . .

Head for your local Citizens' Advice Bureau (CAB). CAB can give advice (and sometimes legal support and help) in welfare areas such as housing and social security benefits for unemployment, sickness, invalids and widows, as well as child special allowances, retirement pensions and death grants.

If you need to consult a **solicitor** and don't know where to find one, your local CAB will be able to help you. A solicitor can tell you what his opinion is of your winning your case, and his services may be paid for under the **Legal Aid Scheme**.

However, for further arguments against going to court, see 'How to avoid a lawsuit', p.343.

If you decide to claim in a county court or to sue someone without using a solicitor, two useful, free leaflets can be obtained from you local library, local CAB or local county court. The free leaflets are: *Small Claims in the County Court: How to sue and defend actions without a solicitor* and *Suing on your own – making a small claim in the county court.*

Be aware that even if you *do* win your case, the court does not enforce its judgement. You will probably have to employ bailiffs to extract any money due to you.

How can you complain about your local authority services? **The environmental health department of your local government** is responsible for keeping the streets clean and emptying the dustbins. Shopping complaints are dealt with by **trading standards officers in local councils** (this network forms the policing system for a lot of consumer law).

Discover who is directly responsible for the service by contacting your **local authority office**. Write your complaint to the responsible person. If nothing happens, write to your **local councillor** (they really do care whether or not you voted for them, so always say if you did). If you are still left unsatisfied, write to your **local MP** (who also cares whether or not you voted for him). You might also send a copy of this letter to your **local newspaper**.

If you feel that a local council's decision is corrupt or unfair, then report it to the **local authority ombudsman**, who *can't* be pushed around by the local council and *can* make a judgement on an individual's case. To contact him, telephone the local council and ask the switchboard to connect you to the local authority ombudsman.

To complain about a **nationalized industry** – such as electricity, trains or post office – first complain at the *local office*, showroom, depot or station. Ask who is in charge, then ask to see him or write to him. If nothing happens, your local gas and electricity showrooms can provide the names and addresses of members of regional **gas consumer councils** and local **electricity consultative councils**. Check the telephone directory to find the local **Post Office Advisory Committee**. Ask at your local railway station for your **Transport Users' Consultative Committee**. You should get their advice *as soon as it is clear that you*

have a problem, rather than try to grapple with it yourself and waste time doing the wrong thing.

If you've tried to get your complaint dealt with by the appropriate organization and find that you're still getting nowhere *because the policy of the industry is unjust*, then contact **your local MP**. (Ask at your local library for the name, and address your letter to the MP at the House of Commons, Westminster, London SW1.)

Should you wish to complain about **the police**, contact the **Chief Constable of your local police force** (ask your local library for the address). If you live in the London Metropolitan Police District, you should complain directly to the **Home Office**.

Should you get no satisfaction from doing this, then complain to the local ombudsman. In order to reach him, contact **your local councillor** (get his name and address from the local library or the town hall) and ask him to refer your case to **your local authority ombudsman**, whose correct title is the Commissioner for Local Administration.

The ombudsman's job is also to investigate complaints from people who think that **their local council** has not acted properly because of an administration problem, incompetence or needless delay.

If your local councillor refuses your request, *then* you can contact the ombudsman yourself.

The equivalent of the **ombudsman in Northern Ireland** is the Commissioner for Complaints, who has a direct responsibility *to investigate and to solve problems*. His responsibilities are greater than the government ombudsman and extend to local government, the Health Service, gas and electricity supplies.

Problems with **banking and building societies** are also dealt with by an ombudsman.

The **government** has certain obligations to its citizens and is responsible for enforcing the law of the land through the **Director of Public Prosecutions**. (For example, under the Department of Trade and Industry, the Office of Fair Trading can investigate a breach in consumer credit law.)

To complain of maladministration in government departments and ministries (but not the Cabinet), you need to contact the **Parliamentary Commissioner for Administration**.

If you want an old law changed or a new one brought in, contact the **National Council for Civil Liberties**.

Some useful addresses

Advisory Centre for Education
18 Victoria Park Square
London E2 9PB
Tel: 081-980-4597

Age Concern
Bernard Sunley House
60 Pitcairn Road
Mitcham, Surrey CR4 3LL
Tel: 081-640-5431

Central Transport Consultative Committee
Golden Cross House
Duncannon Street
London WC2N 4JF
Tel: 071-839-7338

Child Poverty Action Group
1–5 Bath Street
London EC1V 9PY
Tel: 071-253-3406

Claimants and Unemployed Workers Union
120 Standhill Crescent
Barnsley, Yorkshire S71 1SP
Tel: 0226-287776

Commissioner for Complaints
Progressive House
33 Wellington Place
Belfast BT1 6HN
Tel: 0232-233821

Commission for Local Administration
(local ombudsmen)
21 Queen Anne's Gate

London SW1H 9BU
Tel: 071-222-5622

Commission for Local Administration in Scotland
Princes House
5 Shandwick Place
Edinburgh EH2 4RG
Tel: 031-229-4472

Commission for Local Administration in Wales
Derwen House
Court Road
Bridgend
Mid-Glamorgan CF31 9BN
Tel: 0656-61325

Consumers' Association
2 Marylebone Road
London NW1 4DX
Tel: 071-486-5544

Department of Education and Science
Elizabeth House
39 York Road
London SE1 7PH
Tel: 071-934-9000

Department of the Environment
2 Marsham Street
London SW1P 3EB
Tel: 071-276-3000

Department of Health
Alexander Fleming House
Elephant and Castle
London SE1 6BY
Tel: 071-407-5522

Department of Social Security
Richmond House
79 Whitehall
London SW1A 2NS
Tel: 071-210-3000

Gas Consumers' Council
Abford House
15 Wilton Road
London SW1V 1LT
Tel: 071-931-0977

Home Office
50 Queen Anne's Gate
London SW1H 9AT
Tel: 071-273-3000

Institute of Chartered Accountants in England and Wales

P.O. Box 433
Chartered Accountants' Hall
Moorgate Place
London EC2P 2BJ
Tel: 071-628-7060

Institute of Chartered Accountants of Scotland
27 Queen Street
Edinburgh EH2 1LA
Tel: 031-225-5676

Law Society
113 Chancery Lane
London WC2A 1PL
Tel: 071-242-1222

* *Legal Action Group* (research body –
doesn't deal with complaints)
242 Pentonville Road
London N1 9UN
Tel: 071-833-2931

National Citizens' Advice Bureaux
Middleton House
115–123 Pentonville Road
London N1 9LZ
Tel: 071-833-2181

National Consumer Council (research body –
doesn't deal with complaints)
20 Grosvenor Gardens
London SW1H 0DH
Tel: 071-730-3469

National Council for Civil Liberties
21 Tabard Street
London SE1 4LA
Tel: 071-403-3888

* *Parliamentary Commissioner for
Administration* and *Health Service
Commissioner*
Church House
Great Smith Street
London SW1P 3BW
Tel: 071-276-3000 (parliamentary offices);
071-276-2035 (Health Service inquiries)

Pearl Assurance House
Grey Friars Road
Cardiff CR1 3AG
Tel: 0222-394-621

11 Melville Crescent
Edinburgh EH3 7LU
Tel: 031-225-7465

* *Patients' Association*
18 Victoria Park Square
London E2 9PF
Tel: 081-981-5676

* *Post Office Users' Councils*
Caradog House
St Andrew's Place
Cardiff SF1 3BE
Tel: 0222-374-028

Chamber of Commerce House
22 Great Victoria Street
Belfast BT2 7PU
Tel: 0232-244-113

* *Post Office Users' National Council*
Waterloo Bridge House
Waterloo Road
London SE1 8UA
Tel: 071-928-9458

Royal Institute of British Architects
66 Portland Place
London W1N 4AD
Tel: 071-580-5533

* *Scottish Office*
43 Jeffery Street
Edinburgh EH1 1DN
Tel: 031-244-5576

* *Shelter*
88 Old Street
London EC1 9HU
Tel: 071-253-0202

THE PROFESSIONALS

**Where it's still a man's world and
you're at their mercy, how do you
communicate?**

The plumber, the electrician, the painter and similar workmen who visit your
home can be unreasonably uncooperative
and difficult to communicate with because you don't realize that they have a
problem – and the problem is you.

When you hire a man to do a job, *you*
see that as a straightforward exchange of
money for work, but many men don't see

* When writing to any of these addresses, please enclose a stamped, addressed envelope. Do not try to
telephone them. Your case is better put in writing. Keep a copy of your letter.

DOWN WITH SUPERWOMAN!

it that way. They see it as you having money – the power – to hire them and criticize any shoddy work. You Tarzan, him Jane, is how they see it and they deal with it by what the army calls 'dumb insolence' – nothing you can put your finger on and complain about.

If you've ever had **workmen** trample mud through your home in a way that their wives or mothers wouldn't put up with, then look astonished when you complain about it, you are the victim of dumb insolence and it is sexist behaviour based on the fact that a man doesn't like a woman having power over him – as he sees it.

What you can do about it is NEVER CLEAN UP AFTER THEM, *NEVER BE UNDERSTANDING.* Stop the work. Call the foreman. Call the boss. Ask if this is the company's standard behaviour and get his confirmation in writing that it won't happen again, before you let his workmen back into your home. Make a fuss about it, show you're a force to be reckoned with and they will not try it a second time.

This is a tiresome waste of your time, but the alternative is to have a lot *more* of your time wasted, much aggravation and possibly extra cost.

Never allow any workman in your home unsupervised. If you're having your home redecorated, have an on-site foreman *at all times* written into the letter of agreement or contract. It will cost you extra money, but it will save you even more, especially if you're told this is unnecessary extravagance.

Women are generally at the mercy of a **garage mechanic** who is contemptuous of their ignorance of machines – and who often shows his contempt, not only on his face, but on his bill. Always ask for a quotation for repair work and try to check it with the AA, the RAC or a friend who *does* understand mechanics.

Ask specific questions and write down the answers. 'What is wrong with the

car? How much will the replacement part cost? How much will any other material cost? How much will labour cost? How long should the job take? When can you do it? When will my car be ready?'

Try to use a garage that's part of a big chain, because then you'll have some come-back, although I believe that there's a universal male conspiracy to swindle women with car repairs.

Don't get friendly, because then it's even more difficult to query their bills.

Be brisk. Expect respect and you're likely to get respect; if you don't, complain to the management.

Remember that nine out of ten men don't know what's wrong with their car when they take it to be repaired.

When dealing with **people who expect a tip** – such as a waiter, hairdresser or taxi driver – don't tip unless there is a reason for you to tip. In a restaurant always ask if service is included in the bill and, if so, don't tip. If a taxi driver is disagreeable and doesn't help with your baggage, don't tip. If the hairdresser turns you out looking like Ken Dodd, don't tip. You will keep not only your money, but also your self-respect. Remember that these people are *taught* how to make you tip by projecting silent disapproval or blank-faced contempt and thus pressing your guilt button. If someone makes you feel bad, there is even *less* reason to tip him.

Deal with the cast of thousands at the hairdresser by calculating 10 per cent of a big bill or 15 per cent of a small one and handing it over in cash at the desk saying, 'This is for the staff.'

Remember that tipping is degrading and should be wiped out. Waiters, taxi drivers and hairdressers should get properly paid by the people who employ them.

Don't let experts overawe you. What they are *all* expert at is projecting expertise (and disapproval should you query it). Many doctors, accountants and lawyers are experts in Advanced Fog Index Behaviour, otherwise known as professional mystique. This can confuse, complicate and conceal. (The army word 'bull' means throwing a thick smoke-screen around a situation to make things appear as they are not, or more complicated than they are, or to hide mistakes.) Pomposity can also be a smoke-screen for incompetence.

Apart from doctor and dentist, you may not think you need any other professionals. But if you want to buy a home, you may suddenly have to deal with bank manager, accountant, estate agent, insurance agent, lawyer, architect and surveyor. Suddenly you are at the mercy of The Professionals.

Members of a profession belong to a group that protects their interest, just as a trade union does. In order to belong, their members have to pass certain exams – indicated by the letters after their names – which prove they have been properly trained but *not* that they are infallible or even careful.

Just as there are good and bad secretaries, footballers and gynaecologists, there are good and bad architects, lawyers and accountants. Don't expect all professionals to be professional – that is, disciplined, efficient and competent – rather than lazy, muddled, careless and prevaricating to hide this situation.

Some professionals *want* to bewilder you in order to make their job seem more difficult and complicated, because then they can charge you more for it. I have been quoted £30, £200 and £500 by different accountants for the same small job. The £30 quote was the correct one. Over the years I have seen many people lied to, overcharged, cheated by top-rated, top-charging qualified professionals. I have more than once seen chaos caused by professional incompetence and the resultant business and personal problems.

Another trick of The Professionals is to invoke paternalism ('Come to Daddy with your problems and Daddy will solve them'). Their female clients (who like to feel looked after by Daddy) then pay their enormous bills without daring to question Daddy's authority to send them.

Remember that you can't delegate ultimate responsibility for your life to some professional.

If something puzzles you about your professional, if things don't add up . . . remember the small boy who was the only person who spotted that the Emperor was wearing no clothes. Trust your instinct. Don't try to make your mind perform backward somersaults attempting to believe the lies that you may be told. Check your information and get an unbiased second opinion (in writing) from a second expert. Telephone the regulatory body, tell them you want a second opinion and they will give you a list of suitable people in your area.

If you feel anxious at the mere *idea* of querying your professional's authority, if you tremble at the knees at the thought of your professional's disapproval, turn to 'Do you know any doormats?', p. 391.

If you are consulting a professional for the first time, before the meeting, to help clarify your thoughts, write down what you want to ask your professional and what you have to explain about your circumstances.

Take a notebook to the meeting and write down the advice you get, either at the time or immediately afterwards in his waiting room. Ask to have any advice confirmed in writing.

At the meeting act calmly and sensibly. Keep business and friendship apart, otherwise it may be embarrassing when you query his work or his bill – it sounds like querying a friend's honesty. Never use sex (flirting) hoping that you'll get professional advice free. This is an expensive way of paying a bill – and you will get the bill anyway.

DOWN WITH SUPERWOMAN!

Check the billing method *before* you start talking about your project. Discuss money early on in your relationship: ask him what he's going to cost and when you can expect the bill. Always remember who's paying the bills – you, so you have a right to ask for what you want, a right to have it clearly explained, a right to know how your bill will be calculated.

When dealing with professionals, instruct them in writing (or write to confirm your verbal instructions). Always get an approximate date for the next step of the project to be completed. Never stop checking on your professional. You are only one of maybe sixty clients that he has to think about in that limited head space of his.

Remember that you are more interested in your life than any professional can possibly be. *You* are more strongly motivated to see the work finished than he is, so *you* must constantly monitor the project until it is completed.

A word of warning If you consult someone, never give them any power over you, such as your cash, access to your bank account, care of your vital paperwork (deeds, for instance) or belongings. Never let any of your documentation out of your possession. (What would you do if you never got it back? Certainly, you might be able to prove that X had it, but you still might not be able to get him to hand over, say, the deeds of your home.)

Dentist

You may think you have a personal NHS dentist, as you do a doctor, but really the dentist only contracts to give you *one* course of treatment.

Even in an emergency dentists can refuse a patient for NHS treatment and they can do as much private work as they like.

Dentists who have specialist post-graduate training are oral surgeons and orthodontists, who correct wrongly placed teeth.

Before treatment, make sure you know how much of the bill will be paid for by the NHS and how much by you. Before the dentist does anything, you should be given a form to sign for all treatment on the NHS. A dentist can charge his patient for failing to keep an appointment or cancellation at unreasonably short notice.

Doctor

Feel comfortable with your doctor. Because of the bodily functions a woman experiences and a man doesn't (babies, PMT, period pains, menopause), you may feel that a woman doctor may be more effective for you than a man because a man simply won't comprehend what his patient is feeling.

How your doctor should behave He shouldn't be patronizing to his patients. There's nothing more frustrating and depressing than being treated like a small child. The doctor should be patient. A patient never comes to a doctor for nothing, but if her problem is not clearly visible (such as a broken leg), it will take longer to elucidate. A good medical history takes longer than a clinical examination.

How the patient should behave A doctor told me not to expect perfection, any more than speed, of the NHS. There is no great untapped source of funds and treatment waiting for you. Public health care is limited to what is available: don't waste it. Don't waste the doctor's time: always be on time for an appointment, don't ask him to make house calls if you can walk, and don't go out having asked him to call.

Don't rely on your NHS doctor to winkle out what's worrying you or remember everything about you. You are one of a possible 3,500 patients, your

336

entitlement of his time is about ten minutes a year and he is only human. You are far more likely than he is to remember your previous ailments and treatments.

Take responsibility for yourself and remind your doctor if some annual check-up is due.

Tell the doctor of any allergies and what medication you are taking (such as the Pill).

Don't conceal information. Tell your doctor what's wrong with other people in your family; what you have may be inherited. Tell your doctor about any major illness you had before *he* was treating you.

If you are given a prescription, take the complete course even if you feel better immediately. Tell your doctor if you don't follow his instructions to the letter.

Make sure you understand what's wrong with you and ask what can be done about it. If you receive soothing, reassuring palliatives with NO FACTS, beware. Get a second opinion. Don't be too timid to ask for this. If a doctor is ill, he will have a third, fourth or fifth opinion before you can say 'ninety-nine'. This is because *he* knows that doctors, specialists and surgeons can form a wrong opinion. There's a difference between a wrong opinion (which is understandable) and a mistake (wrong leg amputated).

Remember that if a medical man forms the wrong opinion, he hates admitting his mistake – we all do. Accept that medical men, like the rest of The Professionals, cover up for each other.

It's especially difficult to insist on a further opinion if you feel too ill to care, but whoever is closest to you should firmly step in and 'interfere' if it seems necessary.

Travel agent

It's not easy to be a travel agent; they work on very small margins in a field where encyclopaedic knowledge is expected.

There are plenty of reputable travel agents and tour operators; personal recommendation is the best way to find them.

Check on your travel agent's stationery to ensure that he belongs to ABTA – The Association of British Travel Agents (and Tour Operators). This powerful organization can give you advice if you need to make a complaint and, as a last resort, their conciliation department can help you if you cannot reach an agreement with your tour operator or travel agent. But they can act only if you book through one of their members.

Also **check** that your tour operator holds an ATOL (Air Travel Organizer's Licence), which also confirms his financial standing and fitness to operate. All licensed operators must quote their ATOL number in advertisements and brochures. Avoid any travel agent or tour operator who is not a member of ABTA or who has not got an ATOL, because there's probably a good reason for this lack. Having paid your cash for a package, you may find yourself with a worthless ticket or booked into a very poor hotel.

An incompetent or lazy travel agent will try to earn the maximum money for the minimum effort. He won't offer you price alternatives, but possibly the most expensive and roundabout way of getting where you want to go so that he gets the biggest commission.

Ask your travel agent the fare to your destination, then ask if it is the lowest fare he can offer. Telephone another travel agent and check the fares he can offer. In my experience you can save a lot of money with a few phone calls.

In any case, always check if you qualify for the APEX (Advance Purchase Excursion) fare, available on scheduled airlines if you book at least two weeks before you travel.

DOWN WITH SUPERWOMAN!

There are some good 'bucket shops' – a derogatory description of travel agents who sell cut-price tickets, usually with no frills and some restrictions. The main airlines are among their principal supporters, so you can often get a fare on a major airline at a dramatically reduced price from the official fare.

If you're shopping for a package holiday, similarly shop around. Check the small print: 'from £40' means that £40 is the *starting point* – check for extras and surcharges. Check the available discount packages.

Insurance agent

Insurance often puts women in a tizzy of anxiety that is not necessary. All you need do is to check that you are insured by a reliable firm that doesn't overcharge you and that does pay up when its supposed to . . .

How do you choose this reliable firm? By a recommendation from someone who has dealt with the firm for the same sort of insurance for at least five years. I like my agent to be a member of the British Insurance and Investment Brokers Association.

Your insurance agent is a retailer. He deals with many different specialist insurance 'wholesalers' and if you have a claim, he will argue with them on your behalf.

Comparative-shop for insurance by getting quotes in percentages, not money. If one reputable company offers you 2 per cent and another reputable company offers you 4 per cent on the same terms, take the lower offer. It means that your insurance will cost annually 2 per cent of the total amount insured; so if a ring is valued at £100 and is insured for 2 per cent, the insurance will be £2 a year.

Obviously car insurance is more complicated. For instance, restriction of driver and voluntary excess (the amount you contribute to a claim yourself) pro-

visos can make a lot of difference. So make sure you compare like with like.

If you've ever made an insurance claim, you may have felt that the retailer with whom you dealt was putting off settling for as long as possible, using any rubbishy arguments to do so, either because he was trying to beat down the amount for which you would agree to settle (from exhaustion and boredom) or because all the months that he wasn't paying your claim he was getting bank interest on *your* money that he hadn't yet paid to you.

This is not necessarily so. In fact, the man who works for the insurance company has no personal stake in the payment of claims and it's in his interest to get you out of his in-tray as fast as possible.

But it takes a couple of weeks for your insurer to answer your letter requesting a claim form. It then takes a couple of weeks for your insurer to write and tell you that you've filled in the claim form wrongly and haven't included a copy of the valuation. It may *then* take a couple of weeks for the wholesale insurer to decide that they are not liable, because some other party is . . .

A simple claim should be paid relatively quickly with no problems. A complicated claim, or where immediate and full liability is in dispute, is neither simply nor quickly dealt with.

When a claim is made, the relevant company or Lloyds underwriters (the wholesalers) don't consider, 'Are we liable?' but 'Who is primarily responsible?' An unbiased outside assessor (called an adjuster) may be appointed to decide this.

As an example, a hotel once lost a suitcase insured by me that I had left there in store. Was I responsible for the loss or was the hotel? Had I had a receipt, the hotel would have been responsible, but unfortunately I forgot to get one. The underwriters argued with the hotel's underwriters. Eventually, my insurance brokers (Sutton Meears of Croydon) paid me six months after the initial claim, which seems reasonable to me.

(See also 'Beating burglars', p. 199, and 'Asset register', p. 285)

Estate agent

If you are selling, never give an estate agent an exclusive right to sell your property, because *this is then his legal right*. It's logical that he should then make much more effort to sell your property, but supposing he doesn't (and in my experience, they *don't*) – *you can't then go to another agent*.

Always get an estate agent's charges in writing. They will always try to get the highest percentage from you. Again, comparative-shop. Having been quoted a lower rate from a second agent, tell the first agent. (*Don't mention the name of one agent to another*.) The first agent may beat the second agent's offer. Then go back to the second agent and ask if he would like to reconsider his quote. Don't bluff; you don't need to. When you stop this lark is when neither will reduce their quote.

If you're buying, know exactly what you want and put this in writing. Assume that the agent won't pay much attention. To be fair, this is because a client often changes his mind when he sees a house that doesn't answer to his original specification.

Never visit a property without the agent, even if the owner is living in it and is prepared to show you around. This will stop the agent wasting *his* time by showing you unsuitable properties.

Always insist on seeing beforehand a photograph of every property the agent wants you to visit.

Don't assume that the property has anything – not even a lavatory – that isn't on the printed description.

Bank manager

Bank managers aren't pessimists, they are realists. If your bank manager ever disapproves of your plans, listen carefully. He has a lot more experience than you.

Architect

There are three problem areas if you are employing an architect.

1 The money you are prepared to spend.
2 Whether the architect produces a scheme that meets the specification you gave him. (You don't want Bauhaus if you're expecting neo-Georgian.)
3 Whether the architect correctly supervises the job. *Never hire an inexperienced architect*

If you are having any conversion work done, you probably **will** need an architect. If you choose the right one, he will probably save your money and pay his own fees via the supplier's discounts that he obtains.

Always ask for proof that your architect is a qualified architect. If not, *on no account* use him, because you have no professional protection. Ask to see proof of his professional indemnity insurance and his ARCUK registration card (Architects Registration Council of the UK, 73 Hallam Street, London W1N 6EE, tel: 071-580 5861).

The Royal Institute of British Architects (RIBA) offer a free advisory service to help you choose an architect.

The architect's charge is a percentage of the work, on a sliding scale. (The percentage is high for a small job, but lower for more expensive ones.) The scale of fees is laid down in the RIBA pamphlet *Conditions of Engagement* (free from RIBA Publications, 66 Portland Place, London W1N 4AD, tel: 071-580-5533).

Always obtain from your architect

written confirmation of what you are paying for.

In addition, ask the architect to confirm to you in writing that no other expenditure will be incurred unless specifically signed and dated for in advance by his client – the person who is actually signing the cheques.

If you employ an architect to produce a scheme and then decide not to go ahead with it, you will still have to pay the architect. If you alter your specification in any way after he has produced the scheme, you may have to pay him *twice*. Or *three* times, if you alter your specification again.

If there has been negligence or a major design failure, you should report it to the RIBA's Conduct Committee, but the most they can do is expel the member responsible, which may not get your roof back on. You have to sue the architect if you want to try to get compensation.

In order to preserve your legal position (and your sanity) get a 22 × 15 cm (8⅔ × 6 in) office diary and note down every stage of the work – especially if you are let down.

Speaking from experience, I would always have a lawyer check any contract with the architect (to make sure that the architect's specification contains everything on my specification to him and that nothing is left out that I later have to pay for as an extra) and with the builder, and I would hire a quantity surveyor (whom you pay by the hour) right from the start to check both the architect and the builder.

Accountants

If you are a freelancer or have a small business, you may need an accountant. If so, check that he has the correct professional qualifications because *anyone* can call himself an accountant – *I* could call myself an accountant. As with lawyers' clerks, it's amazing how many accountants' clerks manage to give you the impression they are fully qualified accountants. There are three Institutes of Chartered Accountants (England and Wales, Scotland, and Ireland) and the Association of Certified Accountants. Members are fully qualified and subject to the discipline of the Institutes and the Association.

Don't economize by going to a back-street accountant; they can be as dangerous to your business as a back-street abortionist can be to your health. You wouldn't feel happy if an unqualified brain surgeon were about to operate on you. It is a false economy to use a person for a job that he isn't qualified to do, because that means that *he isn't good enough to do it*.

There are good accountants, who think accounting is simple and can explain it as such. I once arranged an accountancy lecture for my younger son as his birthday present. When the accountant, Brian Stapleton, turned up, he was astonished to find that about a dozen of my son's friends had asked to be present – and listened attentively to every word.

There are bad accountants, who make you think that accounting is difficult, so that they can send you big bills and you can't spot their incompetence. If you feel that accounts are difficult to grasp, you may well have a bad accountant.

My management consultant said, 'My worst clients are accountants: their offices are always the most disorganized and untidy.' I would never leave my papers with an accountant after seeing how some of them work. Always instruct, supervise and check on your accountant. It is your own responsibility to keep your affairs in order and you are legally responsible for making your own tax returns.

Choose an accountant in the right area – dealing with people in your income bracket and your type of business. Give him a carefully written briefing. Get it checked by a lawyer. A careless account-ant can get you into deep trouble and a careless letter of appointment can absolve him of *any* responsibility. If you use an accountant, try to use one who belongs to a sizeable firm; you will then have *back-up*, *supervision* and *answerability* (some competent senior partner should be always looking over everyone's shoul-der). Because of this, a sizeable firm will charge more than a one-man business.

If possible, get the accountant to do your accounts *at your place*; then you'll know how long it takes and be able to check his charges. Never let them take your papers away or you risk losing them.

Get a correct briefing from your ac-countant on what he expects you to do – keep receipts, stamp books, cheque-stubs or whatever.

A first-class accountant invoices for clerical work at *six times more* than a secretary's hourly wage. So save the bill by doing the easy, sort-out work your-self.

Most accountants are not trained or qualified to advise you on investment. Their job is to keep your figures tidy and advise you on your tax situation. Don't make the mistake of looking upon your accountant as a financial consultant unless the firm has been authorized by the Financial Services Act specifically to conduct investment business and you have checked his professional indemnity insurance. (In addition, the Institute of Chartered Accountants in England and Wales can compensate each client of its members up to £50,000.)

The Institute of Chartered Account-ants says that if a client reports two or three instances of delay, unanswered let-ters or other unprofessional behaviour, the Institute will investigate and can take disciplinary action ranging from a repri-mand or a fine up to expulsion of the accountant from the Institute. Write for their excellent guidance to the Institute of Chartered Accountants in England

and Wales, P.O. Box 433, Chartered Ac-countants Hall, Moorgate Place, London EC2P 2BJ, tel: 071-628-7060.

Lawyer

Death, wills, divorce, buying a home, being swindled One day you may need a lawyer. All lawyers are ex-pensive, but some are more expensive than others. What's *really* expensive is an incompetent lawyer who is in business on his own.

Pick only a qualified professional and check his or her qualifications with the Law Society. As with accountants' clerks, it's amazing how many lawyers' clerks manage to give you the impression that they are qualified lawyers.

You probably don't want a histrionic, pugnacious lawyer – aggression invites counter-aggression and suddenly two heavy-weight lawyers may be in there slug-ging out their little private boxing match, for which you are paying. A lawyer who sounds reasonable and persuasive may be more likely to reach a settlement.

Aggression amongst lawyers is a game played for the benefit of the client – to make the client feel that his champion is fighting for him. Opponent lawyers know this and take no notice of it. They'll all be playing golf together next week.

Choose a specialist lawyer *each time you want to employ one*. A 'family lawyer' is a Jack-of-all-trades and possibly not master of the expertise you require. You don't want an 'all-rounder', you want an expert, because the other side will have an expert.

When you get your expert lawyer, check his expertise. Ask what experience he has had, what similar *specific* cases he has *won*. Check that only *this* person will be handling your case.

Here's an example of what I mean. Keith Blackburn went into hospital with suspected pleurisy and came out with massive brain damage. The *Sunday*

DOWN WITH SUPERWOMAN!

Times reported that at 45, he had a mental age of 3, was incontinent, needed twenty-four-hour nursing and was confined to a wheelchair. As Keith's wife was dead, his children had to be placed in care. It took twelve years for Keith's father to get his case to court. Three firms of solicitors said that there was no evidence of negligence or that the case would be too difficult to prove. Then Keith's father found a firm of solicitors who *specialized* in the complex field of medical negligence. According to the *Sunday Times*, the health authority was forced to disclose all existing case records and X-rays and – two years later – the health authority was found liable and Keith was awarded heavy damages.

Keith's case might have taken three years, instead of twelve, had Keith's father originally gone to a specialist lawyer. How could he have found one?

Action for Victims of Medical Accidents (Bank Chambers, 1 London Road, Forest Hill, London SE23 3TP, tel: 081-291-2793) is an advice charity run by lawyers and helps claimants to find lawyers specializing in medical negligence.

It's a pity that the Law Society doesn't organize a register of lawyers that the Society can recommend to the public as specialists, like those that already exist in a few areas, such as child-care, mental health and insolvency.

Before you visit your specialist lawyer's office, clarify your thoughts (remember to write things down) and tell him what you want, in note form. At the first meeting ask him what will be involved in his work and how he calculates his charges. A lawyer isn't interested in seeing justice done; he is a hired gun and his interest is winning his client's case, and you need the best gun you can afford. What your lawyer needs is ammunition in the form of provable evidence. A black eye is not provable evidence. Evidence is somebody who *saw* you being given the black eye. Listen to

a lawyer's advice, evaluate it and then *instruct* him – tell him what you want him to do. *After your visit*, brief your lawyer in writing (dated) and, of course, keep a copy. Think carefully before you leave your documents with a lawyer: if you want to dispense with his services, he may suddenly produce a huge bill and refuse to give back your papers (which may include such documents as the deeds to your home) until you pay it.

When the job is finished, write straight away to thank your lawyer and ask him to send his bill immediately.

A good lawyer presents your case as advantageously as is possible and, you hope, spots the weaknesses in the other side's case. Having established his cards, your lawyer plays his hand and either a settlement is reached or you go to court. (Often a settlement is reached only at the door of the court, because this gets the lawyers to concentrate on pulling their case together.) The good lawyer then sends you a big bill.

A bad lawyer is one who forgets the facts of your case, plays his hand badly, irritates the judge and then sends you a big bill.

How can a lawyer let you down? He can overcharge you. He can fail to take any real interest in your case; he can forget the details of your case. He can be unavailable to you even by telephone. If you decide to take your case away from him, he may send you a big bill and hang on to your papers until you pay it. What can you do?

You can ask the High Court or County Court to examine a solicitor's bill for overcharging. However, you may need *another* solicitor to advise you about this, as it can be an expensive and complicated procedure. You should first complain personally and in writing directly to your solicitor and say that you are going to report him to the Solicitors Complaints Bureau, Portland House, Stag Place, London SW1E 5BW.

The Law Society certainly acts. It seems as if almost every day *The Times* reports that some lawyer has been struck off the Law Society's Register for unprofessional or dishonest behaviour.

However, the Law Society cannot insist that a solicitor pays compensation to a client, nor offer any sort of legal advice to that client. The independent Disciplinary Tribunal is concerned with whether the solicitor should be allowed to carry on practising. The Law Society can require a solicitor to reduce his bill if his work has been very badly done.

The Government has set up a body – the Lay Observer – to examine how the Law Society handles complaints, so if the Law Society does not deal with your problem to your satisfaction, write to the Lay Observer, Royal Courts of Justice, Strand, London WC2A 2LL.

How to avoid a lawsuit

Don't go to court if you can avoid it was the advice Judge Maude gave upon his retirement. What he *doubtless* meant was that being in the right doesn't mean that you will win. Additionally, litigation can be risky and ruinously expensive, even if you have a simple, watertight case.

So remember that in litigation the person in the *wrong* always has the advantage, because he doesn't have to take the initial action and the winner of a lawsuit may nevertheless lose in terms of money, time and stress. Of course it's unfair. Bad luck.

It is unreasonable to expect no bad luck in your life. If bad luck is dished out by God, you don't try to sue God. If a small bit of bad luck comes your way – say, you step on a mess in the street, you wipe it off your shoe and forget it – try to treat bad luck caused by nasty humans in the same way.

The disaster scale On a disaster scale of 1 to 10, decide the size of your mess, minimize the damage and get on with your life.

1 Minor exasperation (broken fingernail, zip, tyre).
2 Medium exasperation (dry-cleaning ruins favourite dress, machine breaks down).
3 Major exasperation (a legal problem).
4 Relationship problems (quarrels).
5 Burglary, eviction, flood.
6 Serious financial loss, being made redundant.
7 Serious debt, blackmail.
8 Prison, divorce.
9 Serious illness or accident, or addiction.
10 Death.

So if you're thinking of suing someone, ask yourself:

1 **Do I know I will win?** No lawyer can tell you that you are going to win. He will tell you that you *ought* to win. But life is unfair. A court is not infallible. Both judge and jury may be prejudiced or show bad judgement. Every lawyer knows that it is impossible to guarantee justice.
2 **Can I afford to lose** in terms of money and humiliation?
3 **Will my wrong be righted if I win?** Will going to court undo the damage? (Going to law will get you money only – it won't get you a new leg, for instance.)
4 **How much will it cost to sue?**
5 **Do I know that I will get all the legal costs back, even if I am awarded costs?** (No.)
6 **If I win and I am awarded damages, am I sure of collecting that money from the other side?** Has the other side got that money? Can the other side pretend it hasn't?
7 **Will a lawsuit cost me time?** How many weeks, months or years?
8 **Am I prepared to spend perhaps a year preparing my case?**
9 **Will a lawsuit cost me aggravation?**
10 **Will a lawsuit cost me anxiety?**

DOWN WITH SUPERWOMAN!

11 **Is there any alternative to taking legal action?** Nobody ever really forces a person to sue. When they suffer injustice, people often behave stupidly, through righteous anger. For instance, if you are sold something that doesn't work, it may be cheaper to pay to have it fixed fast rather than incur legal costs and aggravation in order to get your rights.

12 **Can I continue to exist without going to court?** Only sue someone if you can't afford *not* to do so and you *can* afford to lose your case. Otherwise swallow your pride, pocket your losses and don't lose *more* by going to law.

Unless you answer yes to 1, 2, 3, 5, 6, 8, no to 7, 9, 10, 11, 12 and nothing to 4, think seriously about swallowing your pride and ignoring it.

A lawsuit is always a *gamble*. Look upon a potential lawsuit as a molehill-sized disaster that could grow into a mountain! Better to wipe it off your shoes, out of your mind and get on with your life.

Forget revenge. As I said elsewhere, you are not a Sicilian peasant. And the Lord said 'Vengeance is mine', meaning leave it to Him.

Whenever I hear myself saying, 'I'm doing it for the principle of the thing', I know that I am being ruled by my feelings. Better to hit a punch bag, stick pins in a wax image and then forget it/him/her and get on with your life. Long term, your actions will speak for you.

How to pay the professionals

Phrases like 'Don't worry about the bill' don't mean that you won't get a bill; *you will*, no matter how long your eyelashes or pathetic your situation.

Before you buy tomatoes, you check the price. Don't hesitate to do this before you hire a professional, because they are

far more expensive than tomatoes. So don't let your fear of the disapproval of an authority figure put you off ascertaining his price. You wouldn't wake up in the night in a cold sweat of anxiety about the cost of tomatoes. You wouldn't rehearse in your bath what you were going to say to the greengrocer about those bad tomatoes.

It is easy to calculate the price of a professional who charges on a percentage basis or who, like a surgeon, works for a flat fee payable in advance.

The problems lie with professionals like lawyers, who often can't tell you in advance what your total bill will be, because neither you nor they know what the work will entail.

In America a lawyer bills at his pre-agreed rate: 'To fourteen-minute telephone call on 9 May . . . \$ . . .' In Britain some professionals (especially lawyers) bill you only once every six months with one smoke-screen sentence that goes on for a complete page and is unspecific. Because it's unspecific you can't check it. This is the whole point as far as the bill-sender is concerned.

So you should always briskly ask a professional the following question: 'What are your firm's billing-out rates?' If he says, 'What do you mean?', you say 'The hourly rate at which you charge for the services of different staff.'

What he *should* say is, 'Senior partners are billed at £w per hour, junior partners at £x per hour, clerical staff at £y per hour and junior clerical staff at £z per hour.'

Getting the answer to the hourly billing rate *in advance* and *in writing* is the only way you're going to be able to control your costs.

You may well detect irritation in the voice of your professional as you insist on an answer. This merely proves that you are right to ask. If your professional says he can't give you an answer, ask him *how* his firm calculates their bills. (In *his* case the true answer is probably that they bill their clients for as much as they reckon they can get away with, without losing the client.)

Watch out for lawyers who quote what they call their *standard* billing-out rates or expense rates. This means that *on top of their billing-out rates* they may well *also* charge you what they reckon they can get away with.

Go easy on your telephone calls. If you ring your solicitor regularly, the number of calls can mount up, as can the time for which the solicitor will charge you. The time charged may well include time spent examining your file and other work as well as the telephone calls.

Do everything you can to avoid clerical staff work, because *this* is where a bill can soar. See that all your papers (including receipts) are submitted in date order, with the most recent date on top of the pile, and a list of the contents of your file. Because you know the scenario, you can do the work much quicker than a clerk and *you* don't charge yourself a huge sum per hour.

A simple professional scam is when a five-minute telephone call from you is billed out as one hour's work by him if he *says* that he thought it best to check your file afterwards.

Ask to be billed monthly (or even weekly) and to be told in writing immediately your account goes over £x. (*You* decide this amount; allow, say, seven hours of your professional's time per week.) *This puts a limit on your bill*. If the firm waits six months to send you a bill, you might unknowingly run up a huge bill that's uncheckable.

Go over the *first* bill with a fine-tooth comb, then you are less likely to get an inflated second bill. Raise *any* query that you can in writing. (The Law Society suggests this sort of wording: 'I am surprised that you should bill me for six hours of interviews in May. I have kept a note of them and I have recorded the

time at four hours. Please reconsider your bill.')

My management consultant told me that the less the client seems to care, the bigger his bills are. He advised me *always* to question fees and expenses *as soon as the bills appear* and to do so in as much detail as possible. He also advised me always to write on the payment cheque 'in full and final settlement of your firm's total account to (date of bill)'.

One thing you can't blame lawyers for is legal jargon. This is what precisely clarifies a legal agreement and it is *not* Fog Index. I always ask for a one-page letter summarizing any contract – and this is well worth paying for.

THE CON MEN

I would hate to admit to you the number of times I've fallen for a con man's pitch, but you may regard me as an expert by now; even my mother admits that I'm gullible.

Any woman who longs to hear her man say 'I love you' is vulnerable to the glib Latin lover – and the con man in business or on the doorstep.

Con men do not look like con men. No longer are they shabby encyclopaedia or vacuum-cleaner salesmen. No, now they wear Gucci loafers and Savile Row suits and specialize in new up-market areas. The electronic salesman (telephone, word processor, computer, digital watch), the home-money manager, the psychological expert whose expensive course will put your life right in one weekend, the cosmetics or vitamin salesman, the 'business consultant' and the chap who's selling a new way of living or a religion are all charming, reliable-sounding people, who are plausible and persuasive, and who clearly demonstrate their honesty (short-term) in order to gain your confidence.

Closet con men (and women) are con

DOWN WITH SUPERWOMAN!

men *who do not themselves realize* they are con men. Naturally, this is the most successful type.

One sign of a con man is the question 'Don't you trust me?' It never occurs to trustworthy people that others do *not* trust them. The other sign of the con man is his polite persistence: if, exasperated, you are eventually rude to him and he isn't clearly offended, beware.

A con man, who may also be a hustler, does exactly what his description implies – he hustles you! He verbally jostles you, he fast-talks and bewilders you, he makes you feel he's cleverer than you are, he doesn't give you time to think clearly and sensibly. Often he is charmingly amiable – a *lovable* hustler.

The world outside your door is a jungle of hustlers. Every time you buy anything from a box of tomatoes (rotten ones at the bottom) to a lawyer, you are wide open to deception, manipulation, intimidation and outright swindle. The opportunities to bamboozle are so fat and so safe – and the victims are so many, so honest and so unsuspecting (just like you) – that the marginal and crooked operator will, like the Great White Shark, always be with us.

The predator feeds on the Three Is: the Innocent, the Ignorant and the Impatient. The gullible include not only simpletons, but clever professional people.

The con man relies on your good manners. He will make *you* feel guilty if you are nasty to him. His weapon is friendliness and understanding. With polite persistence, he plays subtly on your pride, shame or simple stupidity. Why, Ms Goodbody, what will your neighbours think? Surely you don't want them to see you with a cheap quality carpet? How *can* you ignore this truly fine purchase at a price you must *promise* never to mention? All of which suavely passes over the fact that you were lured to the telephone or into the shop or the salesroom

in the first place by the bargain-priced product at which the hustler now sneers.

How does the con man reach his prey (you)? Every time you sign your name to practically anything, from a wedding licence or a birth certificate to a magazine subscription, your name, address and vital statistics – even in some cases your income – are sold to one or several compilers of mailing lists.

If you answer an unsolicited mailing shot, you may well find a con man on your doorstep waving a discount at you. He may locate you because you've answered a newspaper advertisement or he may turn up on your doorstep because he's simply working the street. There are more sophisticated approaches. I have several times been introduced to con men by so-called friends.

The commonest form of con-man hustling has infinite variations and is as old as time. It is called bait-and-switch. An advertisement for a microwave oven may offer the lowest priced, full-sized model in the world at £19 (REDUCED FROM £120) for £2 down and £1 a week. *Deep down in your intelligence, you know this is ludicrous.* And yet . . . you call the company, which duly sends round a salesman, who – if you insist on that £19 miracle bargain – will explain that the firm has *just run out* of that particular model, BUT he does have an infinitely superior bargain at £149. Two fast-talking hours later, *you* may have swallowed the bait; *he* switched.

Why do you believe someone who promises you something implausibly wonderful? Because you *want* it to be true (a lot of us still want to believe in fairies) or because the con man leads you to think that whatever he is offering is going to fill a lack in your life or improve your general quality of life. But ask yourself WHY ME? WHY NOW? Why should he give YOU this amazing offer, instead of one of his friends or deserving relatives?

So how can you check on a suspected con man?

Look for visible proof that the salesman has delivered (on time) in the past. Get a reference. Check it in person or on the telephone (no sensible person will ever put anything critical in writing, in case he gets sued).

A con man is after two things: your money and the names of your friends – his future victims. A sure sign that you are dealing with a con man is either his request for money ('a deposit') or else his reluctance to put in writing (*dated* and signed by him) the total price of what he is selling.

To summarize: be on your guard. Don't be persuaded by a stranger who appears on your doorstep into buying *anything* that you never intended to buy before he appeared. Never buy a major item in a hurry. Don't be hurried. Take time to make your mind up (overnight, at least). Read the boring fine print on sales documents. Don't hand over any money.

Don't mention the names of your friends or neighbours. Don't fill in any form headed 'confidential'. Don't tell him anything that you wouldn't want the world to know. Some con men are also blackmailers.

TIMESAVERS

HOW TO SAVE ENERGY (YOURS)

Film stars and other famous busy folk sometimes talk about 'quality time', as in 'I'm careful to plan regular quality time for being with my children.' I think they mean *uninterrupted* time. BECAUSE ALL TIME IS QUALITY TIME.

Time-management is the art of getting done what *you* want done rather than being at the mercy of events and other people. However you manage to divide your time between family, work and other interests, a professional business consultant will claim to save you the equivalent of an extra day every week. This is why time-management (which is simply getting yourself organized) has become big business. Executives attend expensive weekend courses in it; lesser mortals buy an expensive Filofax.

Successful time-management depends on spotting the difference between pro-

ductive work, system-support work and unproductive work. Writing a novel is productive work and I get paid for it. Washing dishes is system-support work. Drying the dishes by hand instead of letting them dry on a rack by themselves is unproductive work and a waste of time.

The aim of this book is to cut out unproductive work and cut down system-support work. This leaves more time for productive work and pleasure (often the same thing, as in writing a novel).

A business time-management course – I've attended a couple – will include many things (possibly wrapped in long, executive fog-words) that you can pick up from this book: a personal stress-management plan, a personal goal plan, ways to improve concentration, lectures on delegation, conflict management, body language, efficient note-taking and . . . minimizing work-load management, which means eliminating the time-wasters.

Many women hate being efficient in the home and they tend to feel uneasy if they hear the word 'organization'. Lists and routines simply do not fit into the pink-check-gingham-and-lace mental picture of the soap-opera mother, which so many of us were brought up to be. Many women hate the idea of timetables, because they hate having to account to anyone, especially themselves. 'How have you spent your time today and what do you have to show for it?' is a far more irritating question than 'How can you have spent all that money and have nothing to show for it?'

I see my time as a commodity, like money, that can be wasted, lost or stolen. Anything or anyone that interrupts what you're doing is a time-waster and adds to the stress of what you're doing. Anything that you find yourself doing when you haven't planned to do it is a time-waster. So is doing unnecessary system-support work at the expense of pleasure or achievement.

I budget how to spend my time as I budget how to spend my money and I have a constant battle to eliminate the time-wasters that erode my day. I try to balance my day so that I spend enough time – but not too much – on eating, sleeping, system-support work, achievement . . . and pleasure. Don't underestimate the importance of fun. All work and no play makes Jill a dull lay.

Pleasure is not necessarily doing nothing. Doing nothing for a day is fine if you're exhausted, but if you aren't, then simply wasting a day can leave you feeling tired, aimless and depressed – because you *know* you've wasted the day.

If you want to improve your time-management system, the most difficult part of doing it is keeping your mind open to new ideas, because naturally you think your present system is as efficient as you can manage.

Don't try all the suggestions in this chapter at the same time. **Just try the one that sounds easiest.** And be patient with yourself: doing something for the first time takes ten times longer than doing it for the third time.

Cautionary tale

When I stopped full-time work and started working from home (writing a book), I made one big, basic mistake. As I was my own secretary and cleaner, I used to play these roles in the morning and leave the afternoons free for my writing – the production work that paid the bills. The drawback was that I never finished the morning's work until 6 p.m., by which time I was too tired to write. I had to learn to reverse this procedure, to do productive work in the morning and the system-support work afterwards (with what energy I had left).

Your energy level

Everything you do requires a different level of mental energy to get it done. All human beings have different biological and psychological rhythms, which affect their mind and energy. The lark is most energetic in the morning, the owl gets into her stride only after sunset. You probably know if you are an owl or a lark, but why not analyse your energy levels a bit more thoroughly? Even if you have a full-time job and can't do as you please during the weekdays, being able to predict your energy level will enable you to make the best of your private time.

Psychologists say that we have ten energy levels but I use this four-level system in order to get things done:

Prime time is your peak time, when you are at your best and most brilliant. **B time** is when your concentration is not quite as good (good enough to write a letter, but not good enough to write a book). **C time** is your medium energy

DOWN WITH SUPERWOMAN!

level, useful for routine tasks, and **D time** is passive-participation level, when your brain is barely functioning and can produce only the degree of energy required to watch TV.

Prime time is a level of creativity and concentration that everyone has, but some people *never* use. You *can* watch TV or wash-up in your prime time, but it's a waste of prime time. You probably need prime time to start learning something interesting, but you won't need such a high energy level when you've got the hang of it.

Expect to be irritated if you are interrupted in prime time, because this will break your concentration and it can be as painful as awakening a sleep-walker. The painter Matisse said that if a model interrupted his concentration by merely asking him the time, his drawing was lost.

Use prime time for such occupations as writing, painting, thinking, problem-solving, planning all activities.

Use B time for such occupations as research, study, management, planning the week's menus and shopping list, writing letters, bookkeeping. It's hard to learn anything, except in prime or B time. Perhaps it's easier for a child to get up early to do his homework rather than be forced to do it after tea in his D time.

Use C time for exercise, sport, being with small children, entertaining, being entertained, committee work.

Use D time for housework, simple sewing, walking, swimming, cooking, shopping, gardening, listening to music, watching TV.

To understand your energy levels, try keeping this timetable card for a week and fill in your energy levels; if you can't decide, keep the relevant timespace empty. Incidentally, your energy levels may seem different at the weekend, but they are not.

Don't jeer at the 4–6 a.m. period. It was only by keeping a timetable that I realized why I wake early: unfortunately 5 a.m. is the start of my prime time, and I can't keep my eyes open after 10 p.m.

As a guide, here are my energy levels:

Prime time: 5 a.m.–1 p.m. – my mind is running smooth and fast.

B time: 1–2.30 p.m. – my concentration is slowing.

D time: 2.30–3.30 p.m. – my mind is lying panting by the side of the road.

B time: 3.30–6 p.m.

C time: 6–10 p.m. – my mind is jogging.

Some people can nap in their D time, but unfortunately I can't. Writer Bernard Levin, lucky chap, can nap in the bath in his D time from 6.30 to 6.45 p.m., then go out for the evening as fresh as a daisy.

Check whether any of your prime time is being wasted on sleeping at the wrong hours. Check whether you are trying to do prime time work in C or D time, which is exhausting and means you will not produce your best work. Check that you aren't doing prime time work in C or D time. Why be ironing when you might be writing a play? (In fact, why iron at all?)

Why not try for *one weekend* to fit *your* energy levels? Stop working to someone else's timetable and plan your own – even if it sounds ludicrous. Will it hurt you to try?

If you want to check whether you could better use your energy levels, list the things you want to do next weekend and allocate an energy level to them. Then fill in the activities on your timetable, matching the task to the energy level.

Your energy level is also affected by your attitude to what you're doing – whether you love it or hate it, whether it's done in your home or outside it. It was difficult to get my elder son out of bed until he started his own business, but now he's in the office an hour before it opens.

Your energy level can also be affected

Your energy levels

	Mon	Tue	Wed	Thu	Fri	Sat	Sun
a.m. 4–6							
6–8							
8–10							
10–12							
p.m. 12–2							
2–4							
4–6							
6–8							
8–10							
10–12							
a.m. 12–2							
2–4							

by exterior events, such as the death of a friend (energy DIVES) or a telegram announcing that you've won the pools (energy SOARS).

You can deplete your energy as a result of overwork, dancing all night or eating the wrong things. Illness gives you a twenty-four-hour D time day, too much drink similarly reduces your capability, eating too much pasta makes you sleepy.

Your eating *pattern* may also distort your energy level. If you sag at 11 a.m., check that this isn't ordinary executive slump resulting from only a cup of black coffee and no protein for breakfast. If you sag at 3–4 p.m., check that you haven't got dieter's slump, which is the result of skipping lunch or eating too

little, too late. And if you feel you *need* a drink in the evening, you probably didn't have tea.

WHAT SORT OF TIME-PLAN SUITS YOU?

People who tend to put things off until the last minute often find a time-plan makes life more restful. People who do things only when they become urgent often live in a harassed, permanent state of crisis, which is exhausting and stressful both for them and the people they live and work with.

A very efficient and grand lady told me that she had learnt to time-plan from

DOWN WITH SUPERWOMAN!

watching her mother's head-gardener. Every morning at 7 a.m. the gardeners gathered around him and each one was asked what he planned to do with his day. Getting an overview like this for the day makes you feel calmly in charge of your day, as opposed to being hurtled through it by an outside force.

Self-sufficiency farmer and author John Seymour always plans his life on a timetable. 'We stick to a very tight timetable,' he said, 'otherwise with so much to do, you find your life begins to sprawl.'

The trick is to dissociate the timetable from schools and railways, and see it as an easy, visible time-plan for the week. Think of a time-plan in the same way as a money budget. Keep it flexible and see it as a guide rather than a straitjacket. *You* choose what to put on your plan and *you* can alter it whenever you want to, because, just like underestimating costs in a money budget, what you think may take two hours may well take four hours or even eight hours. I'm wildly over-optimistic in estimating how much time I allow for a project. I no longer bother to think too carefully about this; I simply treble the time I think the project will take.

It's important to keep a written record (in your diary?) of your planned time, so that if, like me, your time guestimates are inaccurate, you can work out *exactly* how inaccurate your guesses are and then allow for this. So if you estimate a job will take two hours, write (2h) before the job and after it, write (fact – 6h).

Be careful not to spend too much time on your planning: allow yourself half an hour to plan a week. You don't want to be the sort of person who spends so much time planning what to do that she never gets anything done.

If you feel that your spare time gets frittered away, then devise a **timetable for your spare time.** (Evenings, perhaps?)

If you've ever felt that the weekend

disappeared and that you just flopped around or were constantly distracted, so didn't do the things that you wanted to do, try a **weekend time-plan.** This can give you a cheerful feeling of anticipation. Plan for pleasure, don't just allocate your time to tasks, family co-ordination and trying to get ahead of things before flopping with the Sunday papers.

Some mothers always have a romantic vision of what their weekend will be like, but are disappointed. A recent American survey on working mothers found that 95 per cent look forward to the weekend but 52 per cent feel exhausted when it's over. Twenty-seven per cent of mothers said that *most* of their weekend was work, 54 per cent reported that half of their weekend was spent working. On average, the women spent only about three weekend hours on themselves. The conclusion of the survey was that mothers should learn to manage their time better, which is what a timetable does.

A timetable works well for a mother when pinned on a felt pin-board (available from Ryman's): then everyone can see what you intend to do with your week, weekend, evenings or other spare time.

Many people prefer to organize their time with a Filofax. This is a good system if you're basically disorganized and can can afford the time to fill in the notes on the different coloured pages, together with the charts and other esoterica. My simple, cheap alternative system is a small notebook and pocket diary, carried in pocket or handbag. I don't have to lug it around and it won't get lost. Even worse than losing your handbag, diary or address book is the thought of leaving your Filofax – your entire life system and method of communication – on some bus.

If you use a Filofax, fill it with a pencil to avoid a lot of messy crossing out. Never *pull* the ring-binders apart or eventually they won't work. Instead, put a thumb on each of the metal end plates and press firmly until it opens.

Recently I switched from a small pocket diary to a Ryman's Langham Desk Diary, which is kept on my work-table. I use this as a diary and a work organizer. The bigger writing area gives me enough space to do several things in one book.

I write appointments on the left. On the right is my TO DO list: phone calls (never more than three), small tasks, re-minders. At the end of the week, I look at the diary and highlight anything that didn't get done. Either I do it first thing the following week or decide that, as it clearly wasn't important enough, I should forget it. First things first and second things never.

If I conveniently 'forget' to do things, I write a reminder on a coloured index card and stick it where I can't help notic-ing it. If it has to be done before break-fast, I stick it by my tooth mug. If it has to be done before lunch, I'll stick it on the fridge. If it has to be done before I go out, I stick the card on the doormat. If it has to be done before bedtime, then the card goes on the bed.

When unexpected things occur or jobs take longer than I had planned or life threatens to swamp me in some other way, I deal with agitation by look-ing at my diary and *taking something off it*. Sometimes the entire day gets slashed.

LIFE PLAN

Every January I put aside a Sunday to sort out my life. This is an exercise that I always enjoy – and that always surprises me. I do the sorting out in an exercise book with a pretty cover and I regard the day as a special occasion.

I peep into the future by asking myself:

What would I like to be doing in ten years' time (one main goal and a few minor ones)? **What do I have to plan to achieve this?**

The answers give me a long overview, into which my next two questions fit.

What would I like to be doing in five years' time (one main goal and a few minor ones) and **what do I have to plan to achieve this?**

These are the areas I consider:

Myself. Health, happiness level, ap-pearance, exercise, leisure, holidays, social life.

Other people. Family, friends, sup-port team, business friends.

My work. Writing, office organiza-tion, business, voluntary work, business travel.

In the back of my New Year diary I now write a list of goals for the coming year, some of which may be very minor.

I then review the past year. I check my last year's diary to see what happened to last year's goals. Some will have been achieved. I consider whether to dump the others or transfer them to the New Year's list.

I notice that I've achieved some things that *weren't* on my previous year's list (when something happens, I scribble it in the back of my diary).

I ask myself if last year taught me any expensive lessons. Undoubtedly it will have done, although these expensive les-sons never seem to be useful because (by now I know) next year's crises will always be different.

I fill in the yearly planner in the front of the diary and highlight holiday space and other dates to remember.

A more advanced form of time-management is *Getting Things Done* by management-training specialist Roger Black (published by Michael Joseph). My elder son sent me this book, which is visually fascinating and easy to read with a zero-rated fog index. It contains hardly any psychobabble and is divided into 100

DOWN WITH SUPERWOMAN!

short sections, each of which is a step towards better management of time and achievement; they include 'Improve your memory', 'How to read faster', 'Handling complex projects' and 'Overcoming fears'.

HOW TO SORT OUT YOUR THOUGHTS

Writing lists is the easiest way to get things done efficiently. They are a painless way of sorting out your priorities, cutting out unnecessary jobs, sorting out your life, cheering yourself up and spring-cleaning your mind.

People who don't make lists often have someone else (who makes lists) to look after them. If not, people who don't make lists either don't have much to do or they forget things and are unreliable.

On those days when you feel you have too much to do, when you panic – do nothing. Have a cup of tea and make a TO DO list. Making a list gets things out of your head and on to paper. A list removes the agitation from your mind, which will then be cool and calm although you won't have done a damn thing on the list. However, your head is clear and you can now calmly decide what to do next by picking something off the list.

In addition: list **work to do**.

List the **cleaning routine.**

List your **shopping requirements.** I photostat some copies of a basic list and every week I simply highlight the items I want to buy; this takes minimal time and nothing is forgotten. (Use the stat machine in your local library.)

List the **books** you want to read and the **films** you want to see.

List **letters** to write.

List **phone calls** to make.

List **birthdays** (by the month).

List **religious and other holidays.**

Write your lists in no particular order, simply jot down whatever comes to your mind. Then number each item in order of priority and rewrite the list. (It's sometimes easier to do this if you cut up your list and shuffle it into priority order and then stick it together with magic tape.) This helps you to clearly establish your priorities in your mind.

A GOOD/BAD list can help clarify your options so that you can make your mind up and take a decision. I am often surprised by the decision my GOOD/BAD list points out to me. Do you want to buy a caravan? Go to China? Buy a freezer? Draw a line down a sheet of paper. On the left list the arguments in favour of the project (GOOD); on the right list the arguments against it (BAD).

Listing her priorities on a GOOD/BAD list helped my friend Cynthia to reorganize her home. Her husband, a Sunday painter, used to stand his easel in her tiny kitchen because he had nowhere else to paint. But *she* had nowhere else to cook. Eventually Cynthia turned her sitting-room into a kitchen and turned the kitchen into a studio.

When my elder son needed a bedroom to himself, I used a GOOD/BAD list to sort out our priorities, then I turned the sitting-room into the sitting/dining/kitchen and the old kitchen into a bedroom/laboratory, because that is what my son needed.

After writing a GOOD/BAD list, if you are still left in an agony of indecision, it might well mean that *it doesn't much matter which decision you take*, because both are equally desirable – the GOOD/BAD sides balance out.

Sometimes you have only a choice between two evils: in which case, decide which choice will hurt you *less* (to check, use common sense and ask a friend). Remember, worse things have happened to other people and it wasn't *their* fault either. Life is *not* fair.

		Deliver MS to publishers			
	Check artwork	Rework as necessary			
Write draft 1	Write draft 2	Write draft 3	Get MS typed & checked	Get editor's criticism	Write final draft
Plan book	Write synopsis	Sell to publishers	Discuss with editor	Do research	Check research

Problem-solver list

On *one* sheet of paper write down the answers to these six questions:

1 What is the problem?
2 What is the reason for the problem?
3 What alternative solutions are there?
4 What is the best solution?
5 What do you have to do to make the best solution happen?
6 How are you going to monitor point 5 and on what date?

HOW TO GET THINGS DONE

If you start a project without clearly planning it first, you risk wasting a lot of time and effort. Start with an *objective* (you've decided to buy the caravan) and then work towards it with a *plan* that outlines every step of the way (visit caravan exhibition, visit bank manager, etc.), the time each step will take and who is responsible for each step. Allow contingency time (and possibly money) for your plan.

Cut a big job into manageable sections, then divide each section into subsections and tackle one subsection at a time. This is a **project plan**.

Remember that the pyramids were built of single blocks of stone. So draw a diagram of your project as a pyramid. Starting at the base, decide that each stone of the pyramid is a series of small tasks. Tackle the bottom row, one block at a time. Then tackle the next row. I draw the pyramid on a card, pin the card to my pin-board and black out each block when I've finished with it until I have a blackened pyramid. In disheartened moments when I feel I'm getting nowhere, a glance at my blackening pyramid proves otherwise.

This is how I plan a book. The contents pages of many non-fiction books, such as this, are also the project *plan*. Plan everything else in the same way.

A project plan consists of an overall aim (the finished manuscript) and a list of the steps necessary to reach it.

List to plan a project

1 Define the project in fifty words (if you can't do that, it's probably too complicated to be successful).
2 What is the main purpose of the project?
3 Define the need for the project.
4 How are you going to meet the need?

5 What else will be achieved by the project?

6 List each part of the project, giving the name of any other person involved and the date of completion.

7 How much will the project cost? (Give a detailed budget that shows how much each part of the project will cost.)

8 Where will the money come from?

9 How long will the project take?

10 When will the project be completed?

11 How will you judge if the project is a success?

For instance, I start to write a book with a clear idea: '*I* can't find a simple, cheerful book on housework, so why not write one?' (Items 1 and 2 on list to plan a project.) 'If I can't find such a book, then maybe other people would buy mine. After all, everyone has to do housework . . .' (item 3).

I list the chapters I want to read in this book (item 4) and I realize that the book I want isn't only on housework but also about running a home (item 5). There are twenty-two chapters on my list at this point.

My final list of thirty-two chapters (I add a few on the way) is also the book synopsis, which is simply a couple of pages saying what the book is going to be about so that the publisher can read the synopsis instead of listening to me mumble about it.

If I'm writing a fiction book, I write a two-page summary of the story (the synopsis) first and then do the list of chapters afterwards.

I pin the chapter list on my pin-board and draw my pyramid diagram, which is my work-plan (item 6). Towards the end of a book I pin a list of research checks (experts) and chapters still to be typed (item 6).

I decide that the project will take twelve months to write and will take two typists six months to type. I work out how much money I will need (item 7) and get a publisher's advance or a bank loan if necessary (item 8). I give my publisher a tentative date (item 9) but I don't give an exact finishing date (item 10) until I'm sure when the book will be completed.

I keep a separate work diary in which I write the hours I have worked each day, the chapter I have worked on, the number of words written that day, the total number of words written so far. This writing diary is useful reassurance for those days when I feel I am wading uphill through treacle and getting nowhere.

The list of chapters is my route map. The diary tells me where I've got to on the road and how much further there is to go (if you're writing 100,000 words, then after 50,000 words you know you're on the downhill path).

I write the messy first draft of each chapter by hand and I cross each finished chapter off the chapter list. I then tidy up the first draft, which thus becomes the second draft. I show this to my editor (my contact person at the publisher), who criticizes the manuscript. I then write the third, final draft.

Writing the book is no problem – the problem is everything else. Every day there are interruptions to my work (for good reason, which makes them all the more exasperating) because, whatever you're trying to do, LIFE GETS IN THE WAY.

If you can't seem to get things done, what's the reason? It isn't lack of will-power or laziness, because they don't exist.

There's no such thing as will-power. It's a beat-yourself-up word. Every woman who has ever been on a diet knows that she hasn't got any. Instead, try using determination. If you decide to do something, don't tell yourself you're going to *try* it, because you won't have switched on your determination at full power.

There's no such thing as laziness. It doesn't exist. There may be lack of motivation and subsequent understandable lack of enthusiasm. There may be lack of self-confidence. If so, wipe it out of your mind because it will distract your concentration.

I've already suggested how to avoid sabotage from housework, interruptions and a family or social life that is too demanding. Are there any other good excuses? Of course there are. Anyone can always find plenty of good excuses . . . (*every day* I can find a different excuse not to do my exercises). Look upon excuses as obstacles on your path, which have to be side-stepped, because these are what stop you reaching your goal.

Do you plan to put aside time *regularly* **for your special project?** Whether you're a pole vaulter or a Prime Minister, the secret of achievement is to establish a regular work pattern and stick to it. Nothing else seems to work.

Do you know how to improve your concentration? Switch on your tunnel vision. You've made your lists – stick to them. Keep looking straight ahead down the tunnel towards your goal and don't be distracted.

As I reach the end of a book, tunnel-vision becomes all-important and all other disciplines fall by the wayside. The slut-rating soars to ten, the exercise plan is discarded, comforting junk food tends to creep on to the menu and after work I have the strength only to watch TV. Oh dear!

Are you prepared to give up something to achieve something? I have found that, just as you can't have everything you want, you can't *do* everything you want. Decide what you want to do *most* and which other pleasant activities you are prepared to sacrifice for it.

International pianist Moura Lympany practises for six hours *daily*. After her arduous work, she needs to rest. She misses a great many daytime social occasions, but says that her true friends understand and accept her self-imposed isolation and that anyone who complains about it isn't really her friend.

ABC FOR ADULTS

Working mothers are often excellent time-managers – because they have to be. Quite often they have a system similar to this ABC list, which worked for me until my sons left home.

List your priorities. I don't mean routine household cleaning; I mean everything *except* that.

How can you ruthlessly simplify your life? How many jobs can you delegate?

Allocate a specific amount of time to each job you can't dump.

Check your job list and tick the priority jobs. Now cut out everything that isn't top priority.

List A: What you want to do long-term.

Your long-term objectives, to be realized after six months (example: go to Greece next summer).

List B: What you want to do this week.

Your short-term objectives, to be realized within six days (example: getting the dress finished in time for the Saturday party).

The things on your A and B lists are the things that will make you feel that you have achieved something for yourself, instead of merely keeping your head above the daily tidal wave of system-support work. Of course, this is no small achievement in itself, but somehow it doesn't seem like it.

DOWN WITH SUPERWOMAN!

Lists A2 and B2: These are lists of the actions that have to be taken to achieve your A and B objectives.

Pin these lists up on your pin-board or behind the kitchen door; if that's already covered with pinned-up lists, use the back of your bedroom door or (if you want to keep quiet about having Aims) your underwear drawer.

I prefer to keep my goals secret, so that no one except myself knows what I'm aiming at. But I write them down so I can't wriggle out of what I'm aiming at.

Every day *for a week* write a **C list** *of what you actually do* (take suit to cleaner, dog to vet, etc). You may well find that most of your day's activities are non-productive, so far as your two sets of goals are concerned.

If so, on the following week, check the things on the A2 and B2 lists and every day **choose one item to do before your daily routine work**. If you find that you have some perfectly normal, mind-paralysing daily block, such as 'What shall I give them to eat tonight?', by all means deal with that first and lay out the chops to defrost before turning to your A2 and B2 lists.

You needn't bother to keep a diary in order to check your performance. Just keep your lists and at the end of the week see what got crossed off and what didn't. Check *all* your lists quietly at the end of the week over a quiet drink. Check *why* certain things didn't get done. Were you not tough enough with yourself? Too easy on other people? Check that you're not striving for perfection (that way madness lies).

Lie on a sofa and work with your brain; use it to eliminate as much work as you can. Learn to look after yourself in this way. This is creative laziness.

Ask yourself whether you are deleting and delegating enough of your housework. Think of a mother not as the family servant, but as the family housekeeper. Traditionally, a housekeeper's job is to organize, delegate and supervise. That's all.

Accept the fact that, like the Sunday newspapers, you are not indispensable. Then you will feel less guilt about your shrinking lists. Believe me, it's more fun having spare time than wearing an invisible martyr's crown.

Another way of lessening your work is to learn to say NO, and to keep saying it cheerfully, but firmly, whenever *anyone* asks you to do *anything* that isn't on your A and B lists. The trick here is to say NO as the first word, followed, perhaps, by an explanation, although no explanation is necessary, just a repetition of your first monosyllabic message, or perhaps 'I'm afraid not' or 'I'm sorry I can't.' Say this charmingly and firmly, then *stop*. Then let the other person speak. If you are immediately asked again, immediately repeat your NO. DON'T ALTER IT THE SECOND TIME.

No matter how worthy other people's problems are, their A and B lists are not your concern. Don't let other people delegate to you.

Always bear in mind Conran's Second Law of Housekeeping, which is POSSIBLE DAILY OUTPUT IS ALWAYS HALVED BY UNFORESEEN INTERRUPTIONS. Halving the things on your list in advance doesn't seem to eliminate this problem, because Conran's Third Law is: HOWEVER MUCH YOU HALVE YOUR LIST, YOU WILL STILL GET ONLY HALF OF IT DONE. It's a mystery, like what is beyond outer space.

A brilliant journalist once wistfully told me that she wished she hadn't wasted so much time in her life. Well, we *all* wish that. So don't waste more time regretting it. Now is the time to stop wasting time, because your time is what you need in order to achieve *any-*

thing. Today's time, that is. Stop wishing you'd done more in the past. Stop daydreaming about the future. Decide on a possible positive project and start planning it TODAY. You have nothing to lose and plenty to gain.

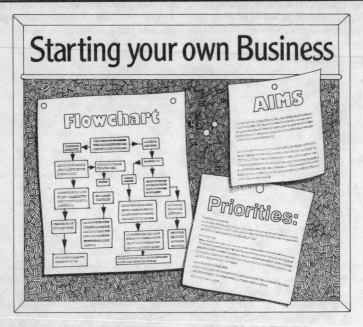

Starting your own Business

Flowchart

AIMS

Priorities:

I was dubious about including this section, as it strays from the subject of household management, but I was outvoted by the other three women in the office. 'Who *else* is going to tell us how to take the first steps if you don't? Look at Laura Ashley and Jane Shaw, starting in their *kitchen*,' they said hopefully. So here it is for when you outgrow the 'Money, Money, Money' chapter. Skip what follows until you need it.

If you're thinking of starting your own business, the most practical way to go about it is simply to *start doing it*.

Like Gaul, any business can be divided into three parts:

1 Thinking of the idea.
2 Putting the idea into practice.
3 Running it.

Number 2 is the rock on which most fortunes founder. So once you've decided what to do, DO IT NOW, WHATEVER IT IS.

GETTING DOWN TO BUSINESS

Do something you know about and are good at and stick to it. Always talk to other people in the same field to learn the pitfalls from their experience.

Listen only to expert advice. If you have very little money, you can afford only the *best* advice, from the best (and probably most expensive) experts. Don't necessarily take it. Don't be intimidated by experts. It is their job to explain and advise you in their specialist areas, but you must make your *own* decisions in your *own* business.

If you're tempted to do dutifully what someone else tells you to do, first check that he's rich and successful.

Don't think there's a market for something merely because you and your friends would like it. Check the market.

Most of the home employment offered to housewives is naked exploitation.

Avoid like the plague any sort of piece-work or commission-based schemes (envelope typing, telephone selling) because you will have to work like a slave, the work may be very disheartening and you may very possibly make very little money or even end up out of pocket.

If you have a special skill – typing, sewing, cooking, translating – advertise it in places where the people who might employ you will *see* your ad. A skilled *qualified* home-worker gets the best deal from people who use her services, so stick to an area that you know. For instance, if you were trained as a secretary, you might start a home typing agency. My last novel was typed by four part-time secretaries; the money to pay for their word processor was borrowed, and my payments discharged their loan in six weeks. They were expensive but worth every penny because they were reliable.

You might start a home industry in your bedroom. Perhaps sew cushion covers, do knitting, with or without a machine, or crochet work. I have seen many simple starts such as these lead directly to success.

Make sure you are efficient, neat, professional and reliable. No jam stains on translations or letters unposted because your husband put them in his pocket and forgot them. Allow no home life intrusions of any sort.

First, *decide how much you can afford to lose* in terms of time and money. Do not be over-optimistic.

Then, clearly define your long-term and short-term goals. Write them down and pin them where you see them often. (You're going to need more underwear space.) Write a report sheet to yourself every month, with a page for good-news and a page for bad-news items. Learn from the bad-news items. They are what is called Experience and comfort yourself with the fact that Experience is always Expensive.

Write down your aims and your priori-ties, and stick them on top of your pin-board. (You will get a pin-board, won't you? It helps to clarify and focus your aims. Ryman's sell cheap pin-boards.)

Don't think that being your own boss is easy.

Be prepared to work all the hours you're awake at all the necessary jobs, including those that you couldn't ask anyone else to do (such as scrubbing filthy warehouse floors).

Be prepared for longer hours, more discipline, far more responsibility and self-control than you've been used to, but a job that may be far more satisfying and rewarding than anything you've done to date.

If you're going to expand to more than a one-woman cottage-industry typing agency, you had better forget all the stories you've heard about overnight success. Any overnight success will confirm that starting a business is sheer hard slog, needing self-discipline, nerves of steel, bulldog stamina and endless hard work. You will have to take the decisions, churn out the publicity, keep the books and beat up the business, cope with the customers, and produce the products, as well as delivering the goods.

You need a fine mixture of optimism (which keeps you going) and pessimism (so that you can shrewdly and realis-tically assess the risks). There is never any guarantee of success, but if you coldly recognize, and are constantly alert to, the possibility of failure, it is less likely to afflict you.

YOUR BASIC OFFICE SYSTEM

Keep your organization simple and you're more likely to keep it in order. The organization is merely keeping track of what's happened to everything. The important thing is that you should under-stand it and your accountant when you get one, should understand it.

DOWN WITH SUPERWOMAN!

See that you have some *reliable* way of dealing with inquiries. One no-answer is enough to put a would-be client off for ever. So is 'Mummyth out thopping, I fink . . .'

Don't be a slave to the telephone. Once you've got started, the cheapest way to be efficient is to have two telephones and one answering machine. One telephone is for your out calls and the other is permanently hitched to an answering machine with an Elastoplast stuck over the dial, so you can easily check if British Telecom sting you for any calls.

Check your answering machine *without fail*, possibly at 9 a.m. daily. Keep your tin-voice message as short as possible ('This is Julia Ross. Please leave a message and I'll call you back after 10 a.m.'). If you use an answer machine, you must use it efficiently, otherwise it puts people off immediately. Don't make whimsical jokes or play music on your answer machine.

Divide your mail into three groups.

Group 1 Put aside letters that need special thought before answering.

Group 2 Answer letters as you read them, with a handwritten, signed, dated reply on that letter.

Group 3 You are entitled to throw away any unsolicited mail.

I read my mail only once a week and answer it all immediately unless it relates to bookkeeping or can be put in my pend tray, which I answer at the end of the month, by which time I find that events may have overtaken the letter and it then doesn't need answering.

Before you send anything out (goods, cheques or invoices) write it down in a bookkeeping book (see p. 365). When you receive a cheque, write it down in a book. The one office rule I stick to is that cheques are dealt with immediately. They are never put down. They are checked off, checked out and put in the envelope to go to the bank.

Send any valuable documents or difficult-to-duplicate documents by recorded delivery, or registered post, if it's abroad, or Datapost (guaranteed 24-hour delivery). Then:

1 The letter may arrive faster. Everyone I know has this touching faith in the Post Office and goes around saying, 'But I don't understand, I sent it first-class mail on Monday; it *must* have arrived by Friday.'

2 The letter is more likely to arrive. The Post Office once mislaid over 200 of my letters, which they later found and returned with an apology, and since then I have always sent letters to lawyers, banks, agents and accountants by recorded delivery.

3 People can't pretend not to have received your letter if it is sent by recorded delivery and clearly marked as such underneath your signature on the letter. You *should* stick the recorded delivery slip on to your copy of the letter, but I find it easier to write 'recorded delivery' on the letter and keep all the slips in date order in a little plastic box.

Your office organization might consist simply of an inexpensive electronic calculator (always double-check your additions and do a mental rough check on it), the cheapest reconditioned second-hand typewriter you can find, and a second-hand filing cabinet.

WHAT YOUR ACCOUNTANT WANTS ME TO TELL YOU

What follows is about accountancy. Don't try to absorb this all at once; dig into it as you need it, one thing at a time. However, don't try to take short-cuts or alter the procedure or insert clever improvements: it has evolved over hun-

Budget

	£	£	£
Annual income			
100 cushions @ £20			2,000
Capital expenditure			
Second-hand van, acquired with money borrowed from the bank. (The cost will be spread over four years: £4,000 ÷ 4 = £1,000 a year as a charge for depreciation in your non-capital expenditure, below.)	4,000		
Non-capital expenditure			
Production costs			
100 cushions @ £4 (see costing sheet, p. 364)	400	400	(400)
Gross profit (income minus production costs)			1,600
Other costs			
Depreciation	1,000		
Overheads	26		
Own salary	130		
Stationery	10		
Total other costs	1,166	1,166	(1,166)
Total production + other costs		1,566	
Contingency (10% of total costs)		157	(157)
Grand total non-capital expenditure		1,723	
Net profit before tax (gross profit minus Other costs and Contingency)			277
Tax	77		(77)
Net profit after tax			200

dreds of years for good reason. If there is a universal language, it is the language of accounts, because accountants all over the world use the same basic system for a small business or a huge international complex. If you start moving away from the system, your accounts probably *won't* account accurately.

Your budget

A budget is to help you keep your eye on where the money is **supposed** to go and where, in fact, it went. A budget should be regularly checked to see if it is accurate (which it won't be) and if you can cut it (especially the tiny sums – all those

tiny sums mount up to a big sum. See above for how to work out the budget). A budget has three basic areas:

1 Expected income.
2 Capital expenditure.
3 Non-capital expenditure.

Capital expenditure is the purchase of a visible asset, such as a motor car, that's going to last longer than a year. Non-capital expenditure is money spent on items for which you have nothing to show after the item has been used, such as petrol for the motor car.

The budget above is a simplified example to illustrate my points. For the purpose of the example you are a cushion

Costing Sheet

To produce 100 cushions style 'The Sahara'

Production Costs	£
Material: Brocade	100
Material: Cotton for back	100
Wages (100 hours @ £1.20 per hour)	120
Packing	25
Advertising	15
Bank interest	15
Telephone	25
Total cost for 100 cushions	400

Cost for 1 cushion £400 ÷ 100 = £4

maker and expect to make 100 cushions a year, which you will sell at £20 each.

Don't forget to include your own salary in your budget, and if you don't take a salary, then *imagine one* at £X a week and add your time into the budget, otherwise your budget will not be accurate.

Your income will pay for your non-capital expenditure if your debtors pay when they are supposed to; if they don't, you will need a further bank loan, upon which you will have to pay interest.

Anything you buy that isn't in the budget is *over* budget, so the money that pays for it comes *off your profit* if it is non-capital expenditure (such as a bigger electricity bill than you expected) and *off your capital* if it is a capital expenditure item (your bargain car needs a new engine).

Remember that there's nothing sacred and unalterable about a budget just because you wrote it down on paper. A budget is a hopeful statement of intention at the time you wrote it. You might have to revise your budget every month to begin with but eventually you should be able to accurately calculate a yearly budget.

Your *costings* are as important as your budget. These are estimates of what each product costs you to produce. If you undercalculate this sum (a classic beginner's mistake), the amount that you have left out will come *off your profit*. Include in the cost of each item an amount for overheads directly related to your production of cushions: this covers light, heat, power and rent of the back bedroom or wherever it is that you assemble your products (the cushions). If you intend to make 100 cushions, divide your total costs by 100 to calculate the overhead cost on each cushion.

Distinguish between variable and fixed costs. *Fixed costs* are those that you *know* won't alter whether you produce one or 4,000 items, such as your rent, the van or a sewing machine. *Variable costs* depend on the things you are making and may include materials, outworkers and packing, advertising and telephone bills.

Don't forget that what your working money (capital) costs is the amount of interest that it would earn in a building society or, if you've borrowed it, what the bank is charging to lend it to you. So include bank interest on capital in your costings, at base bank rate plus at least 3 per cent, or whatever fiendish sum your bank charges you. (If your bank won't reduce their charge to 3 per cent over base, try going to another bank.)

When budgeting, it is vital to make allowance for contingencies: these are mistakes and things you never thought of. Perhaps your sewing machine or calculator breaks down and you have to hire or buy another one. Perhaps somebody *else* goes bankrupt, owing you money. THERE ARE ALWAYS CONTINGENCIES AND THEY NEVER MAKE MONEY FOR YOU; YOU ALWAYS HAVE TO SHELL OUT MORE. Add 10 per cent of your total non-capital expenses for contingencies in your first trading year. (This is a non-asset expense item.)

Now for that *profit margin*. When preparing your budget, decide the profit margin and at first check it monthly. Of course you're up to your eyebrows in vital work, but if you don't show a profit, you probably won't have a business pretty soon, so discipline yourself to check that you really are making the profit you *think* you are.

Your profit can be split into two figures. In this simple example, the *gross profit* is the sale price minus the cost of making the goods, 1,600. The net profit is the gross profit less all other expenses and tax – in this case, £200.

Your net profit margin might be 10 per cent (as in this example), or as much as the market can stand, such as 200 per cent. You might be charging for the genius of your idea as well as production.

Your basic bookkeeping books

Most people shudder at the thought of bookkeeping, because they were badly taught by someone who confused them. If you enjoy crossword puzzles, following a knitting pattern or tapestry, you may well find bookkeeping intriguing.

A Your **order book** (to other people). This is for *all* goods that you order. This duplicate book should be numbered.

B Your **invoice book** (your bills to other people). This duplicate book should also be numbered with a different system to the order book.

C **Money-you-receive book.** A double-column cash-book should do to begin with.

D **Expenditure book** (money you spend). Get an analysis book with more columns than you think you'll need.

E **Expenditure ledger** – vital to stop you paying people twice. I'll explain later.

F **Fixed asset register.** To record all capital items purchased and sold, such as motor vehicles, photocopier or freehold land.

G **Sales ledger.** To record all invoices you send out, the date you send them, the amounts received from your customers and the date your customer pays. This will enable you to know at a glance who owes you money. Use this book to chase payments due to you.

H **Bank paying-in book.** A detailed list of cheques you pay into your bank accounts.

I **Petty cash book.** To record all petty cash expenditure.

Never enter anything into these books without first entering the date.

Your basic bookkeeping

'Women tend to think that they're weaker in finance than men – but they're very often better,' I was told by the Small Firms Information Centre. Whatever your ability, or seeming lack of it, don't try to ignore the bookkeeping side of the business. It is particularly important at the beginning, when you haven't any time for it. And it never gets less important.

In particular, don't write accounts down on the back of envelopes. A lot of small firms fall down on this. Many an accountant turns up yearly to inspect the books, only to find that there aren't any – just this towering pile of old envelopes and scribbled bits. Sorting it out can be very expensive. On the other hand, avoid an elaborate accounting system that you don't use because you have to *think* about it. Better a simple system where you fling everything into the right place because you understand it and it's easier than having it on the kitchen table.

Until you need an accountant, you can keep track of sales and spending, money you are owed and money that you owe other people, by doing three simple things:

1 To avoid confusing your business with

DOWN WITH SUPERWOMAN!

personal finances, open a separate business bank account. If you are making a regular monthly profit and have a steady cash-flow, you might consider opening another bank account. If your calculated *gross* profit is 10 per cent, every month pay 10 per cent of your takings for the month into this account. Pay tax bills from this account.

If you bank with more than one bank, try keeping a duplicate book to record payments to all banks. You then have a record of payments in only one book.

2 **When you receive a cheque,** enter it in Book C, then Book G, then Book H, then shove it off quickly to the bank before it gets mislaid, and to cut down on interest charges.

3 **When you pay a cheque,** enter the details in Book D and Book E, then on your cheque-stub, and *only then* write the cheque.

Always check that your receipts and payments reach your bank account. Get your bank statement sent monthly. When your bank statement comes in, tick off your own cheques on the statement (make sure they return your cheques to you).

Next, tick off the cheques you have received against your bank statement. After checking them, fold in half the relevant pages in your bank paying-in book (H). Anything that hasn't reached your account is instantly visible because it hasn't been folded back. Don't think that you needn't check on your bank. Money is hard enough to make: make sure you keep it.

At this point you balance your books. You take the month's total in your cash-book (C) and check the month's total in your paying-in book (H). They should be the same amount. This should also be the same amount that has been paid into your bank according to your bank statement.

Similarly, check the total amount you

withdrew from the bank with the total in your expenditure book (D).

In theory, the totals in your books should be the same as the totals in your bank account. In fact, this is rarely so, because the amount you paid into the bank on the last day of the month won't be credited until a few days later – in the next month. Not all the cheques you write will be immediately paid into the bank by the recipient. At this stage you write a bank reconciliation.

As the bank statement doesn't give your accurate cash position, you calculate this as follows:

	£
Balance according to your bank statement	+ 100
Less: unpresented cheques	− 50
Plus: cheques paid into your account but not yet cleared	+ 70
Balance according to your books	+ 120

You now know that *your true position* wasn't £100 in the bank on the last day of the month (as the bank statement says), but £120.

Often you will see one line below a subtotal, two lines below a total. Often a series of subtotals are duplicated in a further right-hand column, which makes it easier to consider and add up to a grand total.

Accountants don't bother to write + or −. Any final minus figure has a bracket round it. (Amount in bank = (£20,000) means you have an overdraft of £20,000.) Take a pencil and write in the pluses and minuses on the final column. How do you know? Common sense tells you that all expenses are − and all income, receipts and sales are +. In the example above I have added in the + and −.

Your expenditure book (D) has columns to analyse your expenditure; you can calculate the total of each category.

Why do you need to put your expenditure into different categories? To tot up

Expenditures

Date 19—	Item	Their invoice	Amount £	Office supplies – stationery £	Materials – fixed office overheads £	Materials – to make products £	Workers' wages £	Packing and delivery £
1 Jan	Pickfords		9					9
1 Jan	Liberty's/ fabric	02210 of 10 Dec 89	8			8		
7 Jan	Workers' wages 1–7 Jan		4				4	
7 Jan	Ryman's	0761 of 20 Dec 89	1	1				
7 Jan	Rackman	Rent Jan–Mar 1990	2		2			
10 Jan	Ryman's	0798 of 2 Jan	7	7				
10 Jan	Liberty's/ fabric	02360 of 3 Jan	3			3		
16 Jan	Workers' wages 8–16 Jan		4				4	
16 Jan	Pickfords/ delivery		5					5
	Total expenses for January		43	8	2	11	8	14

monthly what your *total* spending is in each category and to check you're not spending more than you allowed for that item in your budget.

An accountant wants to be sure that your figures haven't been altered or added to by someone other than yourself, so never leave a space between each entry. You're supposed to write accounts in pen. Don't write to the bottom of the page – leave a space for notes *below* the totals. Before turning a page, always total the columns and repeat them at the top of the next page: under 'item' write 'brought forward'.

Notice that you can check the total you've spent at the bottom of column 1. The total of the remaining columns adds up to the same amount – and this is often a check on your arithmetic.

If in your budget you allowed £20 for the year for office supplies and by the end of January you've spent £8 of it, then you will either have to cut down on stationery or alter your budget.

Highlight the firms you do regular busi-

ness with and make *another* entry for each payment to these firms. Allocate each firm a separate page in your expenditure ledger (E), which should have a double cash column.

Then you start again.

You can then easily spot by eye if you are about to pay a bill that you have already paid (which is why you have to note the invoice number).

Ask your accountant not to confuse you at this stage by explaining debit and credit entries. All you need to know for

Liberty's

	Item	You pay £	You owe £
1 Jan	Liberty's invoice 02210		8
10 Jan	Liberty's invoice 02360		3
5 Feb	Cheque paid to Liberty's	11	
		11	11

DOWN WITH SUPERWOMAN!

the moment is that a debtor is someone who owes you money and you may wish that debtors' prisons still existed so that the wretches could be thrown into them. A creditor is someone to whom you owe money and they are hopefully of saintly temperament.

Shove your bank statements and your empty cheque-books in a file.

Each month get receipted bills and any other proof of payment in date order and stapled (so that they stay in order.) Shove them in a big plastic sandwich bag (one for each month) and stick it in a file.

Keep your invoices that you have received but not paid in a lever-arch file. Also keep a section in this file for invoices that you are querying before payment.

Keep a little book for **petty cash** (I). Scribble down the amount in it when you draw the money, say £5. When you next reach for £5, first scribble down what you spent the last fiver on. You can remember small amounts of petty cash without difficulty, although it's better to jot them down in your handbag notebook. But try to avoid paying for things with petty cash, because you often don't have a record of it. Make it as difficult as possible for yourself to get and to dip into the petty cash, otherwise it can be a constant little money leak.

Start with a specific float (say £10). Each month pay back into the petty cash *the exact amount* that was taken out during that month. Do so with a separate cheque. This will stop muddles in your petty cash.

GETTING PAID

When you send someone an *invoice*, or bill, it is an exact account of what they owe you money for. If you don't send an invoice, their accounts department won't know that they owe you money. The invoice should be sent at the same time as the goods, unless you have made other arrangements.

A short summary statement giving the overall sum they owe you should be sent at the end of the month. Business theory says that bills are paid at the end of the month after the first statement has been sent. By invoicing on the 29th, rather than the 1st of the next month, you should, theoretically, get paid a month earlier.

Established businesses with great big accounts departments pay as slowly as they can. But you can often get the buyer you are dealing with in a big store to make special arrangements for payments to you within the month. They understand that as a small supplier you can't afford to hang around waiting for your money for four months or longer because it would cripple you, you'd go out of business and then they would no longer be able to get your products.

You may have sensibly made arrangements that your goods are paid for *before delivery* (*pro forma*), in which case you just bill in advance and don't hand the goods over until payment is made. Don't sell goods on a sale-or-return basis – 'on spec'. Your goods are gone and the shop hasn't invested in them, so it might be less keen on selling them than some other product in which the shop's money is tied up, and getting them to take' responsibility for possible dirt or damage can be tricky. Never allow credit for more than two months for any reason whatsoever. Whatever the story you're offered, try to turn up *without warning* at the place of business of the person concerned and stand there and ask for your money or your goods. Be prepared to wait all day and make a (loud) nuisance of yourself. Embarrass it out of them as a last resort and if that doesn't work, nothing will.

THE VATMAN COMETH

VAT is value added tax – the tax that

makes small people give up their business in despair, gives them ulcers or nervous breakdowns, ensures that no accountant will ever be out of work and guarantees the phenomenal success of the pocket calculator. This is the tax that makes you spend a vast amount of time doing sums on behalf of the government. However, this is the system and you can't avoid registering for VAT if you have a business with a *turnover* (not profit) of a certain level a year. (Ask your local VAT office what it is.)

Briefly, VAT is a tax that is collected on almost anything you buy or sell, do or have done to you. It is collected at each stage of the manufacture and distribution of most goods and services; so, if you are VAT-registered, when you sell your goods or services to your customers, you have to charge them VAT on top of your price. However, *once registered*, you can also claim back VAT that you have paid on goods and services supplied to *you* for your business (telephone, petrol, equipment, machinery, raw materials, etc.).

Every three months you add up the VAT you've charged your customers – this amount is called the output tax. You also add up the amount of VAT that has been charged to you – this is called the input tax. It will have been invoiced to you by your suppliers of telephone, petrol, equipment, etc. You then pay Customs and Excise the amount you have charged (output) after deducting the amount you have been charged (input).

Sometimes, input is bigger than output, in which case you get a repayment from Customs and Excise. This happens when you have paid more VAT for goods and services received than you have charged to your customers for goods or services that you have sold them. The only person who can't claim back VAT is the eventual consumer.

However, even if you are not registered for VAT, you must monitor your business and notify Customs and Excise immediately if the scale of the business or its activities changes to such an extent that registration is necessary.

It is very important to get your record system working correctly from the very beginning because three months can pass very fast and it can seem that no sooner have you dealt with one lot of VAT than the next one is inexorably settling round your shoulders.

You must keep an *exact* record of:

1 All the VAT you have paid on everything that contributes to your business.
2 All the VAT you have collected from the customers to whom you sold your goods and services.

A simple way of keeping track of payments you have made is by never letting anyone have his bill back. When you write the cheque to pay it, scribble on the cheque 'To pay your invoice 0027' and chuck the bill into your receipts file. It is not a receipt, but as far as you're concerned, the matter is settled. Don't let the bank get away with not returning your cheques. Insist, or change your bank.

Your invoices and business stationery must state your registered VAT number. The bills you send out and the bills you pay must all have the VAT clearly separated from the basic cost.

In order to do this you have to keep your expenditure book (D) and your invoice book (B) in three damned columns instead of one. They are:

Basic Cost   VAT   Total Cost

VAT rates go up and down, depending on the whims of the Chancellor of the Exchequer. Some goods and services have no VAT. If so, they are either 'zero-rated' or VAT exempt.

Zero-rated are most food and drink, books, magazines, newspapers, children's clothes, public transport and new domestic housing. When zero-rated,

DOWN WITH SUPERWOMAN!

manufacturers and traders can reclaim VAT that they have paid out to suppliers.

Exempt from VAT Certain trades don't charge VAT and are *not* entitled to claim VAT relief. They include education, insurance, health, postal services, land, rent, burial, cremation and betting.

If you want to know more about VAT, get two books, numbers 700 and 701 from VAT offices. Together they total 300 pages and are *merely* a general guide. There are also books that cover specialist areas, such as export, import and catering. You get these (and any information you need) from your local VAT office, which is in the telephone directory under Customs and Excise. They say that if anyone is worried about how to keep VAT records, an inspector can come round and help, or you can ring them or make an appointment to go to see them.

You're supposed to pay your VAT money when you send in your quarterly return. If not, you will get 'chaser' letters. You can expect one month's leeway if you get in a muddle and can't pay, and after that the penalties can be very severe. 'If someone is badly in arrears, they risk having a distraint put on their goods', I was told. This might easily mean bailiffs knocking on the door and a pantechnicon outside to take away your furniture.

YOUR CASH-FLOW CRISIS

As soon as possible, get an accountant to help you with your costings and then keep your eye open for ways in which profit might trickle away. I once ran a small textile business and when profit started dropping, I traced the leak back to the warehouse, where I found that the bales of fabric were being carelessly measured, so what was paid for as a metre was in fact about one metre plus five centimetres. As my 10 per cent profit on each metre was ten centimetres, that extra five centimetres neatly halved my profit.

Your capital rarely seems an acute problem at the beginning but, ironically, it gets more painful and chronic as you become more successful, when you need to find more money to pay all those outworkers and to buy all the materials needed to make your products.

Whatever your price is, it had better be competitive (discover what the competition charges) and one that people are prepared to pay. Theoretically, you pay for the production of the item and sell it to someone who pays you a bit more and this is your profit margin. If you want prompt payment from retail stores, you offer a discount for payment within fourteen days (ask your accountant what you can afford). Always try to take and give discounts. Always try to buy everything wholesale, even stationery.

Your little profit may be swallowed up by bank interest and the accountant's fees. Meanwhile you need *more* cash to finance *more* materials and outworkers because export orders are now pouring in from all over the world – Saks Fifth Avenue in New York, Galeries Lafayette in Paris, and Harrods in Buenos Aires. This period in your life is called a cash-flow crisis and it is at this point that the amazingly famous new lady tycoon finds herself living on macaroni for months on end. *Because however many orders and ideas you have, you won't be able to put them into practice without sufficient cash.*

Try to avoid being too successful too fast. Try to grow steadily and learn to crawl before you leap. Avoid expanding your business too fast, so that your capital is insufficient. Because people want to buy your goods, don't make more of them than you know you can pay for.

Keep checking your budget, your costings (see further on) and your cash-flow. Try to avoid spending on anything that is non-productive, no matter how good the reason. Don't delegate 'looking after the money'. Don't let anyone else get his hands on the tiller or the till.

Having written that, I'm amazed that anyone ever starts a business. But the even more amazing thing is that you learn all this quickly once you start. And, apart perhaps from having a baby, there is no greater feeling of satisfaction than running your own business, which is why so many people do it and so many people want to do it.

YOUR BUSINESS BRAINS

If you're going into business, you do it in one of three ways: as a *sole trader*, as a *partnership* or as a *limited liability company*. You can trade under your own name without any special permission, but if you want to create a business name by using anything other than your name *alone*, you have to apply to the Registrar of Business Names at Companies House, 55 City Road, London EC1Y 1BB (tel: 071-253-9393). It costs £1 to register and they'll send you free leaflets.

A sole trader is a private person working by herself who bears the entire ultimate responsibility, no matter how many people she employs. She gets all the profits, but if the business collapses, she's liable for all the debts and her personal possessions can be sold to pay them.

Partnership Having tried it with painful consequences, in future I would avoid collaboration or partnership. You may think a partner will be comfortingly available to share your anxiety, your responsibility, your costs, your financial risk and your work. However, what you risk is that he/she won't share, and may well add to, your anxiety, responsibility, financial costs and work – and lawyer's bills. You may risk doing 100 per cent of the work (or even 150 per cent if the partner *makes* more work for you) for 50 per cent of the money and getting bad-mouthed by your partner/collaborator,

who may well claim to have done all the work.

If you're good enough to do it – do it on your own and hire the helpers. At least you can fire them if they don't perform.

If you go into partnership you have no more protection than a sole trader. If your business goes bust, you're actually worse off, because you're liable for the debts of the partnership as a whole, and that includes your partner's share as well as your own. So you may forfeit not only the money you have invested, but also (if the other partner or partners can't or won't stump up their share) any other money you have and personal possessions, which can be seized to pay the entire partnership debts.

If you want to go into partnership, it's vital to have the relevant documents drawn up by a lawyer who is married to neither of you. These should state how much money you're going to invest and when; how much work you're both going to put in and when; what your mutual responsibilities are; who will sign the cheques (both of you preferably); who will make the decisions and whether or not they are to be jointly agreed upon before any action is taken.

You should also state how you should each be reimbursed and who will get what if you decide to split. If you've ever been involved in a divorce, you'll know how easily misunderstandings can occur between two people who once knew and trusted each other. You'll then see how necessary it is in a partnership to get these things straightened out before you start.

To limit the risk of your investment (so that *you* can't go bankrupt), you can form a **limited company**: company debts can be paid only by company money and your personal money and belongings are not at risk unless you personally have given guarantees to the bank on the company borrowings. A limited company may not give you the best tax advantages, but it does protect you from losing everything and having the house sold over your head. However, you have to take on certain obligations (imposed by the Companies Act) and produce properly audited yearly accounts.

It will cost you less than a West End meal for two to set up a limited company and your accountant can do it.

YOUR BUSINESS CONTACTS

It's worth belonging to your local chamber of commerce. I know a girl who was left with £30 and a one-week-old baby. Five years later she had a world-wide soft toy business. She lived in a country town in Leicester and says that the key to her success was joining the local chamber of commerce (ask at your local library where they are). While still making her toys by hand she met other small-business people, bank managers, insurance agents, solicitors and accountants, and was able to discuss her problems and get personal recommendations. Other owner-managers understand what it's like to have no one to share your problems with and how isolated and worried you can sometimes feel.

Such an organization is a good place to ask around for a recommendation for an *accountant* and a *lawyer*. Draw up a list of possibles, then visit everyone on the list. These two professional advisers are going to be very, very important in your life, so don't rush into it. Make sure your sort of business will suit them. Try to get to a partnership rather than an individual; several individuals will have more experience than one and at least one should always be available.

Solicitors must, by law, be professionally qualified but *anyone may practise as an accountant*. So be very, very careful. Whoever you choose, check that he is a member of a professional body, such as the Institute of Chartered Accountants in England and Wales, or of Scotland. Write to them at Chartered Accountants Hall, Moorgate Place, London EC2R 6EQ, or 27 Queen Street, Edinburgh EH2 1LA, respectively. It's a good idea to ask other people who do your sort of work who their accountant is, because specialist knowledge and experience can save much time as well as money.

Draw up your budget before you go to the accountant, and be prepared for him to think of a lot more that hadn't crossed your mind. For instance:

* **Cost of accountant or lawyer.**
* **Cost of premises,** including rent, rates, heating, decorating, light, cleaning.
* **Cost of equipment:** furniture, floor coverings, desks, delivery vehicle, machinery.
* **Cost of telephone and postage:** stationery, photostatting, etc.
* **Cost of insurance** Don't forget to insure for loss of profits in case of fire, flood or theft, which could hold up your business. Also insure premises, stock, equipment, employer's liability. Ask your insurance agent's advice about insurance.
* **Staff salaries.**
* **Cost of stock.**
* **Promotional cost:** cards, catalogues, photographs, brochures, direct mail, advertising and public relations if you have to entertain.
* **Tax:** VAT and otherwise. Also National Insurance. Tax rules change regularly: always consult an accountant to clarify your obligations.

Remember that those seductive 'justifiable expenses' *are still paid for by you out of your money*, not by the Inland Revenue. If you pay for something that is a tax-deductible business expense, IT DOESN'T COST YOU NOTHING: you're *still* paying with your money. How-

STARTING YOUR OWN BUSINESS

ever, you don't pay tax on that money and, as a result, you reduce your tax bill.

Should you need them, you might have a *financial adviser* and a *legal adviser* who are in no way connected with your accountancy firm. The financial adviser should have no control over cash and no self-interest, and he should work for a fee on an hourly basis, like a lawyer. You should define your objectives to your accountant, who should then advise you to set up your bookkeeping system in a suitable manner.

The *bookkeeper* keeps the money records and *the accountant* checks that the bookkeeper is doing this correctly. If you want someone to check on the accountant, you get another accountant to *audit* (double check) the accounts, which, of course, costs twice as much and normally isn't necessary.

Your accountant shouldn't do the bookkeeping (because then how can he check on himself?) or have any spending power. (Accountants have been known to empty the bank account and fly to South America.) The accountant should have no relationship with the bookkeeper (so they don't take off to Buenos Aires together) or with your *manager* if you have one. Before you hire a manager, read all about 'The con men' (p. 345).

To give anyone else power to sign your cheques can be a dangerous act. Don't do it, however plausible the reason. (If you are abroad, get cheques for signing sent to you by courier.)

WHERE TO GO FOR HELP

Everyone who's in business would like someone who doesn't cost a fortune to advise her how to operate more efficiently and profitably. In fact, there's a lot of available help and advice.

The Consumers' Association with Hodder and Stoughton have published two very useful books: *Earning Money at*

Home has ideas of what you might do, and *Starting Your Own Business* gives practical advice.

To the person starting in business, many business words and phrases are puzzling. *The Penguin Dictionary of Commerce* by Michael Greener (published by Penguin Books) is an excellent and fascinating small reference book that defines business terms. It starts with 'Able-bodied seaman' ('strictly one who has served three years before the mast, at least one of them in a trading vessel'). It ends with 'zero-rated VAT'.

Through the Department of Employment and the Manpower Services Commission the government runs several schemes to aid people setting up, or who already have, their own small business. The **Small Firms Service** provides free information on a wide variety of small-business problems and provides free counselling by experienced businessmen and women who can give sound practical, impartial and confidential advice on your project. Your questions might be about money, premises, production or marketing – nothing is too simple to ask them. I know a hairdresser who recently set up her first business and found this service comforting, friendly and invaluable. This service also gives advice on government schemes to encourage small businesses. Contact the service by dialling 100 and ask for Freefone Enterprise.

The **Enterprise Allowance Scheme** will provide some financial help during the first year that you are working for yourself. The idea is that you shouldn't lose out (because you no longer qualify for *unemployment* or *income support*) by taking the plunge to set yourself up in business. Only people receiving either of those benefits and who have been out of work for eight weeks can join this scheme.

Applicants must also have £1,000 to invest in their business – or be able to raise it by loan or overdraft. The other condition is that you mustn't start the business *before* you apply.

Throughout the year you can take advantage of free advisory sessions. Contact your local Job Centre and ask for a *Guide to the Enterprise Allowance* booklet.

The **Loan-Guarantee Scheme** (contact your bank manager) and the **Business Expansion Scheme** (contact the Inland Revenue, your accountant or the Small Firms Service) are schemes designed to make it easier for you to borrow money. New and existing small businesses qualify. (My hairdresser friend had a loan-guarantee scheme.)

The Manpower Services Commission also runs two training courses, the **Business Enterprise Programme** and the **Private Enterprise Programme**. The first is an introductory seven-day course for people who are thinking of setting up a business; the second is a series of seminars for those who have already started and need more help in certain areas. Get more information about both from the MSC Training Division.

There is also the **Woman's Enterprise Development Agency** at Aston Science Park, Love Lane, Aston Triangle, Birmingham B7 4BJ, which gives advice to new and existing businesses.

WHAT ARE YOU WORTH?

Probably a lot more than you realize. When you are calculating what you are worth, draw three columns on the right-hand side of the page. There are three different ways to value your assets and all are useful to you for money-making decisions.

1 **Historic value** This is the original cost of any item, which is used in order to balance the accounts. *Example*: In 1985 a telephone answering machine cost you £X.

2 **Replacement value** This is what it would cost you to replace any item, such as your telephone answering machine. A new machine loses its purchase price value as soon as you buy it (because it then acquires second-hand resale value), but what it is worth to *you* from then on is its replacement value. By 1990 the machine might cost you £2X to replace. I always insure for replacement value.

3 **Resale value** This is what you can get for flogging your 1985 answering machine in 1990, and that sum may be half £X. Resale value is important because if you are calculating how much you really are worth, you must use resale value – the price you'll get for it.

In professional accounts, there is often a note to the accounts giving resale value, in order to clarify the true position. For instance a property may have been purchased in 1970 but by 1990 it is worth twenty times its historic value.

An accountant can advise you on depreciation of assets, which will be shown on your balance sheet.

You can calculate the worth of a company in the same way as your personal worth. Your worth is the total of:

* Any money owed to you that isn't a bad debt.
* Any cash.
* Any money in the bank.
* Any insurance policies, life insurance.
* Any pension calculated at its current value (how much you've paid in).
* The resale value of any assets.
* Any shares.

Add that up and then deduct any money that you owe (such as loans, interest on loans, creditors [unpaid bills] and accountant's fees). The remaining figure is what you are worth at the time you do this

Profit and loss account

	A £	B £	C % Profit
Sales Product X	0		
Product Y	200		
Total	200	+ 200	
Cost of sales Stock at start	nil		
Purchases for X	0		
Purchases for Y	200		
Less: stock at close X	0		
stock at close Y	50		
	150	− 150	
Gross profit margin		= 50	= 25
Overhead expenses			
Heat and light	2		
Telephone	2		
Advertising	1		
Salaries	5		
Wages	4		
Bank interest	1		
Bank charges	1		
Rent	5		
Sundry expenses	2		
Petrol	2		
Stationery	2		
Postage	3		
Total:	30	− 30	
Net profit margin (before tax)		= 20	= 10

calculation. Basically, the balance sheet of a business does the same thing.

YOUR BASIC ACCOUNTS

Your accounts consist basically of three pieces of paper: a profit and loss account, a source and application of funds statement, and a balance sheet.

The profit and loss account

The profit and loss account for the year shows exactly what it says. It is basically about how much it cost you to make the goods and sell the goods, and whether the difference between these two figures was a loss or a profit. Look at the simple example above. Cushion sales were £200. Cost of sales was £150. Overhead expenses were £30. Total costs were therefore £150 + £30 = £180. This gives a profit of £20, or 10 per cent of the sale price of each cushion sold.

The source and application of funds

This shows in summarized form the source of all income received during the year and exactly where it went. As can be seen in the example on p. 376, it also tracks the final profit from the profit and loss account and shows what eventually

Source and application of funds for the
year ended 19—

	£	£
Sources		
Net profit for the year		20
Adjustments for items not involving the movement of funds		
Depreciation *		o
Foreign exchange profit/loss		o
Profit on sale of fixed assets		o
Movements in working capital		
Increase in stock	(50)	
Increase in debtors	(30)	
Increase in creditors	70	
	——	
	(10)	(10)
Funds provided by operations		10
Other sources		
Bank loan received	4,000	
Shareholders' funds	10	
	——	——
	4,010	4,010
Application		
Purchase of motor vehicle		(4,000)
		——
Net increase in net liquid funds		20
		==
Being . . .		
. . . Increase in cash at bank		20
		==

* Note 1. No depreciation allowed for van, as it was purchased towards the end of the year. Depreciation will be charged in next year's accounts.

happened to the profit and how the profit fits into the final cash position. (For instance you might have made £50,000 profit, but it isn't in the bank – because you bought a brand new truck, repaid the bank loan and bought a new warehouse, for which you paid a 10 per cent deposit.)

It shows cash at the bank when you started your business was nil.

Cash at the end of the year was £20, so you increased funds by £20.

It shows that you took out a bank loan for £4,000 to give you capital to purchase the motor vehicle.

The balance sheet

A balance sheet is the last thing you have to worry about in the early days of a business. When the time comes, if you don't already know, ask someone (such as your accountant) to show you how to

Balance sheet as at year-end

	£	£
Fixed assets		
Motor vehicle	4,000	
Less depreciation		4,000
Current assets		
Stock	50	
Debtors	30	
Cash at bank and in hand	20	
	100	
Creditors, amounts falling due within one year		
Bank loan	4,000	
Trade creditors	60	
Accruals	10	
	4,070	
Net current liabilities		3,970
Total assets less current liabilities		30
Capital and reserves		
Your own funds		10
Profit and loss account		20
		30

read a balance sheet. They can look alarming if you don't understand them – *but don't pretend that you do if you don't*: you'll make it worse for yourself in the long run. A balance sheet is a sort of bird's-eye view of a business on a given date (often the end of your trading year) and to produce it is a job for a qualified accountant. It shows your financial position and gives a summary of your assets and liabilities, your capital and profit and loss.

To summarize (which is what a balance sheet does), the balance sheet states the following:

Assets − Liabilities
= Capital + Profit − Loss

It tells you the exact worth of the business at a certain date, and analyses

the make-up of that worth (normally on a historic value basis).

So, for example, your balance sheet at the beginning of the year would be as follows:

Balance Sheet at 1 January 19—	£
Fixed assets: motor vehicle	4,000
Current assets: cash	10
Total assets	4,010
Creditors: bank loan	(4,000)
Total assets less liabilities	10
Capital: your own funds	10

This shows that at the start of the business, the business was worth £10, which you had invested. If the motor vehicle was sold for £4,000 and you repaid the bank loan of £4,000 on day 1, before interest had been incurred, you would have been left with your original £10.

After the business has been running for a year, the balance sheet has altered.

The example on p. 377 shows all the assets of the company and all the debts of the company. The trading profit figure of £20 is taken from the final total shown on the profit and loss account (a disappointing amount after making all those cushions). Also taken from the profit and loss account is the figure for stock.

Taken to the source and application of funds statement are the final profit, increase or decrease in debtors and creditors, cash at bank, your funds invested and the bank loan.

You now see that we have on the balance sheet the fixed assets and capital and reserves (profit is called 'reserves').

Notes to the accounts are what they say. They generally follow the accounts to explain particular items in the accounts or the way the accountant has treated the item.

Whatever and however sketchy your accounting system don't get behind with it. If you've had no bookkeeping or office experience, you might go to evening classes or get help from your Small Firms Information Centre. Check the address in your local telephone book.

Inflation accounting

If the materials and labour for a cushion cost you £X and you sell that cushion for £2X, have you made 100 per cent profit? Yes, so long as the materials and labour for your next cushion also cost £X. But if, because of inflation, the materials and labour for the next cushion cost £2X, then you have *made no profit* unless you put your prices up accordingly.

Bear this in mind when you price your cushions. You might like to include in your costing a percentage for the current year's inflation.

It is not normal UK accounting practice to account for inflation, because nobody could agree on the necessary complicated accounting procedures.

Finally . . . if you really want to understand professional company accounts, read *Understanding Company Financial Statements* by R. H. Parker (published by Penguin Books). It tells you how you can glean information from the accounts of a business, how you can find out whether a company is stable, how you can tell if its dividends show a fair yield, how you know if it's as profitable as can be expected and other information. I picked up this book after a hard day in the office . . . and, absorbed, was still reading it at midnight.

There are two sorts of crisis: there is the personal one, such as the loss of a job or of a loved one by death or divorce, or the communal one, such as a motorway threat to a village, or a war. But there always seems to be some sort of crisis.

There's nothing like being personally machine-gunned on your way home from school (as I was during the Second World War) to make you realize that someone you've never even met is actually – amazingly – unreasonably out to get you, and that you had better do something about it fast. But it's much harder to be wiped out (emotionally, physically or financially) than you ever suspected.

Obviously what you gain from a crisis is self-knowledge and greater independence and self-confidence, since your own resourcefulness has now been tested. You also gain the knowledge that when the time comes to face all the dreaded nightmares, they're not nearly as bad as you've imagined.

Once out the other side of the tunnel, a sort of survivor syndrome sets in. You have come through. Nothing gives you such added strength and confidence as dealing with a disaster and landing on your feet.

CRISIS AVERSION

You can sometimes prepare for material mishaps, or prudently ward them off or deal with them in practical ways. You can, of course, be *over*-prepared; you can have an atomic fall-out shelter in your garden and buy two of everything in case one breaks, in which case you'll have half as much money and twice as many things to look after, worry about and insure, but for disasters that affect your ego and your emotions, you can only prepare a broad psychological strategy. The first thing to realize is that only YOU can mentally prepare yourself for great personal wounds and losses, and you'd also better face up to the fact that in life they are bound to happen.

SURVIVING A CRISIS

When personal disaster strikes, you probably need sympathy and practical help; but there is a distinct possibility (especially if everyone else is also swimming for the lifeboats) that the only person who is always interested in you, and able to provide you with sustained help, is YOURSELF.

Don't think 'somebody ought to do something about it' or 'the government should see to it'. Start thinking in terms of self-reliance: what *you* can do and what *you* can't do – because that may be all you can count on. Whatever your crisis, force yourself to look cheerful. Shakespeare said: 'There is nothing either good or bad, but thinking makes it so,' and Napoleon added that 'the moral is to material as three to one'. I would also say that the quickest face-lift is a smile. Go on – try it, just for today SMILE and try to find something good instead of something bad in every new situation.

What you can do

Look on the bright side, because there always *is* a bright side, however minor. If your husband disappears, at least you won't ever again have to watch *Match of the Day*.

Occasional depression is the reverse side of freedom.

Face your crisis and don't hide your head in the sand, ostrich-wise. Don't cross your fingers and hope for the best. Face what it is here and prepare for what might be coming.

Be constructively selfish. Think of yourself first. If you're not healthy and functioning efficiently, you can't look after your family or do your job. Ignore

accusations of selfishness, egotism or ruthlessness from those who resent that you won't do what they (selfishly) want you to do. The need for self-preservation forces everyone to be selfish.

Don't hope to change anyone or their attitudes: it will probably be an exhausting waste of time.

Don't hate anyone: it's a destructive waste of energy. Try to ignore that person and try to make sure that you are no longer vulnerable to him or her.

Recognize your practical and emotional limitations. If you can't control your temper, look for ways to avoid losing it. Don't allow yourself to be tempted or bullied into any emotionally upsetting situations that you can avoid.

Don't hope. Hope is dangerous if it is over-optimistic, and can stop you viewing your situation realistically.

Try not to worry. It can't do any good and it's often only a habit. ('Your mother's a worrier.')

Don't go on about it. People may get bored or embarrassed. So keep it to yourself.

Don't be self-pitying. You don't need pity; you need clear thought and action.

> Thought must be the harder; the heart the keener.
> Courage must be greater as our strength grows less.

A fighting Anglo-Saxon chieftain said that; whoever he was, he sounds like a survivor.

Make allowances for your weaknesses. It's unrealistic to give up smoking to save money now if that's the only thing that takes your mind off your problem. Just make sure you don't start smoking or smoking more.

Count your friends. Whatever your crisis, it is important to realize that it has happened before. Trust your true friends to understand and sympathize, although it may not be within their power to help in practical matters. Don't mind asking for simple practical help when it is needed. At the worst, they can only say no. Some people in this world *are* selfish, but it *helps* most people to give help when it's in their power. Those who have been through hard times are glad to pay back the help they've had from others. This is the way the help chain works.

Don't ask too much of your rights. The less you rely upon them, the less you risk disappointment – when a few pounds takes months to come through or someone else's inefficiency negates your claim.

Count your resources. Your money, time, talent, possessions and family help. Write them down in a list. Mine started with 'mother' and ended with 'continental quilt'. I looked at this long list (there were other things in between) and thought 'How dare you feel sorry for yourself?'

Once at a low point in my life a medical specialist asked me, 'Haven't you anything to look forward to?' Wondering how I was going to pay him, I shook my head. 'Do you have children?' he asked. I nodded. 'I have only one child,' he said, 'and he is mentally defective.'

I returned home to a pile of bills now feeling not only depressed but ashamed of it. Panic and fear of the beige envelopes made me feel stupid, lethargic and rooted to the ground. My mother made a two-hour trip just to sit with me while I paid my bills, knowing that each cheque put me in deeper debt to the bank. My mother couldn't pay my bills, but she sat there, giving me moral support, then she made her two-hour return trip.

Get expert advice. A survivor must be practical. Assess your immediate problems, write them down and seek objective advice to clarify your situation. No one can think clearly when disaster strikes. You might need to visit a specialist, solicitor or accountant.

A solicitor once wrote to me, 'I deal with an awful lot of divorces . . . I see women particularly when they are feeling that life has nothing to offer them . . . but I know that in three months' time that same woman will be telling me what she intends to do with her life, rather than crying because she does not know what to do.'

You must also realize that you might be in a state of shock, which is a physical illness. Don't hesitate to go to a doctor if you have any unusual symptoms and be sure to tell him the whole problem, not just the physical symptoms. Again, don't be proud or ashamed, or feel that you are wasting his time. He's heard it all a million times before and your problems will obviously be treated as confidential. To pride yourself on *not* going to the doctor or to think you are making a fuss might harm you and might impair your efficiency for dealing with your crisis.

What you should tell yourself if you are depressed for good reason is: '*One day I will get over this.*'

Make your own decisions. Although specialists may be useful to analyse a situation and suggest solutions, they cannot run your life for you. Once your choices are clarified, use your common sense to make your own decisions. Then force yourself to be pessimistic, to look for the snags in the arrangements and face them. Don't opt out because you don't understand your position. Make your adviser explain it all again until you *do* understand it, and so can be responsible for deciding which path you want to take. Be prepared to be responsible for your own decisions. Life is a risk. Nothing is certain in this world and there is no guaranteed security, financial, intellectual or emotional. Security lies in your own self-reliance to deal with the problems of life. You will make some right decisions and some wrong ones. Pay the penalty for the wrong ones, cut your losses and start again.

DOWN WITH SUPERWOMAN!

Make a rule *never to take a decision if you are upset*. Wait at least twenty-four hours until you can think more clearly. Also wait twenty-four hours before sending an emotional letter. Then tear it up.

THE ADVANTAGES OF A CRISIS

A crisis can be a blessing in disguise if it makes you stop and take a long look at your life, and then cut out the clutter.

Cut out waste. Don't waste money, resources, time or friendship. You can now stop feeling obliged to do things just because others expect them from you. There are now plenty of reasons and excuses.

There are a lot of things in life that you needn't do. You don't have to cook a hot lunch on Sunday or return the Jones's invitation, or attend parties if they make you nervous, or functions if they bore you.

Don't waste time. And if you've suddenly got more of it than ever before, try to look upon it as a life-enriching bonus. If you've wished for more time in the past, now's your time to use it.

Use that time for more creative leisure, active sports and hobbies, doing things *with* your children instead of *for* them, or taking an inexpensive, stimulating course. Think of something rewarding to do and start DOING IT NOW.

Stop wanting things. Are you wasting time, effort and money doing things and buying luxuries that you don't really need? After all, your grandparents got along without a freezer or video recorder. Try switching off the sound on the TV commercials for a start and then start trying to tell the difference between a wish and a want. A wish is not a true need, but an artificially stimulated status symbol. In other words, unnecessary.

When recovering from a crisis, you should be somewhat like Hercule Poirot

solving a murder. In trying to figure out What Went Wrong, you can sort out, analyse and examine all the clues (e.g., has anything like this ever happened to you before?) and separate the outside causes of calamity from those that may have come from within yourself. (If in doubt, charge them up to yourself.)

If your disaster involves guilt and self-hatred, however far-fetched and pointless ('But I thought he knew how to swim'), then you should see your family doctor.

If your disaster involves your pride (loss of job or lover), accept the fact that your ego may have taken a terrible blow, that it's just had major surgery and needs time to recover from the wound.

A main problem may be to restore your eroded self-esteem. Just how do you get the gilt back on the gingerbread? Family, friends and lovers can help, but it's sometimes easier to seek objective, professional advice (and I don't mean an astrologer) as well as love and sympathy.

Without being self-pitiful or making excuses for yourself, perhaps it's simply time to be nicer to yourself? Perhaps no one else has been nice to you for some time?

If so, prepare a few little treats for yourself. Buy a stack of paperbacks, buy yourself some flowers, go on a boat trip, *get outside the front door*.

It's good therapy to get involved with something outside yourself. Try working for the community chest or the local cancer drive or your church and you'll not only be helping people, but also you'll maybe see how minor your troubles are compared with those of others! And you'll also find out that casting a little bread upon the waters *often* brings back caviare on toast, just so long as you never count on it.

COMMUNITY CRISIS

Share your troubles and share the solutions to them, whether it's grouping together to buy groceries in bulk or passing on a good recipe. All over the country people may be having the same problems. Pool your resources. Start lending things, the way people did in the war.

Advertise in your local tobacconist's right now for a swap baby-sitter; baby-sitter-swapping is *far* more liberating than wife-swapping. If one person answers the ad, you can take turns to sit for each other. If two or three people answer it, you might as well be a bulk baby-sitter if you're stuck doing it anyway. You could each of you look after three babies a morning, or afternoon or day, and have the rest of the week free. Wouldn't that be nice for a bit? If more than one person answers the advertisement, start a rota.

Don't wait for someone else – *you* do it. Nothing gets started unless somebody starts it, and if nobody else seems to have thought of it, why shouldn't that someone be you?

Today we are threatened on all sides by environmental, financial, industrial and political crises. However, you aren't the Prime Minister or the President of the USA. Let those people continue to shoulder all *their* responsibilities. What *you* can do is mind your own business, check the store cupboard and the hot-water bottles (crises are always cold) and start digging an allotment. Voltaire said, '*Il faut cultiver notre jardin*,' and I'm sure that if that sensible man were alive today he'd tell us to turn it over to chemical-free vegetables.

MIND!

R.I.P.

She made people laugh

YOUR IDENTIKIT

Who are you?

You'll need a notebook and pencil for half an hour. First the facts. The first information that you fill in on a biography sheet (CV) when applying for a job: name, age, occupation. Add any qualifications.

Other people's CVs leave me deeply depressed because they always sound so much better qualified than me. To cheer myself up, I read my own CV. I do not recognize this paragon. Feeling guilty, I again read my CV. Certainly, it's true but ... it doesn't feel like the real me. Everyone has 'bad' and 'good' parts but when writing their CVs, everyone carefully leaves out the bad bits. The picture that's painted on a CV is a masterly personal exercise in accentuating the positive. See yourself this way.

Do you know your own strengths?

Recognize all your strengths and list them. Not only the sort of things that go on a CV (O levels, A levels, swimming certificates and any other recognized qualifications). Mothers have other experience, which doesn't provide a certificate but which may be more essential for survival: I know nobody who has an A level in Tact or Ability To Calm People Down, but these are qualities that every chairman needs.

In order to know your own strengths, spend a pleasant five minutes remembering past compliments – things other people have told you – that pleased you. Write them down.

Where are you vulnerable?

Most people are blind to their weaknesses: after all, if they knew that what they were doing was detrimental, then they

384

probably wouldn't do it. On the other hand, what *you* think of as a weakness may be part of a strength. I consider impatience a strength because it speeds up performance; gullibility, a disadvantage, proceeds from honesty, a virtue. The people who love you and live with you can see your weak areas more clearly than you can – *so ask them*, if you want to strengthen these areas. Expect to stagger under the load that will be hurled at you if you ask the wrong dearest: never ask a brother or a sister. A mother knows you best and tells you gently. But whoever paid any attention to what Mother said?

The irritating thing about hoping to learn from experience is that even when you recognize your weak areas, you can't seem to strengthen them. It's better to confront the weak areas that we all have, but if you can't, then try to avoid them. If you're impatient, don't do careful jobs when you are in a hurry.

If you persist in falling in love with the same sort of wrong man – a bully, a weakling, a parasite – check whether *you* subconsciously invite this. (Twice is a coincidence, three times is a pattern.) If so, discuss it with your doctor.

Your attitude to life

Do you feel proud of yourself? Probably not. A Western upbringing tends to emphasize the negative (*'Don't* do that, you *naughty* girl'), which detracts from your feeling of self-worth. A child then focuses on the need to please others and loses touch with her own rights and, therefore, her own worth. To please yourself is VITAL.

A child's opinion of herself is of primary importance to her relationships. Children who are not treated with respect and love often grow up to have a poor opinion of themselves and lack self-worth. Such children grow up into victims. (The ones who pick the bullies.)

If you have a low opinion of yourself, this isn't modesty, this isn't a virtue, and this isn't a good excuse for not doing better. It is a pity. Compulsive modesty is an exercise in self-denigration.

Life has always been a struggle; human beings have always needed survival skills to survive; the strongest survival tool is a positive attitude.

A positive attitude is energetic and life-enhancing; a negative attitude drains energy and life from you. Try always to twist negative thinking into positive thinking. For instance, if you're about to take an exam or a driving test, try seeing it as an exciting challenge.

What people notice about a positive person is cheerfulness, good nature and concern for other people. Pessimists who are depressed, lack enthusiasm and show a total disregard for other people's feelings don't have many friends. Everyone avoids sour apples.

A person with a positive attitude to life concentrates on the best parts and tries to accept and integrate the bad bits of himself. A positive person enjoys the sight and smell of a rose; a negative person points out the thorns.

A positive attitude needn't cost you a penny – it's acquired by simply deciding to have one.

Don't forget past failures – remember them so that you don't repeat them – but there's no point in dwelling on them. Like guilt, shame and regret, they are negative feelings that serve no purpose whatsoever. Don't waste your time re-enacting the past by watching the video-tape replay in your mind. Those actions are in the past and you cannot change the past. Be positive. Live in the present.

A positive person isn't nice only to other people, she's nice to herself. So cut out the self-criticism and, as you brush your teeth at night, think of something positive that you did during the day, rather than dwelling on the things that went wrong. See yourself as somebody who can *do* things, whether it's baking cakes, writing books or both.

Did you go to the right school?

Most of the things we do in life are work. A good school teaches a child to *enjoy* work; the child doesn't get a sneaky feeling that he shouldn't be enjoying art, because it's a lesson and lessons are work and work isn't fun.

Work can be fun and fun can be work. Ask the nearest mountaineer if climbing is hard work. Ask the nearest dedicated ballerina whether two hours' practice *every day* is fun. Life is not divided into work and play – they overlap. How you behave when working will affect how you behave when playing, and vice versa; the enjoyment of life depends on how you handle *everything* you do.

Most work, however absorbing, has its system-support parts – the boring, necessary parts of the job. Most work also involves responsibility: you can choose to do the job properly or you can do it sloppily.

Men tend to measure their work performance by how much money it brings in. Women, when choosing a job, tend to think more about their quality of life and are influenced by whether or not they think they will enjoy the work; both measure their performance by the approval it generates.

If you don't have a positive attitude to your work, you won't have a positive attitude to your life, because you can't switch BEING POSITIVE on and off. You are either a positive person or you aren't – the choice is yours.

HOW TO DO THINGS WELL

If you do everything as well as you can, you will get into the habit of doing things as well as you can. If you are sloppy

about, say, washing-up and do not scrape mustard off the underside of plates, then you will acquire the habit of being sloppy. If you decide to wash-up with a radio switched on, a dreary job takes on a different aspect – because you have positively decided to eliminate the boring aspect of the job. Listening to Radio 4 while washing-up can be almost as restful as knitting.

Note: Don't train a baby to be neat too early. Babies like making a mess – in every way. Potty training that is too early can result in a reaction later – a deliberately messy adult.

WHAT QUALITIES DO YOU VALUE?

Do you value these qualities in other people? Mark them on a 1–10 scale. An angel gets 10 out of 10 for everything. An incompetent Spanish plumber might score a 0 on every count.

* **Honesty**, including bus fare morality, which is thinking it's OK to steal a ride from an organization without a face.
* **Truthfulness**, including prevarication, which is lying to yourself.
* **Reliability** Doing the things that you said you would do when you said you would do them, even if it's inconvenient or when later you wish you hadn't said them.
* **Punctuality** – a subdivision of reliability.
* **Charity** (not to be confused with buying a poppy.) A charitable nature includes kindness, generosity and sympathy. Incidentally, a mean adult had a 'mean' mother.

Now rate yourself on a 1–10 scale. If you rate a virtue as highly desirable in other people, but score a low mark for yourself, you have a double standard. Why should you expect a Spanish plumber* to be more reliable and truthful than you are? Why should you expect other people to treat you better than you would treat them? Avoid elastic morality, which conveniently stretches to fit *your* requirements.

If you work out your own standards of morality, to replace those that were forcibly fed to you when you were little, you will know how *you* expect yourself to behave. Deciding on your own moral guidelines will stop any unnecessary guilt and strengthen your character. You will not be living up to someone else's expectations, but to standards that *you* have decided are reasonable.

WHAT WOULD YOU LIKE TO SEE CARVED ON YOUR TOMBSTONE?

Write fewer than six words without thinking about it. Some responses I've had include:

> She made people happy.
> She was a good mother.
> She made people laugh.

Your tombstone quickly clarifies how you would most like to be seen by other people and it is probably what you strive hardest to do or be. For you, this is one of life's top priorities.

YOUR OBITUARY

Next, write your newspaper obituary. Allow yourself six sentences at most.

Here's what my friend Nicole wrote: 'She was generous and kind, reliable, conscientious and trustworthy. Her son, Marlo, attributes his success to his original and thoughtful upbringing by a mother who developed her own talents while encouraging his.'

Compare your obituary to your CV. Are your recognized qualifications (such as O levels) on it? They shouldn't be. Qualifications such as these, which are a means to an end, can get out of proportion in the panorama of your life. Your obituary shows the qualities that you have, that you value and that you strive to improve. These are your strengths.

---

* Anyone who has experienced problems with Spanish plumbers will agree that this isn't xenophobia.

Skip this section if your self-confidence never falters and you are entirely happy with the Real You (which is your whole self).

Most people are short on self-confidence, especially if they are starting something new and different and on their own. This is only natural, whether you're a child starting at a new school or the newly elected Prime Minister walking into Number 10. Suddenly, you feel uncertain and wonder whether you're good enough. Your self-confidence falters.

You firmly remind yourself that you were voted Prime Minister because other people had confidence in you, because of your previous record. You think about *that* – and step firmly forward into Number 10.

In moments of uncertainty you need to clearly see your self-image (which is you and your record) and to approve of what you see.

What you've read so far in this book has given you the opportunity to analyse your character, your situation, your strengths, your limitations, your assets and your ambitions. Now is the time to check the accuracy of your self-image – that what you see is the Real You.

THE CRITICS

If you care too much what other people think, you will be at best self-conscious and at worst a doormat. Someone else's opinion may be based on inaccuracies, misconceptions and lack of information.

Listening to accurate criticism can help develop your talents and strengthen your self-control. Listening to inaccurate criticism can shrivel your self-esteem. Too much criticism too early can result in a child's loss of self-confidence: a victim of unfair criticism is driven to high levels of performance activity in order to seek approval.

Always remember that criticism is one person's opinion, and it may not be accurate or true.

Criticism is either requested or not requested, fair or unfair. If it's fair, it may be useful; if it's unfair, don't waste your life over it. Dismiss it as malice and ignore it. Distract your mind by concentrating on producing another success.

Before paying any attention to criticism, ask yourself whether it was:

List 1	List 2
Requested	Not requested
Kind	Unkind
Positive	Negative
Specific	Vague
Fair	Unfair

Pay attention only to those whose criticism falls in List 1. Never pay any attention to someone with a judgmental attitude, who behaves as if he is God Almighty – because he isn't.

I don't read my press cuttings, in case they upset my judgement, but I listen very carefully to the few people I have *chosen* as my critics.

What you should ask a critic for is an objective assessment of your performance. Having asked for criticism, you should listen carefully to your critic. Constructive criticism at an early stage can save you a lot of time, especially if you're attempting to do something in a field for which you are not suited. There may be good reasons why you shouldn't be attempting to run a four-minute mile.

However well intended and however constructive, criticism is more likely to be acted upon if it is served between a sandwich of praise: this part was good, that part could perhaps be tried differently, the other part was excellent.

Don't think of school reports only as a guide to what a child is good at; a school report may be a guide to what a teacher is bad at.

All criticism is a matter of opinion and if it is based on inaccuracy or gossip (there's no smoke without a liar), it is unreliable criticism.

Derogatory criticism *behind your back* almost always happens because the other person feels inferior and dependent on you. The clinical name for this is *contemptuous devaluation*, as in, 'Of course, he couldn't run the office for five minutes without *me*; he's hopelessly disorganized.'

Constant criticism (especially marital) is negative and can be bad for your health. You feel low, then depressed and then possibly resentful. There is no such thing as being cruel to be kind; these people are cruel to be cruel.

If you receive vague criticism, a lot of time can be wasted running around in circles wondering what you did wrong. If another person is so inadequate that he can't clearly explain what you did wrong, then you can't do much about putting it right and you can't treat his accusation seriously. So always ask for chapter and verse if somebody hurls a critical bomb at you (what exactly is he complaining about? When exactly did you do it?). Otherwise, logically, you can do nothing but ignore the accusation and see it only as an attempt to hurt you.

In life you're going to meet some people who like you and some people who don't. Don't pay much attention to people who don't like you or you risk building up your anxiety. The person who can see yourself best is you – if you make a conscious effort to do this. (Most people don't.) If you like yourself, how others feel about you is their problem.

Anyone who is a success, whether it's for winning a school race or a Hollywood Oscar, may well be the victim of unfair criticism. Envy and malice are the price of success in all areas of life. Anyone who is successful (in however minor a way) has to learn to handle criticism, and this can be difficult to begin with.

Aim for self-approval, which leads to greater self-esteem and less dependency on other people's opinions. Don't waste time or agony on what people think about you. You cannot be responsible for other people's interpretations of your actions and there is nothing you can do about it. If you catch yourself at it, firmly twist your thinking into deciding what *your* opinion is of the other person. You'll be amazed how fast this gets the situation in perspective.

YOUR SELF-IMAGE

Like the separate segments of an orange, you can clearly see and assess your advantages and disadvantages, and you have just done this in 'Your Identikit'. However, many people cannot see the whole orange; instead, they see themselves as a wizened little tangerine. It's important to think well of yourself, whether or not anyone else does. (They might be wrong.) Having an accurate self-image leads to self-respect, which is a very private thing, and very precious.

A person's self-image may well have been eroded by years of criticism – by her parents and teachers, by her nearest and dearest, who almost from birth have told her what to do and what to think. She may lack the confidence to develop her own personality, remaining childishly dependent because she has been taught to respond submissively and do as she is told: she is not used to making decisions by herself and has been discouraged from doing so.

A person may also underestimate herself as a complete package because she zooms in and worries about her weak areas and takes the things she does well for granted (doesn't *everyone* make perfect omelettes, speak French and type like a concert pianist?).

Don't have a magnified view of other people's abilities and a shrunken view of your own, because this leads to insecurity.

Careers officers say that low self-image is a problem of many women who are trying to re-enter the work force: they are too apologetic about their abilities, lack belief in themselves and generally hang back. This was certainly the experience of a friend of mine who runs a firm of financial consultants. Some years ago he was looking for a partner. He put an advertisement in a paper, giving full details of the job, including the generous salary. He had over fifty replies – all of them from men, none of whom was good enough. Someone advised him to put the ad in again with a lower salary, which he did. This time he got even more replies – most of them from women, one of whom he chose.

Psychologist Abraham Maslow wrote that people who are happy with themselves find it easier to give love to other people. The more unsatisfied needs and hungers a person has, the more difficult it is to be concerned about other people and the less love one has to give.

If you can't approve of and love yourself, you won't be able to love anyone else well. Jesus didn't teach 'Love thy neighbour'; he said, 'Love thy neighbour *as thyself.*' Whatever your religion, this is why you should look after yourself and see to your own needs: if *you* aren't in good shape, how can you look after all the other people who depend on you?

Did your mother spend your childhood telling you to be unselfish? Then before you left home did she tell you that if you didn't look after yourself, nobody else would? That, in a nutshell, is the problem of deciding when you should be selfish and when you shouldn't.

The secret of successful sex, we are told, is being unselfish. But of course this works only as long as *both* people are. Successful sex is a mixture of selfishness and unselfishness, of knowing what the other person needs but also recognizing what *you* need, and being able to ask for it (unless you're in bed with a mind-reader).

On a scale of 1–10 a well-balanced woman should rate 5 for selfishness, self-centredness and self-indulgence. It's as tedious to live with a too-unselfish person (a martyr) as it is with a greedy tyrant. You should be as unselfish as you can afford – and no more.

DO YOU KNOW ANY DOORMATS?

Doormats are people who give away more than they can afford. Doormat behaviour in women may well be the result of submitting to unfair or harsh parental discipline or violence in childhood.

Doormat behaviour starts in a child who timidly suppresses her natural angry reactions to lack of love and care, because she believes that her parents will withhold their love if she expresses any negative feelings. This child feels inferior, unlovable and defeated; she suppresses all positive, lively tendencies – such as curiosity, get-up-and-go, trust in her own judgement and sticking up for herself. Her self-respect is gradually eroded and then, stripped of her self-confidence, she lives in a permanent, underlying state of humiliation, of which she is unaware.

Nature's bodily response to humiliation is similar to that which occurs when a person is in physical danger: the body prepares itself for maximum reaction – the choice of fight, flight or submission. The stress of constant submission and the suppression of irritation or anger saps energy and can lead to chronic fatigue. A tired child who dare not openly defy her parents may instead defend herself by becoming ill.

In a situation where a self-assured person will refuse to do something and clearly say why, a person who can't say boo to a goose becomes ill and therefore *unable* to do it. Helplessness gives an

invalid a sort of negative power in response to a threat or demand: you can't make an ill person do the washing-up. Helplessness can also check aggressive tendencies in grown-up tyrants: it's socially unacceptable to wallop a child who's ill.

When the child becomes an adult, she *still* feels helpless, inadequate and a potential victim in a world where *everyone else* is entitled to the power and the glory, the money and the happiness. In addition, she feels resentful without realizing that this is the mildest possible expression of her suppressed rage. She may over-react to minor irritations but cower under major abuse.

Since a doormat has received only humiliating attention during childhood, she mistakes this for love in adult life. She is compulsively attracted to bullies – men who abuse her – and this is a variation of the battered wife syndrome.

Shyness stems from timidity, which stems from fear. The timid child can grow into a timid woman who deteriorates into a doormat, a little bit here and a little bit there.

A doormat still feels, and therefore acts, like the unappreciated child she once was. A doormat is a person who believes that she is at fault in *every* situation and that when something goes wrong, she is *always* to blame. Riddled with guilt, she apologizes endlessly and believes that she alone should be the one to solve any problem, because, in some way, she's responsible for it occurring. She feels that in order to consider herself worthwhile she must be 100 per cent competent, adequate and achieving in all possible areas – and, of course, this isn't possible.

A doormat may let her mate abuse her because she reckons that, in some way that she can't see (but *he* can), she must deserve abuse because she isn't coming up to his high standards – which are naturally more important than hers. She feels that he has the right to judge her, but she doesn't have the right to judge him. Of course this is nonsense.

Basically, doormats need love and approval from just about everyone in sight and at whatever cost to themselves; they need it so badly that it takes priority over all their other needs. But however much reassurance they get, it will never be enough to make them feel self-confident.

Loving and giving, gentle and sensitive, self-effacing and self-sacrificing, the doormat does for other people what she secretly wishes other people would do for her. A doormat finds it very difficult to ask outright for anything for herself. She pushes her own needs and dreams to one side in order to help other people reach the top.

The peace-loving doormat rarely loses her temper, but turns her anger and aggression inwardly on herself and blames herself (who else) for anything that goes wrong.

A doormat feels inferior because she shrinks her own self-image, she sees herself only as a wizened tangerine instead of a big juicy Jaffa orange. There's a bit of the doormat in all of us.

How do you stop these negative feelings that are the result of being shoved for so long into the humiliating position? You learn to say no.

CHANGING YOUR PATTERN

A cowed puppy isn't a well-trained good puppy. He is a bewildered puppy who no longer understands how people want him to react. He is cowed because of something that was done to him by another living being – perhaps he was kicked to provide someone else with sadistic pleasure. Whatever the reason, that puppy has been conditioned to a certain behaviour pattern.

All conditioning is physical, verbal or a mixture of both. We are all at the mercy of our early conditioning, and it is important that you should know what your early conditioning was, because it may still affect you.

Remember, twice is a coincidence, three times is a pattern. People never choose their powerful patterns and can rarely see a pattern in themselves unless it is pointed out.

No one can change their past, but by understanding the patterns of the past, it's possible to cope better with the present.

HOW TO BE THE REAL YOU

How nice are you? Perhaps too nice? A woman may *seem* nice when in fact she spends too much time pleasing others, because she doesn't have enough self-confidence to be *less* nice, if that is appropriate.

Being the REAL YOU is simply being yourself, not the person that would suit the other people you know. Often in order to do this, you have to be less nice. The meek will not inherit the Earth; the pushy people will grab it unless someone stands up to them.

In life you will be treated the way you show you *expect* to be treated. If you don't stand up for yourself, you will be pushed around and become a victim. In future make sure that what you want to get isn't changed into what other people want you to get, because you can't afford to attend to other people's wants at the expense of your own. Your aim is to stop other people making you dependent on their approval by stripping you of your self-esteem and making you rely on their judgement of you.

You can't have self-confidence unless you have good self-esteem. *Feeling* that you are a good person, a person of value who should therefore be respected, will gain respect for you from other people, which in turn will reinforce your self-confidence.

Unfortunately, no amount of reassurance will satisfy anybody with serious self-doubts; he will always need MORE reassurance and may need professional help.

Learn to say no.

Do you ever say yes when you want to say no – perhaps because you don't want to offend someone, because saying no might lower someone's opinion of you?

Being unable to say no can lead you into situations where you will lose your self-respect and allow other people to exploit you. Being unable to say no can distract you from your goals and it can lead to communication problems if, instead of saying no at the right times, you say yes and then allow your resentment to build up like a head of steam that suddenly explodes, to everyone's astonishment ('What did I *say*?').

What can you do?

1 *Practise* saying NO. Imagine that you're being asked a few unreasonable requests. Say no to all of them. Now imagine that you're being asked a few reasonable requests ('Can you tell me the way to the Post Office?'). Say no to all of them. (Like other people do to you.) Do not give reasons for saying no. Only children have to account to others.

Next time you want to say NO, say it. *Say nothing else.*

2 Picture yourself having a small argument with someone (you say the bread is stale, the shop assistant says it isn't). Having practised in your head, next time disagree with the shop assistant.

3 Build up slowly to more important disagreements with people who are more important to you than the shop assistant.

Choose one small area of your life and quietly start doing what *you* want to do in that area. If you always find yourself going to a football game when you want to go to a concert, or vice versa, then take yourself; be your own attentive escort.

4 Next, choose another area – and then another.

In these imaginary exercises, picture yourself as firm, purposeful and determined. You stand up for yourself calmly and clearly. You broadcast confidence and expectation of success: you say *nothing* to indicate that you expect argument (such as 'Of course, if you don't agree with me . . .' or 'I don't mind compromising . . .'). Keep your message short and clear; if necessary, repeat it, but don't alter it.

Don't lose your nerve. Don't try to avoid a showdown. Welcome it. It's PRACTICE.

Ignore the bad behaviour of other people, *because the only behaviour that you can change is your own.* You are responsible *only* for your own behaviour and not what other people choose to think about it.

Timid women can often achieve more than they think they can, although at first they don't trust themselves to handle any drama that results. Every one of us can do more than she thinks she can, but not all at once.

Expect:

In yourself	In others
Fear of not being thought nice.	Red-herrings to distract you from your purpose.
Fear of rejection by someone you care about.	Signs of disapproval.
Feeling guilty because you're not perfect.	An aggressive attack.
Anxiety, especially if you don't want a showdown and will do anything to avoid a row.	Bullying.

If you make a start to hang on to what is yours – especially if it's your individuality – it may well irritate other people, who may want to stop your growth so that they feel bigger than you.

Expect people to be surprised by your new and unexpected behaviour. Expect them to push your guilt-buttons by accusing you of being selfish/ungrateful/bad-tempered/unreasonable and so on. Simply – expect disapproval. *Remember that disapproval is what a doormat will do anything to avoid.* But also remember that every single time you stand up for yourself, you are laying another stone on your pyramid of self-confidence.

Our motto: Enough is enough – and not enough is not enough.

WOMAN'S INTUITION

If you trust your intuition (which is a very private part of you that certainly exists), you are *proving* to yourself that you have confidence in yourself. A woman's intuition is the sum of her entire life's experience, recorded on the computer of her unconscious mind, which works faster than the conscious mind. It is the observation, recollection and adding-up of other people's behaviour patterns and feelings, which lead the woman to a conclusion that she cannot consciously explain.

The voice of your intuition speaks when you're not concentrating on something else. It's the little voice in the back of your head that speaks up when you're having a bath or peeling potatoes, or something similarly undemanding of the brain. Never ignore the little voice.

YOUR FUTURE SECURITY

Maturity is an adjustment between the yearning for the safe, protected, lost state of childhood, the defiant aggression of adolescence, and the confidence of realizing your real, proven capabilities.

Self-confidence is simply knowing what you've been capable of in the past and, therefore, being fairly certain that you can deal with that sort of situation in the future. It is also being prepared, as a proven, capable person, to try an equally or even more demanding job: if you can swim 100 metres (or yards) then – if you don't panic – you can probably swim 800 metres (or yards), and if it is vital that you should swim that far, you will. This is truly mature self-confidence, rather than the rash, brash, unknowing and optimistic reaction of the teenager who has not yet experienced life's inexorable demands; this is how, step by step, the office boy becomes the boss.

Life is always risky. Nothing is certain in this world. Fate can fling a spanner in the most carefully laid plans of the most worthy people; there is no guaranteed security, financial, intellectual or emotional.

But you have survived life to date. Your future security lies only in your self-confidence, which is your knowledge of your ability to deal with the problems of life as they crop up – to make decisions and take responsibility for them, to know that not all your decisions will be the correct ones, because you do not have a crystal ball.

Being self-reliant is being able to make your own decisions (even if you decide to do what other people want you to do) and it is the nearest that anyone gets to true freedom. Self-reliance is taking responsibility for yourself and your actions (right or wrong) *all the time*, because you learn what not to do by making mistakes and suffering the consequences, not by blaming fate or other people.

All mistakes have to be paid for. Recognize a mistake; don't try to avoid it. Then recognize your responsibility, both moral and legal (it's very easy to confuse the two). What will it cost to repair the damage and clean the slate? Calculate the price in time, effort, money and discomfort.

CHARM

Diamonds aren't a girl's best friend, her self-confidence is. *Genuine* charm, when accompanied by warmth and kindness, is a manifestation of self-confidence; genuine charm is a sort of benevolent radiance that other people open up towards, like flowers towards the sun.

Be wary of *excessive* charm: like seductive behaviour, this is acquired in childhood as a calculated mechanism for obtaining love and approval from a non-giving parent. Someone who charms you into working for him or always doing what *he* wants and not what is in your interest is dangerous.

In the course of many interviews with famous genuine charmers (both male and female) I noticed more warmth and kindness than anything else. I also noticed:

* They do more listening than talking.
* They are always enthusiastic and appreciative, especially about other people's projects.
* They lavish praise on the efforts of others and never allow anyone to lose face – not even children, especially not their *own* children.
* They don't waste time in criticism and they rarely contradict.
* They are tactful and considerate.
* They never seem to be lethargic or bored.
* They smile a lot.
* They never go out of their way to be popular, they are just themselves; this is what they're best at and it's what you're best at and it's what most people like most.
* They don't worry about making a good impression, they just *assume* success and get on with it; they are totally self-confident.

One of the Pied Piper secrets seems to be that charmers don't mind making themselves vulnerable to others when they are being totally themselves. At times you can't believe that the charmer is taking such risks, in allowing you to see her vulnerability, telling you of her inadequacies and imperfections.

Charmers quietly get their own way, but you rarely notice – it always seems to be someone else's idea.

INSTANT RECOVERY PLAN

Handling humiliation is difficult; the more public it is, the more difficult it is to handle.

We all have disappointments and *everyone* has to face rejection and the consequent self-doubt.

Rejection can make you feel miserable, worthless and lifeless. As you probably still behave in the same way as you did before the rejection, you can't understand why – suddenly and bewilderingly – you are worthless to the person who previously found you worthy. So on top of losing your job, your man or something else you value, you may also have to deal with the loss of your self-confidence.

A positive self-image is the only cure for the loss of self-confidence. It never works to alter yourself, to try to suit someone else in order to get his acceptance, approval or love. This is rejecting your Self and it is devaluing your Self – and it won't work in the long run, although it might work for a bit.

Certainly, if you've been rejected, find out why it happened. On the other hand, the reason may not have much to do with you, whatever the stated reason is.

I asked the most self-assured woman I know whether she had ever lost her self-confidence. 'Oh yes,' she said, 'about once a day I have doubts and once (after being fired from a bad job) I lost my self-confidence for two years. I blamed myself entirely for everything and at the time could not see how much of the job failure was due to other people and circumstances beyond my control.'

So what do you do when your confidence has been destroyed, when anguish and despair turn into self-doubt and when self-doubt turns to self-contempt, which turns to self-loathing? What do you do when you convince yourself that you are a born loser and that you can do nothing about it, except reach for the aspirin and self-destruct?

1 Give in to the emotion you really feel (don't put a brave face on – this is hiding and denying your feelings). Go into mourning for whatever it is you just lost, but not for more than three days unless, sadly, you are mourning a person.
2 Decide whether what you want is realistic. Perhaps you were turned down for the job because you weren't suited for it, in which case it's a good thing that you never started it. Look upon male rejection in the same way. If you weren't right for him, then *he* probably wasn't right for you; good thing that monster is now out of the way.
3 Lack of self-confidence is a sudden failure of nerve – generally when you need it most, perhaps before an important interview. Feelings of inadequacy stem from your lack of confidence in yourself and capabilities. In such moments of self-doubt what you need to get your nerve back is the reminder of your true worth, proven by the many things that you have done well in the past.

Before you need it, list your *talents and achievements* on a card, so that in moments of self-doubt you can whip it out and remind yourself of all the things that are good about you.

Also list the *things that have frightened you before* – being scared of the dark, being afraid to swim, dive, ride a bicycle, being scared of being in the school play. Probably some of the things you were once frightened of are

now included on your list of achievements. You've been frightened before, but it didn't stop you winning through.

Challenge whatever frightens you. Do not *avoid* it. The greatest mountaineers are those who have successfully challenged their fear of heights.

When you feel your self-confidence ebbing away, read both lists (perhaps in the privacy of some lavatory). Concentrate on the truth of what you are reading. It is tangible proof of your capability. You have slain dragons before and you will again. Tell yourself that the coming interview is merely today's test of nerve. In these moments of self-doubt also keep in touch with your own self-esteem by reading flattering letters (keep them in a folder marked CHEER UP).
4 Make a conscious effort to look your best. If your hair needs washing, your shoes are down-at-heel and your hem is dragging, it's not going to help you establish a good self-image.
5 Let people see that you value yourself. Remember that other people tend to see you as you see yourself.
6 In life when you are happy in your situation and don't need any alternative offers, the offers come pouring in. When things aren't going well . . . no offers. Project confidence, because people run a mile from insecurity. Save your glum negative thoughts for the privacy of your bedroom.

Remember that people are unlikely to despise you, scorn you, laugh or jeer at you – that happens only in nightmares: anyone that does isn't worth bothering about. Most people want to be liked, most people want to behave well and most people are a bit shy.

Every success you've ever known or read about has also known failure. In fact, as success comes from building on your failures, successful people are probably the ones with the *most* failures.

THE SEETHING CAULDRON

In small doses, violent feelings can protect you or spur you on to achievement; in large doses, uncontrolled violent feelings are malignantly destructive. For instance, *aggression* is what got us out of the tree-tops and in front of the television. But excessive aggression is best transferred elsewhere – for instance, to a ball; the original football was an enemy head and someone probably externalized a lot of resentment while kicking it around.

A civilized person is someone who can keep violent feelings under control. But why? And which feelings? And what is 'under control'? And what is the difference between controlling your feelings and suppressing your feelings?

Remember that stupidity is the operation of intelligence obstructed by feelings. Your feelings can distort your logical processes into deciding that the best place in the whole world to go for a holiday is Wigan in February – because that's when *He* will be in Wigan. Such

wrong decisions can ruin a lot more than your holiday; they can ruin your life.

The heroine of Daphne du Maurier's *Rebecca* led a miserable life in the midst of luxury because of her **jealousy**. Othello strangled his beloved Desdemona in a jealous rage. Jealous people want what someone else possesses. **Envy** (which is even more destructive) is, in addition, wishing that the other person didn't have the possession; there's a lot of self-hatred in envy.

Terror is a response to a threat that may annihilate you. Rage or aggressive conduct is a response to a threat that doesn't seem to be overwhelming; the aim of **rage** or aggressive conduct is to annihilate the threat.

When you are angry, it's important to admit to yourself how angry you are. If you suppress your anger, the force of your feelings will grow inside you like a volcano until some little thing triggers an eruption.

DOWN WITH SUPERWOMAN!

Many nice women think it's unfeminine – not nice – for a woman to display anger. So many women, ostrichlike, pretend they aren't angry because they don't know how to handle anger – many women would do anything to avoid a row. When faced with someone else's anger, they tremble with fear – which is exactly the reaction that the other person wants.

Many women suppress their rage because they are afraid of losing the person who is making them angry, they are afraid of being abandoned. But the same woman is capable of showing her anger to someone whom she is sure won't abandon her – her mother, for instance.

However, if you suppress your rage, then you risk turning your destructive anger inwards against yourself and it is at moments like these that an 'accident-prone' person cuts herself with the kitchen knife. Clamping down your anger is not healthy and can lead to serious illness: your stomach really does get churned up and you end up with an ulcer.

A Relate (formerly Marriage Guidance) counsellor told me, 'In practically every couple I see, suppressed anger is an area that comes up again and again.' Some examples of semi-suppressed rage are sarcasm, nagging, being upset, being meaningfully silent and being over-polite: these attitudes show that you're angry, but in a weak way that will not annihilate the threat.

The reason that **sarcasm** is so unpleasant is because it is the perfect cover for suppressed anger. Since most people are quickly reduced to apoplexy by sarcasm, they end up by acting out the anger felt by the sarcastic person – to his satisfaction.

Nagging is a symptom of resentment due to suppressed rage. Often the nagger feels insecure because the other party has all the material possessions and she has none, so she has no power to do anything – except nag.

Martyrdom is a form of silent nagging.

'Being upset' is what a weak person says she is when she is angry. It is a recognizably weak thing to say and it puts her in a weak position. Other people dismiss 'being upset' as neurotic and weak. 'I'm very upset' doesn't convey what the speaker really wants to say, which is, 'I am angry.' If you catch yourself saying 'I'm upset', try saying 'I'm angry' instead, and see how much better you feel.

Being **meaningfully silent** can be the best way of making someone else angry and the worst way of talking about a problem. When one partner refuses to talk, quite often the other one goes berserk and lashes out.

Turning the other cheek (in a doormat way, without truly wishing to forgive), attempting to smooth over the situation, responding to rage with **over-politeness** (also known as dumb insolence) can also be a way of suppressing anger.

We are taught to 'turn the other cheek' when someone abuses us. This is bad for your health because every time you do it, you suppress a little anger; the little bits of anger build into a big head of steam, until some little thing blows your safety valve. This may then look like unfair over-reaction on your part, so it can arouse indignation and resentment in the other party (who has probably behaved far worse before and got away with it), and can lead to a never-ending spiral of resentment.

If anger is constantly suppressed, it can develop into depression, accompanied by inexplicable moodiness, tears, outbursts, bad temper or lack of interest in sex. A depression isn't merely feeling down in the dumps for a day – it feels like being trapped in a black hole, all the time.

Often a partner's reaction to your depression is to be aloof, withdrawn, 'not there', not interested – indifferent. Of course, this makes the depressed person feel *more* depressed.

DEALING WITH VIOLENT FEELINGS

Can you remember something that made you angry last year but that no longer has the power to make you angry this year? Why, then, did you allow it to make you angry last year? Perhaps because your strong feelings were distorting your logical processes and turning a mole-hill into a mountain.

What can you do about this? When something makes you angry, you can try to see the situation in perspective by asking someone who knows you and whom you trust what she would do in that situation. Don't ask her what *you* should do; she'll be far more positive about her own reaction.

Take responsibility for your own feelings, because you *are* responsible for your actions and your feelings, and also for your reactions to other people's actions and feelings. Only you can upset yourself by allowing your equanimity to be disturbed.

The most important thing about dealing with all violent feelings is to recognize your feelings and then deal with them. Different ways to deal with them are:

1 Get away from everyone and yell, scream, cry for as long as you like. God gave us tears for a good reason – to get rid of pent-up emotion, rage or grief – and the sooner men learn to cry the better.

2 Transfer the violence out of yourself and on to something else: kick a ball, hit a pillow, make a wax image and stick pins in it – whatever lets off your pent-up emotion.

3 Don't transfer the violence out of yourself and on to someone else by being sarcastic or picking a row. Don't be like the chairman who snaps at his secretary, who then scowls at the office boy, who then kicks the cat. (They all should be playing tennis.) This is dumping your painful feelings on somebody else – externalizing them.

4 Try transferring your anger to paper. Write a furious letter, keep it for two days and . . . then tear it up.

5 It would be nice to think that time wounds all heels, but it doesn't, so wipe thoughts of revenge from your mind. As I've said before, you're not a Sicilian peasant. The way to deal with people who have hurt you is to have your say and express your anger, then truthfully forgive them. (Incidentally, nothing irritates them more.) The alternative is to feel resentful, which is a destructive waste of your time. Instead of saying, 'I shall never forgive X . . .', substitute 'always' for 'never'.

Exiled Russian poet Irina Ratushinskaya said that from her labour camp experience she learnt that hatred is a bad feeling: 'I can testify that only those who do not hate their torturers are not broken by them. Hatred ruins your soul and your personality.'

6 Bitterness is also rust to the soul. Whatever you might feel about your problem, bitterness increases it. If you can't forgive, do yourself a favour and forget.

While you are forgiving other people who don't deserve it, why not forgive yourself for everything you've ever blushed about? Instead, if it's appropriate, say you're sorry (often very difficult, whether you're in the wrong or the right). If possible, compensate for your wrong actions; if not, then simply go out and get on with life. Forget guilt. It is a useless bit of mental baggage; like an empty hat-box on an aeroplane, it only gets in the way.

Historically, girls have never been taught to be alone. Even today many women believe that a woman alone is an object of pity who can't find a man to protect her. Consequently, women are often frightened of being alone, frightened of being left behind and frightened of being defenceless.

However, there is a vast difference between being lonely and being alone. Being lonely is being *emotionally* on your own; you *might* feel most lonely when lying in bed next to the person you're supposed to love. Loneliness is feeling that you are without a close relationship, or being afraid of being without a close relationship.

Being alone is being by yourself, perhaps when you choose to be, perhaps only for short periods. When a woman stops feeling lonely and starts to enjoy being on her own, she will feel a surprisingly strong sense of happiness and security.

It took me seven years to learn to live alone. A woman may find herself living alone for many reasons – a job posting, a bereavement, a divorce, or because life simply turned out that way. Why should living alone be a problem? Surely somebody who hasn't got a family to cope with has plenty of free time to look after and amuse herself?

Certainly a woman living alone hasn't a family to keep her so busy that she hasn't time to notice that she hasn't time to do anything rewarding for herself. But having more free time than you can fill may result in a feeling of aimlessness, lack of direction and – somehow – failure, which leads to depression.

Of course there are advantages. With no one else to consider, you can do what you want *when* you want – eat baked beans on toast at four in the morning or spend the afternoon in bed with a bad book. You don't have to worry whether someone else is happy or not, is pulling his weight or not, or is contributing to family happiness.

But what do you do when you find yourself with a whole free day ahead of you – what you longed for when swamped by family – that threatens to turn into an empty day?

You are no longer being swept along as a reactor to what other people want to do. *You* have to be the one who acts in order to make things happen to you.

How you do this is simple, although it took me a long time to work it out. In your diary, plan to fill your time for the weekend after next, but plan your time *this weekend*. Phone a friend, or an acquaintance, and suggest going to a museum, exhibition, or some other entertainment that you can't get on TV and that will get you *out*. Don't sit at home feeling forlorn because you don't have any invitations and may not speak to anyone from Friday night to Monday morning.

Cautionary tale A beautiful, newly divorced friend from Scotland, who had no money worries, had bought a nice little house in Chelsea. She then telephoned me to say that she was lonely. I arranged for her to help at a hospital bazaar on the coming Saturday and I asked my sister to invite her to a dinner party. I also asked her to spend an afternoon helping me prepare a party for 250 people to launch a book.

My friend met the other people who were helping me to prepare the book party. Afterwards, she complained that she'd spent the entire afternoon making salad and hadn't met anyone interesting at the party. After the hospital bazaar, my friend complained that she was exhausted (so was I, so was everybody). My sister reported that at her dinner party my friend had ignored the women and flirted with all the men, so my sister didn't invite her again.

But what do you do on Friday night if

the cash-point machine flashes 'refer to . . . bank', and you're stuck at home for yet another weekend? Renew your library card. Offer to help in someone's garden, (the only time your offer will be refused is February). Offer to help in the local Oxfam shop. Volunteer to work for some charity that interests you. Don't regard these projects as a way to meet people – although you will.

Where do you go for bank holidays? You don't go anywhere. You take the initiative. You invite people to visit you. Don't feel apologetic if you live in a bedsitter and they don't. They'll either come or they won't.

My friend Maggie told me, 'I take an unconventional view of bank holidays. I plan a special treat for myself for the weekend *before* or *after* the bank holiday – I avoid the crowds and the hype. On the bank holiday I do something mundane but satisfying, possibly something I have been putting off for a long time, such as writing letters or washing my curtains. My feeling of achievement at the end of the day outweighs the Bank Holiday Blues.'

Who do you go on holiday with? Do you go on your own? Do you visit friends and end up exhausted after their children have jumped all over you at six every morning?

A holiday spent with a chaotic family might be just the sort of holiday you need to recognize the advantages of your quiet life. Go on holiday with a friend if you're going to a country where you don't speak the language, but remember that exciting adventures rarely happen if you travel with a friend. One of my best holidays was spent travelling alone around America on a one-month Greyhound bus ticket. However, you don't have to go abroad to see the country by coach. Or try an activity holiday. But avoid cruises full of widows looking hopeful.

Who can you talk to about problems at

work? You shouldn't be talking or thinking about work problems out of working hours. Compartmentalize your work and keep it to working hours, or work problems may swamp your life. Instead, ask somebody at the office out for a drink and talk about *their* office problems. Listen sympathetically (sympathy makes people *feel* better), remind them of what is going well for them in other areas . . . and pay for the drinks.

Who can you talk to about money? The person who does this best is probably your bank manager. Many people don't think of their bank manager as a person, but some of the most important and entertaining men in my life have been bank managers.

How do you cope with married friends who never invite you to dinner unless it's to make up the numbers? Who needs friends like that? Find other friends.

How do you find other friends? You are friendly. Practise being friendly by chatting to people that *you don't know*, so you don't feel embarrassed. Chat at supermarkets, bus stops, in the launderette – anywhere except the library.

Join some sort of physical activity club – and talk to people. Here you just drop the odd remark about the activity, which is a subject that you're both interested in or neither of you would be there.

If you are frightened of meeting other people because you're shy or because you don't want to risk being hurt or humiliated again, choose a charity – everyone will be glad to see another volunteer and you are never at a loss for something to talk about.

When you're making friends, don't immediately look for someone to confide in. Keep your confidences for your bedside journal and don't swamp other people with them. Let them confide in *you*, if they want to. Aim to build up your B-team of friends and hope that some of them will eventually get promoted to the A-team.

Don't think of potential friends as people only in your age or financial bracket. This is very old-fashioned. People today think in terms of mutual interests and the whole person.

What do you do about married men? Or lack of men? You avoid married men like the plague, unless you're prepared for a frustrating, miserable, humiliating relationship in which you will *still* be alone at Christmas and on holidays. As for other men – start thinking in terms of people and not men. You are, of course, unlikely to meet Prince Charming in the launderette, but you are far more likely to meet him through a woman friend who knows the type of person you are, and the type of person you like. If you want to meet men, meet women.

When you're introduced to somebody, don't immediately decide whether or not you might marry him. This is not the way to build up your B-team. Your chances of disappointment in the relationship will then be 99 per cent. However, don't waste your time going out with men you don't *really* like. Remember that your time is precious.

A Short Stress Survival Course

TEMPORARILY OUT OF ORDER

One thing at a time ~ ~ and that well done

FRESHENER

2 MINUTES?
15 MINUTES?
30 MINUTES?

This entire book is about minimizing stress. Stress isn't an illness that can be cured by a doctor; it is a normal bodily reaction to a situation that can be altered only by the owner of the body – YOU.

Knowing what to do about stress is easy; doing it is very difficult. It is even *more* difficult to get a person to realize and admit that he or she is under stress, especially if that person is yourself.

In order to minimize stress you have to know what stress is, why it occurs, recognize the symptoms and know what can be done about them.

Stress is the rate of wear and tear on the human mind and body. Erosion by stress is cumulative – you can't 'catch up on your rest' by staying in bed late on Sunday morning. Any demands (emotional or physical) beyond the general capability of a person will result in stress. Today it is the most prevalent health problem of the faster-moving world, in which we strive to keep up.

Although some doctors call stress the twentieth-century disease, stress has always existed. Nature's built-in fight-flight-or-submission response originally prepared the human body for instant vigilant reaction at times of danger, when facing a charging bull elephant or a taller chap from another tribe with a bigger club than yours.

Anxiety in a human being can occur as the result of a threat to peace of mind as well as to physical safety. You can't fight or escape a crowded, sweaty underground train; you are forced to submit to it, and your stress inwardly turns to frustration, then anger. Excessive stress can lead to serious physical and mental illness.

Popping pills doesn't attack the problem of mental exhaustion or depression; it just covers up the problem temporarily – and there is a risk of getting hooked on the pills. Drugs that reduce anxiety also reduce vigilance, the speed of reaction in

DOWN WITH SUPERWOMAN!

emergency and the efficiency with which you perform difficult or dangerous tasks, such as driving.

WHO SUFFERS FROM STRESS?

Some of the most admirable people I know have fallen apart under stress. *Any* human being will if you overload him, and it can be quite a small thing that triggers stress overload – the last straw really *does* break the stress-laden camel's back.

Some people think that there is something shameful about suffering from stress but most people have, or will have, a stress problem at some time in their life. In a world where the earth, the sea and the sky have been dangerously polluted within a couple of decades, and when all life might end if someone presses the wrong button, modern civilized people live under stress such as their forefathers could never have imagined.

Stress is not confined to dynamic executives; in fact, some executives thrive on their fascinating but stressful hard work.

A person such as Mrs Thatcher might get depressed if her interesting work were taken away from her. Doctors, journalists, lawyers, taxi drivers and others in pressure professions tend to find their demanding job is excitingly addictive. The rush of adrenalin that comes with the thrill of facing a challenge can make you feel more alive, which may well be one of the reasons that so many people furtively enjoyed the Second World War.

In addition, high-powered executives can make decisions and control their own pace of life, so they are less subject to stress than telephone operators, chefs, waiters, policemen and firemen, who have to jump when other people tell them and have no decision-making power over their working life.

A typist working every day in inadequate light for an irritable boss in a polluted, noisy atmosphere after a long journey in a crowded train may also crack under stress.

A 5-year-old child can be severely stressed if he's bullied at school. In fact, stress can affect whole families if they are living in cramped or intolerable conditions.

Stress can be experienced by under-achievers as well as over-achievers; a monotonous, quiet life in which nothing ever seems to happen and over which you feel you have no control can be depressingly stressful.

A quiet old age can be sadly stressful, especially for someone who has to cope by herself with bereavement, illness, poverty and inflation.

Stress isn't always the result of something unpleasant; a happy wedding is a stressful event for the happy couple.

However, as we've all known from years of experience, medical research now indicates that working mothers are the group considered to be under *greatest* stress, because, statistically, the risk of stress-related disease increases with each child.

In addition, twentieth-century women have been pioneers of the emotions. For the first time in history women have openly discussed all the feelings in the seething cauldron. For advice, they can go to self-help groups or friends about problems that their grandmothers would be ashamed to mention, let alone admit; those women either adopted an ostrich attitude or swept the dreadful drama – 'Dad's problem', 'Mum's funny ways' – under the carpet.

Today few women are prepared to put up with what their grandmothers had to endure. Today a woman tries to do something about her problems even if, in desperation, she decides to dump them (hence the wave of divorce in the 1960s). Changing society for the better has been – and still is – a stressful business.

Teenage society is also in a state of change. One of the worst stress areas is in the late adolescent group. When their glands are looping the loop and responsible for tumultuous emotional highs and lows, teenagers are suddenly faced with major stressful personal decisions, which have to be made for the first time: first big exams, first job, first love and so on.

In addition to this there is the stress caused to teenagers by parents who keep them on a leash and order them around like children and then complain that they aren't behaving like adults.

As part of a voluntary working group, I once worked with problem teenage students from underprivileged backgrounds; they were all under considerable stress for reasons beyond their control (such as parental drunkenness, prostitution, violence or molestation). My group found that the teenagers responded positively and almost immediately to being treated with respect and politeness, and carefully listened to: *as soon as* the teenagers felt free to express their worries aloud, their stress decreased noticeably.

Being a parent is the most difficult and important job in the world but nobody prepares you for it, nobody teaches you about it, nobody supports you if you're having problems – and if you're doing it properly, nobody appreciates you. As with housework, most parents learn about parenting only from *their* parents, but the world has changed so drastically in the last generation that the old rules simply don't apply.

Parents who feel inadequate, depressed, under stress or who have a specific problem can consult a nation-wide organization called **Parent Network**, which concentrates on improving communication between parents and children and aims to nip any friction in the bud, before it develops into a nuclear crisis. In its first three years more than 1,500 parents attended the basic twelve-session programme; some of these parents had no problems but simply wished to improve the inter-family relationship. Get details from them at 44–46 Caversham Road, London NW5 2DS, tel: 071-485-8535.

Exploring Parenthood is another organization for parents who are already under stress. Its aim is to help parents who have already reached the serious-trouble stage with their children. Exploring Parenthood offers guidance, introductions to the relevant professionals who can help, and a chance to discuss your problem with other parents who have similar problems. London-based, the head office is at 41 North Road, London N7 9DP, tel: 071-607 9647.

WHAT CAUSES STRESS?

Overload

1 **Emotional overload:** an overdose of any violent feelings (such as jealousy) to be found in the seething cauldron.
2 **Body overload,** such as too much strenuous work or exercise.
3 **Mental overload** resulting from too much responsibility at home or work.

Another type of mental overload is *being in the victim's position*, from which you can do nothing about trouble – the endless, ear-splitting noise from next door or the fact that your bus is always half an hour late when it's raining.
4 **Time overload:** if you rush through the day with not a moment to spare.

Too much pleasure can also result in time overload: 'debutante's stress' really does exist.
5 **Not enough sleep.**

Trying to get a quart out of a pint pot can start a stress spiral. So are you trying to do too much? What is 'too much' for you? Only you can decide.

DOWN WITH SUPERWOMAN!

Stressful situations

These have been listed and graded at enormous expense by highly qualified research teams, but I feel that such things are relative: what you can stand, I can't; one man's stress is another man's excitement.

Here are just a few situations that are seriously stressful for most people:

* **Death** especially the death of a mate or a child.
* **Jail**
* **Physical problems**
  Any health fear.
  Physical injury, an operation or illness.
  Pregnancy.
  Heart disease.
* **Psychological problems** such as:
  Rejection: the end of an affair.
  A bad shock.
  Feeling that you have no control over your future.
  Guilt.
  Over-drinking.
  Smoking (any smoking is over-smoking).
  Drugs.
  Deliberate deprivation of food, drink, cigarettes. (Dieting is stressful.)
  Over-eating.
* **Money**
  A change of financial circumstances, for better or worse.
  An arranged debt, such as a mortgage.
  Over-spending.
* **Relationships**
  Knowing that your child is in serious trouble.
  Marriage fears, such as infidelity.
  Marital rows.
  Divorce.
  In-law problems.
  Being in love.
  Deprivation of affection.
  Lack of a close relationship.

Sex problems.
Having an addict in the family.
The stress put upon you by other people's stress.
* **Aggression**
  Violence from someone you know (family, friends or neighbours).
  Violence from someone you don't know.
* **Work**
  Starting your own business (especially stressful for someone who is running a home and a family, especially if the business is being started in the home).
  Fame.
  Retirement.
  Business problems.
  Job fears.
  Overworking.
  Exams.
  Adapting to modern office techniques such as the computer.
* **Environment**
  Pollution of air, sea, drinking water, food.
  Noise.
  Traffic.
* **Upheavals** such as:
  Moving home.
  Holidays.
  Christmas.
* **Other major events in any area of your life.** Nobody can handle too many changes at once.

THE ABC OF PHYSICAL STRESS SYMPTOMS

The measurable chemical changes that stress causes in your body can make you physically ill. When nature signals your brain to fight-flight-or-submit, there is instant bodily reaction. Your blood pressure rises, your gastro-intestinal system speeds up and your lymphatic system shrinks.

A SHORT STRESS-SURVIVAL COURSE

There are are no stress thermometers or Speak-Your-Stress machines for the layman. Stress can be measured by a doctor.

Various biochemical tests reflect the effects of stress: for instance, a uric-acid test shows an increased level of cholesterol, the pulse rate shows changes in the blood pressure, minor changes in the heart can be recorded by twenty-four-hour monitoring on the electrocardiogram (ECG). Liver tests show alcohol-related changes.

The body's response to extra adrenalin makes things seem to move more slowly, although your heart pumps faster to give you more energy. You are on a high. Perception is sharpened, and so is concentration: only you and the dangerous situation exist. (No wonder some people get hooked on adrenalin and enjoy stress situations.)

When you tremble with fright and your fingertips tingle *after* an emergency, you are paying for that extra effort that produced the extra energy.

People sometimes deny symptoms of stress ('I AM *NOT* SHOUTING!') because it is more difficult to say, 'I DO *NOT* HAVE SEVENTEEN SPOTS ON MY FACE.'

If you have any of the following symptoms, you may be under stress. However, remember the chap in *Three Men in a Boat*: after reading a medical dictionary, he realized that he suffered from everything in it except housemaid's knee.

Allergies
Loss of **appetite**
Asthma
Backache
Blackouts
Breathlessness
Compulsive eating, drinking or smoking
Constipation
Cramp

Diarrhoea
Dizziness
Gynaecological problems
Headaches (severe)
High blood pressure (which can lead to a stroke)
Prolonged stress can suppress the **immune responses**, lowering your resistance to illness.
Indigestion
Irritability
Joint pains
Migraine
Nail biting
Nausea
Nervous tension throughout the body
A nervous twitch
Pain in neck, shoulders or back (which can lead to a slipped disc)
Palpitations
Permanent weariness
Constant **pressure** felt against the top of the head (this is what is *meant* by 'being under pressure').
Increased **sensitivity to noise**
Sexual loss of interest
Skin rashes
Sleeplessness, broken sleep or waking at five in the morning. Because nature has put you on red alert, anxiety is incompatible with sound sleep. If you can't sleep or anxieties wake you in the night, try mixing two tablespoons of dried skimmed milk in a cup of boiling water and adding a teaspoon of runny honey: milk contains natural tranquillizers and skimmed milk puts minimal strain on your digestion.
Spots
Stomach pains
Tense muscles (especially in neck, back or shoulders)
Tingling sensations in hands and feet
Ulcers (including mouth)
Urinary problems and frequent trips to the lavatory
Vomiting

DOWN WITH SUPERWOMAN!

HOW TO TELL IF SOMEONE IS UNDER STRESS

Psychological stress symptoms in women can escalate from mild to extreme, as follows:

* Does she take to her dressing gown?
* Is she sloppy and untidy and can't be bothered to make an effort?
* Is she weepy?
* Is her memory unreliable? Not short-term or long-term memory, but recent memory of things that happened a few hours or a few weeks ago. (Short-term memory is measured in seconds: you use short-term memory when dialling a telephone number that you don't know by heart.)
* Has she lost her concentration? Does she complain that her mind keeps leaping off to some distressing subject that she doesn't want to think about?
* Do her feelings yo-yo from hyper-highs to abysmal lows without any particular reason?
* Does she over-react?
* Is she stubborn or unreasonable, unusually critical or rude?
* Does she experience sudden losses of self-confidence?
* Has she lost her zest for life?
* Is she depressed without any particular reason?
* Does she go to bed earlier than usual?
* Is she becoming reclusive – turning down invitations and avoiding people?
* Does she complain of feeling neglected and lonely?
* Does she say that feelings of apathy and lethargy envelop her like a wet, black fog?

Traditionally, a serious depression was thought by the layman to be either 'melancholia' or 'nerves' or the result of 'madness in the family' – but nothing in between. In fact, depression is a matter of degree. If nothing seems to be going right in your life, if your family seems overdemanding or uncaring, if you feel exploited, exhausted and – above all – if you feel you 'can't cope' any longer, if anyone is telling you to pull yourself together (people tell you to pull yourself together only when you are incapable of doing it), then you might be falling into a state of depression.

Too much stress can lead to mental illness (which is not the same as being mentally handicapped). Consult your doctor, as you would for any other illness, and ask him how long your recovery is likely to take.

When tycoon Margery Hearst, who started the Brook Street employment agencies, wrote about her nervous breakdown, she said that it had been caused by exhaustion as a result of living for too long on her reserves of energy. At one point she asked her psychiatrist, 'Am I going insane? Will I get better?' He said, 'If you can imagine two parallel lines which head towards the same direction but never touch, this is the difference between depression and insanity: the two are not related.' Margery Hearst realized that her illness was coming to an end when her depression was no longer constant, but ebbed and flowed like the tide.

Other psychological symptoms of stress, such as too much frustration and too much anxiety, can also be exhausting.

A little **frustration** can be good for you – nothing would get invented without it. Frustration keeps you striving, although frequent frustration may indicate that you are setting yourself unrealistically high goals. However, the frustration that you feel in a traffic jam only results in exhausting irritability and rage.

If possible, when in a frustrating situation, decide whether or not you can do anything about it. If not, then working up a rage is a pointless waste of energy. It's up to you to decide whether or not you want to waste your energy on irritation, as surely as if you were frittering money from your purse. Will it matter in a hundred years' time? What does it rate on your 1–10 disaster scale? Why not use that wasted energy for something more useful?

Anxiety is a biological function that is necessary for the survival of the human race: it is the internal reaction to outside stressful forces that threaten physical safety or peace of mind; it is an early part of the fight-flight-or-submission response.

Real anxiety felt for good reason is useful, because in the face of danger it triggers the adrenalin reaction that produces the energy needed to act in a fast but calm and deliberate manner.

Once you've decided what to do, you get on with it and stop feeling anxious because anxiety vanishes as soon as you understand the true situation that you face. Anxiety is an emotion that is concerned with the future, not the past (*that* emotion is guilt). People who don't think they've got a future, don't feel anxious, just despondent.

THE ANXIETY HABIT

Anxiety is a heightened sense of awareness of sudden danger, whether or not that danger is real. ('Did I leave the fire on?') However, if there is no real threat, then being in a constant state of readiness is wasteful, stressful and exhausting.

To prove the effect that anxiety *immediately* has on your body, try this trick. Shut your eyes, knot your stomach, tense neck muscles and jaw, tighten chest, hunch shoulders and then put on an anxious face. Now, as in 'method acting', *think tense*.

Not only will you immediately feel un-

comfortable, you may well feel mounting anxiety and although you hold the anxious position only for a few seconds, you will still feel the resultant stress in your body for some time afterwards. So it's easy to see the payment that is extracted from the body for that extra adrenalin and why undue anxiety causes chronic fatigue and exhaustion.

But because it heightens excitement, anxiety can become a bad habit that makes life seem more interesting ('Your mother's a worrier') or more dramatic, as with gossips who make mountains out of molehills to add drama to their drab lives.

Worriers practise worrying until they get really good at it. As alcoholics become alcohol-dependent, worriers can become addicted to the adrenalin produced by the anxiety. If you solve a worrier's problem and empty her cup of worry, she will *immediately* find another problem to fill it up again – because she likes worrying. Tense, highly-strung people are more likely to develop the anxiety habit than placid people.

On a 1–10 tension level, if 5 is normal, how would you rate yourself? Level 2s are very placid, level 9s tend to dramatize everything. If you rate over 7, check any problem on the 1–10 disaster scale, as you may be exaggerating it. Ask yourself whether this matter is an *irritation*, a *problem* that has a solution, or a *worry* that won't go away and can't be resolved, such as a chronic illness.

To counteract anxiety, try the breathing exercise on p. 410 and focus your mind on something else by doing a relaxation exercise (see p. 411).

WHAT TO DO IF YOU CAN'T COPE

This feeling is not confined to women with jobs or women with young children. Historical biographer and mother of eight children Elizabeth Longford says,

DOWN WITH SUPERWOMAN!

'They are all dispersed now and the week-day turmoil of my early writing days has quietened, but there is still such a lot to be done at weekends when grandchildren arrive. Sometimes I wake up early with "morning panic". I survey what's got to to be done in the rest of the week and I (madly) go on to the rest of the month and finally I am in a state of absolute panic and see that I can't possibly get it done at all. But as the day proceeds I will slowly stabilize the situation and realize that things perhaps can be done after all. I make an effort of concentration; it used to be against the children, but now that they are gone it's an effort of concentration against just all the things that keep coming up.'

But what about when an effort of concentration no longer helps?

Try the Conran Power of Negative Thinking. What you should do when you have too much to do is NOTHING. Nothing is good for you. If you must, write a list of the absolutely essential things you have to do. Now stick it over your mirror and decide you'll look at it tomorrow, when you'll be in a better state to sort out your priorities.

Unless you live in a convent in the country, in these stressful times you will need to make a conscious effort to relax, to unwind, to combat tension and frustration. So what can you do when you're exhausted, and shortly have to scintillate again?

Two-minute freshener

If you're tired at any time – even if it's when you wake up – dash to the nearest source of fresh air and take half a dozen deep breaths. Breathe in through the nose as slowly as possible, expanding your stomach. Hold the breath for ten seconds, then slowly expel all your breath through your slightly open mouth, contracting your stomach as you do so. When you think all the air has left your lungs, try to squeeze still more out, with a little push.

Fifteen-minute freshener

Take off your shoes and tights, loosen your clothes especially round the waist.

As you won't have time to re-make-up, damp your face with a cold sponge or tissue wrung out in cold water, or a pad of eau de cologne. *Allow two minutes.*

Use a kitchen timer so that you're not anxious about overdoing it. If you are anxious, you won't relax properly. Draw the curtains, lie on the floor, put a blanket over yourself – relax in the dark and think of black velvet. *Allow five minutes.*

Then, still on the floor, S-T-R-E-T-C-H like a cat, several times. Stand up with legs apart, hold arms over head and stretch again. *Allow two minutes.* Then flop towards the floor, from the waist downwards, until you feel like standing up again.

Now tuck a towel round your shoulders, lean over a basin and lavishly sponge cold water on the back of your neck, then your wrists. If possible, cold sponge your ankles – this is not as inconvenient as it sounds. *Allow two minutes.*

Now adjust your clothes, check your make-up. *Allow four minutes.* If you have time, walk twice round the block slowly, breathing deeply.

Thirty-minute freshener

In a comfortably warm room, draw the curtains. Take off your shoes, loosen or take off your clothes and put on something loose, light and comfortable, such as a dressing-gown. Lie on the floor (on a rug if there's no carpet) with no pillows and no sound, such as radio music. Try and make your mind go blank: concentrate on thinking of grey fog or black velvet or soft white light.

Relax your body, bit by bit, letting each part go completely limp. Concentrate firmly on *relaxing* each bit of your anatomy in turn; start at the toes of the left leg, then foot, ankle, knee and thigh. Follow with the right leg. Follow with left, then right, arm. Now relax the contents of the pelvis, then the rib cage, then the anus. Finally relax the neck, contents of the head (forehead, eyes, mouth, tongue, jaw). *Allow ten minutes*.

Some physiotherapists prefer you to tauten each muscle in turn, then relax it.

Now stand up and, with your eyes shut, stretch *slowly*. Next work through these simple exercises as slowly as possible, stretching and then holding the final position for as long as possible.

Relaxer 1: The balloon exercise

Lie down flat, hands loosely at your sides. Breathe in by nose to a count of ten, pushing your stomach out as far as it will go, as if inflating a balloon with air. Then gently tilt your pelvis forward and slowly breathe out, through the lips, contracting the stomach and squeezing the air out of the balloon.

Relaxer 2: Neckroll

Stand straight. Keep shoulders straight. Slowly roll your head in a circle round your neck, six times clockwise, then six times counter-clockwise. Try to stretch your neck as far sideways as it can go. Repeat twice.

Relaxer 3: Shoulder roll

Stand straight. Hunch both shoulders forward and then slowly rotate both shoulders at the same time. Concentrate on rotating your shoulder blades. Do it six times, then hold your shoulders as far back as they will go and rotate them backwards six times. Repeat twice.

Relaxer 4: The Flop

Stand up without shoes. Flop downwards from your waist, arms and head down – don't try to reach the floor, just let your weight sag towards the floor. Stay there for one minute, then *very slowly* pull yourself up straight again, carefully uncurling your spine from the pelvis. Take a deep breath and stretch your hands to the ceiling. Try to touch it . . . stiffen kneecaps and bottom. Higher . . . now higher. (Don't stand on tiptoe.) Repeat twice.

Lastly, lie flat on your back and do the balloon for a further *five minutes*. You should then rise a new woman, and allow *five minutes* to dress again.

Leaflets on relaxation tape cassettes are available from the British Holistic Medical Association (head office), 179 Gloucester Place, London NW1 6DX, tel: 071-262-5299.

Tension relief

Tension relievers are soothing, slow, repetitive work with a visible end result, such as knitting, tapestry work, embroidery and patchwork. Sewing, painting and writing your journal aren't mindless enough, no matter what Winston Churchill did to unwind.

Some people find gardening is very good therapy as well as a way of getting exercise in the sun and fresh air. Novelist Mary Stewart has an immaculate garden, because whenever she gets stuck on one of her bestselling novels, she goes out and fiercely weeds. Someone else I know invites herself to different friends' homes to do their gardening. She mows and rakes, weeds and prunes, until she is exhausted and can sleep like a log. She is never short of friends.

You might also try to escape the insatiable demands of civilization for a few days. Here's how to do it:

DOWN WITH SUPERWOMAN!

* **How to ignore the telephone:** take it off the hook.
* **How to ignore the post:** put it, unopened, in a basket and deal with it all next Wednesday morning.
* **How to ignore the television:** unplug it.
* **How to ignore the newspapers:** put them also in the basket until next Wednesday morning. Then throw them away.

If you are really near to screaming point, the best tension reliever is to remove yourself from the action. You need somewhere quiet and calm to calm down. Go anywhere, but go. It is only common sense to remove yourself from a situation that is driving you crazy because of pressure, indignation, noise or exhaustion. It isn't easy to suddenly leave a situation if you're surrounded by yowling toddlers, but should that not be the case, then quietly excuse yourself or loudly storm out. But *go*. It may be for a calming walk in the park, an hour's trip on the river or a bus ride, a weekend in the country or Back to Mother, but go – for however long you feel you need.

Whatever you do, don't jump into a car and externalize your feelings on the accelerator.

Alternatively, if you can't get to sleep or if you keep waking up at night, wondering how you're going to cope, try this . . .

HOW TO HAVE A SMALL NERVOUS BREAKDOWN

Mentally stick up a sign on your forehead saying 'I am temporarily out of order.' Then follow this routine.

First day

1 Give yourself half an hour to cancel everything you've arranged for the next three days. If you have children,

delegate them, or hire someone else to look after them. Don't do this too often, but you can't afford *not* to do it if you're really at breaking point.

2 Draw the curtains, take the phone off the hook and warm the room if necessary. Have a warm bath (not hot), then climb into clean nightwear and go to bed.

3 Lie in bed all day. Keep the room dark. Don't read, write, or listen to music or the radio, and *try not to think*. Don't plan revenge, accusations, vacations, how to get him back or your way out of this mess. DO NOTHING. Don't take pills. Don't drink alcohol. Drink orange juice, weak tea or hot milk with a little honey.

Second day

1 Write down the main things that are worrying you. Try to reduce them to three short sentences.

2 Check out any cobwebs in your mind. Forget the words 'if only'. Accept yourself as you are and remember that woman is imperfect, the Bible says so. Accept that you can't do all the things that you'd like to do. Accept that you can't alter time: the past is past. Use the present to do the best you can in the time available; you can't be expected to do better than your best.

Remember that we've all done a lot of 'wrong' things in our lives and we're probably going to do a lot more. We all make mistakes – all the time – and always will. We all have to learn to live with our mistakes and this can be very hard.

Don't waste time by thinking about past mistakes. We *all* have wasted too much time.

Remember that the Prime Minister was elected to look after the country, not you. Other people's problems are not your responsibility at the moment. Lie in bed all day. Keep the room dark in the afternoon. Don't read. Don't talk. DO NOTHING.

Third day

1 Have another look at those three sentences you wrote yesterday summing up what's wrong with your situation. Talk about them to someone you trust. Can she make any helpful suggestions, either small or drastic?
2 Scribble four lists.
A List all the things you want to do.
B List all the things you enjoy doing. Decide exactly when you can do one or two things on lists A and B.
C List all things you don't much like.
D List all the things you hate.

Decide how to eliminate one or two items on lists C and D. Consider whether you can delegate something you hate but can't eliminate and, if so, work out how much it will cost you in terms of money, barter or time.

3 If you feel you can do it without bursting into tears, sit upright in bed, propped up by pillows, and ask yourself:
★ Who am I?
★ What am I doing?
★ Where am I going?
Or maybe leave it until next month. Today remember that from now on your motto should be:
ONE THING AT A TIME AND THAT WELL DONE.

THE TWO-WEEK STRESS PLAN

Work is an emotive word that instantly and adversely affects a person's attitude to whatever occupation it describes. So I define 'work' as *any* output of energy – anything that requires mental or physical effort.

Creative work is life-enhancing. Even if tired, you feel better after it: you are exhilarated, happy, calm and contented. You sing little songs to yourself and whistle a happy tune. You are relaxed and amiable. You enjoy life.

Relaxing work can be a bit demanding – if you're going out to dinner, you have to make an effort, to be part of the gathering – or totally undemanding, as when watching videos.

Physical work can be good exercise. If you aren't employed as a ditch digger, physical work such as gardening leaves you tired but happy and feeling in touch with the Universe. It is therapeutic.

If you don't do any physical work that you enjoy, you should take aerobic exercise, which is exercise that increases your pulse rate.

System-support work is dull, necessary work that is not life-enhancing and may be depressing if you have to do it as a full-time job. I know women whose main reason for going out to work is that they find housework clinically depressing.

However, one man's meat is another man's poison. Things I hate, which other people find relaxing, are: driving, cooking for my family, ironing, washing-up, making beds. I minimize these things. Things other people hate that I find relaxing are: bookkeeping, cleaning a really dirty room, darning.

Administrative work is often exasperating and stress-inducing, whether you're running ICI or trying to get the plumber to turn up when he said he would. You live with Murphy's Law ('If a thing can go wrong, it will'). The more people you have to supervise, the more admin work they actually create by being part of your system.

Because of the attendant frustration (this is the killer), *ration your admin time* in your weekly timetable and don't allow it to leak out of its place – be ruthless with yourself.

Weekly stress chart (mine)

	Mon	Tues	Wed	Thurs	Fri	Sat	Sun
The doings of the day							
Analysis (hours):							
Creative				5	2 6*		
Relaxing							
Physical							
System-support	6	4	6	7	5		
Admin	8	7	4	3	5		
TV	3	4	5				
Sleep	7	9	9	9	6		
Notes	no lunch break	no lunch break	no lunch break	out to dinner; went to sleep over coffee	*read re-search in evening	an aimless day	cancelled lunch party; too tired, watched tennis on TV

This is what my first week chart looked like: all admin and system-support work, hardly any writing time. No lunch break meant I was too tired to do anything but watch TV in the evening and flopped at the weekend.

My second week limited admin to Monday morning and system-support work to one hour on Sunday. Creative work was increased to 4½ days. By the fourth week this was my routine.

Weekly stress chart (yours – copy this if you want to try it)

	Mon	Tues	Wed	Thurs	Fri	Sat	Sun
The doings of the day							
Analysis (hours):							
Creative							
Relaxing							
Physical							
System-support							
Admin							
TV							
Sleep							
Notes							

Sleep is regenerative. Creative and enjoyable physical work seems to mean that you need less sleep. Depressing work adversely affects your sleep pattern.

A ten-minute nap or relaxation period around 12 p.m., 3 p.m. or 6 p.m. may radically alter your life. Why not try it for two weeks?

Winston Churchill's *admin work* was running the war. His *physical work* was building walls. His *creative work* was painting and writing books. He cleverly avoided *system-support* work. He worked from 7 a.m. to lunch-time and from 6 p.m. to 2 a.m. He *slept* when he had a nap after lunch, *slept* from 2 a.m. to 7 a.m. and exhausted his staff, who couldn't do this.

My elder son designed a stress chart for me (see p. 414) and eventually persuaded me to fill it in after I had repeatedly said I hadn't time to do it. After doing it truthfully for one week, I could recognize what he had (objectively) spotted easily: I didn't allow for relaxation, I didn't plan a proper holiday once a year and I spent too much time on admin work. So I planned the second week and found it difficult to stick to my plan. For the third week I changed my entire pattern of work, and firmly stuck to it.

Your first week. At the end of each day fill in the stress chart. Check how much of your time was taken up by depressing work and how much time was spent on cheerful pursuits.

Second week. Pre-plan your time. Ration depressing work. Minimize admin work. Note how you feel at the end of the day. At first, your time allocations may not be realistic.

THE BEST STRESS BOOK

Ploughing through an almost indigestible book by some medical expert on stress can leave you feeling even *more* stressed after you've wasted your weekend reading it.

The only book on stress that I recommend is *The Book of Stress Survival* by Alix Kirsta (published by Unwin Books), which is cleverly planned and laid out, with plenty of good photographs and diagrams. First, questionnaires are used to help analyse the areas of your life that are most stressful. The next part of the book suggests how to avoid stress at home and at work. 'Ways to Relax' include relaxation techniques, exercise, meditation and simple yoga. The final section – high-stress situations – gives crisp but sometimes over-condensed advice on many stress-related problems, which vary from the common cold to lack of sexual desire.

A SUMMARY OF STRESS REDUCTION

Human beings need affection and cheerful contact with other human beings to stay alive; lack of cuddles is a cause of death in babies; even the gruffest old ogre needs tender loving care. So check that you . . .

Your nest

1 Belong to a group other than your family and workmates.
2 Have at least one close friend on whom you can rely and in whom you can confide. *Any* problem can be minimized once it is shared, faced and evaluated.

  Don't work so hard that you don't have time for friends.
3 Never take your family for granted. That old Victorian concept – the family – may be where you feel most safe and protected from the increasing stresses of the outside world, such as muggings, hooliganism, burglaries, granny rape and men lurking in raincoats; these are now so uppermost in some people's minds that they are afraid to use public transport or to go out after dark.
4 Decide where in this world you feel happy and protected; perhaps this isn't where it is supposed to be. When things go wrong in life, go there. (This is why brides in tears rush home to mother.)
5 Develop an outside interest that *really* interests you; learn a relaxation technique; plan adequate leisure, rest and non-competitive exercise (not nearly as easy as it sounds, of course).

Your problems

6 Keep any problem in perspective. Remember that dragons look bigger in the night.

DOWN WITH SUPERWOMAN!

The most difficult and important part of being under stress may well be recognizing tht you *are* under stress.

Never underestimate the snowball effect of stress: overwork leads to stress, stress leads to illness (because people under stress are vulnerable) and illness leads to other problems; other problems lead to anxiety, which leads to further illness and perhaps a breakdown.

7 Think in stress compartments, like tycoons do. I try to keep exasperating admin work for Wednesday morning, and what doesn't get done on Wednesday morning has to wait until *next* Wednesday morning.

8 Remember that you can't do more than you can do. This was neatly summed up by a sports masseuse I met in Hollywood. She told me that she coped with stressful situations by thinking, 'This is the position I'm in right now. I'm coping as best as I can and the rest will have to wait until later.' Then she went off to massage Elizabeth Taylor.

9 Measure your problem. Decide whether it is an *irritation* (baby throwing up on your shoulder), a *worry* (baby breaking your valuable antique teapot) or a real *problem* (baby being badly bitten by the dog next door).

HOW LONG WILL THIS PROBLEM LAST? Will this be important tomorrow? Next week? Next month? Next year? In ten years' time?

10 Is the problem being magnified by your mood (PMT time?)?

11 **Do you seem to have one crisis after another?** Most crises result from:

* Failure to anticipate (so plan in detail).
* Failure to listen to the small warning voice in your head (so trust your intuition).

* Failure to check *at an early stage* the work of other people working on a project. (I'm bad at this.)
* Underestimating the time to allow for a job (so check your guestimates).
* Trying to do too many things at the same time (so list your priorities).

12 **Do things always go wrong when you're in a rush?** When you're in a rush, your brain is racing ahead of your body! You drop, break or tear something because your body hasn't had time to catch up with the brain's instructions. The nurse who told me this had been taught at her training school that:

(a) When you're in a hurry, *do things slower*.

(b) When you're carrying anything, such as a loaded tray, sing aloud 'Here Comes the Bride', because this will slow you down.

(c) If you're carrying an object, always carry it in front of you, not to one side or behind you; in this way you can see that the object is unhampered.

13 Is it a last-straw stress situation, occurring on a day when everything is going wrong? Something that may cause stress on the day when you are harassed, rushed and have just dented the car might not cause stress if it happened on a quiet Sunday afternoon.

14 Are you over-influenced by what other people may think about your problem . . . the Joneses, for instance? This is an unnecessary magnifying factor; turn the telescope firmly round the other way.

15 Before your next emergency, think how you reacted in your last emergency. Did you do anything foolish?

In an emergency don't do anything that could harm you in your stressed condition, such as driving a car. If an emergency affects your mate or children, don't be panicked into action.

16 In times of trouble, try to spend five minutes doing the breathing exercise on p. 410 before doing anything. Concentrate on the breathing and nothing else, because many stressed people hyperventilate – you gasp for breath and your heart beats faster.

17 **Do you seem to have too many things to keep track of?** Respect your headspace; like suitcase space, this is limited. If there are too many things in it, you'll have to dump a few of them or else, of course, the suitcase won't function. In addition, you spread yourself too thinly and risk **gridlock**, which is when you have so many things to think about that you can't think of *anything*. Learn to recognize the impotence and panic of gridlock, which is cured by making a list.

Your brain can keep track of only a certain number of things at a time; with some people it's only one thing at a time, other people can keep track of as many as eight things. Never sub-divide a project into more than eight areas, if you want to keep track of it overall.

18 **Your best weapon to fight stress is** lists. Stress-expert Dr Andrew Mason says that list-makers suffer less than they might from stress, so what you may need to minimize stress and feel more in control of your life is just a cheap plastic folder with a few check-lists shoved into it.

Most people think of lists as a way to avoid forgetting, but lists are also CLARIFIERS and they are the simplest, cheapest aid to help you take decisions calmly and increase your efficiency.

If work and responsibilities are taking more than the time and assets you have available, then lists may prove to be a quick way of analysing your stress situation to yourself or someone who may help, such as your doctor. The most important time to make a list is when, swamped by work, you tell yourself you haven't enough time to make a list.

THE LAST WORD ON STRESS

If you're under stress what you must do is *less* ... BECAUSE THIS IS THE ONLY THING THAT WILL LESSEN YOUR STRESS. Try it. You have nothing to lose – and your life to save.

Overloading your mental capacity is like overloading an electrical socket by simultaneously plugging in the vacuum cleaner, the electric kettle and a hairdryer; when *that* happens, the socket goes on strike, blows a fuse and won't work at all. Similarly, if you are under stress, the only thing that works is to *reduce your load*, because if you don't, the same thing will happen again.

It is often the kindest, most generous, hard-working people who get life's loads dumped on them, while the selfish people happily sprint ahead along life's road. If you are under stress, LEARN TO BE MORE SELFISH.

Start saying NO. Reconsider your obligations. Can you relinquish any of them? No, you say, but imagine that you are suddenly told that you will have to spend a year in hospital. What will happen to those obligations?

Try to reduce your load by subcontracting parts of it and dumping other parts. At first sight this will probably look impossible, because otherwise your overload situation wouldn't have arisen in the first place.

Remember that however much the lady next door can cram into twenty-four hours, what you are doing is *too much for you*. So be sensibly selfish, dump some of your load, plan to do less, learn to say no, firmly stick to your plans and if you are tempted to do anything else, lie on a sofa and murmur ...

'DOWN WITH SUPERWOMAN!'

How to get hold of
the V.I.P.s in your Life

(*You* fill in these telephone numbers)

Police station _____

School secretary _____

Hospital _____

Doctor _____

Dentist _____

Chemist _____

Local gas emergency _____

Local gas service _____

Local electricity emergency _____

Local electricity service _____

Heating fuel supply _____

HOW TO GET HOLD OF THE VIPs IN YOUR LIFE

Heating repairs _____

Railway stations _____

Garage _____

Taxi-cabs _____

Town hall (also refuse collection) _____

Bank manager _____

Insurance broker _____

Vet _____

Milkman _____

Builder _____

Decorator _____

Plumber _____

Carpenter _____

Electrician _____

TV repairs _____

Telephone repairs _____

Domestic machine repairs _____

Special machinery repairs _____

Newspaper delivery _____

Laundry _____

Dry cleaner _____

Drain cleaner _____

Window cleaner _____

Florist _____

Local odd-job agency _____

DOWN WITH SUPERWOMAN!

Fill in the following according to your needs, i.e., piano tuner, contract cleaner, carpet cleaner, curtain maker, baby-sitter, off licence, flower nursery, local paper advertisement department.

_____

_____

_____

_____

_____

_____

_____

_____

_____

_____

_____

_____

_____

_____

_____

_____

_____

_____

_____

_____

_____

_____

_____

A quick guide to the metric system (translations of British Imperial measures into metric measurements) and the most frequently needed transatlantic equivalents.

THE METRIC SYSTEM: A ROUGH CRIB

The great point about the metric system is that it is logical and not based on the length of the big toe, pole or perch of somebody's Saxon ancestor. The French worked it all out according to reason just after the Revolution in 1791.

The decimal units of calculation are: length in metres, area in square metres, solid weight in grams, temperature in degrees, liquid volume in litres. All calculations are made in units of ten,

indicated by such prefixes as milli- (1/1000), centi- (1/100), deci- (1/10), hecto- (100), and are interrelated; for example:

10 *millimetres* (mm)	=	1 centimetre (cm)
10 *centimetres*	=	1 decimetre (dm)
10 decimetres	=	1 metre (m)
10 *metres*	=	1 dekametre (dk)
10 dekametres	=	1 hectometre (hm)
10 hectometres	=	1 *kilometre* (km)

Most people use only the measurements in *italics*.

In the following conversions the measurements have been rounded off for convenience – they are not exact equivalents.

Useful lengths

To translate kilometres into miles, divide by 8, then multiply by 5. To assess short distances *roughly*, simply halve the number of kilometres.

DOWN WITH SUPERWOMAN!

Metric		Imperial
3 mm	=	$\frac{1}{8}$ in
6 mm	=	$\frac{1}{4}$ in
1.3 cm	=	$\frac{1}{2}$ in
2 cm	=	$\frac{3}{4}$ in
2.5 cm	=	1 in
3 cm	=	$1\frac{1}{4}$ in
4 cm	=	$1\frac{1}{2}$ in
4.5 cm	=	$1\frac{3}{4}$ in
5 cm	=	2 in
7.5 cm	=	3 in
10 cm	=	4 in
13 cm	=	5 in
15 cm	=	6 in
18 cm	=	7 in
20 cm	=	8 in
23 cm	=	9 in
25.5 cm	=	10 in
28 cm	=	11 in
30 cm	=	12 in (1 ft)
35 cm	=	14 in
0 cm	=	24 in (2 ft)
90 cm	=	36 in (1 yard)
100 cm (1 m)	=	40 in
1.2 m	=	4 ft
1.5 m	=	5 ft
1.8 m	=	6 ft
2 m	=	7 ft

Distances

Metric (km)		Imperial (miles)
8	=	05
16	=	10
48	=	30
80	=	50
120	=	75
161	=	100

Area

Metric		Imperial
1 sq cm	=	0.15 sq in
6.5 sq cm	=	1 sq in
930 sq cm	=	1 sq ft
0.8 sq m	=	1 sq yd
1 sq m	=	$1\frac{1}{2}$ sq yd
4,000 sq m	=	1 acre
10,000 sq m (1 hectare (ha))	=	$2\frac{1}{2}$ acres

Useful weights

Metric		Imperial
15 g	=	$\frac{1}{2}$ oz
25 g	=	1 oz
40 g	=	$1\frac{1}{2}$ oz
55 g	=	2 oz
70 g	=	$2\frac{1}{2}$ oz
85 g	=	3 oz
115 g	=	4 oz
125 g	=	$4\frac{1}{2}$ oz
140 g	=	5 oz
170 g	=	6 oz
200 g	=	7 oz
225 g	=	8 oz ($\frac{1}{2}$ lb)
255 g	=	9 oz
285 g	=	10 oz
340 g	=	12 oz
450 g	=	1 lb
680 g	=	$1\frac{1}{2}$ lb
900 g	=	2 lb
1 kg	=	$2\frac{1}{4}$ lb
1.25 kg	=	3 lb

Your weight

Metric (kilogrammes)		Imperial (stones)
6.5	=	1
13	=	2
19	=	3
25	=	4
32	=	5
38	=	6
44.5	=	7
51	=	8
54	=	$8\frac{1}{2}$
57	=	9
60	=	$9\frac{1}{2}$
63.5	=	10
66.5	=	$10\frac{1}{2}$
70	=	11
73	=	$11\frac{1}{2}$
76	=	12
79	=	$12\frac{1}{2}$
82.5	=	13
86	=	$13\frac{1}{2}$
90	=	14
92	=	$14\frac{1}{2}$

Useful temperatures

freezing point of water	0 °C	32 °F
cold winter day in Britain	5 °C	41 °F
cool day in summer or very mild day in winter	15 °C	59 °F
warm spring day	20 °C	8 °F
centrally heated living-room	21 °C	70 °F
heatwave	30 °C	86 °F
normal body temperature	37 °C	98.6 °F
		110 °F
hot bath	43 °C	120 °F
hand-hot water	49 °C	

Temperature chart

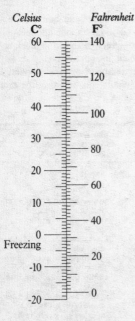

Celsius
C°

Fahrenheit
F°

60 — 140

50 — 120

40 — 100

30 — 80

20 — 60

10 — 40

0 — 20
Freezing

-10 — 0

-20

Sheets and blankets: ancient British and metric

Take this crib with you when you shop.

Sheets should be at least 274 cm (108 in) long.

Blankets should be the same width but need not be longer than 250 cm (100 in) if you have a narrow turnover at the top.

Beds 76 cm (2 ft 6 in) wide need sheets 150 × 260 cm (60 × 102 in).

Beds 90 cm (3 ft) wide need sheets 180 × 260 cm (70 × 102 in).

Beds 135 cm (4 ft 6 in) wide need sheets 230 × 260 cm (90 × 102 in).

Beds 150 cm (5 ft) wide need sheets 230 × 260 cm (90 × 102 in).

The new metric bed sizes are:

Standard single: 100 × 200 cm (sheet size 180 × 260 cm).

Standard double: 150 × 200 cm (sheet size 230 × 260 cm).

Fabric width

Metric (cm)		Imperial (in)
90	=	36
115	=	45
140	=	55
150	=	60

Quietly going metric in the kitchen

For converting your own recipes from imperial to metric. Recipe translators generally use 25 grammes as a basic unit in place of 1 ounce, 560 mililitres in place of 1 pint. Use the new British Standard 5-ml and 15-ml spoons in place of the old variable teaspoons and tablespoons; they will give slightly smaller quantities.

Translated recipes are rounded off – either upwards or downwards – in quantity, but the *comparative* quantities should remain the same.

Never mix metric and imperial measures in one recipe; stick to one system or the other.

To measure cookery ingredients, Talaware manufacture an excellent metal measuring cone with metric and transatlantic conversions on the side.

DOWN WITH SUPERWOMAN!

Useful volumes

Metric	Imperial
1 millilitre (ml)	= a few drops
5 ml	= 1 small teaspoon (standard medicine-spoon size)
15 ml	= 1 tablespoon
1 centilitre (cl)	= 1 dessertspoon
1 decilitre (dl)	= 6 tablespoons
280 ml	= 10 fl oz ($\frac{1}{2}$ pt)
560 ml	= 1 pt
1 litre (l)	= 2 pt
4.5 l	= 1 gal, so a 5-l tin of paint holds just over 1 gal.

Don't think that an average wine bottle is a litre; it's about 75 centilitres: a hock bottle contains even less.

Meat roasting A meat thermometer takes the guesswork out of roasting, but if you don't have one, below is a time-table guide. It allows for wrapping meats or poultry in foil and unfolding the foil during the last twenty minutes of cooking so that the meat will brown satisfactorily.

These times are for average British taste. If you like your meat rare, cross out this timetable and pencil in your own. It's also for meat joints of average family size, i.e. 1.5–2.5 kg (3–5 lb).

Cups In Canada and the United States, most ingredients for recipes are measured by volume, in cups, rather than by weight. How much does a cup hold? How many tablespoons are there in a cup? Amazingly enough it depends in which country you are standing. The standard cup used in Great Britain is larger – 280 ml (10 fluid ounces – $\frac{1}{2}$ pt) – than that used in the United States – 225 ml (8 fl oz). To translate recipes and convert quantities, use your Talaware measuring cone.

Spoons (solids and liquids) The British Standard tablespoon and teaspoon are slightly larger than an American one. You may, like me, have four different sizes of teaspoon in your drawer. However, if you're not splitting the atom for lunch, it won't make much difference.

	Quick roast at high temperature (Gas 7, Elec. 220 °C = 425 °F)	Slow roast at low temperature (reduces shrinkage) (Gas 3. Elec. 160 °C = 325 °F)
Beef and venison	15 mins per 450 g (1 lb) + 15 mins (rare) 20 mins per 450 g (1 lb) + 20 min (well done)	25 mins per 450 g (1 lb) + 25 mins
Lamb or mutton	20 mins per 450 g (1 lb) + 20 mins	30 mins per 450 g (1 lb) + 30 mins
Veal and rabbit	25 mins per 450 g (1 lb) + 25 mins	35 mins per 450 g (1 lb) + 35 mins
Pork	25 mins per 450 g (1 lb) + 25 mins	Can't cook it this way, if you want crackling, but if not 35 mins per 450 g (1 lb) + 35 mins
Chicken and duck	15 mins per 450 g (1 lb) + 15 mins	25 mins per 450 g (1 lb) + 25 mins
Goose and turkey	15 mins per 450 g (1 lb) + 15 mins	25 mins per 450 g (1 lb) + 25 mins (under 6.5 kg (14 lb))
(Before cooking a fat goose stab the bird with a fork so that the fat oozes through and bastes itself)		20 mins per 450 g (1 lb) + 20 mins (over 5.4 kg (14 lb))
Game	(Gas 6. Elec. 200 °C = 400 °F)	
Woodcock	15 to 20 mins	
Grouse, guinea fowl, partridge and young roast-ing pigeon	35 mins for small ones 45 mins for large ones	
Pheasant	15 mins per 450 g (1 lb) + 10 mins	

Oven temperatures

Solid fuel	Gas	Electricity °C	°F	To Cook
Very cool	¼	110	225	Stew
	½	120	250	
Cool	1	140	275	Casseroles, slow roasts or milk and egg dishes
	2	150	300	
Slow	3	160	325	Biscuits
Moderate	4	180	350	Fruit cake
Mod. hot	5	190	375	
	6	200	400	Soufflés, short pastry, flan, sponge cake
Hot	7	220	425	Fast roasts, bread
	8	230	450	Puff and flaky pastry
Very hot	9	240	475	

All cookers aren't the same: some tend to be hotter than the temperature at which they have been set: allow for the idiosyncrasies of your oven in using the table above and follow manufacturer's instructions.

INTERNATIONAL CLOTHING SIZES

The tables below should be used as approximate guides, as actual sizes may vary from one manufacturer to another. It is wise to check all measurements in centimetres.

Women's clothes

Britain (size)	8	10	12	14	16	18	20
Bust (cm/in)	80/31	82/32	87/34	92/36	97/38	102/40	109/42
Hips (cm/in)	85/33	87/34	92/36	97/38	102/40	109/42	114/44
France (size)	34	36	38	40	42	44	46
Bust (cm)	81	84	87	90	93	96	99
Hips (cm)	89	92	95	98	101	104	107
Germany (size)	34	36	38	40	42	44	46
Bust (cm)	80	84	88	92	96	100	104
Hips (cm)	85	90	94	98	102	106	110
Italy (size)	38	40	42	44	46	48	50
Bust (cm)	82	85	88	91	94	97	100
Hips (cm)	84	88	92	96	100	104	108
Portugal (size)	36	38	40	42	44	46	48
Bust (cm)	78	82	86	90	94	98	104
Hips (cm)	84	88	92	96	100	104	110
Scandinavia (size)	34	36	38	40	42	44	46
Bust (cm)	81	84	87	90	94	98	103
Hips (cm)	89	92	95	98	102	106	111
Spain (size)	36	38	40	42	44	46	48
Bust (cm)	78	82	86	90	94	96	104
Hips (cm)	84	88	92	96	100	104	110
USA (size)	6	8	10	12	14	16	18
Bust (in)	32	33	34½	36	37½	39	41
Hips (in)	34	35	36½	38	39½	41	43

DOWN WITH SUPERWOMAN!

Women's shoe sizes

Britain	2	2½	3	3½	4	4½	5	5½	6	6½	7	7½	8
Europe	34	34½	35	35½	36½	37	37½	38	39	39½	40½	41	41½
USA	3½	4	4½	5	5½	6	6½	7	7½	8	8½	9	9½

Swimwear

Britain	8	10	12	14	16	18	20	22	24
Europe	36	38	40	42	44	46/8	50	52	54
bust (cm)	76	81	86	91	97	102	107	112	117

Bras Cup sizes the same throughout (AA/A/B/C/D/DD/E)

Britain	30	32	34	36	38	40	42	44
Europe	80	85	90	95	100	105	110	115
International	65	70	75	80	85	90	95	100

Men's shirts

Britain	14½	15	15½	16	16½	17	17½
cm	37	38	39/40	41	42	43	44

Men's suits

Britain/USA (in)	36	37	38	39	40	41	42	43	44	45	46	47	48
Europe (size)	46		48	50		52	54		56	58		60	62
Europe (cm)	92		96	100		104	108		112	116		120	124

Men's shoe sizes

Britain	4½	5	5½	6	6½	7	7½	8	8½	9	9½	10	10½
Europe	37½	38	38½	39½	40	40½	41	42	42½	43	43½	44	44½
USA	5	5½	6	6½	7	7½	8	8½	9	9½	10	10½	11

Men's swimwear

Britain	SMALL	MEDIUM	LARGE	XLARGE
waist: cm	76–81	84–89	91–96	99–104
waist: in	30–32	33–35	36–38	39–41

And so farewell . . .
with the joke that
never fails

As we bashed out lunch for twenty teen-agers when only seven were expected, an old schoolfriend of mine hissed that what she wanted to read in this book was a joke that she will continue to think funny every time the milk boils over. So here's my favourite.

An astonished husband has returned home from the office to an amazing scene in his kitchen. Two little children are murdering each other while another tot is garrotting the cat. There is a pile of last night's dirty dishes and a heap of dirty laundry. Saucepans are burning, clouds of steam are rising, the floor is covered with smashed crockery and the dog has just upset the litter bin.

In the middle of this chaos is his wife, sitting in an easy chair with her feet up on the table. She is reading a novel and dipping into a box of chocolates. She says, 'I thought that the best way to let you see what on earth I do all day was not to do it.'

Index

INDEX

INDEX

INDEX

FOR THE BEST IN PAPERBACKS, LOOK FOR THE 🐧

In every corner of the world, on every subject under the sun, Penguin represents quality and variety – the very best in publishing today.

For complete information about books available from Penguin – including Puffins, Penguin Classics and Arkana – and how to order them, write to us at the appropriate address below. Please note that for copyright reasons the selection of books varies from country to country.

In the United Kingdom: Please write to *Dept E.P., Penguin Books Ltd, Harmondsworth, Middlesex, UB7 0DA.*

If you have any difficulty in obtaining a title, please send your order with the correct money, plus ten per cent for postage and packaging, to *PO Box No 11, West Drayton, Middlesex*

In the United States: Please write to *Dept BA, Penguin, 299 Murray Hill Parkway, East Rutherford, New Jersey 07073*

In Canada: Please write to *Penguin Books Canada Ltd, 2801 John Street, Markham, Ontario L3R 1B4*

In Australia: Please write to the *Marketing Department, Penguin Books Australia Ltd, P.O. Box 257, Ringwood, Victoria 3134*

In New Zealand: Please write to the *Marketing Department, Penguin Books (NZ) Ltd, Private Bag, Takapuna, Auckland 9*

In India: Please write to *Penguin Overseas Ltd, 706 Eros Apartments, 56 Nehru Place, New Delhi, 110019*

In the Netherlands: Please write to *Penguin Books Netherlands B.V., Postbus 195, NL–1380AD Weesp*

In West Germany: Please write to *Penguin Books Ltd, Friedrichstrasse 10–12, D–6000 Frankfurt/Main 1*

In Spain: Please write to *Alhambra Longman S.A., Fernandez de la Hoz 9, E–28010 Madrid*

In Italy: Please write to *Penguin Italia s.r.l., Via Como 4, I-20096 Pioltello (Milano)*

In France: Please write to *Penguin Books Ltd, 39 Rue de Montmorency, F-75003 Paris*

In Japan: Please write to *Longman Penguin Japan Co Ltd, Yamaguchi Building, 2–12–9 Kanda Jimbocho, Chiyoda-Ku, Tokyo 101*